Praise for *Engineering Trustworth*

MW00852413

"This is the 'bible' for cybersecurity, which needs to be co
solve this enormous threat to our national security."

—John M. Poindexter, PhD, VADM, U.S. Navy (ret.),
Former National Security Advisor to President Reagan

"This book is a technical tour de force! Neatly organized between these covers is a comprehensive review of how to think about designing and building trusted (secure) systems, representing decades of experience and deep thought by the author. Sami presents the material clearly, including diagrams, charts, and extensive pointers to outside references. He has also crafted useful summaries and questions for further thought, making this book useful as either a valued reference or as an advanced textbook. Not only does Sami describe techniques to use in designing trustworthy systems, but he also describes shortcomings—he's not trying to 'sell' a particular method.

This is the book I have wanted for over a decade, for use in my advanced information security systems course. This will occupy an honored position on my bookshelf between Ross Anderson's *Security Engineering* and Michael Howard's *Writing Secure Code*. If you are involved with any aspect of designing or evaluating trustworthy systems, it should be on your bookshelf too."

—Eugene Spafford,
Professor of Computer Science and
leader of the CERIAS Project, Purdue University

"Sami Saydjari is today's cybersecurity Renaissance man. Sami was the first to recognize that failed cybersecurity could one day deliver societal existential change equivalent to nuclear warfare. His early tenacity led to DARPA's first cybersecurity research investment. This book is a definitive textbook on cybersecurity, and will become the instructional foundation for future trustworthy systems. Like the genius of Da Vinci, this book delivers insightful philosophy, deep understanding, practical guidance, and detailed instruction for building future systems that mitigate cybersecurity threats!"

—Dr. Marv Langston, cybersecurity technologies consultant;
former Naval Officer, DARPA office director,
U.S. Navy's first CIO, and U.S. Defense Department Deputy CIO

"Sami is one of the great experts in our field and he has produced one of the finest and most complete works in our field. It should be your priority to purchase and read this amazing book! For anyone desiring a comprehensive treatment of the cybersecurity discipline, this is definitely the book. It's an impressive work that covers the important issues in a complete and accurate manner."

—Dr. Edward G. Amoroso, CEO of TAG Cyber, and former CSO, AT&T

Praise for *Engineering Trustworthy Systems* (cont.)

"Sami Saydjari's career has spanned most of the history of cybersecurity, and in this book he distills the lessons of a lifetime. This book is both comprehensive and easy to read, making its concepts widely accessible. It is notable for its emphasis on looking at a system as a whole, not just an aggregation of components, and for helping readers understand how to value information and how to deal with risk. I urge those building the systems that will be part of tomorrow's critical cyberinfrastructure, which now extends into our factories, airplanes, cars, and homes, to read this book and apply its techniques. Until we learn to build on the lessons of the past, the future of cybersecurity will continue to resemble the present."

> —Carl Landwehr, IEEE Fellow and member of
> the National Cybersecurity Hall of Fame

"Saydjari has written an authoritative, timeless, and practical guide to cybersecurity. The architecture of the book allows the reader to gain knowledge across a wide range of areas from strategy and risk management, to the technical design concepts of engineering a trustworthy system with security and safety at its core. Each chapter concludes with a set of critical thinking questions. If organizations—corporate or government—take a disciplined approach in answering these questions, their understanding of the risks to their mission can only increase. We are reminded that society's dependency on information technology is growing and new technologies are introducing even more risk to our way of life. Saydjari presents multiple methods to assess risk and diagnose an organization's strengths and weaknesses. He then presents a thoughtful approach to effective risk reduction, taking into account cost and mission impact. This book underscores that our opponent's reach, speed, and understanding of our vulnerabilities currently outmatch our defenses, which is why we must learn how to invest in creating/designing/engineering the most trustworthy systems. Our future depends on it."

> —Melissa Hathaway, cyber advisor to Presidents George W. Bush and
> Barack H. Obama, now President of Hathaway Global Strategies
> advising countries and companies around the world

"In *Engineering Trustworthy Systems*, Sami perfectly captures the asymmetrical nature of cyberwarfare. This text will help level the playing field and put the adversary on their heels and is required reading for any organization building or running a security testing team. Focusing on the 'hack' is a mistake, and Sami explains how and why bringing the strategist and tactician together builds a truly effective test team. Following the lessons from this text will transform test teams from hackers to cyber guardians."

> —Jim Carnes, former Chief of Security Testing Center at the DOD

"Sami Saydjari's valuable new book reflects decades of experience in designing and building secure computer systems. His approach to risk management for secure system design is innovative and well worth reading."

> —Steven B. Lipner, member of the National Cybersecurity Hall of Fame

"This book brings together all of the important aspects in cybersecurity design for the first time to include all of the myriad cybersecurity perspectives, the types and impact of failure, and the latest thinking in mitigation strategy. I can see this book becoming an essential and complete reference for the new student of cybersecurity as well as for the well-experienced professional. Sami's thoughts and insights give the book an excellent structure and relevant examples that make even the most difficult concepts easy to digest."

—Tom Longstaff, Chair, Computer Science, Cybersecurity,
and Information Systems Engineering Programs,
The Johns Hopkins University Engineering for Professionals

"As a long-standing proponent of rigorous, first principles design, I can endorse this book with unbridled enthusiasm. Cybersecurity practitioners, designers, and researchers will all find that the lessons in this book add inestimable, tangible value to their missions. The depth and breadth of this book are truly impressive."

—Roy Maxion, PhD, Research Professor,
Computer Science Department, Carnegie Mellon University

"'Yet another cybersecurity book' this is not. Its real strength lies in going beyond the requisite scary attack stories and empty claims straight to the heart of very real operational problems that undermine current defensive capabilities and strategies. It does this to encourage the reader to think more carefully about the kinds of strategic design and planning that are so often lacking in building sustainable, evolvable, and comprehensive cyber protections. I highly recommend this book to those who actually have to make cyber defense work."

—Kymie Tan, Systems Engineer, Jet Propulsion Lab

"O. Sami Saydjari addresses cybersecurity using a comprehensive and straightforward approach that draws on examples from other fields, such as biology and astronomy, to enhance clarity and purpose. *Engineering Trustworthy Systems* is a well-timed tome that strikes a balance between Saydjari's many years of experience as one of DARPA's top cybersecurity experts and the ubiquitous nature of technology in our daily lives. His style is personable and digestible for those without any formal computer science training. Read this book—and learn from one of the best."

—Teri Shors, Professor, Dept. of Biology, University of Wisconsin Oshkosh;
Author of *Understanding Viruses*

"This book provides a refreshing look at cybersecurity by acknowledging the need for systems engineering. The book also emphasizes that cybersecurity is important for the sake of mission assurance, which is very important, but all too often overlooked by IT security personnel."

—Joe Weiss, PE, CISM, CRISC, ISA Fellow, IEEE Senior Member,
Managing Director ISA99 (Industrial Automation and Control Systems Security)

ENGINEERING TRUSTWORTHY SYSTEMS

Get Cybersecurity Design Right the First Time

O. Sami Saydjari

New York   Chicago   San Francisco
Athens   London   Madrid   Mexico City
Milan   New Delhi   Singapore   Sydney   Toronto

Library of Congress Cataloging-in-Publication Data

Names: Saydjari, O. Sami, author.
Title: Engineering trustworthy systems : get cybersecurity design right the
  first time / O. Sami Saydjari.
Description: New York : McGraw-Hill Education, [2018] | Includes index.
Identifiers: LCCN 2018019355 (print) | LCCN 2018020821 (ebook) | ISBN
  9781260118186 (ebook) | ISBN 9781260118179 (pbk. : alk. paper) | ISBN
  1260118177 (pbk. : alk. paper)
Subjects: LCSH: Computer networks—Security measures.
Classification: LCC TK5105.59 (ebook) | LCC TK5105.59 .S318 2018 (print) |
  DDC 005.8—dc23
LC record available at https://lccn.loc.gov/2018019355

Engineering Trustworthy Systems: Get Cybersecurity Design Right the First Time

1 2 3 4 5 6 7 8 9   LCR   21 20 19 18

ISBN   978-1-260-11817-9
MHID   1-260-11817-7

Sponsoring Editor	**Technical Editors**	**Production Supervisor**
Wendy Rinaldi	Earl Boebert	Lynn M. Messina
	Peter G. Neumann	
Editorial Supervisor		**Composition**
Patty Mon	**Copy Editor**	Cenveo Publisher Services
	Margaret Berson	
Project Manager		**Illustration**
Ishan Chaudhary,	**Proofreader**	Cenveo Publisher Services
Cenveo® Publisher Services	Lisa McCoy	
		Art Director, Cover
Acquisitions Coordinator	**Indexer**	Jeff Weeks
Claire Yee	Karin Arrigoni	

This book is dedicated to Andrew Saydjari, my amazing son, and his brilliant peers who will shape the future during what will surely be a tumultuous time in human history.

About the Author

Mr. O. Sami Saydjari has been a visionary thought-leader in cybersecurity for over three decades, working for elite organizations, including the Defense Advanced Research Projects Agency (DARPA), National Security Agency, and NASA, among others. He has published more than a dozen landmark papers in the field, provided consultation to national leadership on cybersecurity policy, and educated the public through interviews with major media such as CNN, PBS, ABC, the *New York Times*, *Financial Times*, the *Wall Street Journal*, and *Time* magazine. Follow the author on Twitter @SamiSaydjari and visit www.samisaydjari.com and www.EngineeringTrustworthySystems.com for more information.

About the Technical Editors

Earl Boebert wrote his first computer program as an undergraduate at Stanford in 1958. He then served in the U.S. Air Force as an EDP Officer, where he was awarded the Air Force Commendation Medal for an Air Force–wide project. He then joined Honeywell, where he worked on military, aerospace, and security systems, and received Honeywell's highest award for technical achievement. He was the Chief Scientist and technical founder of Secure Computing Corporation, where he led the development of the Sidewinder security server. He then finished his career as a Senior Scientist at Sandia National Laboratories.

He is listed as an inventor on 13 patents and is coauthor of a book on formal software verification and another which analyzes the causes of the Deepwater Horizon disaster. He has participated in 11 studies and workshops of the National Academies of Sciences, Engineering, and Medicine and in 2011 was named a National Associate of the Academies.

Peter G. Neumann (Neumann@CSL.sri.com) is in his 47th year at SRI International, where he is Chief Scientist of the Computer Science Lab. Prior to that, he was at Bell Labs in Murray Hill, New Jersey, throughout the 1960s, with extensive involvement in the Multics development. He has AM, SM, and PhD degrees from Harvard, and a Dr rerum naturalium from Darmstadt. He is a Fellow of the ACM, IEEE, and AAAS. In 1985, he created the ACM Risks Forum (http://catless.ncl.ac.uk/Risks/), which he moderates. His 1995 book, *Computer-Related Risks*, is still timely! He has taught at Darmstadt, Stanford, U.C. Berkeley, and the University of Maryland. See his website (http://www.csl.sri.com/users/neumann/) for further background and URLs for papers, reports, testimonies, and musings.

Contents at a Glance

Contents

Table of Figures

Table of Tables

Foreword

If you are a cybersecurity professional of any type, read this book; study it, reread it, and you will find yourself keeping it close at hand.

Engineering Trustworthy Systems has layers of subtlety, breadth, depth, and nuance that will continue to yield wisdom to the readers on each reading at various stages of their careers.

It carefully builds from the most foundational elements of cybersecurity to the most complex and nuanced topics that will bring deep and lifelong understanding that can make your performance in cybersecurity more effective, efficient, and stronger.

Understanding this book can place the readers head and shoulders above their peers and will offer a key strategic advantage to the individuals and organizations that are lucky enough to have them.

Whether you are a designer, evaluator, accreditor, tester, red teamer, cyber emergency response team member, or a manager of information technology, you need this book, now. *Engineering Trustworthy Systems* offers the most comprehensive coverage on the topic of cybersecurity engineering that is available in even a combined library on the topic. It is a profound technical book, coherently covering some of the most important unpublished cybersecurity engineering material available.

The book is carefully crafted by the author for completeness, breadth, and depth in the field. It is designed to fill gaping holes in the literature and is structured to allow the reader to grasp this complex discipline in digestible chunks that build on each other. Its organization allows it to act as a guide to cybersecurity engineering as well as a compendium.

This book is for the maven and the newbie alike. True wizards will find that they must have it on their shelf and refer to it often as a definitive source of cybersecurity knowledge when they face challenging situations. Aspiring cybersecurity professionals will find it an invaluable grounding available nowhere else, which will serve to frame all other learning and experience in the field. It is for students of cybersecurity as well as for professionals who are lifelong students of their chosen discipline.

As Sami's professional mentor, I had the pleasure of both observing him and working alongside him on major initiatives. His performance, insight, and creativity never ceased to impress me and often stunned me, both in the depth and breadth of his knowledge.

Many senior leaders at the National Security Agency were equally impressed, causing him to be in extraordinarily high demand. His stellar reputation went well outside of the walls of government, extending to the commercial sector, academia, and to the leadership of technical conferences seeking his wisdom on a multitude of cybersecurity topics.

I can think of no person better qualified to write this sorely needed tome. Sami is one of the leading conceptual innovators in the cybersecurity field, with over three decades of experience in all aspects of cybersecurity engineering. He is internationally recognized and trusted as a talented cybersecurity architect. His understanding of this complex topic is both expansively wide and impressively deep in many areas. Despite that, or perhaps because of it, he has a unique ability to communicate the most complex and subtle content in terms that are clear and easily understood. He is part of the world's brain trust on the topic and cares deeply about passing on the collection of wisdom and deep insights to help make cyberspace a safer place.

This book will be *the* reference go-to book in cybersecurity engineering for decades to come. After benefitting from reading this book, propagate it to everyone you care about in the field. The information in this book needs to be quickly spread as far and wide as possible because we are woefully behind where we need to be, and this book can help us keep pace with advancing attacker capabilities.

—Brian Snow, former National Security Agency,
Technical Director of three different key components,
Research and Engineering, Information Assurance,
and the National Cryptologic School

Acknowledgments

Teri Shors for being my dedicated author mentor and trusted advisor throughout the process of writing my first book. She has invested innumerable hours patiently coaching me on both process and content, for which I am deeply grateful.

Brian Snow for hundreds of invaluable conversations on the principles of cybersecurity design throughout my career as my primary mentor and very good friend.

Earl Boebert and Peter G. Neumann for their comprehensive technical review and Steve Lipner for his additional technical input, helping to ensure the highest-quality content delivered to you, the reader.

I also acknowledge the following individuals (in alphabetical order) and many others who prefer to remain anonymous for deep and insightful conversations that have contributed to my thinking in the field.

Scott Borg, Cyber Consequences Unit
Dick Clarke, Formerly NSC
Debbie Cooper, Independent
Jeremy Epstein, National Science Foundation
Don Faatz, Mitre
Wade Forbes, Independent
Tom Haigh, Formerly Honeywell
Jerry Hamilton, Formerly DARPA SETA
Sam Hamilton, Formerly Orincon
Will Harkness, Formerly DoD
Melissa Hathaway, Formerly NSC
Cynthia Irvine, Naval Postgraduate School
Jonathan Katz, University of Maryland
Dick Kemmerer, UC Santa Barbara
Carl Landwehr, Formerly Naval Research Lab
Marv Langston, Formerly DARPA
Karl Levitt, UC Davis
Pete Loscocco, DoD
John Lowry, Formerly BBN
Steve Lukasik, Formerly DARPA
Teresa Lunt, Formerly DARPA
Roy Maxion, Carnegie Mellon University
Cathy McCollum, Mitre

John McHugh, Red Jack
Bob Meushaw, Formerly DoD
Spence Minear, Formerly Honeywell
Carol Muehrcke, Cyber Defense Agency, Inc.
Corky Parks, Formerly DoD
Rick Proto, Formerly DoD
Greg Rattray, Formerly Air Force
Ron Ross, NIST
Bill Sanders, UIUC
Rami Saydjari, Physician
Razi Saydjari, Physician
Dan Schnackenberg, Formerly Boeing
Fred Schneider, Cornell University
Greg Schudel, Formerly BBN
Dan Stern, Formerly TIS
Sal Stolfo, Columbia University
Kymie Tan, NASA Jet Propulsion Lab
Laura Tinnel, SRI
Bill Unkenholz, DoD
Paulo Verissimo, University of Luxembourg
Jim Wallner, Formerly CDA
Chuck Weinstock, Software Engineering Institute
Jody Westby, Independent Attorney
Joel Wilf, NASA JPL
Ken Williams, Zeltech
Brian Witten, Symantec
Mary Ellen Zurko, Formerly IBM

Introduction

Content

This book is about how to engineer trustworthy systems using timeless principles. Trustworthiness is a delicate and complex property concerning confidence that a system meets its requirements. The focus of this book will be on cybersecurity requirements. Trust is granted by a human user, by faith, or due to reasoned evidence, perhaps in the designer of the system. One trusts for some specific purpose. For example, you might trust someone to fix your plumbing, but you are not likely to trust the same person to manage your finances. This book is about how trust can be *earned* through sound system design principles.

The reader will learn the principles of engineering trustworthiness from a practical perspective.

These principles are complementary to basic engineering principles—an understanding of which is expected of the reader. Further, the book assumes that readers have a basic understanding of the mechanisms of cybersecurity, such as access control, firewalls, malicious code, cryptography, and authentication techniques. This book is about how to architect such mechanisms into a trustworthy system. By analogy, books on architecting physical buildings assume understanding of basic material science, physics, stress mechanics, and the properties of bricks, glass, mortar, and steel.

Audience

The book's intended audience includes various kinds of systems engineers and information technology professionals. Cybersecurity professionals, computer scientists, computer engineers, and systems engineers will all benefit from a deeper understanding of the principles of architecting a trustworthy system.

The goals for this book are to

- Educate cybersecurity engineers and systems engineers on the principles of assuredly achieving cybersecurity properties.
- Focus on practical engineering and not just theory—giving lots of examples.
- Inform system architects who already have a basic understanding of cybersecurity mechanisms such as cryptography and firewalls.

Foci

There are two important foci that the reader might note in this book that I should explain: a military focus and a respect for "old ideas." The military focus takes the form of sometimes explaining cybersecurity in terms of nation-state adversaries and potential global-scale warfare in cyberspace. Although I have experience in cybersecurity in the commercial world, the vast majority of my experience in cybersecurity has been in the military and intelligence communities. This experience bias is partly because this community was the first to recognize and embrace the need to address this important problem area. Another reason for the military focus is that in many cases (certainly not all), the military version of the cybersecurity problem is often a superset or harder version of the same problems that the commercial sector has. Therefore, addressing the military context allows one to scale down the solution to a commercial context where the stakes are usually lower. I compensate for this military focus by offering commercial and nonprofit examples to broaden and clarify the application of the principles to cybersecurity problems in other than military arenas.

The second focus that the reader may notice is references to "old ideas" alongside new ideas. Some have a tendency to dismiss ideas that are older than x years, where x seems to be getting smaller and smaller as the pace of technology development continues to increase at an exponential rate. There is a tendency among some to think that cybersecurity is purely a technology problem—that if you just build the right widgets (device or piece of software), the problem will be solved. I call this the "widget mentality." Widgets are certainly important, but knowledge and deep understanding are essential. Indeed, developing widgets without an understanding of the nature of the problem and what constitutes a real solution to the problem is ineffective.

The purpose of this book is to focus on the form of principles that underlie cybersecurity so that designers can understand what widgets to build, to what requirements they should build them, how they should be deployed and interconnected within cyberspace, and how to operate them when under attack.

Terminology

The field of cybersecurity is still relatively young (about 60 years old) and so terminology is still in flux. This can interfere with understanding what people are saying today, as well as reading papers from as little as two years earlier. Even the field itself has been called by many different names, including computer security, information assurance, information operations, digital security, security and privacy, and cybersecurity (the term I have chosen to settle on for this book). To counter this, I try hard to pick a term and remain consistent throughout the book and note when there might be variation in terminology in the current field and with historical literature. I may not have done this perfectly consistently, particularly when there is a strong historical basis in the use of one term over another. Also, I provide a glossary in the back of the book to help the reader through what sometimes appears like a Tower of Babel.

In the use of terminology, I have fastidiously steered clear of the use of the prolific number of acronyms that appear to plague the cybersecurity field. The tendency to use acronyms upon acronyms frustrates me immensely because it seems to intentionally impede understanding.

Some seem to use a string of acronyms to create a secret language to make them feel more knowledgeable than they are and to make others feel less knowledgeable than they really are. I see it used all too often to exclude nonexperts from a conversation. It has gotten so bad that sublingos have developed where cybersecurity experts do not even understand each other. Where the acronym has become extremely important in the vernacular, I will include it on first use and in the glossary so the reader can understand other texts. Cybersecurity concepts can be quite sophisticated, yet well worth understanding. I try hard to make concepts accessible and understandable to the widest possible technical audience.

Analogies

People learn very effectively using analogies. It provides an anchor to things they already know and provides a rich connection between fields. I make ample use of analogies throughout the book, including biological analogies, physical attack analogies, aviation analogies (possibly because I am an avocational pilot), and game analogies. I sometimes get teased for my use of analogies as an oversimplification. I believe, instead, that it provides a useful starting point to help understand the most complex ideas. Analogies are never meant to be taken literally and, of course, deviate at some point from what is being explained. Savor them for as far as they take you and know when to let go of them when you use them as a springboard to deeper understanding.

Presentation

I have included several features to help both visual learners like myself and nonvisual learners.

- Each chapter starts with a detailed outline of the chapter so that the reader can see the topic sequence and understand the flow and logical order.

- Each chapter states upfront learning goals so the reader can understand the value of reading the chapter in the bigger picture.

- Panels are included throughout the text to summarize the essence of important attacks and defenses.

- An extensive glossary with all keywords specially marked through the book, to facilitate grasping of key terminology.

- Ample use of tables and figures, most of which are original to this book.

- Each chapter includes a summary to help the reader understand the key points from the chapter that align with the learning objectives.

- Each chapter ends with a set of critical thinking questions that will help solidify the reader's knowledge and understanding of the topics.

- The book has been reviewed and improved by some of the most experienced and well-known experts in the field of cybersecurity.

- Much of the information in this book can be found nowhere else and represents the distilled experience of over three decades of work as a cybersecurity researcher, architect, and engineer.

Organization

The book is organized in five major parts that group chapters logically. I have done this to help the reader build a strong foundation of knowledge on which their career can firmly stand.

- "Part I: What Do You Want?" is about defining the cybersecurity problem and all of its aspects. The first and most important step in understanding how to solve a problem is understanding the problem itself.

- "Part II: What Could Go Wrong?" is about understanding attacks, failures, and the attacker mindset. Cybersecurity engineers must deeply understand the nature of attacks in order to properly design defenses against those attacks.

- "Part III: What Are the Building Blocks of Mitigating Risk?" explores the solution space for the problem described in Parts I and II.

- "Part IV: How Do You Orchestrate Cybersecurity?" discusses the principles of addressing the cybersecurity problem and attack space holistically and lays out the principles of cybersecurity architecture, including dependability and intrusion tolerance.

- "Part V: Move Cybersecurity Forward" prepares the reader to understand where the field is headed and how to best apply their newly gained knowledge to improve cybersecurity wherever they go.

Depth and Breadth

I have endeavored to cover the broadest set of the important topics in cybersecurity from a principles perspective. I have asked dozens of my most esteemed colleagues to review my topic list to ensure that I did not leave anything important out. I stress breadth in this book because design principles are necessarily holistic and must be understood together and at once to gain the full value. As I reach the end of each chapter, I think of a hundred questions that I could and would like to answer, particularly on the whys and hows of what I discussed. I have had to resist the urge to answer them all for two reasons. I see the publication of this book as urgent to help the next generation understand some very important principles that are found nowhere else. More material equates to further delay as there are only so many hours in a day. Many of my colleagues have commented that each chapter could, on its own, be a book, and that I should write a series. I *love* that idea, though I can feel the great weight of expectation on my shoulders as I write this sentence. It will be a project of mine to create a series of books that further explain each chapter. For now, please know that I have done my best to keep the book broad and provide the reader with the most essential knowledge regarding the principles of the field.

Engineering Change

Those who master the material of this book will be in the upper echelon of all cybersecurity engineers in the field. You will be able to define the vision of cybersecurity architecture for your organization—the so-called to-be architecture. Defining such an aim point on the horizon will be challenging and exciting. At the same time, human psychology and therefore, organizations led by humans, naturally resist change because there is an inherent fear of the unknown. There is a sociotechnical art to helping people and organizations overcome their fears and resistance, to holding their hands through scary changes, and implementing those changes in a minimally disruptive way to mission. I forewarn you that engineering change is at least as hard as defining to-be architectures that meet the challenges of the ever-evolving adversary and constantly changing technology. It is worth investing some of your time and energy to understand the way to affect changes without breaking the system that you are trying to serve and injuring and frustrating yourself in the process. This topic is beyond the scope of this book, but one that I intend to write about in the near future. In the meantime, I recommend that cybersecurity engineers learn the basic principles of industrial psychology such as those discussed in Daniel Pink's book, *Drive*.

Motivation

Why did I write this book? My career spanned a good portion of the development of the field of cybersecurity. Much of it grew and evolved as I was learning and applying it. Acquiring knowledge and applying the theory was on-the-job training for important systems with high stakes attached. It was a bit like building an airplane while flying it—sometimes a bit too exciting.

There are many good books on aspects of cybersecurity, many of which I cite and extol in this book. At the same time, there are none that really address the problem holistically, practically, and in an organized manner that starts with a foundational understanding of the problem. I feel it is important and urgent to confer this essential knowledge to the next generation so that they can stand on the shoulders of those that came before and build on it to solve important and emerging problems to come.

Cyberattacks pose an existential threat to our entire society, and addressing this problem has been a lifelong passion of mine. I hope it becomes yours as well.

—Sami

PART

I

What Do You Want?

"Part I: What Do You Want?" is about defining the cybersecurity problem and all of its aspects. The first and most important step in understanding how to solve a problem is understanding the problem itself.

CHAPTER 1

What's the Problem?

Overview

Learning Objectives

- State the nature of the cybersecurity problem.
- Enumerate key operational questions and state their importance.
- Describe ways that cybersecurity is asymmetric compared to conventional security.
- Define the scope of various aspects of the cybersecurity solution landscape.
- Describe the trade-off between prevention and detection-response in cybersecurity.

Designing and building trustworthy information systems is difficult. The field is relatively young, having started in the late 1960s spurred by the military need to control access to classified data at differing levels from users at differing clearance levels [ANDE72]. A rough timeline of important historical events in cybersecurity in given in Figure 1-1 [CORB65] [MULT17][WARE70] [TCSE85] [SPAF88] [MILL09] [CERT04] [ICAN07] [LANG13]. *The state of the art is still immature. Nonetheless, much can be accomplished toward designing more trustworthy systems.* This chapter examines the nature of the design and operation of trustworthy systems and explains why they are so critical.

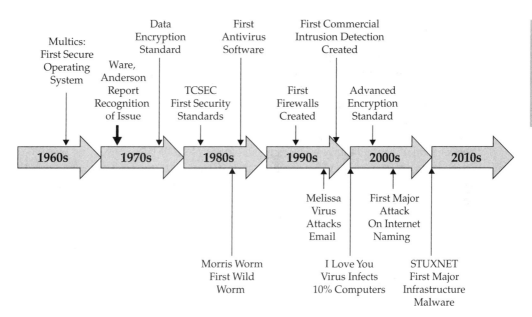

Figure 1-1   History of cybersecurity technologies and attacks

1.1 Baking in Trustworthiness: Design-Time

The title of this book is *Engineering Trustworthy Systems*. First of all, what is a **system**? A system is a collection of components that operate together to achieve some larger function. Most generally, the universe is a system, the Earth is a system, a nation is a system, the election process is a system, your body is a system, and an organization is a system. Although this book's principles generalize to almost all systems, the book focuses on collections of networked computers as systems—also known as information technology (IT).

When the word "system" is used throughout the book, it generally refers to the system being defended (also called the mission system, depending on context) or the cybersecurity subsystem of that defended system. If the term "system" is not qualified with "defended," "mission," or "cybersecurity," then it usually refers to systems in general, or the qualification will be clear from context.

1.1.1 What Is Trust?

Trust is confidence that a system has certain specified properties. One must ask: **trusted** for what? There are a large variety of potential properties including those of reliability. This book focuses on three specific cybersecurity properties: (1) **confidentiality**—trust that the system does not easily leak data deemed by the user to be sensitive (e.g., passwords to one's online bank account), (2) **integrity**—trust that data and the system itself cannot be easily corrupted (which makes integrity the most foundational property), and (3) **availability**—trust that the system will operate in the face of attempts to stop its operation (known as **denial of service** attacks). Taken together, these three essential security properties are known by the acronym CIA—confidentiality, integrity, and availability. Notice that the wording of the definitions is not absolute.

The more general concept under which trustworthiness falls is called **dependability**. Dependability is concerned with properties beyond those of cybersecurity, including reliability, privacy, safety, and many more. As we shall see, a student of cybersecurity is necessarily a student of dependability because cybersecurity must be dependable, and therefore the underlying system must be dependable. This book focuses on the cybersecurity aspect of dependability, which we will refer to as trustworthiness. Further reading on the broader field of dependability is strongly encouraged [NEUM17].

We note up-front that cybersecurity stands in stark contrast with the random failures involved in reliability because cybersecurity involves the more challenging problem of intelligently guided, intentionally induced system failure—what we call cyberattacks. Said another way, trustworthiness is achieved in an environment of active threats, not passive failures.

Realistically, none of cybersecurity properties can be achieved with 100 percent certainty. The ability to achieve them depends on engineering trade-offs made during design (more on this later) and on the resources an **adversary** is willing to invest to defeat these properties. So, trustworthiness refers to the confidence one has that a system dependably achieves its **cybersecurity** properties. The basic anatomy of a top-down attack design is given in Figure 1-2 to help the reader understand the nature of the challenges that a **defender** faces when trying to achieve the desired properties.

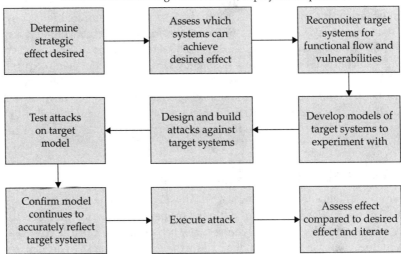

Figure 1-2   Anatomy of a top-down attack design

1.1.2 Trust and Belief

Why do we use the word "trustworthy" and not "trusted"? Historically, the term "trusted systems" arose from the world of computer security, enshrined in documents such as the "Trusted Computer Security Evaluation Criteria (commonly known as "the orange book") [LIPN15]. Trust involves belief. Beliefs can be based on strong evidence or on faith. The term trusted is about a conclusion that someone or some group has drawn about a system. Sometimes conclusions are well-founded, but other times they are not. *Most people trust their computers because they have trouble conceiving that it might not be worthy of their trust.* People often assume that system designers would not sell them an untrustworthy system, or people simply do not pose the question at all. This book uses the term trustworthy to indicate that a system is worthy of being trusted with respect to its stated requirements based on evidence, including the use of cybersecurity engineering principles laid out in this book.

> *Trustworthiness is about well-founded belief.*

1.1.3 Engineering

Why "engineering"? All systems have some level of trustworthiness. It can be explicitly designed in or it can be an accidental side effect. This is true of all system properties. Unfortunately, for many systems, the trustworthiness is a side effect. *The purpose of this book is to enable system designers to explicitly achieve some degree of trustworthiness, dictated by how much is needed for their mission and what they can afford in terms of money and less tangible things such as the impact to mission, time to market, and usability.*

1.1.4 Why Trust?

> *There are only nine meals between mankind and anarchy.*
> —Alfred Henry Lewis

Why do we need to trust systems? Computers have become so ubiquitous that many people do not realize how much society and individuals depend on them. Some people's primary experiences with computers is to send email to their friends or surf the Web, go shopping online, or interact with friends through social media such as Facebook®. It may seem to these people that computers are useful and trustworthiness is nice, but perhaps not essential. *In reality, the most critical of society's functions, including banking, power, telecommunication, oil, and gas, are all critically dependent on computers and increasingly so.* In other words, a severe lack of trustworthiness in systems that operate these critical areas could result in a catastrophic loss of those services.

> *Society inexorably depends on trustworthy systems.*

While emailing one's Aunt Susie may be a nice-to-have item, the power to heat one's home in the winter in the northern latitudes can be a matter of life and death. While losing access to one's bank account for a day may be no big deal, losing the assets in those accounts or destroying the faith in currency is a critical issue with major societal consequences. Therefore, *all systems engineers must have a strong grasp of cybersecurity engineering principles and know when to call in a cybersecurity engineer for help in explicitly engineering trustworthiness in cybersecurity properties.*

1.2 Operational Perspective: Basic Questions

No matter how secure a system is, that system will come under attack. Some attacks will succeed. Table 1-1 gives a sampling of some of the most historically significant, successful attacks [JAMA16][ARN17][STRI17][WEIN12][SPAF88][RILE17][STRO17]. The table is sorted by date of attack and is intended to show a wide range of

- **Types of attack**   confidentiality, integrity, and availability
- **Targets of attacks**   government, industry, and infrastructure
- **Classes of adversaries**   lone hackers, hacktivists, and nation-states
- **Motivations**   experiments gone awry, warfare, espionage, and retribution
- **Levels of damage**   embarrassment, billions of dollars of damage, and assault on sovereignty

#	Name	Description	Target	Year	Effects
1	Morris Worm	Buggy out-of-control net crawler	Internet	1988	$50M
2	Solar Sunrise	Teens hack 500 govt Sun Solaris systems	Govt Sun Solaris	1998	SecDef chagrin
3	DoD/NASA attack	Teen hacks DoD servers; NASA ISS SW	DoD/NASA	1999	Chagrin
4	Melissa Virus	Word virus via attachments/Outlook	Word/ Outlook	1999	$80M
5	MafiaBoy DDos	Targeted attack on commercial websites	Websites	2000	$1.2B
6	Internet Cripple	DDOS on 13 root domain name servers	Internet DNS	2002	Almost huge
7	"Titan Rain"	Enduring and pervasive espionage attack by China on the U.S. government and industry	Government and industry data	2003	Secrecy loss worth billions
8	Estonia Cyberattacks	Sustained cyberwarfare attack from Russia on Estonia banking and government	Estonia	2007	Experiment?
9	Google China	Chinese government allegedly hacks Google	Google	2009	Privacy, IP

Table 1-1   Some Historically Important Cyberattacks (*continued*)

#	Name	Description	Target	Year	Effects
10	Credit Card Fraud	Payment Card Net hacked, millions CCs	Credit cards	2009	Unknown
11	Cyberattack-ROK	DDOS botnet targeting government, finance, news	S. Korea/U.S.	2009	220K infected
12	Stuxnet	1000 Iranian nuclear centrifuges control	Iran	2009	Two-year setback
13	Aurora	China attacks software vendors to modify source	Yahoo, Juniper	2009	Distrust
14	PayPal Payback	Revenge attack on PayPal for suspending WikiLeaks	PayPal	2010	Unknown
15	Cyberattack-CDN	Espionage from China targeting classified data	Canada	2011	Classified data
16	Flame	Windows virus for eavesdropping on victim	Middle East	2012	Unknown
17	Opi Israel	Anti-Israel widespread DDOS to "erase" Israel	Israel	2012	Destabilizing
18	OPM Hack	Probable Chinese compromise of security clearance application forms	OPM	2015	Privacy
19	Wanna Cry	Ransomware worm exploiting a known vulnerability in Windows, with a known patch	Healthcare	2017	230K infected
20	Equifax Hack	143 million people's financial data compromised	U.S. Credit Bureau	2017	Privacy, identity theft

Table 1-1   Some Historically Important Cyberattacks

Cybersecurity is not just a matter of good design; it is also a matter of good operations. When a system comes under attack, it raises some important questions that are important to both operations and design of systems. Let's examine these questions. Table 1-2 summarizes them.

1.2.1 Am I Under Attack?

This seems like a simple question, but answering it can be quite complex and filled with uncertainty. *Modern enterprises of any scale are constantly failing in some way*—some minor, some significant. There is a tendency to assume that all failures are unintended errors in the system design (bugs), often initially resulting in the inability to properly identify a **failure** as resulting from an **attack**. This can delay response, which can lead to more extensive damages than would have otherwise occurred.

#	Question
1	Am I under attack?
2	What is the nature of the attack?
3	What is the mission impact so far?
4	What is the potential mission impact?
5	When did it start?
6	Who is attacking?
7	What are they trying to do?
8	What is their next step?
9	What can I do about it?
10	What are my options and how effective will each be?
11	How will my mitigation actions affect operations?
12	How do I better defend myself in the future?

Table 1-2 Basic Operational Questions Regarding a Security Breach

One can further ask how operators can determine when their system is under attack. This is partly a matter of good design and understanding the residual risks of a system design (where and how it is vulnerable). Good diagnostic tools to determine the locus and nature of system failure are invaluable in addressing the question. Also important are good **intrusion detection systems** (see Section 14.1) that are specifically designed to detect attacks in progress. By **intrusion**, we mean a cyberattack that gains unauthorized access to a system.

As in all systems, *the defender must understand the characteristics of the intrusion detection system itself to understand how to operate it and interpret its results.* One must understand its capability under various conditions of computer and network operations (e.g., traffic load and types) and its **vulnerability** to attack. For example, if an intrusion detection system is blind to certain classes of attacks [TAN02, IGUR08], it is meaningless and indeed misleading to say that the system has detected no attacks without the disclaimer of the attacks that it cannot possibly detect. The dynamics of attack execution are shown in Figure 1-3 to help the reader understand how attacks proceed in general. The attack execution method involves a series of steps, each building on the success of the previous step, guided by strategic goals established as depicted in Figure 1-2. This approach follows what is called a flaw hypothesis methodology that generates plausible event chains to gain access [ABRA95]. See Section 6.1 for further discussion on adversaries and attacks.

> *Understanding cybersecurity mechanism performance is essential.*

1.2.2 What Is the Nature of the Attack?

Assuming operators identify a system failure as an attack, it is important to quickly discern what type of attack it is, where in the system it has succeeded, what it has accomplished, the **mechanism** it is using, and what vulnerability it is exploiting. This information is essential in

Attack execution follows a dynamic pattern that can include gaining a toehold onto a system, escalating privilege to gain more access, reconnoitering to find targets within the system, and then attacking to get to the targets and then attack the targets themselves.

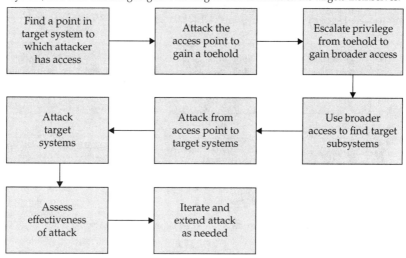

Figure 1-3   Physiology of a bottom-up attack execution example

planning and executing a response to the attack. Responses to attacks take time and resources, and can significantly impact **mission** operations. For example, if a computer **worm** (Figure 1-4) is spreading throughout the network, a response may be to shut down all the routers to prevent further propagation, but that would essentially bring all services to a halt, potentially causing more damage than the attack itself.

Attack Panel: Code Red	
Name	Code Red
Type	Worm
Identified	2001
System Target	Microsoft Internet Information Service
Vulnerability	Buffer Overflow
Mission	Distributed denial of service of specified addresses, including the White House
Prevalence	1-2 million servers (17-33%)
Damage	$2B in lost productivity
Significance	Attack on government infrastructure

Figure 1-4   Attack description: Code Red Worm

Determining the nature of an attack involves being able to capture attack actions in attacking packet sequences and attack code that may be resident or propagating on the defender's enterprise, having tools to quickly analyze packets and code to determine their targets and mechanisms, and having a significant knowledge basis on the nature of existing known attacks from **forensic** organizations that perform that sort of function (e.g., US-Computer Emergency Response Team [CERT]). See Figure 1-5 for a summary of this workflow.

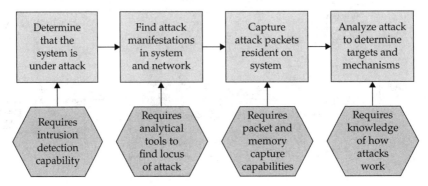

Figure 1-5   Determining the nature of a network-based cyberattack

1.2.3 What Is the Mission Impact So Far?

As an attack unfolds, there is often a "fog of war"—uncertainty over what is going on and how severe the impact is. Further confusing matters for top decision makers is the fact that IT professionals often speak in terms of what servers or devices are affected, not in terms of how mission is impacted. That is because the connection between servers and devices, and their ability to support mission, is not well understood. It is easier to report that server 327 is down and device 18 is not responding—both concrete facts—than it is to say that the **domain name system** (DNS) is run on that server and without DNS, the system cannot operate; therefore, all online retail sales are suspended until that server can be brought back up again. The latter is what a chief executive officer needs, not the former. If one of a thousand servers is down, it is often unimportant, except when it is the only server running a critical function.

The ability to determine mission impact of a system's problem is known as the **mission-mapping** problem. Mission mapping requires having an *a priori* firm understanding about how all subsystems in a system support mission function. It is a hard problem. Fully understanding it in a given system is beyond the state of the art, but with a little know-how, operators can do much with what exists today. This requires an inventory of all devices, computers, and software their location (physical and network) and some description of how mission depends on them and what happens if they are no longer available. Such inventories are useful to plan continuity of operations contingencies and recovery, which are in turn important to improve designs to build in better automated failure recovery, such as moving critical services such as DNS to other computers when their hosts go down.

Knowing mission impact is important in determining viable courses of action in response to the attack. If the impact is minor, the defender must take great care not to overreact and cause more damage than an attack. For example, if a college math major breaks into an enterprise system to "borrow" some supercomputer time to improve the fidelity of one of their simulations, and that enterprise has spare supercomputer capacity, then it would be foolish to do something as draconian as cutting the enterprise off from the Internet in response to that attack.

> *Mission impact assessment is essential to cybersecurity.*

1.2.4 What Is the Potential Mission Impact?

When assessing damage to the mission so far, *it is important to understand how damages can be cascaded.* For example, gaining control of one computer system in the enterprise when there are 10,000 computers is insignificant. If that computer is the master computer for the distribution of all software updates within the enterprise, that minor damage significantly changes the vulnerability profile of the enterprise system. Therefore, *potential damage assessment must be part of the mission impact assessment.* If an adversary is on the cusp of serious damage to mission, then higher-cost and higher-impact actions become viable. *Decision makers must understand not just where the attacker is, but where the attacker is going.* Wayne Gretzky, a famous hockey player, once said, "I skate to where the puck is going to be, not where it has been." Great **mission impact** assessment is the same way.

Predicting mission impact requires defenders to have a firm understanding of mission maps (as described earlier) as well as cascading failure models (an understanding of how one failure can lead to other failures in mutually dependent systems). If an organization "games out" (predicts an opponent's actions and counteractions against defender actions through several moves ahead, using game theory concepts and techniques) a series of critical attacks, this will help them understand how to predict where attacks might be headed [HAMI01, HAMI01a]. This is called a **cyber** playbook [SAYD02] (see Section 23.3 for elaboration).

1.2.5 When Did It Start?

Knowing when the attack started is important to determining damage to the mission that might have been incurred (e.g., what data might have been stolen or what systems may have been corrupted) and when was the last "good" state of the system. Knowing the last good state is essential to determine what system state to **roll back** to, as well as for diagnosing how the attacker got into the system.

1.2.6 Who Is Attacking?

Attribution of cyberattack is one of cybersecurity's top hard problems [IRC05, NICO12, NRC10]. *Just because an attack is coming from a specific machine does not mean that the owner of that machine is malicious.* In fact, more often than not, that attacking computer has been compromised and then used by the attacker; the computer that attacked that computer also is likely to have been attacked, and so on. Knowing the path of the attack is nonetheless helpful because it may be possible to stop the attack by specifically filtering out its packets (by targeting its source Internet Protocol address and ports) at an upstream router in the path from the attacking computers to the victim computers. This may involve eliciting the assistance of a system administrator within the enterprise network, an Internet service provider, or the owner of another system that is upstream of the attack.

Occasionally, it is possible to identify the attacker or attacking organization. Sometimes this can be done by **fingerprinting** the code used—*just like people have fingerprints, attackers have preferred software coding styles and techniques that could identify them.* This is useful to try to hold the attacker accountable through law enforcement, international treaty, or some form of diplomatic public shaming.

1.2.7 What Are They Trying to Do?

Attacks usually come in sequences of attack steps, each of which can itself be considered a separate, but related, attack. The attack sequence usually has some specific goal or function that may, in turn, be part of a larger plan to reach some strategic goal. Rarely do attackers attack just to see if they can get into the system (though that often was the case in the 1970s, when hacking was a hobby of the computer science elite). Rarely is the first step in an attack the only step. Often the attacker is simply trying to "own" the computer so that the attacker can use it in future attacks such as a massively distributed denial of service attack. Sometimes, it is simply an access point (way into the system) to the next access point, to another access point, to increasingly privileged and protected parts of a system. By analyzing the attack sequence so far, it may be possible to predict what subsystem the attacker is going after and what goal they might be trying to achieve.

> *Discerning the attacker's goal improves defense posture.*

1.2.8 What Is the Attacker's Next Step?

As part of attacker goal analysis, it can be important to hypothesize an attacker's next step. Predicting attacker next steps can help optimize the effectiveness of defenses, such as altering preventative rules such as those in firewalls (Figure 1-6) to block the step, or increasing the sensitivity of intrusion detection systems to better detect the step while it is in progress (to either better record it or to shut it down before it succeeds).

Defense Panel: Firewalls	
Type	Perimeter Defense
Capability	Block attacks from outside of system network from coming in.
Means	Filters network traffic from rules-specified Internet addresses, ports, and sometimes with content.
Limitations	Only filters attacks that have been previously identified and for which rules have been written.
Impacts	Restricting network traffic can cause legitimate applications to fail in hard-to-predict ways.
Attack Space	Intended to stop known computer network attacks that come from the outside the system network.

Figure 1-6   Defense description: Firewalls

1.2.9 What Can I Do About It?

Attack sequences take a certain amount of time to execute, as does each attack step. At each stage, there is a potential opportunity for the defender to take action. *The defender has a large repertoire of dynamic defense actions such as changing firewall rules, changing router configurations, changing host security settings such as operating system security settings, and altering intrusion detection settings.* Not all actions are relevant to all attack steps. For example, if a worm is already inside an enterprise system, it does little good (in fact, it could do more harm than good) to disconnect the enterprise from the network from which the worm entered.

With knowledge of how an attack sequence is succeeding and where it is going, a defender can generate a list of possible actions to take, evaluate each in terms of cost and benefit, and decide what action to take. The defender must keep in mind that the clock does not stop during the decision-making process or during the defense execution process. Certain actions may end up being too late. More on the timing of defense tactics will be discussed in a later chapter (see Section 23.3.2).

1.2.10 What Are My Options and How Effective Will Each Option Be?

The previous analysis on possible dynamic actions to take in response to an attack should generate a set of defense options (called **courses of action**). Evaluating how effective each will be depends on the level of knowledge the defender has gained about the mechanism of the attack (how it is succeeding and what it is exploiting) and where the attack seems to be headed. Both of these estimates will have significant uncertainty associated with them. The defender must make the best decision possible given what is currently known. A defense action could be to gain more information about what is happening before or during some other defense action. *The defender should keep in mind the tyranny of time—waiting for certainty could mean total loss of mission.*

1.2.11 How Will My Mitigation Actions Affect Operation?

As part of the cost-benefit analysis of possible courses of action, understanding each action's potential negative mission impact is essential. For example, blocking all web traffic on port 80 could block revenue-generating sales or cause real-time control systems to fail unexpectedly. *The time to figure out the mission impact of possible courses of action is prior to having to use them.* To do that effectively, the defender must understand how their mission depends on the underlying information technology infrastructure [HAMI01, HAMI01a]. See Section 22.4 for details on this point.

1.2.12 How Do I Better Defend Myself in the Future?

As important as it is to successfully defend against a given attack, it can be even more important to extract important lessons learned from the attack to help defend against future attacks. How did the attack proceed? What defense choices were made? Why? Were they effective? What was the level of damage? What would the level of damage have been if action was swifter or different? How should the defense be altered to prevent similar classes of attacks in the future, and how can detection and response systems be amended to improve the decisions made next time? *These are all questions that must be answered after each major attack if a defender hopes to be on a cycle of continuous improvement and to get ahead of the escalating attacker capabilities.*

1.3 Asymmetry of Cyberspace Effects

Cyberspace is a complex hyper dimensional space that is much different than physical space, which is three-dimensional. This makes dynamic cybersecurity control (see Section 23.1) extraordinarily difficult.

The human mind often grasps new ideas by analogy. Analogies can be an effective way of quickly learning concepts with many similar subconcepts. At the same time, analogies have limitations and can cause errors in thinking about a problem like cyberspace. Table 1-3 enumerates some of the important ways that cyberspace differs from physical space. These attributes will be discussed in turn.

	Physical Space	**Cyberspace**
Understandability	Intuitive	Nonintuitive
Dimensionality	Three dimensions	Thousands of dimensions
Nonlinearity	Kinetic munition effects are well understood	Nonlinear effects (e.g., area/sphere of influence, persistence, "yield")
Coupling	Interdependencies generally understood	Complexities of information use complicate interdependency issues
Velocity	Most attacks exist at perceptible speeds	Attacks may aggregate too slowly to be perceived, while others occur in milliseconds
Manifestation	Most attacks have physical manifestations	Often no physical manifestations until it is too late
Detectability	Overrun and compromise are easily detectable	Compromise may not be detected at all

Table 1-3   Asymmetric Nature of Cyberspace Compared to Physical Space

1.3.1 Dimensionality

Contrasted with three-dimensional physical space, cyberspace has dimensionality in the thousands. This makes it difficult to conceive of how attacks move and how defenses can prevent and control attacks. For example, the physical borders of a country are distinct. An invasion must cross one of those borders. Whereas in cyberspace, systems are connected by networks without much regard for borders. Software in a system comes from hundreds of different sources, all of which could have been compromised somewhere in the life cycle of that software. So, attacks can seem to come from nowhere when they emerge from inside the defender's own system. It is a sort of "fifth column" where the citizenry (in this case, computers) can be co-opted against the defender [REMY11].

1.3.2 Nonlinearity

Nonlinearity refers to the property that outputs resulting from a series of system inputs do not increase proportionally. There are two distinct aspects of nonlinearity—causes and effects. By causes, I refer to the investment that it takes to mount a cyberattack. For nuclear war, there is a significant "barrier to entry"—investment required to be able to perform some activity such as waging nuclear war. For cyberattacks, the investment is primarily one of time and a modicum of skill. *One can download malicious software from the Internet, customize it, and point it at a target and immediately do significant damage with little risk.* Similarly, there is a nonlinearity of effect. In physical space, a bomb has a specific range of effect. In cyberspace, the footprint of damage within cyberspace can be highly unpredictable, especially when self-propagating attacks (e.g., worms) are used. The effects of unleashing a simple program can be quite large [SPAF88].

1.3.3 Coupling

Systems are coupled in ways that are difficult to understand—that is, their behavior is connected because of subtle interdependencies. A humorous description of distributed systems is "one in which the failure of a computer you didn't even know existed can render your own computer unusable" (attributed to Leslie Lamport). A famous example of this is the dependency of modern networked systems on the domain name system (DNS). The DNS translates human-understandable names such as "en.wikipedia.org" into a computer-understandable Internet address that is a hierarchical set of numbers much like a phone number. *Without DNS, much of the Internet comes to a screeching halt.* There are many other examples such as license servers for licensed software, authorization and authentication servers, routers and routing tables (paths to other computers) to access the network beyond your local computer, and cloud providers that host critical content. *This coupling of systems creates the increased dimensionality of cyberspace and is one of the key factors that makes nonlinear effects possible* (such as changing one entry in a routing table or falsely advertising a shortcut path that could crash large swaths of the Internet).

> *Cyberspace interdependencies breed nonlinearity.*

1.3.4 Velocity

Data travels on networks at nearly the speed of light. In theory, data could travel around the Earth 7.5 times in one second. With switches and routers, data travels a bit slower than that, but this sets the right order of magnitude. Attacks are generally somewhat slower than that because they often need to attack multiple computers in sequence, and so they are limited by the amount of time required to take over a computer and then set up and perform the next attack step in the sequence. This all creates an order of magnitude slowdown from seconds to minutes, but *attacks are still incredibly fast compared to human decision and reaction times.* For example, it is possible to have an attack propagate worldwide in 15 minutes [STAN02].

As another example, the average computer is attacked within four minutes after being connected to the network [HUTC08].

> *Cyberattacks can propagate beyond human decision speeds.*

1.3.5 Manifestation

For a nation to engage in a ground war, they have to reposition assets such as tanks and mobilize troops. This takes time, and the signs are pretty clear. Mobilizing for a cyberattack can be done quite stealthily. The attacker can take over many computers in preparation for attack and can pre-position malicious software (**malware**) inside of the defender's systems that can be exploited when it comes time to perform that attack. Attacks can hide within network traffic by going "low and slow"—riding on other network traffic and performing actions such as **network reconnaissance** slowly enough to not trigger alarms from intrusion detection systems. Once an attacker has successfully compromised a computer, the evidence can be erased from audit logs, and the software code implementing the attack sequence can be hidden on the compromised computer (e.g., by ensuring that the attacker's process does not appear in the process table listing or so that the attack code only appears in the running image of software, never on disk).

1.3.6 Detectability

When a physical attack succeeds, the effects are often obvious, the damage is clear, or the presence of occupying forces is clear. Cyberattack effects are much less obvious. **Espionage**—stealing data—can be hard to detect. *The loss can be amplified by the defender not even knowing that the data was lost, so that the attacker can exploit the data as well as the element of surprise that they know the data.* For example, if a company's negotiating position is known to a company with whom they are making a deal, that data can be exploited to create a much better deal for the company that possesses the other company's position. Had the losing company known that their negotiation position was stolen, they would at least have had the option of withdrawing from a deal or completely changing the nature of a deal. Similarly, for **sabotage**—whereby a system's integrity is undermined—an attacker can completely "own" (i.e., control) a defender's system and do what they intend without the defender knowing that the attacker has achieved that level of sabotage.

1.4 The Cybersecurity Solution Landscape

There are many important aspects of the cybersecurity solution landscape. With the bewildering array of different products and the explosion of terminology, sometimes just for marketing purposes, it can be difficult to see the forest for the trees. This section provides a quick high-level overview of the types of solutions. Figure 1-7 shows how these types of solutions relate and build on one another.

1. Information Assurance Science and Engineering forms the foundation of the solution space "map," (see Section 25.4).

2. Defensive Mechanisms such as firewalls and encryption are the building blocks of security (see Section 8.1).

3. Cyber Command and Control constitutes the brains and muscles of cybersecurity, making and executing decisions to dynamically defend against evolving attack situations (see Section 23.1).

4. Cyber Situation Awareness provides a broad strategic view of what is happening in the system as far as possible attacks and what the implications to mission might be.

5. Cybersensors and Exploitation solutions provide the data to detect relevant attack events to feed Cyber Situation Understanding (see Section 22.1).

6. Cyber Defense Strategy represents knowledge developed through experience, experimentation, and theory on how to understand and control a system to properly defend it (see Section 23.2).

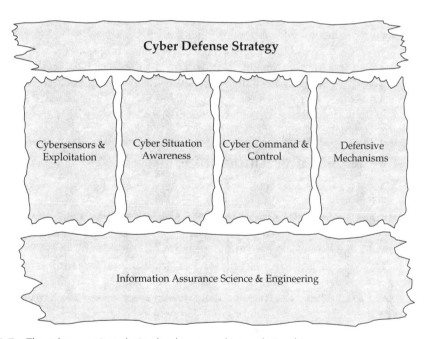

Figure 1-7   The cybersecurity solution landscape and interrelationships

1.4.1 Information Assurance Science and Engineering

At cybersecurity's foundation is knowledge of what cybersecurity is and how best to use its mechanisms and principles. This is an often-neglected aspect of the field. Indeed, that is one of the main motivations for this book. The codification of systems engineering knowledge is needed to understand how to use cybersecurity technology and techniques effectively to thwart attacks and preserve mission. It is here where one explores how attacks manifest so that **cybersensors** can be properly designed to detect manifestations (see Section 13.2), for example.

1.4.2 Defensive Mechanisms

The collection of all cybersecurity mechanisms installed throughout the enterprise constitutes the defense mechanisms. Defense mechanisms include subsystems such as firewalls, audit, **authentication**, **authorization**, malware detection, intrusion detection, intrusion prevention systems, and operating and system configurations. Some mechanisms are static, some are configurable at boot time, and some are dynamically reconfigurable during the operation of the system. Some are preventative systems that block attacks, some detect attack, and some recover from attacks. Those that detect are part of the cybersensors; those that are dynamically reconfigurable are part of cyber **actuation**, which adjusts configuration in response to attacks (see Section 23.1).

1.4.3 Cybersensors and Exploitation

A cybersensor detects some manifestation of a cyberattack (see Section 13.2). All **sensors** have their strengths, weaknesses, and blind spots, all of which can vary with the dynamically changing environment. Cybersensors produce data that needs to be exploited by correlation with other sensor data and to distinguish true attack detection from false alarms. The union of all sensors needs to cover the full breadth of the attack space. Further, the way the sensors are placed and configured within the system, the sensor architecture (see Section 15.1), is highly relevant to detecting attacks. It needs to be carefully considered. The state of the art is such that only a small fraction of attacks is detected [SANTI15]. These issues will be discussed in detail in later chapters.

1.4.4 Cyber Situation Understanding

Knowing that an attack has occurred or is occurring is only the beginning of the process [ONWU11]. As discussed in the earlier section on questions that must be answered, the defender must understand the gravity of the attack in terms of mission impact, potential impact to mission in terms of what further attacks the attack opens up, what the adversary's goals might be so the defender has insight into the attacker's next "move," and the courses of action that are available to the defender. **Cyber situation understanding** requires a deep understanding of how an enterprise system connects to the supporting mission, what the attack space is, and how the attack interacts with the enterprise system to change the risk profile by changing the vulnerabilities to the system as the attacker succeeds with each new attack step.

1.4.5 Cyber Actuation

In the same way that sensors form the foundation of situation understanding, cyber actuation forms the foundation for actions formulated by **command and control**. Actuators perform actions to alter the dynamic configuration of the system defenses. Actuation could include changing a firewall rule, reconfiguring a router or switch, reconfiguring an operating system to change how it responds, altering the security subsystem to require different levels or types of authentication or authorization, or changing the parameters of intrusion detection systems to increase the sensitivity to better detect attacks. Actuation is often a series of **human-in-the-loop** actions (those that require human intervention as opposed to fully automated) that must be manually run to accomplish some change. This can be slow and error-prone. *Errors in actuation can have grave consequences,* such as misconfiguring a router that causes the entire enterprise to go offline. Previously thought-through scripts encompassing multiple actions need to be developed in advance and properly secured so that only highly privileged and highly authenticated users can invoke them, and so that they can be executed quickly.

> *Actuation infrastructure needs to be set up in advance.*

1.4.6 Cyber Command and Control

Having a palette of possible actions that can be executed quickly and in a properly orchestrated manner is a good foundation, but a decision-support process to decide *what* to do, particularly under the stress of an ongoing attack, is the higher-level brain function of the system. Command is about properly issuing the decision, once made, to the right actuation systems. Control is about ensuring that the command is properly executed and that it's effective; this assessment is fed back into another command and control cycle. The actual decision-support process is also part of command and control. It consists of a playbook to determine the strategies that would be effective as a function of the situation the enterprise is in. The playbook is therefore deeply connected to cyber situation understanding, since certain plays make sense only in certain situations and since the criteria for deciding the best play also depend on the state of the system and the state of the attack.

1.4.7 Cyber Defense Strategy and Tactics

The knowledge to determine which commands will be most effective in which situation is the crux of defense **cyber strategy and tactics**. An old saying is that *wisdom comes from unwise actions.* Similarly, strategy and tactics knowledge comes from the analysis of attack-defense encounters—what worked, what did not. The notion of gaining the high ground in a physical battle almost certainly came from ancient conflicts where those who did not have the high ground lost. Similarly, *analyses of attack encounters are the basis of strategy and tactics knowledge.* This includes the epidemiological knowledge of other people's encounters (that is why it is important to openly share the essence of these experiences as publicly as possible) as well as simulated encounters in exercises or even gedanken encounters (hypothesized thought experiments). This knowledge, combined with knowledge engineering and game theory, forms the basis of this emerging cybersecurity arena that is still in its infancy.

> *Strategy and tactics knowledge comes from attack encounters.*

1.5 Ounces of Prevention and Pounds of Cure

Certainly, an ounce of prevention is often worth a pound of cure. To the extent that attacks can be easily prevented, they should be. Detecting attacks and recovering from damage caused by attacks can be very expensive.

At the same time, there are two cases where the old adage cannot be applied blindly. First, preventing certain attacks can simply be too costly in terms of cost or mission impact on the system (performance or functionality, for example). An analogy holds with the computer operating system design problem of deadlock prevention versus deadlock detection and recovery. The performance impact of preventing operating system deadlocks is often unacceptable [PETE83], but it turns out that if deadlocks are caught quickly enough and recovered from, the users never even notice and no harm is done [COUL12]. One must consider this sort of trade-off in cybersecurity design.

Second, even when an ounce of prevention is applied, it still can be valuable to invest in a pound of cure—the ability to detect and respond to an attack that was intended to be prevented. Prevention mechanisms can sometimes fail or even be successfully hacked, and so detection-response, which appears to be redundant, may save the day when it is the last line of defense. Also, sometimes prevention mechanisms such as firewalls can be bypassed by insiders who inserted malicious code directly on an enterprise computer within the boundary of the firewall.

In summary, prevention and detect-response techniques are not mutually exclusive and work best when used in concert and sometimes in overlapping manners to achieve the best results, as will be discussed in the sections on layered architecture (see Section 13.1 and 20.5).

Conclusion

This chapter gave a 50,000-foot overview of both the cybersecurity problem space and the solution space with broad brushstrokes. The intention is to give the reader an idea of the big picture and how aspects of cybersecurity cohesively hang together. The next chapter continues the big picture with setting the right frame of mind and perspective needed to become an effective cybersecurity strategic thinker.

To summarize:

- Trustworthiness of a system is a fundamental property of a system that must be designed into the system from the outset.
- The quest for trustworthy systems raises many questions relating to cybersecurity and other attributes, including operational questions relating to dealing with attacks.
- Compared to physical attacks, cyberattacks are unique in speed, magnitude of effect given small effort, and stealth.
- The cybersecurity solution space involves a complex mix of design and dynamic control.
- Cybersecurity engineering involves many delicate trade-offs with mission.

Questions

1. Why must cybersecurity be designed into a system as opposed to being added after a system is created? Discuss how to make legacy systems secure given this principle.

2. What are the operational questions that must be answered by cybersecurity? Discuss other important operational questions and considerations and why they also might be important to answer.

3. Why is cybersecurity particularly challenging to a defender compared to physical security? What does asymmetric threat mean and how does it apply? Discuss the implications of asymmetric threat to the problem of architecting an effective defense.

4. What are the aspects of the cybersecurity solution space and how do they relate to one another? Discuss the nature of the relationship between all the pairings of solution aspects and their implication to design.

5. What are some of the important engineering trade-offs between cybersecurity and other aspects of system function? Discuss the nature of these trade-offs and the criteria that one might use to make trade-off decisions.

CHAPTER 2

Cybersecurity Right-Think

Overview

Learning Objectives

- Learn that the primary metric of cybersecurity is risk and its components.
- Understand the trade-off space between security and aspects of mission.
- Describe the connection between understanding attacks and how to defend systems.
- Understand the nature of the especially high risk at interfaces between systems.
- Define how top-down and bottom-up design approaches are both useful in cybersecurity.

This chapter is about how to *think* about cybersecurity. It will give you a perspective on how to keep sight of a forest in the midst of millions of trees and how to distinguish the issues that matter most from those that can be safely ignored. The idea is to help create a mind-set that will serve you in all aspects of what you learn about cybersecurity in order to give you a frame of reference on which to hang the knowledge.

2.1 It's About Risk

In the end, understanding cybersecurity is about understanding risk, where it comes from, and how to effectively reduce it for reasonable cost and small impacts to mission. **Risk** is the bottom-line metric of cybersecurity. When looking at a **countermeasure** and deciding whether it is useful, one should ask to what degree it decreases risk in both the near term and the long term.

Risk has two important components: likelihood of something bad happening to mission and how bad those somethings are. System designs can decrease the probability and reduce the quantity and degree of bad outcomes. Probability can be affected by defenders making the attacker's job harder, more expensive, or riskier to them. Quantity of bad outcomes can be altered by the way the system is architected—for example, one could decide to not store the most sensitive information on computers at all. There will be more discussion about how to manage risk in sections to come (see Sections 4.1 and 7.1). The point of this section is to convey that risk is the bottom-line goodness metric of system cybersecurity. *If a defense is not measurably either decreasing the probability of successful attack or decreasing the damage that can result from a cyberattack, then one must question the utility of such defenses.*

> *Cybersecurity is about understanding and mitigating risk.*

2.2 The Cybersecurity Trade-off: Performance and Functionality

Cybersecurity experts like to believe that security is the most important part of a system—that is a delusion that leads to wrong-headed thinking that will likely have the opposite effect of what a designer seeks. *The reality is that cybersecurity is always in a trade-off with mission functionality, which has two important dimensions: performance and functionality.*

Funds spent on cybersecurity are resources not spent on mission. Secure systems engineering is about optimizing mission, which is about minimizing risk to mission, not about maximizing cybersecurity.

> ## *Cybersecurity is always in a trade-off with mission functions.*

Even for cybersecurity zealots who mistakenly believe that cybersecurity is the number one requirement of any system, a design always ends up at some point in the cybersecurity mission trade-off space. Engineers can either design to a specific point or a dynamic range of points that can be carefully controlled, or they can be stuck with wherever this trade-off falls from the set of decisions they make. Good engineers will work with mission owners to understand the right trade-off and will engineer a system to achieve the desired points in the trade-off space. Figure 2-1 notionally depicts that trade-off space.

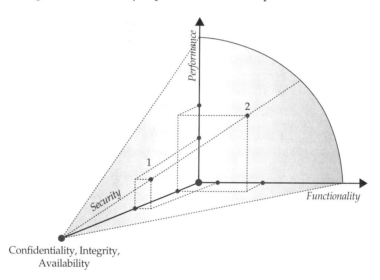

Figure 2-1   The cybersecurity-functionality-performance trade-off

A system reconfiguration or dynamic change of parameters should be able to move the system smoothly from one point to another in response to a dynamically changing situation. Because the defender's situation is highly complex and varying, there is no one optimized trade-off that is best for all situations. The defender must allow the system a wide range of maneuvers and must enable operators to know when and how to move between those trade-off points.

Other aspects of mission that are traded off against security are user-friendliness, time to market, employee morale, missed opportunity, opportunity cost, quantity of service or product, quality of service or product, cost of service or product, and limited resources such as computing and power, space, and cooling (see Table 2-1). Carefully considering these trade-offs as part of the upfront engineering process can turn typically contentious battles into productive dialogue between mission and cybersecurity experts that can significantly improve the system design to better satisfy both sets of requirements.

#	Aspect	Example
1	User-friendliness	Having to remember passwords is inconvenient and cumbersome.
2	Time to market	Some security requirements could delay time to market.
3	Employee morale	Reviewing security logs can be mind-numbing and frustrating for some employees.
4	Missed opportunity	Because cybersecurity can impact both performance and functionality, some mission opportunities may no longer be viable.
5	Opportunity cost	Often, investment is a zero-sum game, so resources invested in cybersecurity means resources not invested in mission functionality.
6	Quantity of service or product	Cybersecurity is an overhead and typically takes away some fraction of system resources that could be used to produce more product or service.
7	Quality of service or product	Cybersecurity is an overhead and typically takes away some fraction of system resources that could be used to produce a higher-quality product or service.
8	Cost of service or product	Cybersecurity is an overhead and therefore increases the cost of a service or product.
9	Limited resources such as computing and power, space, and cooling	Cybersecurity consumes system resources, which are often a zero-sum game such that use for cybersecurity means that those resources are unavailable for mission.

Table 2-1   Factors that Trade Off with Security

2.2.1 User-Friendliness

Cybersecurity can make systems harder to use. For example, users having to carry around a special token, such as a smart card, to authenticate themselves may seem like a minor burden, but it is an added inconvenience that makes the system less easy and less pleasant to use. Tightening down security so that users can access only what they can prove they need to know creates a burden to identify the need, prove the need, then register the need, and administer the authorizations. In addition, such tightening severely reduces the opportunity for discovery of key data that may be needed, but the need cannot be known upfront. For example, perhaps the marketing department could mine the customer service database to discover how to make the organization's product better. Unless that synergy is understood and planned for upfront, that synergy will be lost. Many modern architectures are starting to leverage and enable the notion of facilitating discovery of both data and services to make systems more adaptable and evolvable as mission and technology change.

Cybersecurity can impede some of the advantages of information sharing and collaboration innovations. As the 9/11 Commission observed [NCTA04], failing to share can be disastrous in causing the failure to correlate important data that might have averted the 9/11 attack on the U.S. twin towers. Lastly, the requirements for vetting employees to establish their trustworthiness can be so intrusive as to repel highly qualified workers from even applying for jobs, thus restricting an organization's labor pool and reducing potential innovation and productivity improvements.

Trade-off Example   Requiring authorization prior to accessing data and services is both potentially important and cumbersome. A balance might be to require pre-authorization for the 5 or 10 percent of the most sensitive data and services, and simply allow audited, but free, access within an enterprise to the remainder. The audit logs can be analyzed in near-real time, and abuses can be investigated and discussed with employees on an as-needed exceptional basis. This allows the enterprise to reap the majority of the benefit gained by trusting employees and by serendipitous discovery, while preserving the majority of important parts of authorized access to data and services.

2.2.2 Time to Market

It is well known that time to market can make or break a product or service—particularly when the business objective is to establish market dominance by becoming a de facto standard (e.g., Windows). Imposing security requirements often leads to delays in creating new capabilities supporting the organization's mission. The reason is simple: adding new requirements to a system of any kind makes it more complex, requiring more effort, more review, and more testing. Sometimes, security expertise within an organization is backlogged because there aren't enough experts to go around, and so this can also lead to further delay. Each day of delay translates into missed profit or missed accomplishment of mission that could be critical to the future success of an organization. Given that security is about managing risk, adding onerous security requirements, if not balanced properly, can have the effect of increasing the risk to an organization.

Trade-off Example   Often, requirements are placed on new software to interface with the cybersecurity authorization and authentication services and enforce their decisions and audit all access transactions. This can delay time to market, particularly if the developer has to find a security consultant to do the development. A trade-off can be made to perform the **authentication**, **authorization**, and auditing through a proxy service that front-ends the service and performs these functions for it. Later, when there is more time, the security services can be better integrated into the service itself.

2.2.3 Employee Morale

Creating a secure environment through personnel security processes, such as background investigations, and cybersecurity processes, such as registering to use services and data, can create an atmosphere of distrust and repression. Further, in addition to the natural need to want to feel trusted, employees want to feel productive [PINK11] and enabled. Cybersecurity constraints can limit productivity because of both the need to perform security-related tasks (such as taking security reminder courses every year) and because the security-related tasks can get in the way of other mission tasks that need to be performed (waiting for an approval to use some new data or service). Employees can eventually feel untrusted and thwarted from realizing their full potential. *This feeling can be lethal to creativity and innovation*. People with such tendencies could either suppress their creativity or leave the organization entirely. The loss is hard to measure, but it can be very real and can suck the life out of a great organization.

Trade-off Example Allowing employees to prove their cybersecurity awareness through passing an exam achieves the desired goal of ensuring that employees understand how to conduct themselves properly while sparing them having to review the same material over and over again each year. Also, minimizing the number of services and data sets for which they need to get pre-authorization, as discussed earlier, gives them a sense of being more trusted and can improve morale.

2.2.4 Missed Opportunity

Sometimes, opportunities have narrow time windows—a now-or-never moment. For example, there may be a launch window for a spacecraft relating to the configuration of planetary orbits that comes around only every few decades, or observation of an event such as a supernova that is unique. A more commercial example would be an action-figure product release timed with release of a movie when interest is highest. Such requirements place timing constraints on the development of a new capability. Delaying could mean that the opportunity window would be missed. Other requirements may impose a certain level of computational performance, such as real-time rendering of animation or music. If security requirements were to degrade performance below a certain threshold, then it is no longer possible to create the capability. In such cases, security actually can block the creation of an important new capability if not properly thought through.

Trade-off Example Often performance is an important issue, and adding fine-grained security controls could make performance unacceptable. A trade-off would be to either create coarse-grained security controls or create dedicated operation. One can achieve dedicated operation by using virtualized environments so that users at different sensitivity levels are architecturally separated from one another. Such a design means obviates the need for security to be checked on a per-transaction basis.

2.2.5 Opportunity Cost

Resources, including human capital, spent on security are not spent on mission. Security is an investment and should be held to a standard of return-on-investment to mission in the same way that all other investments are held—though the return is not just in terms of profit. If 5 percent of a company's talent pool is working exclusively on security, might they have invented some new interesting mission capability if they had the chance? Similarly, if all workers are spending 10 minutes each day feeding the security machine (performing security-related tasks such as logging on or refreshing their security identification material), that is 10 minutes not thinking about mission. That 10 minutes multiplied by thousands of employees multiplied by thousands of days adds up to a significant investment. What important opportunities are missed by that investment? Is there a way to make it 9 minutes or 8 minutes? Can one apply the **Pareto 80/20 Rule** [KOCH11] and find a way to get 80 percent of the security value for 20 percent of the cost—in this case, cost being time?

Trade-off Example As enterprises are applying more and more policies and restrictions on login, the login process is taking more and more time. Systems could be designed to immediately allow users access to local resources and commonly available network resources until the entire network **policy** and checks are done. This way, the user can become immediately productive while waiting on some of the more sensitive resources on the network.

2.2.6 Quantity of Service or Product

In today's information economy, the quantity of service or product that can be created is often a function of the information technology resources brought to bear in support of creating the product or service. If one is in the business of selling information technology services directly, such as cloud or computational services, then the effect is very direct and apparent. Any resources used for cybersecurity (indeed, system management of any type) are unavailable to be sold as a service to consumers and therefore represent a loss of profit. As another example, if an organization performs intense data analysis and its value is the product of that analysis, overhead such as cybersecurity directly subtracts from the pool of resources available—including storage, network bandwidth, and computation. Cybersecurity can have significant storage requirements for audit and intrusion detection data, significant bandwidth requirements to transmit such data within the enterprise, and significant computation to analyze the data for attacks and abuse. The requirements can sometimes rival the resources required by the mission itself.

Trade-off Example   *The organization should consider defining and enforcing "budgets" on the cybersecurity components' use of system resources.* Such budgets ensure that the trade-off is made explicitly and force thought and planning and rationale behind the budgets. Such budgets can avoid cybersecurity slowly eating far into mission resources, well beyond what decision makers realize and want. Such budget policies also ensure that the trade-off is controllable and dynamic to adjust to changing situations and environments. Such budgets may drive innovative solutions whereby data is at least partially analyzed at the edge of the network where it is collected, and only the most pertinent "golden nuggets" are communicated for further analysis.

2.2.7 Quality of Service or Product

Similar to quantity, the quality of an organization's product or service can be a function of its available system resources. Often analyses are bounded by the resources available. For example, algorithms to find the optimum solution are often exponential with the number of elements in the set being analyzed. As the size of the number of elements gets into the thousands, hundreds of thousands, or even millions, calculating the true optimal solution is often not feasible. Heuristics are then used to calculate approximate optimums. Optimization plays a key role in business success—such as minimizing overhead of material used in manufacturing or planning the least expensive path to travel to multiple cities (known as the traveling salesman problem [CORM93]). Often, the quality of the approximation of optimal is a function of the amount of computing resources dedicated to the process. Decreasing that amount due to any overhead activity, such as security, can lead to suboptimal solutions, which can reduce the quality of result and create waste and losses for an organization. For the reasons discussed under the section on quantity, cybersecurity's use of systems resources should be carefully managed and policed to ensure that it is an optimal or near-optimal trade-off with mission goals.

Trade-off Example   In some cases, cybersecurity processes are allocated their own dedicated hardware to run on, instead of pulling from the same pool of resources that the rest of mission systems use (a regimen called elastic computing [YADA10]). The upside of the scheme of dedicated resources is (a) better cybersecurity because potentially malicious software running within mission software could "break out" of the virtual environment and attack the security mechanisms, which could have catastrophic consequences to the enterprise; and (b) the security system cannot consume more resources than are allocated to it and therefore cannot interfere with mission (at least in terms of storage and computation, network bandwidth is almost always shared). The downside is that the IT budget is almost always a **zero-sum game**, so funds allocated for cybersecurity resources are not allocated to mission resources. When functionality is segregated, it usually leads to more idle time because the resources have to be sized to handle load surges, and such surges are not the common case. Therefore, the segregation (a) creates inefficiency in the utilization of resources, depriving mission of resources it could have had (the residual capacity of the dedicated resources of security), and (b) limits the level of surge the cybersecurity system can use in case there is a serious emergency that absolutely requires it to consume additional mission resources (e.g., there is a major attack going on, and more data collection and analysis are needed to find its source and shut it down).

2.2.8 Cost of Service or Product

In the same way that there is an opportunity cost for non-monetary resources discussed earlier, there are similar opportunity costs associated with monetary resources. If an organization spends $1M on cybersecurity, that represents $1M that is not being invested in mission, and some new capability or improvement is blocked. These costs take many forms and should be accounted for in all of their forms. There is the obvious direct cost of cybersecurity mechanisms themselves, such as authentication and authorization systems, antivirus software licenses, and firewalls. There is the additional development cost imposed by security requirements on mission systems to properly integrate security. Additional operations and maintenance costs are associated with the cybersecurity subsystems as well as the aspects of the mission systems that have security elements in them. For example, a myriad of security mechanisms on the network, hosts, and devices can make debugging a network access failure (meaning one system that needs access to another suddenly loses the ability to communicate) extremely difficult and thus can increase cost, delay, and mission impacts substantially.

Trade-off Example   Security mechanisms often achieve overlapping coverage of the **attack space**—the sphere of all possible attack types and instances against an enterprise. Although overlap can be good in creating backup and **defense in depth**, an enterprise can only afford x dollars of security. It is more important to ensure the best possible coverage of the attack space, particularly the high-probability attack space, than to redundantly cover some portions and leave other portions unprotected entirely. In trading off with mission functionality, it is important to understand the difference between the marginal gain from redundant covering of a portion of the already covered attack space compared to covering a gap area. The relative gain should be stacked up against the return on building mission functionality with competing investment. This topic will be covered more deeply in Sections 8.2 and 8.3.

2.2.9 Limited Resources

Sometimes an organization's information technology infrastructure is limited by factors other than just money. For example, a government organization may be limited to a certain number of square feet per employee. Another example might be that the local electrical company cannot deliver more power due to limits in the distribution or generation infrastructure. A third example may be that there just is not enough cooling capacity to cool all the computers within the space allowed. This triad is sometimes known as the power, space, and cooling (PSC) constraint. There are certainly other such constraints. Cybersecurity, by virtue of taking up system resources, uses up these finite resources and blocks mission from using those resources, irrespective of financial budgets.

Trade-off Example   Sometimes additional funding gets earmarked for cybersecurity in reaction to some cybersecurity crisis in the world or in that organization. These funds, in some sense, do not come out of the mission budget since it is "found money." Because of limited resources such as power, space, and cooling, such investments can still displace mission because the limitations cannot be expanded with money. Limited resources become a zero-sum game and create a cybersecurity-mission trade-off that needs to be carefully considered, as discussed earlier.

2.3 Theories of Security Come from Theories of Insecurity

The notion of cybersecurity requires the defender to answer the question: "defend against what?" *To understand cybersecurity, one must understand how systems are breached.* This means the defender must understand system vulnerabilities and attacker capabilities against those vulnerabilities. *Ideally, expert defenders are expert attackers.* One must understand attacks from both a strategic and tactical perspective. A strategic perspective means understanding how to accomplish some high-level adversarial goal by a series of plausible attacks made in combination against specific target systems. A tactical perspective means to understand how specific attack steps are accomplished, such as how to breach a firewall or how a self-propagating worm works. *In short, theories of security come from theories of insecurity* [PROT84]. See Section 18.3 for further discussion on this topic.

> *Theories of security come from theories of insecurity.*

2.4 They Come at You Through the Weeds

Systems are difficult to design. Implementations of any appreciable size are full of undetected bugs. There are always misunderstandings between engineers designing two subsystems that are meant to work together in a particular way. Even for well-designed systems, there is always some subcomponent that is broken at any given time [GALL77]. These facts taken together are exploited by attackers. *Attackers thrive in the murky waters of poor design and implementation and in the turbulence of partial system failures.*

> **Attackers await and leverage faults of all types.**

A simple, non-security-related example would be one system calling a square-root function offered by another system as a service. The designer of the square-root function implicitly assumes that any caller of the service is going to only supply positive numbers. The caller, on the other hand, being an electrical engineer, knows that the square root of negative numbers is indeed defined on the imaginary number line and this is part of complex numbers, which play a key role in understanding wave propagation. So, in this case, the caller expected a completely general implementation of the square-root function, whereas the service provider incorrectly assumed that it would be called with the more common limitation of positive numbers. This mismatch in assumptions could cause the square-root function to fail catastrophically, particularly if (a) the service provider does not check the sign of the input provided to the function before performing operations on it, and (b) the caller of the square-root service does not check the returned value to ensure that it makes sense before using it.

In the realm of cybersecurity, another type of assumption failure leads to what is known as a **buffer overflow vulnerability**. If the provider of a service does not check the length and type of input before processing it, the caller can exploit this error by providing it an unexpected string, such as a very long string. That long string could have malicious code at the end of the input that can then find its way into the execution stack of the service provider, thus enabling the caller to take control of the service.

2.5 Top-Down Meets Bottom-Up

Put two or more engineers in a room and they will argue endlessly about the virtues of top-down or bottom-up design—whichever happens to be their favorite. Feuds will start and objects will be thrown around the room.

The reality is that good designers of both attacks and defenses must use both, seeing a system from many different perspectives, with each perspective bringing an important part of the system into best focus. Top-down design is excellent when the engineer is starting totally from scratch—a rare luxury. Even for systems with substantial legacy or systems that are out of scope of the system designers, it is essential to have a good top-down understanding of system requirements and how cybersecurity requirements fit within those system requirements. A good designer should be able to summarize the entirety of the cybersecurity requirements in one page to ensure that the big picture stays in focus even as they are further refined. For example, if one has a lab in which one is analyzing malicious code to understand how it works to better defend against it, one might have a requirement that says "don't let bad stuff out, but let the knowledge gained by examining the bad stuff freely flow out." Of course, a good cybersecurity engineer must iteratively elaborate the cybersecurity requirements into multiple layers of abstraction, but the top level keeps the cybersecurity goals in focus (see Section 19.2 for discussion on modularity and abstraction).

> *Good cybersecurity engineering requires multiple perspectives.*

Bottom-up design is required because at some point there is only a certain palette of building blocks from which to construct a secure system. These building blocks, or even combinations of building blocks forming a design pattern, may be the components of the system from which the design is realized. These building blocks must be well-characterized, and it must be clear how they interface so that the cybersecurity engineer can architect them to meet the top-level requirements. See Section 19.2 for details on design patterns.

It is where top-down refinement of mechanisms and components meets the bottom-up reality of the available building blocks, tools, and design patterns that makes for a practical realistic design that coherently meets its requirements.

2.6 Cybersecurity Is a Live Orchestra, Not a Recorded Instrument

When thinking about cybersecurity, *think immune system, not a single white blood cell.* Think science, not talisman. There are three classes of instruments in the cybersecurity orchestra: prevention, detection, and reaction.

Prevention is about stopping attacks through thwarting one or more mechanisms exploited by an attack sequence. For example, limiting the computers that can talk to a system using restrictive firewall rules can substantially narrow the **attack surface** (vulnerabilities that an attacker can directly reach) available to an attacker.

Detection simply determines that an attack step happened and that perhaps a larger attack sequence of steps is in progress. Detection by itself can be valuable if the entire value to the adversary derives from the defender not knowing that the attack happened. For example, if an attacker steals a defender's war plan for a region, the defender can change the plan, and so the element of surprise is not lost.

Reaction is done in connection with detection—it is the action taken to thwart the attack and repair damage to ensure continuity of system function.

These classes of cybersecurity instruments are then arranged to play the music of defense. No one instrument suffices, and the instruments must work together to create an effective defense. The music must be well-planned and it must be continuous. Cybersecurity is not just some property of a system that you build in, such as coloring a toaster silver; cybersecurity is an organic process of system management in the moment and technology evolution over time.

Conclusion

This chapter sets the right frame of mind and perspective needed to become an effective cybersecurity strategic thinker. It is part of the upfront picture of understanding the nature of the problems and of approaches to solutions to those problems. To continue the big picture, the next chapter discusses how we need to stay focused on what system are supporting—the mission.

To summarize:

- Cybersecurity is about effectively reducing risk for reasonable cost and mission impacts.
- Cybersecurity requires a trading off mission goals, performance, and functionality.
- To understand cybersecurity, one must understand how systems are attacked.
- Risk is particularly high at interfaces between systems because of bad assumptions.
- Top-down and bottom-up design work together to design effective cybersecurity.
- Cybersecurity requires well-informed orchestration of dynamic aspects of mechanisms.

Questions

1. What is the relationship between cybersecurity and risk? Discuss where risk comes from and ways of mitigating it.

2. What is cybersecurity traded off against in system design and why? Discuss other important system trade-offs with cybersecurity and how those decisions might be best made.

3. What is the connection between cybersecurity defense methods and cyberattack methods? Discuss ways that defenders can test their systems using an understanding of attack methods.

4. Why is risk particularly high at system interfaces? Discuss some examples of invalid assumptions that one system may make about another system that could lead to a cybersecurity problem.

5. How are top-down and bottom-up design used in concert to design large enterprise security systems? Discuss how system engineering tools, such as architecture specification languages, can be used to support this hybrid design approach.

6. Why is cybersecurity dynamic in nature? Discuss how the dynamic nature of cybersecurity might manifest during system operation.

CHAPTER 3

Value and Mission: Know Thyself

Overview

Learning Objectives

- Identify what organizations value in cyber infrastructure and how that affects cybersecurity.
- State the role of cybersecurity in optimizing mission, not optimizing cybersecurity.
- Discuss how system design can make systems more or less attractive targets.
- Understand the nature of secrecy and the implications for how to defend it.
- Describe why and how to minimize secrecy and an organization's dependence on it.
- Describe the nature of trust in a system and how it can be misplaced and evolve.
- Understand why integrity is at the foundation of all cybersecurity.
- Explain why availability is the most tenuous cybersecurity property.

The concept of cybersecurity requires an answer to the question of what exactly needs to be secure. Since the context of this book is the cybersecurity of organizations, the answer becomes the cyber infrastructure of an organization based on how that infrastructure supports the organization's mission. Typically, organizations are broadly concerned with the confidentiality of sensitive information, the integrity of critical information, and the availability of the service. The nature of the concern and relative weight of these concerns depend entirely on the mission of the organization. Organizations such as open source foundations that distribute free software may care little about confidentiality, while the integrity of their software may be critical. Military organizations tend to highly value secrecy in many different forms for different reasons, but they also have strong integrity and availability concerns that are sometimes overshadowed and thus given short shrift because of the importance placed on secrecy.

This chapter begins with a general discussion on what it means to focus on mission and value, then proceeds to discuss the value of confidentiality (in three sections), integrity, and availability.

3.1 Focus on Mission and Value

Cybersecurity is not the mission, although it can be important to it. The mission of many information systems is decision support. The value of information would be significantly reduced if (1) sensitive information is leaked, (2) critical information is manipulated, and (3) the system were not available during the times when it is needed most. These correspond to the essential cybersecurity properties of confidentiality, integrity, and availability, but in the context of the mission.

The important point is that notions of cybersecurity-at-all-costs and all-or-none cybersecurity are misguided. Cybersecurity is always in an engineering trade-off between system functionality and performance. Sometimes functionality and performance take precedence over cybersecurity when we consider the mission. For example, a control system for a fly-by-wire airplane must be reliable for the airplane to remain safe. If one has to temporarily give up availability of the airplane's Internet communications of its passengers so that the fly-by-wire functionality is assured to work, it is a good trade-off.

Cybersecurity architects and system designers must allow for explicit trade-offs such as these, both during design-time and the operation-time of systems. We must involve and trust system owners and users to help make these trade-offs during both design and operation.

> *Cybersecurity's goal is to optimize mission effectiveness.*

3.1.1 Avoid Concentrating Value

Adversaries calculate their cost/benefit in the same way that defenders do. Whether an attack is worthwhile to them depends on the value that the attack returns. *If the value protected by any given mechanism or system is high enough, the adversary will make significant investment and focus a great deal of energy on a single point—making it hard to defend.* An example would be to use a shared network key for encrypting large volumes of traffic. That key becomes a **high-value target** for the attacker because it unlocks a huge amount of sensitive data. If the system design spreads value out, such that the adversary does not get significant value with any given attack, the attacker's cost is significantly increased to achieve the same result, and he cannot concentrate his resources at a single point. On the other hand, if each subnetwork uses a separate key and that key is changed frequently, then very little data is revealed by the compromise of any one key, and so it becomes less worthwhile for the adversary to target a key.

> *Avoid creating high-value targets for the adversary.*

Similarly, architects must be careful not to create powerful control and management mechanisms that an adversary can exploit. For example, we often create powerful management subsystems to control networks and sometimes the cybersecurity mechanisms themselves. Such systems are great for reducing the complexity of managing the system but can create a high-value target for the adversary if defeating that one system can allow them to defeat multiple mechanisms. In other words, management mechanisms can unintentionally defeat the value of defense in depth of multiple mechanisms if the management mechanism creates a common attack mode that controls all of the mechanisms. The old "root access" on UNIX to facilitate administration is an example—though somewhat obsolete. This has been largely eliminated by most modern certification and accreditation processes, only to be replaced by automated management systems protected by weak passwords.

3.1.2 Beware the Complacency of Trust

An old saying is: "Just because you are paranoid does not mean that they are not out to get you." [HELL10]. *Trust is something to be earned, not given lightly.* Everyone involved in systems, from sponsors, to designers, to administrators, to users, should have a healthy skepticism in trusting a system. One should always ask, "Why should I trust the system to do X?", not "Why shouldn't I?"

> *Trust is to be earned, continuously.*

Even if a system earns trust at one point in its life cycle, for example, when it is brand spanking new, everyone should keep in mind that systems transmogrify over time, and the trust once earned can be eroded. Continuing to trust a system that is no longer worthy of trust can have dangerous consequences. For example, entrusting one's secrets to a system that is not trustworthy to keep them runs a high risk that one's valuable secrets will be lost to cyberattack.

3.2 Confidentiality: Value of Secrecy from Adversaries

There are four different types of confidentiality value—value derived from keeping a secret. There are also two important aspects of secrecy: (1) preventing the loss of secrets and (2) detecting the loss of secrets. Each aspect has different value depending on the nature of the secret. The types and aspects will be described next. They are summarized in Table 3-1, including priorities on prevention and detection.

The four types of secrets are as follows and will be explained further in subsequent sections.

1. **Acquired-knowledge secrets**   Those gained through processes such as research and development—are expensive to gain; losing them is irreversible and costly, and detecting their loss is useful, but not critical.

2. **Planning secrets**   Those created through the planning processes in a competitive environment—are high value to prevent loss, but even higher value to detect because not knowing that the competitor knows one's secret could be lethal to an organization.

3. **Stolen secrets**   Those acquired from a competing or opposing organization—are often moderately important to keep secret (depending on the type of stolen secret) and moderately important to detect that the secret was stolen.

4. **Means-of-stealing-secrets secrets**   Secrets that are typically the most highly valued secrets, and detecting their loss is high priority because of the damage an adversary can do by feeding deceiving information into compromised sources or channels of communication.

#	Types of Secrecy	Prevention Priority	Detection Priority
1	Acquired-knowledge secrets	High	Low
2	Planning secrets	High	Very High
3	Stolen secrets	Medium-High	Medium
4	Means-of-stealing-secret secrets	High	Very High

Table 3-1   Types of Secrecy

3.2.1 Acquired-Knowledge Secrets

Knowing something that one has learned that nobody else has independently learned is of potentially high value. Keeping such information secret is valuable because it offers a competitive advantage (including economic, political, or military advantage between nation-states). Keeping a trade secret, such as the formula for Coca-Cola®, or the proper settings for crude-oil "cracking"—an industrial process to break crude oil into its constituent products (e.g., gasoline, kerosene, diesel, etc.), are both examples of this type of secret. Military examples include knowledge for advanced technology such as aircraft stealth or submarine stealth—operating without being easily seen by detection technology such as radar and sonar.

In addition to losing competitive advantage by losing the secret, there is a significant competitive loss because the organizations acquiring the secret information do not need to invest the same money (which could be in the hundreds of millions of dollars) that the losing organization did to create the secret. This frees the funds of the acquiring organization to invest in some other way to create a further competitive advantage in some other area. Therefore, a loss of such secrets (Figure 3-1), in a sense, is a double loss and should be accounted for that way when deciding how much it is worth investing to protect that secret.

Attack Panel: Secrecy Attack	
Name	Data Compromise
Type	Confidentiality
Identified	Since computers were invented
System Target	Data in storage and in transit
Vulnerability	Cleartext data; weak operating system and server security
Mission	Copy valuable data without being detected
Prevalence	Widespread, particularly industrial secrets
Damage	Billions in lost competitive edge and lost research advantages
Significance	Strategic damage in the information age

Figure 3-1   Attack description: secrecy attack

The loss of knowledge-acquired secrets is irreversible in the sense that one cannot re-create the value other than through a new investment process to create a new knowledge-acquired secret. Detecting that such secrets have been lost can be useful if learned early enough, but generally it will become obvious when the competitor exploits the acquired-knowledge secret to gain advantage, so reality often acts as the detection method of the loss of this class of secret.

3.2.2 Planning Secrets

The value of planning secrets is in competitors not knowing an organization's plans before the plans are executed. This is sometimes called the element of surprise in the military context. Consider a chess game where the opponent knows every move their opponent is going to make before they make it. That foreknowledge clearly places the opponent at a major disadvantage. It does not necessarily mean that the player will lose the game, but it does mean that it will be much harder to win, because the opponent does not need to consider all the move options and can focus resources and energy on the one move that he knows the player will make.

The Normandy invasion in World War II is another example. Had the Nazis known precisely where the Allied forces were going to land, they could have concentrated all of their military might at that single point, making it nearly impossible to succeed [BARB07]. Therefore, the Allied forces spent considerable resources in a cover and deception campaign to mislead the Nazis as to where an invasion of the European mainland would land. Nonmilitary examples would include product release timing of new phone or computer features that competitors could try to beat to gain market share and therefore profit, or knowing the positions of competitors during negotiations, thus potentially gaining more value than one would have ordinarily gained.

The loss of a planning secret has three aspects:

- The value that the plan has to others because it is a good plan that can be adapted and used.

- The losses incurred because the competitors knew the plan and the organization did not know they knew.

- The cost to alter the plan sufficiently to regain the element of surprise because the organization knows that the competitors know before beginning execution of the plan.

The third aspect has two subtle subscenarios: one in which the competitors know that the organizations know that the competitor has gained the secret, and the other where the competitors do not know. In the first scenario, the organization and its competitors are back to a level playing field of neither knowing the other's plan. In the second, the organization may be able to gain value by exploiting the fact that the competitor does not know the organization knows its secret is lost. The advantage comes from the organization's ability to better predict what the competitor may do, thinking that they have secret knowledge of the organization's plan, so effective counterplans can be put into place.

The value of the loss of a planning secret is related to the timing of the loss. Losing a planning secret in the early stages of a plan tends to be less damaging because the investment in the detailed planning has not yet been made. So, detailed mature plans that are close to the time of execution of the plan, when there may be insufficient time to create an equally good and detailed plan, are generally much more valuable. For planning secrets, detecting that the secret is lost (e.g., through intrusion detection) is extraordinarily important. That is because value loss associated with a lost plan that is not known could be several orders of magnitude higher and could be lethal to the organization. This fact informs the cybersecurity design and places high importance on attack detection and forensics and exactly what needs to be detected.

3.2.3 Stolen Secrets

In addition to types of secrets created by an organization, there are types of secrets associated with organizations being on the receiving side of secrets from other organizations. We will loosely refer to these as stolen secrets because the losing organization typically does not want those secrets known, and they are typically gained through some method that violates the rules, policies, or laws of the losing organization. For example, consider a reporter who has a source inside an organization that leaks an embarrassing fact about that organization. When information from that source leads to a published news story, the leaker is almost certainly violating the policies of the organization that employs them. Similarly, when an intelligence organization gains a secret from another government, it almost certainly involves at least the leaker breaking the law by revealing nationally classified information.

Stolen secrets have different components to their value. As discussed earlier, stolen knowledge-acquired secrets are intrinsically valuable, and keeping the fact that one knows that secret has relatively low value, at least in the long term, because exploitation of the secret generally makes it obvious that the losing organization lost the secret.

Stolen planning secrets, on the other hand, have some intrinsic value in knowing the planning capability and style of an organization, but the bulk of value comes from knowing the planning secret and keeping that knowledge secret. So, protecting stolen planning secrets is critical to retaining the value of such secrets. So, acquirers of such secrets must place high value on avoiding detection in the process of acquiring the secret and then later protect the secret from being acquired, at least from the organization from which it has been acquired.

3.2.4 Means-of-Stealing-Secrets Secrets

The way that an organization gains secrets is a particularly important type of secret. One reads about journalists choosing jail time over revealing their sources. That is because the means of gaining information is almost always much more important than the secret information gained. This is for the obvious reason that the means can continue to be a source of additional secrets. In addition, if a human source is revealed to the detriment of that source, other such sources are much less likely to act as sources in the future, and so there is a broad loss of value in addition to the loss of the one source.

There is an interesting connection between stolen secrets and the means-of-stealing secrets. Sometimes, secrets are kept so tightly among a small number of people and systems, that the loss of the secret implies a particular means (or a small set of means) of loss. For example, if only two people know a secret and it is leaked, it is pretty easy for the other person to know who leaked it. Sometimes the means is not a person, but a system. In World War II, Winston Churchill found himself in the unenviable position of not being able to act on intelligence to save Londoners' lives from a rocket attack, because acting would reveal knowledge and the Nazis could have concluded that their cryptographic communication system (code-named Enigma) had been compromised [RATC06][HODG14].

On the other hand, if a means of stealing secrets is compromised, then it may be possible to learn all the stolen secrets that have been lost through that means. For example, if some encrypted communication path is discovered to have been compromised, then the discovery can lead one to know that all data transmitted across that communication path has been stolen. This can be useful to a defender because knowledge of lost secrets is valuable, as discussed earlier.

So, in summary, protecting the means-of-stealing-secrets secrets is high priority. Identifying the loss of such secrets can also be very important. If a means is lost, then if a defender is "lucky," they learn of the loss through further secrets stopping from that particular means—such as a source being fired from an organization from which they are leaking information. It is also possible for an opponent to keep the loss of means a secret. They do so by continuing to allow that means, such as a human informant, to work. Indeed, they may even allow some true low-level secrets to continue to leak, but then intermix deceptive false information to cause the opponent to make poor decisions that could lead to high-value loss.

3.3 Confidentiality: Beware the Tyranny of Secrecy

Three can keep a secret, if two of them are dead.

—Benjamin Franklin

Maintaining secrecy, achieving confidentiality, is complex and tenuous [BOK11]. Secrecy tends to breed more secrecy, and an organization can become too dependent on it—almost as an addiction. Once a secret has been learned, one can keep that secret and exploit it for oneself (e.g., blackmail someone or make better strategic decisions knowing a secret) or reveal the secret to destroy value for some sort of competitive gain (e.g., revealing the Pentagon Papers to bring scrutiny on a hidden process that might be destructive [ELLS03]).

There are many problems with secrecy, as summarized in Table 3-2. Each will be discussed in turn.

#	Problems with Secrecy	Description
1	Tenuous	Once created, secrets are hard to keep.
2	Expensive	Protecting secrets has high direct and indirect costs.
3	Self-defeating	Identifying and labeling secrets create an obvious target.
4	Self-breeding	Secrets proliferate because of disincentives.
5	Corrupting impediment	Secrets impede communication and cooperation.

Table 3-2   Problems with Secrecy

3.3.1 Secrecy Is Tenuous

Once a secret is created, it is only a matter of time before it is revealed. As information technology improves, it will become increasingly difficult to maintain any secrets for any significant length of time. *Once search engines such as Google start to routinely make deep inferences in addition to just finding published data, it will be difficult for any secret to have no inferable footprint in cyberspace.* See Section 25.1 for details.

For example, if an organization wants to keep it quiet that there is some big planning operation going on, but someone notices that the expected delay time on all pizza restaurants in the area has gone up due to a high demand in the late evening, it is possible to infer that something is going on. Inference means taking known facts that are available and deriving on the facts that, taken together, are implied or suggested by those facts. Logical rules of deduction and induction are used to learn new things that are not explicitly available.

3.3.2 Secrecy Is Expensive

Keeping something secret requires special processes, special and separate cyber infrastructures, and separate vetting processes for personnel that can be onerous and limit the pool of talent to work a given problem. As an example, the U.S. Defense Department estimates the annual cost of maintaining secrecy to be in billions of dollars [DODI13], as summarized in the "Panel: Report Summary" sidebar. In addition, there is the opportunity cost of funds spent on protecting secrets to spending it on the primary mission of the organization.

Panel: Report Summary

Title: DoD Evaluation of Over-classification of National Security Information (2013).

1. Management was not properly held accountable for proper classification and procedures for challenging over-classification were unclear and not properly incentivized.

2. Some original classification authorities are not making many or even any classification decisions, leading to a waste of allocating security resources.

3. Ineffective management and updating of security classification guides leading to potential over-classification.

4. Ineffective security education and training in some cases.

3.3.3 Secrecy Can Be Self-Defeating

The mere act of identifying and labeling something as secret flags it to potential adversaries as highly valuable information worth stealing. It is like painting a big red target on data or a system containing such data. The adversary is able to focus resources on that data and those systems and not waste any resources on trying to decide what is important to the defender.

3.3.4 Secrecy Is Self-Breeding

Once an organization creates special rules and processes to handle secret information, and once those rules and processes establish negative consequences to people responsible for protecting secret information, there is an unavoidable effect that people will be overly conservative in identifying information as secret when it really is not. There is generally no consequence to human authorities to over-identifying sensitive information. Information that *could* be sensitive, and may be related to data that is *actually* sensitive, will tend to be labeled sensitive "just to be on the safe side." Then that data is incorporated into reports that are mostly not sensitive, but one might be able to infer the data from the surrounding nonsensitive data, so the entire report becomes labeled sensitive "just to be on the safe side."

Similarly, once one creates a special protected infrastructure to protect sensitive information, these infrastructures tend to grow and incorporate nonsensitive data to integrate with the sensitive data, commingling and causing even further overly conservative labeling. This drives cost up and actually makes the truly sensitive data less well protected because the defenders can become cavalier about it since there is so much of it. It is the equivalent of the management saying that "if everything is priority one, then nothing is"; so, "if everything is sensitive, then nothing is."

If everything is sensitive, then nothing is.

3.3.5 Secrecy Creates a Form of Corrupting Power and Impediment to Operation

If one person knows a secret and another does not, that fact can be used to create a sort of currency to trade within organizations and perhaps even between organizations. That can disrupt the flow of information in an organization and can decrease the efficiency and effectiveness of executing mission. Lives can and have been lost in this way. It exacerbates the well-known bureaucracy phenomenon where the right hand does not know what the left hand is doing.

3.4 Confidentiality: Changing the Value Proposition

In subsequent chapters, we will discuss how to achieve confidentiality—depending on the loss of secrecy. Prior to that, the cybersecurity engineer must consider the nature of the value proposition of secrecy and work to strategically address its role in the mission of the system. It may be important to change the nature of the role of secrecy to improve the ability to maintain secrecy. See Section 25.1 for further discussion on how the world may inherently change the nature of secrecy.

3.4.1 Minimize Secrecy and Dependency on Secrecy

For reasons discussed earlier, secrecy should be kept to an absolute minimum and its proliferation should be actively and intentionally resisted. Secrecy can be engineered, just as trustworthiness or reliability or any other system property can. How does one minimize secrecy? First, one should enumerate what data they believe is sensitive, why it is sensitive, what type of secret it is, what its half-life is, the consequences to mission if the sensitive data is lost, and an alternative way of achieving mission without the need for that secret. See Table 3-3 for an example worksheet.

Minimize secrecy and dependency on it.

#	What	Why	Type	Half-Life	Loss Consequence	Can You Live Without It?
1	Invention	Competitive advantage	Knowledge-acquired	1.5 years	Market share	Patent protection
2	Personal identifying information	Legal liability	Other	Until deleted	Lawsuit or fines and reputation loss	Outsourcing human resource management

Table 3-3   Secrecy Minimization Worksheet Example

Once an organization has identified its prioritized and ranked list of sensitive information, it should consider applying the 80/20 rule. Can the organization achieve 80 percent of the value of keeping the most sensitive information secure by only labeling and protecting the

20 percent most important data? Often the answer is yes. Another important question for the most sensitive data on the top of the list is, "Does it really need to be stored on a connected system or a computer system at all (e.g., can it just be written down and stored in a safe)?" Storing information offline can significantly reduce its vulnerability by reducing the attack paths available to the adversary.

Even further, *an organization should explicitly attempt to engineer itself so that it does not rely so heavily on secrecy*. Certainly, minimizing secrecy as described earlier reduces dependency on secrecy. Are there ways to reduce dependency on secrecy other than by reducing the number of secrets? Yes, one can have alternative processes, parallel to the one requiring secrecy (see Section 25.1 for further discussion). For example, if an organization manufactures a product that depends on secret ingredients, perhaps it can develop an alternative product that succeeds because it is less expensive or uses the highest-quality ingredients.

Another way to reduce dependency on secrecy is to reduce the half-life requirements for secrets—in other words, the requirement for how long a fact needs to remain a secret from adversaries to have little value to them. If a company develops a culture of fast innovation and fast product development to get to market first, it may not need to keep its innovations secret for as long as other less fast-paced companies, thus reducing the cost of preserving those secrets and reducing the time that the secrets can have other negative effects, as discussed earlier. For example, 3M® is reputed to be unconcerned about giving public tours of its factories because it says that by the time a competitor copies one of its technologies, it is already on to the next idea [PETE12].

3.4.2 Minimize Impact of Loss of Secrecy

Because secrets are known to be so ephemeral, all organizations should design themselves to be highly tolerant to the system "failure" of the secret being revealed; the value loss should be minimized.

Reducing an organization's dependency on secrets, as discussed previously, is one good way to minimize the impact of secrecy loss. Sometimes secrets are created by illegal or scandalous actions by individuals in an organization such as embezzlement [MCLE13] or inappropriate and risky sexual behavior [BERL01] [KAPL12] [WEIS17]. These secrets, once discovered, are often kept by an organization with the misguided intention of protecting the mission of the organization from distraction or a loss of stakeholder or public confidence. Such secrets can rarely be kept because of the ephemeral nature of secrets. Organizations should divest themselves of these secrets themselves by making them public and controlling the timing and the spin to minimize damage to the organization and its mission.

3.5 Integrity: The Root of All Trustworthiness Value

Without integrity, no other cybersecurity properties matter. Given that the system supports the mission, the system and its data are of no use if you cannot rely on them. This is analogous to building a house on a poor foundation. Integrity comes in two important flavors: data integrity and system integrity. Data integrity refers to the confidence that the data in the system has not been maliciously modified. System integrity refers to the confidence that the system itself (hardware, software, operating system, devices, etc.) has not been maliciously modified.

> **Without integrity, no other cybersecurity properties matter.**

Maintaining secrecy of corrupt data is pointless since the data has no value if the defender does not know if the data is valid. Consider the case of an attacker modifying the defender's system to include malicious code that essentially gives full control of the defender's system to the attacker. If the defender cannot trust that their system has not been modified in this way, then the defender no longer really owns their system and cannot rely on it for their mission. Availability of the system is an illusion and is granted as a temporary favor by the adversary who becomes the true owner (controller) of the defender's system. Of the two types of integrity, system integrity is more fundamental because an attacker can use system integrity attacks to mount any other attacks, including data integrity corruption. For this reason, it is the author's experience that integrity *is one of the most undervalued aspects of* cybersecurity *by most defenders today.*

3.6 Availability: An Essential Yet Tenuous Value

Availability refers to the system being up and available for supporting the mission. In today's information age, disabling an organization's information infrastructure is often the same thing as disabling the organization itself. If the organization's operations and survival are time-critical, this could be lethal to an organization. For example, retail stores make a large percent of their profits between Thanksgiving and Christmas, and sales value can be in the hundreds of thousands of dollars per hour. If the retail system of a marginally profitable company is down for an extended period of time, it could literally kill the company.

Unfortunately, availability is very difficult to ensure. A modern system often depends on many other systems outside of its control to operate correctly. For example, if an organization's **Internet service provider's** service is down, they have no access to the Internet. Often applications now depend on real-time access to validate a license or call an online service such as the domain name system, which translates human readable names such as www.ibm.com into computer-understandable addresses.

Similarly, with modern just-in-time-everything, suppliers and customer systems are tied in so tightly with a producer's system that the entire connected system can break if one system goes down in any aspect of the connected system of systems. So, a supplier's system that you do not own could be attacked and stop working, and your production line halts because you do not get the parts you need in time. See Section 24.2 for further discussion.

Conclusion

In this chapter, we learned what it means to give primacy to mission and how cybersecurity supports mission and how value is derived from confidentiality, integrity, and availability. In the next chapter, we will see how to identify and focus on the most important potential harm to mission.

To summarize:

- Organizations weigh the needs for confidentiality, integrity, and availability of data.
- Cybersecurity protects mission as the body's immune system protects the body.
- Take the attacker's perspective and seek to minimize the value an attacker will derive.
- Avoid concentrating valuable data in one place to avoid creating a high-value target.
- Secrets are difficult to protect, tend to proliferate, and can hamper mission.
- The mission role of secrecy should be carefully evaluated throughout a system's life cycle.
- Minimize dependency on secrecy and mission loss from the loss of secrecy if it occurs.
- Trustworthiness must be proven to stakeholders throughout a system's life cycle.
- Without system integrity, confidentiality and availability are pointless.
- Availability depends on systems that are not under the designer's operational control.
- Avoid outsourcing critical functionality and data to potentially untrustworthy entities.

Questions

1. Name three very different types of organizations and predict how they are likely to weight the value of the three essential security properties and why.
2. Describe how cybersecurity goals relate to mission goals and their relative priority. Give an example where cybersecurity may need to be suppressed in favor of mission goals.
3. Give two examples of systems decisions that might aggregate too much value in one place and what alternative decisions could be made to avoid such aggregation.
4. List five aspects of secrecy that make it complex and difficult to manage and give examples of these aspects in organizations that you know about.
5. Why should an organization reduce their dependence on secrecy? Suggest three ways to decrease dependence on secrecy.
6. Describe two examples where loss of a secret could have severe impact on the success of an organization.
7. How do system integrity and data integrity relate to one another? Which is more fundamental and why?
8. Why is integrity the most fundamental of the three properties of cybersecurity?

4

Harm: Mission in Peril

Overview

Learning Objectives

- Define harm and state how it relates to mission.
- Define strategic risks and describe why it is important to focus on them.
- Discuss how expected loss calculations drive strategic risk.
- Describe how concerns about strategic harm are elicited from senior leadership.
- Summarize how the principle of "wisdom of crowds" applies to estimating total harm.
- Describe what a "belief harm" is and why is it particularly hard to address.

What is harm and how does it relate to value? The previous chapters established the primacy of risk as a bottom-line metric of cybersecurity. Recall that cybersecurity *is about risk to mission*. Risk to mission can be thought of as the probability of bad outcomes that would be a significant detriment to mission. That collection of bad outcomes is what harm is about. **Harm** is a measure of how bad each of the outcomes in the collection would be if it occurred. It can be measured in dollars or some qualitative metric such as utils [SALV99] (a measure of utility), but each must be clearly thought about and conclusions must be drawn about how bad bad can be with respect to each unwanted outcome. In this section, the terms "harm," "loss," "consequence," and "impact" are used interchangeably.

4.1 Focus on Strategic Risks

Cybersecurity architects sometimes lose sight of the big picture. Sometimes they focus on cybersecurity mechanisms because they are easy to deploy and count. By analogy, they have a cybersecurity hammer and so everything looks like a cybersecurity nail. Programs take a life of their own, and then the focus shifts to sustaining and extending that deployment. This can be to the detriment of working on other, possibly more important, risks. *Resisting this natural tendency and staying focused on the strategic risk is difficult.*

4.1.1 What Is Strategic Risk?

By strategic risks, we mean risks that could be catastrophic to the mission of the organizations. For example, if the mission of a nonprofit organization is to motivate donations (both monetary and food), collect donations, and distribute food to the needy, then strategic risks would be ones that directly degrade any one of these stages. If a scandal or even a false accusation jeopardizes the motivation donors have to donate, then it is a strategic risk to that organization. Similarly, if the website that collects monetary donations is down for a month due to a **distributed denial of service attack** (Figure 4-1), that could seriously jeopardize financial resources, which in turn jeopardizes mission.

The way to focus on strategic risk is to look at jeopardy to each of the elements of an organization's mission and to the overall mission. In this case, an example of a nonstrategic

Attack Panel: Distributed Denial of Service	
Class	Availability Attack
Type	Network Flooding
Mechanism	Typically a botnet of hijacked computers sending an overwhelming number of network packets to a target system from multiple locations.
Examples	Code Red, Mirai botnet targeting the domain name servers.
Damage Potential	Billions of dollars in lost revenue due to preventing access to key online resources such as retail ordering sites.

Figure 4-1   Attack description: distributed denial of service

risk (noncatastrophic) would include hackers breaking into the organization's system and disrupting operations for 10 minutes during a noncritical period.

Strategic risk is about jeopardy to mission.

4.1.2 Expected Harm

A quantitative measure of risk is the expected harm from a successful attack. This expected loss can be found by simply multiplying the likelihood by the consequences of an attack. Table 4-1 summarizes this notion and places attacks into nine broad classes. Shaded cells are those classes of most concern as measured by the expected loss. One can argue how accurately one can estimate probabilities and expected losses and how easy it is to classify attacks into these categories. The point of the table is to *establish the conceptual context to make qualitative engineering and managerial decisions about return-on-investment and to bring focus to the most important categories.* One can also infer that cybersecurity engineers must put energy into increasingly better estimation of risk so that the basis of these decisions improves continuously.

		Consequence ($)		
		Low ($<10^4$)	Medium (10^4—10^8)	High (10^8—10^{12})
Probability	Low ($<10^{-6}$)	$0.01	$100	$1M
	Medium (10^{-6}—10^{-2})	$100	$1M	$10B
	High ($>10^{-2}$)	$100	$1M	$1000B

Table 4-1   Risk is calculated by probability of an event times the consequences; shaded cells show potentially strategic risks; and values are given in exponential format. A probability of 10^{-6} means 1 chance in 10 with 6 zeros after it, or 1 in a million.

4.1.3 The Range of Risks

Continuing the earlier example of a nonprofit that distributes food to the needy, an example of a low-probability–low-consequence event might be an attacker breaking strong cryptography used to secure email traffic to learn the content of the emails. Commercial **cryptography** is now quite strong and difficult to break with an **exhaustion attack** (a cryptanalytic attack in which one attempts all possible keys to see which correctly decrypts the message). One might estimate the probability of such a successful brute force attack to be on the order of one in a million. For most nonprofits, privacy of email content is not a high priority because transparency is one of their intended modes of operation. So, a loss of email confidentiality is not likely to have serious consequences. One can then estimate the consequences to be worth less than $10,000. Therefore, the risk is on the order of one cent and therefore is not worth investing substantial resources in attempting to mitigate.

> ### *Don't over-sweat the small stuff.*

On the other hand, a local warlord using a cyberattack to reroute a major food convoy through his territory so that he can hijack the shipment, to sell or barter it, is a significant risk in certain countries and poses a major risk to the mission of successfully distributing food to the needy. Indeed, *publicity about such hijackings has a multiplying effect* because donors might conclude that it is futile to try to distribute food in such countries and stop donating altogether.

4.1.4 The Meaning of Focus

Focusing on strategic attacks means that resources should be dedicated to mitigating strategically important risks, and the quality of cybersecurity solutions should be at least partly measured against mitigation of these risks. The risk should be spelled out through scenarios, and solutions should be examined to determine if they mitigate the risks of the representative scenarios.

4.2 Harm Is About Mission

Statements of strategically important harm can come from the organization leadership's statements of what keeps them up at night—sometimes humorously referred to as "resume updating events" (meaning that the event is so bad, even senior executives would not be insulated from being fired, which would require them to update their resumes before searching for another job). Said a different way, one asks "what are the cyberattack-related headlines that leadership fears the most?"

We note that there is risk beyond the organization as well. The Equifax [RILE17] and Office of Personnel Management [STRO17] breaches of millions of sensitive data records are examples where the consequences reach far beyond the institutions that are the source of the breach. This is a type of tragedy of the commons, in which society collectively bears the cost of the actions of its members. These institutions do not typically bear the full costs of their failure, and so there is insufficient incentive for them to invest to avoid such massive breaches on personnel confidentiality, creating long-term risk for millions of people. This lack of bearing consequences is known as a "moral hazard" and creates a serious societal issue. The only way to properly consider such overarching risks is for higher-level institutions, such as parent companies or the government, to create a form of accountability and required investment to factor in such harm.

4.2.1 Elicitation of Harm

Engineers should carefully elicit these statements from a diversity of senior leadership that are in charge of key aspects of the organization's mission—not just the chief information officer. For example, the chief operating officer and chief financial officer as well as the chief executive officer should be included. These statements should be elicited in a session apart from the influence of other seniors who may bias the input of their colleagues.

It has sometimes proven useful to prompt leadership with the three major categories of attacks corresponding to the three pillars for defense: confidentiality, integrity, and availability. If they draw a blank, which can happen when they are not used to thinking about worst-case scenarios, it helps to have an example of each type to get their thinking going. There is some risk that an engineer-provided scenario would bias the executives' input, but generally, such prompts have rarely caused an executive to adopt the suggestion—rather, they usually come up with a new one that is similar but much worse.

4.2.2 Aggregating Harm Statements

Ideally, one would get at least two harm statements in each of the three categories (so six total) from each executive. Given three to five executives solicited, one ends up with somewhere in the neighborhood of ten to fifteen harm statements after eliminating duplicates and combining similar ones. The aggregate set should contain clear statements of each harm outcome and at least one concrete example of the harm, including a plausible scenario. The aggregate set can be shared with the group of executives for one final set of improvements.

4.2.3 Representative Harm Lists

Note that the harm list is not intended to be exhaustive, but rather representative of the harms that would be of strategic concern to the organization. This suffices for cybersecurity engineering purposes because it motivates countermeasures that cover the related attack space that is in the family that "surrounds" each element on the list. If the list does not span the attack space by some qualitative measure, it ought to be revisited to fill in any gaps.

4.3 Critical Asset Inventory: Data

Missions depend on critical assets to operate. A critical asset inventory is simply an enumeration of assets (information technology assets in this case) on which the organization critically depends to achieve its mission. For example, an organization may depend heavily on its front-door gateway and firewall to deliver its service; its lack of availability makes the entire system unavailable to consumers. This could be particularly critical in online retail.

Often the dependency can be subtle. Take, for example, infrastructure systems such as the domain name system (DNS). It can be critical to accomplish anything, but DNS is a service that most, including IT people, do not think about often. How to develop a full inventory will be discussed in Section 22.4. This section focuses on an important subpart of the inventory—data assets.

4.3.1 Data Asset Types

There are two types of critical data: (1) executable data, including software, and (2) passive data. The difference is important from a cybersecurity perspective. Software is active, meaning that it contains instructions that affect operations of the computer, including changing data files or other software. Data, on the other hand, is passive and is usually operated on by software.

Software in the form of data includes source code, object code, linked files, executable files, and even configuration data such as files (sometimes called "config files") used as input to determine how software will run (e.g., telling the software to run with high privilege or to output diagnostic data). Some languages, called interpreted languages, directly execute the source code. Such languages are sometimes called scripting languages (e.g., Visual Basic for Applications [VBA] in Microsoft Excel). Such scripting files can often seem like data files and be embedded within data files, but they are in fact software since they can be executed.

Data includes objects like user files such as Word documents and Excel spreadsheets and application files that are used to control processing and to communicate from one application to another (e.g., Unix pipes). Data is read, written, modified, or deleted by software. For example, when a user opens up a text file to look at it, some active software (such as Microsoft Word or EMACS) reads the data and presents it visually to a user on the computer monitor. A database is an example of a data object that is usually read, written, and modified, usually by a database application (e.g., Oracle's Database Management System).

4.3.2 Data Value Spectrum

Not all data is equally important. The league bowling scores and lunch menu data objects are not as critical as the secret formula for Coca-Cola, for example. Modern computer systems have terabytes of data, bordering on petabytes. Going through the expense of protecting all data equally does not make much sense. *The more highly data is protected, the more it costs per bit to protect it. This leads to the notion of prioritizing data in terms of levels of criticality.* Organizations sometimes refer to the "crown jewels" as their most important data and thus create a two-tier system of "crown jewels" and everything else.

> *Prioritize data protection, or the adversary will do it for you.*

4.3.3 Criticality Classes

The question of criticality depends on context—critical for what? *It is useful to think of criticality in terms of the three pillars of cybersecurity—confidentiality, integrity, and availability.* One can speak of confidentiality-critical data, integrity-critical data, and availability-critical software or data. Tables 4-2 and 4-3 summarize the types and offer some examples.

Criticality Types	Software (Active)	Data (Passive)
Confidentiality	Confidentiality-critical software	Confidentiality-critical data
Integrity	Integrity-critical software	Integrity-critical data
Availability	Availability-critical software	Availability-critical data

Table 4-2   Criticality Types of Software and Data Based on the Three Pillars of Cybersecurity

Criticality Types	Software (Active)	Data (Passive)
Confidentiality	Industrial control software that encodes highly proprietary algorithms for controlling petroleum cracking process settings	The secret formula for Coca-Cola, any trade secret, nationally classified defense plan, personally identifiable information, protected health information
Integrity	Infrastructure software such as operating systems, the microcode within processors, or software within routers	Banking data that keeps track of account balances and financial transactions or military weapon targeting information
Availability	Order taking or credit-card processing software on a retail website or infrastructure software such as the domain name system	Time-sensitive public data such as the Federal Reserve bank posting the updated prime lending rate

Table 4-3   Examples of Criticality Types for Six Categories

4.3.4 Criticality Levels

How many levels of criticality should one attempt to identify? Three is a good starting point. Start with identifying important data that is essential to mission accomplishment in the six categories defined in Table 4-2. It is worth separating this set into two groups—merely important and so critical that it could lead to the demise of the entire organization—this creates two levels. The third level is all the other noncritical data.

The 80/20 Pareto Rule (80 percent of effects come from 20 percent of the causes) is always useful. Noncritical data should be 80 percent of data; critical data should be 20 percent. Only 20 percent of that 20 percent (4 percent) should be deemed hypercritical. In some cases, such data or subsets of such data should be considered so sensitive that they should be stored offline (not on any connected computer system) if at all possible. The pyramid in Figure 4-2 illustrates this principle.

> ***Reserve the strongest protection for the most important elements.***

Noncritical data constitutes the vast majority of enterprise data and consists of data that is not essential for accomplishing the organization's mission—such as the lunch menu.

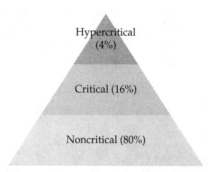

Figure 4-2   Levels of data criticality

Critical data is important to accomplishing some key mission element; bank account data is an example. Hypercritical data is data whose loss could jeopardize the existence of the entire organization.

4.4 A Template for Exploring Mission Harm

Understanding how to focus on strategically important harm can be a challenge. This section discusses an approach to doing so, including a template for getting started. Before proceeding, it is useful to have a variety of sample missions to make the abstract ideas more concrete in the examples discussed next. Table 4-4 lists sample missions for a commercial company (a bank), a nonprofit organization (a charity), and a government organization (a national military). These are meant to be sample organizations and sample elements of mission to foster the examples. The mission elements, important subordinate missions, are by no means exhaustive.

Mission Elements	Bank	Charity	Military
1	Gain deposits	Collect donations	Defend homeland
2	Lend money	Buy and select goods	Protect interests internationally
3	Maximize profit	Distribute goods to needy	Support humanitarian missions

Table 4-4   Sample Mission Elements for Three Sample Organizations

With sample critical data and sample missions in hand, a template for identifying harm can be discussed. Table 4-5 offers two examples for each of the three cybersecurity pillars. The notation of "<critical data x>" is used to indicate that an element of the set of critical data for the corresponding organization can be inserted to create a concrete attack for the organization that is being analyzed. Similarly, "<mission element y>" symbolizes that one of the mission elements for the corresponding organization can be inserted. Note that not all combinations of critical data and mission elements make sense for every organization. Table 4-5 is meant to create a starting point to help formulate strategic harm. The following text describes each row of the table in turn and discusses how it might be instantiated.

#	Type	Description	Scenario
1	**Confidentiality**	Loss of *<critical data 1>* jeopardizes *<mission element 1>*	Attacker hacks into system, steals *<critical sensitive data 1>*, and reveals to world
2	**Confidentiality**	Loss of *<critical data 2>* requiring major reinvestment to regain capability for *<mission element 2>*	Attack uses insider attack to steal *<critical sensitive data 2>*, which organization relies upon to enable *<mission element 2>*
3	**Integrity**	Corrupt integrity of *<critical data 3>* so that consumers of data lose trust in *<mission element 3>*	Attacker uses a life-cycle attack to insert malware that discovers and corrupts *<critical data 1>*
4	**Integrity**	Corrupt integrity of *<critical data 3>* to cause erroneous decisions to damage *<mission element 4>*	Attacker analyzes system and selectively corrupts the output *<critical data 3>* after they leave producer's system but before they enter the consumer's system
5	Availability	Deny service to *<critical subsystem 1>* to make *<critical subsystem 2>* unavailable for more than x days.	Attacker does a distributed denial of service attack on *<critical subsystem 1>*, which is required by *<critical subsystem 2>*
6	Availability	Corrupt system integrity of *<critical subsystem 3>* and its backups required by *<critical subsystem 4>* to operate	Attacker does a computer network attack on organization's enterprise system and corrupts key infrastructure *<critical subsystem 3>* as well as its backups to disable *<critical subsystem 4>*

Table 4-5   Example Template for Cybersecurity Harm Statements

Row 1   Loss of *<critical data 1>* jeopardizes *<mission element 1>*. As an example, if you take a national military organization's mission to defend the homeland from Table 4-4 as "mission element 1" and "nationally classified defense plan" from Table 4-5, the result is the following harm statement: "Loss of classified homeland defense plan jeopardizes the military organization's capability to defend the homeland (because knowing the defense plan could give an adversary an overwhelming advantage)."

Row 2   Loss of *<critical data 2>* requiring major reinvestment to regain capability for *<mission element 2>*. As an example, take a nonprofit organization protecting endangered species with a mission element to protect the last remaining handful of white rhinos in the wild, all of whom they have radio tagged and for which they keep a constant location position to protect them against poachers. The "critical data 2" in this case are the geographic coordinates of the animals. The "mission element 2" is protecting the white rhinos from poachers. So, the harm statement becomes, "Loss of geographic coordinates of white rhinos to poachers requiring a major and urgent activity to relocate all of the individual animals before the poachers kill them all, which is catastrophic with respect to the organization's goal."

Row 3   Corrupt integrity of *<critical data 3>* so that consumers of data lose trust in *<mission element 3>*. As an example, let's take a bank that posts incorrect balances and incorrect transactions on all customers' bank statements online as a result of a hacking incident. In this case "critical data 3" would be "banking data that keeps track of account balances and financial transactions" from Table 4-3 and "gain deposits" from Table 4-4. The harm statement then becomes: "Loss of substantial deposits as a result of losing integrity of account balance and transaction data and the consequent loss of trust from depositors causing a significant fraction of customers to move their money to competing banks."

Row 4   Corrupt integrity of *<critical data 3>* to cause erroneous decisions to damage *<mission element 4>*. For an example in this case, let's take a bank again, but focusing on the lending function. The bank has to set its interest rate based on the prime rate updated periodically by the U.S. Federal Reserve Bank. If the prime rate is read from the reserve's computer into the bank's computer and is intentionally subtly corrupted in transit, the bank could erroneously decide its revised rate and post that erroneously low rate to its customers and then either be forced to lend at an unprofitable rate or suffer the public embarrassment regarding the bad decision based on bad data. The harm statement would be: "Corrupt integrity of newly posted prime rate from U.S. Federal Reserve Bank causing an erroneously low bank lending rate to be posted, resulting in losses from public embarrassment or from being forced to lend at an unfavorable rate."

Row 5   Deny service to *<critical subsystem 1>* to make *<critical subsystem 2>* unavailable for more than x days. For this template instantiation, let's take a charity organization's mission to collect donations on its website. Often, there are very critical date windows during which the majority of such donations happen—let's say between Thanksgiving and Christmas. If the website taking donations is unavailable for a large portion of the critical date window, the donation collection would be seriously jeopardized. This could be accomplished by a distributed denial of service attack on a network gateway just upstream (last router in a sequence of routers between the most donators' computers and that of the charity) of the charity's website. So, the harm statement would be something like: "Deny service to proximal router to make charity organization's donation collection website unavailable between Thanksgiving and Christmas to reduce collections by over 50 percent."

Row 6   Corrupt system integrity of *<critical subsystem 3>* and its backups required by *<critical subsystem 4>* to operate. In this case, let's return to a national military example seeking to support an emergency relief mission that is time-critical, such as a flood. If the military's logistics planning group's operating systems were all corrupted, as were their backups, they would be prevented from planning the support mission, which could in turn scuttle the entire humanitarian relief effort. In this case "critical system 3" includes all of the operating systems used by "critical system 4," which is the military organization's logistics planning system. So, the harm statement becomes: "Corrupt the system integrity of the logistic system's operating systems, causing the logistics planning systems to become unavailable for a critical three-day planning window, making support for a humanitarian mission impossible."

4.5 Harm Is in the Eye of the Beholder

Once an agreed-upon harm list is created, the organization must reach consensus on the gravity if a harmful outcome occurs. Estimates are often based on a comparable event. The risk assessment discipline often uses dollars as a convenient measure because it makes it easier to then carry over risk analysis into decision support for investment [PELT01]. Non-monetary risks, such as loss of life (though seemingly callous, the insurance industry does this as a matter of standard business) or mission, are translated to the equivalent dollars as best as possible. We will proceed with that metric. Others such as "utils" are available [STIG10].

4.5.1 Gravity of Harm: Consensus

Reaching consensus on harm is an interesting process. Once again, it is much better to elicit harm values from each of the executives separate from each other to avoid biasing. One can then combine the data and use a geometric mean as a starting point for consensus. The combined data can then be presented to the group of executives for directed discussion.

4.5.2 Drawing Conclusions

Often, it is useful to discuss the events with the most variation first, because the variation usually stems from differences in assumptions or difference in knowledge between members of the group. For each event, it is useful to give the floor to the outliers first to state their assumptions and give a rationale for their score. In that process, outliers need to be made to feel safe, so the leader of the group needs to help with creating that atmosphere.

　　Once the assumptions and differences of knowledge are fully discussed, members can be given the option of changing their scores in response to newly acquired understanding. They are not required to change their score and no pressure should be created to do so. Variation is useful to create a "wisdom of crowds" [SURO05] to get better estimates. Parenthetically, the discussion on differences of opinion can itself be quite illuminating to leadership and be the source of many interesting follow-up strategic conversations apart from the cybersecurity engineering process.

4.6 Sometimes Belief Is More Powerful than Truth

In considering harm, one should consider a class of harm that we will call "belief" harm. The damage is not tangible in the sense of damage to equipment or data, but rather the harm comes from inducing a belief in stakeholders of the mission. The belief can be a true belief that the organization did not want its stakeholders to know, but more often these are false beliefs that are induced though calculated misinformation—so-called deception attacks, to use military parlance.

4.6.1 Destroying Value

These beliefs often involve undermining the faith in the organization and its ability to perform its mission in a safe and reasonable way. *Make no mistake; faith can have huge impact on value.* For example, if investors lose faith in the value of a stock, billions of dollars can be lost overnight [RAPO17].

> *Belief attacks can be worse than actual ones.*

For example, if a cyberattack occurs on an organization, supporting organizations, or organizations that credibly report news (or their sources), the attack can plant false data about mismanagement or fraud that has been over-reporting value. A successful attack of this type could literally wipe out the equity in a company and could cause it to fail completely. Similarly, one can destroy a product brand by spreading rumors that it is tainted in some fashion and planting credible evidence that supports that false accusation.

4.6.2 Frustrating to Address: Life Is Unfair

These attacks can be very powerful, and all lists should include some. The attacks are also frustrating for both executives and engineers alike. Executives dislike them because they see such attacks as punishing them for something that they did not actually do wrong. The bad news is that life is not always fair. Executives need to be helped to overcome this reluctance.

Engineers dislike belief attacks because they can be extraordinarily difficult to counter. It may not be about better defending the system since the attacks are rarely on the defender's systems, so few, if any, of the proposed technical solutions do much to mitigate these attacks. *They must be considered nonetheless, if for no other reason than to understand the nature of the residual unmitigated risks after all solutions have been applied.*

Conclusion

This chapter gives the reader an understanding about what it means to focus on strategic risks and specific approaches to identify and prioritize them. The next chapter will begin to examine the nature of the systems that underlie missions and those that would do harm to missions.

To summarize:

- Focus on strategic risks by focusing on ways that mission elements can fail.
- Don't sweat the small stuff—it's a distraction that only serves the adversary.
- Strategic harm stems from what damages keep the C-suite up at night with worry.
- Partition data into tiers of criticality based on the degree to which mission depends on it.
- Criticality determines the relative importance of confidentiality, integrity, and availability.

- Examine cross-product of the mission and the critical data elements to find strategic harm.
- Agreeing on the key strategic harms is enlightening and leverages the "wisdom of crowds."
- Belief attacks are serious, frustrating, and are likely to grow in the future.

Questions

1. Explain why focusing on mission elements creates a focus on strategic harm.

2. Under what can conditions can a high-consequence attack have a relatively low risk; under what conditions can a medium-consequence attack have a high risk? Give examples.

3. Given that harm estimates are subjective, why are they useful? What could make them better? What is the alternative?

4. What is a critical asset inventory and how does it relate to data? What are the types of data and some subtypes within each type? What is the key difference between the two major types of data?

5. Give an example of each of the six categories of criticality and explain why it might be critical to the mission of an example organization of your choosing.

6. Pick an organization not described in the chapter, state three elements to its mission and two critical data elements, and then give three strategic harm statements using some combination of the mission elements and critical data elements, using the pattern discussed in this chapter.

5

Approximating Reality

Overview

Learning Objectives

- Explain the concept of system state and why it is too complex to understand without modeling.
- Explain why abstraction is needed and how to pick the proper levels of abstraction.
- Explain why abstraction by itself is not enough.
- List the elements of a system model and explain how they relate to one another.
- Summarize what can go wrong in modeling and the consequences.
- List the elements of a defender's view of the model and over which they have the most control.
- List the elements of the attacker's view of the model and over which they have the most control.
- Explain the forms a "view" takes and why it is a valuable target for the opponent.
- Describe the interdependency between trustworthiness and cybersecurity.
- Explain the design implications of assuming an adversary knows your system.
- Explain the design implications of assuming an adversary is inside your system.

5.1 The Complexity of State: Why Model?

Computer systems are incredibly complicated. In computer science, one speaks of the state of a system. System state can be a difficult concept to fully grasp, partly because it can be at many different levels of abstraction. In the most fundamental form, the state of a memory cell is either one or zero. Indeed, in the transition between these two states, there are other intermediate states, but the computer "hides" those states by not allowing a read operation on a memory cell until it is electrically stable in a definite binary state.

At the hardware level (see Section 9.1), the system state can be thought of as the aggregation of the state of all of its primary memory cells. **Primary memory** is the memory that the computer accesses first or directly to enable execution of programs (it is sometimes called random access memory, or RAM for short) and to store data. Today this is measured in gigabytes. In addition, there are several levels of faster memory called caches that are measured in megabytes. This is on top of the terabytes of **secondary memory** (e.g., hard drives) and sometimes petabytes of tertiary memory (e.g., backup media such as tapes and optical media).

Beyond this complexity is the fact that it is really the combinations of memory locations that have meaning (and therefore potential security implications), so one cannot look at memory values in isolation. So, one must examine the power set (i.e., the set of all subsets) of memory to fully understand what is going on. The number of subsets of any given set (where the set refers to the collection of memory cells) is 2 raised to the power of the size of the set—in this case petabytes. This gives 2^{30}—a big number indeed—10,000 times more than the number of drops in the oceans.

The other issue one encounters is that all of memory in a single computer, and indeed across the many computers that comprise modern systems, does not change synchronously. So, at any given instant, some memory is in a transition state and is not readable with a sensible value. This is not to mention the problem of the time delay of reading each memory cell and communicating its value to some place, each read operation and communication having different **latency** (delay) to reach some central point to view all of state.

The human mind can only hold and understand so many things at the same time—about seven, plus or minus two [MILL56]. *Clearly, knowing, let alone understanding, the full state of a modern system is beyond human faculties at the lowest level of details.* That is the purpose of abstraction and the mathematical equivalent of abstraction—modeling (see Section 19.2).

> *Abstraction makes incomprehensible system state intelligible.*

5.2 Levels of Abstraction: At What Levels

In addition to determining which combination of state elements to focus on, one can ask the question: What are the right levels of abstraction in modeling the design of a desired system? The right level of abstraction depends on the aspect of the system that is being designed and assessed. As we shall see in Section 19.2, there are many abstraction layers to consider.

The state of a computer can be as simple as on or off, too hot or not too hot, under attack or not under attack. In a large system of systems, just knowing what fraction of systems are "down" (not operating due to some unexpected failure) can be important and useful information, particularly if those systems have something in common—such as part of the same subnetwork, or perhaps they all share the exact same operating system release and patch level.

At the other end of the spectrum, to perform attack (and failure) forensics, an analyst may examine a "system dump" of a portion of primary memory to find an attack that exists only in primary memory and perhaps took advantage of a **buffer overflow attack** (see Figure 5-1). That is because the attack may not ever exist in anything other than primary memory, or the mechanism by which it gained control of the computer would only become apparent by examining primary memory of the application that had a vulnerability that it exploited.

Attack Panel: Buffer Overflow	
Class	Integrity
Type	Error Exploitation
Mechanism	Provide an input to a program that is larger or of a different type than expected such that input overwrites important memory to degrade data or gain control of process execution.
Examples	SQL Slammer worm exploited a buffer overflow in Microsoft SQL Server 2000.
Damage Potential	Billions of dollars in lost revenue due to the attacker being able to take control of machines and do further damage.

Figure 5-1   Attack description: buffer overflow

Alternatively, one can focus on the dynamics of control and data flow between major subsystems of a large system if the concern is about attacks that manifest at interfaces. For example, one can look for attack signatures or anomalous levels of traffic at the interfaces between a data collection subsystem, a data processing subsystem, and a data distribution subsystem.

5.3 What to Model and Why

Now that you know that *you must model to understand* and that there are choices regarding level of abstraction, the next question regards what to model. Given the astronomical size of state, there are a mind-boggling number of choices. Examining each possibility from the bottom up would take decades. Instead, one asks: What question is the model attempting to answer?

Often, broader questions result in the need for more complex models. The question "Is the system secure?" is a simple question, but very broad. It raises the question of what it means for the system to be in a **secure state** and what it means for a state transition to preserve security. One can simplify the definition of security to simplify the modeling requirements. For example, defining security as meaning "does not leak sensitive data to unauthorized users" can lead to a simple model of state—on or off. If a system is "off," then it is secure. If it is "on," it may leak data with some probability. So, to achieve a secure state would mean turning off all the systems. Of course, this is a cartoon to illustrate the point of model oversimplification and the possible absurd conclusions one might draw when the model is incomplete. In this case, the model fails to take into consideration that much value is brought to an organization by their systems being "on" and functioning properly.

Before proceeding with discussing what to model, it is important to distinguish between prevention and detection of a transition into an insecure state. If one is only concerned with detection, then only operations that result in reading and writing to memory are directly relevant. If one cares about preventing insecure transition, then it matters what **objects** can be executed as well (objects are called "programs" or sometimes "scripts"). One develops a theory of how to limit transformations to only those that are secure—either by limiting each and every operation, or by generally blocking certain types of operations to certain classes of objects. In general, one needs to model the target system, the users, the adversaries, and the measures/countermeasures. Each is discussed in turn.

5.3.1 The Target System

Only the security-relevant portions of the system are modeled since that is the focus of cybersecurity engineering. By security-relevant, we mean relevant to proving the cybersecurity properties of the system, including the correctness of the underlying components on which those properties depend. When trade-offs between cybersecurity and functionality and performance are required, functionality and performance may also need to be modeled in some fashion—often informally and qualitatively. *To decide what is security-relevant, one can examine the three states of data: data at rest—memory or storage, data in motion—communications and networking, and data in transition—computation.*

This means that storage, communications, and computation must be modeled. An example of modeling storage is modeling data objects such as files and binding **metadata** (e.g., security sensitivity labels, such as the military's unclassified–confidential–secret–top–secret schema as depicted in Figure 5-2) to those objects, which are then used by access control rules governing access to those objects. An example of modeling communications is modeling inter-process communications and the network socket abstraction used in some operating systems. An example of modeling computation is to create a process abstraction whose execution is controlled and monitored in terms of rules governing its access to resources, such as storage and communication channels. These are the basics. System modeling is a long and complex topic warranting its own book. More detail can be found in [LEVE12][SMIT08].

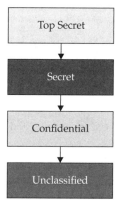

Figure 5-2   U.S. classification hierarchy in which a person cleared at a given level can see data at that level and lower.

All security controls are, by definition, security-relevant. Therefore, devices such as firewalls, access-control routers, intrusion detection appliances, authorization and authentication systems, and security subsystems of operating systems and applications are all part of the defenses and therefore all are security-relevant.

5.3.2 Users

Technically, users are part of the broader system, but are treated here separately because they are a particularly complex and sometimes problematic aspect of system security. Sometimes cybersecurity engineers exclaim a half-serious lament that *security would be so much easier without users*! Of course, the irony is that the system has little purpose without users. A complete model must include users. **Social engineering attacks** (Figure 5-3) that focus on tricking users are almost always successful. Users often make serious mistakes that create vulnerabilities. Sometimes, users intentionally bypass security, such as creating unauthorized network connections with the honest intention of "getting the job done" without fully appreciating the risk they create for the mission of their organization. Modeling users means at least understanding and allowing for these sorts of attacks and security-relevant failures.

There is one special class of user worth calling out separately here—the **defense operators**, including system administrators, network administrators, and intrusion detection system monitors. These operators are the privileged users who have the knowledge and ability to command the defensive subsystem against attack, to reconfigure the system and adjust its operation to keep the mission safe. These special users, like normal users, are human.

Attack Panel: Social Engineering and Phishing	
Class	Access
Type	Psychological Operations
Mechanism	An attacker uses some ruse such as an urgent situation or keeping someone out of trouble to get an authorized user to violate security policy such as giving out their password.
Examples	Reveal password over phone to help fake IT department solve some crisis. Phishing and spearphishing use similar techniques, but typically through email.
Damage Potential	Attacker gains a toehold on the system and can then escalate privilege to gain complete access to all systems on a network.

Figure 5-3 Attack description: social engineering and phishing

That means they are also subject to social engineering attacks, make mistakes, and sometimes do risky things in the name of mission that they should not do. *If these special users succumb to social engineering attacks, the damages can be grave.*

> *Defense operators are high-value targets for attackers.*

5.3.3 Adversaries

Adversaries are another special class of user. Adversaries have many characteristics that will be discussed in detail in Sections 6.1 through 6.3, including capabilities, resources, and risk tolerance. Adversaries also have goals with respect to the target systems such as stealing the data, destroying the integrity of the data, or making the system unavailable for a period of time. Adversaries take a sequence of actions to accomplish their goals and need to understand the target system and the degree to which their actions succeed or need to be adjusted.

5.3.4 Measures/Countermeasures

Systems have inherent security measures that are intended to thwart attacks. These measures are sometimes called countermeasures because they are designed to counteract the measures that an attacker might take to achieve some attack goal. They are effectively actions, or "moves" in the sense of a game analogy (e.g., chess). With respect to modeling, static measures are part of the system model. Often these measures have a dynamic component such as changing the rules of a **firewall** to make the **security policy** more conservative in response to an apparent attack. This dynamic nature must be captured in the model. When an action is taken, whether by the attacker or the defender, these actions affect system state and move the system closer to or further from the attacker's goal state of compromise. This dynamicism is complex because actions often take time to complete and transition the system state. Actions sometimes fail.

The system state can change during action execution, making state transition difficult to predict or fully analyze.

The elements of the model come together to form a complex model as depicted in Figure 5-4. This is intended to show the reality of the state of the system as it exists in reality. As discussed earlier, these states in their most detailed representation are incomprehensible, so a model or approximation of the state must be created to understand it. Such models are discussed in the next section.

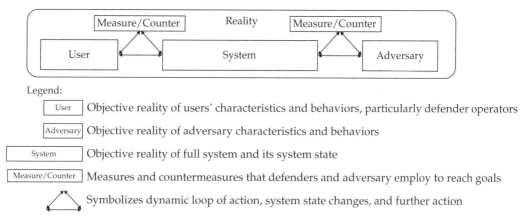

Legend:

User	Objective reality of users' characteristics and behaviors, particularly defender operators
Adversary	Objective reality of adversary characteristics and behaviors
System	Objective reality of full system and its system state
Measure/Counter	Measures and countermeasures that defenders and adversary employ to reach goals

Symbolizes dynamic loop of action, system state changes, and further action

Figure 5-4   A model of a system including users, adversaries, and dynamic measures/countermeasures. Users (defense operators) apply measures/countermeasures to keep the system in a secure state, while the adversary applies measures/countermeasures to achieve their attack goals.

5.4 Models Are Always Wrong, Sometimes Useful

Because models are approximations, they are always necessarily wrong in some way [BOX87] [TOUR52]. *The goal is to model systems in such a way that their wrongness is not essential to the purpose the model is intended to serve.* For example, if one is trying to simply model **uptime** (amount of time each component in a system is operating), one need not bother with the details of which operating system it has, what patch level, and all the configurations of all the loaded applications. Including such details unnecessarily complicates the model.

There are at least three ways models can be wrong: incompleteness, inaccuracy, or non-timeliness. Each is discussed in turn.

5.4.1 Incompleteness of Essentials

Incompleteness does not refer to nonessential elements that are appropriately and intentionally left out. Incompleteness refers to aspects of a system that *are* in fact essential, often subtly so, that were *mistakenly* left out. As an example, if one were concerned about availability attacks and became too focused on **flooding attacks** on the border of a system, they could easily mistakenly omit modeling **domain name attack** or **logic time bombs** internal to the system border.

Failure to model what turn out to be important aspects of a system can have surprising and sometimes disastrous effects. As an analogy, let's say that there were extra dimensions of the physical universe that enable one to travel between any two points of the three-dimensional universe instantaneously. A defense plan that assumes a three-dimensional universe would be completely ineffective against an alien race that understood and could exploit extra-dimensional travel. To put this in cybersecurity terms, if one were not aware of **supply-chain attacks** (Figure 5-5), it could be quite surprising for an attack to start occurring from inside one's own network, perhaps even from inside one's own cybersecurity subsystem (e.g., a firewall has a **backdoor** that allows that adversary to take control of the firewall at will).

Attack Panel: Supply-Chain Attack	
Class	Integrity
Type	System Integrity
Mechanism	An attacker attacks a development or distribution channel of a program to insert malicious code allowing later activation when the program is deployed in some end system.
Examples	Inserting a backdoor malicious code by hacking into the development system on which an operating system like Windows or Unix is developed.
Damage Potential	Varies, but could be mission-ending damage.

Figure 5-5   Attack description: supply chain attack

5.4.2 Inaccuracy

Most simply, the system model may not reflect the system as built and operating. How could that be? The design process is complex, interactive, and prone to errors and evolution. Systems typically are refined from user requirements, to high-level design, to detailed design, to implementation, to testing, to deployment, to maintenance. This is essentially true, though contorted, even for Agile design methods, as discussed further in Section 19.1.6. Further discussion of good design principles is included in Section 19.2. *Each of these steps should undergo review and analysis internally and between steps to ensure that one step accurately reflects the previous step.* This process, as shown in Figure 5-6, is highly prone to human error.

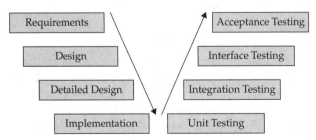

Figure 5-6   Systems engineering "V" showing steps of design and mapping in which faults can be introduced

The artifact of each step could itself have errors, as could the mapping to the next step. For example, a designer or engineer may inaccurately capture a user requirement, making all subsequent steps related to that requirement incorrect. At the same time, even if the requirements are perfect, an engineer can make an error in design process such that the design does not meet the requirements. Each step and mapping are prone to similar issues.

In addition, the system evolves during the design process and even after deployment. Testing may reveal an implementation flaw that is really a design flaw that possibly stemmed from an ambiguous requirement. Ensuring that all documents are properly updated in the heat of the project deadlines within mandated cost constraints requires extraordinary discipline that most teams fail to muster. As a result, operations and user manuals are created based on inaccurate documentation and are therefore themselves inaccurate.

Once the system is deployed, system owners and operators often make adjustments to the system configuration and operation without updating the original system design documentation. As a simple example, users often add new computers to meet a mission need for additional computation or resources. The design makes such additions as simple as plug-and-play. Unfortunately, that means that many people do not take the trouble of updating the network diagram to reflect the additional computers on the network, or worse yet, a new router that connects the internal network to an external network such as the Internet. Therefore, the defenders may use the designer's network diagram that is beautiful but inaccurate.

5.4.3 Non-Timeliness

Lastly, even in the rare case that a model is accurate and complete with respect to the static components, it is difficult to keep it accurate with respect to changes in dynamic state. In addition to the complexities of capturing system state discussed in the beginning of this chapter, there can be delays in both the implementation of changes and reporting of changes to the system. For example, say that a defender issues commands to all border firewalls to shut off all traffic on port 80 (web traffic) temporarily. That command must go through many steps and must go out to many firewalls for implementation, and then their reports of completion must be returned. These many steps are abstractly depicted in Figure 5-7 and discussed in more detail in the following paragraphs.

The following unexpected delays or errors may occur in the complex processing sequence shown in Figure 5-7:

- **Non-instantaneity** People have gotten so used to events happening so close to instantaneously (relative to a human time scale) that they confuse the act of commanding a change with the change actually occurring. Computers, particularly under high load, can take time to assemble the commands, communicate the commands down through a busy operating system on a network socket, through a network interface, out onto a busy network, and back up through a similar stack on the receiving side, which also could be heavily loaded.

- **Translation delay** The high-level command may require manual translation by human operators to device-specific command sequences to accomplish the change.

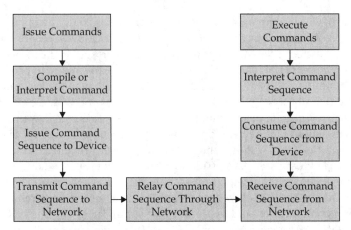

Figure 5-7   Issuing cybersecurity commands involves a complex and hidden sequence of actions that are subject to attack, error, and delay at each step.

- **Alternative configuration setting**   Often these command sequences involve the creation of an alternative configuration with the new rule set and then a command to switch from the existing rule set to the alternative configuration.

- **Wait-to-complete**   The firewall may wait to complete certain transactions and connections before executing the switch. So, the operator may incorrectly assume that once the firewall acknowledges receipt of the command sequence, the implementation of those commands is instantaneous or at least determinate.

- **Not expecting report**   Because programmers often do not adequately anticipate delays and errors, they sometimes do not even wait for or expect any report on whether an action was successful or not. This can lead to an incorrect belief that a command has been executed when it is still pending or perhaps never was received by the device.

- **Device blocked**   Communication between the transmitter and the recipient on a network can be blocked. This could happen because the network is overloaded, possibly intentionally with a denial of service flooding attack either at the transmission device, the recipient device, or the network in between. Networks often drop packets (i.e., do not transmit) as a matter of standard operating procedure when the network becomes congested. Using unreliable protocols such as **user datagram protocol (UDP)** is highly efficient and fast, but is subject to undetected failure due to dropped packets (a subset of data packets that are not relayed in the network because the load is too high). Use of **Transmission Control Protocol (TCP)** is far more appropriate when the message delivery reliability is important—as is almost always the case in cybersecurity. Even TCP can fail in the case of flooding, but at least the transmitter knows that a message did not get through.

- **Reporting delays**   Once the device has completed a command, it could determine that reporting is a low-priority activity and schedule it for a time when it is less busy. If an attack is ongoing, waiting for a relatively free moment could take a long time.

- **Error**   Despite most people experiencing computer failures on their home computers, many, including programmers, seem to not realize that computers fail in a myriad of ways. There are design and implementation flaws in all systems. Some can lead to incorrect or delayed execution and reporting of commands. For example, a recipient device could report receiving a message and executing as a matter of efficiency and then spawn a process to actually execute the command, only to find insufficient process memory to do so.

- **Compromise and lying**   At any point in the data packet transmission chain, as depicted in Figure 5-8, there could have been a successful attack in which the adversary has gained control of that element of the system. Thus, it is possible for that element to simply lie and say that the command was issued or communicated, when it was not; that it was transmitted, when it was not; that it was received, when it was not; or that it succeeded, when it did not.

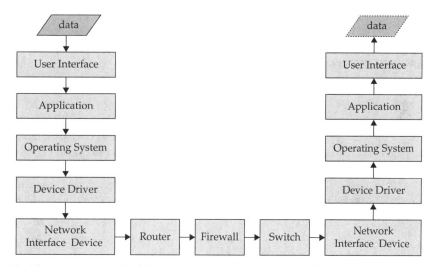

Figure 5-8   The processing path of data packet showing delay, error, and attack opportunity to consider

5.5 Model Views

So far, the discussion has centered around what to model and what can go wrong in modeling a real system. Now, the discussion turns to a "view"—modeling of a system from a specific perspective. While there are many possible perspectives that are interesting and worth considering, the focus here is on the defender views and the attacker views.

5.5.1 Defender's View

The defender must formally or informally model all of the aspects of a system discussed previously: the system, the user, the adversary, the action of measures and countermeasures, and more. Because models are abstractions, they can be thought of as a projection of the real complex system onto a much simpler model system. This projection is depicted in Figure 5-9.

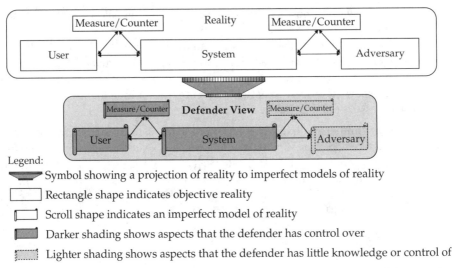

Legend:

Symbol showing a projection of reality to imperfect models of reality

Rectangle shape indicates objective reality

Scroll shape indicates an imperfect model of reality

Darker shading shows aspects that the defender has control over

Lighter shading shows aspects that the defender has little knowledge or control of

Figure 5-9 A defender's model of a real system can be thought of as a projection of the complex real system onto a simpler abstract model system.

Notice in Figure 5-9 that there is an important difference between the left-hand side of the defender's view and the right-hand side. The left-hand side includes the defender's system users, the cybersecurity measures and countermeasures that are available to the defender, and the system itself. All of these are under the direct control of the defender. *This can be an important strategic advantage because the defender has the opportunity to design and operate the target system in a manner that makes the adversary's job harder while making the defender's mission easier.* Of course, these two aspects are sometimes in a trade-off, and the method of making that trade-off explicit is complex and not yet well understood.

> ### *Defenders can shape the cyber terrain in their favor.*

The right-hand side of the view is completely out of the defender's control and totally within the adversary's control: the adversary users and the measures and countermeasures that are available to them. Indeed, although it is not depicted for simplification of the figure, there is also an adversary system, which is also subject to attack, possibly by the defender. To take that to one more level of detail, the adversary system generally has at least two parts: an attack development system where they create general attack components, and an attack integration and testing system in which they generally operate an actual system that is a working model of the defender's system, so that the tests are realistic. This detail bears on strategies such as cyber maneuver and cyber deception to prevent the attacker from gaining an accurate model to test against, and cyber network attack intelligence to gain insight into attacks that an adversary is planning, and the defender mounting a cyber network attack against an attacking system.

Because the defender has little control over the adversary and their actions, it is important to develop generic models of a range of different classes of adversaries, their characteristics, and goals so that the range of possible actions and the strategies may be thought through in advance of an actual attack. Armed with such models, it may be possible to predict an adversary's next action and reconfigure the system to thwart the action before it is initiated. It is also possible to predict the adversary's preferred targets, attack methods, likelihood of attempting certain attacks, and likelihood of success if they try. *This is all invaluable information in optimizing both the static defense design and the dynamic defense posture at any given time.*

Lastly, the defender must develop courses of action (command sequences) that respond to attack scenarios in advance of actually encountering those scenarios. This is important for many reasons:

- First, for every second of delayed response, the defender is likely to incur damages at an increasing rate. Thus, pre-computed actions and pre-evaluation of when those actions (measures and countermeasures) are used to speed the decision cycle and reduce damages from the attack.

- Second, one can take the time to analyze each command sequence in advance and test it to determine how long it takes to execute and how it reacts under various system loads.

- Third, certain defense strategies may call for actions that have not yet been defined or are not supported by the underlying defense mechanisms. This gives an opportunity for the defender to develop a new capability to design the scripts to execute the actions and perhaps to update the defense mechanism infrastructure to ensure that it is able to perform some of the important functions needed in a defensive response.

Similarly, by having generic models of classes of adversaries and their potential attack actions and scenarios, defenders can (a) improve detection of those actions, and (b) evaluate the best defensive courses of actions against those attacks in advance and be ready to deploy those actions once the attack is detected. The generic models can be improved as the defender learns more about various attackers' actual attack operations through being attacked directly by them, or by learning from attacks on others from those adversaries—using the cyber epidemiological data available for organizations such as **computer emergency response teams (CERTs)**. It also motivates one to direct intelligence gathering against the adversary cyber capability and attack system to further improve the model.

5.5.2 Adversary's View

Just as the defender has their view or projection of the target system, the adversary has their own view of the same system. Each view or model is intended to be optimized for the purpose for which it is intended, and therefore, the models will be inherently different from one another. For example, *an adversary needs to find only one vulnerability in a system to exploit, whereas a defender must be aware of and defend all of them*. This truism alone can drive each to very different models. The adversary view is added to the accumulating model of models as shown in Figure 5-10.

> *Defenders must close all attack avenues; attackers need only one.*

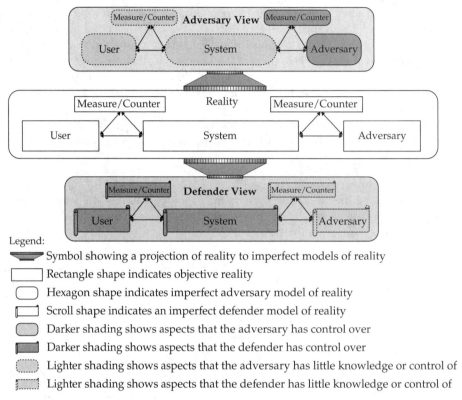

Legend:

 Symbol showing a projection of reality to imperfect models of reality

 Rectangle shape indicates objective reality

 Hexagon shape indicates imperfect adversary model of reality

 Scroll shape indicates an imperfect defender model of reality

 Darker shading shows aspects that the adversary has control over

 Darker shading shows aspects that the defender has control over

 Lighter shading shows aspects that the adversary has little knowledge or control of

 Lighter shading shows aspects that the defender has little knowledge or control of

Figure 5-10   Cybersecurity-relevant security state is complex and dynamic. The adversary and the defender both have models approximating the state that are inaccurate in some ways and useful. These models drive decision making.

Similar to the defender's view, the adversary's view has two distinct sides with two different levels of control and information. In this case, the adversary has knowledge and control of the right-hand side of the figure: adversary users (and the non-depicted adversary system) and the actions he may take against the target system. The left-hand side includes the target system, the target system users, and the actions that the defender can take to try to stop the adversary attack. Although there is a similarity in the lack of control and information from one side to the other, as there is in the defender's view, there is an important difference. The adversary has the element of surprise and potentially covert action. *The adversary knows they are going to attack the target system. They know when. They know how. They know why.* The adversary can surreptitiously reconnoiter the target system and develop a detailed model of the target system, defense, and even the actions that the defender is capable of. They can search for and find vulnerabilities using the flaw hypothesis methodology as mentioned in Section 1.2.1 and verify them through experimentation.

> *The attacker has the big advantage of the element of surprise.*

The adversary may go as far as monitoring the live system to watch how the defender reacts to attacks from others that happen serendipitously. More proactively, the adversary may construct and conduct experimental attacks to learn exactly how the defender reacts under specific aspects of scenarios the attacker is intending to use. Such attacks would, of course, be **anonymized** or intentionally made to be **misattributed** to come from a different attacker (for example, by hijacking computers in a different country and launching the attacks from there to make it look like hackers in that country are launching the attack).

All of this adversary **reconnaissance** means the attacker can develop excellent models of the defender's target system, its verified and potential vulnerabilities, and the defender's tactics and strategies in the face of attack. *The more an attacker learns, the better the chances that their attack will be effective against the target and will account for defender behavior.* Indeed, the attacker may even be able to use the defender's behavior against themselves by inducing the defender to take some action such as taking themselves off the network to try to prevent further attack—and effectively successfully mounting a denial of service attack against themselves such that their system is no longer available to support mission.

> *Deny attackers knowledge of target systems when possible.*

Ironically, because the adversary's model of the target is developed from the system as it really exists—with all of the post-deployment modifications and the intended and unintended security and functional flaws compared to the design—*the adversary's model of the defender's target system is often more accurate than the defenders' model since the defender often relies on outdated design documents, flawed designs, and buggy implementations for theirs.* The adversary has the advantage of looking coldly and objectively from the outside of the system, unbiased by the wishful thinking and delusions of the system designers.

5.5.3 Attacking the Views Themselves

As models have been discussed so far, the reader may have inferred that these models are all explicit and that there are some great tools that allow the exploration of the models. While it is true that some tools are emerging for this purpose [LEMA11], these models are often informal models that are sometimes in documents, sometimes in PowerPoint slides, and sometimes just in people's heads (sometimes humorously referred to as **wetware**—a play on the word software, but using the brain, which is wet). So, models are a hybrid of many different artifacts and beliefs. As time progresses, it is likely that models will become more sophisticated, increasingly comprehensive, and supported by tools that allow the users to explore alternative paths of attack and defense.

Such hybrid models, the attacker and defender views of the systems, are themselves subject to attack by the opponent and valuable targets. As we have seen, defenders depend deeply on their models to properly and effectively defend their systems (whether they realize it explicitly or not). Similarly, adversaries even more critically depend on their models to develop and execute effective attacks. Therefore, it stands to reason that *these valuable models are excellent targets of attack by either side to deprive the user of the model and the huge benefit the model provides.*

> ### *Models themselves are valuable targets and deserve protection.*

Attacking views can come in two forms: attack the artifacts (manifestation of models in the form of documents or simulation systems) or attacking the beliefs. The notion of attacking the artifacts themselves is relatively straightforward. One simply attacks the system on which the artifact exists and executes an integrity attack against that artifact. Again, this can be done by either the adversary or the defender. Confidentiality attacks against the opponent's model may also prove useful to learn what they know and what they think they know about their opponents.

Alternatively, one can attack the beliefs of the other. For example, the defender can try to induce the belief that the defender's defenses are stronger than they are. A good analogous example of attacking beliefs is purchasing and posting a sign outside of your residence that it is protected by an alarm system when in fact it is not. This effectively deters a lot of would-be robbers who find it easier to locate an alternative non-protected residence to rob than to determine the veracity of the sign. Similarly, if a system displays a banner upon network connection that all users are subject to monitoring by an advanced anomaly-based intrusion detection system—the banner may have a similar effect to the house alarm placard.

As another example, adversaries could, and sometimes do, make their attacks appear like normal system failures when part of the value of the attack is the defender not knowing that an attack happened and was successful (such as when compromising secret information). As mentioned, *attackers may design the attack so that it appears to come from a different source and cause the defender to take retaliatory action against the supposed attacker.* That retaliation may itself be the goal of the attack. For example, if it is in the best interest of a country to not have two other countries become allies, then such a country could fake an attack in either or both directions between the two countries to increase tension and decrease the likelihood of future collaboration.

Belief attacks are powerful and important. They will become increasingly important over time as will be discussed in subsequent chapters.

> ### *Defense against belief attacks will become increasingly important.*

5.6 Defense Models Must Consider Failure Modes

Reliability and cybersecurity are closely related, but separate, systems engineering disciplines. Reliability addresses avoiding, detecting, and recovering from unintentional failure. Security addresses avoiding, detecting, and recovering from intentional failure toward some specific goal. Clearly, the difference is about intentionality. This means that the techniques for one cannot be easily applied to the other without significant adaptation. What one can say is that *achieving security requires reliability and achieving reliability requires security.* That close interdependency is why the term dependability was created to cover both disciplines because they are best considered together [ALVI04].

> ### *Security requires reliability; reliability requires security.*

Why does cybersecurity require reliability? If security measures and countermeasures are completely unreliable, then they actually do more harm than good. That is because system owners and users will operate and conduct themselves with the mistaken belief that they are secure when they are not, thus taking risks on the system that they would otherwise not take. No matter how well a system is engineered, designers never achieve 100 percent reliability. Therefore, designers must anticipate unintentional failure of the system and particularly cybersecurity mechanisms. Adversaries are constantly watching for such failures and will take advantage of them when they occur. *If a security designer does not anticipate these failures, they will not do adequate reliability engineering to avoid those failures, they will not detect them, and they will not have methods to quickly recover from them before they are exploited.* This principle is succinctly summarized humorously in a book called *Systematics* [GALL77] with the theorem: "Systems that are designed to be fail-safe often fail by failing to fail safely."

> ### *Failure avoidance, detection, and recovery are essential.*

Reliability is concerned with **faults**, errors, and failures [ALVI90], which relate to one another, as shown in Figure 5-11. Faults represents flaws in a system design or implementation. These faults can remain dormant and not cause any deviation from correct operation until they are activated, such as when a little-used branch of a program case-statement is reached. This creates an active fault, which causes an error in the system state. That error causes a failure when the error or some subsequent propagated error causes the software to provide incorrect service. An error that has not yet caused a failure can be said to be a latent error and can eventually cause a failure under the right conditions. For example, if a system has a fault that provides an incorrect value for pi in the tenth decimal place, then that is a dormant fault. It becomes an error when an actual incorrect value is returned to a program. If that program rounds to the hundredths place, then the error does not become a failure because it is rounded away anyway. However, in a highly precise calculation such as in calculating rocket trajectory, that error becomes a failure when the wrong thrust is used because the program returned an erroneous value of pi in the tenth place.

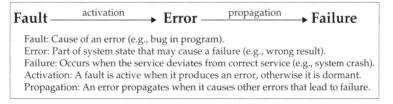

Fault ———activation———▶ Error ———propagation———▶ Failure

Fault: Cause of an error (e.g., bug in program).
Error: Part of system state that may cause a failure (e.g., wrong result).
Failure: Occurs when the service deviates from correct service (e.g., system crash).
Activation: A fault is active when it produces an error, otherwise it is dormant.
Propagation: An error propagates when it causes other errors that lead to failure.

Figure 5-11 Chain of dependability threats [ALVI90]

A good cybersecurity engineer must deeply understand the concepts of failure and take them into consideration during design. They should know enough to avoid faults, detect errors and failure, and recover from errors and failures quickly. They should know basic reliability engineering techniques such as hazard analysis as discussed in [REAS90, DORN96, WIEG03]. They should know when the stakes are high enough to consult a reliability engineer to ensure that reliability properties that the cybersecurity engineer thinks they are achieving are actually achieved. See Section 20.5 for more discussion on designing systems to tolerate failure.

5.7 Assume Adversaries Know Defender's System

I was in a high-level government meeting one day and posited a devastating attack scenario against a critical system. The response was "nobody would think of that." When I pointed out the obvious—that I just did think of it—the retort was that that was only because I understood the system deeply. I found that perspective disturbingly naive. *Secrecy is never a reliable means of ensuring the security of one's system.* This is a principle that is long-known, tried, and true.

> *Design secrecy provides ineffective protection.*

Secrets are fleeting, and we must also assume they will eventually be revealed. Therefore, *systems must be designed under the assumption that the adversary knows your system at least as well as you do, and possibly better* [KERC83].

> *Assume that your adversary knows your system better than you.*

As a basic example of this, *never include a secret key or a password in the code or data structures of a program.* Assume that the adversary has a copy of the program and so that secret is instantly lost, as is any authentication or secrecy that that password or secret afforded. In cryptography, more subtly, this means that the secrecy of the encryption process cannot depend on the secrecy of the encryption algorithm. Instead, the secrecy depends on a small bit of data called the **cryptographic key**.

This principle is not to say that secrecy of design has no role. For example, the algorithms that protected classified data were still classified by the U.S. government for an added degree of supplemental security. This is because getting cryptographic algorithms correct in both design and implementation is extraordinarily difficult.

Similarly, *it is unwise to advertise the exact nature, configuration, and settings of one's defensive systems as well as one's risk management analysis and plan.* For example, if a defender were to publicly post the detection threshold settings on their intrusion detection system, it would be easier for the adversary to design attacks that would go undetected. Extending this idea further, it could prove useful to vary the configuration of the system unpredictably so that the adversary faced uncertainty of the defense model, thus increasing the risk that the design attack would not succeed and could possibly be detected.

> *Protect system defense parameters.*

Finally, **zero-day attacks** are attacks that have never been seen before on the defender's system or any other known system. Zero-day attacks are generally created by adversaries finding or learning about security faults in a system design or implementations [BEUR15]. They are usually found through careful analysis by the attacker or some third party that makes the attacks available to the attacker. One way that attacks are made available is through selling the zero-day attack on the black market [RADI09].

This is why it is a high priority for attackers to break in and steal the source code to popular systems software such as Windows [EVER04] and popular applications. Stealing the code gives them ample opportunity to carefully examine the code for flaws in the privacy of their own systems, which may also have specialized tools and analysts to conduct the analysis.

Often, developer systems for software, particularly those of smaller vendors, are poorly protected on the grounds that they are "just development systems" and are not involved in production or operations of the mission. The problem is that they are feeders into such systems and could be a source of vulnerabilities that can be exploited by zero-day attacks, which are difficult to defend against, since the nature of the exploitation is not known in advance of the attack, particularly if the zero-day attack is in the defense mechanism itself.

> *Poorly protected development systems lead to zero-day attacks.*

5.8 Assume Adversaries Are Inside Defender's System

In modern system design, cybersecurity engineers must work with an even more difficult assumption in their model: that *the adversary not only knows the target system, but is inside the defender's system.* This assumption is fully warranted given the highly complex nature of the system of systems that modern systems represent and the myriad of opportunities that adversaries have for successfully attacking those systems at nearly any point in their life cycle and supply chain.

In addition to attacking development systems as discussed previously to insert **malicious software**, *the adversary can attack the development tools themselves* as is pointed out in the classic paper "Reflections on Trusting Trust" [THOM84]. As shown in Figure 5-12, the adversary can attack the **compiler**, the linker, the loader, the libraries, or the configuration build files. Detecting and stopping these sorts of attacks are very difficult.

> *Software development tools and processes may be vulnerable.*

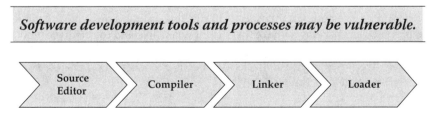

Source Editor: Programming tool used to enter source code
Compiler: Translator from high-level language to object code
Linker: Links pre-compiled program libraries into the object code
Loader: Places executable code into memory and prepares for execution

Figure 5-12   Programming tools used in the creation of executable programs are all subject to attack.

The implication of this design principle and model assumption is that the designer must isolate compromise, a type of cybersecurity failure, to prevent it from propagating throughout the entire system. This means the architecture must extend the principle of **least privilege** (that users get the minimum privilege they need to do their job) to the system itself and ensure that a piece of malicious code inside one component cannot propagate to another. *This is done by minimizing intersystem trust and by making interfaces between systems clear, the minimum for what is needed, and requiring authentication and authorization to use.*

> *Minimize intersystem trust requirements.*

Another implication of this principle is that the system must be designed to detect malicious code operating inside the security perimeter of the system, using **covert channels** of communication (i.e., communication mechanisms not specifically designed to communicate so that the communication cannot be easily detected, like banging on the pipes in Morse code in prison; see Section 12.1.3), escalating privilege without apparent reason, and the movement of data to and from unexpected parts of the network.

Specifically, the principle of attacker-inside-your-system gives rise to the *requirement to not only monitor the system border for incoming attacks, but also for outgoing exfiltration (malicious and usually covert transmission of stolen data from inside of a system to outside of a system for an adversary to have easy access), incoming command signals to the malware, or covert communications between instances of the malware inside the system attempting to coordinate activity toward an attacker goal.*

> *Exfiltration monitoring is equally important as that of infiltration.*

Conclusion

This chapter concludes the first part of the book, giving a broad overview of the problem and solution space, which will be detailed in future chapters. We discussed the best perspective to take when considering cybersecurity design and analysis. We then discussed the importance of focusing on the mission of systems and the core of the value that is at risk by cyberattack. The chapter on harm then showed how the mission can be imperiled by cyberattack and how to focus on the most important aspects. Lastly, this chapter taught how to model incredibly complex modern systems to make them comprehensible and to use those models to guide effective cybersecurity engineering. The next two chapters go into much more detail on the nature of adversaries and their attacks as a means of educating cybersecurity engineers as to what they must defend against.

To summarize:

- Systems are too complex to understand without modeling in some way.
- Abstraction helps focus attention and foster better cybersecurity design and operation.
- System models include the technology, human behavior, and their palette of actions.

- Models can be inaccurate, incomplete, or obsolete, causing design and operations errors.
- Defender models have the advantage of controlling and knowing their system.
- Attacker models have the asymmetric advantage of the element of surprise.
- Defender and adversary models are themselves valuable targets.
- Cybersecurity and reliability are interdependent aspects of trustworthiness.
- Assume that an adversary deeply knows the target system's design and implementation.
- More strongly, assume that adversaries are inside the system in the form of malicious code.

Questions

1. Describe the size of a detailed system state, the complexities of state transition timing, and the difficulties in taking a state snapshot.

2. Pick a simple cybersecurity aspect of a system you are familiar with, and describe a good level of abstraction and the elements of the model at that level. Provide a rationale for your choices.

3. What are the aspects of a system to model when considering static and dynamic attacks and defenses? Why is it important to model human behavior?

4. Describe how and why a model can be incomplete. Inaccurate? Obsolete?

5. Explain the level of fidelity of the elements of a defender view of the model and what can be done to improve them.

6. Explain the level of fidelity of the elements of an adversary view of the model and what can be done to improve them.

7. List two forms a defender or adversary view can take and why they are valuable targets to an opponent. Describe how they are valuable from the confidentiality, integrity, and availability perspectives and how they fit together. Which is most important and why?

8. Describe the relationship between reliability and cybersecurity. Define the terms fault, error, and failure and how they relate to one another.

9. Why should a designer assume an adversary knows their system? What are three different types of knowledge that an adversary may have?

10. Why should a designer assume an adversary is inside their system? What exactly does that mean? Give two examples of being inside a system and discuss the design implications.

PART

II

What Could Go Wrong?

"Part II: What Could Go Wrong?" is about understanding attacks, failures, and the attacker mind-set. Cybersecurity engineers must deeply understand the nature of attacks to properly design defenses against those attacks.

CHAPTER

6

Adversaries: Know Thy Enemy

Overview

Learning Objectives

- Discuss characteristics of adversaries and understand the implications for cybersecurity design.
- Describe what assuming a smart adversary means and why it is important to design.
- List ways in which adversaries don't play fair and the implications for cybersecurity design.
- Summarize trends in cyberattacks and how cybersecurity engineers can anticipate new attacks.
- Discuss the nature of red teams and their important role in cybersecurity assessment.
- Contrast the purposes of pure cyberspace and cyber-physical exercises.
- Define the phrase "red-team work factor" and how it is used as a quality metric.
- Consider the limitations of red teams.

We have met the enemy, and he is us.

—Pogo

Just as theories of security come from theories of insecurity, as discussed in Chapter 2, theories of *proper defense come from a deep understanding of adversaries*. Ideally, a defender would have perfect information about the intentions, capabilities, resources, risk tolerance, strategic plans, and attack tactics [SALT98] of each and every adversary that a defender faces and may one day face. Because all of these characteristics are subject to change over time, this perfect information would have to be instantaneously updated continuously in this ideal world. For example, in a world where all adversaries are so risk-intolerant that they would never dare attack for fear of being discovered, security would be a waste of resources. Of course, the world of perfect information and hyper-cowering adversaries does not exist; therefore, defenders must develop the best possible information they can.

It is often said that we are our own worst enemies, as highlighted by the opening Pogo quote. Discussion of the consequence of poor design, operations, and maintenance practices that create enormous risk will be the topic of subsequent chapters and is the focus of the book "Computer Related Risks" [NEUM94]. For this chapter, we focus on the adversary that is not within us all.

> *Proper defense comes from a deep understanding of adversaries.*

6.1 Know Your Adversaries

Adversaries have characteristics that help to predict their strategies, preferred targets, and attack methods, so it is well worth understanding as much about the adversary as possible. Each adversary characteristic is discussed in turn.

6.1.1 Intentions

Different adversaries can have vastly different goals leading to diverse types of attacks against different aspects of a given mission. For example, take a nation-state that richly participates in the heavily interdependent international trade and commerce world. Such a nation is not likely be keenly motivated to destroy the economy of a key nation such as the United States for fear of a cascading wave of economic damage that could actually damage the attacker as much as or more than the defender. On the other hand, a disenfranchised transnational terrorist group with minimal infrastructures and meager wealth that does not participate in and benefit from the world economy has little to lose and much to gain if their intention is to gain international recognition of their plight, or perhaps only to punish the world, or to return to a simpler time, where they are not so disadvantaged by circumstance.

There are three broad categories of intentions: espionage, sabotage, and **influence operations**. Espionage is about stealing information to gain an advantage; sabotage, the doing of intentional damage to cause disadvantage; influence operations, altering beliefs and decision making, including deceit, to achieve some nefarious goal. *Espionage often precedes sabotage and influence operations as a means; however, it can be an end in itself.* Influence operations includes a number of other disciplines, including psychological operations, information warfare, cover and deception, and disinformation—which will be discussed in later sections. Although influence operations have been occurring for millennia, social media and the speed of the Internet have caused them to become a much more powerful and targeted weapon, as evidenced by the Russian influence campaign in the United States and Western Europe in 2016 [PRIE17].

All adversaries are motivated to do a combination of activities to execute these three categories of intentions. One could propose to model a single espionage adversary, a single sabotage adversary, and a single influence operations adversary, but, as with other characteristics, this would be a bit too simplistic.

> *Espionage, sabotage, and influence are goals underlying cyberattack.*

> *Espionage is often a precursor to sabotage and influence operations.*

The political and international environments play a role in the intentions of the mix between espionage and sabotage. For example, if a country is at peace, it is more likely to lean toward espionage to improve its decision-making processes and influence operations to impose its will on its target. If a country is at war, sabotage will rise in importance; influence operations and espionage may change goals. We can generalize *country* to any organization and generalize the notion of war to a conflict or competition of some sort. For example, if a company is under extreme duress and is in danger of failing, it is much more likely that they would risk sabotaging a competitor than if they were healthy and had much to lose if caught engaging in acts of sabotage.

6.1.2 Capabilities

There is a significant difference between the capabilities of lone hackers operating out of their basements in their spare time for **hacktivism** (the use of hacking for an activist cause) versus an elite superpower military organization with thousands of cyber-warriors operating as an effective team. As an obvious example, a superpower organization will have a highly developed **Signals Intelligence** (SIGINT) capability enabling it to intercept communications and to run **cryptanalytic** attacks using algorithms, specialized hardware, and experience that a lone hacker simply does not possess. Capabilities involve knowledge, methods, and processes developed through concentrated effort and experience, as well as the training of personnel to use that knowledge, the methods, and the processes.

Such vast differences are why one cannot model just one espionage adversary. This leads us to consider candidate adversaries to model: a nation-state and a lone hacker. There are certainly many capabilities in between these extremes. For example, a transnational terrorist organization or rogue nation may have significant capabilities—realizing that it gives them asymmetric advantage over wealthier and stronger entities. Organized crime has developed special capabilities for extortion such as **reversible sabotage** with systems held hostage for ransom—so-called **ransomware** [LISK16] (see Figure 6-1). Organized hacker groups or clubs such as Anonymous [OLSO12] and the Elderwood Gang [GORM13] have also developed impressive capabilities over time.

6.1.3 Attacker Resources and Defender Resources

Resources come in at least two forms, people and money. Having a budget of $100 for an attack is very different from having a budget of $100 million. Resources, in some cases, can buy access to capabilities. For example, there is a black market of cyber-warriors that a rogue organization could potentially hire if it had access to significant funds. A Fortune 500 company can muster more funding for corporate espionage than could a mom-and-pop private business. Organized crime often has access to significant funds. Nation-states often supplement funding of organized crime and hacker groups that loosely work toward their strategic goals, thus giving those nation-states some plausible deniability in involvement in particularly egregious cyberattacks.

Attack Panel: Ransomware Attack	
Class	Integrity
Type	Data Integrity
Mechanism	Malicious code is installed and executed on a target computer, often by a worm or virus. The malicious code disables the computer typically by encrypting key files under a key only known to the attacker. The attacker then demands money in exchange for restoration.
Examples	The Wanna Cry attack of 2017 exploited a known vulnerability in old unpatched versions of the Microsoft operating system.
Damage Potential	Ransoms vary depending on what the attacker believes the target can afford—hundreds for home computers, tens of thousands for institutions like hospitals, hundreds of thousands for banks.

Figure 6-1   Attack description: ransomware

6.1.4 Risk Tolerance

Some people are willing to jump off cliffs with nothing more than a wing suit and a parachute, racing down mountains at 200+ mph mere inches above the ground, while others are afraid to leave their homes. Therefore, there is considerable variety of risk tolerance among adversaries. Some adversaries are completely unconcerned with being caught in attacks and by the diplomatic consequence of public admonition by other countries. Adversaries have ready-made cover stories for their attacks by using cut-out organizations (also known as state-tolerated organizations) such as organized crime (e.g., the Russian Business Network [NEWS09]) or hacker clubs (e.g., China's hundreds of hacker clubs that feed both valuable information and experts to the Chinese military [CHIN15]).

6.1.5 Strategic Goals

If an adversary's strategic goals call for complete control of an adversary's critical systems, then that requires long-term planning and substantial resources. On the other hand, if the strategic goal is to gain membership in an elite black hat hacker (a hacker who attacks systems for illegal purposes, such as stealing money) group by demonstrating hacking prowess by breaking into a major bank's system—then that simply requires a one-time effort and proof that the deed was accomplished without necessarily doing any damage to the target at all.

Strategic goals to wreak wanton destruction are far simpler than subtle attacks altering data in nearly imperceptible ways to adversely affect the decision making of the consumer of that data or use of that system. Such variation in strategy can determine which attacks an organization will attempt and what time horizons they will accept to accomplish their goal.

So, *the adversaries can be short-term or long-term oriented, subtle or brute force oriented.* There are certainly a number of other strategic planning characteristics that could create even more subclasses of adversary [DSB13].

6.1.6 Tactics

Finally, there are the actual tools, techniques and procedures (TTP) an adversary uses. These can be a by-product of the skills, individual preferences, mentors, background, and organizational style of a group. For example, organizations tend to develop general malware approaches and reuse the same software by enhancing it and repurposing it for the next attack. This can create attributable **attack signature** data in attack software since it tends to implicate a single organization that tends to use that particular attack code base. Of course, knowing this may lead another attacker to steal that code base and use that code in *its* attacks to cause **misattribution** of the attack.

The common weakness enumeration [CWE17] provides a list of common software security weaknesses in systems. Different adversaries have different preferences for exploiting such weaknesses that are well-known.

Some organizations tend to prefer the use of zero-day attacks and seem to have stockpiled a significant quantity [ABLO17]. Some groups use extremely **high-stealth** techniques such as serious encryption or low-probability detection communication techniques such as super-slow **port scanning** to stay below the **detection thresholds** of intrusion detection algorithms. Some use covert signaling for communications, and they will tend to use similar types of channels in different attacks. Certain tactics call for deeply hidden implanted code in the life cycle, to be activated only in an emergency when there is a serious crisis.

If one takes all of these attributes and analyzes all of the values that each can have, hundreds of distinct adversary classes result. Hundreds of adversary classes can be too many to manage reasonably, which will become apparent later in discussions of risk assessments and comparing architectures with probability estimates on attacks for the various adversary classes (see Section 17.6).

What is needed is a representative set of adversary classes with specific profiles that is diverse enough to span the set of actors and actions with which the defender is concerned. For example, if a designer is developing a commercial system, then defending against nation-states may not be in the adversary set of concern. More adversary classes give a higher granularity analysis but are significantly more work and could lead to too much emphasis on certain attack classes because of the inclusion of multiple adversaries that employ very similar techniques and have similar goals. Fewer adversary classes simplifies the analysis, but could cause the defender to neglect an important problem. Table 6-1 gives a reasonable list of adversary classes for risk assessment, but it is highly tailorable to the specific type of analysis that is being sought.

#	Adversary Class	Key Characteristics
1	Nation-state at peace	Long-term, espionage and influence focused, well-resourced, risk-averse
2	Nation-state at war	Short-term, sabotage and influence focused with targeted espionage, well-resourced, risk-tolerant
3	Transnational terrorists	Short-term, sabotage-focused, well-resourced, risk-tolerant
4	Organized crime	Well-resourced, risk-averse, financial-focused
5	Hacktivist	Very high skills, activist-oriented, modest resources
6	State-tolerated hacker groups	Very high skills, nation-state type goals, modest resources, though sometimes subsidized by nation-states
7	Lone hacker	Innovative, determined, risk-averse

Table 6-1   Examples of Representative Adversary Classes

6.2 Assume Smart Adversaries

That which can be thought of by one individual can be thought of by another [YARD13]
—H. Yardley

In the process of evaluating defenses from an adversary's perspective, we should *never make the mistake of underestimating adversary capabilities*. We must assume adversaries are at least as sophisticated as we are. Even if they do not have an indigenous capability, they may be able to buy or borrow it from another adversary working in conjunction with them. Specifically, we must not assume that transnational terrorist organizations are backward and ignorant because they come from developing nations; this would be hubris and folly. A few insiders, some help from their allies, and the use of mercenaries can go far to instantly create a capability that did not exist before.

> ### *Never underestimate the adversary.*

In addition, as discussed in Section 5.8, we must *assume adversaries know as much about the defender's systems as the defender does and may have even implanted malware in that system and so have some partial degree of control.* These assumptions will not always be completely true, but making a slightly overly conservative assumption is far better than the opposite, which could have disastrous consequences to the mission of the system. These assumptions are similar in nature to Pascal's wager regarding the existence of God. He figured that it was better to believe in God just in case there is a heaven and hell than to not believe and risk eternal damnation. Similarly, when one banks on some assumption being true, good cybersecurity engineers should always ask themselves what the consequences would be if they are wrong.

> ### *Assume your adversary knows your system well and is inside it.*

6.3 Assume Adversaries Don't Play Fair

One aspect of being smart is playing unfair—finding surprising attack avenues not considered by the defender. Said a different way: attackers never cheat, because there are no rules. Some types of unfairness include

- Going around security controls
- Going beneath security controls
- Attacking the weakest link
- Violating a design assumption
- Using maintenance modes
- Compromising initialization, especially after forcing a system crash
- Using **social engineering**
- Using bribery and blackmail to subvert insiders
- Taking advantage of temporary bypasses
- Taking advantage of temporary connections
- Taking advantage of natural system failure
- Exploiting bugs you did not even know you had
- Compromising external systems that a system trusts

6.3.1 Going Around Security Controls

Sometimes designers have excellent authentication and authorization controls to system resources but do not notice that there is an alternative way to address those same resources. Take a block of memory, for example, in modern systems such as cloud computing; memory can be accessed directly or through a network interface (e.g., storage area networks). A good security engineer will almost certainly address direct addressing, but may not adequately understand cloud architectures well enough to know that alternative memory addressing is possible. Conceptually, if you think of security controls as a series of slats in a fence, as shown in Figure 6-2, this unfairness is about simply going around the fence or through the gaps.

6.3.2 Going Beneath Security Controls

Using the fence analogy shown in Figure 6-2, there is a technical analog of digging underneath a fence of security controls. Security controls are built on top of operating systems, which are built on top of device drivers, which are built on top of hardware devices, which contain microchips that have their own micro-operating systems, which depend on other hardware devices on a system bus (which itself is a device), which also have their own subdevices and operating systems.

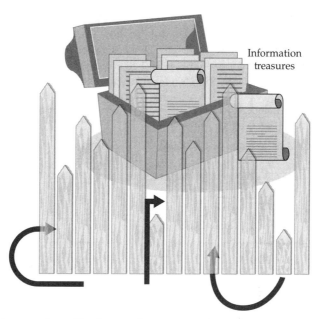

Information
treasures

Figure 6-2   Security controls are like slats in a fence; attacks from outside a system can go around the fence, through the lowest slat, or underneath the fence.

For example, to a user, a hard drive is a place to store files. Files are an abstraction made up of blocks of memory on the disk. Those blocks of memory can be read or written only when the arm of the disk moves to that location, generally guided by processors and software on the device controller for that hard drive device. That device is accessed by low-level software at the bottom of the operating system. That low-level software knows how to address the hard drive controller memory to ask it to do low-level tasks such as seeking to a memory block, reading or writing to it, and verifying that the writing operation worked correctly.

Many security controls depend on a file abstraction, for example. Security control programs assume that if they store data in a file, the file will not be changed the next time the program accesses it unless the control program itself changed it. *If an attack changes file content below the file level abstraction, then the file abstraction assumption is violated, and an attacker can completely change how a security control works.*

> *Attacking below operating system abstractions bypasses controls.*

The attack options include disabling it completely or allowing just the attacker to bypass the security controls so that it appears to continue to work. Allowing the attacker to bypass gives the defender an even bigger surprise when an attacker seems to be able to violate access rules without leaving a trace.

The opportunities for attacking a system below the security control layer of abstraction are shown in Figure 6-3, for both the computer and all of the connected devices, which are specialized computers in their own right. Devices, especially third-party add-on devices such as graphics processors, occupy highly privileged positions within the system and thus can be particularly damaging. See Section 9.6 for further discussion.

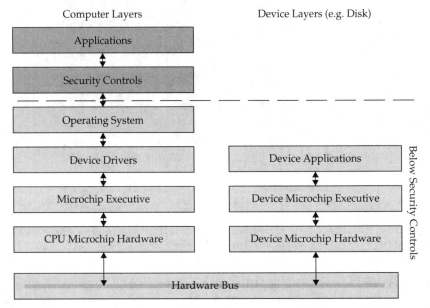

Figure 6-3   Degree to which security controls depend on a variety of different underlying mechanisms to work correctly

This notion of having dependency layers on which security control depends means that security controls themselves need to be properly layered. Such a **layered security** control architecture follows a recursive structure, at the bottom of which needs to be a foundational kernel of security at the microchip level on which all other security is built and ensuring that those layers cannot be violated by non-security-control software.

6.3.3 Attacking the Weakest Link

Once again, returning to Figure 6-2, the adversary is likely to evaluate each of a defender's security controls and attack the weakest control. In Figure 6-2, the height of each slat represents the relative strength of a corresponding security control compared to the other controls. It is necessarily true that there is always a weakest and a strongest control. The strength is relative to a given attack class, so there is no universal ranking of all security controls. Strength depends on its position in an architecture and how a control is implemented, in addition to the type of attack that is attempting to defeat that control.

A competent adversary planning an attack will have done a complete and careful analysis of all of a target system's security controls that are relevant to that attack and will know their vulnerabilities, which are weakest and strongest, and will plan accordingly. *If a defender has not evaluated their strengths and weaknesses in this fashion with respect to a wide range of attack scenarios, the defender opens themselves to many surprises in successful attacks.*

> ### *Know your strengths and weaknesses, because your adversary will.*

This leads us to another important principle: *checkbox security engineering is dangerous.* Evaluation criteria or security standards enumerate a set of possible controls to consider. **Checkbox security engineering** means having non-security engineers ineffectively attempt to address each control. An inadequately trained assessor then agrees that it is relevant and checks off a box that such a control exists in the system as if it were a binary value—the control exists or does not exist. Such a superficial approach is in contrast to recognizing that design, implementation, and position of controls in the architecture matter deeply.

> ### *Checkbox security engineering is dangerous.*

As a final observation in this area, there is an important investment bias to point out here. One may ask why the slats of the fence are so uneven—that is, why security controls have such diverse strength given the **weakest link principle**. Certainly, one reason is that some security controls are inherently harder to get right and to assure than others. Another is that there is an investment bias in working on security controls that are more familiar [ZAJO01] and on which it is easier to measure progress. So, if the chief information security officer's background is primarily in developing firewalls, that organization will likely be biased toward investing too heavily in firewalls and give short shrift to other controls that the executive understands less. This is not a criticism of ex-firewall-developer security officers; it is a statement of natural human psychological biases that must be carefully managed in the security engineering process—especially by the security engineers themselves, who need to consider their own backgrounds and consequent biases.

6.3.4 Violating a Design Assumption

All system designs, including security subsystem designs, involve a wide range of assumptions about the surrounding and underlying environment as well as the users. *These assumptions are almost never documented, and when they are documented, they are woefully incomplete.* Even when they are documented, there is rarely a process to ensure that those assumptions are met by the implementation in the process of mapping an implementation back to a design. Even if that is done, maintaining these assumptions as the system evolves and is patched brings us into the realm of the unicorn in terms of likely existence.

There are many typical design assumptions that security engineers make that are rarely true, including

- Rational users
- Perfect users

- Perfect data input
- Perfect command input
- Well-behaved calling programs and services
- Well-behaved called programs and services
- Correct operation of the operating system and underlying hardware
- Correct operation of the libraries
- Correct operation of the development tools such as compilers
- An uncompromised host computer
- Correct operation of all security controls

This is a very short list from a much longer set of bad assumptions. Adversaries know the full list well and will immediately probe for violations of these unrealistic assumptions (e.g., buffer overflow attacks by providing imperfect inputs to programs), and they have a very good chance of finding one or more such violations, which can be useful in the context of an attack that exploits a series of vulnerabilities.

6.3.5 Using Maintenance Modes

All good programmers design in testing and debugging modes of operation to diagnose problems more easily during development time and later in operation time when maintenance may be required. During development time, programmers make it easy to enter such modes because there is little at risk, and optimizing for development ease is the right thing to do. Such modes often bypass security and other important features to ease diagnosis. Once a system goes into production, it is imperative that these modes be reduced and require special authentication and authorization to enter and that entry is permitted in a very limited manner under very special circumstances.

As an extension of this idea, programs often have a specific maintenance mode and special access port for developers to gain deep access into the bowels of a program and its data structures. This port is for debugging and patching purposes, after deployment. Such ports and accesses are typically extraordinarily risky and sometimes can be escalated to privilege on other parts of the system. Great care should be taken in limiting access to these ports of entry and monitoring them very carefully when they are entered to ensure that access is authorized and that authorized access is not abused. Remote entry to these ports should be allowed only if there is no other practical option. Such ports present high risk because millions of hackers have potential access to try to hack a remote port. Without such ports, attackers would have to gain access to a physical **machine room** to access restricted maintenance ports.

6.3.6 Using Social Engineering

Social engineering is about doing things such as calling users on the phone or sending them email, pretending to have a dire and urgent need for the user to take an action that will end up resulting in the compromise of a system. It is surprisingly easy to convince someone to share their password, or type in a command sequence, or load a program as a favor. Success is highly likely. Furthermore, in the field we see that when attractive people conduct the social engineering, they are even more likely to succeed. In a user population, there is almost always some subset of less-aware users who will fall for these ruses. Social engineering *almost always works.*

Designers can roll their eyes and wish it weren't so and blame "stupid users" for the security failure, but in reality, blame lies with the cybersecurity engineers for designing systems without an adequate understanding of this reality. *Like any other attack, it is impossible to make it impossible, but it is plausible to make it implausible.* If users revealing passwords in a social engineering attack is a problem, then designers should consider getting rid of passwords and using a different form of authentication that is less vulnerable to social engineering (e.g., **biometrics**, token-based schemes, or multifactor authentication).

> *Anticipate that social engineering attacks will succeed.*

6.3.7 Using Bribery and Blackmail to Subvert Insiders

People are, after all, only human. They have flaws, problems, ideology, and unmet needs. These can be exploited by adversaries to recruit insiders, particularly well-placed and highly privileged insiders such as executives, system administrators, and investigators paid to find such insiders. Insiders with system access can do enormous damage and can initiate attacks from within the system, which is particularly bad for organizations that focus their defenses at the perimeter, such as at firewalls. Insiders can cover the tracks of their attacks if they have access to monitoring systems such as audit logs. If they are aware of intrusion detection thresholds, they can ensure that attacks operate below such thresholds.

6.3.8 Taking Advantage of Temporary Bypasses

For the sake of mission, security controls (and sometimes even safety controls) are temporarily bypassed to "get the job done" because security "is in the way" or causes a performance issue of some sort. For sure, the dynamic trade-off between security and mission is a very real requirement of operations. Unfortunately, attackers are waiting for such an opportunity, constantly scanning systems for such weakness.

Designers must come to understand that *the human time scale is not the same as a computer's time scale.* The smallest time increment that a human can perceive is about 10 milliseconds or 10^{-2} seconds. A computer time increment is around 10^{-12} seconds. Therefore, in a human time increment, there are 10^{10} computer increments. Said a different way, a perceptible tick of time to a human is about 1,000 years to a computer. So, even if a security control is bypassed for only 10 milliseconds, it is a millennium in terms of what a computer can do in that time scale. Further, temporary bypasses often last hours, sometimes days, and sometimes they are forgotten about and remain in place for the lifetime of the system. The average time until a newly Internet-connected computer is attacked is minutes [CERT17].

An example of a temporary bypass is setting firewall rules to "any" access, bypassing all rules on the mere possibility that a network connection is not working because a firewall rule set may be too restrictive. Sometimes all authorization control is similarly bypassed due to the possibility that security controls are impeding access needed by mission exigency. Another example occurs when organizations are in transition between information infrastructure such as a move to the cloud, such as appears to be the case with a breach at a major accounting firm [HOPK17].

Unfortunately, one of two things happens after such controls are bypassed. The bypass solves the problem, in which case the controls are left open for the duration of the critical operation that was taking place. Alternatively, the bypass fails to solve the problem, and people are scrambling to find the real problem, leaving the security controls open "just in case" they were contributing to the problem or just because the operators are frantically busy and forget. *In both situations, there is significant risk that the temporary bypass will be left open way longer than is needed and possibly indefinitely until a major problem occurs and someone figures out that they unintentionally left the controls wide open.* It would be great if the firewall gave out a recorded loud human blood-curdling scream the entire time that it is left wide open, just as a reminder that the organization is doing a very dangerous thing. Unfortunately, that is not likely to be a feature in high demand any time soon.

Once an attacker has gained access due to the temporary bypass, they are certain to leave in a backdoor or **Trojan horse** so that even after the controls are reinstated, they will be able to easily regain access through the control. Therefore, although a security operator may feel good about diligently closing the control after a mere few hours, this could be the equivalent of the proverbial closing the barn door after the horse has escaped.

Security engineers must assume this sort of security bypass *will* happen and not declare system breaches that result from such bypasses as the fault of the bad users and operators. If it is known ahead of time that these bypasses are operationally necessary, then pretending that they aren't is bad design that leads to unnecessarily high risk. A root problem is that security devices (and most devices on networks today) are abysmal at participating in a collaborative process to diagnose connection and access problems, and so the operators have little choice but to bypass. Furthermore, because security engineers do not provide partial and controlled bypass, the operators are left with a binary choice and the burden to remember to undo it. Clearly, there is a major opportunity for design improvement here in many dimensions.

6.3.9 Taking Advantage of Temporary Connections

In a similar vein as the previous discussion, system operators and even users create temporary network connections that they know are risky, but, again, they do so in the name of mission and expediency. As an example, people have been known to connect an internal company network with a carefully controlled interface through a firewall that has hundreds of carefully controlled rules to an external network such as the Internet. They do so because they cannot get a needed working connection to a colleague or because the connection through the normal interface is too slow. What they may not realize is that the reason that they cannot make the connection is that the larger enterprise owners have determined that that destination network poses too high a risk (e.g., because it is known to have **cross-site scripting attacks** on its website; see Figure 6-4).

Attack Panel: Cross-Site Scripting (XSS)	
Class	Integrity
Type	System Integrity
Mechanism	A popular website is first compromised using some other attack. The attacker then modifies the website to send malicious scripts (programs) to the browsers of unsuspecting users visiting the site, thereby compromising the computers of all such users.
Examples	The Samy attack of 2005 compromised over a million users within 20 hours. The TweetDeck attack of 2014 propagated through Twitter spreading like a worm.
Damage Potential	Damage potential is substantial. Once an attacker has control of a victim's machine, they can use passwords to gain access to sensitive information such as bank sites.

Figure 6-4   Cross-site scripting attack description

This brings us to another important principle: *users and project leaders should be prevented from unilaterally taking on local risk (i.e., risk to them or their project).* If they choose to take on such risks, they must (a) completely understand the risk they are taking, (b) understand how that risk propagates to the enterprise and larger mission, and (c) gain concurrence from the larger mission that they are willing to accept that propagated risk. This almost never happens, partly because of a lack of controls and partly because of a lack of security education of the users and project owners.

> *Local risks aggregate into global risk; control them carefully.*

6.3.10 Taking Advantage of Natural System Failure

In the same way that attackers are just waiting for a temporary bypass or a temporary network connection that they can exploit, they are on a constant lookout for natural system failures. For example, let's say that an adversary wants to eavesdrop on network encryption that is properly encrypted and keyed using the strong **Advanced Encryption Standard** (AES) [FIPS01]. Cryptanalysis of such traffic is quite difficult and may well be beyond the adversary's means. Does that mean that the adversary should simply give up? No. Encryption sometimes fails and it sometimes fails open, meaning the data continues to be transmitted in the clear. Often, there is no alarm on the failure, and so the clear communication is now totally vulnerable to the adversary simply directly reading the traffic, and the system operator may never realize that the encryption failed.

Similar failures could happen on access control, intrusion detection systems, firewalls, etc. *Persistence and patience can pay off for adversaries.* Cybersecurity system engineers must assume an adversary is waiting and watching for the aforementioned opportunities and place great emphasis on preventing such failures, alarming them when they happen, and recovering from them by engineering systems to fail in a way that does not cause a serious security breach.

> *Adversaries actively search for and exploit failures.*

6.3.11 Exploiting Bugs You Did Not Even Know You Had

Developers have limited time and budget to find and eliminate inevitable bugs. For code of any appreciable size, *it is an absolute certainty that residual hidden bugs will remain*—many of them—some of them serious and some that could cause serious security breaches. There are development coding practices to reduce these bugs [HOWA06, GRAF03], but even with such practices, bugs remain.

Adversaries do not have similar time and budget pressures regarding finding bugs. Indeed, to find bugs, adversaries may have better and more specialized tools such as both static analyzers (tools that review source and executable code to find bugs) and dynamic analyzers (tools that monitor programs in execution to find bugs or to understand behavior). Adversaries may have specially trained experts in finding security bugs with skills that the developer simply does not possess. *This is how adversaries find* zero-day attacks.

> *Anticipate bugs and consequent zero-day attacks.*

Cybersecurity engineers must take great care to prevent bugs, using the best tools and techniques available and gaining or hiring the skills needed to eliminate such bugs. Further, *a good developer will dedicate up to 50 percent of code to error detection and error handling* [BENT82, GOOD07]. If a programmer's code is well below that level, they are probably missing something important. Even still, *some errors will go undetected and will be exploited.* That is a fact.

If the cybersecurity engineers assume such a failure will happen, then they will look for signs of exploitation of such failures and build in diagnostic capabilities to learn where and how these exploitations are taking place so they can be shut down quickly. A designer who does not acknowledge or understand this possibility will never look, and an unpleasant surprise surely awaits them.

6.3.12 Compromising External Systems that a System Trusts

A modern system depends explicitly and implicitly on many external systems and services. A good example is the multiple bugs and vulnerabilities found in the Border Gateway Protocol, which can cause exploitable vulnerabilities in how network traffic is routed in the

Internet [ALAE15]. As another example, a system may depend on **Network Time Protocol** (NTP) as a source for time of day. If an access control role involves time of day (e.g., "access to this system is only allowed from 9 AM until 5 PM"), then altering the time can have a direct effect on security. Also, setting the clock to prehistoric time or a time in the distant future could cause systems to crash because they do not expect such values.

Certain programs depend on external security services for authentication and authorization. If these services are compromised, then the access control of all of those programs using that service are compromised, making these services high-value targets to adversaries. Unix has a built-in notion of specifying trusts of other computers for the purpose of easily sharing file structures. This creates an environment ripe for cascading failure when one machine is compromised and the **transitive closure** of all machines mutually trusting one another is then compromised.

The totality of the discussion earlier leads us to another important design principle: *always expect the unexpected*. This principle encourages designers to a mind-set that examines assumptions and failures and prepares for them by architecting the system to detect and recover from such failures, so that damage is reduced.

> ***Always expect the unexpected.***

6.4 Anticipate Attack Escalation

Cybersecurity engineers must not only prepare for attacks that are known today but must also anticipate improvements in attack technology during the lifetime of the systems they create.

In the early days of cybersecurity, hackers were mostly kids learning systems and demonstrating their skill. Today, hacking is a serious business used by organized crime as a major source of revenue. Ransomware is now big business, and defenders must prepare for more and better attacks of this class.

In the early days, attacks were relatively unsophisticated code that attacked a single vulnerability and performed a single task. Now, attack code has built-in detection evasion, self-encryption techniques, uses covert channels, is capable of exploiting multiple vulnerabilities, and is capable of reaching back through **command and control** channels to enable the exploitation of even more vulnerabilities of new systems that it encounters. As code becomes stealthier and more sophisticated, reliance on **signature-based** attack detection schemes will become increasingly unreliable. Defenders will need to learn how to make use of **anomaly detection** and other techniques that do require having seen the attack before.

As time has progressed from the early days, attacks have spread down the system abstraction layers from application attacks on programs and services such as mail and web servers, to operating system–level attacks, to attacks on network infrastructure that connects those operating systems, to router attacks and domain name system attacks that support that infrastructure. The reason for this progression is that attacks at lower layers in the layered stack of functionality, although harder, give much more access from which to springboard more types of attacks and reuse attacks for different purposes. *We can expect that attacks will continue down the stack to device drivers and device controllers.* Because the software is under the security control layers, we can call this low-level software "underware."

> ### *Expect increasing underware attacks.*

Lastly, attacks started in the pure digital world because it was the most obvious first target and because computers were not often connected to physical systems. There has been a dramatic increase in **cyber-physical systems** (CPS), in which a physical system such as a power grid or a chemical process control system is controlled directly and irrevocably by computers (see Figure 6-5). This opens up a whole new level of damage that cyberattack is can wreak on the world.

Attack Panel: Cyber-Physical Systems	
Class	Cyber-Physical System
Type	Availability through System Integrity
Mechanism	Malicious code is installed and executed on a target computer, often by a worm or virus. The malicious code is later activated or triggered to produce some damaging physical effect by manipulation of control commands.
Examples	STUXNET which attacked a nuclear centrifuge control to destroy it for the ostensible purpose of setting back a nuclear development program in Iran.
Damage Potential	Damage from attacks on critical systems like banking, power grids, and phone systems could approach a trillion dollars and could erode national sovereignty itself.

Figure 6-5   Attack description: cyber-physical systems

The **Stuxnet attack**, in which a nuclear centrifuge was intentionally damaged by an attack on the control software, represents an infamous step in that direction. Cybersecurity engineers must prepare for the likelihood of more and more sophisticated attacks on cyber-physical systems such as the smart grid and smart homes.

The **Internet of Things (IoT)**, in which almost everything from toasters, to refrigerators, to your person is being measured, controlled, and connected to the networks, is going to present a special problem in this area, partly because the devices have very low power and price points.

6.5 Red Teams

What's a **red team**? The origin of the phrase comes from the Cold War when Soviet Russia was the primary opponent of the West. Russia, and Communism in general, adopted red as a color symbolizing the blood spilled by the working class within capitalist societies.

Therefore, the flag of the Union of Soviet Socialist Republics (USSR) adopted red as its background color, as did Communist China. Hence, the term "reds" was adopted as a derogatory shorthand by the Western world to describe Russia in particular and other Communist countries such as China (e.g., "Red China").

6.5.1 Opposing Force

To improve training of Western troops against the Soviet threat, military leadership felt it wise to simulate the Soviet **opposing force**—sometimes called the **OPFOR** (because everything in the military has to sound cool and be maximally hard to understand). To do so, Western forces would train segments of their troops in what was known about Soviet tactics. They would even go so far as to capture Soviet equipment such as tanks and military aircraft, such as Soviet MIGs, and train selected pilots to fly them using Soviet tactics. This was consistent with the military principle of "*Train as you fight; fight as you train*"—attributed to George S. Patton. These Western forces that had specialty training to simulate Soviet tactics became known as "red teams" because the opposing force they typically simulated were the Communist "red forces." The term red team has come to be used synonymously with any opposing force, not just the Communist forces.

> *Train as you fight; fight as you train.*

Many terms from the military **kinetic** world have been adopted and adapted for use in cybersecurity. This adoption is for two important reasons. First, the military and intelligence communities were the first to understand the gravity of cybersecurity and the so-called **digital domain** of operation. The military recognition came early in the form of concern for **multilevel security**—the simultaneous use of the then-scarce computing resources for data at multiple classification levels and the concern that data from a higher level could be intentionally leaked to a lower level to personnel who were not cleared for knowledge of that data, therefore posing significant risk. The second reason for the connection is that cybersecurity has strong analogies to kinetic conflicts where there are competing forces, attacking and defending, toward a strategic goal, using tactics based on experience and theory.

6.5.2 Red Team Characteristics

The military principle of "train as you fight; fight as you train" clearly applies to the digital domain as well as the physical domain. Therefore, one definition of *an ideal cyber red team is a team trained in and capable of simulating a cyber opposing force for whichever adversaries are of most concern for the defender.* Unfortunately, most red teams do not have this characteristic, and the term "red team" is used inconsistently to mean at least two other things discussed in the next section.

Under the proper definition of red team, most fall short in several ways:

- Their attacks are not strategic toward some adversary goal.
- Their thought process is not really adversarial, in terms of modeling a real attacker.

- They have no training in the tools, tactics, and procedures of real adversaries.
- In the rare case that they do use real attacker tools and professional attackers, such teams are typically trained only in their own techniques and are under the mistaken impression that real adversaries act just like they do.
- They tiptoe around the system, using very carefully crafted "**rules of engagement**," to ensure there is no chance that they do any unintentional damage.

Most red teams comprise a set of individuals who have been trained in the use of **vulnerability testing** tools such as Red Seal [REDS17] (tools that check for a list of known vulnerabilities). Such tools are undoubtedly important, and having people trained in their use is also important, but such groups of people are not true red teams. They are partial bottom-up vulnerability testers or sometimes called doorknob turners (because they do the analog of trying to open every cybersecurity door and just see which are unlocked, or vulnerable). We use the word "partial" because they only test vulnerabilities that (a) someone designing the tool thought of and (b) someone found easy and practical to implement in a tool. We use "bottom up" because it essentially looks for known things that can go wrong without any reference to damage to mission or the strategic goals an adversary might have.

Good red teams are adversarial thinkers, students of attack tactics used by their adversaries, and who consider strategic damage to mission as a primary driver. Often it is useful to have two types of individuals on a red team—the out-of-the-box-thinking strategist who understands strategy, mission, and how to damage mission from the top down. Their function is to propose and sketch attack scenarios at a high level. The second type of individual is more of a **Class A** hacker—someone who deeply understands attack tactics and all of the tools and techniques that are available, and how to creatively adapt and apply those to achieve an important tactical result in a strategy. The strategist and the tactician work together to develop a series of prioritized attack scenarios and estimate the damage they would do and the likelihood that they would succeed. The tacticians would implement a subset of those attacks where there is either a need to concretely demonstrate an important idea to the system operators or if there is some disagreement or uncertainty regarding the attack itself.

6.5.3 Other Types of Red Teams

There are two other important misuses of the term "red team" that can cause confusion. The first, and most common one, is to use the term interchangeably with a **penetration testing** team (also called **pen-test** team for short). Penetration testing, as it is used today, is most often associated with vulnerability testing, though testers sometimes work at a higher level of tactics and strategy. Penetration testing can sometimes include software code analysis, but rarely does it include a search for zero-day attacks, which are typically due to faults in the design or implementation of the system. An example process for a vulnerability assessment team is shown in Figure 6-6.

Vulnerability Assessment Team—A Process

1. Meet with client and agree upon the nature of the threat to be simulated, including what resources they may bring to bear.
2. Establish duration and budget for simulation of that threat.
3. Using the set of threat resources, perform a flaw-hypothesis-methodology analysis of target sites.
4. Develop attack plan and present to client. This will be in the form of an event chain, exploiting a series of vulnerabilities.
5. With client agreement, tag certain steps in the chain as "gimmies" that do not have to be demonstrated.
6. Demonstrate other steps, either in lab environment or on actual target system.
7. Celebrate success, because this approach never fails.

Figure 6-6   An example process of a vulnerability assessment team

The other interesting use of the word "red team" comes from the **intelligence and military community** and is associated with an **alternative analysis** and out-of-the-box thinking with respect to a situation or predicted situation. Such red teams often develop one or more scenarios or plausible interpretation of events—"what-ifs"—that might cause decision makers to make dramatically different decisions if those scenarios are true. People on these red teams are typically out-of-the-box thinkers, highly creative, and generally have a broader education that allows them to consider ideas that others who are more narrowly trained may not come up with. Such red teams can help high-level decision makers avoid serious strategic errors and at least open their minds to other possibilities so that strategies can include contingencies and preparations for these alternative possibilities. Such red team thinking can actually play an important role in the opposing-force style red team that this book takes as the preferred definition. Specifically, they can help generate ideas for the strategic attack components of the opposing-force red teams to consider.

All of these forms of red teams, despite the confusion caused by the multiplicity of usages, represent important skills and aspects of assessing the quality of cybersecurity defenses and should be used in combination to provide effective assessment. At the same time, it is important to understand that just because a group is called a red team does not mean that it provides all of the various aspects discussed earlier. See [HOFF17] for further reading on red teams.

6.6 Cyberspace Exercises

With an understanding of what red teams are and are not, we turn to the topic of cyber exercises. Under the proper definition of red team that is most true to the original physical analog from the military, if there is no intention to carry out a cyberspace exercise or assessments, then there is little point in having a true red team.

6.6.1 Red Versus Blue

Returning to the military analogy, the military runs exercises to improve training and preparedness. In these exercises, there is a designated opposing force made up of specially trained portions of the nation's own forces. The exercise is typically conducted in as close to realistic conditions, environments, and scenarios as possible, with limitations put in place for safety and cost. For example, military exercises do not typically use live ammunition since both sides are part of the nation's forces. Exercises restrict themselves to a well-defined terrain set aside for the purpose. Exercises also have a clear beginning point, an end point, and clear rules of engagement of conduct during the exercise. Exercises also have regular national forces, often called the "**blue team**" to distinguish them from the red team.

Organizers take great pains to clearly identify all activity as an exercise to everyone involved to avoid the possibility of someone taking aggressive action against a real adversary under the mistaken view that an attack is real. Indeed, *actual adversaries are almost always advised of an exercise if there is any possibility of them seeing an exercise event and misinterpreting the events as a real attack.* To be sure, exercises are risky endeavors. For major exercises, it is not uncommon for soldiers to die due to an accident that would not have otherwise occurred.

During military exercises in which red teams are included, often, any and all failures are attributed to the red team, with an intention to shut them down. It is ironic in a military with the great slogan of "train as you fight, fight as you train" that they often constrain or exclude cyber red teams because their effect on the exercise is so disruptive that it interferes with the training value of the kinetic portions of the training. This can make sense in one or two exercises, but it represents a serious strategic flaw in exercises if this becomes a standard way of operating all exercises. It is the equivalent of burying one's cyber head in the sand.

6.6.2 Pure Versus Hybrid

There are pure cyber exercises that take place solely in cyberspace and hybrid exercises in which physical exercises have a cyber component that is an inherent part. These exercises have similar characteristics to purely physical exercises discussed earlier. Such exercises have defending forces with clear goals, opposing forces with clear goals (e.g., capture the flag [KNOW16]), and clear rules of engagement. Let's take each in turn.

Hybrid exercises should really become the norm and be called regular exercises because there are virtually no military exercises that do not have a cyberspace component to them. There is a significant issue about how cyberattack is treated in hybrid exercises. Many military leaders have in their mind that the primary purpose of these exercises is to train soldiers in the art of kinetic combat. Offensive **cyber network operations**, if done well, can be highly effective at bringing the entire exercise to a grinding halt. Such an outcome defeats the primary purpose of these exercises, and the tremendous resources laid out for the exercise are, in some sense, wasted. At the same time, if cyber operations can truly be that effective, then there is clearly a strategic problem worth addressing, perhaps outside of the context of the immediate exercise so that the next one can be more realistic in its treatment of Offensive cyber network operations. Restricting cyber operations from midnight to 1 AM in the morning while nothing "important" is happening is not very realistic. In the end, cyber operations must be included under the umbrella principle of "train as you fight; fight as you train."

Pure cyberspace exercises can also be very valuable, particularly for non-nation-state entities such as commercial companies that do not typically engage in physical conflict. In such exercises, the red team is as described previously. The blue team is the set of cybersecurity operators in charge of the security controls on the defended system.

Additionally, there is usually a **white team** that acts as the referee and ensures that the rules of engagement are maintained. The white team will often document the exercise to gain the maximum lessons learned to improve defenses and tactics for real scenarios.

Some refer to an effective melding of red team and blue team activity as a **purple team**. The purpose of a purple team is to encourage sharing between red and blue teams to ensure that cybersecurity is optimized, not the egos of the two teams. To this point, a red team that cannot or will not share how it succeeded with the defenders is of little value.

Some red teams withhold their techniques on the grounds that they are so sensitive that they cannot be shared for fear that the free world will be destroyed. There is, of course, some value in knowing that a system is vulnerable to a Class A (meaning a high-quality and high-skilled red team familiar with the latest and most effective attack techniques) red team, but true value comes from knowing what to do to improve defense. Collaboration between red and blue is best done before an exercise during planning, and after, in collecting lessons learned and improvement plans for defenses, as well as for the next exercise. Collaboration during an exercise is generally unwise because it interferes with the realism of the exercise and works at odds with its purpose. Table 6-2 summarizes the variously colored teams and their roles.

#	Team	Role
1	Red	Simulates adversary.
2	Blue	Simulates defense team.
3	White	Referees in exercise to ensure compliance with rules.
4	Purple	Limited collaboration of a joint red and blue team.

Table 6-2   Summary of Roles of Red, Blue, White, and Purple Teams in Exercises

6.6.3 Purple Collaboration

One effective pre-exercise "purple" collaboration involves **whiteboarding** attacks—identifying attack measures, defense countermeasures, and counter-countermeasures to discuss how a series of attack scenarios is likely to unfold. *If both teams agree that the attack would be wildly successful and that the defender could do absolutely nothing to stop it, both can agree to simply not run it and include this agreement in the lessons learned.* After the exercise, the two teams can collaborate by brainstorming the most effective way to defend against such attacks for future exercises. Similarly, if the two teams agree that there is no way a particular attack can possibly work, there is little value in carrying through with the attack. In this way, a *highly significant value is extracted from the red teaming process before anyone even touches a keyboard.* For attack scenarios, where there is disagreement on the outcome or the difficulty of attack or defense, then it is likely to be worth running instances of such attack classes to learn more.

Some may be concerned that this pre-exercise discussion degrades the realism of the element of surprise that adversaries enjoy. While this is partly true and represents a trade-off, the red team is not necessarily bound to use only attack scenarios discussed, and has the benefit of the element of surprise in the exact timing of the attack.

Post-exercise collaboration takes the form of both teams sitting in the same room directly after the exercise (to ensure ideas and information are fresh) and analyzing the entire scenario, usually led by the white team since they can see both sides and best organize the discussion. Then, at each significant point in the scenario, each team comments on less obvious parameters, such as:

- What was each team thinking at that point?
- What ideas did each team have but did not try?
- Why did they not try them?
- How successful was the attack or defense perceived to be, how successful was it actually; what were elements of the "fog of war" (uncertainty due to the confusion of all the things that were happening)?
- What is realistic and what might just be an artifact of the exercise?
- What lessons were learned to improve defenses?
- What lessons were learned to improve simulated attacks?
- What lessons were learned to improve the next exercise?

6.7 Red Team Work Factor: Measuring Difficulty

The previous section mentioned measuring the difficulty of an attack. Not all attacks are equally difficult or likely to succeed. Indeed, often the rules of engagement are written such that if the red team does not gain the first level of access after a certain period of time, the white team gives them that access on the grounds that either (1) with enough time and effort that cannot easily be simulated in the exercise, they would eventually gain that access, or (2) more information will be gained by giving the red team access in the event that some more creative real adversary can solve that problem or has a zero-day attack that gives them that access.

Understanding the relative difficulty of attacks helps the defender make better decisions about which defenses to improve and which residual risks to tolerate. This will be discussed more with the topic of risk assessments in subsequent chapters.

This means that red teams need to take careful notes and document what they are doing, why they are doing it, how long it's taking to do it, what tools and techniques they are using, what their sequence of attacks is, and how they are adapting to defenses along the way. All of this documentation gives insight into how difficult an attack sequence is to accomplish and why it is difficult and how it can be made more difficult.

The measures of time and resources it takes a red team to accomplish each step in an attack sequence are known as "**red team work factor**." It is a practical and directly useful metric on the quality of a given defense against a good red team. Red team work factor plays into evaluating defense mechanisms and alternative architectures and configurations. Of course, this metric is limited by the talents and skills of a specific red team, who have both biases and blind spots. That means that such metrics are imperfect, but they are useful in guiding defense strategy and analysis, and no better practical metric has been proposed to date.

Conclusion

This chapter explains the nature of adversaries and how that affects cybersecurity design. The next chapter completes the picture by explaining how attacker goals are realized through attack techniques.

To summarize:

- Adversaries have a variety of attributes and ranges of values each can take on.
- Adversaries are smart, skilled, and knowledgeable despite our wishing otherwise.
- Adversaries do not play fair and violate unrealistic or poorly understood assumptions.
- Attacker knowledge and capability will continue to improve and become more aggressive.
- Attackers will begin targeting cyber-physical systems and underware.
- Red teams, as model adversaries, play a critical role in assessing designs and mechanisms.
- Cyber exercises are essential in both guiding design and operational preparedness.
- Red team work factor is a useful measure of difficulty to compromise system security.

Questions

1. List three adversary attributes and discuss the range of values each attribute can take on.
2. Describe why it is important to assume a smart and knowledgeable adversary, and state at least two aspects of this smartness.
3. List five ways that an adversary may not play fair and how each affects cybersecurity design. List an additional way that is not discussed in the chapter.
4. Describe how attacks have evolved over the years and how they might continue to evolve. Discuss how a design can accommodate such an evolution.
5. Define a red team and its role in assessment. Distinguish the proper definition of a red team from two other usages, and describe the valid role those types of red teams might have.
6. What are the purposes of a cyber exercise and what might one expect to learn from them? What is whiteboarding, and how can it improve the efficiency of cyber exercises?
7. Define red team work factor. How it is calculated? Is it analytically calculable? Is it quantitative or qualitative? How it is used? What are its limitations?

CHAPTER

7

Forests of Attack Trees

Overview

Learning Objectives

- Describe **attack trees** and attack forests and their purpose.
- Discuss why understanding failures provides insights into attack trees and **attack forests**.
- Summarize how the five-whys approach applies to cybersecurity.
- Explain why forests must be representative and not exhaustive.
- Describe both the art and science of attack tree goal refinement.
- Explain the stopping criteria for goal refinement in attack trees.
- Summarize external dependencies in attack trees and why they matter.

7.1 Attack Trees and Forests

Section 4.4 covers how a series of attacker strategic goals can be generated to represent the ways in which mission can be strategically damaged. Such goals help drive a prioritized security analysis. The next important question revolves around how these goals can be achieved. That is where attack trees come into play. There are many different types of attack trees, which creates some ambiguity for the term. This book focuses on goal-directed attack trees, which will simply be called attack trees from now on.

7.1.1 Attack Tree Structure

The top of an attack tree is an attacker's strategic goal as developed in Section 4.4. This top-level goal is called the root. Each subsequent level of the tree below (by convention, the tree grows downward from the root) consists of a set of subgoals called nodes that together or separately achieve the previous level's nodes in the tree. Consider the children's fairy tale of "The Three Little Pigs" in which the attacker is the big bad wolf and the defenders are the three little pigs, with the edifices of straw, wood, and stone representing the system being defended. In this example, the root strategic goal is to "blow your house down," and the subordinate goal nodes implemented by the attacker might be "huff" and "puff." When completion of subgoals like huff and puff both must be done, we call it an "AND" relationship. We borrow both the term and the symbol from the subfield of computer science called digital logic as shown in Figure 7-1.

Figure 7-1   The OR and AND symbols borrowed from digital logic gates

This simple breakdown of a goal into two subgoals that must both be done is shown in Figure 7-2. It indicates that the goal nodes connected below it must both be done to achieve the goal indicated inside that node (which, in this case is a root node since it is at the top of the tree). The node that is broken down into subgoals is sometimes called a parent to the children subnodes.

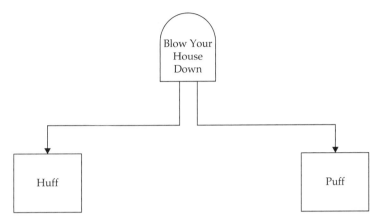

Figure 7-2   Simple example of a goal-directed tree using the "Three Little Pigs" fairy tale story

For a particularly clever and resourceful big bad wolf, the huff-and-puff combination of subattacks may have an alternative of "using dynamite." That makes the attack tree a bit more complex. First, the direct subordinates of the root node are now alternatives in the sense that the wolf needs to do only the huff-and-puff method *or* only the dynamite method. Again, we borrow from digital logic and use the OR operator and the corresponding symbol. As a convention, to make the tree clearer, we also have to create some other intermediate node that characterizes the huff-and-puff attack method. This creation of an intermediate node creates another level of the attack tree. Perhaps we can call this new parent node the "destructive-wind method" node. The new attack tree with the alternative is shown in Figure 7-3.

Now, we know that all of the points in the tree are called goal nodes. The special node at the top of a tree is a root node. The nodes in "the middle" that are neither top nor bottom nodes are sometimes called internal nodes. What about nodes at the bottom? Using the physical tree analogy, these are called attack leaf nodes. The tree terminology is borrowed from a part of computer science called graph theory, about which it is well worth reading more [AHO74].

7.1.2 Deriving Attack Scenarios

We now know that attack-tree leaf nodes are fundamental attack steps, but how exactly do they relate to the root—the strategic attacker goal of the tree? By examining the tree, and particularly the AND and OR relationships between the nodes, one can derive attack scenarios that accomplish the root. In the case of the simple example earlier, there are exactly two attack scenarios that accomplish the root goal: (1) huff AND puff and (2) use dynamite. This can be algorithmically calculated from any given attack tree using the graph theory concept of a **minimal cut set** [AHO74].

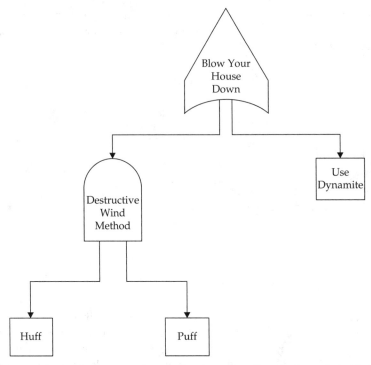

Figure 7-3   The simple attack tree example with the alternative of using dynamite added to the mix, making the tree deeper and more complex.

7.1.3 From Trees to Forests

Now that you know what attack trees are, we can extend the tree analogy a bit. Because we generate a variety of strategic attacker goals to create a representative set to drive cybersecurity design, there must be a set of trees, one for each goal. This collection of trees is called an attack forest because a collection of physical trees is called a forest. The attack forest represents the methods by which the representative strategic attacker goal set can be accomplished. One often finds that there are common subtrees between the attack trees, so it is often useful to name the subtrees and copy them from one tree to another.

Why go through the trouble of breaking down all of the strategic attacker goals into an attack forest? This takes us back to Section 2.3, where we learned that *theories of security come from theories of insecurity*. In general, the more a defender understands the potential goals of an adversary and how they might achieve them, the more a cybersecurity engineer will understand how to design proper defenses. Therefore, the exercise of creating attack trees is invaluable in and of itself. At the same time, an attack forest can be used to further understand how to prioritize attacks and thus prioritize defense options.

7.2 System Failures Predict Cybersecurity Failures

A student of security must be a student of failure. As discussed in previous chapters, security requires reliability because the unintentional failure of a security subsystem necessarily creates a vulnerability that an adversary can exploit. There is another reason why understanding failure is so important.

> *A student of cybersecurity must be a student of failure.*

7.2.1 Inspirational Catastrophes

As we learned in earlier chapters, developing a list of representative strategic attacker goals is an art. One inspiration of strategic attacker goals and subgoals within attack trees is historical catastrophic failure and near-failures—in one's own organization or, better yet, in someone else's organization. By catastrophic failure, I mean a failure that placed an essential mission of the organization or the organization itself in serious jeopardy. A near-failure is similar, except that events were such that a catastrophe did not actually occur, but had fortune gone slightly differently, most realize that a catastrophe was imminent.

7.2.2 The 10x Rule

As a general rule of thumb, *any failure that has occurred in a system by accident can be induced intentionally by an adversary with an effect that is significantly worse than that of the accidental failure—sometimes orders of magnitude worse.* Failures generally happen as a result of a triggering event exposing a design flaw in the system that has led to errors that manifest themselves. Generally, the triggering events are not so complex that an adversary could not create similar conditions given sufficient access.

> *System failures predict security breaches—times ten.*

When a failure occurs, it is detected at some point by a system administrator who will act to mitigate the damages if possible. Often, during post-mortem failure analysis, cybersecurity engineers observe that the damages could have been much worse if the failure mode was slightly different or if an operator had not caught it as early as they did. Therefore, if an adversary can influence the triggering event and the ability of operators to see the consequence early, then the adversary would significantly increase the damages.

Unintentional failures generally occur at a somewhat random time and so the chances of their causing maximal damage are low. On the other hand, if the adversary can trigger a failure at a time of their choosing, they can determine the worst possible timing and ensure that a failure is triggered at that point. For example, imagine if an adversary could trigger a radar system failure just as their bombing raid is coming across a monitored area to strike strategically important targets, causing catastrophic damage.

7.2.3 Feigning Failure

In addition to taking advantage of existing failures, adversaries can affect the life cycle of a system to insert subtle flaws that create new failure modes or exacerbate existing ones. This ability has two important benefits to the adversary: (1) by choosing the type and position of a failure, the adversary can multiply damage much further than exploiting an existing error; (2) the failure can be made to appear to be an unintentional failure, and so the adversary avoids detection and potential retribution. This is an important point. *When conducting failure analysis, analysts would be wise to not too quickly conclude that a failure is unintentional if the damage is greater than one would expect, or has a very specific effect that one would not expect to happen at random.*

> ***Treat security-relevant failures as attacks until proven otherwise.***

7.3 Understanding Failure Is the Key to Success: The Five Whys

Architects should study the historical failures that have happened to a system and its predecessors. Such analysis helps them understand the damages possible from intentional attacks and understand how to detect and mitigate the consequent damages through good designs using dependability techniques.

7.3.1 Why Five Whys?

Organizations should study cybersecurity failures within their own institution using an approach similar to that used by the National Transportation Safety Board (NTSB) when investigating aviation accidents [WIEG03]. It is insufficient to know the superficial proximal cause of an aviation accident—the aircraft was destroyed because it hit the ground going really, really fast. One must ask why that happened, and for every answer, ask why that happened, until one has worked backward at least five levels to determine the root cause [BOEB16].

This iterative analysis sequence is depicted in Figure 7-4. On the example on the right-hand side of the figure, we see that the airplane crashed because it ran out of fuel. It ran out of fuel because the fuel service request read "pounds" when the pilot was expecting "gallons" (a gallon of gas weighs about 6 pounds). The pilot made that error because the Fuel Service Request form was unclear, using a small font and the check boxes for pounds and gallons were scrunched right next to each other. The form was poorly designed because the designer of the fuel request form had no training in failure avoidance.

> ***Understanding failure is a key to success.***

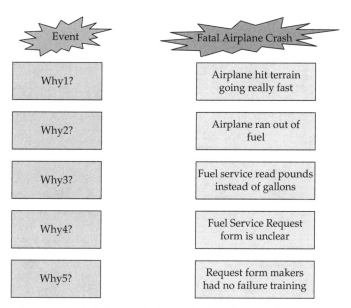

Figure 7-4   Linear five-whys style failure analysis on a fatal airplane crash

7.3.2 Projecting Fishbones

It is also useful to project those answers onto many systems of interest and ask how each contributed to the failure. This creates more of a fishbone causal chain than a linear chain. For the NTSB, systems of interest include the pilot, the aircraft design, the cockpit operations, air traffic control, and maintenance (Figure 7-5). With that information in hand, the NTSB has systematically been involved in a long-term quality control feedback process to make aviation one of the safest modes in existence by recommending changes in each of the relevant systems to reduce the chance of the failure occurring again.

A similar regimen in cybersecurity would be highly valuable. For cyberspace, systems of interest on which to project include system designs, system design processes, system designer training, system operators, rules of operation, operational user interface, inter-system interfaces, policies and directives, leadership, and organizational culture. Each should be examined for the role they may have played in the five-whys failure analysis.

7.4 Forests Should Be Representative, Not Exhaustive

When developing attack forests based on a set of strategic goals, it is important to remember the key point that the strategic attacker goals are intended to be representative, not exhaustive, of all possible strategic attack objectives. In fact, one can always come up with dozens of variations of a given strategic attack goal by varying a parameter involved with the attacker goal. Consider an abstract space of all possible strategic attacker objectives where a dot represents each attacker objective. The space would look something like that shown in Figure 7-6.

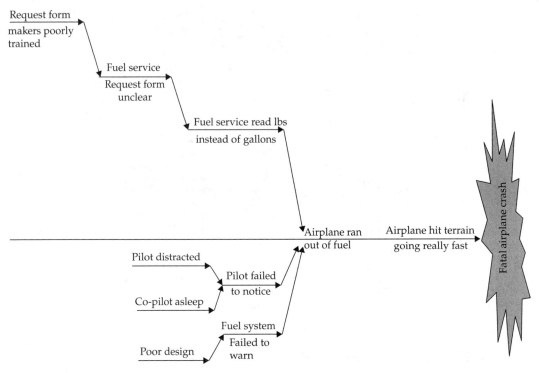

Figure 7-5   A more complex fishbone-style five-whys analysis considering multiple systems

Now consider the distance between dots to represent how similar one attack tree is to another. For example, if one attacker objective is to disrupt an organization's mission for more than seven days, nearby nodes could vary the number seven, or could reference key submissions. One could create hundreds of nearby neighbors whose attack trees would be

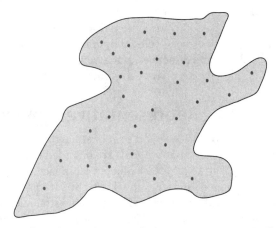

Figure 7-6   Abstract view of attacker goal space, where proximity means similarity

very similar. Thus, one can create neighborhoods or regions of similar attacker strategic goals. These groupings are sometimes known in computer science as an **equivalence class**—meaning that all members of a set are equivalent with respect to some attribute or method that one would apply to the elements of the class. Conceptually, such equivalence classes are shown in Figure 7-7.

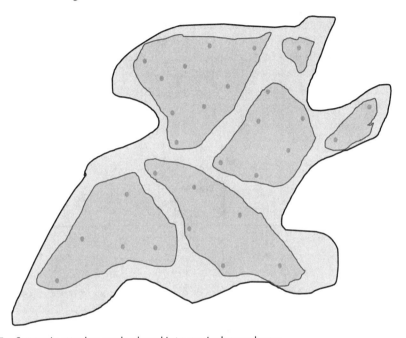

Figure 7-7 Strategic attacker goals placed into equivalence classes

Once again, there is a bit of art and a bit of science in how to group attacker goals into equivalence classes. Also, as depicted in Figure 7-7, there is no fixed number of goals that must be in a set, and it will surely vary from set to set. As a general rule, two trees are equivalent if addressing the attacks in the tree would cause a cybersecurity engineer to select and weight the palette of possible defenses in nearly the same way. From a practical perspective, if the attack trees look very similar to one another, that is a good indication that two trees should be treated as equivalent.

7.5 Drive Each Attack Tree Layer by Asking How

How do you know how to break a node down into subgoals when refining from one level to the next? This, too, is as much art as it is science. The primary driving question to ask is "How could a given goal node possibly be achieved by an adversary?" This is a time in which creativity and out-of-the-box lateral thinking [BONO10] is useful. In small groups, use brainstorm rules to generate as many ideas as possible and only then evaluate and consolidate ideas. Being a good student of attack and failure is also helpful. One must adopt an adversary's mind-set for this activity.

On the science side, there are two important properties that should be true of the subgoals in a layer; they should be (1) mutually exclusive (that is, the nodes should not overlap in any way) and (2) exhaustive (meaning that the analyst creating the level should consider all ways of achieving the parent goal).

A couple of patterns may be useful to consider in breaking down a level to ensure that it is exhaustive: process sequence and device type enumeration. For process sequence, if a goal is to attack the integrity of data, one could use the data pipeline in a sequence of ORs as the basis for the breakdown of that node. One has to find data, collect data, store data, process data, and then report data to decision makers. An attack could occur at any of these exhaustive stages of data, so each element in the list becomes part of a sequence of five ORed nodes. Figure 7-8 graphically depicts how such a process-sequence subgoal decomposition would look in an attack tree.

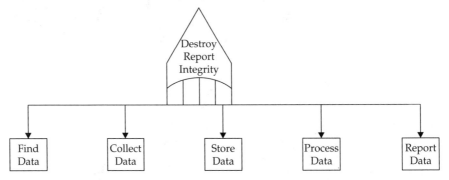

Figure 7-8   Example of using a process-sequence pattern to refine a goal from one level to the next

As an example of device type enumeration, when one considers how a computer such as a firewall might be attacked, one can look at the various layers of a computer system and place those in an ORed relationship: firewall application, firewall middleware, firewall operating system, firewall device drivers, device controllers, or hardware attacks. Figure 7-9 shows graphically how such a device type enumeration subgoal decomposition would look in an attack tree.

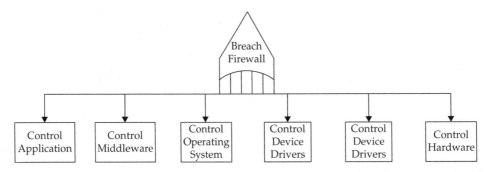

Figure 7-9   Example showing a device type enumeration analysis pattern for refining an attack goal

Which analysis pattern one uses depends on context. When there are equally good options, then it can be a matter of the preference of the analyst making the decision on how to break down the levels.

7.6 Go as Deep as Needed and No Deeper

You might ask at this point how one knows when to stop successively refining the goals into subgoals and, so, how do you know that something is truly a leaf? Well, the unsatisfying answer is that one person's leaf node is another's internal node. It depends on what the tree is trying to accomplish and how it will be used.

A basic rule of thumb is that one stops when an attack step is reached that the audience understands and can assess in some way. More will be discussed about the assessment in future chapters. In the simple example from the preceding section, it is clear to most people what huffing and puffing means and how to do it (though most probably do not know how to do it at sufficient strength to destroy edifices, but they are willing to suspend their disbelief for the sake of the story).

> *Tree goal refinement stops where analyst understanding begins.*

7.7 Beware of External Dependencies

When developing attack trees, you must consider the widest possible definition of your system that accomplishes your mission, including systems on which your system depends that are beyond your immediate control. The Parnas "uses hierarchy" describes the development of such dependency trees. We say that A "uses" B if the correctness of A depends on the correctness of B [PARN72].

It is tempting to say that such systems are "out of scope" and "we can't do anything about them anyway." Ignoring such systems can be a serious mistake. For example, most organizations that have an enterprise system depend on an Internet service provider. If an adversary successfully mounts an availability attack on the provider, then the enterprise services will not be available to anyone outside of the enterprise. This could be a serious problem for an online retailer, particularly between Thanksgiving and New Year's (the heaviest shopping season, where the vast majority of sales are made). Of course, the Internet service provider may also in turn depend on the telephone company for communication lines and on Internet services such as domain name system.

7.7.1 Just in Time

In today's world, a mantra seems to be "just-in-time everything" [ALCA16]. What this means is that manufacturers and service providers alike seek to minimize their costs. One way to do that is to reduce the need to store parts by having the parts appear from suppliers exactly when they are needed. Similarly, in the ideal world, when a product comes off the manufacturing line, it is shipped directly to a client who has already ordered it so that nothing is produced for which there are no orders.

This sounds great and even sometimes works great, except when things go wrong. The system brittleness this creates is not the subject of this book, but the reader may notice that today, more things seem to go wrong than they did in the past. In any case, *one consequence of this just-in-time strategy is that organizations must intimately connect their systems with their suppliers and their distributors in order for suppliers to know the demand in advance and in order for the organization to know about orders so as to time the production line.* This intimate interconnection of systems creates significant risk because the risk from one organization can more easily propagate from one system to another. It is similar to how communicable diseases spread much faster in cities because people are in closer proximity to one another on a frequent basis.

> *Just-in-time requires interconnection of systems and their risks.*

7.7.2 Information Dependency

Not all organizations are in the manufacturing business, but there are analogs for organizations in the information business. Information comes from suppliers of information. After information is stored and processed by an organization to add some value, they then distribute that information in some fashion, perhaps in the form of reports. One interesting example of external dependency occurs when an adversary actually attacks the systems of the distributors or end consumers of the information (systems that tend to be less well-protected in many cases). Just because an integrity issue happens in the distribution or consumption systems does not mean that the producer will not be blamed and will not suffer irrevocable harm in reputation and eventual sales. A good example of such a phenomenon happened in 1972 when people actually died due to in-store tampering of Tylenol bottles [BART12]. It did not matter that it was not the manufacturer's fault; the damage to the reputation caused serious harm. A similar event could happen to reports that are on distribution or consumer computers.

So, when considering attack trees, think about all the ways your system depends on other systems and particularly in the context of just-in-time strategies [LEVE12]. Even though such systems may be beyond your control, mission is equally disrupted. One can childishly decry that "it wasn't my fault" when mission fails and perhaps even the organization fails, but it is no consolation.

7.7.3 Creating Redundancy

In point of fact, even though one does not have direct control of external systems, one can do something useful. One can create redundancy and quality of service agreements to improve the situation and reduce the chances of a bad outcome. For example, if power is very important, automated backup systems are often used. If communications are essential, an enterprise may want to use two independent Internet service providers.

In creating redundancy, cybersecurity engineers must take care to ensure that the redundant systems do not have a **common mode of failure**. This means that even though two things appear to be independent, they depend on something in common whose failure could cause both to fail simultaneously, thus violating the tacit assumption of system independence and the decreased probability of failure that one gets from independence [WYMAxx]. This sort of dependency can be made visible by the Parnas uses hierarchy [PARN72].

A good example of pseudo-independence is when two apparently separate power feeds into a building go through the same buried conduit or across the same bridge. If the ditch is accidently dug up or the bridge is damaged by a natural or man-made disaster, both services will be cut simultaneously. A subtler example occurs when two providers use exactly the same operating system and router infrastructure and one or both of those has a serious problem that is being exploited by an ongoing attack. Again, both provider systems will go down simultaneously. This means that the cybersecurity and systems engineers must ask tough and deep questions when attempting to create redundancy for reliability and security purposes.

Conclusion

This chapter concludes this short two-chapter discussion on the nature of adversaries and the attack strategies they use. The next part of the book deals with countermeasures and how to thwart adversaries and mitigate the risks from the space of possible attacks.

To summarize:

- Attack trees help defenders understand the "how" of the strategic adversary goal.
- Failures can predict attack—with significantly higher damage.
- Root cause analysis uses a five-whys approach that allows defenders to improve design from failure.
- Attack tree forests need to be representative of the attacker goal space.
- Attack trees successively refine attacker goals into subgoals, increasing the level of detail.
- Attack trees go as deep as needed based on what they are needed for.
- Leaf nodes of attack trees are attack steps that are well understood by the tree's audience.
- Include critical suppliers, distributors, and service providers in system analysis.

Questions

1. What is an attack tree and why is it important?
2. What is a cut set and how does it relate to strategic attacker objectives?
3. Why do failures predict attack and why can the damage be so much higher?

4. What are attacker goal equivalence classes and how do they drive the selection of an attack tree forest?

5. What does each layer below a given layer in an attack tree signify? Explain how one creates a lower layer from a higher layer.

6. How deep should an attack tree go and why?

7. Discuss why ignoring external systems on which a system depends will degrade an attack tree analysis. What might the consequences of that choice be?

What Are the Building Blocks of Mitigating Risk?

"Part III: What Are the Building Blocks of Mitigating Risk?" explores the solution space for the problem described in Parts I and II.

8

Countermeasures:
Security Controls

Overview

Learning Objectives

- Discuss the history of countermeasure design and its implications on the future.
- Explain the notion of attack space and how to cover the space with countermeasures.
- Define and compare the concepts of defense in breadth and defense in depth.
- Define and explain the historical significance of multilevel security.
- Compare and contrast the types of integrity policies.
- List and define the factors involved in the usability of cybersecurity countermeasures.
- Discuss how cost affects cybersecurity design in several different ways.

Up to this point in the book, we have discussed the nature of the cybersecurity problem and its underlying roots—adversaries and attacks. This chapter begins the discussion of how to counter the attacks using countermeasures aimed clearly and directly at the source of the most important risks. Said more directly, *countermeasures counter specific attacks within a threat space; they are not mere mysterious talismans to ward off evil cyber spirits.* Countermeasures, also known as security controls, must be designed to purpose, deployed in a specific way and in specific places in the architecture, and combined in such a way as to effectively cover the attack space and complement each other's strengths while bolstering each other's weaknesses to reduce risk. Furthermore, security controls must be considered an investment of precious and finite organization resources toward optimizing mission. *The development of security controls is about return on investment in terms of risk reduction.*

> **Security control is about risk-reduction return on investment.**

8.1 Countermeasures: Design to Purpose

When the cybersecurity problem first emerged in the late 1960s and early 1970s as a military confidentiality issue, engineers confronted it by applying existing technology and techniques toward this new problem area. They used mechanisms such as system audit to try to detect attacks based on the premise that attacks would surely have manifestations in system audit. They adopted weak login and password mechanisms as their primary human-to-machine interface and even used hard-coded passwords in programs (passwords that were embedded in the source code of a program and easily compromised just by inspecting the code) to authenticate programs to one another. This was a reasonable first step to try to leverage existing solutions to begin to address the problem. It was a struggle to use these tools, meant for a completely different purpose, for cybersecurity. Much energy was and, to some extent continues to be, poured into adapting the aforementioned non-cybersecurity mechanisms for cybersecurity purposes.

The attack space should be considered part of the essential requirements for driving security control design. For example, driving detection requirements from attacks is likely to show that highly specialized custom sensors are required for sophisticated high-stealth attacks of the type expected on highly protected segregated enterprise networks. It may be that certain commercial sensors are better than others for detecting events relating to these classes of attacks, and so they should be used. Custom sensors in plug-in-capable systems should also be developed and integrated into detection architectures that are more open. See Section 15.1 for more discussion on detecting the breadth of attacks.

8.2 Ensure Attack-Space Coverage (Defense in Breadth)

Cybersecurity engineering is about covering the attack space. The attack space is an abstraction that characterizes the totality of attacks that can be mounted against a system, by adversaries of concern, weighted with some sense of probability. Similar attacks can be grouped into attack classes, and the collection of attack classes make up the attack space. Pictorially, think of the attack space as an amorphous blob as depicted in Figure 8-1. Note that there are some parts of the space that are not depicted in specific attack blobs. This interstitial space represents as-yet-undiscovered attacks, of which there are many.

The space of all possible attack avenues is large, complex, and generally not well understood. Still, it is important to describe the space as best as possible and to ensure that the countermeasures and the architecture features map into the attack space such that all of the attack space is covered in some way. This can also be thought of as the principle of

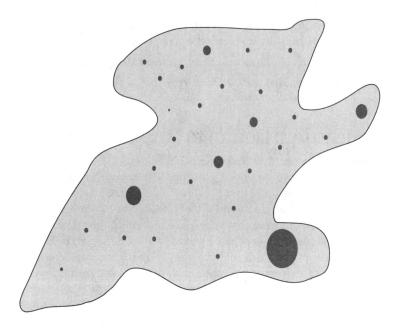

 Attack space

• Attack class within the attack space where size corresponds to number of attacks in the class

Figure 8-1   Abstract representation of the attack space where dots represent attack classes and size represents attack likelihood

defense-in-breadth. The concept of defense-in-breadth is shown in Figure 8-2. In the figure, a shaded grouping of attack classes represents all the attack classes that are addressed by a given security control. Ideally, some security control addresses every known attack class in some way. The figure shows that ideal condition. Often, practice falls short of that ideal.

8.3 Defense in Depth and Breadth

Defense in depth means to ensure that multiple independent mechanisms address a given class of attack. This is important for several reasons: (1) an attack class can be quite broad and so a given mechanism may strongly address part of a class and weakly address another; (2) defensive mechanisms can fail just like any component; (3) defensive mechanisms can themselves be attacked and defeated, so multiple robust mechanisms are often harder and more expensive for the adversary to defeat.

Figure 8-3 illustrates the concept of defense in depth. Each shaded region represents the subset of attack classes that are addressed by a security control. As shown, some attack classes are covered by multiple security controls, meaning that an attack from that class will be handled by multiple security controls at the same time. Note that a security control can address an attack by preventing an attack, detecting an attack, recovering from an attack, or tolerating the attack. We do not specify at this level of discussion what type of coverage it is.

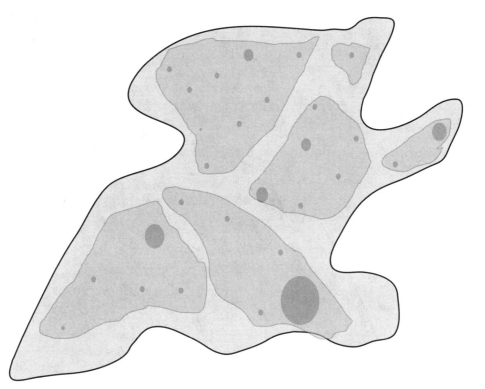

 Attack space

• Attack class within the attack space where size corresponds to number of attacks in the class

◇ The subset of attack classes covered by a security control

Figure 8-2   Illustration of the concept of defense in breadth with the regions showing coverage of a subset of the attack space that each of several security controls address

Detailed cybersecurity engineering would require an understanding of the type of coverage and how the types interplay.

When planning defense in depth, it is important to (a) choose and specify the granularity of attack class being addressed, (b) argue as to the manner and degree to which a given mechanism covers that class, and (c) argue that the mechanisms and their failure modes are truly independent from one another. One final note: We add the implied principle that defense-in-depth without defense-in-breadth is of limited use, because the adversary will pick the easiest attack avenue. Therefore, the expense of adding depth of mechanism in only a few areas may not be worth it if many attack classes exist without similar depth or strength.

Depth without breadth is useless; breadth without depth, weak.

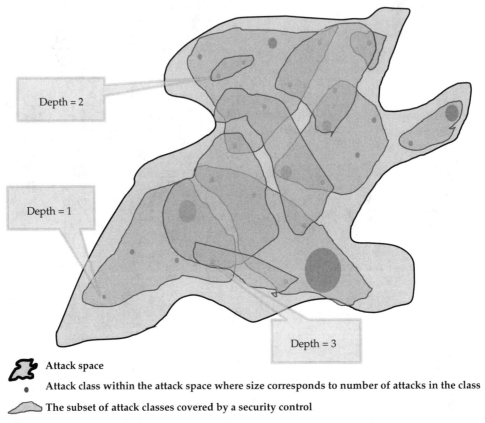

Depth = 2

Depth = 1

Depth = 3

🗿 **Attack space**

● **Attack class within the attack space where size corresponds to number of attacks in the class**

◣ **The subset of attack classes covered by a security control**

Figure 8-3 Illustration of defense-in-depth where each region represents a security control's coverage and overlaps show multiple coverage and therefore depth

8.4 Multilevel Security, Trusted Code, Security Kernels

Two concepts, **multilevel security** and **trusted code** [ANDE01], will not be deeply covered in this book, but they are of considerable historical importance. This chapter gives cursory knowledge of them to help explain some important ideas in trustworthy hardware and cybersecurity in general that the reader will come across in the accumulated literature.

8.4.1 Multilevel Security

In the late 1960s, the U.S. military sought to process information at multiple classification levels at the same time, to get maximum utilization out of what were, at the time, very expensive machines. Soon, it was learned that such attempts at multiplexing multilevel processing were risky business [ANDE72], because classified data could potentially be stolen from the system. The primary concern was that a malicious user who did not have a security clearance could gain access to classified data and that the concentration of classified data provided a high-value target for adversaries. The malicious user could potentially hack the security controls of the operating system or could potentially entice a cleared user to execute a Trojan horse—a seemingly useful application that also performs malicious activity. *Such a Trojan horse could simply write classified data into an unclassified file, and the uncleared malicious user could simply walk out with the file—nobody the wiser.*

In theory, every piece of software executing on the computer system could be certified to not contain a Trojan horse or other malware, but that is in fact impractical in reality, and, in the most general form, undecidable in theory (meaning that it is theoretically impossible to prove, in general, the absence of a Trojan horse in a program) [HOPC79]. This led to the notion of **mandatory security policy**, which stated that no process operating at a given clearance level could write to any objects (files, memory blocks, etc.) that were at a lower level than that of the process (for example, a Top Secret process could not write to a Confidential file). This became known by unusual name of the *-property [BELL76]—named so because the authors could not think of a clever name at the time of first draft and so the "*" was a placeholder character for a good name that never came to them before publication. System enforcement of the *-property meant all processes had to be labeled, as did all storage.

A companion property called **simple security** prohibits processes at a given clearance level from reading any objects at a classification level higher than their clearance (for example, a process operating at the unclassified level could not read an object labeled Secret). Simple security corresponded to how things worked in the paper-and-pencil world of classified documents—where people held clearances and documents had classifications (Figure 8-4). The two properties together meant that a malicious user could neither access classified objects above their clearance level nor could they downgrade classified data to a lower level without proper authorization to do so.

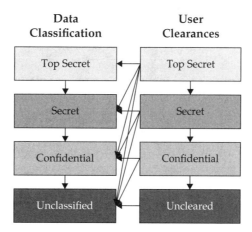

Figure 8-4   Simple security—users with a given clearance can read data classified at their clearance level or below.

The goal of attaining multilevel security is of historical importance because it led to a substantial volume of research and development that created the field of cybersecurity. It motivated research into improved processors, hardware memory management, robust operating systems, and security policies to protect systems from adversaries using malicious code and employing malicious users as insiders.

8.4.2 Trusted Code

Malicious software was recognized early on as a critical problem. The inability to prove that the vast majority of programs were free from malicious code presented a huge challenge. A good **assurance case** could be built for the correctness of small programs or abstract high-level specifications. Building such assurance cases requires substantial resources and highly specialized expertise despite having tool support from theorem provers such as the Prototype Verification System [RUSH81] and Gypsy [GOOD84]). It was cost-prohibitive to do such assurance cases for more than a tiny fraction of software. For example, general operating systems are way too massive in size and complex for such analysis and proof of the software code.

8.4.3 Security Kernel and the Reference Monitor

Operating systems were essential to system security and particularly to implementing the mandatory policies discussed earlier, operating in the most trusted hardware mode—the **supervisor mode**. Yet they were too complex to prove correct. The solution was to divide operating systems into three layers: the **security kernel**, **trusted extensions**, and untrusted libraries operating in user mode. This layering is shown in Figure 8-5.

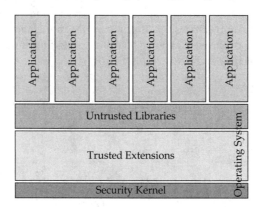

Figure 8-5   Layering of traditional operating system to create differing trust requirements

Security Kernel   At the very foundation of an operating system is what is called a kernel—meaning the core. That core was all security-relevant because it was the part that mediated control of the hardware resources. Therefore, this kernel in the secure system became known as the security kernel. Only the security kernel would need to run in the trusted supervisor mode, and it could be made relatively small and simple. Being small and simple made it possible to construct strong correctness arguments. In addition to being correct, it would need to be **tamperproof** (so it cannot be changed once proven correct) and **non-bypassable** (so that no program could gain access to operating system resources other than through the kernel). These three properties taken together are called the **reference monitor** properties.

Trusted Extensions   There were other parts of the operating system that required reference monitor properties, but were much less critical because they were not directly involved in processor and memory allocation. These parts were called trusted extensions because they extended the core functionality of the security kernel—but had limited and verifiable functionality. This layer typically consisted of programs that controlled external devices such as printers, displays, and removable media. Such data moving to and from external devices needed to be properly labeled, based on the clearance level of the process and the data that was imported out of or exported into the computer system. Because trusted extension software had to create objects at various levels, depending on the level of the data imported, the software had to violate the letter of *-property (no write down) to perform its function. The extension therefore had to be proven to not violate the spirit of the *-property—to not intentionally downgrade classified data to a lower level for the purpose of intentionally leaking it.

It was important that operating system trusted extensions be provably correct, non-bypassable, and tamperproof. For example, if malicious code operating at the Top Secret level were to bypass the trusted extension in control of the printer, *it could write the label "unclassified" on the top and bottom of every page, and a malicious user could simply pick up the Top Secret document and walk out the door with it.* So, the trusted extension code is security-critical, even though it does not need to necessarily run in supervisor mode. As we will learn in Section 9.3, one could run trusted extensions in a privileged mode of the processor that is less privileged than supervisor mode. So, security kernel code might run in the most privileged processor mode, sometimes called protection ring 0, and trusted extension code might be placed in a second protection ring, while user code is run in the least privileged mode or outer protection ring. Figure 8-6 depicts this ringed configuration.

Libraries   Lastly, there are portions of the operating system that exist for convenience, such as most libraries, that require no trust at all. The math libraries and string-handling libraries are good examples. Such software requires no special privilege to operate and can essentially run in user mode as normal user programs. As a result, the library software requires no special verification of properties. In fact, untrusted code could have, in theory, been written by the defender's strongest adversary and be riddled with Trojan horses, and the computer system should be able to operate without violating mandatory security policy.

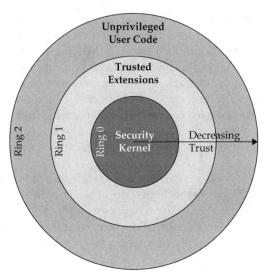

Figure 8-6   Depiction of rings of trust and privilege in hardware modes supporting software of varying degrees of trustworthiness

8.5 Integrity and Type Enforcement

While confidentiality garnered much of the U.S. Defense Department's attention, the integrity problem was more foundational and at the root of all the other properties. One cannot have confidentiality without system integrity. The mechanism of many availability attacks (other than **network flooding attacks**) is based on system and data integrity attacks.

8.5.1 Multilevel Integrity

Multilevel security properties depend on the integrity of the underlying system. The concept of **multilevel integrity** [BIBA75] parallels that of multilevel security (which really would be more aptly called multilevel confidentiality, since it focuses exclusively on that one-third of cybersecurity). Whereas multilevel security dictates that information be prevented from flowing to lower sensitivity levels, multilevel integrity dictates that portions of the system with an established high level of integrity (e.g., through careful design and analysis) not depend on systems of lower integrity (e.g., software applets downloaded and executed on-the-fly from some website of unknown pedigree).

As an example of the need to take in what programs a system depends on, malicious code detection programs tend to be integrated deep into operating systems, giving them high degrees of privilege. These programs are integrated at these low levels to help prevent the malicious code they are designed to detect from getting underneath the detectors and subverting them. Thus, the computer systems highly depend on these malicious code detection programs being trustworthy. Unfortunately, there is little evidence that these companies offer to demonstrate that they are trustworthy. In 2017, strong suspicions arose that the detection program by Kaspersky was indeed not worthy of that trust, and many users discontinued using it [GOOD17a].

Similar to system dependencies, data of established high integrity (e.g., through careful input and verification procedures) must not depend on and be corrupted by the inclusion of data of lower or unknown integrity (e.g., unchecked human inputs through untrustworthy software).

Implementation of the principles of multilevel integrity is complex and involved, as will be discussed in later chapters, but the idea is conceptually clear, whether for system or data integrity: never depend on anything deemed less trustworthy.

> *Never depend on anything deemed less trustworthy.*

8.5.2 Type Enforcement

A key problem with multilevel integrity is that it does not provide granular enough control, particularly over **data integrity**. Security experts observed that data integrity flowed in narrow pipeline structures with particular programs having access to particular data sets, which performed transformations on data before handing it off to the next program. Because of the similarity that this bears to data abstraction in programming languages (also an aspect of what is called object-oriented programming), the alternative non-hierarchical model was called typed objects [FEIE79] and then later refined into **type enforcement** [BOEB85]. A generic pipeline of data flow is shown in Figure 8-7.

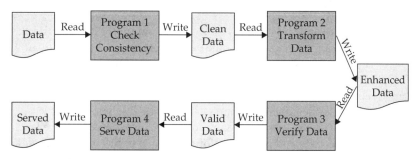

Figure 8-7   Generic data processing pipeline that is difficult for multilevel integrity policy to handle

In type enforcement, the pipelines of data flow are directly supported. Programs are assigned a **domain** and data containers (e.g., files) are assigned **types**. One then could create a type enforcement **access control matrix** with entries allowing the data to flow in one direction in the pipeline. An example of an access for the generic example is given in Figure 8-8.

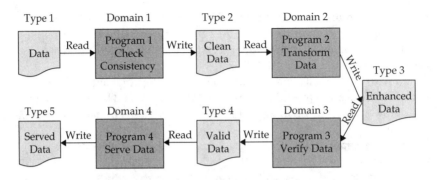

Figure 8-8 Generic data flow pipeline with a corresponding access control matrix in which programs have been assigned domains and data have been assigned types

Domain	Type 1	Type 2	Type 3	Type 4	Type 5
Domain 1	Read	Write	--	--	--
Domain 2	--	Read	Write	--	--
Domain 3	--	--	Read	Write	--
Domain 4	--	--		Read	Write

To make the data flow pipeline more concrete, consider the problem of creating a labeled document that is to go to a printer. We have one program that applies the classification labels to the top and bottom of each page of the document. We have a separate program, called a spooler, that queues the document for printing. In a multilevel security system, as discussed in the previous section, labeling a document for printing is a security-critical operation because failure to mark it properly can result in someone walking out of a physically secure building with a classified document improperly marked as unclassified.

Because of the security-critical requirement, the program doing the labeling is considered trusted code and must therefore be shown to be correct in function, non-bypassable, and tamperproof. Such proofs are onerous, expensive, and complex; therefore, the smaller the program that does the labeling, the better. This is one reason why one does not just modify the spooler to do the labeling and printing. Additionally, off-the-shelf programs are much less expensive to manage and maintain than custom programs or even customized programs, so keeping the spooler unmodified is the preferred solution.

It is possible that the spooler could maliciously change the labels before printing, so one would need another program that checks the documents in the print queue to ensure they were not changed from the version output by the labeling program. This is a very simple property to prove by producing and comparing **digital signatures** between the output file and the one on the queue. The proof that all printed files are properly labeled therefore comes in two parts: (1) a proof that the labeler has reference monitor properties and performs its labeling function correctly and (2) a proof that the labeling is preserved before the actual printing of a document. This is called **proof factoring** because a complex proof is factored into two parts. Actually, the third part of the proof is that the pipeline mechanism provided by type enforcement also works correctly for the two-part proof to be valid. This processing example is shown in Figure 8-9.

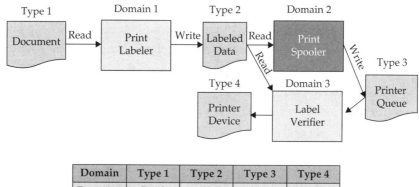

Domain	Type 1	Type 2	Type 3	Type 4
Domain 1	Read	Write	--	
Domain 2	--	Read	Write	
Domain 3	--	Read	Read	Write

Figure 8-9   Type enforcement example of a print labeler and spooler pipeline

David Clark and David Wilson similarly pointed out the limitation of a multilevel integrity model with respect to commercial data integrity [CLAR87] and proposed a **Clark-Wilson integrity mode**, which was focused on transforming data from lower-integrity during the input process to higher-integrity data and having verification rules to check for consistency of data before and after transformation. Only one or two programs would be trusted to perform each transformation. This conceptually created a pipeline of data transformations and verification procedures. This pipeline, with very limited process access to reading and writing data for their specific pipeline and the need for role separation of duty, made the hierarchical multilevel integrity model a poor fit. Type enforcement accommodates the commercial integrity concerns directly, demonstrating its flexibility and power. Implementations of type enforcement include SELinux [LOSC01] and the Sidewinder firewall [BOEB10].

8.6 Cybersecurity Usability

No chapter on countermeasure design would be complete without discussing the usability of cybersecurity, which, to date, has been nothing short of abysmal. One of the most prominent and early observations of this fact comes from a paper entitled: "Why Johnny Can't Encrypt" [WHIT99]. In this paper, the authors point out that users need to know what to do, how to do it without making errors, and they have to want to do it. This book expands on those useful starting requirements.

Modern cybersecurity mechanisms are highly configurable and flexible with many options. Although this flexibility can be a good thing, the myriad of options can be confusing to users in terms of which options are best under which circumstances. Indeed, often the doctrine has not been worked out by the experts as to which options are best under which circumstances.

To be usable, cybersecurity mechanisms must be

- Invisible, when possible
- Transparent, when not
- Clear in presenting options and implications of options and basis for choosing
- Easy to understand using language that everyone can comprehend
- Reliable in selection process
- Fast
- Reversible when possible
- Adaptable
- Reviewable
- Traceable for diagnosis

8.6.1 Invisible

In the ideal world, cybersecurity would be completely invisible—meaning that it would be constantly operating on your behalf, adapting to your changing needs depending on the circumstances, and you would not even have to be aware of its existence. For example, all network connections transmitting data from one system to another should be encrypted by default, using system-to-system strong encryption so that eavesdroppers cannot read data in transit between systems. In circumstances where there is system policy against the encryption so that intrusion detection systems can inspect the content in some places, the system should figure that out and not use encryption for those network connections. That analysis, decision, and implementation should not involve the user, or even most programmers. Designers need to find a way to minimize the burden placed on users to make sound cybersecurity decisions and execute them.

8.6.2 Transparent

When the user really must make a choice in cybersecurity mechanisms use or configuration, it must be made obvious when and how the mechanism is engaged. For example, if a user engages an email encryption service, they must be given some sort of reliable and independent feedback that it is working. Why? Because maybe they did not invoke it correctly. Maybe they thought they clicked the right option, but they missed and did not notice. Maybe the encryption service itself failed for some reason. There needs to be an independent program sampling the output of the email verifying that it is encrypted, and there must be very clear feedback to the user that it is working and unmistakable feedback if it fails in any way.

8.6.3 Clear

Sometimes, the user has options in configuring the security service they seek, maybe to be involved in a cost/performance/functionality trade-off. Nothing is more exasperating than being presented options in gibberish without a clear indication of the implications of one's choices or a basis on which to choose them. In the 1980s and early 1990s, there was an operating system called Microsoft® Disk Operating System (DOS). Whenever it got confused, it would regurgitate the most annoying choice onto the user screen: "Failure: (A)bort, (R)etry, or (I)gnore", exhorting the user to press the A, R, or I button to give it guidance on how to proceed. It was never clear exactly what failed, what the meaning of each of the options was in the context of whatever failure occurred in whatever subsystem that is unidentified, or what were the implications of choosing any one of the three selections. "Retry" always seemed like the best choice, but never worked. "Ignore" sounded incredibly dangerous, but was the next least horrific choice when "retry" failed, because the user wanted whatever result they were waiting for. Finally, and almost inevitably, the user had to select "abort" because it was the only thing that worked and it was the exact action they did not want because it meant that they were not going to get what they had asked for. This is an outstanding example of how *not* to design a decision support system for a user when they truly do need to make a meaningful decision.

A system may ask a user to pick a password. There are millions of passwords they could pick. What is the trade-off among the choices? Is a shorter one that you can remember better than a longer one that you have to write down? What support do modern systems give you for this important decision? As another example, do you want to encrypt your disk or not? Well, gee, I don't know; if I forget my key, do I lose all my data? Why might I want to encrypt my disk? What threats does it protect against? What happens to backups? Will it slow my system down? Few of these questions are posed, let alone answered, by any of today's systems to help the poor uninformed user make a good decision. *This is an unacceptable circumstance that adds substantial risk to the system and to the users for little reason.*

8.6.4 Easy to Understand

When a cybersecurity decision is made, it should be easy to implement that solution. Having to go through complicated processes and scripts to get the system or application to perform a security service makes mistakes likely and certainly decreases the user's willingness to use cybersecurity. For example, take using public-key infrastructure. One has to go and present themselves to some registrar, who has to generate a public-private key pair, and the private key must be securely transmitted to the user. The user then has to receive the private key and then install that private key in their system account. The user then has to inform each application about it and where to get it. In the process, the users must back up their key, and if they do it wrong, they may accidentally save their private key **in the clear** in their file system, which would then be an easy target for an attacker to steal and then masquerade as that user.

When using encryption on something such as email, one should not have to go six levels deep on submenus to find the option to encrypt. It should be crystal clear, and the button should be large, obvious, and provide some sort of visual and audio feedback that it has been engaged.

8.6.5 Reliable

Making a decision on the use of some cybersecurity mechanism is hard enough. In addition to making the selection easy as described earlier, the selection process must deeply and explicitly consider error avoidance in the interface design. We have all seen the insane user interfaces where the delete-all button is right next to the save button. Another common issue is that an option is in six-point font and so close to another menu button that it requires an incredible amount of attention and care to just select the right option. If a user is given a choice to encrypt their disk or not encrypt their disk, two radio buttons that are right next to each other, in the same font and color, is a bad interface design. All cybersecurity engineers should take a course or at least a course module on human-machine-interface design to avoid these types of circumstances.

8.6.6 Fast

If engaging a cybersecurity mechanism slows the system to a crawl, particularly the human-machine interface, it will be avoided like the plague. There is nothing more frustrating than a user interface that takes multiple seconds to respond to a typed or clicked input. Turning on heavy auditing of user actions can have this effect. Heavy auditing can also sop up too much of network bandwidth and cause slow response times to computer services and slow the entire system down and cause errors by forcing the network to drop packets to try to keep up with the load.

Cybersecurity takes system resources, which necessarily will slow the system down some. Designers should establish design policy and goals regarding limiting allocation of resources to cybersecurity functions. *A good rule of thumb is that the totality of security mechanism (not just a single aspect) should collectively take up no more than 10 percent of system resources.*

> *Cybersecurity designers should impose no more than 10 percent overhead.*

8.6.7 Reversible

When taking a cybersecurity action, there is an enduring angst about the implications of the decision. For example, setting very conservative firewall rules for incoming and outgoing connections sounds like a great idea, and it is. At the same time, operators worry about whether they will unintentionally interfere with mission operations by adopting such rules and cause severe damage to the organization. This happens in real life, and it could be career-ending for the poor soul who is just trying to protect the organization. *This type of irreversibility of damages creates decision paralysis for some operators.*

An alternative approach would be to set conservative rules and automatically add new rules for any new connections (other than those that are on a blacklist) while each connection is automatically analyzed and the persons responsible for those connections are contacted. This approach risks some damage from an attack on an unauthorized connection, but the trade-off is with a risk of doing significant damage by unintentional self-inflicted **denial of service**.

8.6.8 Adaptable

Sometimes, cybersecurity engineers imagine that they know exactly what a user needs in the way of cybersecurity mechanism and configuration, and therefore they do not give the users and system owners configuration options. For example, an authorization system making access control decisions to all system services seems like a fantastic idea, until it fails catastrophically. Then what? If there is no adaptation built into the system, the entire mission comes to a screeching halt until someone diagnoses the source of the problem and fixes it. Meanwhile, the defender incurs massive damage from a self-inflicted denial of service. A fallback mode where all services require only authentication would obviate such a problem.

The system also needs to be designed in a way consistent with how a user actually operates the system. This includes giving the user the ability to trade-off between cybersecurity and system performance and functionality when that dynamic trade-off is critical to the success of the mission. For example, in a communication confidentiality service provided for air-to-air combat, the user (pilot in this case) may favor performance over the confidentiality service under some circumstances. An example of such a circumstance is when an airplane is in a dogfight and one plane needs to quickly warn another of a fast-inbound threat (such as a missile); in this case the user does not want to wait the few seconds for cryptographic synchronization to guard his communication because the adversary certainly already knows about the incoming threat since they probably launched it.

One needs to be careful about automated adaptation and deeply consider the implications of alternative modes of operation. For example, if cryptographic protocol exchanges fail to create a secure connection, should the system just fall back to create an unprotected link? The answer is that it depends on what is at stake. If it is an email to your Aunt Susie about the great weather you are enjoying, then that would be fine. If the subject matter is the time and date of an operation against a terrorist cell, then such a fallback would be disastrous. This is known as the **fail-open** or **fail-closed** alternative. Both are valid depending on the circumstances, but one must choose one or the other. Whichever is chosen, there should be a clear and loud announcement when entering into that mode so that the user understands the nature of the risk change that has happened.

8.6.9 Traceable

A key aspect of the problem associated with reversibility is that the negative effects of cybersecurity mechanisms on mission do not always manifest themselves immediately. Sometimes it takes months or even years. Why? There are several possible reasons:

- Some missions are intermittent in nature and therefore may not be active when new cybersecurity mechanisms are introduced; for example, an annual software update from a vendor.

- New mission systems get created or modified as part of normal ongoing operations, maintenance, and development work; for example, a new application needs to communicate with a new partner involved in the distribution of a new product.

- New non-cybersecurity mechanisms get deployed, such as network management systems, that could negatively interact with the cybersecurity mechanisms in unanticipated ways; for example, a new network management system pings all application services and is mistaken for malware doing reconnaissance.

- The network or system topology changes due to the organization growing, shrinking, or reorganizing; for example, a new router and subnetwork get added and the implementers fail to update the security filters in the existing routers to accommodate the change.

- New cybersecurity mechanisms get deployed, which have an unknown negative synergy with existing security mechanisms; for example, a new mechanism that encrypts all network connections gets flagged by the intrusion detection system as malware.

Identifying cybersecurity mechanisms that are interfering with mission is a serious problem that costs organizations a lot of wasted resources. In general, when a mission system fails in some fashion, diagnosis is a nightmare because each separate system must be independently diagnosed, and there could be dozens of them on which the mission system depends (e.g., application, operating system, network device driver, network device controller, the domain name system, the routing infrastructure). It should be possible to interrogate all cybersecurity mechanisms to report the existence and cause of blocked actions to facilitate diagnosis of the issues described previously.

One problem that we often see is that cybersecurity mechanisms are the first to be blamed and they are immediately reconfigured to the most permissive settings to ensure they are not in the way. When it is found that the cybersecurity mechanisms are not the issue, they are often left in the permissive configuration for the remainder of the diagnostic process, just in case they were somehow contributing to the problem. One issue is that, even after the diagnostic process is finished, the system manager often forgets to put the cybersecurity mechanisms back to the proper settings and so the system remains wide open for an extended period. That happens way more frequently than people like to admit. Support for timed temporary reconfiguration would be useful to address this aspect of usability.

8.6.10 Reviewable

Security settings range from straightforward and obvious in their meaning to completely unfathomable. For example, deciding to encrypt email or not is straightforward, though perhaps choosing the Advanced Encryption Standard with 256 or 512 bits or the old Data Encryption Standard (which has been deemed insecure) is less clear.

Refereeing means to have an independent review of something to verify that it is correct. Journal articles are refereed by peers prior to publication for this purpose. The same applies to security mechanisms. They accrete over time and are modified, updated, and temporarily changed many times throughout their life cycle. An independent review is needed periodically. Unfortunately, that is nearly impossible if nobody can understand the meaning and purpose of a configuration anymore, not even those who put it there.

Firewall rule sets are a perfect example of this problem. They grow a few at a time as the system configuration changes and new elements are added. Eventually, the firewall ends up with hundreds of rules, sometimes tens of thousands of rules. Nobody remembers why any given rule is there, what it does, and how it interacts with the other rules. Such a situation is completely unreviewable. Nobody wants to even touch it because they fear that something will break. This calls for higher-level languages to specify rule sets, support for documenting rule sets, and accountability for each rule set to a human user who must periodically validate it.

8.7 Deploy Default Secure

A corollary to the principle of usability is that of default secure deployment. Systems are often delivered with default settings that are not secure, and security must specifically be turned on for them to work. Further, systems do not indicate that they are operating in an insecure mode, and so users do not realize that cybersecurity features are not enabled. Also, systems delivered with default passwords to user accounts must ensure that the passwords are changed before allowing the system to enter an operational mode.

8.8 Costs

Cybersecurity countermeasures cost money to develop, operate, and maintain. They cost time in delayed mission capability and time of personnel to perform security functions. They cost a loss of mission function in that cybersecurity sometimes means not being able to perform some mission because of impacts to performance or resources. These costs are an essential part of the cost-benefit trade-off that must be calculated as part of the cybersecurity design engineering trade-off.

8.8.1 Cost Always Matters

Just as there is an important engineering trade-off between cybersecurity and mission functionality and performance, there is a trade-off with cost. A key part of systems engineering is proper cost estimation for various aspects of the system design—cybersecurity being one of them. These estimates help determine whether a proposed solution is worth it. Cost estimates should include

- Development cost
- Deployment cost
- Operations cost

These classes of costs together make up the **total cost of ownership**. Many engineers only calculate the development cost, which grossly underestimates the total cost of ownership, which invalidates any cost-benefit analysis. Knowing the cost of each component is important because often each is done by a different suborganization and must be planned in separate budgets. In addition, and for similar reasons, it is often useful to have two larger buckets that are broken down in the three components of cost. The two buckets are infrastructure costs and application costs. Infrastructure costs are typically born by the information technology department, whereas application costs are born by the mission elements. Again, this division is important for planning purposes, and sometimes there are ways to design the system to move costs around between the two larger buckets and between all the components of costs within the buckets. This is helpful in the planning process.

8.8.2 Time-to-Deploy Matters

As the saying goes, "time is money" or, more generally, "time is mission" to encompass nonprofit organizations. In the for-profit world, this is called time-to-market for new products and services. To generalize to nonprofits, we will call it **time-to-deploy**. In the for-profit world, imagine that a new product or service will make the company $1M per month. That means that every month of delay costs $1M. If the imposition of cybersecurity requirements causes a multimonth delay in deployment, it costs the company multiple millions of dollars. This must be considered in the decision cost-benefit analysis. Further, sometimes first-to-market timing could mean the difference between getting adequate market share or getting no market share. This means that a critical delay of deployment time beyond the first-to-market window could kill a product line, which could in turn kill a company if it is on the edge of profitability. *A highly secure system that is shut down because the company no longer exists is of no value.*

For government organizations and nonprofits, there are similar critical windows. For example, for interplanetary space exploration launches, there are specific time windows when the planets are aligned perfectly to both minimize distance and to use the gravitational pull of some planets to help propel a spacecraft toward its destination (called the slingshot effect). Adding cybersecurity to the point that it delays a launch beyond the window kills the opportunity to do the science for months, years, or even decades until similar alignments happen. For celestial events that are very rare, such as some comet transitions into the solar system, the window could effectively disappear for generations. As another example, a nonprofit providing relief for an ongoing drought has urgency because every day of delayed relief means that x more people die of starvation. *Time can literally be a matter of life and death.*

8.8.3 Impact to Mission Matters

Cybersecurity sometimes impacts mission functionality—often negatively, though sometimes it can be positive. If intrusion detection takes up 20 percent of network bandwidth and the organization's value is in the data it collects, then that could translate directly into a 20 percent reduction in value because of the displaced network capacity. This same impact applies to all resources. For example, if an organization depends heavily on computation to generate its product and service, then any computational resource taken up by cybersecurity displaces mission capability tied to that computation. The cybersecurity engineer must take care to consult closely with the mission owners to properly understand the range of possible mission impacts of existing and proposed new cybersecurity solutions. The cybersecurity engineer alone cannot estimate this impact.

Impact to mission can be positive as well as negative. For example, integrating authentication into applications can obviate the need for separately logging in to each and every service on the system. This security feature actually saves users time and improves operations. Cybersecurity also has positive impact to mission in terms of **human safety**, preventing loss of life, and ensuring continuity of mission, but these are accounted for as benefits and not as costs. They are significant factors and will be discussed in more detail in the context of risk assessment in Section 18.3.

8.8.4 Pareto Rule: 80/20

Once a cybersecurity engineer has a good and thorough estimate of the cost of a cybersecurity mechanism, they need to ask themselves how the costs relate to the risk-reduction value that the mechanism delivers. The question should also be asked if there is an alternative whereby it is possible to achieve 80 percent of the risk-reduction value for 20 percent of the cost. It may not always be possible, but it is at least partially achievable in more cases than most engineers realize.

Note that, as pointed out in the previous sections, cost is not just about money. It may be possible, for example, to achieve 80 percent of the value while halving mission impact by making the slightest adjustment in the design. This is possible and has happened quite successfully in practical system design examples. *Look for 80/20 opportunities in all the flavors of cost for all countermeasures.*

Always seek 80 percent of countermeasure benefit at 20 percent cost alternative.

8.8.5 Opportunity Cost Is a Key Part of Cost

During development and deployment, a dollar spent on cybersecurity is a dollar not spent on the primary mission. Further, a dollar spent on mission may return more than a dollar in value. The cost of cybersecurity is therefore the loss in value not just of the $1 that could have been invested in mission, but the full value of what that dollar would have contributed. This is known in economics as the **opportunity cost**. So, when considering the cost-benefit of cybersecurity, the full costs should be considered, including opportunity cost.

8.8.6 How Much to Invest in Cybersecurity

The issue of opportunity cost brings up the important question about how to invest in cybersecurity. Most organizations have no clue. Skeptically speaking, the algorithm for determining investment appears to be something akin to

1. Use last year's budget (typically around 5 percent of the information technology budget) [FILK16].
2. Add 1 percent if something bad happened to someone else.
3. Add 10 percent if something had happened to us, 11 percent if it was particularly bad.
4. Subtract 10 percent if nobody can recall anything unusually bad last year.

So, how does one answer this question? Let's start with a couple of questions that will help anchor the conversation. How much are you willing to pay for homeowner's insurance?

How much are you willing to pay for health insurance? The average American pays around $600 per year for insurance on a median home worth around $189K; $18,000 per year for health insurance. This suggests that Americans value their quantity and quality of life about 30 times more than their things. That makes sense since things have no value if you are unable to enjoy them. But where precisely do these numbers come from?

There are specialized accountants called actuaries who collect and analyze data that boils down to probabilities of bad events times the cost damage if those bad things happen. For example, they calculate the probability that your house will catch on fire and then the average damage from a fire. The product of these two numbers is the average loss (also called expected harm). They use these numbers to then determine the price for insurance policies. This same approach can and should be used by organizations. They need to look at the value that is at stake from cyberattack, the likelihood of such attacks, and then determine the expected loss. Investment should be around that level.

Most organizations fall well short of that level and therefore are operating at unnecessarily high risk. We will discuss more on how to estimate likelihood of bad events in future chapters. For now, we just need to understand that *cybersecurity investments should be based on sound engineering analyses, not arbitrary guesses.*

> *Cybersecurity investment must be commensurate with risk.*

8.8.7 Optimizing Zero-Sum Cybersecurity Budgets

Overall budgets are almost always a zero-sum game, though justification should be given for budgets that are commensurate with the needed risk reduction. A zero-sum game means that the budget is usually fixed at some value and often cannot be easily supplemented. Assuming some fixed budget that can be spent on cybersecurity, choosing expensive solutions may mean that some aspects of the system go without risk mitigation at least for a while, thus the system vulnerability is higher than it might have been if multiple less expensive solutions were chosen (or custom made). This will be discussed in later chapters, but, for now, the cybersecurity engineer should see that they should explicitly generate and evaluate a wide range of solutions and not just try to design the full-featured expensive system that will end up being prohibitive to implement.

> *A range of cost options should be generated in cybersecurity.*

Conclusion

This chapter gave an overview of some of the key building block concepts to mitigate the adversaries and their attacks discussed in the previous two chapters. The next chapter focuses on a very important building block—gaining a strong foundation with trustworthy hardware.

To summarize:

- Countermeasure design-to-purpose maps countermeasures to attack space.
- Broadly cover all important attack classes with some mechanism or architectural feature.
- Defense in breadth is brittle without defense in depth; depth is useless without breadth.
- Early days of multilevel security research had a profound influence on trustworthiness research.
- Integrity policy and control are the foundation of all cybersecurity.
- Cybersecurity measures are ineffective if they are not usable.
- Cost, in a variety of forms, is a key factor in cybersecurity engineering trade-offs.

Questions

1. What does design-to-purpose mean for countermeasures? Give an example, picking some attack and describing how the countermeasures cover that attack.
2. Define attack space and describe its characteristics.
3. Why does a security engineer need to cover the attack space?
4. What does defense in breadth mean and how is it achieved?
5. What does defense in depth mean and how is it achieved?
6. How do defense in depth and defense in breadth relate to one another?
7. What are the two basic properties of multilevel security mandatory policy? State each property and why each is needed. Why are they both needed at the same time?
8. What is the historical importance of multilevel security? Does the commercial world have similar issues to that of the military classification separation problem? How? Give examples.
9. What is a security kernel? How does it relate to an operating system? What fraction of an operating system would you say a security kernel is? Why?
10. Name the three properties of a reference monitor and provide a rationale for each property. What does the correctness property mean; correct with respect to what?
11. What is trusted code and what is it trusted to do and to not do? Why is it needed at all? Give examples.
12. Describe parts of the operating system that require no privilege at all and why.
13. What is a Trojan horse and how did it drive security policy requirements?
14. Why was it possible in theory to allow an adversary to write user code and not be concerned about it violating mandatory policy? How can an adversary potentially circumvent mandatory policy? What does the system do about that possibility?

15. What is multilevel integrity and how does it relate to multilevel security? Summarize the subordinate properties and contrast them.

16. What is type enforcement and how does it work? Give an example not included in the book.

17. What is Clark-Wilson integrity and how does it relate to military-style policies?

18. List and define five aspects of cybersecurity usability and explain why they are important.

19. Why do we say that cybersecurity countermeasures with poor usability are ineffective?

20. List and explain three different types of costs associated with cybersecurity design.

21. Why does cost matter?

22. Along what two dimensions should cost be estimated and why?

23. Why can delays in delivering mission function be lethal to an organization?

24. Explain opportunity cost and how it relates to cost-benefit calculations for cybersecurity.

25. How does the Pareto Rule of 80/20 apply to cost in the design of cybersecurity countermeasures?

26. How does one decide how much to invest in cybersecurity? How might the right investment level be different for a plumbing firm with $1M of revenue per year versus a web hosting service at the same revenue level?

27. What is a zero-sum budget and how does it relate to investing in cybersecurity mechanisms in the defense of a system?

28. When one considers the cost of cybersecurity, list some non-monetary costs. List some non-monetary costs of not implementing cybersecurity.

Trustworthy Hardware: Bedrock

Overview

Learning Objectives

- Explain why hardware is the foundation of trustworthy systems.
- Compare how hardware security relates to the two types of processor instruction sets.
- Describe how supervisor mode and rings support a trustworthy system.
- Explain memory protection techniques and how they work with supervisor modes.
- Describe how multilevel security, security kernels, and reference monitors shape system trust.

- Explain why hardware is softer than we think and what risks that poses.
- Summarize a computer's bus and microcontroller system and its cybersecurity implications.

In the days when single applications had dedicated use and control of all of a system's resources for a period of time until another application was given control, there was no need for hardware separation mechanisms and trustworthiness for that separation. In the early days, computers did not have the capacity to run dozens or even hundreds of processes. As computers became more advanced, multiple applications and multiple users could make use of the increasingly large set of computer resources. This required that the uses and users be separated so that they did not accidentally or intentionally interfere with each other's processing. A supervisor had to act as a cop to keep resources and processing separate while allowing controlled interaction. To prevent the supervisor itself from getting trounced, a special operating mode was required that could not be interrupted or overridden by any other guest program. This led to the birth of increasingly sophisticated operating systems whose job was to perform this supervisory function between the multiple applications running, the processor, and other system resources.

9.1 Foundation of Trust

Application software runs on operating system software, which runs on a low-level kernel, and device drivers, which run atop hardware (Figure 9-1). Security services (such as authentication and authorization services) and mechanisms typically run on top of operating systems, within operating systems (e.g., a security kernel), and sometimes within device drivers. Hardware is the foundation of all systems and therefore must necessarily be the foundation of trustworthiness. *If the hardware is not trustworthy, nothing running on that hardware is trustworthy.*

> *Hardware is at the foundation of trustworthiness.*

Figure 9-1 shows the conceptual layers of a computer system. We see that there is user software, supported by **system software**, supported by hardware. The system software is often portrayed in two layers: a basic foundational layer that interfaces directly with the hardware and a more complex set of functions built on top of that basic foundation. Because the layers are often portrayed as a stack of boxes (as seen in the figure), the foundational software is often referred to as **low-level system software**; the more complex system software is sometimes called **high-level system software**. The operating system implements the high-level system software. Low-level system software is usually executed by **firmware** such as Intel's® **Basic Input/Output System (BIOS)** and **device drivers,** such as disk device drivers that abstract a disk storage device into a series of memory blocks that can be allocated and connected together to create files.

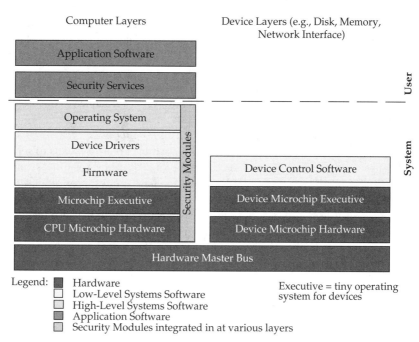

Figure 9-1   Computer system layers with hardware at the foundation of trust

The hardware layer consists of devices for computation, storage, or communication. A computer's **central processing units (CPUs)** are a prime example of such a hardware device that is the heart of modern computers. These devices often have very low-level software that orchestrates the intricate details of the internals of the device. Generally, this software is considered part of the hardware and is not directly accessible to higher-level software running on the device. This orchestration software is like a tiny operating system for the device itself. It is sometimes called an **executive** because it executes the low-level code. The **master bus** is another example of hardware. It is essentially a small network inside the computer to allow communications within the computer between the various devices. Like all networks, it is not just a passive wire, but a subsystem in its own right that needs to be controlled and operated. A third example of hardware is a disk drive. Such a device is depicted as a shorter software stack on the right-hand side of the figure. It has its own processor, its own executive, and even its own software that runs on the executive to control the device. It communicates with other devices such as the central processing units through the master bus.

Application software data and control flow typically starts at the top of the computer stack and flows downward to eventually cause hardware instructions to execute on its behalf. When devices outside of the central processing units (but still within the computer bus) are accessed, control passes through device drivers, through the processor, out onto the master bus, then up the device stack—received by the device's microchip hardware under the direction of the device's executive and to the **device controller** software to perform the requested function (e.g., creating a new file on a disk device).

Security control must be maintained, at least in some form, through the entire stack of control and data flow throughout the thread discussed earlier. This control is shown in the form of a vertical box labeled "security modules" spanning multiple layers to indicate that the security software at these lower levels are not separate pieces of self-standing software code, but rather integrated aspects of the software at those various layers. Security services are special application software that leverage these lower-level security controls to provide a cybersecurity architecture.

Trustworthiness requires both security-critical functionality and assurance so that functionality operates correctly. The functionality must create a means of separating both computation and memory access. For computation, the processor must separate the **instruction set architecture** into at least two separate modes: user mode and supervisor mode. The memory must be tagged so that access to that memory can be restricted. Without both of these features, one cannot build a trustworthy system because malicious applications could simply execute instructions to perform arbitrary actions on system resources and could read or corrupt all memory contents, thus making confidentiality, integrity, and availability attacks trivial. These basic functions must be **provably correct**, tamperproof, and non-bypassable—the three properties of a reference monitor [ANDE72].

9.2 Instruction Set Architectures

We start by discussing the instruction set architecture of the hardware—this refers to the instruction set the processor is capable of executing. The instruction set represents the language that the processor understands. At its heart, the set includes memory access (e.g., load contents from memory location, store contents to memory location) and mathematical operations (e.g., add, subtract). Most tasks that a general-purpose computer needs to do are built upon these few foundational instruction types.

There are two distinct philosophies in developing instruction sets for processors—minimalist instruction sets that operate quickly versus larger, more complex instruction sets that do much more. The first is aptly called a **reduced instruction set computer (RISC)** and the second is called a **complex instruction set computer (CISC)**. Abstractly, it does not matter from a cybersecurity perspective which type one uses as long as they have the requisite functionality and assurance. Practically speaking, reduced instruction set computers can be easier to provide assurance for because they are simpler. There will be more on assurance when we discuss assurance cases in Section 21.3.

9.3 Supervisors with Rings and Things

Let's first discuss how we create separate processing modes within the processor—one supervisor mode and one user mode. The user mode is easy; it is simply all the functional instructions that the computer needs in order to perform. Supervisor mode basically needs just two additional instructions—"enter supervisor mode" and "exit supervisor mode." The machine boots up in supervisor mode. The operating system is the first program to be executed. The operating system sets up all of the sharing structures it needs and initializes the system state and then stands ready for applications to request execution.

When applications request startup, they are given system resources such as primary memory and a set time slice of the processor. When the application's time slice is up or when it requests additional system resources, control automatically passes back to the operating system in supervisor mode suspending the application [MACE80]. The operating system in supervisor mode can then directly access the pool of resources, give another application an opportunity to execute for a while, and then eventually pass control back to the original application. This processing sequence is shown in the universal markup language sequence diagram shown in Figure 9-2.

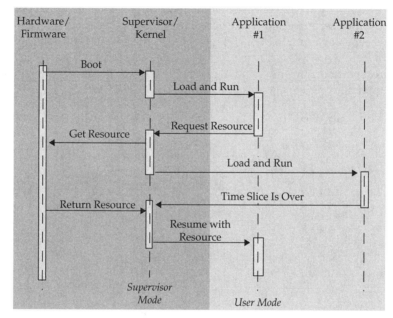

Figure 9-2   Processing sequence diagram for supervisor/kernel operation with user applications

Once a separation of modes is created, additional modes can either be supported directly in hardware or can be emulated using the basic separation. Additional modes can be useful in setting differing levels of supervisory privilege and control, thus making it possible to structure layers of abstraction with controlled interfaces, making assurance arguments easier. These layers are sometimes called protection rings and were experimented with in the early days on a progenitor trustworthy system like Multics [CORB65][MULT17].

This user-supervisor mode separation enables the foundation of trustworthy sharing of system resources. It is necessary, but insufficient. The memory must be labeled and controlled in some fashion.

9.4 Controlling Memory: Mapping, Capabilities, and Tagging

Programs are executed by fetching instructions out of memory into the processor. So, if user-mode programs could write to any part of primary memory, they could not only interfere with one another, but they could replace the code that the operating system is executing and cause it to do whatever they wanted, making the separation of user mode and supervisor mode ineffective [KAIN96]. Therefore, it is imperative to carefully control access to memory using techniques such as memory mapping, capabilities, and tagging.

9.4.1 Memory Mapping

One solution would be for supervisor-mode processes to have separate and exclusive access to their own memory. This would help, but user-mode processes could still interfere with one another. We can basically extend the model of allocating dedicated portions of primary memory into user space and create boundaries around that space so that if the user tries to reference memory outside of that range, the system hardware will issue an error and will prevent it from occurring. The mapping scheme is depicted in Figure 9-3. If two users want to share a portion of memory, they can arrange through the supervisor-mode process to create partially overlapping memory space.

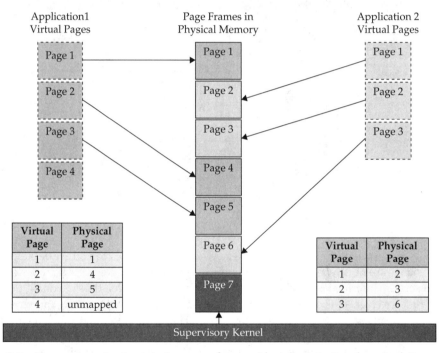

Figure 9-3 Memory mapping to protect memory from accidental or intentional manipulation

This process of allocating memory in a protected way is called memory mapping or memory management and is often assisted by specialized hardware called a memory mapping unit to ensure that it is done as quickly as possible.

9.4.2 Capabilities

When programs want to share segments of memory (a variable-sized page of memory), they can ask the system to create an unforgeable ticket to that memory that names the segment and states the type of access allowed (e.g., read access or write access). The program can then pass that ticket to another program to grant it access to that page of its memory. This ticket is known as a **capability**. Note that the capability resides exclusively in memory under the control of the supervisor, and so the user programs cannot alter the content of these tickets once they are created. Programs can, however, sometimes pass capabilities on to other programs for further sharing, depending on the policy regarding the capability propagation. The scheme of capability creation and sharing is shown in Figure 9-4.

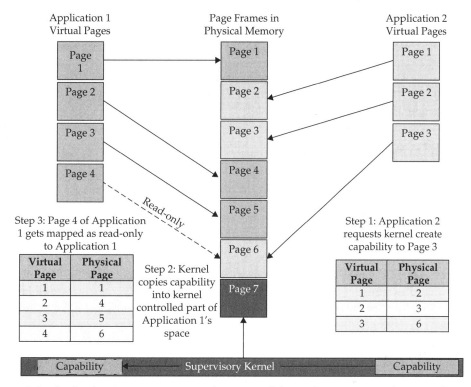

Figure 9-4   Application 2 creates a memory sharing capability and passes it to application 1 through the kernel. The capability generated by application 2 for its virtual page 3 enables application 1 to request access and gain access via physical page 6.

The mapping scheme is depicted in Figure 9-3. If two users want to share a portion of memory, they can arrange through the supervisor-mode process to have partially overlapping memory space. Application 2 requests that the supervisory kernel generate a capability to its virtual page 3. The kernel creates the capability, but keeps it inside the kernel's memory space to protect it. The kernel hands a reference to the capability to application 2, which communicates that capability reference to application 1 (not shown in the figure). Application 1 then asserts that capability to the kernel. The kernel responds by finding where application 2's page exists in physical memory, page 6 in this case, and maps the next available open virtual page in application 1 to the same physical page in a read-only mode. Thus, memory sharing of the physical page through overlapping memory maps is the mechanism by which the capability for sharing is implemented in this example.

9.4.3 Tagging

Notionally, memory can also be tagged with metadata indicating how access is to be controlled to the data content in that memory [FEUS73]. For example, one can imagine tagging data with the Department of Defense classification hierarchy of Top Secret, Secret, Confidential, and Unclassified. Then, the supervisory kernel software could control access to that memory based on the clearance of the program attempting to access the data. A research example of such a system was the Secure Ada Target [BOEB85a][KAIN87]. Although some tagged architectures were produced commercially, such as the Lisp machine that used tags to aid garbage collection, this did not ultimately prove to be an effective approach. The tagging overhead, particularly if done on every word in memory, was considered prohibitive for all but the narrowest of applications. Recent advances in information technology hold promise for implementing hardware-based tagging in a way that is efficient enough to eventually become commercially viable [WATS17][JOAN17].

9.5 Software in Hardware

In modern systems, we should note that hardware is not as hard as it might seem. It is actually operated by software within the hardware, creating a potential vulnerability that few cybersecurity engineers realize. This section discusses this special software and how it controls hardware.

9.5.1 Microcode

Processors have **microcode** that controls the behavior of the processor. The microcode is really software—a type of tiny operating system and integrated application all in one—that is at the heart of the processor. Minor adjustments to the instruction set architecture can be made by reprogramming the processor's microcode.

9.5.2 Firmware

On top of that, there is often code outside the processor that helps to orchestrate other integrated circuits and chips on the computer motherboard. This outside code is sometimes called firmware and can be thought of as somewhere between the processor and the operating system. The Intel Basic Input/Output Services (BIOS) is an example of such firmware.

Such low-level software exists to allow vendors to fix bugs and issue updates without having to replace chips, saving millions of dollars and improving the time to market for the benefit of the consumer. At the same time, it is important for cybersecurity engineers to be fully aware of this low-level software and its potential risks [CERT17a]. *It represents a soft underbelly that could be attacked and undermine the security of the entire system in very surprising ways.*

9.5.3 Secure Bootstrapping

The amount of software that drives the hardware below the operating system raises concern for attack, as discussed previously in this section. This gave rise to the need for a **secure bootstrapping** standard to at least be sure that the low-level system software configuration is as delivered and signed by the vendor. That does not mean it is free from malware introduced at the vendor's development site, but at least it means that it was not tampered with after installation.

This feature of the module is called **remote attestation**. The vendor signs the internal low-level software, which can then be checked by the hardware prior to loading and executing that low-level system software. This allows what is called secure bootstrapping processes, in which each succeeding layer can be checked by the underlying layer that checks the integrity of the next-higher layer before loading and executing. This allows some confidence that the operating system that the computer system boots into has not been subverted from underneath. The current commercial standard for this process is called the **Trusted Platform Module** (TPM).

9.6 Buses and Controllers

Believe it or not, there is actually a layer below, or at least beside, the processor. The processor is but one device in a tiny network inside your computer. The network backbone is called a master bus. There are sub-buses and dedicated channels between devices as well. It is a complex world of computers inside computers talking to other computers (devices) inside the innards of your computer (Figure 9-5). For example, memory chips reside on the master bus and so memory is addressable on the bus by the processor. Another example is the hard drive (secondary memory), which provides most of the computer's file storage. The network device is yet another important example.

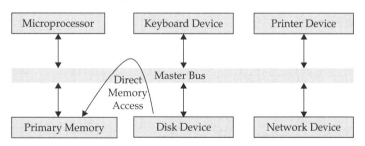

Computers as Tiny Device Networks

Figure 9-5   Internally, a computer is really a system of active computer elements connected by a master bus.

Each of the device controllers often has its own processor driven by its own microcode, executing its own embedded operating system called an executive and an embedded application to actually control the device. These processors (sometimes called microcontrollers) often can access the master bus without impediment or access control of any kind. In fact, for speedup, they can often directly access primary memory in what is called **direct memory access** (DMA) mode on the master bus. *If little alarm bells are going off in your head about the potential for malicious code operating at this level and the difficulty in detecting and stopping it, then you are developing the adequate level of paranoia to become a good cybersecurity engineer.*

Conclusion

This chapter explains the nature of the foundation of all trust within the hardware and its many complexities and subtleties that have important cybersecurity implications. In the next chapter, we switch gears to another foundational yet somewhat mysterious building block of cybersecurity that is used in many ways—cryptography.

To summarize:

- If you cannot trust the hardware, then the work required to trust the software is futile.
- Both complex and reduced instruction set architectures support trustworthiness.
- Processor uninterruptible privileged mode forms a foundation for trustworthy software.
- Memory must be protected using techniques such as memory mapping and capabilities.
- Hardware has some software driving its operation, posing a little-known cybersecurity risk.
- Inside a computer, devices often communicate freely on a tiny network called a master bus.

Questions

1. Why do we say hardware is at the foundation of trustworthiness and therefore at the foundation of cybersecurity?

2. Why is trustworthy separation of processing needed? Was it always needed? List some trustworthiness properties that one might need on a dedicated computer and explain why they might be needed.

3. What prevents user code from entering supervisor mode?

4. What is the purpose of supervisor mode? How does it differ from protection rings? Describe how to create protection rings if you have a supervisor mode.

5. Why isn't supervisor mode sufficient to protect privileged operation?

6. What is a capability and why are capabilities needed? Why must they be unforgeable? How does the system make them unforgeable? What problem does unlimited propagation of capabilities create with respect to the *-property?

7. Give some examples of how and where software is inside hardware. Why does this pose a risk? What can we do about that risk?

8. What is secure bootstrapping and what sort of mechanisms does one need to accomplish it? How can an adversary gain control of the hardware even though the bootstrapping process worked flawlessly? What can be done about those issues?

9. What is a device controller? How does it work?

10. Compare and contrast a master bus and a data network.

11. What is the trust model for devices that are on the master bus? Why might this be a security problem?

Overview

Learning Objectives

- Explain the purpose and fundamental nature of cryptography.
- Discuss the desirable characteristics of the key space of an algorithm.
- Summarize the requirements of **key generation**.
- Explain why **key distribution** is a problem and describe ways of solving the problem.
- Describe the nature of public-key cryptography and how it is applied.
- Summarize how cryptography is applied to address integrity issues.
- Discuss how cryptography has both a positive and negative impact on availability.
- Explain the limitations of cryptography and potentially disruptive technologies.
- Describe why cryptography is not a panacea for security problems.
- Discuss why homegrown cryptography is a bad idea.

Although this is *not* a book on security mechanisms, cryptography warrants special coverage because of its foundational role in cybersecurity. The goal of this chapter is to familiarize the reader with the fundamental properties and principles behind cryptography as opposed to attempting to make the reader a master **cryptographer**. Cryptography is an important topic and well worth further reading [FERG10][SCHN15].

10.1 What Is Cryptography?

The goal of cryptography is to protect data from compromise—allowing it to be read exclusively by authorized persons. The data can be anything, including programs, stored files, and messages sent across communications channels. The goal is accomplished by scrambling the data so that only authorized parties can unscramble it. The scrambling, called encryption, is accomplished with a cryptographic algorithm in conjunction with a cryptographic **key**. An algorithm is a mathematical transformation process from the original data, called cleartext, to the encrypted data, called **ciphertext**. A key is a string of bits that dictates the details of processing to ensure that the encryption is unique for different keys. Secure distribution of the key is the means of authorizing parties to unscramble the data, called decryption. The encryption process is intended to have the property that unauthorized parties cannot decrypt the data without the key. See Figure 10-1 for a graphical description of the encryption-decryption process.

Using a key also has the desirable property that if the key is **compromised** (discovered by an adversary), then only the data encrypted with that key is compromised. This, of course, means that the sharing parties would be wise to change their key periodically so that not all of their data is encrypted under the same key. The requirement for frequent key changes also creates a problem of properly generating and distributing the keys to the senders and authorized recipients. These are known as key-generation and key-distribution problems, as discussed in the next sections.

Traditional or Symmetric Key Cryptography

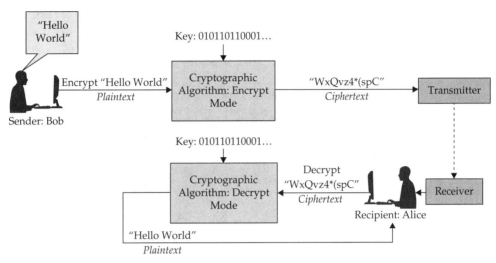

Note: Keys are identical and were pre-distributed to Bob and Alice.

Figure 10-1   Basics of the cryptographic encryption and decryption process

10.2 Key Space

It is important that the adversary not be able to guess the selected key used to protect data. This means that there must be a very large set of possible keys. If, for example, a key was 1 bit only, an encryption system would only have two possible keys (0 or 1), and the adversary need only try both keys. Because the decryption process is designed to be fast to facilitate the functionality of the encryption system, the adversary could **decrypt** the encrypted message in seconds. The number of possible keys for a given encryption algorithm is called the **key space**. The key space is not something that is specifically stored, but rather is abstractly specified, as discussed later in this section. So, the key space must be large, but how large?

An attacker attempting to decrypt encrypted data by applying all possible keys is called an **exhaustion attack**. This is because the attacker must exhaust all possible keys in the key space until they find the right key. The attacker knows that they have found the right key when data decrypts to sensible data depending on the language and type of data it is. The attacker could get incredibly lucky and find the right key on the first try; terribly unlucky and not find it until their last try; or anywhere in between. Intuitively, you can see why the attacker will have to, on average, exhaust half the key space. Obviously, the attacker can stop once they find the right key.

The question of the required size of the key space boils down to two questions: (1) how fast the adversary can try keys and (2) how long, on average, the defender wants to keep their secrets secret. How to answer these is a matter for other more technical books on cryptography. As an example, the National Institute of Standards and Technology's (NIST) strong encryption standard called the Advanced Encryption Standard (AES) [NIST01] has possible key lengths of 128, 192, and 256 (Figure 10-2). Because keys are strings of bits, the key space sizes are $2^{key-length}$. If one had a key length of 2, there are 2^2 possible keys—00, 01, 10, and 11. So, for a 128-bit key, the key space has 2^{128} keys, which is $3.4 * 10^{38}$. If an adversary could try a million keys per second, it would take $2 * 10^{27}$ years to exhaust. As a point of comparison, the estimated age of the universe is about $4 * 10^{17}$ seconds (13.7 billion years).

Defense Panel: Advanced Encryption Standard	
Type	Cryptography, Symmetric
Capability	Encryption process to encrypt sensitive data.
Means	Mathematically transform plaintext data into ciphertext using a key from the encryption algorithm's key space.
Limitations	Cryptography is subject to failure in the same way all other components are. The encryption process must be done carefully and securely. Cryptographic algorithms and implementations are complex and difficult to get right.
Impacts	Enables sensitive data to be transmitted and stored in areas where adversaries have potential access—such as commercial Internet service or telecommunication providers.
Attack Space	Intended to stop exploitation of sensitive information transmitted and stored in high-risk environments.

Figure 10-2   Defense description: Advanced Encryption Standard (AES)

You might ask whether such key lengths are overkill and a waste of time. If the encryption algorithms and implementations and operations were provably perfect, then they might be. Sometimes, clever mathematicians find ways of determining the key that don't require full exhaustion of the key space. These are called **subexhaustive attacks**. If, for example, an attacker could somehow find a way to reduce the search to one-half of the key space, it would not do them much good because a space of 2^{128} divided by 2 is still 2^{127}. On the other hand, if they could somehow reduce the key space down by a whopping factor of 2^{127}, then they could find the key immediately because there would only be two keys remaining that needed to be tried. Of course, attacks might exist anywhere between these extremes that could allow the attacker to practically exhaust over the reduced key space.

Cryptographers spend a great deal of time looking for subexhaustion attacks before proposing a cryptographic algorithm for use. Unfortunately, mathematically proving that an algorithm is not open to such attacks is not practical. So, even with Herculean effort to avoid such subexhaustive attacks during algorithm design, sometimes they are found. If the flaws are minor, the algorithm can continue to be used. *If subexhaustion attacks are major (cutting the key space down such that an attacker can practically find the key by searching the reduced key space), then the algorithm must be revised, and data previously encrypted using that algorithm is compromised.*

> *Cryptographic algorithms must resist subexhaustion attacks.*

10.3 Key Generation

Now that we understand the nature of keys, the question arises regarding how to select a key from the large pool in the key space. You might think that a person can just choose any key they want, perhaps all zeros to begin and, subsequently, increment up one for every new key that is needed. That approach has the property that key generation is simple and easy to keep track of. Unfortunately, it means that the adversary can also guess and predict the keys quite easily. The reason that an adversary has to exhaust the key space is because they have no idea which key the defender chose. If the defender introduces any predictability in the key selection process, they run the high risk of significantly reducing the key space. For example, you might somehow use your birthday, or Social Security number, your pet's name, or even your significant other's name so that it is easy to generate. Letters can be translated into numbers using standard codes such as the American Standard Code for Information Interchange (ASCII) and then converted from numbers into binary strings (Figure 10-3).

Letter	ASCII Code		Letter	ASCII Code
a	01100001		n	01101110
b	01100010		o	01101111
c	01100011		p	01110000
d	01100010		q	01110000
e	01100011		r	01110001
f	01100110		s	01110010
g	01100111		t	01110011
h	01101000		u	01110100
i	01101001		v	01110101
j	01101010		w	01110110
k	01101011		x	01110111
l	01101100		y	01111000
m	01101101		z	01111001

s	a	m	i
01110010	01100001	01101101	01101001

Translating string "Sami" to binary using ASCII Codes
from table above

Figure 10-3   Example showing how one might translate letters into binary to create a key (don't do this!)

Adversaries know that humans will tend to pick familiar names and numbers and will research extensive personal information about the operators. Also, the mere use of names constrains which bits are possible and reduces the key space tremendously (because bit codes for letters are a much smaller set of possible binary sequences). Historically, this sort of operator sloppiness is what helped the Allied Forces break the German Enigma code during World War II. The machine operators chose nonrandom parameters as input into the encryption process [HINS01].

> ### *Key selection must be random to ensure there is no predictability.*

The bottom line is that key selection must be random to ensure there is no predictability. You might think that you can just pick a **random number** off the top of your head by randomly choosing ones and zeros until you have the key length. It turns out that humans are abysmal at choosing random numbers such as keys [SCHU12][MUNG07] and will always create keys that contain predictable regularity that an adversary can exploit. As Figure 10-4 shows, people avoid certain numbers and disproportionately gravitate toward others, as compared to an even distribution of 5 percent across numbers from 1 to 20, as would be expected if choices were truly random. For example, humans will resist creating runs of more than two or three ones or zeros because that does not "seem" random, so they eliminate a

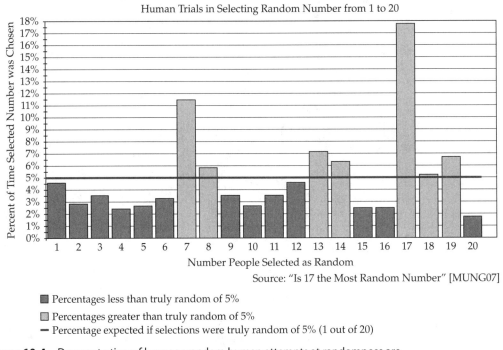

Source: "Is 17 the Most Random Number" [MUNG07]

- ■ Percentages less than truly random of 5%
- ▨ Percentages greater than truly random of 5%
- ▬ Percentage expected if selections were truly random of 5% (1 out of 20)

Figure 10-4   Demonstration of how nonrandom human attempts at randomness are

large part of the key space that way. Therefore, we employ computers using **random sources** to produce random numbers for us. This process is called key generation.

> *Random key generation requires random sources, not humans.*

10.4 Key Distribution

Amateurs attack the algorithm; professionals attack key management.

—Anon

Even if the cryptographic algorithm is perfect, if the keys are poorly generated or distributed, the cryptographic system is poor. Therefore, it is just as important to get key management right as it is to get the cryptographic algorithm right. Both are very complex subsystems with ample opportunities to get an important aspect wrong.

> *Amateurs attack the algorithm; professionals attack the key management.*

Part III

Once a random key from the key space is generated, it must be securely communicated to all parties intended to share in being able to see the encrypted data. If all parties happen to be in the same room, you need only yell out the bit sequence to everyone and they can securely enter that key into their encryption device to create the shared transformation. Unfortunately, the convenience of co-location is almost never the case, partly because one would not need to securely communicate electronically if everyone was in the same room.

Key distribution is the system by which a generated key is delivered to the intended parties to share in the encrypted data. Key distribution has three steps: (1) transmission to the intended recipients, (2) storage prior to loading into the encryption device, and (3) loading the key into the encryption device. The three steps of key distribution are discussed in the following three sections. The overall process of key generation and key distribution is overviewed in Figure 10-5.

10.4.1 Transmission to Intended Recipients

The first step in key distribution is transmission to the intended recipients. The communication of a key to one of several parties carries risk. This is an opportunity for an adversary to gain access to the communication by stealing or copying the key in transit. Because the key is likely to encrypt large volumes of data, it becomes a high-value target to the adversary—meaning that compromising just a few hundred bits gives the adversary access to potentially trillions of bits of sensitive data. A high-value target is one that gives a high **return on investment**. This return motivates the adversary to spend significant resources to acquire the target—in this case, a key. A human courier could be bribed by the adversary. Physical mail can be intercepted, opened, and resealed. Email, although it might seem private, is worst of all because it can be easily copied in any of dozens of computers that are involved in storing and forwarding your email through the Internet to get from the sender to receiver.

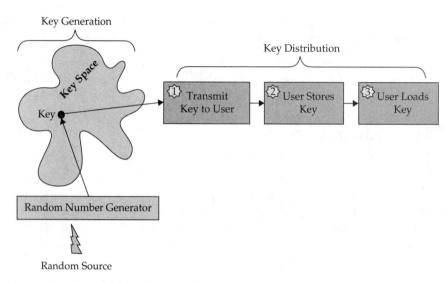

Figure 10-5 Cryptographic key generation and the three steps of key distribution, with compromise possibilities at each step

To reduce the risk of compromise in transit, often the key itself will be encrypted using a separate key called a key-encrypting key. One can use extraordinary protections to get a key-encryption key to all parties (such as a two-person control in which two couriers are used to ensure the other is not malicious, making it much harder for an adversary to succeed in attack or bribery) and then use that key to encrypt all subsequent keys for periodic key changes. If the key is encrypted, it can be transmitted conveniently and easily through any means, including email, because stealing a strongly encrypted key does the adversary little good. Of course, if the adversary somehow compromises the key-encryption key, all data encrypted with all keys encrypted with the key-encryption key are compromised. This means that the key-encryption key becomes a super high-value target. Also, the adversary need only compromise one instance of the key-encryption key and all data shared between all parties is compromised. There must be a better way. Along came public-key cryptography, as discussed in Section 10.5.

10.4.2 Storage

Step 2 of key distribution is storage of the key. Distributed keys almost always need to be stored prior to being loaded into the encryption device. Storage is required for two reasons. First, the users of the device often cannot wait for the delivery of a key to begin encrypted sharing. Such sharing is often time-sensitive. Second, the processes associated with protecting keys in transit can be expensive, so transmitting many keys at one time spreads the fixed costs out over many keys, which improves cost-efficiency of transmission. *Storing such keys* in the clear *(without being encrypted) poses significant risk for adversaries stealing the keys while being stored. The consequence of having an entire* **key store silently compromised** *(meaning without the defender detecting the compromise) is similar to having* *a* key-encryption key compromised—*all data encrypted with all keys in the key store is compromised.* Therefore, it is wise to encrypt stored keys to reduce the risk of compromise. Of course, one must carefully guard the key-encryption key from compromise, but that is an easier problem because it is only a single key. It could even be stored offline and used only when needed. *If keys could be generated and transmitted in real time, there would be no need for storage and therefore storage protection.* Public-key cryptography, once again, offers a solution, as discussed in Section 10.5.

10.4.3 Loading

Step 3 of key distribution is loading the key into a cryptographic device for use. Once a key is transmitted and retrieved from storage for operational use, it must be loaded into the encryption device or software that will use the key to decrypt shared data. This loading process is also a point of vulnerability since adversaries might have a limited presence on the defender's system. Ideally, the key remains in encrypted form prior to showing up within a protected perimeter of the device or software that receives it. This requires the encryption device itself to have a key-encryption key so that it can decrypt the encrypted key before use.

If the processes of transmitting, storing, and loading keys sound complex and risky to you, you are right. *Real-time generation and use greatly simplifies key distribution.* That observation, again, brings us to the next section on public-key cryptography.

10.5 Public-Key Cryptography

Public-key cryptography is a form of **asymmetric-key cryptography** in which closely related **key pairs** are generated and assigned to users [STAL16, DIFF76, ELLI70]. In a key pair, there is a private key and an associated public key. The user to whom the private key was assigned holds the key and keeps it secret. The private key is the secret that keeps the secrets—meaning that public key still requires some key distribution of the private key. The associated public key part is published widely.

> *It takes a secret to keep a secret.*

The notion of sharing a key widely seems counterintuitive because usually one views keys as being shared secrets, as previously described. In public-key cryptography, the encryption and decryption keys are different. The decryption key is the private key held securely by the owner; the encryption key is the public key published to a public directory. Knowledge of the public key provides no information about the private key, allowing it to be safely published. Because the encryption key is different from the decryption key, public-key cryptography is sometimes referred to as asymmetric-key cryptography. In contrast, with traditional cryptography, the encryption and decryption keys are identical—which is why *traditional cryptography* is sometimes referred to as **symmetric-key cryptography**. Figure 10-6 depicts the basics of public-key cryptography, which stands in contrast to secret key cryptography, shown in Figure 10-1.

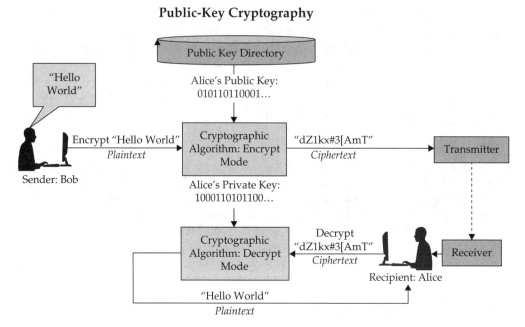

Figure 10-6   Public-key cryptography process flow, also known as asymmetric-key cryptography because the decryption key is different from the encryption key

10.5.1 The Math

Public-key cryptography relies upon a class of mathematical equations called one-way transformations. An example of such transformations is the problem of factoring very large integers into their constituent prime factors. One can quickly generate a series of prime numbers and multiply them together to get a very large prime number. It turns out that reversing that process is computationally hard. Specifically, it is exponentially hard relative to the number of digits in the number to be factored. Thus, one can create a relatively small number (around a thousand bits) and make the prime factorization into its constituent primes computationally impractical in a reasonable time scale.

Using one-way transformation algorithms makes it possible to publish the public key without compromising the associated private key. This, in turn, allows senders to encrypt data using the recipient's public key and be assured that only the receiver can decrypt the data with the corresponding private key. Similarly, the recipient can reply using the sender's public key to encrypt the reply and be assured that only the sender can decrypt the data. This enables a pair of users to establish secure communication and data sharing. This is sometimes called pairwise secure communication because it is effective for a pair of users establishing secure communication.

10.5.2 Certificates and Certificate Authorities

The binding (i.e., association) between a user and their public key is security-critical. If an adversary can subvert a server that makes that association, they can essentially masquerade as a user of their choosing by simply generating a key pair and substituting the public key that they just generated for anyone's (or everyone's) public key. This would be a very devastating attack. In addition, a server is not always available, such as in the disconnected devices on separate networks or totally off any network.

The solution to preserve the integrity of the binding between a user's identity and their public key is to cryptographically bind them. This essentially means to digitally sign the two together, combined with some other attributes, such as the period during which it is valid. The data and the digital signature is what is called a public-key certificate. Someone certifies that a particular user identity is indeed associated with a specific public key and implicitly certifies that the private key was somehow securely distributed to the user (and a hope that the user properly protects that private key from disclosure).

The someone that makes this certification is called the **certificate authority**. The certificate authority is a very highly trusted user and subsystem that generates and signs the certificate as described earlier in this section. How does one know who the trustworthy certificate authorities are? This is another sort of key management problem. One has to tell all applications and systems that use public-key infrastructure who the authorities are and provide their public key. This allows those systems to check the signature on certificates to make sure they are valid.

How does one know that the binding between the certificate authority and their public key is valid? Again, there is a parent certificate authority that signs the certificate authority's certificate. This creates a chain or tree of authorities that must at some point end in a root certificate authority. The root's certificate is essentially self-signed, and so the security of the chain really depends on the root's public key being widely known and rarely, if ever, changed.

If a certificate authority's key is compromised, it can compromise the identities of all the certificates that it issued. For efficiency's sake, designers often create a large span of control for each authority because it reduces the number of signatures in a chain that need to be checked (each signature check taking some time to accomplish). Thus, the span of damage from a certificate authority compromise is often enormous [GOOD17]. If the root is compromised, the damage would be extraordinary.

What if someone becomes a criminal, is fired, or simply leaf nodes an organization? The certificate must somehow be revoked because the certificate often also contains the organization the person is associated with, and there is an implication that the person is a member in good standing and is authorized to take actions at some basic level. Historically, **certification revocation lists** have been used for that purpose. Some authorized user, such as the head of the organization's human resources department, contacts the certificate authority that issued the person's certificate, and the authority puts that certificate on a list of revoked certificates. That certificate authority then periodically broadcasts or publishes this list, and all users of that infrastructure are supposed to ensure they have all the lists. Part of their validity check includes ensuring that the certificate that is being provided is not on a revocation list. Managing these lists, distributing them, and checking them can be quite cumbersome.

What if the user has stored important data with their private key and then loses their key? Bad news. All of their critical data could be lost. To mitigate this problem, public-key infrastructure systems generally have an emergency key recovery capability, allowing the private keys to be **escrowed** in some trusted service. This escrow capability creates a significant high-value target and thus a vulnerability. So, public-key cryptography is well-suited for the exchange of volatile messages, but works less well for long-term storage of data.

10.5.3 Performance and Use

One problem with encrypting data using public-key cryptography is that it is relatively slow compared to symmetric key encryption. Another problem is that to share data with a group of N people requires that the data be encrypted N times—once for each recipient. A method to address both problems is to use the best of both worlds. The method is to generate a symmetric key and use public-key encryption to send only the encrypted key. Thus, the public-key encryption becomes a form of key distribution. Pairwise communication is speeded up enormously because a symmetric key is generated (by the sender, receiver, collaboratively by both, and sometimes by a third party), and then the pair of users use the faster symmetric key algorithms to encrypt all further data traffic. Similarly, for a group of N, one can encrypt the data once using a single symmetric key and then send the key to each of N recipients separately, encrypting that symmetric key in their public key. This ensures that only the N recipients have the shared symmetric key.

Figure 10-7 shows how the two types of cryptography can be combined for maximum effect. In this example, Bob generates the key and distributes the key securely to Alice by encrypting it using her public key. Even though public-key cryptography is much slower than symmetric key cryptography, the key is relatively short and so the operation is fast. Alice receives and decrypts the symmetric key using her private key. At this point, Alice and Bob share a common symmetric key that they can use for further communications, employing symmetric key cryptography, until they decide they need to change it. In the example, Bob sends Alice a big file, which could take a long time to encrypt using public-key cryptography, but he can just use the key that he just generated. He can then send that encrypted file to Alice. Alice can decrypt the file using the symmetric key algorithm, employing the key that Bob sent her earlier. Notice that if Alice then wants to send Bob a different big file, she need only encrypt it using the shared symmetric key; there is no need for further key exchange.

As you may have inferred, public-key cryptography enables real-time generation, distribution, and use of symmetric cryptographic keys. It does so with very little delay or computational cost. Such real-time operations cut out the need for specialty key generation facilities, cumbersome key distribution schemes, and protected key storage. This is why public-key cryptography is enormously popular and used throughout the world.

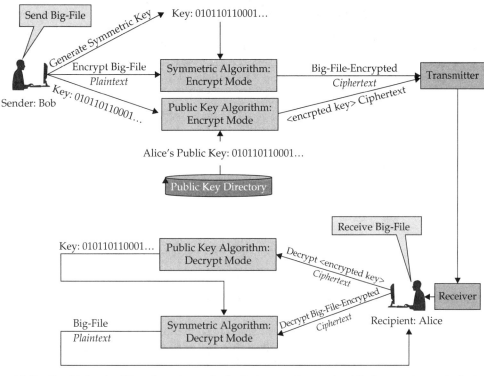

Figure 10-7   Combining traditional cryptography for fast encryption and public-key cryptography for key distribution offers the best of both worlds.

10.5.4 Side Effect of Public-Key Cryptography

Public-key cryptography has another useful property, almost as a side effect of the process. *Because the user to whom the private key belongs is the only one that knows the private key, proof of possession of that private key proves the identity of the user.* This, of course, depends on proper generation of the key pair, secure transmission of the private key to the user, and proper handling and storage of the private key to ensure that it remains private to the user for whom it was intended. Proving possession of the private key is built into protocols such as transport layer security. This proof of possession of the private key is called authentication and is discussed further in Chapter 11.

10.6 Integrity

Cryptography is most often thought of in the context of protecting sensitive data from being compromised. Cryptography is also useful for ensuring data integrity. Because data transmission and storage are subject to error, including dropped bits and bits that are flipped accidentally due to noise or hardware failures, it has been historically important to detect and correct such errors to improve reliability [SHAN48].

The process of detecting errors is aptly called **error detection**. Similarly, the process of correcting errors is called **error correction** [PETE72][LIN70]. One way to handle errors is to send the same data several times for redundancy. Then for each bit, one could compare the values from each copy and use a majority vote. For example, if the data is sent three times and two out of the three copies have a "1" and one copy has a "0," then under relatively low error and noise conditions, it is reasonable to conclude that the original and intended bit was a "1." Thus, the error in that bit position is detected and the correction is immediately available. The process of error detection and correction is shown in Figure 10-8.

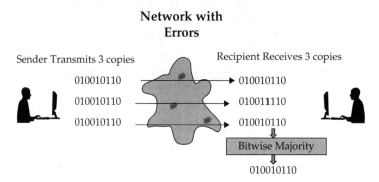

Figure 10-8 Example of error detection and error correction using complete redundancy

If the error rate is high, then the strategy is to send more copies. For example, human deoxyribonucleic acid (DNA) uses a fully redundant copy (complementary base pairs) to aid in error detection and correction during replication. Exactly how many copies need to be sent for a given error rate is calculable using a field called **information theory** developed by Claude Shannon [SHAN48]. Information theory is at the foundation of cryptography and many other important aspects of cybersecurity. The dedicated security engineer is strongly urged to read Claude Shannon's original treatise as well as more modern interpretations [STON15] of the timeliness principles.

Sending multiple redundant copies costs a lot of extra bandwidth and storage, which translates into extra cost and complexity. It turns out that one can do better by creating shorter representations of the full data by doing some calculations. These shorter strings of data are generically called **checksums**. They are computed using a specified algorithm designed to maximize error detection while minimizing the length of the additional string of data that needs to be transmitted. Detection can be accomplished with relatively short checksums. If one wants both detection and correction, the checksum needs to be longer. Standard checksum algorithms have been developed and used for over a half-century [PETE61]. These checksums are typically part of metadata (i.e., data that describes the corresponding data) and are often prepended or appended to the data. For accidental errors, which tend to be random, it suffices to store or transmit the checksum along with the data.

For malicious and intentional attacks, simply accompanying the data with the checksum does not suffice. The reason is that an attacker can intercept the data, change it to whatever they want, and then recalculate the checksum, and then send the data and the revised checksum, and the recipient would be none the wiser. Additional measures are required to stop this so-called **man-in-the-middle attack**. A man-in-the-middle attack is one where the attacker places himself between a sender and recipient of data, unknown to both. The attacker intercepts the sender's communication, alters it, and then retransmits it to the recipient in such a way as to fool the recipient into thinking that it came from the original sender (Figure 10-9).

Attack Panel: Man-in-the-Middle Attack	
Class	Cryptographic
Type	Confidentiality and integrity
Mechanism	An attacker intercepts the setup of a secure communication between two parties. The attacker masquerades to each party as the other legitimate party, relaying messages between the parties and eavesdropping and potentially changing the messages.
Examples	If there is no authoritiative source for public keys, parties can provide their own public key to the other party as part of the protocol. This allows the attacker to intercept the protocol and send their own public key to both parties instead.
Damage Potential	Lost confidentiality and integrity of all data exchanged during the session.

Figure 10-9   Attack description: man-in-the-middle attack

To address the man-in-the-middle attack, one needs a way to prevent the attacker from merely recalculating the checksum and passing it off as the original. This is a job for cryptography used for authentication. A pair of cryptographic functions called sign and verify are used. The signing process computes over the input data using the sender's private key, producing an output called the digital signature. The recipient uses a corresponding verification process that takes in the data, the digital signature, and the sender's public key and outputs "valid" if the data matches the digital signature, or "invalid" if it does not. If the signature is determined to be valid, then the message has integrity—that is, the message has not been maliciously (or accidentally) modified from what the sender intended. Thus, *the man-in-the-middle attack is defeated by* a digital signature.

> *The man-in-the-middle attack is defeated by a digital signature.*

Notice that digital signature schemes do not require that a message be encrypted; the digital signatures are sent with the data, which can be in the clear. There are many examples of data that needs integrity but no encryption. For example, most National Aeronautics and Space Administration (NASA) data is publicly available to scientists for analysis. It is important that it *not* be encrypted so that access is easy. On the other hand, to ensure the validity of scientific results, it is essential that the data have integrity. As a second example, it is important that software distributed from the vendor to the customer system have high integrity, but confidentiality is rarely important because the executable code of most systems is not sensitive. In such cases, a cybersecurity engineer might request that the vendor digitally sign the software before distributing the software or a software patch and ensure that the signature is checked before installation. This prevents an attacker from accomplishing a supply chain attack in the communications portion of the process.

Some data could require both protection from disclosure and integrity. Bank and other financial transaction data would be an example of that. Clients want their banking transactions to remain private, and it is critical to maintain the integrity of the data indicating the details of a transfer—you would not want a $10 transaction to a vendor for a small retail item to suddenly become $100,000.

The important thing to observe is that *sensitivity protection and integrity protection are independently applied and can be used separately or together*, though both depend on cryptography.

10.7 Availability

Cryptography can have both positive and negative effects on availability. This section discusses each and the nature of the engineering trade-off.

10.7.1 Positive Effects

From a positive perspective, cryptography can be used to ensure the integrity of the systems, application software, and corresponding configuration information during life-cycle distribution of software and updates. Without such systems integrity mechanisms, the system is vulnerable to supply chain attack and **computer network attacks** that involve altering system code, causing the system to crash.

In addition, cryptography is at the heart of authentication. With authentication, the system can better prevent unauthorized system use. For example, the system could refuse all network connections except from strongly authenticated clients. This reduces the probability of a network-based attack succeeding, which could in turn prevent the attacker from mounting a panoply of different attacks, including availability attacks. Similarly, a router could filter out all packets from sources that are not from authenticated sources, which could reduce the chances of a successful network flooding attack.

10.7.2 Negative Effects

On the negative side, cryptography inherently uses valuable system resources, including computational resources, storage resources, and network bandwidth. This is because cryptography is an added step to whatever functional process is planned, so that step has resource costs associated with it. In modern systems, the resource costs tend to be low, in the 5 percent range, but this can add up for large and expensive systems. Such resource requirements can be prohibitive for systems limited to minimal resources because of size, power, or weight considerations, such as in some classes of Internet of Things (IOT) devices.

In addition to direct resource costs, cryptography impacts timeliness. Cryptographic processes involve many operations and often involve multiple communication exchanges.

Each exchange causes roundtrip communication delays (called latency) that can dominate the delay associated with computations.

For most applications, such as email and most web traffic, these delays are inconsequential. In other applications that require real-time or near-real-time transactions, even the minor delays imposed by cryptography can be problematic. As an example, imagine an air-to-air battle when two friendly airplanes are engaged by enemy aircraft. Let's say that one of the enemy aircraft launches a missile at the friendly planes. The first pilot to notice needs to able to very quickly communicate the situation because they both only have a few seconds to react by taking evasive maneuvers and deploying countermeasures such as metal chaff or flares to confuse the incoming missile. Although establishing a strong cryptographic connection can take only a second or two, this delay in being able to communicate could mean the difference between life and death for the pilots.

It is not particularly important to maintain confidentiality in this case because the adversary is perfectly aware that they have just fired a missile and so there is little point in trying to protect messages about that fact. Therefore, it is sometimes valuable for users to be able to opt not to engage cryptographic mechanisms to protect some communications. This option is known as cryptographic bypass, since those mechanisms are sometimes interposed in the communication path—particularly in military applications. *Situations such as the example given are why* **cryptographic bypasses** *are almost always necessary when encryption is built into the communication path; they also are a major source of vulnerability since users can invoke a bypass inappropriately.*

> ### *Cryptographic bypasses are a necessary evil requiring great care.*

In addition to the indirect impact on timeliness, there is an important impact on reliability. Adding cryptography means additional hardware or software or both to execute the cryptographic functions. These cryptographic functions are interposed in important functional processes such as communications of data across the network. If the cryptography fails, then, often, the entire system fails.

In addition to normal component failures that happen to all devices and software, including cryptographic ones, failure could happen even when all components are functioning properly. Although modern cryptographic protocols are relatively fast, this is only true under relatively good conditions on the network or communications media (such as wireless communications). If the communication path has high noise or high congestion, this could cause the protocols to continually fail and ultimately to give up. This, in turn, makes the system even more brittle. Furthermore, such failures may be particularly difficult to detect, leading to long delays in diagnosing and mitigating the failures. The increased system failure rate and the increased time to recover could significantly impact overall system reliability.

Encrypting data can also have other important negative consequences that could result in reduced reliability and availability. If a user loses their key and there is no retrieval or recovery mechanism, all of the data encrypted by that key is lost. As a dramatic example, consider encrypting your computer's entire hard disk with a key, losing the key, and having no means to recover the key. Such a loss would be catastrophic because even though the backed-up data is encrypted, all the data becomes completely unavailable.

Another availability problem with cryptography is that it can sometimes make it harder to detect attacks within an enterprise. Consider intrusion detection systems and firewalls that monitor incoming and outgoing traffic for potential threats. Neither can perform their protective function unless they share in the key of all such traffic, which is generally not acceptable since that creates a single point of vulnerability for all protected communications. This opaqueness of communication can also be leveraged by attackers to encrypt their malicious communication. In most systems today, firewalls and intrusion detection systems tend to ignore and allow such encrypted communications on the assumption that they are secure and therefore good. Ironically, *encrypted communications can pose significant overall risk and could decrease reliability and thus decrease availability.*

Lastly, encrypting certain data and not other data tells an adversary exactly where to look for the most sensitive and valuable data. This motivates the adversary to put substantial resources toward breaking the cryptography, the cryptographic protocols, and the end systems involved in the communication. *Therefore, encrypting data can have the opposite effect of its intent by increasing the probability of compromising the very data it is trying to protect.* This suggests that encrypting as much data as possible would help to reduce this effect, but could have other consequences as discussed early in the section. What this demonstrates is that cybersecurity is always an engineering trade-off, even *within* a given capability such as cryptography.

> *Encrypting data can actually make it a high-value target.*

10.8 Chinks in the Cryptographic Armor

All of cryptography depends on the computational impracticality of breaking it. In the case of symmetric cryptography, the impracticality is in the form of exhausting over the key space. In the case of asymmetric-key (also known as public-key) cryptography, the impracticality concerns the difficulty in reversing some transformations such as factoring the products of large primes. This impracticality must hold true even in the face of expected advances in computation capability. For example, Moore's Law predicts a doubling in speed and capacity every 18 months [MOOR75]. Also, massively parallel computers promise to reduce the time the adversary needs to perform the difficult calculations.

10.8.1 Quantum Cryptanalytics: Disruptive Technology

One possible disruptive technology which could create a serious issue in these assumptions is quantum **cryptanalytics**. *Quantum computing has the potential to become so fast that what was impractical to compute may become practical.*

> *Quantum computing may break existing cryptography.*

Quantum computing is now mostly theoretical, though prototype minimally capable proofs of concept already exist. It is only a matter of time and a handful of required breakthroughs before quantum computing becomes practical [COFF14]. This means that the cryptographic community must immediately begin to research cryptographic methods that are impervious to quantum computing. The main approach today to address this potential new vulnerability is to create quantum cryptography in such a way that quantum cryptanalysis would not succeed.

10.8.2 P=NP

In addition to a vulnerability to quantum computing, public-key cryptography has a special potential vulnerability. Public-key algorithms are based on what are called Non-deterministic Polynomial-time Hard (NP-Hard) problems [AHO74]. Such problems are exponentially hard in practice, but there exists no proof that such algorithms are inherently so. That means that it is theoretically possible for someone to one day discover a **polynomial-time** (non-exponential) solution to reverse these transformations. Such a discovery would cause a collapse of public-key cryptography based on NP-Hard problems and all data encrypted using public key cryptography. Such a discovery would be a global security disaster given the prevalence of the usage of such public-key algorithms, as discussed in Section 10.5.

10.9 Cryptography Is Not a Panacea

Wise cybersecurity engineers have said, "Those who consider cryptography the solution to all their security problems do not understand cryptography and do not understand their security problems."

Cryptography is an excellent tool in the repertoire of the cybersecurity architect. It is at the heart of authentication protocols, which are the basis of **identity certification**, which in turn is the basis of authorization. Cryptography is also essential to protecting data at rest and in transit over networks.

Cryptography has negative effects on the system as described earlier in this chapter and therefore is part of a trade-off that must be done within the engineering process. There is a temptation to apply cryptography blindly because it seems like a good idea and more of it seems like it would always be better. That is a naïve perspective.

Assuming cryptography is designed and implemented correctly, it is unlikely that the attacker will often successfully break the cryptography itself. On the other hand, properly invoking cryptographic functions is difficult. Cryptography functions must be invoked securely and through a **trusted path** so that the caller knows that the cryptography is properly invoked. Such important properties are hard to achieve and require good security engineering of the entire system employing the cryptography.

Using strong cryptography without an equally strong system ensuring that it is called and used correctly is a waste of time and money. The attacker will simply attack the calling system. For example, if the attacker has complete control of the calling system, it could simply lie to the calling application and say that it performed operations that it did not. Similarly, consider the case where the system has access to the private key and the adversary has control of the system. As you recall, possession of a private key in many systems is the basis for proving identity. Thus, the adversary can easily masquerade as anyone who has accounts on that system because all of their private keys are compromised.

> *Strong cryptography embedded in a weak system is a waste of time.*

10.10 Beware of Homegrown Cryptography

Cryptography and cryptographic protocols are very subtle and hard to get correct. When one first studies cryptography, one is tempted to first implement some of the basic algorithms such as single substitutions [GAIN14] and then more advanced algorithms. Such implementations are excellent teaching devices to better understand the nature of the algorithms. *Designing one's own algorithm or key management system, even based on the best theories of cryptography, should be approached with extreme caution.*

Like mathematical proofs [LAKA76], new algorithms must undergo vigorous analysis by a large skilled community of professional cryptographers before one can even begin to consider trusting algorithms to protect important data. Even then, the defender should be prepared for the possibility of an adversary discovering a clever attack that could render the cryptography ineffective and reveal the data that was protected by it.

Cryptographic applications are also complex and difficult to get right. A long-standing wireless security protocol called WiFi Protected Access (WPA2) was recently found to be vulnerable [GOOD17b], allowing nearby hackers to eavesdrop and insert malicious code to connections that were supposed to be secure. In addition, the flaws in the implementation of a commonly used cryptographic library left millions of users with high-security public-private pairs of cryptographic keys vulnerable to having their private key easily derivable from their public key [GOOD17c].

> *Cryptographic design—do not try this at home!*

Conclusion

This chapter overviews the fundamental concepts and principles of cryptography—a key building block of cybersecurity mechanisms such as protecting communications, protected storage, and authentication. The next chapter further discusses authentication and its role in the larger cybersecurity picture.

To summarize:

- Cryptography protects data, using a key, so that only intended recipients can read it.
- Cryptographic strength relates to key-space size, which relates to the key length.
- Key generation must be truly randomly chosen from within the key space—it's hard.

- Keys must be securely distributed to intended recipients of encrypted data.
- Public-key cryptography enables real-time key generation and usage.
- Public-private key pairs ensure that knowledge of the public key does not divulge the private one.
- Proof of possession of a private key can be an effective way of proving identity.
- Cryptography can protect data integrity in transit or storage using digital signatures.
- Cryptography has weaknesses and uncertainty with respect to technology advances.
- Cryptography is a useful tool, but is worse than useless if used incorrectly.
- Cryptographic algorithm design is a complex art that should not be done by amateurs.

Questions

1. What is cryptography and how does it work?
2. Describe the difference between symmetric-key and asymmetric-key cryptography and explain how they can work together.
3. Explain why a key length of 16 bits is almost certainly too small to be secure.
4. Explain why we cannot rely on people to make up random numbers in the key generation process.
5. Define public and private keys and explain how they are used to secure communications between parties.
6. What is a digital signature and what is it used for?
7. Define error detection, contrast it to error correction, and explain why one requires more redundancy than the other.
8. Describe three ways that cryptography could have a negative impact on availability, and explain why.
9. Discuss approaches and vulnerabilities that can lead to compromising cryptographic implementations of strong algorithms.
10. List a technology advance that could have a serious impact on all of cryptography and explain when you think that advance might happen.
11. Define what "non-polynomial hard" means and what happens if such problems are found to have polynomial solutions.

Authentication

Overview

Learning Objectives

- Explain the authentication problem and how cryptography is applied to solve it.
- Discuss the phases of authentication and how they relate to one another.
- List and describe the three types of unique identifying schemas.
- Compare and contrast strengths and weaknesses of identity schemas.
- Explain the value of multifactor authentication and its value to cybersecurity.
- Differentiate between entity identification and identity certification.
- Summarize the identity assertion and proving process.
- Describe the identity decertification process and when and why it is done.
- Explain machine-to-machine authentication and how it relates to that of human-to-machine.

One important application of cryptography is authentication. There are at least two different types of authentication. There is **human-to-machine authentication** and there is **machine-to-machine authentication**. Although separate, they often work together to create a **chain of authentication** in a similar manner to the concept of a chain of custody for legal evidence. Human-to-machine authentication concerns proving to a computer that a person is who they say they are—or at least that they correspond to the identity of the person who is registered with the system. Human-to-machine authentication is commonly called **login** or **logon**. Machine-to-machine authentication concerns non-persons (active computing elements) proving that they are the same entity (e.g., a system such as a bank website or a service such as the domain name system) that was originally registered and can serve as a valid proxy for a person. The authentication chain concept is shown in Figure 11-1.

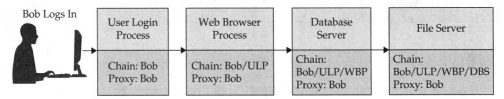

Figure 11-1 Authentication chain concept in which a user action goes through four non-person entities acting as proxies

As a point of vocabulary, a **non-person entity** is an active computing element (e.g., a process) that has a distinct identity within a system, but is not a human. Devices such as routers and application programs in execution (called processes) are examples of a non-person entity. The term **entity** is a more general term that covers both persons and non-person entities. Accordingly, sometimes a person is referred to as a **person entity** to clarify that a person is being referred to as a system-identifiable entity in the context of authentication processes. This reference also makes it clear that a person identity is a subclass of the term entity.

Authentication has several important distinct phases, each of which is sometimes incorrectly and confusedly called authentication:

1. Entity identification
2. Identity certification
3. Identity resolution
4. Identity assertion
5. Identity proving
6. Identity decertification

These six phases in the life cycle of authentication are shown in Figure 11-2 and described in Sections 11.2 through 11.5. The six phases are grouped into three major functions:

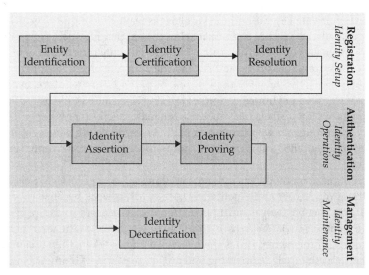

Figure 11-2   The six phases of the authentication life cycle shown in three groups: registration (which sets up identity), authentication (which proves identity during operations), and management (which updates or deletes identities)

- **Identity registration**, in which entities are made known to the system and given the ability to demonstrate their identity.
- **Identity authentication**, in which entities assert and prove their identity to other entities during operations.
- **Identity management**, in which entities are decertified from the system and perhaps recertified differently (e.g., when a name changes after marriage).

11.1 Entity Identification: Phase 1 of Authentication

Entity identification is a registration process that generally happens outside of the technological system for person entities. A person provides physical proof, such as a driver's license, to prove to a system registrar that they are who they claim to be.

The registrar, a specially designated, trained, and privileged person, then certifies the person's identity. They do so by generating identifying data that is unique to each person. An example of unique identifying information is a secret password. A password is essentially a secret known by both the system and the one person who holds it. This is another instance of the principle that it takes a secret to keep a secret. A private key of a public-private pair is another example of unique identifying data.

11.2 Identity Certification: Phase 2 of Authentication

Identity certification is the second phase of authentication and is the second step in the registration process. *There are three types of unique identifying schema: something you know, something you have, and something you are.* Something you know is a unique secret such as a password or private key. Something you have is usually a unique version of a device, sometimes called a physical **authentication token**, that is issued exclusively to you [e.g., Google's token [AXON17]. Something you are is usually referred to as biometrics, and it involves the system measuring and registering a unique physical aspect of a person, such as their fingerprints, the image of their retina, or perhaps, in the future, even keyboard typing rhythm (also called **keyboard cadence**) [HOLO11]. There is a hybrid of the first two types, which is essentially "something you get"—such as a secret that is generated on the fly and transmitted through some trustworthy path. An example is a bank sending you a one-time code, sometimes called an out-of-band authentication, for you to enter in addition to a password.

Each of these methods has inherent weaknesses, as well as weakness in implementation. "Something you know," implemented as passwords, is weak because short passwords are easy to break and long passwords must be written down by users—usually in easily guessable places (e.g., under their keyboard). "Something you have," in the form of a token, can be stolen or lost. If the owner writes the password on the token, then it can be used to masquerade as the user. "Something you are," in the form of biometric measurements compared once on login, have three weaknesses:

- Tolerances must be set sufficiently high to prevent users from becoming annoyed at being locked out; this makes them susceptible to false positives, in which the system misidentifies a similar person.

- Replay, in which an attacker uses the same device to create an identical digital string that is representative of the biometric measurement; this string can then be sent directly to the authentication system, bypassing the measurement device.

- Registration issues, in which the biometric device can be tricked into measuring the wrong thing (e.g., a contact lens instead of a retina, or a latex glove with an embedded fingerprint instead of a real finger).

These types of unique identifying schemas are sometimes called factors. Each has its strengths and weaknesses. Traditionally, the three factors are thought of as being listed in increasing strength (and increasing difficulty and cost): something you know being the weakest, something you have being stronger, and something you are being strongest. This is not exactly true in general and, of course, it depends heavily on implementation details. The hierarchy of the authentication factors is shown in Figure 11-3.

There is an unwritten assumption that the more factors that are used, the stronger the process is. This is based on the reasonable intuition that the strengths of one factor will complement the weaknesses of the other. This assumption is rarely, if ever, supported with evidence and argument beyond the intuition. Of course, it is theoretically possible for the strengths and weaknesses of each to align perfectly so that two factors are no stronger than just using one. It is even possible that one mechanism could weaken another such that two together would be weaker than one. When a security engineer is designing an authentication system, a structured argument (called an assurance case) should be made about how strengths and weakness may synergize or even negatively synergize.

Figure 11-3   The three types of unique identifying schemas or authentication factors and how they combine to create multifactor authentication (human-to-machine)

The use of more than one factor is called multifactor authentication. The term two-factor authentication refers to using exactly two out of the three factors. Usually, two-factor authentication refers to adding the something-you-have schema to the something-you-know schema—so it involves both issuing secret information and issuing an authentication token or device. Similarly, **three-factor authentication** refers to using all three factors together. Figure 11-3 depicts this most common interpretation of two- and three-factor authentication. Technically, using two different mechanisms within an authentication factor can be referred to as two-factor (e.g., using a password and having to know the answers to three questions, such as in online banking). This makes a term like two-factor authentication highly ambiguous—it is not clear which two factors are being proposed, whether there are two instances from within the same factor or one instance from each of two separate factors, or how they will be implemented to ensure complementary and effective synergy.

11.3 Identity Resolution: Phase 3 of Authentication

Identity resolution is the final step of the registration process within the six phases of authentication. Once identity certification is complete, **identity resolution** is performed. This step simply refers to the process of getting the unique data and devices set up and conferred to the person in such a way as to maintain the assumptions about uniqueness. For example, emailing a user their password, in the clear, potentially compromises the password to any intermediary that happens to eavesdrop on the email while it is in transit from the sender to the receiver. This, in turn, violates the uniqueness assumption that only the intended recipient knows the secret data. Once the data and devices are conferred to the user, they often must make some local system changes such as making applications and system programs aware of where to get the data and how to interact with devices. Once that is done, the resolution process is complete. The first three steps together are what can be referred to as the initialization, setup, or **registration** process.

11.4 Identity Assertion and Identity Proving: Phases 4 and 5 of Authentication

Phases 4 and 5 of authentication represent the operational-use phase, which is most properly termed authentication. One entity asserts its identity to another entity. If there is little at stake, such as providing the time of day service, the entity to whom the original entity was asserting its identity may choose to just trust the assertion. More often, and built into protocols such as Transport Layer Security (TLS) [DIER08], the recipient of the **identity assertion** attempts to verify the assertion by checking for **identity proof**. For example, if a person claims an identity by asserting possession of a private key corresponding to the published public key bound to that identity in the system, the recipient of the claim can check this assertion by sending an encrypted **nonce** using the sender's public key to that original sender. The recipient can then ask the sender to decrypt it and send it back to the recipient to check for correspondence to the nonce that they sent.

11.5 Identity Decertification: Phase 6 of Authentication

Identity decertification is the final phase of authentication and is the primary process within the management grouping. **Identity decertification** is the process of removing a registered identity from the system, typically because the person has left an organization or their identity was somehow compromised. This involves communicating the decertification decision to any entities that may be currently trusting the original identity certification, and removing any trace of the person's identity certification from the system (other than for archival and forensic purposes). The process involves removing their public key from the public directory, posting a **certificate revocation** notice for a public-key certificate (Figure 11-4), and removing a person's account from the system, or at least deactivating it so that nobody can use it. Depending on the system, the delay between when the revocation occurs and when all users get notified could be hours, days, and even months.

Identity data sometimes changes, such as a name change when a person gets married. One can have a separate process to update an identity certificate, but conceptually, it is the same as decertifying the original entity identity and creating a new one with the same attributes (including the same private key).

In addition to identity changes, new certificates may need to be issued if the certificate authority's signature key is compromised. The decertifications are needed particularly when it is not possible to determine precisely when the key was compromised. All certificates have to be presumed to be invalid. All legitimate certificates must then be reissued under a new certificate authority key. The same private keys and attributes can be used, unless the certificate authority device itself was completely compromised along with all the private keys (which is possible, but less likely). The invalidation of all existing certificates and the subsequent reissue of all legitimate keys is known as **emergency rekey**.

Defense Panel: Public Key Certificate	
Type	Identity Management, Cryptography, Asymmetric
Capability	Identity certification through a distributed system.
Means	A strong cryptographic binding between an entity system identity, some essential attributes, and a public key that is part of a private-public key pair. The binding is achieved by creating a message hash of the elements and having a recognized authority digitally signed.
Limitations	The strength of the binding depends on the entity keeping their private key secure and secret from others.
Impacts	Enables an effective identity certification, authentication, and management across a large distributed enterprise.
Attack Space	Addresses attackers spoofing the identity of an authorized user to gain access to accomplish some attack mission.

Figure 11-4 Defense panel: public-key certificate and identity management

11.6 Machine-to-Machine Authentication Chaining

Once a person authenticates their identity to the system during a login procedure, the system must be able to operate on the user's behalf. The user takes no direct action on a system other than login. At the point after successful login, any action taken on a computer is done by a process that is operating on behalf of the user, sometimes called the **user** process. When that process requests a system service (e.g., open a file) that requires authentication, the process must assert a claim that it is operating on behalf of a user. Sometimes it does so by simply asserting the unique system identifier in its request. If the requestor of the service and the provider of the service are part of the operating system and therefore trusted, the mere assertion of the identity of the original user may suffice. The user process, operating on behalf of the user, is said to act as a **proxy** for the user—analogous to granting a power of attorney to another person to act on your behalf in legal matters.

Sometimes, when a login proxy requests a service, that service must request support from other system services. These system services must, in turn, use the originator's identity to determine whether to provide access. Thus, one ends up with a chain of proxies, each asserting the identity of the originator. *This proxy chain carries some risk*. It assumes that each entity in the proxy chain correctly conveys the originator's identity without error and without malicious action, such as asserting a more privileged identity to gain unauthorized access. Each entity in the authentication chain must be shown to be correct in its functional operation, and must be tamper-resistant (hard to compromise its integrity) so that an adversary does not modify its correct operation. This level of evidence and analysis is sometimes not done, and so trust of the proxy chain is more a matter of faith than of reason.

Conclusion

This chapter covered authentication of users to machines and authentication between machines, applying concepts of cryptography from the previous chapter. The next chapter discusses the concept of authorization, which builds on authenticating identity to establish the privileges associated with that identity.

To summarize:

- Human-to-machine identity authentication (login) is chained with machine-to-machine authentication to create a chain of trust between a user and the system services.
- Proof of possession of a private key proves identity associated with that private key.
- The six authentication phases are entity identification, identity certification, identity resolution, identity assertion, identity proving, and identity decertification.
- Entity identification uses three schemas: something you know (e.g., passwords), something you have (e.g., an authentication token), and something you are (e.g., biometrics).
- The something-you-know schema, represented by passwords, is weak.
- Multifactor authentication combines multiple schemas to improve authentication's strength.
- Proving identity is proving possession of a private key through a challenge-response action.
- Identity decertification when a person leaves an organization must be quick and thorough.

Questions

1. What are the two fundamental types of authentication involving man and machine and how do they work together to create a chain of trust?
2. What are the six phases of authentication and which one is truly authentication?
3. What is multifactor authentication? What are the three factors and what are their strengths and weaknesses? Why is it good?
4. Distinguish entity identification from identity certification and describe how they relate and depend on each other.
5. What is a non-person entity and how does it relate to authentication?
6. What is an identity registrar and how are they involved in entity certification?
7. Name three types of biometrics that can be measured. Discuss how each might be defeated by an adversary. Propose countermeasures to these attacks and argue why they are effective and state their limitations.

8. If a system has fingerprint recognition and a password, is that multifactor authentication? What if either one suffices to gain access? Is it still multifactor? Is the system stronger than either of two alternative schemes? Why or why not?

9. Give an example of two-factor authentication.

10. Describe how the identity is conferred to users once their identity is certified.

11. Define a nonce and how it is used in identity assertion and in identity proving.

12. What is decertification and why must it be done promptly?

13. What is a proxy and how does it relate to the authentication chain?

Part III

CHAPTER 12

Authorization

Overview

- 12.4 Authorization Adoption Schemas
  - 12.4.1 Direct Integration
  - 12.4.2 Indirect Integration
  - 12.4.3 Alternative Integration

Learning Objectives

- Compare and contrast discretionary and mandatory access control approaches.
- Compare and contrast identity-based access control and attribute-based access control.
- Explain the three aspects of attribute-based access control and relate them to one another.
- Describe the aspects of the attribute management process and why it is security-critical.
- Differentiate between syntactic and semantic validity of attribute data.
- Discuss the issue of freshness in attribute management and policy management.
- Define digital policy and describe the life cycle of a digital policy.
- Explain why policy decision making and policy enforcement are separate functions.
- Explain the assurance obligations on developers for protecting the subsystem.
- List and compare the three modes of authorization adoption.

12.1 Access Control

Access control refers to controlling whether and how active entities (e.g., processes) within the system can interact with passive resources within the system (e.g., files and memory). For ease of reference, we will refer to active entities as **subjects** and passive resources as objects. If one considers a matrix listing all subjects in rows and all objects in columns, it forms a matrix, called an access control matrix [LAMP71]. Entries at the intersection between a given subject and object state the type of access the subject is allowed for that corresponding object. Examples of **access rights** include

- "read" (allowing the subject to see data in the resource, e.g., read a file)
- "write" (allowing the subject to write to a resource, and usually read it as well to verify that the write operation happened correctly)
- "execute" (allowing the subject to execute the contents of an object as a program)

- "null" (prohibiting all actions)
- "own" (allowing a subject to set access rights for other subjects to a given object)

There are many other types of access rights that can be fine-grained, depending on the ability of the system to properly interpret and enforce that access. Table 12-1 gives an example of an access control matrix. Recall that subjects are active entities like system processes that act on behalf of users, so we can think of a column of the table as being an access list to the object at the top of the column for four users on the system (subjects 1, 2, 3, 4).

	Object 1 Access	Object 2 Access	Object 3 Access	Object 4 Access
Subject 1	Read, Write, Own	Read	Write	Null
Subject 2	Null	Read, Write, Own	Write	Execute
Subject 3	Null	Read	Read, Write, Own	Execute
Subject 4	Null	Read	Write	Read, Write, Execute, Own

Table 12-1   Example of an access control matrix. The upper left-hand cell means that subject 1 has read, write, and own access to object 1.

To make the matrix more concrete, it may help to think of subject 1 as Bob, subject 2 as Alice, subject 3 as Harry, and subject 4 as Sally. Similarly, we can think of the objects as passive entities such as files, so we think of object 1 as file 1, object 2 as file 2, etc. We see from the matrix that Bob owns file 1, Alice owns file 2, Harry owns file 3, and Sally owns file 4. Looking at the first column, we see that Bob does not play well with others and grants no other users access to his file 1. Looking at column 2, we see that Alice likes to share her file with everyone to see, granting all other users read access, but does not want to allow anyone to change her file 2.

Note that a system can have tens of thousands of users. There can be thousands of processes spawned for each user (a user can have multiple subjects operating on their behalf), so there are hundreds of millions of subject rows in a real-world access control matrix. Similarly, there are generally large numbers of files that are in the millions on a sizable enterprise system. So, there are potentially tens of billions of cells in a realistic access control matrix.

With the concept of an access control matrix in hand and an appreciation for its enormous size, the key question arises as to who sets the values in the cells and how the values are updated for new subjects and objects. The following subsections answer those questions.

12.1.1 Discretionary Access Control

An obvious first answer is to have the owners and creators of objects set the entries in those access control matrix cells associated with that object with respect to all other subjects. We say that the access control matrix entries are at the discretion of the owning user, and so this is called **discretionary access control**. Creating an entry in the access control matrix is an act of authorizing an access, so we call this an authorization capability or service. Historically, discretionary access control was implemented with **access control lists** associated with each object [DALE65]. Each access control list is essentially a column out of the access control matrix, so the aggregate of all the columns makes up the access control matrix. Figure 12-1 shows an example of how access control lists are defined using the same example access control matrix shown in Table 12-1.

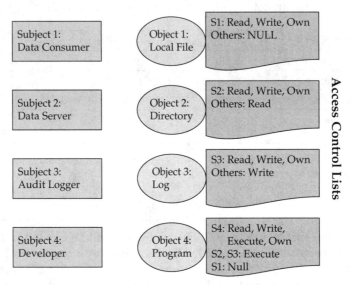

Figure 12-1   Example of discretionary access control for authorization using access control lists, shown on the right, where the access rights for each subject to that object are explicitly listed. "Others" means all subjects other than the owner.

In this example, we elaborate by suggesting that subject 1 is a consumer of data such as a data analyst, thus explaining his behavior of reading other objects, but not widely sharing his own. Subject 2 is a data server (operating on behalf of its owner and operator, Alice), thus explaining why subject 2 allows all the other subjects to read its object (perhaps it is a library of electronic books). Subject 3 is an audit logger, which takes in data from all other subjects' activities for diagnostics purposes, thus explaining why it lets all other subjects write to the object that it owns. Subject 4 is a developer, and its file 4 is really an executable program, which explains why it gives execute access to two other subjects (2 and 3), withholding any access to subject 1 because he has no real need to execute the program in this fictitious example.

Assigning access-right decisions for each and every existing subject and all possible new subjects that get created later is a burdensome task. One solution, implemented by the Unix operating system, has been to create three classes of access—user, group, and world. The user access refers to the rights the user grants to all their own subjects for objects they create. Group refers to a small number of pre-established privileged groups such as system administrators. World refers to everyone else. *This makes the specification process more compact and manageable, making the matrix implicit.*

Discretionary access control sounds like an elegant solution to the problem. Who better to decide access to objects than the creators of those objects? *There is one key problem with the discretionary access control approach; it cannot control propagation of sensitive data.* If a malicious user, such as an insider, gains access to sensitive data, there is nothing stopping that user from copying sensitive data, creating a new object, and granting access to whoever they please. The **insider threat** is real and worthy of addressing. *In addition, there is the more pronounced threat of a Trojan horse within a program that the unwitting user executes.* When a user executes a program, it operates with all of their privileges, including the privilege to create objects and set access control matrix entries. This could be done surreptitiously without the user even knowing that it is being done by some program that they are executing to perform a legitimate function such as word processing or creating presentation slides [KARG87].

> *Discretionary access controls are vulnerable to Trojan horses.*

12.1.2 Mandatory Access Control

Mandatory access control was introduced precisely to counter the weakness of discretionary access control in controlling the propagation of sensitive data. The approach first requires that all data be labeled with the appropriate sensitivities. These **sensitivity labels** are called metadata in the sense that it is data about other data. Sensitivity is one type of metadata. A similar labeling scheme (called clearances) is placed on the users themselves and all of their subordinate subjects, such as processes created on their behalf when they execute programs.

One then creates system access **policy rules** about reading and writing data that adhere to an appropriate policy to control the flow of data that is not at the users' discretion. One rule might be that users at a given level cannot create objects of less sensitivity than their sensitivity label. This rule would prevent the problem described at the end of the previous section regarding discretionary access control. To read sensitive data, a user would have to operate at or above that level (another rule). From that level, they would not be able to create an object of lower sensitivity to share with an untrusted user. Problem solved.

There are a variety of different types of mandatory access control policies to handle different types of problems. That is why the description earlier in this section was kept generic. The astute reader may have noticed that mandatory access control sounds a lot like multilevel security discussed in a previous chapter. Indeed, multilevel security is an example of a mandatory access control policy—as are multilevel integrity and type enforcement. In multilevel security, the "no write down" rule prevents users from exposing classified information to uncleared (and therefore untrusted) users, and the "no read up" rule prevents users from reading classified information above their clearance level.

A problem with mandatory access control is that it is not very granular. To keep the system manageable, there are usually only a handful of sensitivity labels. One can extend the sensitivity labels from a **strict hierarchy** to what is called a **security lattice**, which effectively creates a special type of group, sometimes called a **compartment** or category. This lattice extension improves the coarse controls offered by strict hierarchies.

Figure 12-2 shows a simplified lattice structure where A and B represent compartments. Notice that having a "Top Secret A" clearance does not grant access to "Top Secret B" classifications—the A and B compartments are said to be in a noncomparable relationship. Similarly, having a "Top Secret B" clearance does not give access to "Secret A" classified data. Compartments A and B can be thought of as different mission areas, and so only users assigned to a mission area should be able to access that data, even if they are highly trusted and possess a high clearance level. Note that even though it is theoretically possible that the compartments at a lower sensitivity level extend beyond those from a higher level, it is most typically the case that they are a subset.

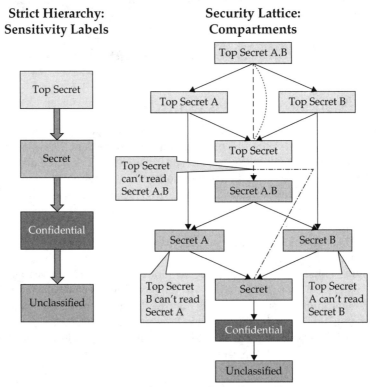

Note: Distinctive lines are used to make tracing easier.

Figure 12-2   Sensitivity labels in a strict hierarchy (on left) versus a simple security lattice with compartments (on right)

Introducing security lattices improves granularity some, but the problem of excluding particular users remains. That is the topic of the next section.

Discretionary access controls can handle individual access exclusion well. *So, discretionary access control mechanisms are often combined with mandatory access control to get the best of both worlds.* Of course, with discretionary access control, there is no guarantee that excluded users will not eventually be able to see data if other users that are included collude and copy the data and provide it to excluded users, but at least there is a guarantee that data will not flow to users without proper clearances.

> **Mandatory and discretionary access controls are often combined.**

12.1.3 Covert Channels

The statement that mandatory access-control authorization service prevents lower-level users from gaining access to higher-level data is not completely true *in the face of active collusion between subjects at a higher level and subjects at a lower level.* The specific case we are considering here is a Trojan horse program (executable object) being unintentionally executed by a higher-level user. The Trojan horse program could be emailed by the malicious user to the higher-level user or placed in a system location (e.g., cool website) that would entice the higher-level user to download the program into their directory. The malicious uncleared user would have a corresponding program on the lower level trying to communicate with the Trojan horse program. This pair of programs attempting to covertly communicate with one another is depicted in Figure 12-3.

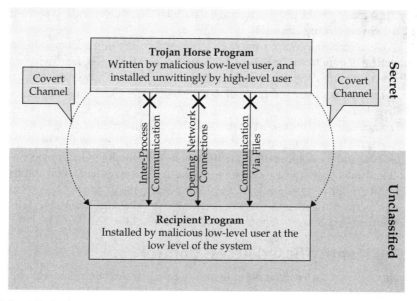

Figure 12-3   A Trojan horse program unwittingly installed at a high level by a high-level user (Secret) attempting to establish covert communication with a receiving program at the lower level (Unclassified)

All operating systems have a variety of ways that programs within the system can communicate with one another: inter-process communication channels, network connections between the processes, or writing to files that are commonly accessible to both programs. Such normal channels of communicating are controlled by the mandatory access control policy as part of the security design. So, when a program (subject) operating at the secret level attempts to open a two-way inter-process communication channel with another process (subject) operating at the unclassified level, the channel creation is blocked by the mandatory access control policy to prevent secret data from leaking through that channel. All such overt communication channels are controlled directly by the security policy of the system.

There are, however, unusual channels of communication analogous to prisoners banging on the pipes in Morse code to communicate with one another. The equivalent of the pipes is shared resources within the system, such as the disk drive. When one user is accessing a shared resource, other users are temporarily blocked from using it by the operating system to prevent a conflicting operation of the disk resource. The other users can detect their being blocked as an event. The event of being blocked or not blocked can be translated into a "1" or a "0," and a binary message can be signaled using the detection of these blocking events by programs at a lower level. These **covert storage channels** [KEMM02][HAIGH87] are depicted as dotted lines in Figure 12-3.

Similar communication channels can be created out of other resources and, as a result, messages can be sent at significant speeds in some cases [WU12]. In addition, covert channels can be created by adjusting the timing of events, such as manipulating the time spacing between sent network packets. For instance, if packets are normally sent at one packet per millisecond and the sending program delays it by 0.1 millisecond, that program is covertly signaling a "1." If the program delays it by 0.2 milliseconds, it is sending a "0." This is called a **covert timing channel**.

One can combine covert storage channels and covert timing channels and communicate a great deal of data from the Trojan horse operating at a higher sensitivity level to the malicious program receiving the data at the lower level. Such transmissions potentially bypass security controls and could violate security policy and cause the leakage of sensitive data.

The approach to this covert channel problem is for systems designers to eliminate as many covert channels as possible during the design and implementation process [KEMM02] and to monitor the remainder as best as possible to alarm on their usage, enabling the defender to shut down the offending processes (subjects) and catch the user attempting to subvert system security policy. Identifying all possible covert channels is extraordinarily difficult, and so there is always a risk that the attacker will find surprising covert channels that were neither prevented nor monitored.

12.1.4 Identity-Based Access Control

Completely separate from the decision as to whether access control is discretionary or mandatory is the issue of the basis of the control. Take an **embedded system**, for example. An embedded system is a system that is contained within a larger system such that there is no external (e.g., user) interface. Software that runs airplane avionics, your car electronics, or even your thermostat are all examples of embedded systems. In such systems, all subjects and all objects are set up when the system is deployed; there are only a small number of each; and *no new objects or subjects are needed.* In this case, one can easily imagine the system designers setting an access control matrix based solely on the identity of the subjects and objects in the system. Thus, very fine-grained control can be established. Furthermore, since no new objects can be created and since the access control matrix itself is static, the policy is a form of mandatory access control. *It is important to understand that there are two separate decisions—one is who gets to set the entries in the access control matrix, and the second regards the nature of the rows in the access control matrix, subject identities, or something broader, as we will discuss next.* Table 12-2 shows how the difference on what access rules are based on (identity versus attributes) and who decides the access (users versus system) results in four separate policy classes—each with strengths and weaknesses with respect to access control goals.

		Who Decides Access?	
		Users/Owners	**System**
Access Rules Based on What?	**Identity**	Identity-based discretionary access control (typically just called discretionary access control)	Identity-based mandatory access control (sometimes just called identity-based access control)
	Attributes	Attribute-based discretionary access control (typically just called discretionary access control)	Attribute-based mandatory access control (most often just called attribute-based access control)

Table 12-2   Types of access control based on two independent properties: (1) who decides access and (2) at what granularity are those decisions. The result is four separate policy classes.

12.1.5 Attribute-Based Access Control

Subjects   For dynamic systems, a mandatory **identity-based access control** scheme can quickly become completely unmanageable when you consider that the access control matrix could have hundreds of millions of cells. One can consolidate by grouping all of a user's subjects together and giving them the same access. One can consolidate further by logical groupings of users. Such groupings can follow organizational boundaries. For example, it is highly likely that most people in the marketing department need similar accesses to system resources—such as read-write to an access file of client lists, but no access to human resources or research and development files. This gives a quick way of putting everyone in groups and assigning access in large swathes of users with a handful of assignments to everyone in the group. Of course, there is a subgroup in each organization that has a management role, and so a separate group can be established that has exclusive access to performance appraisal files for their group. This means that users can belong to multiple groups. Figure 12-4 illustrates with a concrete example of how groups are formed.

In this example, there are three large groups of users: marketing, human resources, and research and development (R&D). Subgroups are created for users with management roles and system administration roles. Users 2, 7, and 12 are system administrators, and users 4, 8, and 12 are managers. User 12 has the highest level of access because they have access to both the manager and system administration subgroups. The lower part of the figure shows group-membership associations.

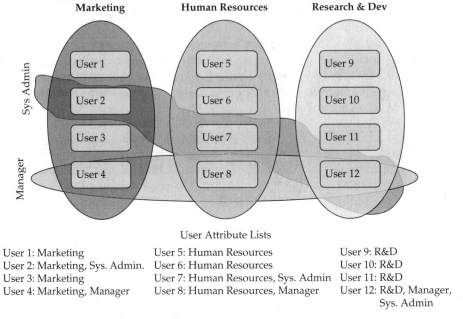

Figure 12-4   Formation of user attributes based on mission and function associations

The most obvious representation of a group is a sorted list of all users in the group. A decision to determine if someone is a member of a group is a matter of searching a sorted list which takes n * log(n) operations, where n is the length of the list (using the most efficient sorting algorithm, called *quicksort*). For a large organization, a group could have 10,000 users in it. Searching the sorted list would take 10,000 * 13,287 = 132,877 operations. That is a lot of work just to figure out if someone should be granted access to a resource! An alternative representation that yields a much more efficient lookup is to associate a list of groups with each user, indicating whether it is a member. This group-membership indicator can be thought of as an attribute of the user. Each membership that the user possesses is a different attribute. Figure 12-4 shows the translation of group association to attribute lists at the bottom of the figure.

Let us take a different sort of grouping as a concrete example—the level of trust an organization places in its users based on vetting processes that it puts them through. The U.S. Defense Department clearances have this characteristic—top secret being most trusted, secret trusted, confidential somewhat trusted, and uncleared not trusted. These clearance levels essentially form groups. So, one's clearance is an example of a user attribute and metadata associated with a user—creating a binding between the user and the attribute.

Objects   For the same reasons as for users, we want to group resources in a similar way, using similar attributes. For example, if we created a group attribute called Human-Resources for everyone in the Human Resources Department in an organization, then we could create an attribute with the exact same name for resources owned and controlled by the Human Resources Department. We could also create a couple of other attributes that are more specific, such as `Personally-Identifiable-Information` and `Protected-Health-Information`, each of which is governed by specific rules and privacy laws in the United States. Personally identifiable information (PII) is data that can be used to identify, contact, or locate a single person. Protected health information (PHI) is any data about health status, provision of health care, or payment for health care that can be linked to a specific individual. The definition gives the semantics or meaning of the attribute and therefore it would indicate which resources would receive this attribute. An example of resource labeling is shown in Figure 12-5.

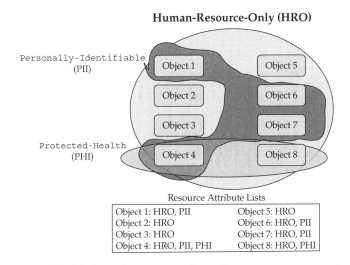

Figure 12-5   Example of the labeling of resource attributes (`Personally-Identifiable-Information`, `Protected-Health-Information`, and Human Resource Only) to the resources (Objects 1 through 8)

From a performance perspective, it is important that the number of attributes assigned to a given user does not approach the number of people in an organization. If that were to occur, the determination of whether a user has an attribute would be an equally slow search of the list of all of their assigned attributes. In most practical systems, users end up with about five or six attributes that reflect their organization mission, perhaps their suborganization mission, maybe a cross-organizational group, and their particular role or function within the organization.

Policy Rules   Now that we have learned about associating attributes with subjects and objects, there is one last important aspect of **attribute-based access control**—policy rules. A policy rule governs accesses between subject attributes and object attributes. For example, there might be a rule that "if subject clearance attribute = Secret and object attribute = Secret,

Confidential, or Unclassified, then access = read." You might notice that this is a rule that captures multilevel security's **simple security property**. Notice the attributes that can be read are explicitly enumerated. One could create a generic rule that states "if subject clearance attribute is-greater-than-or-equal-to object classification attribute, then access = read." This rule is more compact, but then also requires that the relationship "greater-than-or-equal-to" to be formally defined and applied whenever the generic rule is applied.

Policy rules are typically applied at the time of attempted access by a program that has control over the resources that are being sought. That program must retrieve the attributes of the accessing subject, the attributes of the object, and the policy rules that have been established for the resources that are being sought. Note that this means that those attribute associations *must be stored by the system (not by the users) and must possess very high integrity* because the system relies completely on the integrity of the enforcement of those attributes for deciding the access rights. Similarly, the association of the policy rules for the objects must have high integrity for the same reasons. We discuss these aspects of attribute integrity in the next sections.

> *Attribute associations with users must have high integrity.*

12.2 Attribute Management

In the previous section, we discussed the need for user attributes and noted that the association with users must have high integrity and thus neither the attributes nor the association are modifiable by the users themselves. So, who is authorized to create attributes and who is authorized to assign attributes to users?

12.2.1 User Attributes and Privilege Assignment

There needs to be an overall attribute manager who decides when new attributes are needed and creates those attributes. That person is the only one authorized to create new attributes. When a new attribute is created, one or more users are designated as authorized to assign those attributes to other users. So, even though management of the existence of attributes is centralized, the actual management is typically distributed to privileged users to manage. The sequence diagram for the process is shown in Figure 12-6.

The authorization to assign (and unassign) attributes to users is a highly privileged function since it grants access to large sets of sensitive data. Similarly, if some users accumulate too many attributes, they can become risky to the organization if they become an insider. Therefore, sometimes there can be policy rules about which combinations and number of attributes can be assigned to a given user. Also, if users have certain attributes, it may trigger an intrusion detection policy rule to monitor those users more closely than other users to ensure that they do not abuse their privilege. For example, user 12 in Figure 12-4 has accumulated three attributes, including the powerful system administrator

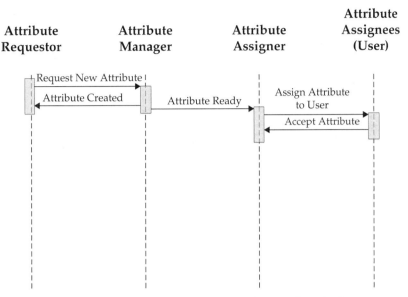

Figure 12-6   Attribution creation and assignment sequence diagram showing the process to create a new attribute and assign it to a user in preparation for making access control decisions based on that attribute

and manager attributes. User 12 bears watching more closely than the average user because of the level of damage that he (or an attacker hijacking his account) can do.

12.2.2 Resource Attribute Assignment

Those who create resources typically assign the attributes required to access those resources and the rules that govern access. Like user attributes, it is usually straightforward regarding how to assign resource attributes based on the mission that the data relates to, the laws and regulations that govern the data, and perhaps the role of the data in a larger mission flow.

12.2.3 Attribute Collection and Aggregation

Attribute data can be assigned in multiple systems throughout the enterprise, given the distributed nature of the attributes themselves. This means that the data, at some point, needs to be collected and aggregated in one place for analysis and distribution. There are typically multiple authoritative sources for different sets of attributes because different organizations may have purview over different types of attributes. For example, the Human Resource Department might have purview over personnel-privileged attributes, whereas the Research and Development Department may control attributes for handling sensitive data about future product releases. The collection and aggregation process is shown on the left side of Figure 12-7.

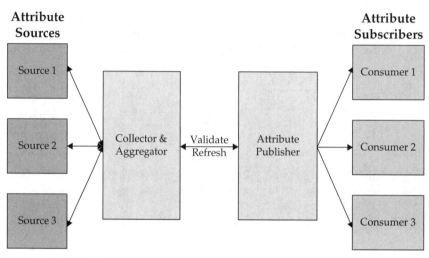

Figure 12-7 Attribute collection and aggregation of sources (left), validation and refreshing of attributes (center), and the publication and distribution process to consumers (right)

We noted in the previous section that attribute data and its association with each user must be of the highest integrity because *a successful attack on attribute data could give the attacker complete access to system resources.* This means that the attribute assignment systems must

- Be highly trustworthy to perform their functions correctly
- Be non-bypassable
- Be tamperproof
- Require strong authentication for the users creating attributes
- Require strong authentication for the users assigning attributes
- Require strong authentication and high integrity in communicating attributes with other trustworthy entities
- Ensure that their attribute data must be syntactically correct
- Ensure that their attribute data must be semantically correct

> **A successful attack on attribute data can subvert all access control.**

We have come across most of these concepts in previous chapters, so their interpretations should be clear to the reader. The syntactic and semantic correctness of attribute data requires a bit more explanation in this context and will be discussed in the next section.

12.2.4 Attribute Validation

There is an abstract space of all valid attributes, identified typically by their unique name. The authoritative source for the list of such attributes is the attribute management system described in the previous sections. Each attribute has a set of valid values that it can take on. For example, the user clearance attribute value can be defined to take on the values "Top Secret," "Secret," "Confidential," "Uncleared." We further specify that a user can only have one of these values at a time. A valid attribute assignment is a pair of the form (<user digital identity>, <attribute name>:attribute value). For example, the pair (JoeSmith, Clearance:"Secret") indicates that the user identity of Joe Smith has an attribute called clearance tied to his identity and the value of that clearance is "secret." Figure 12-8 shows an example of attribute definition and assignment.

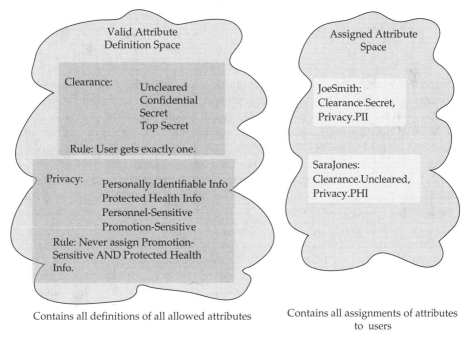

Figure 12-8   Valid attribute *definition* space (left) versus *assigned* attribute space that uses defined attributes (right)

Syntactic Validity   **Syntactic validity** means that the data conforms to the grammar and format specified for the data set. What could go wrong? Here is a partial list:

- The user digital identity may not exist in the set of valid identities.
- The attribute name may not exist in the set of valid attribute names.
- The attribute value may not exist in the set of values that the attribute can take on.

- The pair may not have a proper header and separator (e.g., a comma) between them.
- The checksum in the header may not be valid, indicating possible tampering or bit errors.

All such grammar and format errors should be checked at all stages of the attribute assignment: generation, storage, propagation, aggregation, and distribution. Cross-checking at all stages makes it easier to detect and correct errors when they first occur and damage is minimal. As a concrete example, if an authoritative attribute source for personnel private data, such as a human resource database, puts out a record that says (Sara Jones, Privacy: "PIJ") when they really meant (Sara Jones, Privacy, "PII"), this typographical error needs to be caught immediately or at least as soon as possible. *Attribute syntax errors can and do happen. Anticipate them; detect them and fix them at all stages.*

> *Attribute syntax errors can cause major, yet subtle, disruptions.*

Semantic Validity   **Semantic validity** addresses whether the data is actually true. If the system asserts that Bob has a "secret" clearance, there is meaning behind that statement. It means that some authorized official decided that Bob has a valid need to access "secret" data; submitted Bob to a well-defined vetting process; Bob successfully passed the vetting process; Bob was granted a "secret" clearance; and that "secret" clearance has not since expired or been revoked for some reason. That is a lot to verify. The system clearly cannot dispatch investigators to review Bob's security paperwork and spot-check the granting process upon every access request. Verifying that Bob is still employed at the organization and that his name is not on a revocation list is in fact practical, and such fast checks can and should be done wherever possible. *Each attribute must have a formally specified meaning, and the assigners must be accountable to ensure that all assignment conditions are met.* Furthermore, a process must be in place to quickly determine when the conditions are no longer met (e.g., the person left the organization or moved to a different division and his mission changed). It is also useful if each specification states ways in which the information can be partially corroborated periodically, at least in a sampled fashion (e.g. "Hey, your system told me that Bob is cleared 'secret'; can you please verify that fact today?").

Freshness   Attributes that were once valid can become stale, meaning that it is no longer true. This happens when people change names (e.g., people who get married can choose to have a legal surname change), leave organizations, move around, or are ejected from an organization for misbehavior. Some attribute data is more volatile than others, and the damage from stale data varies depending on the nature of the attribute and the associated policy rules. For example, if a person is fired for criminal behavior and is escorted out of the building in handcuffs, even though their identity certificate and all their attributes are no longer valid, they can do no damage from a jail cell. Similarly, if a highly trusted person moves from one organization to another and changes mission, does a one- or two-day delay in removing attributes pose significant system risk? *Deciding how much time and energy to* *put into rapidly refreshing data is an important judgment call that should be based on the risk that comes from delaying a refresh.*

> ### Fresh attribute data is important to access control.

The collection and aggregation system must be given a sense of what it means for data to be stale from the definition of each attribute. The system then must recheck that definition periodically and ensure that it is met. If not, the collection and aggregation system must cease distributing the stale data and seek an update from the source.

Figure 12-7 summarizes the role and processing of attribute collection, aggregation, and validation in the middle part of the figure, taking inputs from the assigners that create authoritative sources and distributing attributes to subscribers, which is described in the next section.

12.2.5 Attribute Distribution

Once attributes are assigned, collected, aggregated, and validated, they then need to be made available to the programs that make access decisions using attributes. This is called attribute publication (or distribution) to those that subscribe to (or consume) those attributes. The subscribers or consumers often perform policy decisions that will be discussed in the next section. Attribute publication (or distribution) is shown on the right-hand side of Figure 12-7.

We have come across a similar notion in authentication based on public-key cryptography in which a user's public key needs to be published so that other users can use it to verify identity. Therefore, abstractly, *a user's public key is essentially an attribute and its distribution is a type of attribute distribution.*

> ### Public keys can be thought of as user attributes.

Access control decisions to data are frequent and time-sensitive, so

- Attribute distribution points must be as close as possible to the consumers.
- The service itself needs to be fast to maximize performance on the first access request.

In addition, in the round-trip time required to request a subject's attributes over the network to a network service, a computer can perform millions of operations. Therefore, programs making access control decisions must cache the subject attributes so that subsequent accesses by that entity do not have to incur the delay of an attribute fetch over the network. **Attribute caching** is typically effective because of a phenomenon called **locality of reference**, which means that if a program references an object once (in this case, seeks access), it is highly likely to reference it many times within a brief time span. Thus, tremendous speedups are possible using caching strategies.

Attribute caching has a drawback. If an attribute value is updated centrally, the cached value can become obsolete. We saw in the previous section that the collection and aggregation system must monitor for staleness indicators and update the attributes as required so that further distributions are fresh. What about the attributes that have already been distributed? Two possible solutions are to

- Cause published attributes to expire, requiring the subscribers to get updated values from the attribute distribution service, or

- Keep track of all subscribers and push updated values to them.

12.3 Digital Policy Management

Digital policy management is about managing the policy rules associated with **attribute-based access control**. We use the term digital policy to distinguish policy specified and used in computers from policy stated in natural languages by people as derived from laws, rules, and regulations. Policy rules are conditional statements comparing subject attributes and object attributes, and these statements determine allowed access rights between the subject and object in question. Policy rules are in the form of "if A and B or C then allow access D," where A, B, and C are logical expressions that compare attributes, and D is some access such as read, write, or execute. The comparative statements are of the form "subject's attribute list contains X attribute of value $x1$" and "object's attribute list contains Y attribute of value $y1$". The comparative statements are logically related by standard logic operations of AND, OR, and NOT. Returning to the standard classification-clearance schema, a policy rule expressing simple security (see Section 8.4.1) might state "If subject's clearance attribute is greater-than-or-equal-to an object's classification attribute" then permit "read" access right else permit "null". This rule is shorthand for a much longer explicit rule that says:

"if (subject's clearance is "Top Secret" AND

(object's classification is "Top Secret" OR object's classification is "Secret" OR object's classification is "Confidential" OR object's classification is "Unclassified")) OR

(subject's clearance is "Secret" AND (object's classification is "Secret" OR object's classification is "Confidential" OR object's classification is "Unclassified")) OR

(subject's clearance is "Confidential" AND (object's classification is "Confidential" OR object's classification is "Unclassified")) OR

(subject's clearance is "Uncleared" AND (object's classification is "Unclassified")) then permit "read" else permit "null.""

12.3.1 Policy Specification

Who is authorized to specify policy rules? The authorized persons are called **policy authors**, and they are granted the authorization when new **resource abstractions** are added to the system through a policy administration service that has the same foundational status as the attribute management service. A resource abstraction simply means that there is a software program that acts as a reference monitor for a set of newly created resources such as files or databases. We call this the **protecting subsystem** for the resources that are encapsulated by it.

Often, policy is specified in layers by separate policy author types: a universal policy that applies to all access control within an enterprise, and an owner policy that can further restrict that control as determined by the mission owners of the resources. The first layer must always be present and cannot be overridden by the resource owners. This mandatory layering is essential in policy authoring. Like cryptography, security policies can be complex and difficult to get right. Policies need significant analysis and testing. Therefore, authors should not be given the option of overriding well-thought-out mandatory policy because doing so is extremely risky.

For example, an organization may have a multilevel security policy in place for their enterprise. This is a universal policy. The resource owners can create additional rules and related attributes to limit access beyond this universal policy. This relationship between the two classes of policy should be enforced by the policy authoring subsystem. Figure 12-9 shows the policy authoring from multiple sources on the left-hand side of the diagram.

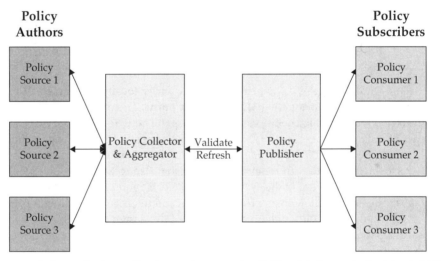

Figure 12-9   Policy authoring, collection, and aggregation (left); validation and refreshing (middle); and publication process to policy consumers (right)

12.3.2 Policy Distribution

Policy distribution refers to the communication from the policy authoring service to the entities that must evaluate those policies at access-request time to decide how to grant access to a requesting entity. Like attributes, policies may be updated, and so there is a question of freshness of policies that have been distributed to consuming decision entities. Therefore, a policy distribution system must have a means of advising consumers storing those policies that the policy is stale and needs updating. Like attributes, distributed policies can have expirations on them, which then trigger the consumer to check for updates. Alternatively, the policy distributor can keep track of all consumers of every policy and push a revised policy upon update. Because human policies tend not to change very often, digital policies tend to be much less volatile than attribute assignments. Therefore, the requirements and risks of policy distribution delay are different from attribute distribution delay and must be considered when deciding how best to address the freshness issue. Figure 12-9 shows the policy collection, aggregation, validation, and refreshing aspects in the center of the diagram. The figure also shows the distribution of policy on the right-hand side of the diagram.

12.3.3 Policy Decision

Policy decision refers to the process of evaluating access policy rules with respect to a given access attempt by a specific subject and a specific object. Policy decisions are triggered by a subject seeking access through a protecting subsystem. The protecting subsystem must evaluate the policy to determine access. Notice that nothing forces the protecting subsystem from triggering the evaluation, which is a highly security-critical function. This means that *the protecting subsystem must be demonstrated to function correctly and always perform the evaluation; otherwise, it could simply decide on its own whether to grant access, which would violate specified policy.*

> *Policy decisions must be demonstrated to be always invoked.*

Policy evaluation can be done in one of two places: locally or remotely. We call the place where the decision is made the **policy decision point**. The protecting subsystem can call an external remote policy decision service across the network. That service can handle all the issues of policy freshness and all the complexities of properly evaluating the policy rules. The downside is that there is a long network round-trip delay in getting an answer.

Performance issues with remote policy decisions led to the alternative approach of the protecting subsystem doing the evaluation itself. This requires the protecting subsystem to subscribe to the policy, ensure that it is fresh, and to execute it correctly. Correct execution is the most difficult and risky aspect of the design choice to gain the speedup of local evaluation. This risk can be mitigated by using a standard language for policy specification and a standard embeddable software module for performing this evaluation. The Extensible Access Control Markup Language [OASI13] is an example of such a language, and there are several execution engines available for use to ensure standardized evaluation [LIU08].

12.3.4 Policy Enforcement

Finally, after the policy is evaluated and a specific access determined, the protecting subsystem must enforce that decision. The location where enforcement is done is sometimes called the **policy enforcement point**. The policy enforcement process interprets the granted access and enforces the intent behind the specified access. It must take care to grant access to only the objects requested and not ancillary data. For example, to respond to a user request, a protecting subsystem may query a database resource using its own privileges. The protecting subsystem may then need to filter out some of the query response due to its interpretation of the meaning of the access granted to the requesting user.

Generally, policy enforcement processing must be fast. Therefore, similar to attribute caching, a decision-caching strategy can be employed to gain substantial speedup. Such speedups come at the trade-off cost of delaying decision updates due to policy or attribute changes. Techniques already discussed would have to be applied to ensure freshness of cache entries. *Like policy decision processing, policy enforcement processing is equally security-critical and must be proven to be correct, non-bypassable, and tamperproof.*

> ### *Correct policy enforcement is security-critical.*

The entire policy decision and policy enforcement process is shown in Figure 12-10 and described step-by-step as follows:

Step 1.   An application, on behalf of user ID, requests read access to resource 1.

Step 2.   The policy decision function of the protecting subsystem ensures that its policy for its resources is the most current policy by checking the policy publication service. The connecting line in the figure is shown as dotted to indicate that the check will not likely be performed on every access attempt, but rather will be done periodically or will be pushed upon update. Note that steps 2, 3, and 4 are conceptually simultaneous because those steps are simply retrieving the data needed to make an attribute-based policy decision.

Step 3.   The policy decision function fetches the user attributes of the user that is seeking access. It does so by calling the attribute publication service.

Step 4.   The policy decision function similarly fetches the attributes of the resources being sought as input into the policy decision process. Although the attributes are depicted as being attached to the resource itself (bottom), it could also be part of the attribute publication service.

Step 5.   The policy decision function now has all the information it needs to evaluate the policy for the resources it is protecting. It either does it locally or does an external service call, as shown in the figure, to the policy decision service. The connection is shown as a dashed line to indicate that this call is not always present, depending on the implementation choice.

Step 6.   The policy decision function at this point has the access right for the user to the requested resources. It passes the decision and processing over to the policy enforcement aspect of the protecting subsystem to interpret and execute the access right.

Step 7.   The policy enforcement subsystem then accesses the resource, obtains the data, and possibly transforms or filters the data according to its interpretation of the access granted.

Step 8.   The protecting subsystem then returns the data to the requesting application (not shown in Figure 12-10). As mentioned, this decision can then be cached and used for subsequent accesses by the same user on the same resource.

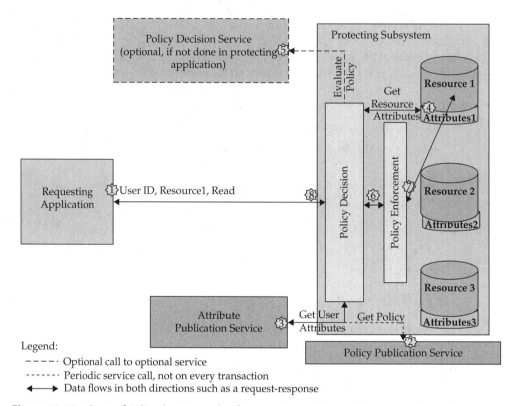

Figure 12-10 Steps of policy decision and enforcement processing within a protecting subsystem

12.4 Authorization Adoption Schemas

Creating an authorization cybersecurity service is only the first step. The authorization service must be integrated into all of the protecting subsystems that protect all the system resources that require protection. This means that an organization must

- Identify the resources that need protecting
- Encapsulate them with a protecting subsystem
- Prove reference monitor properties for that protecting subsystem
- Properly integrate policy decision making either remotely or locally
- Properly design and implement policy execution
- Ensure that its sources of identity are trustworthy and channels to them are secure

12.4.1 Direct Integration

Authorization integration poses a substantial task list that costs time and resources to accomplish. The protecting subsystem can be an existing subsystem that already services the resources or a new subsystem. It can be custom developed by an organization, free and open-source software, or a commercial product. In the first case, the developers must work closely with cybersecurity engineers to carefully accomplish the task list. *Software engineers without security training are not qualified to perform the requisite cybersecurity engineering.* In the case of open-source software, the system owners must learn the software well enough to make the requisite modifications carefully—another skill that is less common among developers than one would like.

> *Integrating security services requires specialized training.*

12.4.2 Indirect Integration

In the case of commercial software, the software consumer must either convince the vendor to make the required changes (a difficult proposition) or encapsulate the commercial product in a custom protecting subsystem that performs the access control functions. This is typically called a proxy because the custom protecting subsystem is *standing in* for the commercial product in performing the required access control functions.

12.4.3 Alternative Integration

There is one vestigial authorization integration mode that is important to mention. It is one focused around authentication. Authentication certificates often carry both implicit and explicit user attribute data. An example of implicit attributes is the certificate's issuing authority. That issuing authority often implies that those that possess the certificate have undergone a defined vetting process, have executed nondisclosure agreements, and are therefore members of a community that is served by that issuing authority. Explicit information might include a user's organization, nationality, and the nature of one's affiliation with their organization (employee, contractor, etc.). All of this information can be used to make basic authorization decisions. For example, it may be that certain data is not so sensitive that everyone in the company can't see it, but the company would prefer that competitors not access the information. A **certificate** that contains organization information can suffice for this level of authorization decision without an appeal to the attributes distribution system. It is a rougher granularity authorization process to be sure, but much of an organization's information does not need fine-grained controlled access. *In addition, this authorization process can be a useful fallback even for critical data if the primary authorization system becomes unavailable for a time.* To plan and accept such a fallback is a matter of a risk trade-off decision.

> *Authorization processes should have fallbacks in case of failure.*

Conclusion

This chapter extended identity authentication to establishing the actions that a user is allowed to perform on a system. Together, authentication and authorization form a foundation for cybersecurity capabilities. In the next chapter, we transition to a sequence of three chapters that discuss how attacks that are not prevented can be detected. An attack detection capability creates a second layer of defense that begins to weave a defense architecture.

To summarize:

- Discretionary access control is useful, but does not prevent the leakage of sensitive data.
- Mandatory access control determines access based on rules about user and data attributes, but may need finer-grained controls as well.
- Identity-based access control provides fine-grained control, but can be unmanageable.
- Attribute-based access control offers scalable access control at the expense of granularity.
- Attribute management is a security-critical function because attributes drive policy decisions.
- Freshness ensures distributed attributes and policy data remains current.
- Digital policy is the set of rules that governs access to resources.
- Like attributes, policies have a life cycle that needs to be managed.
- Application of digital policy is separated into a decision process and an enforcement process.
- This separation facilitates policy updating without having to change software.
- Policy decisions and enforcement are critical and must meet reference monitor properties.
- There are many alternatives for integrating authorization into protecting subsystems.

Questions

1. What does access control manage?
2. What's an access control matrix and what is it made up of? How large are they?
3. Describe how discretionary access control works and its strengths and weaknesses.
4. Describe mandatory access control and how it counters the weakness of discretionary access control. What does it trade off for this strength?
5. How can discretionary access control be combined? If one permits access and the other denies it, how should the conflict be resolved?
6. What type of policy is type enforcement as discussed in previous chapters?

7. What is a covert channel and how does it relate to the goals of mandatory access control?

8. What are the two types of covert channels and how do they work? Give examples for each that are not included in this chapter.

9. How does one address the problem posed by covert channels?

10. Is identity-based access control the same thing as discretionary access control? If not, how are they different? What fundamental question does each answer about the nature of the access control?

11. In what sort of system might identity-based control be manageable?

12. What are the three aspects of attribute-based control?

13. Why are group lists not the most efficient way to implement subject attributes? What does this statement assume about the number of attributes that a subject is assigned?

14. Who assigns attributes to users and how is this authorized?

15. What do we mean by the semantics of defined attributes? Give two examples.

16. What is an access control rule and how does it relate to policy specification?

17. How do rules affect the semantics of attributes?

18. Why might there be policy rules about assignment of certain combinations of attributes to any given user? Where might such policy rules be enforced?

19. How do resource attribute assignments relate to subject attribute assignments?

20. What is attribute collection and aggregation and why is it important? What are desirable properties of network connections between the aggregators and the authoritative resources? Why?

21. What could an attacker do if they gained control of the attribute assignment process? What about if they gained control of the attribute distribution process?

22. How does an identity-public-key pairing in a certificate differ from an identity-attribute pairing in the attribute management subsystem?

23. List the eight properties that must be true of attribute assignment subsystems, and provide a short rationale for each requirement in terms of what would happen if the requirement were not met.

24. Define the two types of attribute validation and why they are both important. Which is more important? Why?

25. What does it mean when we say that attribute consumers often cache attributes that they need? Why would they do that? What issues arise from doing so? How are those issues resolved?

26. What is attribute distribution and why is it needed? Can anyone subscribe to the attribute distribution service? Why or why not?

27. What form do digital policy rules take?

28. Write a digital policy rule for the multilevel security *-property discussed in a previous chapter.

29. Who can specify digital policy? What are the two classes of specifiers?

30. What happens when data-owner–specific policy contradicts universal policy required by the organization? Where is that detected and resolved?

31. Why is policy enforcement separated from policy decision in cybersecurity architecture? What advantages does it bring?

32. What is the trade-off between local and remote policy decision making by the protecting subsystem?

33. What is a protecting subsystem and what must be proven about its properties? What do we mean when we say it encapsulates its resources?

34. What is a way of avoiding the complexity of the protecting subsystem performing the policy decision function? How does this help?

35. What are the three different authorization adoption schemes and under what circumstances would you apply each?

36. What conditions might require the use of attribute assignment revocation?

13 Detection Foundation

Overview

Learning Objectives

- Explain the synergy between prevention and detection techniques.
- Enumerate and describe the seven layers of detection systems.
- Define feature selection and its pivotal role in attack detection.
- Explain how feature extraction relates to feature selection.

- Define event selection and how it relates to a given attack and selected feature.
- Distinguish between event detection and attack-related events.
- Describe how attack detection works and what a false positive and false negative are.
- Discuss the issues of attack classification and the role of probability.
- Explain attack alarms and the human element of attack detection.
- Describe the nature and importance of sensor operational performance characteristics.

It's hard to defend against what you can't see. An honest report to most organization leaders should be something like this: "The good news is that we have seen no attacks today. The bad news; we are blind to most attacks that matter." Detection is an essential arrow in the defense quiver. This chapter covers the important foundations of attack detection. This foundation is then extended into the next chapter to discuss how to engineer cybersecurity attack detection systems.

> *You can't defend against what you can't see.*

13.1 The Role of Detection

If attack prevention were perfect, we would not need attack detection. The reality is that attack prevention is far from perfect. Attacks will succeed because

- No preventative measures cover that aspect of the attack space.
- The preventative measures were not deployed in the right places within the system.
- The right preventative measures were not deployed for a given system.
- The preventative measure failed.
- The preventative measure itself was successfully attacked.

> *Detection is needed because prevention is imperfect.*

There are holes in the **attack coverage** of the sum of all existing prevention measures. One might be tempted to map those holes and simply detect attacks in the holes. This synergistic approach is depicted in Figure 13-1. *Mapping the defense strengths and weaknesses is always a good idea, for defender and attacker alike.* Knowing how the strengths and weaknesses align is also essential. At the same time, because of the long list of reasons why attackers will succeed against a prevention-only system, it is important to consider how to cover the entire attack space, not just the perceived holes in the prevention capabilities.

> *Map defense strengths and weaknesses.*

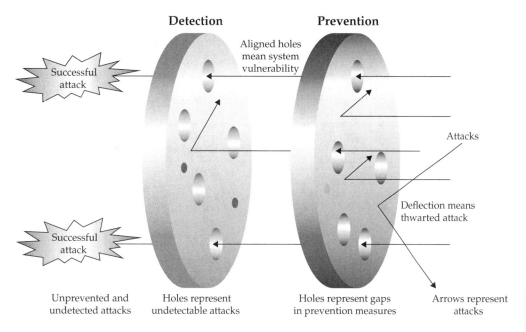

Figure 13-1   Synergy between prevention and detection measures in terms of covering the attack space, represented by the attack arrows traversing from right to left. Aligned holes represent system vulnerabilities.

Historically, a first step in **attack detection** was to simply see what could be seen with the capabilities and tools that already existed—primarily system **audit logs**. It turned out that system audit logs could detect a good variety of different attacks, including attempts to guess passwords from the login interface, malicious file system activity, and malicious system process activity. Essentially, anything that operating systems were monitoring for health and performance reasons, in which attacks might manifest, had the potential of being seen. This was a boon to those who were involved early in the systems to detect attack. Unfortunately, it was also a limiting trap because system audit logs could only go so far. They could not detect attacks above the operating system abstraction (e.g., middleware and application software) or below the operating system abstraction (device drivers, device controllers, processor firmware, etc. See Figure 6-3). Sometimes having an existing solution in hand can blind one to the entire space of solution possibilities and requirements.

13.2 How Detection Systems Work

Before proceeding, we must cover how detection systems actually work. There are several important layers, as shown in Figure 13-2. *Truly understanding the nature of attack detection requires an understanding of all seven layers.*

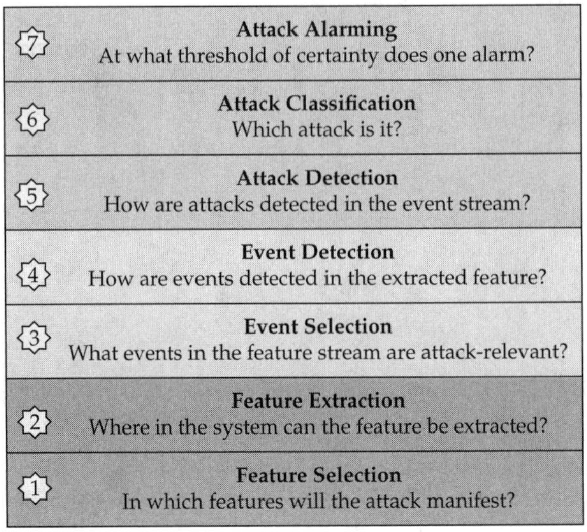

Figure 13-2   Intrusion detection system layers of abstraction. The layers are ordered into three different groupings: features at the foundation, events built on features in the middle, and attacks at the top.

First, notice that there are three groupings of layers. The foundational layers concern **features**—aspects of the system operation where attacks might manifest. The second layer grouping involves **attack-relevant** events—sequences in the monitored features that are relevant to detecting attacks. The third and top layer involves the actual attacks. Too many cybersecurity engineers focus only on the top layer without an appreciation of the importance of the underlying layers and how they contribute to detection success and failures [TAN02]. Each intrusion detection system layer is discussed, starting from the bottom and proceeding to the top layer in Figure 13-2.

> *Understanding attack detection requires understanding all layers.*

13.3 Feature Selection

In the first and foundational abstraction layer, the fundamental question is how an attack will manifest. What is useful about this conceptual layer is that it opens the mental aperture to the entire system and all of its layers of abstraction, not just the operating system and the application layer in which most intrusion detection systems operate. **Feature selection** is typically done offline through analysis of each instance of an attack in an **attack taxonomy** for which one is trying to gain coverage. As an example, a worm may manifest in the operating system's active process table (a table of running processes that the operating system keeps track of). The active process table becomes a feature to look at for this attack.

13.3.1 Attack Manifestation in Features

Each attack may manifest in multiple features (called a **one-to-many mapping**) that can be combined to increase certainty in attack detection. For example, a worm might manifest in the application layer in a mail program as an unusual volume of outgoing emails, at the operating system layer as an odd pattern of network socket utilization, and at the network device driver as an uncharacteristic burst of data to an uncharacteristically wide variety of destinations. Similarly, multiple attacks can all manifest in a given feature (called a **many-to-one mapping**), though the events (discussed next) may be different for each. For example, an insider attempting unauthorized access to protected resources (such as sensitive human resources files) and a Trojan horse trying to discover sensitive data would manifest in the logs of an authorization system in the form of multiple failed authorization attempts.

13.3.2 Manifestation Strength

The mapping of an attack to a feature may have different strengths representing the degree and clarity of the manifestation. The clarity of the manifestation is analogous to signal quality in communication (such as static on your radio when you dial in a radio station). So, we say that a strong and clear manifestation is a strong **attack signal** and a weak manifestation is a weak attack signal. There will be a bit more on **signal processing theory** in the next chapter.

As an example, a **virus** that does not change (nonmutating) has what is a called a **signature string**—a sequence of bits that is unique to that viral code. So, before newly imported code is executed, the file can be checked for that attack signature string. If the signature string appears, that would be a strong signal or indication that the virus is present. On the other hand, if the feature involves network activity and unusual characteristics of outgoing traffic (as described earlier), those features could be confused with benign and perfectly authorized activity (such as an all-hands email to everyone on staff announcing that everyone has the rest of the day off in recognition of National Pi Day), or it could be confused with a variety of different kinds of attacks.

It becomes clear that part of *the feature selection process is to define exactly how each attack will manifest within that feature, how it will be distinguished from normal activity, and how it will be distinguished from other attacks.* These notions of one-to-many mapping, many-to-one mapping, and mapping strengths are summarized graphically in Figure 13-3.

> *Intrusion detection starts with good feature selection.*

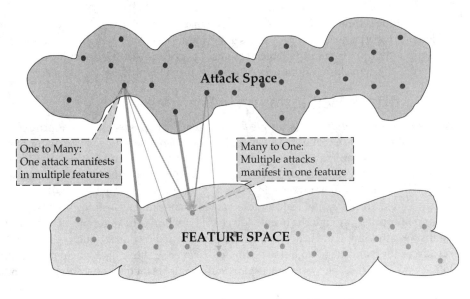

- Attacks like buffer overflow attack or a man-in-the-middle attack
- Portions of the attack space without dots represent attacks not yet discovered
- Features like opening files or log of access requests
- Portions of the feature space without dots represent potential features not yet selected

Figure 13-3 Attacks map to and manifest in the feature space. One attack can manifest in many features (called one-to-many); many attacks can differently manifest in the same feature (called many-to-one). The thickness of the line represents how strongly the attack manifests in that feature.

13.3.3 Mapping Attacks to Features

At end of the process of analyzing all (or at least a representative subset) of the attacks in the attack space, one ends up with each and every attack mapped to one or more features. Each mapping has a description of the strength of the mapping and a description of how the attack is likely to manifest and how it is to be differentiated in that feature. There will be some features to which no attacks map.

13.3.4 Criteria for Selection

One might imagine that the next step would be to instrument each of the features. This **instrumentation** of a feature is called a sensor, though a sensor may end up collecting data on multiple features. Proceeding in this way is not practical for several reasons. Some features may be redundant and therefore unnecessary. Collecting data from some features can cost significant system resources and performance, so ideally, *the attack-detection designers should choose the minimum set of features that have the highest aggregate attack signal and the most reliable attack detection potential. Because some important features may not be selected for cost or practical reasons, it is important to keep this analysis out of the hands of an attacker; it gives them a map of precisely where the defender is blind.*

13.4 Feature Extraction

Once the analysis of the foundational feature selection layer is completed and a cybersecurity professional has a list of features that they want to monitor, the question arises as to where and how they can be monitored in the system and, by extension, whether it is practical to do so. The question of where depends on the nature of the feature and at what layer of abstraction it resides. For example, if one wanted to monitor all of the instructions issued to the CPU, it cannot be done at the application level. It may be possible to do it at the operating system level, but that would potentially exclude CPU instructions issued below the operating system level. Ideally, this would be monitored directly in the CPU instruction cache. The question of how concerns whether it is possible to obtain the feature data without a significant modification to the software or hardware and without a significant impact on performance and functionality. The act of making system modifications to monitor the feature is called **instrumenting** the system.

In the example of the active process feature mentioned in the previous section, the way to extract (i.e., monitor) this feature is to query the operating system's active process table. Most operating systems have this as a built-in capability so that users and system operators can diagnose and correct problems such as hung processes (those that are no longer responding to commands and thus are probably crashed).

Note that some attacks will actually go in and modify the operating system process table listing functionality (an example of a system integrity attack, as mentioned in Section 3.5) *to specifically hide the running malicious process to intentionally reduce the likelihood of detection*. Therefore, the feature extraction designer must consider such attacks and develop countermeasures. That being said, most operating systems have more fundamental process management functionality on which the process-listing functionality is built. The feature extractor would be more robust if it used the most foundational building blocks within the operating system and ran consistency checks to ensure that it is getting a valid data stream.

13.5 Event Selection

Once a feature is selected and the system is instrumented to monitor that feature, one must analyze the resulting stream of data to determine what events in the feature stream are attack-relevant (event selection layer). Just because an attack might manifest in the data stream does not mean that all of the data in that stream is attack-relevant data. In fact, under ideal situations where prevention mechanisms are working well, only a tiny fraction of the data stream will represent possible attack-relevant sequences. During the original analysis of the attacks of concern and the identification of the feature, the detection designers would also specify the nature of manifestation in the monitored feature, not just the general notion that it would somehow manifest—but how precisely it would manifest in terms of events. An event in this case is one or more discrete outputs from the feature detector. For example, if one were monitoring instructions sent to the CPU as a feature, the stream of data might look something like this (given in high-level pseudocode)

```
Load location x with value y
Add 5 to location x
Compare location X with 500
If Result < 500, JUMP to first instruction
Otherwise EXIT
```

Each instruction can be taken as an event, or sequences of two or more instructions can be taken as an event, or only instructions of a certain class (say, input and output instructions) can be taken as events from this stream. In the example instruction sequence, we might take only memory loading instructions as potentially attack-relevant. Notice that load instructions happen all the time in normal programs and are usually completely benign, so that event alone cannot indicate an attack, but it could be flagged as an important event to be further examined higher up in the stack or to create a history state that then looks for another command within some number of instructions that could indicate malicious activity.

Modern computer systems use heavy multitasking, switching often between process threads that are executing. This makes the task of finding attack threads very challenging. Also, multitasking is generally non-deterministic (meaning that the ordering and slices of execution can vary depending on what is happening within the computer). This non-determinism makes testing very difficult, creating potential opportunities of attack. It also makes it nearly impossible to have sequence repeatability, so circumstances that created an event sequence containing attack events will be hard to properly investigate.

13.6 Event Detection

In the previous layers, we established which events are attack-relevant. In this layer, these events are detected in the extracted feature and reported to the next higher layer. This is called **event detection**. Recall that these events are not necessarily attacks, but rather evidence that suggests that there *may* be attacks going on that are worth exploring. In rare instances, when the event is itself a 100 percent indicator of an attack, such as is the case when matching a virus signature, then no further analysis is needed. In most cases, further analysis is needed.

13.7 Attack Detection

The event-detection layer reports bits of evidence from the event stream to the attack-detection layer that can be assembled into a case for the existence of an attack (analogous to the case that a police inspector builds for a crime having been committed by a person). That case can be simple, such as the detection of a virus signature string, or highly complex, as might be the case for a zero-day attack in which there are dozens of weak signals from many different sensors. Often, a correlation (connection of related information together) among different weak attack signal events is required [AMOR99].

Just as in the case of crime investigation, the evidence is not always certain and must be weighed carefully. Reporting normal activity as an attack can waste valuable resources in tracking it down and can disrupt mission and operations. Similarly, failing to report suspected attacks could have bad outcomes in the same way as letting criminals go free to commit other crimes. Once the evidence reaches a certain **alert** threshold—a value that is often adjustable as a parameter—an attack is reported to the next higher layer, attack classification.

13.8 Attack Classification

The **attack classification** layer receives the attack reports from the attack detection layer. The task of automated attack classification is difficult and quite limited in current systems—supplemented by smart human operators. We can expect this to improve over time, but the problem remains complex.

It helps to think of the underlying attack detection layer as hundreds of parallel attack detectors. Any subset of these can be going off at any given time, at various levels of confidence. So, detector one could be saying: "Hey, I think attack #37 is going on with a probability of 52 percent" and detector two, at the same time, could be saying: "Well, I think attack #422 is going on with a probability of 75 percent." Why would that happen? It could happen because many attacks share similar characteristics, making it hard to unambiguously determine which attack is going on. In the previous fictitious example, there are two competing hypotheses—three if you count the low, but non-zero, probability that both attacks are happening coincidentally. In addition to this ambiguity, there are often multiple instances of attack detection across a span of time. Therefore, one could theoretically receive hundreds of reports within a span of minutes that are really about the same attack. Attack classification output requires consolidation of events for human consumption, which happens at the top of the next higher layer.

13.9 Attack Alarming

The reports from attack classification come into this top-most layer where a human defense operator interfaces to the system. An **attack alarm** is a report from the system to a human that indicates that there is enough attack signal to warrant human investigation and possible intervention. Human operators have only so much time and patience in a day to analyze and react to attack alarms. If the system reports too many false alarms, human operators will simply start to ignore all attack alarms, like the boy who cried wolf in the children's story by the same name. Hence, it is important that cybersecurity operators monitoring intrusion detection systems only deal with likely attacks. When attacks are reported by the system, the system should provide as much information about the attack alarm as possible to minimize analysis time.

13.10 Know Operational Performance Characteristics for Sensors

Each sensor, the mechanism monitoring a selected feature, has a performance characteristic for a set of performance metrics that include

- Resources consumed to accomplish its data collection task under various configurations and settings.
- Resources consumed under a spectrum of **system loads** (levels and types of high usage of system resources such as computational resources, storage, and network bandwidth), particularly when close to the limits of those resources.
- Resources consumed under a variety of attack loads (differing types and quantities of attacks going on within a system).

- Typical outputs under various system loads.

- Robustness against various kinds of attack.

- Their potential failure modes and what happens in these modes.

- How one recovers a failed sensor and what data and functionality are lost in the process.

Why does knowing all of this matter? In point of fact, knowing all of this is not unique to sensors. It is a requirement for *all* system components in a dependable system design. It is not that hard to design a working system when it has twice as many resources as it needs and nothing ever goes wrong within itself, its inputs, or the systems it depends on. That, unfortunately, is not how reality works. *System design is hard because components fail all the time, sometimes in ways we do not expect. Characterizing sensors is essential so that when resources are constrained, we know what to expect*—and it would be good if we could expect partial service and not total system failure. Too often total failure occurs because designers did not think of graceful degradation.

Characterizing sensors is essential so that when they fail, we know how they fail and how to recover from the failure. This is particularly important in embedded systems (a system without direct user interfaces), such as those that control systems such as the power grid, cars and tanks, airplanes and missiles, or your pacemaker and toaster. It is even more important when the vehicle is a space vehicle and it is located near the outer planets of Jupiter or Pluto—where sending in a human technician is a multibillion dollar and multiyear activity that essentially means mission failure.

> *Systems design is hard because of many and unexpected failures.*

Conclusion

Transitioning from prevention techniques in the previous two chapters, this chapter begins a series of three chapters on detecting attacks. This chapter focuses on the foundation of selecting features in which attacks might manifest and how to build from there into sensors that detect potentially relevant attack sequences. These sequences can then set off alarms that garner human attention. The next chapter discusses how sensors can function for a system to detect attacks and misuse of the system.

To summarize:

- Detection complements prevention, focusing on attacks that cannot be easily prevented.

- Detection starts with good feature selection and proceeds up a hierarchy of seven layers.

- Feature selection examines where an attack manifests for all attacks in the attack space.

- Attacks map to features in a many-to-one and one-to-many relationship.

- Features are extracted using sensors to collect a stream of data.

- A sensor can stream data from multiple features.

- Events are sequences of data in an extracted feature stream; only a subset is attack-relevant.

- Event detection occurs when an attack-related event is encountered.

- Subtle attacks require correlating multiple events; one event rarely gives definitive proof.

- Attack detection is a type of binary attack classification—is-an-attack versus is-not-an-attack.

- Detection often requires classification of a specific attack to mount a proper defensive reaction.

- Attack detection and classification lead to an alarm to a human operator for further action.

- Alarms are prioritized because there are more alarms than an operator can possibly handle.

- Sensors perform differently based on system loads, attack loads, and failure modes.

- Characterizing sensor performance is essential to creating a dependable detection system.

Questions

1. What does it mean for prevention and detection to be synergistically related for a given set of attacks? Provide examples in your answer.

2. Under what circumstances can preventative mechanisms fail, and how can detection systems help in that regard?

3. Enumerate the seven layers of a detection system and describe the role of each layer and how it relates to the layer above and below.

4. Explain why the mapping between attacks and features is one-to-many and many-to-one. What are the implications of this property?

5. Explain why all possible features of interest may not be practically extractable. Give two examples not provided in the book that would be impractical to extract and explain why.

6. How is event detection different from event selection?

7. When is event detection equivalent to attack detection? When is it not equivalent and why?

8. What is attack classification as contrasted with attack detection and why can it be hard?

9. What is an attack alarm and how does it relate to attack detection and attack classification? What additional information is added to an alarm?

10. Name three important sensor operational performance characteristics and explain why they are important to know for a given sensor.

11. What happens to sensor data when the network is nearly 100 percent loaded?

14

Detection Systems

Overview

Learning Objectives

- Distinguish and contrast the two basic types of detection systems.
- Explain false positives, false negatives, and the trade-off in a receiver operating characteristic.
- Describe how to combine feature sets in creating an efficient and effective detection system.
- Explain the effect of a high false-positive rate on trust in the detection system.
- Determine how to derive detection requirements from attacks.
- Discuss how detection systems fail and the implications for design.

14.1 Types of Detection Systems

There are two basic types of intrusion detection systems: signature-based and anomaly detection schemes. Abstractly, they both adhere to the layered model described previously, but the processing and capabilities of each are quite different. We discuss each in turn.

14.1.1 Signature-Based

Signature-based schemes were historically the first to emerge and remain the dominant type in the market, though they are limited to detecting previously seen attacks. Signature-based detection requires the attack having been

- Observed somewhere before
- Identified
- Captured
- Analyzed (possibly by a third-party lab)
- Assessed to identify some unique part that sets the attack code apart from normal programs and other attack code

The unique part, called the attack signature, usually involves a static aspect such as a sequence of bits that is novel to the attack code, or a pattern of records in an audit log. By analogy, an attack signature is similar to unique deoxyribonucleic acid (DNA, the hereditary genetic code for all cells) that identifies a particular bacterium (analogous to attack software such as computer worms), or a particular subsequence of a biological virus that inserts itself into cellular DNA (analogous to computer viruses). For example, the bit string "000011110011100010101000011101" may be unique to the malicious code. That unique string becomes the malicious code's attack signature. That is what the analysis produces.

Companies such as McAfee®, Norton®, and IBM X-Force®, who are in the business of antivirus software and malware detection, do such analyses to find these attack signatures to incorporate into their products. Organizational computer emergency response teams and some universities also perform this type of analysis. Attack signature strings are sometimes called static attack signatures because they can be captured without respect to the attack software actually executing to observe its behavior.

One can generalize the notion of static attack signatures by examining the attack software during execution. For example, one could observe the operating system call sequences or other resource utilization patterns. Note that observing attack software in execution is a risky proposition because the attack software can attack the system that is used to observe it. Therefore, special precautions, such as isolation of these laboratory environments, are required, analogous to isolation labs required for analyzing dangerous biological pathogens. These dynamic behaviors can also be unique and therefore can be considered dynamic attack signatures. Practically speaking, most signatures today are static, based on what is contained in the malicious code itself. This dominance of static signatures is likely to change in the future as attack software becomes increasingly sophisticated and capable of masking its static signature.

Once an attack signature is obtained, it becomes analogous to an inoculation (or vaccination)—an inert (not active) distillation of the essence of the malware that may then be distributed throughout the population of networked computers. Computers must be uninfected and must be able to receive the inoculant. This capability typically requires installation of malware detection software and a subscription to the service of distributing new malware attack signatures as they are encountered. This updating processing is usually accomplished by periodic polling of a product's distribution point for new attack signatures, and any new ones are downloaded to a local copy that can then be used for comparison with activity on that computer. That process takes some time. The process from the initial attack infection to broad-scale distribution of inoculant and a corresponding attack signature is summarized in Figure 14-1.

"Computer patient zero" is analogous to a biological "patient zero." Patient zero is the first infected patient in an epidemiological investigation who is likely responsible for the spread of a particular infectious disease. After malicious code spreads from computer patient zero to other computers within the network, local cybersecurity engineers (CERT) copy the affected code for analysis in the malware laboratory to determine its attack signature. This process can take hours, sometimes days, and even weeks. The attack signature is used to inoculate uninfected computers so that future attacks by the same malicious code can be detected. This is analogous to vaccination. A vaccine is an inoculant of a harmless pathogen that causes the body's immune system to react and counter new infections by the same pathogen.

Not all computers have software capable of receiving and using attack signatures. Not all computers with such installed software update them as frequently as they should. Further, attack signatures are not always freely and openly shared between companies. This means that a significant portion of the population of computers are vulnerable at least for some period of time after the malware has been released and is available to other attackers to copy and reuse. Even after signatures have been propagated, some organizations significantly delay patching their systems for operational reasons. Significant damage can and has occurred in that delay period such as with the WannaCry attack [WOOL17].

Another drawback of the signature-based method is that it requires an initial detected attack. Such initial infections often affect many system sites simultaneously, with the potential of causing millions and sometimes hundreds of millions of dollars of damage before an attack signature can be developed and distributed. The entire population of computers is vulnerable to novel attacks.

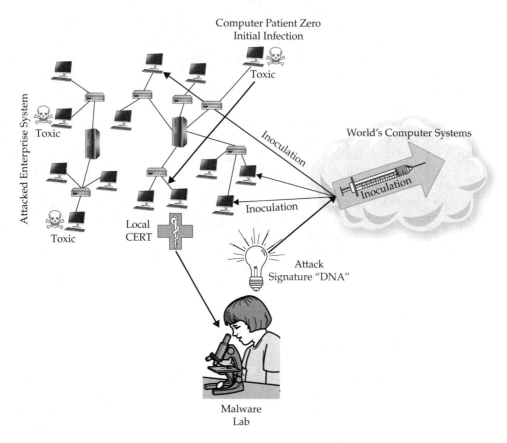

Figure 14-1   Signature-based epidemiological model of discovery and widespread inoculation of attack signatures

One important point about attacks and countermeasures to attacks is that it is an ever-increasing escalation and evolution. In response to signature-based schemes, developers of malicious codes have created stealth techniques and **rapid mutation techniques**. An example of a stealth technique is self-encryption with varying keys. *This means that the majority of the code content appears different when it passes through detection systems.* So, even if an attack signature exists within the code, it is hidden by the encryption process. By varying the key, the attack signatures are constantly changing.

Self-modifying code is code capable of rewriting portions of itself, generally to adapt to a changing environment. Malicious code developers sometimes use self-modifying code techniques to create rapidly mutating viruses, analogous to biological rapidly mutating viruses, such as the influenza A virus. These sorts of techniques of hiding or changing attack signatures are sometimes collectively called **obfuscation techniques**. Such obfuscation techniques, such as the inoculation delay issue, limit the utility of signature-based schemes. These limitations led to an alternative scheme called anomaly detection.

> *Attacks and countermeasures are always escalating and evolving.*

14.1.2 Anomaly Detection

Signature-based *schemes detect some specific list of bad events*—known as attack signatures. Anomaly detection *schemes detect events that are potentially not good.* The difference may seem semantically subtle, but the approach is substantially different. The notion of "potentially not good" is captured in the word "anomaly." An anomaly is something that deviates from what is standard, normal, or expected. Anomaly-based schemes are good at detecting novel attacks, but tend to have a high fraction of false alarms and take substantial resources.

Measuring deviation from the norm requires that the norm be characterized. Usually this characterization is unique to a specific system and must be measured for a defined period of time to establish what is normal. This period is called the **training period**. The measurement has to measure a specific aspect of the system—some feature as described previously in this chapter. An example at the operating system level would be the number of simultaneous network connections opened by a given user. An unusually large number of network connections might indicate a virus attempting to propagate. An example at the application program level would be the number of different recipients from a contact list that a user has sent mail to in a given day (typically, it is a tiny fraction, called a clique [STOL06]). For this feature, sending email to a large fraction of one's contact list could indicate a worm trying to propagate.

Once a feature has been selected and measured during a training period, the system monitors for deviations from the measured value or range of values that feature took on during training. For example, if training data determines that the average system user sends email to less than 1 percent of their contact list in a given day, and a user is monitored sending email to 100 percent of his contact list, this would surely be an anomaly. The example deviation is extreme to make the point, but what if a user sends email to 50 percent of their contact list? 10 percent? 1.00001 percent? Technically, those are all anomalies, but they are vastly different in quantity and perhaps attack relevance.

Anomaly detection schemes must set alert thresholds as to the degree of deviation that is reportable. The thresholds are typically tunable depending on the needs, dynamics, and resources of the organization of the enterprise system being monitored. Sometimes very tiny deviations can be the tiny thread to pull on to find a major attack [STOL89], so that might suggest setting the thresholds very low. Unfortunately, that can lead to **threat fatigue** in which the operators monitoring the system grow weary of spending countless hours tracking down reports, only to find out that they are not really attacks. For example, an email anomaly may be because the salesperson sent out an email blast to all his clients to advise them of a new company product release. Such fruitless wild-goose chases, called **false positives**, can cause the operators to lose confidence in the intrusion detection system and simply start to ignore it. In addition to wild-goose chases, setting the alert threshold too low can cause an overwhelming number of alarms, to the point that only a tiny fraction can be pursued in a day. For this reason, most anomaly detection systems sort the anomalies on priority and set priority based on the degree of variation and known abuse patterns that have been seen before in interpreting anomaly data.

There are several other problems inherent in anomaly-based systems:

- Ground truth difficulties
- Operational mode shifts
- Drift
- Attacker conditioning
- Performance and bandwidth

Truth When an anomaly detection system is first trained on the system, there is no guarantee that the system does not already have active attacks that have infiltrated the enterprise system and comprise part of the resource utilization pattern, including computing, storage, and network traffic. This means that the *training process is learning to recognize that attack activity as normal and therefore to be ignored.* That is, of course, a serious problem that requires serious discipline to mitigate. The good news is that it may be able to detect new attacks that are not too much like existing attacks on the system, but that is a small consolation to the defender. Nonetheless, there is little that can be done about this problem, and so most anomaly detection system users simply live with this risk.

Shift The other problem with training is that the training period represents only one mode of system operation. By mode, we mean a type of operation—a rhythm of activity. There can be high deviation within that mode. For example, activity on weekends and nights tends to be substantially different than activity during normal business hours. So, one may end up with too large a normal range in which attacks can hide, or the anomaly detection system has to have different norms for each submode. This certainly can be addressed, but it adds complexity to the system.

On the other hand, organizations can sometimes switch into a very different mode or operational rhythm than anything seen during the training period. Examples might include a defense department system that transitions from peacetime operations to wartime, a retailer transitioning from normal season sales to holiday season sales, or a nonprofit relief organization transitioning from normal operations to massive relief effort in response to a global disaster.

Major mode changes essentially invalidate the training data almost entirely. It is possible to observe a huge spike in false alarms because what was abnormal under one mode becomes completely normal in this new mode. Most of these radical mode changes happen due to a crisis, emergency, or stressor on an organization—all of which tend to make organizations and their systems more vulnerable. So, just when the anomaly-based intrusion detection system is needed most, it predominantly fails. Of course, the system can be retrained on the new mode, but this takes time "during which the system is vulnerable," resources, and patience, which the organization is not likely to have because it is stressed. In addition, these sorts of stressed modes will tend to have much higher variation, submodes, and unpredictability, all of which will either lead to higher false alarm rates or higher false negatives (as discussed in the next section). In short, just like in life, *shift happens*.

> ### *Anticipate that operational shift happens, complicating detection.*

Drift   In addition to operational mode shifting, the system norms will naturally drift as the system changes in tune with organization changes. For example, organizations grow and shrink all the time due to market conditions. Markets change. Suppliers and distributors change. Management changes. All of these changes lead to drifts in the norms of system behavior. This means that the system must be retrained periodically. Each time that is done, the system runs the risk of training on an infiltrated system and thus training to consider existing attacks as normal. Further, the retraining effort takes time and resources that could be spent on company mission.

Conditioning   Because of the changing nature of systems, operators come to expect changing levels of alarms as the training data gets stale. For a while, threshold parameters can be adjusted to reduce false alarm rates (at the risk of elevated **false negatives**). In addition, *the attacker can take advantage of feeding the system events that just come up to and barely over the threshold.* When the operators find nothing, they are likely to increase the alert threshold. In this fashion, the attacker can condition the anomaly detection system such that their attacks, when they are ready to do them for real, will not be detected. Insidious.

> ### *Cybersecurity operators must beware of attacker conditioning.*

Resource Hogging   Lastly, anomaly detection systems tend to take up substantial system resources. Essentially, organizations are running a digital network intelligence system on their own network. This can take substantial computational resources to collect and process the data, substantial storage to store the data for trend analysis and forensic purposes, and network bandwidth to pass around all the collected data to central analysis points. These are all resources that are not available to perform mission functions. If not controlled carefully, the amount of resources used can grow to rival the resources used by the mission itself (no joke, this can and has happened).

So, signature-based systems have significant drawbacks when it comes to damages from novel attacks and have difficulty with obfuscation. Anomaly detection systems can monopolize lots of resources, give less certain results leading to high false-positive rates, and are subject to shifts and drifts. Just as the human immune system responds to foreign invaders or cellular anomalies (e.g., normal cell division going awry, resulting in cancer), effective intrusion detection systems have to use both in an attempt to cover the weaknesses and leverage the strengths of each. Table 14-1 compares both approaches with respect to the layered model presented back in Figure 13-2. Then, Table 14-2 provides a summary of strengths and weaknesses of each approach.

Layer	Signature-Based	Anomaly Detection
Attack Alarming	Report attack classification and existence immediately to human operator. Possibly take some automated isolating action as a protective temporary measure.	Attack alarms are based on the strength of the attack signal, which is related to the degree of deviation from norm and a priori experience with which deviations are most reliable attack detectors.
Attack Classification	Classification is immediate unless multiple attack variants contain the same unique identifying string.	Often uncertain and ambiguous. It may be possible to narrow the attack to a certain class, but that is the best that can be done in most cases.
Attack Detection	Report when unique string is found.	When deviation from norm exceeds a specified threshold set by operators.
Event Detection	Search from unique string in relevant data stream.	Events that deviate from the norm.
Event Selection	Unique string from attack is found through forensic analysis of attack instance.	The difference between a measured norm and any other events.
Feature Extraction	Based on attack.	Based on attack.
Feature Selection	Based on attack.	Based on attack.

Table 14-1   Comparison of Signature-Based Versus Anomaly Detection Schemes with Respect to the Layered Detection Hierarchy

	Strengths	Weaknesses
Signature-Based	Fast, efficient, unambiguous, low false positives, pre-damage inoculation.	Requires sacrifice of computer-patient-zero systems, delayed inoculation, blind to novel and obfuscating attacks. Signature lists can grow quite large.
Anomaly Detection	Can detect novel and obfuscating attacks, no computer-patient-zero damage.	Resource hogs, ambiguous and uncertain classifiers, high false positives, subject to drifts and shifts.

Table 14-2   Summary of Signature-Based Versus Anomaly Detection Schemes with Respect to Strengths and Weaknesses

14.2 Detection Performance: False Positives, False Negatives, and ROCs

How does one measure detection performance? Certainly, speed and resource utilization are fairly standard performance metrics, but the deeper questions are speed of what and resource utilization compared to what? More importantly, how good is the attack detection system at detecting attacks by real adversaries (or those that can mimic real adversaries such as red teams, discussed in Section 6.5)? For this, we must return to the fundamentals of how detection works in terms of the seven-layer intrusion-detection-system layers-of-abstraction model presented in Figure 13-2:

1. Feature selection
2. Feature extraction
3. Event selection
4. Event detection
5. Attack detection
6. Attack classification
7. Attack alarming

14.2.1 Feature Selection

Feature selection is primarily a human analysis process that maps attacks into system features. That does not necessarily mean that there are not performance or quality metrics on the process. For each attack in the set of attacks of interest in the attack space, there exists a set of system features in which the attack manifests with different signal strengths as depicted in Figure 14-2.

Feature Vector   The **feature vector** is a one-dimensional matrix (called a vector) representation of all possible features within a system. As discussed earlier, this space is quite large and so the 24 features in the figure are illustrative. The features in which the attack under consideration will manifest are shown in solid outline, the others in dotted outline. Of course, the features in which attacks manifest are not known a priori, and there is no existing methodology to exhaustively find them all.

Manifestation Subspace   The subset of all features in which an attack has some manifestation, however weak, we will call the **manifestation subspace**. This subspace exists but is not fully known. In the example of the 24 original features, 6 are identified in this subspace (4, 9, 11, 14, 18, and 23).

Feature Identification   The next layer down in Figure 14-2, **feature identification**, is where the human analysts conduct their search for the features (e.g., audit logs, network activity, etc.; see Figure 13-2) in which the attacks manifest. The analyst identifies all the features they can in which the attack might manifest. In the illustrative example, only four of the six features are identified due to limitations of the analysis process and perhaps knowledge of the analysts

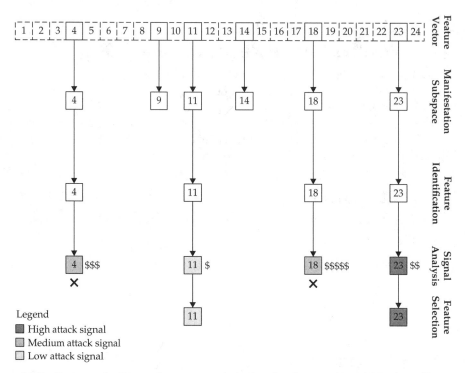

Figure 14-2 Feature selection performance analysis showing features 11 and 14 selected because many attacks manifest in those features (signal analysis) and their implementation is plausible and cost-effective.

themselves. Notice that the analysts' failure to notice features 9 and 14 represents a potential blind spot vulnerability in the detection system. We can look at the performance of this sublayer as 67 percent since that is the fraction of features that were found. We can only come up with the number in the hypothetical example because we simply stipulate the objective manifestation subspace. In reality, that is not known, so the actual performance number will be hard to estimate. It is important, however, to know that *it is always less than 100 percent and that this identification process is faulty and can create vulnerability*—particularly if the attacker can analyze the system and the detection system better than the defender.

Signal Analysis   The transition to the next layer down is called **signal analysis**. This is where the human analysts determine the strength of attack signal for each of the features identified in the previous layer. In the illustrative example, the attack manifests in increasing strength from 11 to 18, to 4 to 23, represented by the increased level of shading in Figure 14-2. In addition to signal analysis, other types of difficulty and cost analysis are done regarding each feature.

Feature Selection   This finally brings us to the actual selection of the set of features for the given attack under consideration. In the example, features 4 and 18 are eliminated because of excessive cost and difficulty of extracting the feature. The analyst is left with features 11 and 23, with 23 having a much stronger attack signal. The analysts could pick only feature 23, but there are a couple of problems with this. Feature extractors can fail or be blocked as discussed earlier. So, picking a single feature is quite brittle. Further, the system generates background noise from which the signal needs to be extracted. That noise can differentially affect different features. Lastly, having more than one feature gives the opportunity for corroboration and amplifying the attack signal to higher levels of certainty that an event is actually an attack.

Keep in mind that the process just discussed is for one attack. It must be repeated for the hundreds of attacks that are in the attack set of concern. If there are N attacks, the analyst ends up with N feature sets. Figure 14-2 shows a simple example in which we are concerned with three attacks labeled Attack A, Attack B, and Attack C. Attack A manifests in six different features: 3, 7, 13, 18, 21, and 24. Attack B manifests in features 2, 3, 7, 11, 14, and 18. Attack C manifests in features 2, 5, 6, 13, and 18. We immediately notice from the figure that features 2, 3, 7, 13, and 18 offer the ability to observe multiple attacks. Feature 18 has the very fortunate characteristic that all three attacks manifest in the overly simplified world of three attacks of concern. To find the full list of features in which attacks manifest, should the analyst take the union, the intersection, or something else among these sets?

The combined feature set to start with should be a non-duplicate union of all feature sets. This is illustrated in Figure 14-3 shown in the bottom middle with the expression $A \cup B \cup C$. A non-duplicate union means that if a feature is listed in the union more than once, it is only taken once, since we are only deciding whether or not to include a feature in the final set. Intersections are interesting in that they identify features that are useful in detecting multiple attacks. That makes them particularly high value.

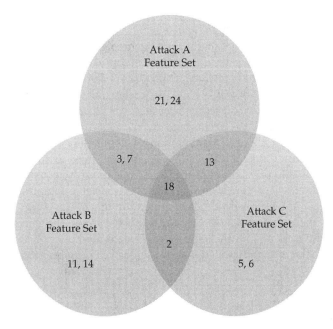

$A = \{3, 7, 13, 18, 21, 24\}$ $B = \{2, 3, 7, 11, 14, 18\}$ $C = \{2, 5, 6, 13, 18\}$
$A \cap B \cap C = \{18\}$ $A \cup B \cup C = \{2, 3, 5, 6, 7, 11, 13, 14, 18, 21, 24\}$

Figure 14-3   Combining feature sets determined by the attack space

What happens if you cannot afford to implement the union of all relevant features? Note that the meaning of cost here is broader than money. *It includes resources required to develop and implement the corresponding sensors; the impact to system functionality, performance, and limitations; and the cost to maintain and operate the sensors.* With an insufficient budget to implement all feature extractors, one is faced with a knapsack-type optimization problem [CORM93], where the utility of each feature relates to the value it brings to detecting a given attack and the importance of that attack in the attack space. Discussing that optimization process is beyond the scope of this book, but the readers are encouraged to explore the idea on their own.

> *Feature selection is a detection optimization problem.*

In closing this section, it is important to note that *if the wrong features are chosen, then no matter how good the remaining layers are, the attacks cannot be detected.* The foundations must be well thought out. At the top layer, one might say that the detection system performs badly, but it is more appropriate to say that the feature selection was done badly and so the remaining layers had no chance of getting it right.

> *Poor feature selection destroys the foundation of attack detection.*

14.2.2 Feature Extraction

With the combined feature set that is implementable within the resource limits of the organization, one then develops the software and possibly hardware to create the sensors that extract and report these features. One or more features can be extracted and reported by a given sensor. If a set of features is closely related in that they are located within the same functionality of the same abstraction layer (e.g., the file system functionality of the operating system layer), there is a basis to combine them.

Sensors, like any other security component, should be designed to be reliable and robust against attack. In addition, it is likely that sensors will need to operate in at least two modes: normal mode and **hypervigilant mode**. In normal mode, sensors report those events needed to detect an attack signal for the feature that is a reasonable compromise regarding the system resources (e.g., storage, bandwidth, and computational power) that it takes up. Later, we will discuss how there may be times when one needs to turn up the gain on a sensor while an attack is in progress—hence the name hypervigilant mode.

Feature extractor implementation into a sensor layer can be done well or poorly in terms of

- The speed to implement the sensors
- The reliability of the implementation
- The cybersecurity of the sensors
- The placement of the sensors

Speed to implement is important because the longer it takes to develop and deploy sensors, the longer an organization is vulnerable to attacks that are detectable by the sensors that are to be built. A pretty good sensor that can be built in a month is often better than a great sensor that takes three years. A sensor does little good if it is unreliable and buckles under high load, just when it is needed most. Similarly, if a sensor is easy to attack, then it does little good if one cannot trust the sensor output, particularly since we know that security infrastructure is one of the first targets of a competent attacker. Lastly, if all the sensors are placed in one small corner of the enterprise network because it is easy to deploy there, then even the best sensors will be of little value since they will not be placed in a position where they can detect most of the attacks.

14.2.3 Event Selection

Event selection is actually performed concurrently with the feature selection process. The analyst must answer the question of what output from the feature extraction process will be attack-detection relevant. This is a matter of deeply understanding precisely how the attack will manifest in the feature stream output by sensors. If the analysis is incorrect, attack detection performance will be very poor or nonexistent. This is another critical point in the determination of the system performance.

14.2.4 Attack Detection

The performance of attack detection depends on how the attack signal is synthesized from the bits of signal from all the features and how well that signal is raised above the **noise floor** under a variety of noise conditions. If the algorithms do not do proper correlation and signal enhancement, the attack signal can be easily lost. Performance here is best measured against the ideal of what is possible, but this is rarely available since a theoretical analysis is generally not performed.

If the attack detection layer reports an attack but there is no attack, it is called a false positive—a type of error. False positives are problematic because they waste resources tracking them down and trying to stop attacks that don't exist. For this reason, operators may begin to lose confidence in the detection system and start to ignore it.

False positives erode trust.

If an attack goes undetected, the error is called a false negative. False negatives are bad because the attack proceeds undetected and is then able to do potentially significant damage to the system. When an attack is correctly reported, it is called a **true positive**.

To understand the performance characteristics of an attack detector, one can plot the true positive rate versus the false positive rate into what is called a Receiver Operating Characteristic curve [MAXI04] as shown in Figure 14-4.

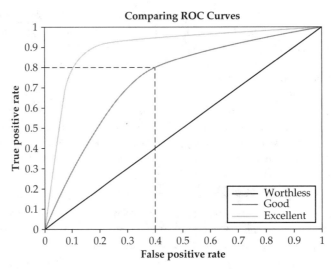

Figure 14-4 Receiver Operating Characteristic (ROC) curves indicate the notional performance of a binary classifier. The intersecting point at the dotted lines indicates a sample point with an 80 percent true positive detection rate and a 40 percent false positive rate.

The attack detection problem is known as a binary classifier in the sense that it classifies an event or event sequence as being an attack, a possible attack, or not an attack. A perfect classifier provides 100 percent true positives with zero false positives. A useless detector is no better than a coin toss. Real detectors are somewhere between these two performance extremes, and one generally trades off increasing false positive rates to get increasing true positive rates.

The sample point shown in Figure 14-4 indicated by the intersecting dotted line shows a point with an 80 percent true positive rate with a corresponding 40 percent false positive rate. That means that if there are 1,000 events of which 100 are actual attack events, then 80 of the 100 attacks (80 percent) will be correctly detected and 360 (40 percent) of the 900 benign events will be incorrectly flagged as attacks. Notice that to get an additional 10 percent attack detection yielding 90 percent true positives, one must accept (in this notional curve) a whopping 80 percent false positive rate, which is normally completely unacceptable. *Receiver Operating Characteristic curves are a critical measure of attack detector performance.*

> *ROC curves are a critical measure of detector performance.*

14.2.5 Attack Classification

Once an attack is detected, the system must identify which attack it is. This moves performance measurement from a **binary classifier** to a multivalue classifier with a more complex operating curve. *Incorrectly classifying the attack can have serious consequences.* The defender could end up taking the incorrect mitigating actions, possibly making the situation even worse. Attack classification is a difficult problem, particularly for novel attacks. In some cases, it can be sufficient to narrow down the attack to several possibilities, particularly if each has similar mitigation actions. For example, if an attack classifier determines that the attack is a type of computer worm that is spreading quickly through the network, it is not immediately essential to determine precisely which worm it is; the mitigating actions to stop the spread of the worm are urgent and can be similar in each case.

14.2.6 Attack Alarming

Expert human operators are one of the most valuable and limited resources within the system. Once an attack has been detected and classified, it is alarmed to a human operator for further analysis and possible action. The attack alarm layer needs to ensure that it aggregates events that are really from the same attack to avoid incorrectly alerting and wasting the operator's valuable attention cycles. Attack alarms are prioritized in terms of potential damage to the system and urgency.

Finally, the cybersecurity system in use must do as much as possible to track down the source of an alarm to determine if it is truly malicious or a false alarm. The goal here is to remove all rote tasks from the human operators that the computer can do and employ human skills for what humans do best—creative analysis and sleuthing for a complex pattern or causal sequence. Note that if the computer can run the vast majority of alarms to ground (i.e., investigate their origins and causes) to determine them to be false positives, then that significantly lowers the impact of a higher false alarm rate. The performance at this top-most layer of intrusion detection systems is about minimizing false negatives and reducing false positives to a reasonable workload for human operators.

14.3 Drive Detection Requirements from Attacks

As attack detection moves forward from its historical roots, it must reach beyond using existing system sensors off the shelf, detecting only those attacks that those sensors can detect. Today's commercial intrusion detection systems are not designed to detect the wide-ranging types and classes of attacks—the full attack space. Commercial systems tend to be motivated by maximizing what can be detected while minimizing costs and impacts to systems, thereby maximizing profit. This trade-off works fine for the multibillion-dollar intrusion detection business, but it does not lead to attack space coverage. Two important attack classes are omitted by these systems: (1) attacks that are not well understood in terms of existing detection methods, and (2) attacks that are too expensive to detect or have too big of a performance or cost impact on the system. Unfortunately, consumers of such products often assume that they have complete attack space coverage and are shocked to learn that many attacks such as zero-day attacks can easily evade such products.

What is called for here is a detection designed from the top down—proceeding from requirements through design to implementation. Detection requirements should be derived from a library of attacks and attack scenarios (which come from multiple sources; see Section 23.2) that are of most concern to the system owners. Such an analysis should then lead to requirements for the sensors and the detection-response system using those sensors. What is needed to do this well is a good attack space taxonomy that breaks attacks down into classes and then characterizes each in terms of where in the system the attacks manifest.

Although there have been several attack taxonomies [LAND94] published that can act as useful guidance in this regard, a full taxonomy for the purpose of detection has yet to be published.

> *Detection should be geared toward attack space coverage.*

14.4 Detection Failures

As with preventative techniques, detection techniques can fail to detect attacks for many reasons, such as

- Underlying attack sensors are blind to the attacks.
- Attack signal is lost in the noise of normal system activity.
- Attack signal is below the alert threshold for the detection algorithm.
- Intrusion detection system was not deployed in the area of the system where the attack occurred.
- One or more critical components of the detection system naturally failed.
- One or more critical components of the detection system was successfully attacked.
- Sensor data was blocked from the attack detection component.
- Attack reports were blocked from being sent.

Each reason is discussed in turn.

14.4.1 Blind Sensors

As discussed previously, sensors can be completely blind to attacks due to a lack of correct feature selection, poorly implemented feature extraction, poor event selection, or incorrect or inadequate event detection. Because of the limitations of technology, even if the seven-layer intrusion detection system is designed perfectly, there will be a certain level of sensor limitations. *It is important to properly characterize exactly where sensor blind spots occur.* Therefore, when the detection system reports no attacks seen, one must always caveat that report with the list of all attacks that are not detectable by the system due to such limitations. *Broad testing of the full attack space is needed to confirm the sensor characterization and to explore possible blind spots that the designers are not aware of due to bugs or design flaws.*

> *Know your detection blind spots; your adversary will.*

14.4.2 Below Noise Floor

Using an analogy from signal processing, the attack signal can be lost in the noise. **Noise** can come in many forms. In anomaly detection systems, noise is related to the data stream from the extracted features. If background activity is highly regular and stable, it can be easier to detect attacks. For example, consider an embedded system of computers in a car. Only a handful of applications are running, performing narrowly defined tasks having to do with operating the vehicle systems. There are no Excel spreadsheets or newly downloaded apps that the user is checking out. If the system begins to make a lot of network connections to systems outside of a predefined set needed to perform its functions, it is a clear indication of malicious activity. Contrast this with a research system at a university computer science department where researchers are trying to stretch computers to the very limits of what they were designed to do. An extraordinarily wide range of weirdness happens on such networks—such as dynamically reconfigured networks, virus-like propagation of software updates, self-modifying code, etc. This weirdness becomes normal, which makes detecting attacks in dynamic research environments difficult.

14.4.3 Below Alert Threshold

Detection systems have receiver operating characteristic curves, as discussed earlier (Figure 14-4). There is a trade-off between the false-positive and false-negative rates. Typically, that trade-off is tunable. If an operator is encountering too many false positives, they can retune the trade-off to yield fewer alerts. Alternatively, only high-priority alerts will be processed, which achieves a similar result. This action effectively lowers the alert threshold, which raises the false-negative rate (an attack happens and it is not detected by sensors). Unfortunately, attacks near threshold are typically the most serious and dangerous attacks in this category because they are well-crafted to remain below normal detection thresholds using stealth techniques. *This means that raising the attack alert threshold ignores the very attacks that may be most important to detect.*

> *Raising alert thresholds to save time can hide critical attacks.*

14.4.4 Improper Placement

System designers with a castle-and-moat mentality focus (historical way of protecting people with strong fortifications on the external city walls) on strongly protecting the boundaries of an enterprise system sometimes ignore or do little to protect the internal system. Such a mentality leads some security engineers to focus their intrusion detection systems on the *border firewalls and routers* to the enterprise—protecting from "outside" intrusions. Such placement is indeed important and wise. At the same time, what happens when an insider launches an attack from a system within the enterprise? The border systems may never see it. *Therefore, it is important to deploy detection systems both inside and on the borders of enterprise systems.* Not doing so is sometimes disparagingly referred to as the crunchy-on-the-outside-soft-and-chewy-on-the-inside approach (referring to certain kinds of candy), meaning that once an attacker gets through the perimeter, there are few internal defenses.

> *Prepare for both insider and outsider attacks.*

The insides of an enterprise system can be quite large and lumpy (meaning lots of subnetworks and sub-subnetworks, sometimes called **enclaves**). Placing sensors and feeding data from those sensors in every system enclave can be expensive both in terms of license cost and resource utilization such as network bandwidth.

Putting intrusion detection systems in only a few places and hoping that the adversary will blunder into them is an ineffective strategy. A good adversary routinely does exploratory reconnaissance scanning of a system to locate and identify detection systems and steer around them or under them (meaning, below their detection thresholds or using features to which they are blind). *Sensors should be deployed in an intentional grid to maximize the attacker's difficulty in evading detection.* This will be discussed later in more detail (Section 15.1.1).

> *Sensor grid designs should maximize evasion difficulty.*

14.4.5 Natural Failure

Like preventative components and any system component, *detection system components fail for all the same reasons.* Failure avoidance techniques are essential in the design of detection systems. For example, code inspection and heavy testing are important aspects of the development process. Failure detection and recovery techniques are also important. For example, detecting stopped processes and automatically restarting them is a useful way of self-healing a transitory failure.

It is also important to design a system such that when it fails, it fails safely into a failure mode that is not harmful to the system. For example, suppose an important sensor stream fails and stops flowing into an event detection layer that has multiple streams feeding it. The output of the sensor stream would still appear to be properly functioning, but, in fact, it would be crippled by the lack of an essential feed. The system needs to check all of its sensor feeds for existence and integrity to ensure that when they fail (or are attacked), the system flags these failures and either alerts a human operator or attempts to fix the problem immediately. Until a failure is repaired, all intrusion system reports should be accompanied by an indication of an impaired capability as a result of the partial failure.

14.4.6 Successfully Attacked

Detection systems and their components, like any other aspect of the system, are subject to attack—indeed they can be a priority attack target. If an adversary gains control of detection system components, then the detection system's inputs, internal processing, and outputs can be manipulated to provide false information. For example, if an adversary gains complete control of critical sensors, it can suppress any evidence of ongoing attacks. Similarly, if the detection system outputs are successfully attacked, then attack alarms can be suppressed at will. The detection system becomes worse than useless; it becomes a tool of the adversary to give the defender a false sense of security by false reports on the absence of attacks.

14.4.7 Blocked Sensor Input

In addition to a sensor failing, resulting in impaired functionality, the sensor stream, which often transits the network, can be blocked by a network failure or an intentional attack (such as a network flooding attack). In a complex enough system, there is always a component that is broken at a given moment. Subnetworks can be temporarily isolated when routers or firewalls fail. Routing tables can be corrupted, leading to misrouted or dropped data. Congestion on the network can cause a swath of network packets to simply be dropped on the floor.

All of these problems can lead to suppression of sensor input. These situations need to be closely monitored and corrected as soon as possible. *Priority needs to be given to sensor traffic, particularly when under attack. Designers should consider creating a dedicated network for system traffic like sensor data to minimize this issue.* Again, until the sensor input is restored, the impaired detection capability should be clearly and prominently reported on all output reports.

14.4.8 Blocked Report Output

For all the same reasons, detection system output reports and alerts can be blocked so that operators do not see them. Similar countermeasures as described in the previous sections should be taken for these outputs as well.

Conclusion

This chapter is the second in a series of three chapters on detecting cyberattacks. Building on the previous chapter, which discusses how to properly design attack sensors, this chapter focuses on constructing detection systems from sensors and assessing the systems' performance. The next chapter then discusses attack detection strategies.

To summarize:

- Signature-based and anomaly detection are the two basic types of intrusion detection.
- Signature-based schemes detect lists of previously seen bad events that indicate attack.
- Anomaly-based schemes detect events that deviate from the norm, and *might* indicate attack.
- Anomaly detection requires training in pristine systems to establish norms.
- Established norms can drift and shift as mission evolves and sometimes changes modes.
- False positive and true positive rates are traded off and represented in a Receiver Operating Characteristic curve.
- Good detection starts with good feature selection and extraction in which attacks manifest.
- Choosing features to monitor involves attack signal as well as practical issues such as cost.
- Attacks drive detection requirements to gain complete attack space coverage.
- Detection systems fail in numerous ways, necessitating multiple sensor coverage.

Questions

1. What are the two types of intrusion detection systems and how do they work?

2. What is an attack signature and how are they developed and distributed?

3. How is malware like a biological pathogen, and how are intrusion detection schemes like biological countermeasures?

4. How does malware evade signature-based schemes? How could signature-based schemes counter these evasions?

5. Why are weak signals from anomaly detection schemes sometimes very important?

6. What is threat fatigue and how does it relate to false alarm rates?

7. List five problems with anomaly detection systems and state why they are problems.

8. Compare and contrast the two types of intrusion detection systems with respect to the seven-layer model of intrusion detection.

9. What are the primary strengths and weaknesses of the two types of intrusion detection?

10. How are false positives and true positives traded off? What is the name of the curve that characterizes that trade-off? Draw a curve showing excellent performance and explain why it is excellent.

11. Describe the feature selection process. What is a feature vector? Why is the set of identified features smaller than the feature manifestation space? Give some reasons why the selected features may be a subset of identified features in which the attack will manifest.

12. Is the set of features that should be monitored the union or intersection of all attack feature sets? What does the union mean? What does the intersection set indicate?

13. Why is a high false alarm rate a problem?

14. Give "five whys" on a detection system failure and explain each one. How can each failure be avoided? How could it be detected? How could it be recovered from?

15. What is a blind sensor and why is it blind and to what is it blind?

16. What is a noise floor and how does it relate to attack detection?

17. What is an alert threshold and how does it affect attack alarming to human operators? What happens if the threshold is set too high? What if it is set to be too low?

18. What is an enclave and what is the implication with respect to the placement of intrusion detection systems?

19. What happens if a sensor input is blocked?

15

Detection Strategy

Overview

Learning Objectives

- Define detection in depth and breadth along two dimensions—network expanse and attack space coverage.
- Describe how to engineer cyberspace to a defender's advantage, such as herding.

- Define and describe attack epidemiology and how it contributes to system safety.
- Summarize post-detection actions that can refine the detection itself.

15.1 Detect in Depth and Breadth

Just as we have a design principle for defense in depth, detection in depth *is needed for the same reasons: sensors can fail, can be evaded, and can have blind spots for given attack classes.*

> **Detection in depth and breadth is essential.**

Detection depth and breadth are in two dimensions—coverage of the various corners of the enterprise network, as discussed earlier, and with respect to the attack space. Table 15-1 briefly describes each of these four areas. The remainder of the section discusses each in detail.

	Network Expanse	**Attack Space**
Depth	Multiple sensors for a given attack between boundary and inner core where the most valuable data and services reside.	For each attack, have multiple types of sensors to detect that attack.
Breadth	Have detection systems in all enterprise system nooks and crannies (i.e., enclaves).	Cover the entirety of the attack space with the union of all sensors.

Table 15-1   Detection in Depth and Breadth in Two Dimensions: Network Expanse and Attack Space

15.1.1 Breadth: Network Expanse

Like the universe with planets in solar systems in galaxies in clusters and superclusters, an enterprise system has structures and substructures. There are legitimate control flows and data flows that define proper processing paths within the system. For example, a retail system might present an online catalog, receive orders from the catalog, process payments, then schedule a shipment of the ordered product. This process entails control and data flows from a client through a series of servers, which may traverse routers to subnetworks and even external systems.

Similarly, an attacker must create and follow an attacking flow—a series of attack steps needed to accomplish a goal. The types of paths attackers might follow are summarized in Figure 15-1 and enumerated as follows:

1. Establishing a toehold on the system (a successful attack that gives the attacker some low-privilege access), typically on an external boundary device such as a router or an external server.

2. Escalating from low privilege such as a low-level user account to high privilege such as a super-user account.

3. Hacking from one system or server with certain accesses and trust relationships to another until a goal system is reached.

4. Disabling or defeating preventions and detection cybersecurity capabilities along the way, in advance of an attack.

5. Hacking through firewalls and other internal boundary devices.

> *Attackers must follow an attack flow path; leverage this fact.*

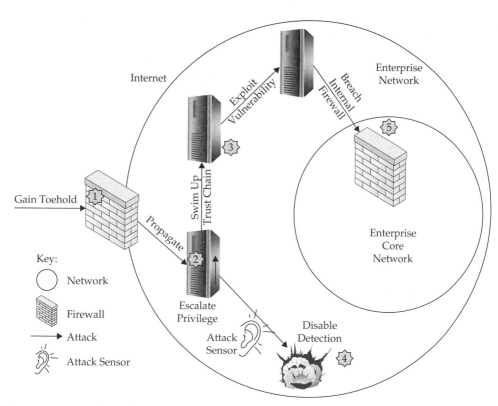

Figure 15-1   Attacking flow path representation from gaining a toehold through breaching internal firewalls

It is most effective to have detection capability along the entire set of attack paths so that the attacker is challenged at each step of the way. Because the adversary will seek to disable these detection capabilities in advance of their attack, it is essential that the *detection systems themselves be robust against a wide variety of attacks and deceptions and will alarm when there is an attempt to tamper with them.*

> *Detection systems, a primary target, must be robust: challenging the attack at each step of the intrusion.*

15.1.2 Depth: Network Expanse

Often, enterprise systems are organized in layers of defense with the first line of defense being in the outer layer, and the last lines being in the inner core(s). Each layer is protected by a boundary protection device, such as a firewall and filtering router. This concept is illustrated in Figure 15-2. An attack must traverse and breach each network layer. In the traversal, the adversary should be subject to detection by an intrusion detection system. Such systems within each layer provide a depth of detection. If security engineers put detection systems exclusively on the core because of its high value, there is no detection in depth and the attacker's mission is made much easier.

> *Detection systems must monitor all subnetworks.*

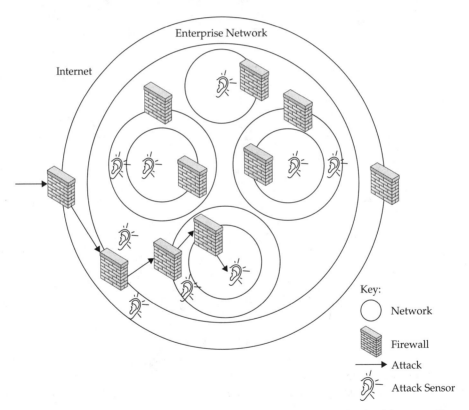

Figure 15-2   Abstraction of successive network detection layers giving a depth of detection along the attacker's entire attack path through successive subnetworks of increasing trust and protection

15.1.3 Breadth: Attack Space

Breadth attack space coverage simply refers to the union of all of the attacks that are reliably detectable by the detection system in place. As discussed in the previous chapters, this depends on the efficacy of all seven layers of the detection system. If an attack manifests in no feature that is monitored by the system, there is no coverage for that attack. By the same token, if an attack manifests strongly in a monitored feature, but the attack detection layer does not identify it as an attack and does not alarm, then there is also no coverage for the attack despite the presence of some activity below the surface in processing attack-related events. Figure 15-3 depicts broad coverage conceptually. Each shaded rectangle represents a set of attacks detected by a given sensor. A sensor feeding the upper layers of the detection system can detect multiple groupings of attacks; therefore, the diagram includes several shaded areas representing the sets. No single sensor can detect all possible attacks, so the white space represents portions of the attack space not covered by the sensor—meaning that the sensor is blind to those attacks. We call the portion of the attacks that is covered **detection breadth**.

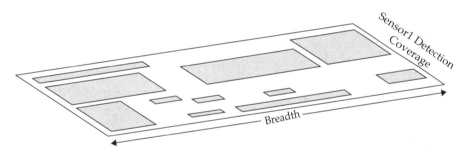

Figure 15-3 Detection in breadth by a sensor or set of sensors, covering portions of the attack space (shaded rectangles) and leaving others not covered (white area)

It is important to have as broad a coverage as possible because the uncovered portion of the attack space represents a significant vulnerability that could be potentially lethal to the system. Further, it is essential to know precisely where detection coverage gaps exist in order to attempt to cover them through prevention or tolerance techniques (discussed in more detail in later chapters). One thing is for sure: *a skilled and strategic adversary will certainly have a detailed map of your detection gaps and will design their attacks to navigate through those gaps.*

> *An adversary will map and navigate through detection gaps.*

15.1.4 Depth: Attack Space

Because detection system components fail, depth of attack space coverage is important. **Detection depth** means that more than one sensor can detect the same attack or set of attacks. If one sensor fails or is successfully attacked, there are other sensors to back that one up with respect to detecting that attack. Of course, having depth for one out of a thousand attacks in the attack space is a bit absurd. As discussed in the previous section, the adversary will develop and use a map of the breadth and depth of your system's detection coverage. The adversary is sure to navigate around depth (good sensor coverage of a single attack class), so detection depth must be applied broadly throughout the attack space. Applying to an exactly uniform depth may not be practical because of costs or impracticalities of certain sensors, but having some depth broadly is essential. *Having a map of where the shallow coverage areas exist is also important for the same reason discussed for breadth—you can count on the adversary to create and use such a map for attack!*

Figure 15-4 depicts detection in depth (and breadth) conceptually. It shows a depth of three, two, one, and even zero in some areas of the attack space. This is a practical reality that is manageable so long as the defender has a plan to cover the weak detection areas.

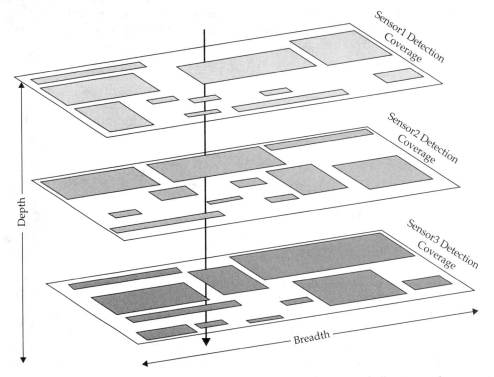

Figure 15-4   Defense in depth and breadth with respect to attack space is challenging to the adversary.

15.2 Herd the Adversary to Defender's Advantage

The defender always has the home field advantage. The defender not only has the potential of knowing the defended system better than the adversary, but they actually get to design that system and thus the environment in which the adversary must conduct their attack operations. To gain this advantage, cybersecurity engineers must work in collaboration with systems engineers in the early stages of design. Together they must define requirements explicitly to design the system to maximize this advantage, and then they must design to those requirements. Unfortunately, this is rarely done.

> ### *Engineer cyberspace to the defender's advantage.*

In the previous sections, we learned that the defender should have a good map of the gaps and depths of their detection capability. *One use of such a map is to manipulate the adversary to avoid areas of weakness.* How do you do that? The cybersecurity engineer can manipulate the adversary through a series of incentives toward areas of the system with good coverage and disincentives away from areas with weaker detection coverage. Such constructions accomplish what is called "herding the adversary."

Disincentives could include tighter and more preventative security controls such as authentication and authorization systems. This not only increases the adversary's work to get to those areas of the system, but also increases their risk because being deflected by a preventative technique is a primitive type of detection.

Incentives to entice an adversary to parts of the system that have better detection capability would be to create the appearance of high-value targets such as files containing keywords that might be of interest (e.g., filenames called "bank-account-passwords" or "nuclear launch codes"). This is a type of useful deception that will be discussed in more detail in later chapters.

> ### *Herd the adversary to the defender's advantage.*

15.3 Attack Epidemiology

In Section 7.3, we discussed using the five-whys analysis to squeeze out all of the important knowledge and understanding from an attack on one's own system (a process that is too rarely followed). That same process applies to learning from attacks on other defenders' systems—indeed, it is much less painful that way. In the same way that humans are a part of a larger interconnected societal fabric subject to infectious disease propagation, computers are part of an interconnected networked population subject to cyberattack propagation.

In the world of human society, when a person falls ill to an unknown disease, the patient is closely examined and subjected to a barrage of tests and analysis to quickly determine the nature and origin of the disease-causing agent. The disease is first noticed by local medical personnel, lab tests yield negative results for all known potential causative agents, and then the case is flagged as an atypical disease of unknown etiology. Once specialists are able to identify and isolate the infectious agent, they quickly work to develop a drug to treat or cure the disease and a vaccine (an inoculation) that will prevent the infection in the remainder of society to minimize the impact of the disease. The U.S. Centers for Disease Control and Prevention (CDC) and the World Health Organization (WHO) play a key surveillance role in monitoring for new or emerging disease outbreaks and overseeing the process to completion for the benefit of the larger society.

Similarly, when a system falls victim to a new cyberattack, the local computer emergency response team (CERT) often identifies it as an unknown agent and begins its investigation. They often simultaneously alert regional or national response teams who help with the analysis. Once the attack has been isolated, the team often issues a bulletin on the attack to make system owners aware of the problem. If the attack exploits a system vulnerability, the vulnerability is identified, along with a system patch to fix the vulnerability if possible. The vendor of the part of the system with the vulnerability (e.g., the operating system vendor) then sends the patch through normal distribution channels as quickly as possible. If possible, the analysts extract an attack signature—identifying the unique aspect of the cyberattack— and share it widely. Antivirus vendors distribute the attack signature through their normal subscription update process.

In this way, the *epidemiological community studying cyberattacks can leverage attacks to real-world systems to minimize societal damages.*

15.4 Detection Honeypots

One can create fake systems to even further minimize damages. A fake system is one that appears real and is attractive to an adversary. Attackers expend resources to mount real attacks to gain what they mistakenly believe is valuable data or services. These fake systems are called honeypots. They can help identify attacks before they do significant damage worldwide. *Fake systems can be extremely well-instrumented and architected to cause adversaries to reveal their attack methods.* Honeypots are a valuable tool in the defender's repertoire.

A variation of the honeypot is to produce fake data which, if publicized by the attacker (e.g., emails) proves to the defender that a breach occurred. This proof is gained without suffering the damage of valuable data being compromised. Also, the volume of fake data could overload the adversary in terms of verifying the data or acting on it. This was evidently a strategy used by the Macron campaign in France to defeat Russian interference [NOSS17].

> *Honeypots are valuable tools to discover attack methods.*

15.5 Refining Detection

When a detection system alerts that there is an attack, it is time for action, but what action? In general, we call the action response **cyber command and control** (Section 23.1). There are some specific high-value reflexive actions that can, however, be taken immediately: running alerts to ground and gaining more information about the attack.

15.5.1 Running Alerts to Ground

Not all alerts are certain, as discussed in previous chapters. Some are false alarms; in fact, often there are many more false alarms than true ones. Each **alarm** requires a certain amount of resources to determine if it is a false positive or true positive. Different alarm types use varying resources to investigate an alarm. Many of the activities to investigate each of these alarms are fairly routine and automatable. Table 15-2 provides a listing of the types of questions an analyst will seek to answer running alarms to ground. These questions come from a history of investigating false alarms and knowing which data tends to support evidence of a false alarm. Answers to all of these questions can be easily mined from existing systems, circumventing the need for a defender to type a series of queries. *A lack of specific evidence that an alert is a false alarm should be treated as an attack.*

> ### *Treat attack alerts as true attacks until proven otherwise.*

#	Question	Purpose
1	What systems were involved?	Some systems are more prone to false alarms than others because of what they do (e.g., a software testing computer can behave unusually compared to a production computer doing routine tasks).
2	What mission are those systems assigned to?	Some missions are more prone to false alarms than other because of what they do (e.g., the research mission tends to push the edge of computer capabilities and therefore behave anomalously).
3	Which users were involved?	Some users are more prone to false alarms (e.g., a user investigating insider activity may have suspicious-looking access patterns).
4	Are those users on vacation?	Inactive accounts often become targets of attack because the users will not as easily notice that someone else is logged on as them when they try to log on.
5	What is the apparent attack path?	Does it seem to be an insider attack or an untrusted user coming from the system boundary?

Table 15-2   Questions and Rationale Used to Run Alerts to Ground when Investigating Suspicious Activity

15.5.2 Learning More About an Attack

Attack detection sensors often have to be attenuated during normal operation as part of an engineering trade-off to ensure that the sensors are limited to a reasonable portion of shared system resources (e.g., 10 percent of network bandwidth). The trade-off during normal mode of operation could and probably should be different from the trade-off when the system is determined to be under attack (which should be a small fraction of the time). Therefore, the trade-off requires dynamic adjustments to sensors to increase their outputs when attacks are occurring. This does not require all sensors to be placed in full throttle, but rather those sensors specifically involved in the hypothesized attack. This enables the system to gain more information about the attack and how to stop it. Tunable sensors, and the means to decide how and when to tune them, must be built into detection systems by cybersecurity engineers.

15.6 Enhancing Attack Signal and Reducing Background Noise

The notion of considering attack detection as a signal that may be hidden within the noise of a system's normal activity is an important recurring idea. In the field of **signal processing**, one has a sender and a receiver cooperating to communicate information across a communications channel (e.g., data network or telephone line) that contains a fraction of random noise. Information theory tells us that for any specified amount of noise (for example, spurious electrical signals), there exists a way of encoding the data (for example, voice data on a telephone line) using redundancy to both detect and correct errors in the data stream, amplifying the data above the noise floor and creating a reliable communication path. *That is an important theoretical result with extraordinarily useful practical implications.*

In the case of attack signal, the situation is a bit different. The communicators are the opposite of cooperating—they are adversarial. The "sender" is the attacker. The "receiver" is the defender. The attacker is actively engineering their attack to be below the noise floor to avoid "communicating" the existence and nature of their attack to the defender. The communication channel is essential to the very large system state. If the attacker is to achieve a goal, they must have an effect on the system, which in turn inherently alters the system state. The attacker therefore cannot help but communicate or signal their attack in the system state space. The question is whether the defender can find this communication signal in the state space by selecting, monitoring, and correctly processing data from the right features, which tap into that state space. Table 15-3 summarizes the mapping between normal communications and attacker-defender interactions.

Aspect	Normal Communications	Attacker-Defender Interactions
Sender (Attacker)	Entity intending to send a message to receiver.	Attacker intending to negatively affect system and system state and thereby unintentionally signaling its activity to defender.
Receiver (Defender)	Entity intending to receive a message from the sender.	Defender seeking to find an attacker signal within the very large state space that is continuously affected by normal system activity as well.
Relationship	Cooperative.	Adversarial.
Channel	Data or telephone network.	System state space.
Noise	Random.	Background system traffic, which can be shaped by the attacker to some extent.
Encoding	Redundancy to overcome random noise.	Attackers modulate activity to have minimum impact on state space and to fall below the noise floor to avoid communicating with the defender.

Table 15-3   Summary Contrasting Normal Communications with Attack-Defender Interactions

The attacker's objective is to have a minimum footprint within the system state space while achieving their attack goals. The objective is also to have any attack footprint which does appear show up in portions of the state space that are unmonitored or unmonitorable (for practical reasons). For the footprint that appears in the monitored state space, the objective is to ensure that the attack signal stays below the noise level of normal system activity, or to have the signal above the noise floor be too weak to cross the alert threshold. *The defender's objectives, on the other hand, are to drop the noise floor to expose more attack signal, amplify the attack signal to the extent possible, and drop the alert threshold as far as possible.* This attacker-defender dynamic is shown in Figure 15-5, which shows these actions to improve detection. The defender's detection enhancement options are discussed in Section 15.6.1.

> ***Drop the noise floor; amplify attack signals; drop alert thresholds.***

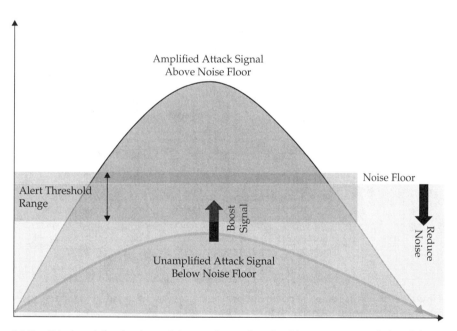

Figure 15-5   Attacker-defender dynamic interaction and goals with respect to attack signal detection

15.6.1 Reducing the Noise Floor

Noise is created by normal system activity. The more chaotic that activity is, the higher will be the noise floor, making it more difficult to detect an attack signal. What creates chaos? *Diversity of activity on the system creates chaos.* Of course, organizations need a diversity of activity to function and thrive. They need business systems such as human resources and financial management systems. They need the wild and wooly world of research and development. They need manufacturing production systems. They need programming development systems for their next-generation capabilities. They need network control and systems administration for operating the system effectively and efficiently. *What they do not need is to host all of these systems and activities on the exact same infrastructure.* The chaos of each adds and perhaps even multiplies when the capabilities cohabitate on the same computers and networks. It may sometimes be prohibitively expensive to create dozens of separate *physical* infrastructures with needed controlled interactions between them.

> ### *Separate different mission activities into controlled subnetworks.*

A useful tool to accomplish controlled separation while sharing common information technology resources, gaining the best of both worlds, is called **virtualization**. Computers can be virtualized using **virtual machine** software—sometimes called a **hypervisor**. Virtual machines (historically rooted in the **separation kernel** [RUSH81] concept) are a low-level operating system. Their function is to give the *appearance* to "guest" operating systems (e.g., Microsoft Windows® or Linux®) that they are running directly on hardware with exclusive use of system resources. This virtualized structure is shown in Figure 15-6. Virtual machines related to one subcommunity can be allocated to that subcommunity, even though it may be sharing the same hardware with another community.

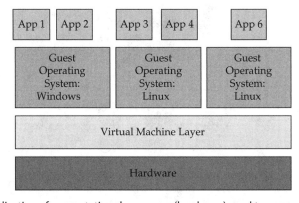

Figure 15-6   Virtualization of computational resources (hardware) used to separate user activity types and thus lower the attack noise floor

Similarly, the network can be channelized using encryption technology to create separate subnetworks on top of the same physical network infrastructure. This is accomplished using specialized router modes, network devices, or communications software on the computers. The resulting subnetworks are called virtual private networks (VPNs). This notion is depicted in Figure 15-7.

With these two virtualization technologies, both processing and network traffic can be separated, yet connected through controlled interfaces. This makes authorized activity on the system much more stable and predictable and drops the noise floor to the point that attacks will be more difficult to hide.

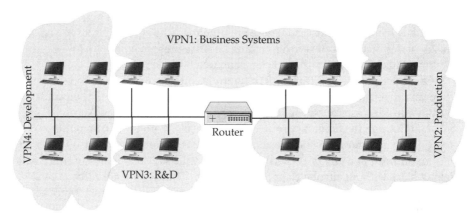

Figure 15-7   Virtualization of networks to separate network traffic to reduce attack noise floor

15.6.2 Boosting Attack Signal

In addition to dropping the noise floor, one can boost the attack signal. By doing so, we can make the attacker work harder in each step of the attack flow. For example, if the system has multiple wide-open known vulnerabilities, the adversary can simply apply a known **exploit**. On the other hand, if a system is promptly and completely up to date on all issued patches, then the adversary will have to do additional reconnaissance, probing, and testing to develop a novel attack. Those activities create fingerprints that boost the overall attack signal of the attack flow. Unfortunately, many systems are not patched, and many known vulnerabilities do not yet have patches.

Similarly, if a system has lots of unneeded services running on numerous system ports, then attack activity on these ports is hard to detect. On the other hand, if the system is locked down tight (called **hardened**) to use only the bare essentials of services and ports needed to serve the mission, an attacker's use of ports can appear very loud indeed; thus, again, boosting the attack signal.

The defender can also use filtration to boost attack signals in the same way unwanted frequencies can be filtered out and wanted frequencies can be amplified in radio communications (e.g., the human voice appears primarily in the frequency band around 300–3,400 hertz, so those frequencies can be selectively enhanced). To filter, the defender needs a logical basis to do so. For this, **misuse cases** are useful. A misuse case is a special type of use case where a particular type or class of attack scenario is postulated and its implications on design and detection are analyzed.

An example of a misuse case is the use of the "reserved for future use" fields in network protocols. There should be no content in those fields. Filtering out all of the network traffic except for the part of the headers that contain reserved fields would boost attack signals tremendously. Of course, some application developers unwisely and improperly use reserved fields sometimes, so such abuses will be caught up in the dragnet as a side effect of the search for an attack. Another example of a misuse case is the **exfiltration** of stolen data to a remote portion of a dedicated network that is less physically protected. Therefore, filtering all traffic except to such remote sites and focusing on volume anomalies in network traffic would be potentially fruitful for this case. There are potentially hundreds if not thousands of such misuse cases that are well worth pursuing because they each potentially amplify the signal of multiple attacks and make the attacker's job much harder.

One last example of filtration is to filter out known and registered communications. Over time, an organization can accrete millions of connections to tens of thousands of network destination addresses outside of the enterprise network boundary. All such communication must go through the boundary routers and firewalls. A policy can be put into place to begin to explicitly register each and every one of these communication paths (source address, destination address, and port used). Over time, what will be left are communications that are taking place without anyone claiming ownership. These connections can then be investigated as possible alerts. Many will be legitimate paths that someone simply forgot to register. The remaining ones after that, though, may well be attacks. For Star Trek fans, this is analogous to an interesting episode entitled "Court Martial" (Star Trek: The Original Series, Season 1, Episode 20, which first aired February 2, 1967) where they find someone hiding in the engineering section of the ship by filtering out the sound of the heartbeats of all the registered crew members; the remaining unregistered heartbeat is that of the rogue crewman thought to have died in an ion storm.

15.6.3 Lowering the Alert Threshold

The last approach to the defender enhancing attack signal is reducing the alert threshold. This is useful because it can expose weak attack signals that are intentionally hiding just below the existing alert threshold. Attackers count on defenders not having the resources or patience to run all of the resulting false positives to ground. If the defender occasionally surges resources to track down these false alarms or decreases the cost of running down each through automation, there is a chance that the defender will catch attacks that they would have otherwise have missed.

Conclusion

This chapter completes the trilogy of chapters on attack detection, from sensor development, to attack detection systems, and, with this chapter, a discussion of detection strategies. This chapter discusses how to deploy and operate detection systems to be most effective at detecting attacks.

To summarize:

- Detection in breadth and depth at the same time is imperative to effective detection systems—with respect to the network expanse to covering the attack space.
- Cyberspace can and should be engineered to the defender's advantage.
- Herd the adversary to areas where the detection systems are stronger and deeper.

- Attack epidemiology can bring the benefit from the attack on one to the many.
- Post-detection can be improved by running alerts to ground and by gaining more information on the nature of the attack.
- Attack signal can be boosted through techniques such as filtration.
- Noise floors can be reduced through processes such as virtualized process and network separation.

Questions

1. Define "detection in depth" and state how it is achieved.
2. Define "detection in breadth" and state how it is achieved.
3. Explain how detection in depth and detection in breadth relate to one another.
4. Name and explain two dimensions of detection depth and breadth.
5. What is an attack flow and how does it relate to detection placement strategies?
6. What is one of the first and most important targets of an adversary when attacking a system in which it is important to keep the attack success a secret?
7. Why should you assume that your adversary has a complete map of your detection gaps and shallow areas?
8. What does "herd the adversary" mean and how do you use this strategy to improve system defenses?
9. What is attack epidemiology? Explain how everyone benefits from it.
10. Name two ways that attack detection can be refined in terms of follow-up action.
11. Compare and contrast aspects of attack signals with those of normal communication.
12. How can an attack signal be boosted? Describe an additional way not provided in the book.
13. How can background noise be reduced? Describe an additional way not provided in the book.
14. How can alert thresholds be reduced? Why would a defender want to do that?

16 Deterrence and Adversarial Risk

Overview

Learning Objectives

- Explain the three requirements to achieve deterrence and how to meet them.
- Define an adversary's risk threshold and discuss how it affects their behavior.

- Determine how a defender can modulate adversary risk and thereby thwart attack.

- Discuss the role that uncertainty and deception play in the attacker-defender dynamic.

- Summarize when and why detection and deterrence are sometimes ineffective in system defense.

In the previous chapter, we discussed ways of optimizing intrusion detection as a means to detect and recover from cyberattacks that are missed by prevention techniques. In addition, and somewhat ironically, detection techniques can have an important prevention effect. Why? It is for the same reason that surveillance cameras can prevent crime—criminals are concerned about being caught, and they are particularly concerned about the legal consequences of being caught (jail time). We say that intrusion detection has a slight **deterrence** effect.

There is much more to be said about deterrence theory, such as applying mutually assured destruction to cybersecurity at a national policy level. Although such discussions are beyond the scope of this book, the reader is actively encouraged to read further on this topic to gain insights on how to become a better cybersecurity engineer [NRC10][RATT01] [SCHW10].

16.1 Deterrence Requirements

For deterrence to work, three things must be true: (1) the attack can be reliably detected, (2) the attack can be reliably attributed to the attacker, and (3) the potential consequences are sufficiently severe so that the attacker would be harmed by the consequences in a meaningful way. We discuss each in turn.

> *Deterrence requires detection, attribution, and consequences.*

16.1.1 Reliable Detection: Risk of Getting Caught

Experts estimate that upwards of 70 percent of attacks go undetected [THOM15]! That is an appalling state of affairs. This is partly because not all systems have performed the basic hygiene of applying patches to well-known attacks [WOOL17]. Some have not deployed even basic intrusion detection, which is readily available as both a commercial product and as open source. Some deploy intrusion detection systems, but do not configure them correctly or actively monitor their alerts. Further, we know that even with the best intrusion detection capabilities that are well-monitored on systems that are well-patched, some attacks will succeed due to gaps in the detection capability—particularly zero-day attacks and unpatched known vulnerabilities. *Still, the defender must make a best effort to maximize the adversary's risk of detection.*

> *Defenders must maximize adversary detection risk.*

16.1.2 Reliable Attribution

For deterrence purposes, it is necessary but insufficient to detect an attack or even to properly classify its specific type. The defender must know who is perpetrating the attack in order to know from whom to exact the consequences. This is known as **attack attribution**. It is difficult because the adversary works hard to obfuscate the source of their attack to specifically avoid **attribution** and consequent retribution if they are caught. Attackers use techniques such as attacking through multiple hops of computer systems, **phreaking** (hacking phone systems) through telecommunications networks, and hacking through multiple countries' systems with preference for countries that have no cybersecurity laws and that lack resources to track and prosecute cyberattacks [MITN11][MITN17] (Figure 16-1). Attackers also use techniques such as **source address spoofing** for obfuscation and **misdirection**, which involves address spoofing to a particular false address to shift blame onto a specific person, group, or country.

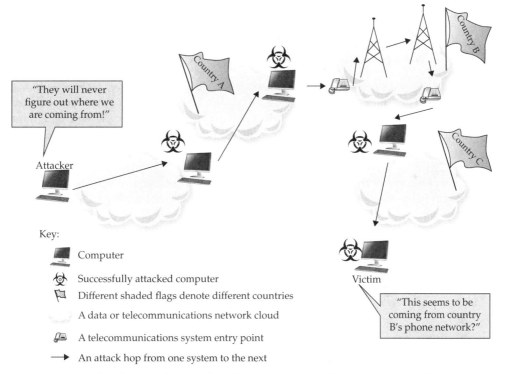

Figure 16-1 Attackers hopscotch through multiple systems in multiple countries to make attribution difficult.

Despite the difficulties, it is sometimes possible to attribute attacks, often with the cooperation of Internet service providers and telecommunication providers, by tracing back each hop of an attack sequence though the routers that each hop passes through. Certain attackers may lack the skills to obfuscate their attack paths by using tools such as anonymizers (e.g., Tor), which make it difficult to determine paths. Therefore, the defender should not assume that attribution will always be difficult.

There is also an ability to examine the attack code itself and find standardized and reused coding patterns that could be highly suggestive of the original source of the attack. Finding reused coding patterns is related to **n-gram analysis**, used to establish authorship and other similar interesting applications by looking at reused phrases and sequences [LOVE02]. Of course, *for every measure, there is a countermeasure.* Because this technique is well known, sophisticated attackers can spoof the **n-grams** of various attackers and can cause false attribution.

> *For every measure, there is a countermeasure.*

16.1.3 Meaningful Consequences

Lastly, the defender must be

- Capable of imposing a meaningful and proportionate consequence on the attacker.
- Willing to impose the consequence.
- Willing to risk retaliation for imposing that consequence.

The interpretation of meaningful and proportionate consequences depends on the system that is being defended, the attacker, and the nature of an attack. Take, for example, a cybersecurity engineer who is defending a critical national security system, and the adversary is a powerful nuclear-capable nation-state, and the adversary is attempting to perform espionage. A meaningful and proportionate response may be first a diplomatic objection. Failing that, a country might want to try public embarrassment. Failing that, the defending country may want to consider a computer network attack on the perpetrating systems. If the target system is instead a major portion of a country's power grid and the nature of the attack is sabotage, then the situation is substantially more grave. Some political leaders of countries have stated that they would take such an attack as an act of war and would consider physical retaliation, including nuclear retaliation (scary stuff!) [CRIS17].

> *Meaningful consequences depend on system, attacker, and attack.*

Consider another example in which the target is a corporate retail system, the attacker is organized crime, and the nature of the attack is extortion. If the ransom is small enough, some companies will pay it. Alternatively, the meaningful and proportionate response could be to engage law enforcement to arrest and prosecute the perpetrators for their crimes, although that can be difficult if they reside in other countries.

In addition to the issue of developing proportionate and meaningful consequences, the defender must understand that attribution *is a matter of probability and almost never one of certainty*. So, one can say that with a probability of 75 percent, we believe the attacker is person XYZ, but that is about all. Further, the defender must consider the possibility that, not only is the attacker trying to prevent attribution to themselves, but may be actively trying to cause misattribution to someone else who they want to inappropriately receive the consequences of their attack. *The defender should be particularly careful when the attack seems too easy to attribute and it seems like it was fed on a silver platter.*

> *Attribution is usually a matter of probability, not certainty.*

16.2 All Adversaries Have Risk Thresholds

Although we have painted a somewhat bleak picture regarding reliable detection, reliable attribution, and meaningful response to the right attacker, all is not hopeless. Attackers always have a risk of being discovered, even by accident due to a failure in their attack or attack process or an insider in the attacker's organization revealing the attack. *The attacker's risk is never zero*, though it can be small enough as to not pose a significant barrier to action, as North Korea, China, and Russia have demonstrated quite clearly.

> *Attacker risk is never zero.*

Attackers have a **risk tolerance**, the amount of risk they are willing to take. An adversary's risk tolerance is related to their estimate of

- The probability that their attack will be detected.
- The probability that their attack will be properly attributed.
- The capability to exact serious consequences that the defender can muster.
- The probability that the defender has the will to exact the consequences.
- Their capability to retaliate against a defender's imposed consequence.
- The probability that they would actually retaliate.
- The level of risk for which individual leaders have an appetite.

Different adversaries have different risk tolerances under different circumstances. *For all adversaries, there is some level of risk beyond which they are unwilling to go.* We call this their **risk threshold**.

> *All adversaries have their risk threshold.*

16.3 System Design Can Modulate Adversary Risk

A defender's goal is to increase the attacker's risk as much as possible by addressing each of the factors listed in the previous section that affects the attacker's risk tolerance. These factors are discussed each in turn.

16.3.1 Detection Probability

Increasing an adversary's probability of being detected is related to

- The capabilities of the detection systems deployed within the defender's system.
- The defender's ability to operate properly.
- How well detection in depth and breadth is accomplished.
- The degree to which a system is well patched.
- The extent of known vulnerabilities for which patches are not yet available.
- How novel the defender's system is.

We have discussed these topics in the context of the detect-recover defense to an ongoing attack. The same factors apply to deterrence. If the attacker knows either through external intelligence or through initial probing that the defender is rated highly on several of these factors, they know that their probability of detection is substantially increased. On this basis alone, the attacker could simply choose a different, easier target.

16.3.2 Attribution Probability

Attribution relates to the **forensic capability** of the defender and their ability to work closely with other experts and service providers to track attack sources. A highly technical organization such as a software developer is almost certainly going to have a better capability than a lower-tech company such as a construction firm. Also, close relationships with regional and national computer emergency response teams can extend an organization's native capability.

In addition, close relationships with Internet and telecommunication companies create a much stronger capability. Therefore, attacking an Internet service provider company will have significantly different attribution implications than attacking a hardware storage system.

Lastly, close relationships with law enforcement and government can significantly extend the capabilities of what can be done with proper warrants, particularly when the cooperation of other countries is needed. Forming industry alliances that then form relationships with organizations such as the Federal Bureau of Investigation through programs like Infragard (www.infragard.org), or with the Department of Homeland Security [NIPP13], can be a good move toward signaling to attackers that you have an extended team and you have the help of the government [GERM14].

16.3.3 Consequence Capability and Probability

A defender can have clearly stated and public policies that make consequences clear to would-be attackers. A company policy against paying ransom to attackers, under any circumstances, sends a clear signal. A policy that says that the company will quickly and immediately cooperate with law enforcement to seek full prosecution of any perpetrators sends a clear signal of a capability. It is important to follow through on such policies and do so loudly and publicly, whenever possible. A lot of bravado in policy without follow-through is not particularly convincing to an adversary.

Making consequences significant enough to deter attackers, and being sure enough in attribution to enforce consequences, is extraordinarily difficult. To date, making this formula effective in deterring attacks has met with very limited success.

16.3.4 Retaliation Capability and Probability

Retaliation capability and probability are in the hands of the attacker. It is important, however, in the attribution process for a defender to know the nature of the attacker and their capabilities. Incurring the wrath of a hacktivist group such as anonymous or foreign organized crime can have serious consequences for an organization. Risking escalating to a kinetic war should be part of the consideration in deciding consequences in the case of a nation-state action.

16.3.5 Risky Behavior

Some people enjoy taking more risk than others [PARK08]. Again, this is almost entirely under the control of the attacker. It can be possible, though, to subtly convince the leadership of an attacking organization that they are taking too much risk and putting the adversary's organization at risk beyond what it would prefer. For example, if a leader of a cyberattack unit of a country habitually and recklessly attacked other countries' systems without much concern for attribution, it *may* be possible to cause sufficient fuss through private diplomatic channels, and even possibly public embarrassment, to cause that leader to be quietly replaced. Countries such as Germany are beginning to form bilateral agreements to disincentivize such risky behavior [PAND15].

16.4 Uncertainty and Deception

As mentioned, risk is a matter of *estimated* probability times *estimated* consequences. Such estimates are based on behavior models that attackers and defenders develop of one another. As discussed in earlier chapters, these models can and should be manipulated to the extent possible to one's advantage. Uncertainty and deception are two ways of accomplishing such manipulation.

16.4.1 Uncertainty

Making it hard for the adversary to be sure about any of the factors discussed in the previous section works to the defender's advantage. For example, if an adversary believes that a defender has an effective intrusion detection system with a probability of 60 percent, but with an uncertainty interval of plus or minus 20 percent, the attacker will need to treat the system as if there is an 80 percent chance of an effective intrusion detection system. A defender creates such uncertainty by not publicizing the details of its product choices and certainly not the details of its configurations and operations. Having a hardened firewall with minimal open ports will also deny the adversary significant reconnaissance and thus will further increase uncertainty.

Attacker uncertainty is the defender's friend.

Uncertainty is not only about whether the attack will be discovered, but about whether the attack will be discovered in time to thwart the attackers' goal. Sophisticated attackers often invest significantly to accomplish a complex attack, so early discovery of their attack steps can cause the attacker to waste significant resources. This potential to waste investment can act as one of the most significant deterrents.

16.4.2 Deception

Taking uncertainty to another level, the defender can use **deception** techniques. For example, the defender can create honeypots that appear to be the defender's system, but are not. The defender can imply in a system banner (message that is automatically transmitted when a program opens a port to a service listening on that port) that they are monitoring every keystroke and are testing a new experimental intrusion detection system or claim to have a high-end commercial system that they do not have (similar to posting a sign saying "This House Is Protected by So-and-So's Alarm System" when, in fact, it is not). A deception can be mounted for each factor, creating both uncertainty and incorrect inflated estimates.

16.5 When Detection and Deterrence Do Not Work

Under what circumstances are detection and deterrence ineffective? It is important to know both where detection helps and where it does not. The theory behind the detect-recover approach counts on attacks being multistep processes that take significant clock time to execute. This is often the case, as shown in Figure 16-2. The graph is similar in theory to the damage avoidance of catching bugs early in the development process [NIST02]. Note that damage can include lost revenue, cost to recover from the attack, damaged reputation, lost mission, or any number of values. Similarly, the time scale is relative to the rate at which the attack can do damage. For these reasons, the notional graph does not provide quantities on the axes.

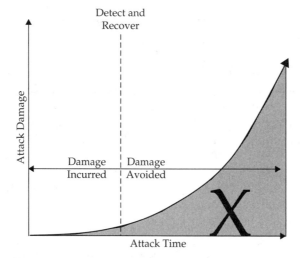

Figure 16-2   Notional graph of exponentially increasing attack damage as a function of attack time, with early detection being able to avoid the bulk of the damage

At the same time, there are instances when attacks are single-step and too fast to do much in the way of damage mitigation. Such attacks are sometimes called "**one-packet-one-kill**." For some vulnerabilities, it is literally true that sending an attack network packet to the right port of an application can cause the application and possibly the entire system to shut down. Hence, the one packet "kills" the system. This term is sometimes generalized to refer to an attack situation that is sufficiently fast that the damage is done before the defender even realizes the attack has started. Also, the notion of "kill" only applies to an availability attack, but more generally, it is about accomplishing the attack mission with a small enough number of steps to be very difficult to detect and thwart in a timely fashion.

For fast attacks, the **detect-recover** model is effective in the circumstance where reversal of the damage is possible. For confidentiality attacks, if the data is compromised, there is not much good closing the barn door after the horses have left the barn. For integrity attacks, recovery is possible as long as backups exist and rollback to a safe state is possible. For availability attacks, recovery is possible through a system reboot. In most cases, the damage is limited to the period of time that the system is down. Of course, the damage can be significant in the face of an urgent situation. For example, an antiaircraft system going down as the adversary airplanes fly overhead is difficult to recover from.

Lastly, deterrence is not effective when the attacker is impervious to most consequences. Nation-states can and have claimed that attacks launched from their countries really came from someplace else or that it was criminal hackers in their population and not the nation-state itself. There is a distinction, although a fine line, between state-sponsored and state-sanctioned cyberattacks. In the first case, agents of the country, such as military personnel, fund and execute the attacks. In the second case, members of a country's population execute the attacks and the state either turns a blind eye or indirectly rewards the actors through recruiting or indirect financing.

With the fuzzy line on who is taking action and on whose behalf, it can be difficult to refute a state's claim of non-involvement. This makes it nearly impossible to impose consequences—particularly if that country is a superpower or, at least a nuclear power, which creates the specter of escalation from cyberattacks to kinetic conflict to the unthinkable nuclear exchange. In addition, if two countries are already at war, then deterrence becomes difficult because it would surprise nobody that a country uses cyberattacks in that context. This occurred in the case of the Russia-Georgia conflict in 2008 [BUMG09][MARK08] in which Russians attacked Georgian government and news media web servers and rerouted Internet traffic in concert with Russia's physical attack on Georgia. The situation becomes even more muddied when the targets of attack are civilian systems such as news sites, banking, or the power grid.

Conclusion

This chapter transitions from the three chapters on attack detection to the strategic attack prevention technique of deterrence. Deterrence deals with dissuading an attacker from even attempting an attack because the consequences are too serious. This chapter discusses the circumstances in which deterrence can work, and those in which it cannot. This chapter rounds out the series of chapters on the building blocks of cybersecurity for mitigating risk. The next chapter begins a new part on orchestrating these building blocks using principles of design and architecture.

To summarize:

- Deterrence requires reliable detection, attribution, and meaningful consequences for attackers.
- Adversaries have risk thresholds that guide their attack actions.
- Defenders can alter adversary risk by increasing the adversary's probability of detection and attribution, and by developing strong consequence options and making it clear that they will be used.
- Defenders can increase adversary risk by increasing the adversary's uncertainty about the detection capabilities of the defender and by deceiving the adversary about it.
- Under circumstances such as open warfare, deterrence plays a very small role.
- Under circumstances of the attack damages being irreversible and happening before detection, the detect-recover model fails to add value to the defense of a system.

Questions

1. What is the deterrence effect?
2. How is deterrence different from a detect-recover capability in terms of intrusion detection?
3. When does detection perform a prevention function? When does prevention perform a detection function?
4. What are the three requirements of deterrence and what does each mean? Are the three all necessary to achieve deterrence? Why? Are the three together sufficient? Why or why not?
5. List at least three defender challenges in achieving reliable detection. What is the one class of attack that is particularly problematic to detect? Why?
6. What does attack attribution mean?
7. Why is attack attribution difficult?
8. If the evidence of an attack is overwhelming and easily points to one possible source, what might you suspect? Why?
9. What organizations may you need to collaborate with to achieve attribution?
10. Why can't one trust the Internet protocol source address in examining the network packets? What do you think you can do about that problem?
11. What is misattribution and why might it be in an attacker's interest to cause it?
12. What is n-gram analysis and what does it have to do with attribution?

13. Describe two different scenarios not mentioned in the book and discuss what proportionate and meaningful consequences might be in those two scenarios.

14. What is an attacker's risk threshold and how is it determined? How does it affect adversary behavior?

15. Name and discuss the rationale for five factors that affect adversary risk tolerance.

16. What is an alert threshold and how does it affect attack alarming to human operators? What happens if the threshold is set too high? What if it is set too low?

17. Discuss three ways that a defender can modulate adversary risk and evaluate which ways you think would be most cost-effective.

18. How does model hacking as discussed in earlier chapters relate to deterrence?

19. How can defenders amplify attacker uncertainty? Why is that useful in terms of decreasing the likelihood of attack?

20. List two examples of how a defender might use deception to increase attacker risk. Discuss how to implement your approach in a practical way.

21. When does the detect-recover model of protection break down?

22. Under what conditions is deterrence least effective?

IV

How Do You Orchestrate Cybersecurity?

"Part IV: How Do You Orchestrate Cybersecurity?" discusses the principles of addressing the cybersecurity problem and attack space holistically and lays out the principles of cybersecurity architecture.

Overview

Learning Objectives

- Discuss the merits of quantitative probabilistic risk assessment in cybersecurity engineering.
- Explain why risk is the primary security metric.
- Describe how metrics are used in engineering systems.
- Discuss the difference between defender and attacker value perspectives.
- Summarize the role of risk assessment and metrics in the defender's design process.
- List and describe the analysis elements on the risk assessment process.
- Explain how resource limitations and risk tolerance affect adversary behavior.

What gets measured gets done...sometimes to the exclusion of all else.

—Anonymous

This chapter overviews a systematic quantitative **risk assessment** process for analysis and how it guides design toward better cybersecurity architectures. It draws on material presented in previous chapters and places it into the context of a process flow.

17.1 A Case for Quantitative Risk Assessment

This chapter and the next represent an application of quantitative probabilistic risk assessment to cybersecurity—a controversial topic. This section states a brief case for this type of risk assessment as an essential part of cybersecurity engineering and addresses some of the objections. Some will continue to object. The question to pose to the critics is: What is your alternative?

If one does not have a unifying measure of goodness such as risk, how can one decide when a system is good enough, or even if one system design is better than another? Certainly, one could argue that the absence of badness, in the form of vulnerabilities, is useful. That is true. Unfortunately, cybersecurity badness has a multitude of dimensions and degrees, making it a poor metric.

Here are some objections to quantitative risk assessment in cybersecurity:

- Cybersecurity is too complex to be quantified.
- Risk measurement is too hard.

- Risk measurement is too imprecise.

- Qualitative assessment is better.

- Cybersecurity is too immature.

Cybersecurity is indeed highly complex, making risk measurement extraordinarily difficult and imprecise in the early stages of the cybersecurity discipline. Throwing one's hands up and declaring it too hard is unhelpful. The mere act of trying to quantify risk helps both cybersecurity engineers and stakeholders begin to understand the nature of risk, where it comes from, and how to efficiently mitigate it. This outcome has been demonstrated dozens of times with the successful application of this methodology to many large-scale and complex systems in the Department of Defense and **intelligence community**.

Documenting assumptions about the source, degree, and nature of risk allows cybersecurity experts to properly debate the important topics, disagree, perform experiments, and drive toward deeper and better understanding. This understanding will lead to improved estimates with higher precision over time. The alternative is to remain ignorant, keep these discussions suppressed, and not advance the discipline. *The alternative is bad engineering and bad science.* Certainly, cybersecurity engineers should take great care to understand the limitations of quantitative risk assessment, as they must understand the limitations of all models and tools.

If the imprecision of estimates deeply disturbs some readers, then they are invited to replace numbers with qualitative values such as high, medium, and low. If the use of dollars is a concern, then one can use some other quantity that measures value. The important aspect of this approach is the analytical techniques and the deep understanding and insights that they yield.

Cybersecurity must go down this rocky and difficult road. These chapters give the reader a foundation in understanding this essential part of the cybersecurity engineering process and how to apply it to analyze and design systems.

> *Quantitative risk assessment is essential to cybersecurity.*

17.2 Risk as a Primary Metric

Some people will incorrectly assert that you can't measure cybersecurity. On the contrary, *cybersecurity can be effectively measured using risk.* As discussed in Sections 2.1 and 16.4, risk is the likelihood of bad events happening multiplied by the probability that they will happen. Understanding cybersecurity risk is about understanding the nature of the bad events that can happen and estimating the likelihood of them happening, based on an understanding of system vulnerability and the adversary's capability and value proposition. This chapter explores a process to define the bad events that may occur and systematically estimate the probability with which they will occur.

> *Cybersecurity is measured using risk.*

17.3 Why Measure?

Why measure? Measurement is essential to

- Characterize the nature of what is and why it is that way.
- Evaluate the quality of a system.
- Predict system performance under a variety of environments and situations.
- Compare and improve systems continuously.

Without measurement there is no compass, no quality **metric**, and no clear way of improving cybersecurity. *Measurement is at the foundation of science and science is at the foundation of engineering.*

> *Risk measurement is foundational to improving cybersecurity.*

17.3.1 Characterize

A cybersecurity metric enables us to understand the processes, artifacts, resources, and environments of a system and all of its defenses. This characterization gives a baseline to understand why system cybersecurity is the way it is. Understanding acts as a springboard for improvements.

For example, we might say that a cybersecurity prevention mechanism is effective for only a specified subset of the attack space because of the nature of the actions it can take. This is a characterization of defense in depth and breadth (Section 8.3). To be even more specific, we can say that firewalls cannot stop insider attack infiltration because firewalls are designed to protect the perimeter of an enclave and an insider, by definition, is on the inside of the perimeter. Similarly, an intrusion detection system that only analyzes network packets is incapable of detecting attacks within a host operating system because those attacks stay within that computer, never trying to communicate or spread from that one host (Section 15.1).

Characterization is about describing the behavior of a given characteristic of a cybersecurity system. In the previous examples, we chose attack space since it is highly relevant and one the reader will be familiar with based on discussions in previous chapters. Other characteristics might include **time complexity** analysis of the mechanism's underlying algorithm. Time complexity is a way of characterizing how much time an algorithm will take to execute as a function of an element of scaling. For example, if a firewall scans content of incoming files for malware, is time complexity a linear function of the size of the file, is it polynomial (meaning file size raised to some power), or is it exponential?

Knowing time complexity is critical to determine limitations of the system in terms of how the system will operate under different conditions. **Space complexity**—the amount of storage a system requires as a function of inputs—is also highly relevant and important. *How does this system react if it does not get all of the time or space that it requires to operate?* Does it still work, but in a gracefully degraded fashion; does it totally fail; or worse, does it cause the entire system to crash? These are important questions of characterization.

17.3.2 Evaluate

A cybersecurity metric allows cybersecurity engineers to determine performance levels of a system to decide their value in guiding investment [JAQU07]. Such a metric also enables a comparison between two alternative designs to guide the system toward better performance. Cybersecurity metrics enable engineers to assess the impacts of new technologies, changing environments, and other important variables so that the system can be designed to perform well under a large variety of different circumstances. Evaluation can be empirical or theoretical. Both have their strengths and weaknesses, and both are valuable in performing any serious evaluation.

Empirical   An **empirical metric** is one that is *directly measured.* For attack detection, an empirical measurement would be evaluating detection performance against an **attack load**—a set of well-understood and characterized attacks. How many attacks are prevented? How many are detected? What is the damage to the system? These are important measurements to make in an empirical evaluation.

Theoretical   A **theoretical metric** is one that is determined by an analysis of the mechanism design and its underlying algorithms and inputs. An intrusion detection system is inherently blind to certain classes of attacks because it simply does not examine the features in which those attacks would manifest (Section 13.3). A prevention technique such as **content filtering** may be inherently limited by the time complexity of the underlying algorithm. The device doing the content filtering may be unable to perform its processing due to data rate or data size constraints. In such an event, the mechanism has to decide whether to block the content (**fail closed**) or allow the content to pass through (**fail open**). In either case, determining that decision point is a theoretical characterization based on an analysis of the design and its implementation.

The use of empirical and theoretical measurements together is valuable. It is a waste of resources to empirically measure aspects of cybersecurity system performance that are known in theory in advance. Why include attacks in the attack load to which the system is known to be theoretically blind or incapable of preventing? *Empirically testing system aspects that theory suggests will perform well is almost always a good idea.* Such testing generally demonstrates that systems perform less well than theoretically predicted due to inadequacies in the models used to do the analysis or due to some gap in the designer's knowledge of the attack process. Such testing is almost always worth doing, particularly what is known as **edge testing**—testing of the system performance at the limits of what the theory suggests. For example, measuring attack detection performance empirically in a high-noise (lots of variable data traffic) environment could be useful because defender models of performance under noisy conditions are often primitive and therefore not reliable because noise models are complex.

17.3.3 Predict

A good cybersecurity metric allows designers to extrapolate trends in risk under a variety of scenarios and to develop cybersecurity mechanisms to counter predicted circumstances before they occur. This creates much more robust systems with higher longevity. Predictions based on risk trends allow engineers to establish achievable quality (e.g., reliability, availability, speed, and accuracy), cost, and schedule goals in projects.

> ***Good metrics predict risk, enabling designers to mitigate it.***

As previously discussed, for a given system, one could predict a system's performance under unusual circumstances of high traffic load, high attack load, noisy conditions, **mission** mode changes (e.g., high sales traffic during holiday season for a retailer), or failure modes under resource starvation scenarios (insufficient computation time, storage, or network bandwidth). At a macro scale, *one can predict adversary behavior based on previous behavior by constructing models.* One could also study industry damage trends and determine that national investment, laws, research and development, and cybersecurity architectures need to fundamentally change to avoid a point at which the system becomes too untrustworthy to conduct any type of serious business.

> ***Previous behavior often predicts future behavior.***

17.3.4 Improve

Quality security metrics enable cybersecurity engineers to identify obstacles to better security, identify root cases of high risk, and identify inefficiencies in designs that impact cybersecurity performance. Identifying these causes is essential to improvement, particularly in areas that yield highest risk reduction for the lowest cost. See Section 7.3 for a discussion on the Five Whys analytical technique and how it can be applied to diagnose design problems that can then lead to significant improvements.

Metrics also help designers avoid making apparent improvements that yield little or no benefit because the risk simply moves to another area of the system where the adversary has equally good opportunities. *In the end, the cybersecurity engineer seeks to make the adversary's life miserable, not simply redirect them to an equally easy target.* In following through with this holistic approach to cybersecurity, risk is reduced across the entire system. Designing systems to reduce risks will be discussed further in Section 18.4.

> ***Risk must be reduced, not just moved around.***

17.4 Evaluate Defenses from an Attacker's Value Perspective

Understanding risk to a system means understanding the attacker's value proposition. *This means that good defenders understand how to get inside an attacker's head and think like an attacker.* If no attacker is interested in a specific aspect of a system, then the defender need not expend resources defending it. At the same time, if an attacker identifies exceptionally high-value targets *from their perspective*, they are willing to expend extraordinary resources to attain that value and to look for multiple creative ways into a system that perhaps the defender did not consider. In the end, though, attackers, just like defenders, have budgets to work within to achieve their goals. Those budgets are not infinite. Defenders can use this fact to *push the cost and risk of attacks sufficiently high to make it beyond the attacker's budget.*

> ### *Push attacker cost and risk beyond their budgets.*

For example, organizations that produce information hold two attractive targets to an attacker: the information-producing apparatus and the information produced from that apparatus. Two items of value to adversaries of such organizations are the impairment of the information-producing apparatus with respect to its ability to gain further information and stealing the information itself for their own use and to learn what hidden information may exist about the information-producing organization.

An adversary will spend only up to one dollar for one-dollar's-worth of value to the adversary. If the defender can increase the adversary's cost, then the adversary will choose to invest elsewhere (perhaps on improving their own attack or defense apparatus in some other way). *The adversary's cost to achieve a gain against a defender's system is equal to the lowest-cost attack available to them to achieve that gain.* Such an attack could be anything from buying an insider to a sophisticated technical **life-cycle attack**. The defender cannot count on the adversary to attack in the most secure places (e.g., attempting to break high-grade cryptography on **communications security**) and *one cannot therefore judge the goodness of defenses from the strength of one's best defenses.*

Therefore, *the value of the defenses mounted by a system is not the sum of the costs of all of the investments made in the system defenses by the defender.* Say the defender invests $1M in the deploying cybersecurity services and widgets. Prior to that deployment, let's suppose that the attackers' best attack costs $100. If afterwards, the adversary is able to find an attack that costs $1,000, that cybersecurity service provides substantially less than sum of its costs in defensive value. In other words, as with buying consumer products, just because you pay $100 for something does not mean it is worth $100. *In cybersecurity, the defender must justify the cost with the cybersecurity benefit in terms of risk reduction.* Risk reduction is a function of how far the measure raises the bar for the attackers.

> ### *Risk reduction is the driving cybersecurity benefit.*

It is hard for defenders to think up all possible clever unexpected attack entry points into a system. Even if defenders systematically look widely for the spectrum of all possible attack classes, there is always the possibility of missing one and therefore significantly overestimating the value of defenses. Employing continuous reassessment by out-of-the-box thinkers is therefore a good idea (see Section 6.5 on red teams).

17.5 The Role of Risk Assessment and Metrics in Design

Measuring **risk** is a key part of the design process. Design begins with requirements analysis. How much risk are the system owners willing to take? *The requirements analysis process should determine the maximum acceptable risk goal.* We see this represented in the lower left-hand corner of Figure 17-1. The maximum risk becomes the risk goal. As the design progresses and iterates, the risk is evaluated, and the resulting risk is compared to this maximum acceptable risk. If the current design risk is less than the maximum risk, then the design process is complete with respect to the risk goal (other considerations could drive the design to continue to iterate, such as reliability). If the system's design risk is greater than the maximum tolerable risk, then the design process continues into an analysis phase in which the risk sources are identified from the evaluation. The results of the analysis are then fed in as additional requirements, which then results in an improved design. This design loop iterates until the resulting design has lower-than-maximum risk. This loop is shown in the middle and right-hand side of Figure 17-1.

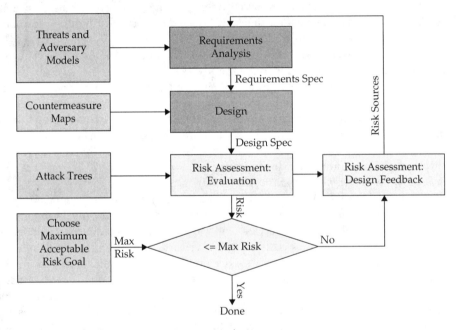

Figure 17-1 Role of risk measurement in iterative design process

Figure 17-1 integrates design process concepts from various portions of this book. Threats and adversary models (Section 6.1) are created, and the information is included with the requirements analysis. Countermeasure mapping (Section 8.2) informs the defender's design. Goal-directed attack trees (Section 7.1) are created to determine attack scenarios and are further used to perform a risk assessment evaluation to determine the maximum acceptable risk goal. Requirement analysis, design, and risk assessment evaluation are part of the iterative design process (Sections 5.4 and 20.4).

The risk assessment process contributes the risk evaluation and the risk design feedback depicted in the iterative design loop. This chapter focuses on the evaluation aspect; the next chapter, on the design feedback aspect. The risk assessment evaluation process itself is a complex series of analyses that can be represented as a flow chart. It is depicted in Figure 17-2. Each element is discussed in the next section.

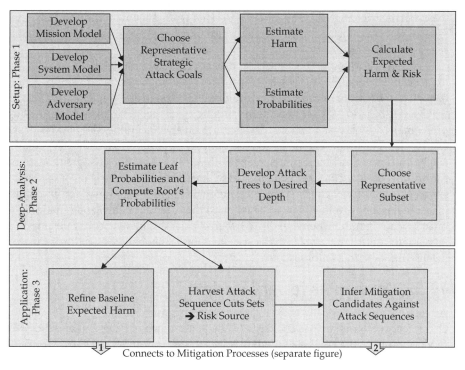

Figure 17-2   Risk assessment analysis tasks and flowchart shown in three phases (connects to risk mitigation process in Figure 18-1)

17.6 Risk Assessment Analysis Elements

The top row of Figure 17-2 represents Phase 1, the risk assessment setup, resulting in models and requirements for what is sought. The middle row depicts Phase 2, the deep analysis using the models to estimate risk through attack trees and predictions of adversary behavior. The bottom row is Phase 3, the application and harvesting of information from the analysis for input into the design feedback subprocess of the risk assessment, which will be discussed in the next chapter.

17.6.1 Develop Mission Model

The first step in the first phase of the risk assessment process is to develop a **mission model**, which can be an informal statement of the organization's missions that are supported by information technology. These statements are important in understanding later steps, which involve discerning where the value and pain-points are for the organization in terms of adversary objectives.

17.6.2 Develop System Model

Another parallel initial step is to develop a model of how the system operates from a life-cycle, control, and data flow perspective. It is done to a sufficient level of detail to facilitate the cybersecurity analysis. The model is derived from documentation and discussions with system experts. Interfaces with external systems are captured as needed depending on their relevancy to the analysis.

Section 5.3 discusses the issues and process of system modeling in detail. A system model can be as simple as one page of prose or a set of PowerPoint briefings. On the other hand, it can be as complex as a set of multivolume design and implementation specifications that span thousands of pages, including requirement specifications, concepts of operation, preliminary design specifications, detailed design specifications, simulations, test plans, and test results. The model can be up to date, though it is usually partially obsolete. The model can be complete, but could contain gaps with respect to ad hoc changes that were made since the original design. Uncertainty along these lines must be seriously taken into account by a good cybersecurity engineer. The system model should be examined for potential inaccuracies, improvements must be made to the extent possible, and remaining uncertainty must be kept in mind when creating a cybersecurity design to account for possible vulnerabilities that exist because the specification is inadequate (see the discussion of defense in depth in Section 8.3).

17.6.3 Develop Adversary Models

Adversary models are generally selected from a standard library of typical adversary characteristics based on the concerns of the system owner. Selection of which adversary models to use in the risk assessment involves understanding the means, motive, and opportunity for real adversaries to damage the mission. To gain this understanding, cybersecurity engineers can study historical attacks against similar organizations and systems.

Section 6.1 covers the construction of adversary models in detail. The result of this modeling activity is essentially a list of adversary types and their primary characteristics. Often, red teams supplement the high-level model by simulating adversary tactics and preferred attack methods. Business intelligence organizations supplement adversary models with information about leadership and budgets and strategies of adversaries. The result of this modeling activity is essentially a list of adversary classes and their primary characteristics. Table 17-1 gives an example of a high-level adversary, derived from a library of adversaries that is sketched in Table 6-1.

#	Adversary Class	Example	Time Horizon	Focus	Resources	Risk Tolerance	Skills	Goals
1	Organized Crime	The Russian Business Network	Medium Term	Extortion	High	Low-Medium	High	Financial, Intelligence
2	Elite Hacker Group	Anonymous	Short Term	Hacktivism	Low-Medium	Low	High	Exposure, Social Change
3	Lone Hacker	Kevin Mitnick	Short Term	Proving something	Low	Very Low	Low-Medium	A cause, gain hacker group entry

Table 17-1   Classes of High-Level Adversary Models

17.6.4 Choose Representative Strategic Attack Goals

The next step of risk assessment develops a set of strategic attack goals that are intended to span the most important threats to mission. They are derived from a combination of mission understanding and classes of cyberattack that might apply to the various aspects of mission. It is not possible to exhaustively enumerate all possible strategic attack goals. The set chosen is intended to be sufficiently representative that it encompasses large classes of related attacks. The representative set is also chosen such that the mitigations of the attacks correspond to mitigations of elements in those classes.

Section 4.4 further details how to select adversary strategic attacks in the context of exploring mission harm. This key step deeply involves mission stakeholders, including senior leadership of an organization. The analysis results in around 10 representative adversary goals, similar to the generic banking system shown in Table 17-2. It is an instantiated version of the general template provided in Table 4-5. This exemplar will be carried forward throughout the chapter to ground the discussion in a common and concrete application.

#	Attack Class	Resulting Harm from Attacks	Scenario
1	**Confidentiality**	Loss of *user account data* jeopardizes *existing and future accounts staying at bank.*	Attacker hacks into system, steals *user account data,* and reveals to world or sells it on the black market.
2	**Confidentiality**	Loss of *borrower-sensitive data* requiring major reinvestment to regain capability for attracting new borrowers.	Attacker uses insider attack to steal *borrower-sensitive data,* which the organization relies upon to enable *confidence in the bank to protect borrowers' most sensitive information about the state of their finances.*
3	**Integrity**	Corrupt integrity of *account transactions and balances* so that consumers of data lose trust in *bank's ability to correctly administer financial data.*	Attacker uses a life-cycle attack to insert malware that discovers and corrupts *user account and transaction data.*
4	**Integrity**	Corrupt integrity of *loan status information* to cause erroneous decisions to damage *cash reserves* in the event of loan failure.	Attacker analyzes system and selectively corrupts the output *loan status information.*
5	**Availability**	Deny service to *online banking subsystems* to make *online banking* unavailable for more than 14 days.	Attacker does a distributed denial of service attack on *online banking subsystem* that is required by *online banking.*
6	**Availability**	Corrupt system integrity of *Fed Wire Interbank transfer system* and its backups required by *interbank settlement system* to operate.	Attacker does a computer network attack on bank's enterprise system and corrupts key infrastructure of *Fed Wire transfer system within bank* as well as its backups to disable *interbank settlement system operation.*

Table 17-2　Exemplar of a Strategic Attacker Goal List Applied to Generic Banking System

Part IV

17.6.5 Estimate Harm Using Wisdom of Crowds

For each of the strategic attack goals, mission experts develop an estimate of harm that would occur if the strategic goal were realized. Refinements of those estimates can be done with the application of additional resources doing further analysis that can then drive refinements of the analysis and conclusions. Such estimates are a matter of expert opinion, but the method uses the "wisdom of crowds" to gain as accurate an estimate as possible [SURO05].

Wisdom of crowds requires two obvious factors: wisdom and a crowd. Here, *wisdom* means that the person estimating has a reasonable basis for the estimate and is familiar with the organization, its mission, and its operations. *Crowd* refers to a diverse group of experts capable of providing estimates for a particular quantity such as the cost associated with an adversary achieving a strategic goal. The diversity requirement suggests that around about five senior leaders in the group *independently* estimate harm. This generally means that the estimates must ideally be done in writing at the same time during the same meeting if possible. It is important that the estimates be made completely independently from each other. Otherwise, more junior employees fear contradicting the boss and tend to just agree with the most senior person in the room. This also means that senior leadership and meeting facilitators must make it absolutely safe (no repercussions) to have different opinions from each other—indeed, that it is essential to do so.

Harm estimates are generally given as order of magnitude values in dollars. An order of magnitude means 10^n where n is an integer. We express estimates this way to indicate an understanding that the estimates are imprecise—rough estimates. We are essentially saying that we are estimating to the nearest power of 10 because that is the best we can do given all of the uncertainties. For example, a value of 10^4 means 10 with four zeros after it, so 10,000, which translates to $10,000 dollars of harm done to the organization.

The use of dollars (or the currency of your choice) is intended to represent both economic costs that are directly measurable and more intangible values such as human safety and human life. The translation of intangibles into dollars is controversial for several reasons: (1) it seems cold and heartless to place a dollar value on items as important as human life and safety, (2) it is hard to make such translations precisely, and, therefore (3) quantitative methods give the illusion of precision that does not exist. These are fair criticisms. On the other hand, society trades off human life and dollars as a matter of standard practice in disciplines such as civil engineering. For example, the decision to put a curve in a road (e.g., to save money in buying land) is a decision to kill x people per year because curves are inherently more dangerous than straight roads. That is a real trade-off that must be made. One can bury one's head in the sand and say that human life is infinitely valuable, or one can treat such intangibles explicitly and debate what the proper value should be. Similarly, arguments that say that one cannot be precise about placing value on intangibles never offer an alternative to how to treat intangibles from an engineering perspective. Currency is merely a convenient means of having a common means of comparing and thus trading off all things of value.

With several estimates in hand for each potential harm, one then can calculate a geometric mean of the supplied estimates—the geometric mean tends to deemphasize the extreme high and low values. Table 17-3 gives an example of combining estimates for one row of the running example we have been using in this chapter.

#	Attack Class	Resulting Harm from Attacks	E1	E2	E3	E4	E5	Mean	Geo. Mean
1	**Confidentiality**	Loss of *user account data* jeopardizes *existing and future accounts staying at bank.*	10^7	10^9	10^5	10^8	10^6	10^8	10^7
2	**Confidentiality**	Loss of *borrower-sensitive data* requiring major reinvestment to regain capability for attracting new borrowers.	10^{10}	10^6	10^8	10^9	10^7	10^9	10^8

Table 17-3   Application of Wisdom of Crowds and Combining Function for Harm Estimates in Dollars for Generic Banking System

Note that the harm values are given in dollars of damage *if the strategic attacker goal is fully realized.* It is important to strongly emphasize to the estimators that *the probability of the attacker goal being realized is a completely unrelated judgement.* This can be hard to separate in most defenders' minds, particularly for *low-probability high-impact events.* For example, if the true likelihood of an event is one in a million, but the harm would be a billion dollars, estimators have a hard time specifying a billion dollars as the harm value. This bias occurs because, in their heads, it is not likely to happen, so they want to somehow downgrade the billion-dollar estimate to something lower and perhaps less scary to them psychologically. So, this estimation process requires a bit of extra coaching using extreme examples, like a meteor striking the Earth. If they estimate the harm is low on the grounds that it is unlikely, then they need further reminders of the independence of the judgements.

After independent estimates are given, it is useful to bring the group that provided the estimates together to discuss the potential causes of variation in their estimates. The point of such a discussion is not to find out who was right or wrong. The point is to discern if some estimators had important misunderstandings about the organization mission and operations or of the estimation process itself. Once estimation assumptions are exposed through conversation, estimators can be given an opportunity to alter their input based on a better understanding of assumptions and the process. It must be made clear that the purpose is not for all estimators to converge on one value; that would defeat the purpose of the wisdom-of-crowds process.

17.6.6 Estimate Probability Using Wisdom of Crowds

As an initial exercise, it is useful for system and mission experts to assess the probability that strategic attacks would succeed, based on their knowledge of how the system works and how the mission depends on the system. Again, notice the probabilities are given as exponentials on a base of 10—orders of magnitude values. As with harm estimates, we use them to indicate the lack of precision on the estimate. In this case, the values are negative, meaning that the exponents are in the denominator. Therefore, for example, 10^{-2} means $1/10^2$, which is 1/100, which represents a 1 in 100 chance or a 1 percent chance of a successful strategic attack occurring.

Estimates at this level of abstraction tend to be overly optimistic. They are significantly biased toward lower probability estimates compared to a more detailed analysis—sometimes underestimated by an order of magnitude. At the same time, the bias is generally consistent between goals, and the purpose of this estimate is to guide the selection of strategic goals to focus on in the remainder of the analysis. The one exception here to be careful with is the **black swan** event [TALE10]. A black swan is a very low-probability event with very high impact. People do not handle these well at an intuitive level, and this error bias can literally kill people and organizations if missed. This is why one cannot rely on estimates at this level. Estimates at this level just provide a gross starting point for comparison purposes later in the risk assessment process.

As noted in Section 4.5, expected harm is simply the damages that one expects given the probabilities. To be clear, the harm outcome either happens or it does not, and so *actual* harm is whatever the harm of the events that do happen.

The product of the estimated harm and estimated probability gives the initial expected harm estimate, which is refined in later steps. Table 17-4 shows an example of fictional estimated probabilities along with the estimated harm values discussed in Section 17.6.5. The first two harm values are carried forward from the geometric mean column of Table 17-3, continuing the same generic banking exemplar through the chapter.

#	Attack Class	Resulting Harm from Attacks	Harm($) (H)	Probability (P)	Expected Harm $ (H*P)
1	Confidentiality	Loss of *user account data* jeopardizes *existing and future accounts staying at bank.*	10^7	10^{-3}	10^4
2	Confidentiality	Loss of *borrower-sensitive data* requiring major reinvestment to regain capability for attracting new borrowers.	10^8	10^{-2}	10^6
3	Integrity	Corrupt integrity of *account transactions and balances* so that consumers of data lose trust in *bank's ability to correctly administer financial data.*	10^{11}	10^{-4}	10^7
4	Integrity	Corrupt integrity of *loan status information* to cause erroneous decisions to damage *cash reserves* in the event of loan failure.	10^6	10^{-3}	10^3
5	Availability	Deny service to *online banking back end server* to make *online banking* unavailable for more than 14 days.	10^9	10^{-2}	10^7
6	Availability	Corrupt system integrity of *Fed Wire Interbank transfer system* and its backups required by *interbank settlement system* to operate.	10^{10}	10^{-3}	10^7
	Sum				10^7

Table 17-4   Calculating the expected harms based on geometric means of harm costs multiplied by the probabilities that a strategic attack will succeed, using a generic banking system exemplar.

The bottom row of Table 17-4 gives the sum of expected harms. Notice that the sum is totally dominated by the values in the rows 3, 5, and 6. Anything less than 10^7 is a rounding error in this case and does not significantly contribute to the calculated expected harm estimate. Using orders of magnitude makes this apparent. It tells cybersecurity professionals to focus attention on the expected harms in the aforementioned three rows because they represent the primary source of harm and thus risk to the organization's mission.

The sum of these expected harm values gives the *minimum* total expected harm for the system being analyzed. Why the minimum? Recall that the strategic attack goals of the adversary are representative goals, not an exhaustive list. Section 7.1 discusses this issue in more detail. Each adversary strategic goal represents a family of attacks in that class; therefore, if one wants an absolute risk value, one would have to come up with a multiplier representing an estimate of the number of instances within a represented class. Based on past experience, the value 10 would be a good starting multiplier.

As will be discussed later in the risk assessment process, *the absolute expected harm is important because it establishes the risk-reduction benefits, which helps determine the value returned by various alternative risk-reduction measures.*

17.6.7 Choose Representative Subset

Based on the estimates of harm and probability and on spanning the space of possible attacks, the analyst may choose a subset of attacks to drive the remainder of the analysis. Generally, this requires a minimum of three strategic attack goals (often one for confidentiality, one for integrity, and one for availability attacks), but can require more depending on the complexity of the attack space, which depends both on the complexity of mission and the ways in which the system supports that mission.

Section 7.4 describes the process of picking a representative subset of strategic attack goals. For the purpose of the continuing generic-banking example, we will stay with the full set of six that was described in Table 17-2.

17.6.8 Develop Deep Attack Trees

Once the representative set of attack trees is chosen, the strategic attack goals are successively refined in goal-directed attack trees. The strategic goal is the root of the tree. The root's subordinate nodes create a layer of subgoals which would achieve the strategic goal at the root. Each of the subordinate subgoal nodes is further refined by sub-subgoals that achieve that subgoal. Each layer ideally contains mutually exclusive and exhaustive subordinate nodes of all possible ways that the goal at the tree root can be met. Each layer of refinement can be broken down from several perspectives—technology (e.g., networks, firewalls, computers, operating systems, etc.), necessary attack sequences (e.g., break into network, find interesting data, get it back out of the network), and aspects of mission (e.g., collecting, processing, analyzing, and disseminating information), to name a few. The choice of which perspective to take is a matter of expert judgment on which facilitates understanding and analysis as well as the next level of goal refinement. Refinement continues until subject matter experts are comfortable that the bottom-layer leaf node probabilities can be easily estimated as singleton events (attack steps), based on their knowledge of systems and missions and how they are connected.

Sections 7.5 and 7.6 describe the successive refinement process and the criteria for when to stop refining into further layers, creating a final bottom layer of leaf nodes. In following through with the current example, refining strategic attacker goal #5, subgoals of hypothetical decomposition are used to create an attack tree. The attack tree is necessarily incomplete, partly for brevity and partly because this is not a book on how to knock over banks. Figure 17-3 shows the exemplar attack tree. Note that a "front end" is a computer that usually runs a web server that is accessible from the Internet so that clients can reach it, and also connects to other systems that are internal to the banking enterprise system—called the "back end" systems.

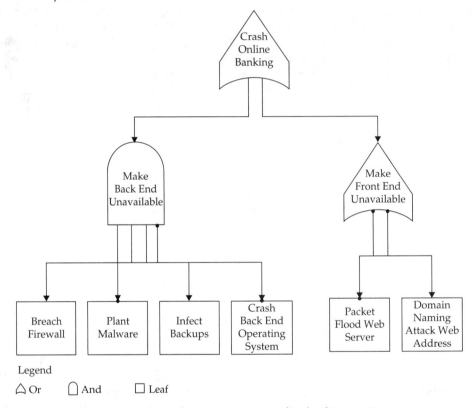

Figure 17-3 Example availability attack tree on a generic online banking service

In the example attack tree in Figure 17-3, the first decomposition is based on the architecture division between the two main components of the generic online banking system and leads to two alternatives for internal nodes in an OR relationship. The internal node on the left, "Make Back End Unavailable," is decomposed by attack step sequencing (an order of attack steps needed to accomplish a goal), which leads to an AND relationship for the attack steps. The steps often need to be accomplished in a specific order, which is not well represented in such trees. The right internal node, "Make Front End Unavailable," covers two types of attack techniques, represented by leaf nodes. The breakdown is inadequate in terms of being exhaustive or detailed, but it suffices for the example.

17.6.9 Estimate Leaf Probabilities and Compute Root

The attack tree leaf nodes from a complete tree are the subject of estimation of the probability of success given that an adversary attempts them. The same approach is used here as with estimating harm: the geometric mean of wisdom-of-crowd estimates. It is useful to have a variety of different experts on the estimating team, including those with red team experience, experts in the various technologies, out-of-the-box thinkers, and organizational heretics. Table 17-5 shows the continuing example, translating the attack tree based on attack goal #5 into a spreadsheet.

#	Attack Tree Nodes and Leafs	E1	E2	E3	E4	E5	Geo. Mean
1	Crash Online Banking						
2	Make Back End Unavailable						
3	Breach Firewall	1E-02	1E-05	1E+00	1E-01	1E-02	1E-02
4	Plant Malware	1E-01	1E+00	1E+00	1E-02	1E-02	1E-01
5	Infect Backups	1E-01	1E-01	1E-02	1E-01	1E+00	1E-01
6	Crash Back End OS	1E+00	1E+00	1E+00	1E+00	1E+00	1E+00
7	Make Front End Unavailable						
8	Packet Flood Web Server	1E-01	1E-02	1E-01	1E-01	1E+00	1E-01
9	Domain Naming Attack Web Address	1E-01	1E-01	1E-02	1E-01	1E+00	1E-01

Shaded field means the score is an outlier

Table 17-5   Wisdom-of-Crowd Attack Leaf Probability Estimates Showing Outlines with Shading

Notice in Table 17-5 that only the leaf nodes, also called the **attack steps**, have estimates associated with them. That is because the probabilities on the internal and root nodes are all mathematically calculated from the leaf probabilities, as will be discussed next. Notice also the shaded leaf-probability estimates. These are what are called **outliers** in statistics. *Outliers are particularly interesting because they could indicate either misunderstanding or keen insight.* Whether an outlier represents misunderstanding or insight is ascertained at an assumptions-leveling discussion among the estimators (after providing their initial independent estimates). The estimators who provided the outliers are usually given the floor to speak first to explain their assumptions, including the detailed attack path they are considering. After a brief discussion and a common understanding is achieved, new estimates can be submitted, as long as the goal is not to achieve consensus, which would undermine the wisdom-of-crowds approach.

> *Outliers suggest misunderstanding or keen insight.*

The **probability of attempt** is the likelihood that an attack effort would be undertaken by an attacker based on attributes of the attack, attributes of the defender, and value of the goal.

Part IV

The probability of attempt, for this analysis, will be assumed to be the value 1 (meaning 100 percent) for purposes of simplification. Probability of attempt models are based on detailed knowledge of potential adversaries, which is often difficult to come by. **Probability of success (given attempt)** is the likelihood that an attack will succeed given that it is attempted by an attacker. Probability of success given attempt is driven by the skills of the adversary and the vulnerability of the system as assessed by the estimating subject matter expert. Henceforth, we use the term "probability of success" or simply "probability" to mean "the probability of success (given attempt)."

After the leaf probabilities are determined, then it is straightforward to mathematically calculate the probability of success of the attack-tree root, and thus the probability that the strategic attack goal would successfully be reached. If nodes are in an AND relationship, then the probability of success is the product of the probabilities. This makes intuitive sense since the attacker must achieve each and every attack step; therefore, it must be at least as hard as the hardest attack step. We say that the minimum probability attack step is the upper bound of the probability of success of the sequence. Mathematically, we say: $P(A \text{ AND } B) < \text{MIN}(P(A), P(B))$. If there are two attack steps, A and B, where A has a 1 in 10 chance of succeeding and B has a 1 in 100 chance, then achieving both is 1 in 1,000. Mathematically, we express this as $P(A \text{ AND } B) = P(A) * P(B)$. Notice that the actual probability can be much worse (lower) for the attacker than the worst (lowest probability) step because of the multiplication. In the example, we see that the best (highest probability) attack step has a 1 in 100 chance of succeeding, but the *chances of the entire attack succeeding is 1 in 1,000.*

If nodes are in an OR relationship, then intuitively, achieving the goal is no harder than achieving the easiest of the alternatives. For example, if the probability of breaking into the front door is 1 in 100 and the probability of breaking into the backdoor (which is, say, a sliding glass door) is 1 in 10, then the probability of an attacker breaking into the house is at least as good as 1 in 10 since that is the best attack. We call this the lower bound of the probability of success. Mathematically, we say: $P(A \text{ OR } B) > \text{MIN}(P(A), P(B))$. Why isn't it exactly the minimum? How could it be better for the attacker?

The key here is to recall that we have a simplified probability of attempt model that says that an adversary will attempt all attack steps, independent of their probability. In our example, imagine two burglars working together. One tries to break in through the front door while the other tries to break in through the back. It is possible for the burglar at the front door to get lucky and find the door open, even though that is highly unlikely. So, the attack goal is achieved if any one leaf node is achieved or any combination of nodes is achieved, which, in some sense, is overkill, but could happen. In the case of our example, it is possible that both the burglar at the front door and the one at the backdoor will succeed.

For various reasons, mathematically, it is better to consider the likelihood of neither A nor B happening and subtracting that from 1. We have four possibilities with respect to attack success: A only, B only, A AND B, and neither A nor B. Because one of these outcomes must be possible, their probabilities must add up to 1. If any of the first three outcomes happens, the attack succeeds. Therefore, instead of calculating the first three values, it is better to take 1 minus the fourth value. Mathematically, we say: $P(A \text{ OR } B) = 1 - (1-P(A)) * (1-P(B))$ where the expression "$1-P(A)$" means the probability of attack step A not succeeding; similarly for attack step B.

Table 17-6 shows the same continuing example from previous sections. The root node probability of success is calculated using the OR formula of two internal nodes: #2 and #6. Node #2 is calculated using a product because the AND relationship requires all the subordinate events to occur. Node #6 is calculated using the OR formula because the leaf nodes are in an OR relationship.

#	Attack Tree Nodes and Leafs	Probability	How
1	Crash Online Banking	2E-01	1-(1-P(#2)) * (1-(P(#6))
2	Make Back End Unavailable	1E-04	Product(#3,#4,#5,#6)
3	Breach Firewall	**1E-02**	Estimated
4	Plant Malware	**1E-01**	Estimated
5	Infect Backups	**1E-01**	Estimated
6	Crash Back End OS	**1E+00**	Estimated
7	Make Front End Unavailable	2E-01	1-(1-P(#8)) * (1-(P(#9))
8	Packet Flood Web Server	**1E-01**	Estimated
9	Domain Naming Attack Web Address	**1E-01**	Estimated

Table 17-6   Calculated Probabilities Using the Leaf Nodes, Showing the Combining Functions for AND and OR

This can be compared to the original estimate at the root node given in the earlier step for a sanity check. From Table 17-4 we see that the root-probability estimate for attacker strategic goal #5 was 10^{-2} when directly estimated. This contrast exemplifies the phenomena discussed in Section 17.6.9, that defenders tend to underestimate the probability of successful attacker events by at least one order of magnitude. Therefore, we use the calculated value as the better estimate going forward. The comparison helps key stakeholders understand why the detailed analysis is important and often surprising.

17.6.10 Refine Baseline Expected Harm

The baseline expected harm is the product of the probability of each strategic attack goal succeeding with the estimated harm if the goal succeeds. So, if the probability is 10 percent and the harm is $1M, then the baseline expected harm is $100K. The calculated number is considered the "baseline" expected harm because further steps in the process estimate how probabilities might change as various mitigations are applied—to help guide improvement investments.

For the sake of the continued example, Table 17-7 shows the revised expected harm table. We only show a detailed recalculation for adversary strategic goal #5. The other values are simply manufactured for the example. We use an order of magnitude higher probabilities to be consistent with the rule of thumb that people tend to be off by at least one order of magnitude on their top-level estimates without the benefit of the attack trees. Notice that the resulting sum of the baseline expected harm estimate changed from 10^7 ($10M) to 10^8 ($100M).

#	Attack Class	Resulting Harm from Attacks	Harm \$ (H)	Probability (P)	Expected Harm (H*P)
1	Confidentiality	Loss of *user account data* jeopardizes *existing and future accounts staying at bank.*	10^7	10^{-2}	10^5
2	Confidentiality	Loss of *borrower-sensitive data* requiring major reinvestment to regain capability for attracting new borrowers.	10^8	10^{-1}	10^7
3	Integrity	Corrupt integrity of *account transactions and balances* so that consumers of data lose trust in *bank's ability to correctly administer financial data.*	10^{11}	10^{-3}	10^8
4	Integrity	Corrupt integrity of *loan status information* to cause erroneous decisions to damage *cash reserves* in the event of loan failure.	10^6	10^{-2}	10^4
5	Availability	Deny service to *online banking back end server* to make *online banking* unavailable for more than 14 days.	10^9	10^{-1}	10^8
6	Availability	Corrupt system integrity of *Fed Wire Interbank transfer system* and its backups required by *interbank settlement system* to operate.	10^{10}	10^{-2}	10^8
	Sum of Baseline Expected Harm				10^8

Table 17-7   Calculating revised baseline expected harm estimates based on detailed tree analysis, and the resulting improved probability estimates, using the chapter's generic banking system example.

17.6.11 Harvest Attack Sequence Cut Sets => Risk Source

From completed attack trees, one "harvests" the set of all attack step sequences (leaf node sets) that achieve strategic goals—these are known as the **cut sets**. For the purpose of the generic banking system example, Figure 17-4 shows the three cut sets for strategic attack for goal #5. One would have similar cut sets for all of the attack trees in the attack forest—a tree for each strategic attack goal, so a total of six attack trees are generated for the chapter's running generic bank system example.

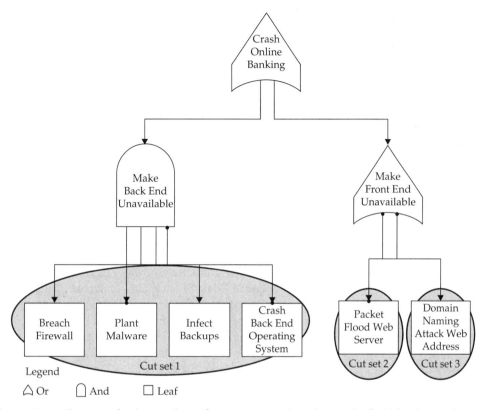

Figure 17-4   Three cuts for the attack tree for strategic attack goal #5, each of which achieves the goal, in the chapter's running generic banking system example

Notice that the collection of all leaf nodes in a cut set suffice to achieve the strategic attack goal. In the case of cut set 1 in the lower left of the figure, all four attack steps must succeed for the parent node (Make Back End Unavailable) to be achieved. Achieving the "Make Back End Unavailable" internal node automatically achieves the root mode because the parent node is in an OR relationship with its sibling. On the right-hand side of the figure, cut sets 2 and 3 are single-element cut sets because either leaf suffices to achieve the parent internal node, which suffices to achieve the root because of the OR relationship of the parent with its sibling. To be completely explicit, the three cut sets are: {Breach Firewall, Plant Malware, Infect Backups, Crash Back End Operating System}, {Packet Flood Web Server}, and {Domain Naming Attack Web Address}.

Often, the same leaf nodes appear repeatedly in multiple nodes and across multiple trees. Many are prerequisites for further steps. These linchpin leaf nodes then become the focus of attention for inspiring mitigation opportunities during design, deployment, and operation of systems. These lynchpins are important to the risk mitigation process discussed in the next section.

17.6.12 Infer Attack Mitigation Candidates from Attack Sequences

Each leaf represents the potential opportunity for changing the attacker's probability of success by improved design, implementation, or operation of the system. *The same knowledge that goes into estimating the probability of success attacks—knowledge of the mission and how it depends on the systems and the way those systems are vulnerable— highlights potential mitigations.* For example, if an attacker must breach a firewall to begin entire classes of attacks, it suggests strengthening that firewall and increasing detection of attacks on and around the firewall.

> ### *Knowledge to estimate attacker success informs mitigation.*

Table 17-7 shows the dominant expected harms come from three strategic attack goals: #3, which corrupts user accounts; #5, which denies service to online banking; and #6, which denies service to an inter-banking settlement service. For the chapter's running banking example, we only analyze strategic attack goal #5, with the attack tree shown in Figure 17-4. Table 17-6 shows that the cut sets of the internal node "Make Front End Unavailable"(Figure 17-4) have the largest effect on the root probability: cut set #2 (Packet Flood Web Server) and cut set #3 (Domain Naming Attack Web Address). Note that both nodes are at a 1 in 10 chance that the adversary succeeds.

What happens if we improve the cybersecurity design such that the Packet Flood Web Server Attack is 1 in 100? How does that change the root probability of a successful attack? The answer is that it does not change in a significant way at all. That is because the adversary can still execute the Domain Naming Attack Web Address attack with a 1 in 10 chance of success. Because that node is in an OR relationship with the one we hypothesized improving, we are not better off because the adversary is likely to succeed through the easiest attack. This is a mathematical instance of the principle that a chain is no stronger than its weakest link. We must improve both leaf nodes if we are going to significantly reduce the root probability.

To what level would these two leaf nodes have to improve for the adversary to be pushed to another attack scenario, represented by a different cut set? We see from Table 17-6 that the next path represented by line #2 ("Make Back End Unavailable") is the ANDed subtree of four leaf nodes on the left side of our attack tree in Figure 17-4. It is achieved with cut set #1 and its probability is 1 in 10,000. This means that we would need to improve both the leaf nodes in cut sets #2 and #3 to 1 in 10,000 before the attack scenario represented by cut set #1 would become an attack path that would affect the likelihood of overall attacker success.

When considering mitigations (Section 18.1), it becomes clear looking at the dominant attack leaf nodes that we must somehow address network flooding attacks and domain naming attacks if we want to change the probability of the root, which in turn changes the expected harm estimates of attacker goal #5. We must do the same analysis for goals #3 and #6 because they are on the same order of magnitude, and therefore have equally large impact on the bottom-line revised baseline expected harm. We augment this approach with red teaming to validate assertions about probability, as discussed in Section 6.5.

17.7 Attacker Cost and Risk of Detection

The discussion so far in this chapter has examined the probability of attacker-success-given-attempt under the assumption that the attacker will always try all attacks. There are two other important considerations that refer back to the adversary model: resources and risk tolerance.

17.7.1 Resources

Each attack costs the adversary resources. Some attacks are orders of magnitude more expensive than others. When the cost of each attack leaf is not modeled, then we make the oversimplifying assumption that the attacker has infinite resources. One can adjust the previously mentioned model to include cost and consider adversary budget constraints. This is a relatively straightforward extension of the model. A simpler alternative would be to filter out any attacks that are beyond the resource level of the adversary set that are being considered in the analysis. This is an imperfect approximation that may cause issues for defending against attacks that are near the adversary's budget limitations, but it is a reasonable first approximation.

17.7.2 Risk Tolerance

A risk-intolerant adversary will not attempt certain attacks, and so countermeasures that improve intrusion detection may get inadequate attention. The model can be extended to include a probability of detection for each leaf node. One can then use weighting functions to prefer attacks with lower risk to properly model adversaries that are highly risk-averse. Alternatively, one can build detection probability into the estimate of attack probability of success. Many attacks must go undetected to succeed. So, the probability of successful attack can be reduced if there is a good chance that the adversary would be detected prior to completing their attack. Therefore, *the introduction of an intrusion detection system countermeasure would cause the probability of success to go down because of the threat of detection combined with the adversary's risk aversion.* Again, it is imperfect, but it gives a reasonable approximation that effectively guides cybersecurity design.

Conclusion

This is the first chapter in this part of the book dealing with orchestrating cybersecurity building blocks into a cybersecurity system capable of defending a mission system. This chapter focuses on risk assessment and determining how much risk a given system is taking on. The next chapter then discusses how to use this risk assessment to guide system design in mitigating the risk and optimizing risk reduction.

To summarize:

- Risk is a practical and useful metric for cybersecurity engineering in analysis, guiding design, evaluating quality, and predicting performance under a variety of challenging situations and environments.

- Measurement is valuable in engineering to characterize systems, evaluate their performance, predict their performance and failure modes, and improve systems.

- Measurement is key to understanding how to reduce risk and not just move it around.
- A key to understanding risk is understanding how attackers gain value from attack.
- A defender's goal is to push the cost and risk of attacks beyond what the adversary can tolerate.
- The value of a cybersecurity architecture has to do with how the attacker's return on investment is decreased, not with how much the defender spent on the cybersecurity system.
- Measuring risk of proposed designs and comparing it to an established maximum tolerable risk guides design iteration to a system design with an acceptable risk level.
- Risk assessment analysis occurs in three phases: setup of models and requirements, deep analysis on probabilities, and harvesting of information for guiding design.
- The collection of cut sets of attack sequences that achieve the attacker's strategic goal, and their associated probabilities, gives insight on how best to mitigate risk because the source of the risk becomes quite apparent.

Questions

1. What is the primary cybersecurity metric and why?
2. What are the four main uses of metrics in engineering? Describe each briefly and give an example of how it might be used in everyday life.
3. How is a risk metric used to drive improved cybersecurity design?
4. Why is the worth of a cybersecurity system not evaluated by how much the defender spent deploying it?
5. How does the attacker value perspective differ from that of the defender?
6. What is the driving cybersecurity benefit when doing cost-benefit analysis?
7. Why do we say that cybersecurity design is an iterative process? What determines when to stop iterating?
8. What are the various models developed in setting up the analysis phase of risk assessment? What role does each play in the analytical process?
9. How are estimates of probabilities developed in the analytical process? What if estimators disagree? How should their estimates be combined mathematically? What if estimators are wrong?
10. What is the upper bound of probabilities of a sequence of attack steps that are in an AND relationship? Why? How do you interpret the AND relationship in terms of what the adversary has to do to achieve the parent node (goal)? What is the formula for probability of the attack steps in an AND relationship?

11. What is the lower bound of probabilities of a sequence of attack that are in an OR relationship? Why? How do you interpret the OR relationship in terms of what the adversary has to do to achieve the parent node? What is the formula for probability of the attacks in an OR relationship?

12. What are attack cut sets and how are they harvested? What form does the harvest take and what do you do with the result? How is ordering of attack steps represented?

13. What does "wisdom of crowds" mean and how does it work?

18 Risk Mitigation and Optimization

Overview

- 18.1 Develop Candidate Mitigation Packages
- 18.2 Assess Cost of Mitigation Packages
  - 18.2.1 Direct Cost
  - 18.2.2 Mission Impact
- 18.3 Re-estimate Leaf Node Probabilities and Compute Root Node Probability
- 18.4 Optimize at Various Practical Budget Levels
  - 18.4.1 Knapsack Algorithm
  - 18.4.2 Sensitivity Analysis
- 18.5 Decide Investment
- 18.6 Execute

Learning Objectives

- List and describe the risk mitigation elements in the risk assessment process and discuss how they relate to risk assessment analysis elements.
- Explain how risk mitigation packages are formulated and how they are used in the process.

- Define, compare, and contrast attack direct cost and indirect mission impact costs and describe how they are derived.

- List the six aspects of risk mitigation package cost and explain why it is important to break down costs in this fashion.

- Explain how revised attacker probabilities of success are developed and applied to baseline probabilities and how this relates to the value of mitigation packages.

- Describe how one optimizes combinations of risk mitigation packages at various budget levels to create the best possible solution sets.

- Summarize how to use optimization curves to drive cybersecurity investment decisions to the most effective outcome.

- Discuss how proper execution of cybersecurity investment is important and how it relates to the basis of the original investment decision.

Risk is the primary measure of cybersecurity and therefore *cybersecurity engineers are in the business of risk reduction to an owner-defined acceptable threshold*. As in the safety arena, risk is measured in terms of probabilities of a spectrum of possible outcomes. In the case of cybersecurity, the negative outcomes are not accidental, but rather intentionally induced by adversaries.

> ### *Engineer risk to owner-defined thresholds.*

Risk reduction is about reducing the risk across the entire spectrum of attacks open to an adversary. Increasing the adversary's cost in defeating one mechanism does not increase the adversary's overall cost if there are other means for the adversary to achieve the same outcome, such as attacking another weak mechanism—a poorly protected workstation, for example.

Further, looking at the big picture from an economic perspective, if the defender must spend $10 to increase the adversary's costs by $1, that is not a favorable financial situation for the defender. Cybersecurity architects should make arguments to organization stakeholders as to the value of their solution in terms of the attacker's cost increase as compared to the investment it takes to increase the adversary's cost.

Whereas the previous chapter detailed the analysis phase of the risk assessment process, this one discusses the design feedback phase where the analysis informs and guides the design toward lower-risk and improved cybersecurity architectures [BUCK05]. The set of steps is shown in Figure 18-1 and described subsequently. The connecting numbered arrows for the design feedback phase show feed-in connection points from the risk assessment analysis phase shown in Figure 17-2.

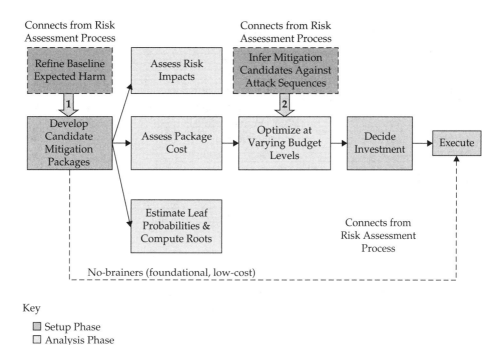

Figure 18-1   Design feedback portion of risk assessment process; connects from risk assessment in Figure 17-2 from numbered arrows

18.1 Develop Candidate Mitigation Packages

The design feedback portion of risk assessment begins with the setup phase, consisting of developing candidate risk mitigation packages—groupings of related countermeasures to cyberattacks. Such packages can be inspired by the attack trees, as discussed in Section 17.6.12. Alternative sources include subject matter expert intuition based on historical experience with actual attacks or on hypothesized attack exercises conducted by red teams to determine vulnerability. Packages can also come from external sources such as industry best practices. A package needs to be fully described in terms of concept, implementation, and scope, as well as the mechanisms by which it impacts risk, cost, and mission.

In this chapter, we continue using the generic bank cybersecurity system example introduced in Section 17.6. The reader should review that section before proceeding to become familiar with the example and the analysis, particularly: the strategic attacker goals presented in Table 17-4, the attack tree associated with the strategic attack goal #5 (availability of a generic online banking system) in Figure 17-3, and the calculated root-node probabilities of success in Table 17-6. Table 18-1 shows a potential mitigation package for the packet-flood-web-server attack step in leaf node #8, identified in Table 17-6, toward attack goal #5, identified in Table 17-4.

Mitigation Aspect	Description
Designator	Package **A**
1. Attack Category Addressed	Availability.
2. Technology	Router and intrusion detection.
3. Description	Buy network flooding detection module for all organization edge routers that detect pack flooding attacks and automatically filter all packets from the originating Internet Protocol (IP) address.
4. Timeline	Two months.
5. Risk Impact	Specifically addresses strategic attack goal #5, node #8 (Packet Flood Web Server). Solution expected to decrease the probability of successful flooding attack by one order of magnitude.
6. Cost Impact	$2K/year in additional license fees for the added module.
7. Mission Impact	Negligible performance impact.
8. Variation (80/20)	Use a free and open-source software network appliance to detect packet flood attack and transmit a rule to the router. Saves the $2K/year in license cost, but creates a one-time development cost of $1K to install and configure the software with a recurring cost of $100/year to maintain the software package with improvements and up-to-date patches. Call this variation A1 (or Alternative 1).

Table 18-1   Example Mitigation Package Using Generic Banking System Example Introduced in the Previous Chapter

The packages generally are assigned letter designators to make it easier to refer to them (e.g., A or A1 in Table 18-1). The following list describes the purpose and intention for each of the fields in the example shown in Table 18-1.

1. **Attack Category Addressed**   is one of confidentiality, integrity, or availability. It indicates the general attack type that the mitigation is addressing and orients the reader.

2. **Technology**   indicates what technology areas are affected. This helps those who need to review the package for potential impact and costs to their areas of responsibility.

3. **Description**   a brief description of what the mitigation plan is and what it involves in enough detail so reviewers understand how the proposed countermeasures impact risk, costs, and the organization's mission.

4. **Timeline**   the estimated amount of time it is expected to take from the time money is committed to the project to completion. *This is important because each day the countermeasure is not deployed is a day of additional risk.* An amazing solution that takes two years to deliver may not be as effective as a good solution that can be deployed in two months.

5. **Risk impact**   the proposer's view of how the countermeasure is intended to mitigate risk and a basis for the claim. The analysis will also be re-evaluated separately by subject matter experts later in the process, but it is important for those risk experts to understand the intention of the proposed solution.

6. **Cost impact**   the proposer's best estimate of the cost of the mitigation package. Cost impact estimates should itemized for all six categories of cost enumerated in Section 18.2.1, Table 18-2. These costs estimates require vetting by the stakeholders who actually have to implement the countermeasure solution, so these cost estimates will be refined in subsequent steps.

7. **Mission impact**   the proposer's idea of how the proposed changes affect the mission as supported by the information technology. As with cost impacts, the actual mission stakeholders must review and refine these estimates because they have the best understanding of potential subtle impacts.

8. **Variation**   identifies potential variations or countermeasure solutions guided by the Pareto 80/20 Rule to try to gain 80 percent of the risk-reduction value of the mitigation with only 20 percent of the cost or 20 percent of the mission impact.

> *Every day without a countermeasure is a day of added risk.*

The candidate **risk mitigation packages** are often developed by the information technology organization in response to the risk assessment analysis phase or in response to other requirements (e.g., an upgrade or technology refresh). That is why packages require vetting with other stakeholders, to ensure that the proposer's ideas of impacts and costs are correct. It is particularly important to communicate with and make the mission owners key stakeholders, who have substantial influence on the planning process. A failure to do so is a formula not only for conflict, but also for mission failures that are avoidable with upfront coordination.

Typically, about a dozen alternative mitigation packages are developed so that the organization has investment options. In the continuing generic online banking example, we present only two for brevity (the original package A and a variation A1). If an organization only develops one package, then they are hampering themselves. *A structured brainstorming session should be held with stakeholders to develop more solutions, particularly out-of-the-box innovative solutions.* Some solution designs may even involve research and development for future capability.

18.2 Assess Cost of Mitigation Packages

Cost impacts include direct monetary costs for the countermeasure solution as well as the costs associated with mission impact. Both are addressed in this section.

18.2.1 Direct Cost

After candidate risk mitigation packages are fully described, the analysis phase begins. The packages are assessed for cost incurred during development, deployment, and sustainment of the solution. For each of the elements, it is often helpful to separate costs that would be incurred by the information technology organization versus those that would be incurred by the mission itself. Therefore, one usually creates a 3×2 matrix of costs for each candidate risk mitigation package—two rows for IT infrastructure costs versus mission cost, and three columns for the three portions of the solution life cycle (development, deployment, and sustainment). Table 18-2 and Table 18-3 give examples of cost matrices for hypothetical mitigation packages A and A1 as described in the previous section.

Package A	Development	Deployment	Sustainment
Information Technology Infrastructure Cost	$0K	$0.1K	$2K/year over 5 years
Mission Cost	$0K	$0K	$0K/year over 5 years

Table 18-2 Cost Breakdown Matrix for Candidate Risk Mitigation Package A to Aid in Budget Planning

Package A1	Development	Deployment	Sustainment
Information Technology Infrastructure Cost	$1K	$1K	$0.1K/year over 5 years
Mission Cost	$0K	$0K	$0K/year over 5 years

Table 18-3 Cost Breakdown Matrix for Candidate Mitigation Package A1 to Aid in Budget Planning

Separating costs between infrastructure and mission costs is often useful because the budgeting and impacts of such investments can have different opportunity costs—therefore the cost-versus-benefit trade-off space can be different for each. Costing analysts can often apply the Pareto 80/20 Rule, whereby 80 percent of the risk reduction can be gained by strategic and selective application top 20 percent of mitigations to the most important parts or aspects of the system. This can result in a separate trimmed package or the replacement of the original package, depending on how many packages are to be examined.

18.2.2 Mission Impact

Assessing package cost includes mission impact—a type of indirect cost. Table 2-1 gives nine different impact factors that can be considered for each mitigation package. These impacts must be monetized to be used in a calculation involving return on investment, which we will discuss in the next section. How might we do that? Let's take an example using our running example of securing a banking system and examine only two of the nine example mission impacts outlined in Table 18-4.

#	Aspect	Example Trade-Off for Cybersecurity
1	User-friendliness	Having to remember passwords is inconvenient and cumbersome.
2	Employee morale	Reviewing security logs can be mind-numbing and frustrating for some employees.

Table 18-4 Two Example Mission Impact Factors from Table 2-1 for the Online Banking Exemplar Problem

Because the two example risk mitigation packages A and A1 do not have significant mission impacts, let's hypothesize two new packages, B and C. These packages will be attempting to mitigate the strategic attack goal #1 (confidentiality; see Table 17-2). Confidentiality of use-account data is lost because of an adversary using a computer network attack to break into the bank system (using a compromised user account or a compromised bank employee account) and **escalating privilege** from one of those toeholds. The risk mitigation objectives of packages B and C will be to tighten authentication processes and tighten security policies in firewalls and systems within the online banking enterprise.

Next, we ask the stakeholders to estimate mission impact for each aspect and for each mitigation package. We use the same elicitation methods as we have used throughout the risk assessment process—independent estimates, followed by **assumption-leveling** discussion to determine if some estimators made inconsistent assumptions, followed by possible revision of estimates based on improved understanding. We do not show the averaging process since it follows the same pattern done previously (Section 17.6.5). Instead, Table 18-5 contains representative final impact on two mission impact factors, expressed as percentages on packages B and C. Estimates are given in terms of relative percentage changes in mission effectiveness as a result of implementing the four risk mitigation packages. The minimum and maximum percentages are recorded to give the range of values.

	Mission Impact Factor	A	A1	B	C	Min	Max	Range
1	User-friendliness	0	0	10%	5%	0	10%	10%
2	Employee morale	0	0	15%	2%	0	15%	15%

Table 18-5   Expert Assessment of Impact on Mission of the Proposed Mitigation Packages, Expressed as Percentages

With the percent mission impact assessments in hand, we return to the senior leadership of the owning organization and ask about the value of these mission impacts. We solicit the same or similar group of senior leaders as was solicited in estimating the harm of adversaries achieving the representative attack goals (see Section 17.6.5). The same wisdom-of-crowds approach is used. For each mission impact factor, the leadership is asked, "What would you pay to move this mission factor from the maximum impact to the minimum impact?" For example, for the user-friendliness factor in Table 18-5, leadership would be asked how much they would be willing to pay to move a solution from 10 percent degraded user-friendliness to no impact. In their minds, they are making a complex calculation having to do with lost customers from frustration over user interface inadequacies and increased expenses from calls to the customer support line to deal with the resulting frustrating issues. Table 18-6 shows the range of impact carried over from Table 18-5 and example estimated mission impact values in dollars from the solicitation process. One can then divide the mission-impact value by the percentage mission-impact range and determine the incremental value of each percentage point of mission degradation for that factor, as shown in the last column of Table 18-6.

	Mission Impact Factor	Range (R)	Mission Impact Value $ (MI)	Value $ per %age (MI/R)
1	User-friendliness	10%	$10M	$1M
2	Employee morale	15%	$5M	$0.33M

Table 18-6   Cost Values Ascribed to the Mission Impact Factors and Calculation of Incremental Cost Values

The calculation of the incremental cost values then allows one to monetize the percentage of mission impacts, given by the experts captured in Table 18-6, by multiplying the incremental cost value times the mission impact value. In the case where the minimum mission-impact percent is non-zero, one uses the following formula to derive the general cost impact multiplier, which is then multiplied by the mission impact value:

$$\text{Cost Impact Multiplier} = \frac{\text{Impact Percent} - \text{Minimum Percent Impact}}{\text{Impact Percent Range}}$$

Carrying forward with the generic online banking example, Table 18-7 translates the percentage of mission impacts, listed in Table 18-5, to mission impact costs associated with each of the four mitigation example packages. The translation is done by multiplying the package's percent mission impact times the mission impact percent. For example, the percent mission impact of package B is 10 percent; the value of the user-friendliness factor is $10M; package B has the maximum possible impact, so its cost is the full mission-impact cost of the user-friendliness factor: $\frac{10\% - 0\%}{10\%} * \$10M = 1 * \$10M = \$10M$. Similarly, package C causes only a 5 percent impact, and so the mission-impact cost is only half the $10M, or $5M. The resulting values will be used in the next section to determine the worth of each package.

	Aspect	A	A1	B	C	Value/%
1	User-friendliness	0	0	$10M	$5M	$1M
2	Employee morale	0	0	$5M	$0.66M	$0.33M

Table 18-7   Translation of Example Factor Percentages into Values Using the Incremental Value

18.3 Re-estimate Leaf Node Probabilities and Compute Root Node Probability

The next task of Phase 2 analysis (Figure 18-1) is re-estimating leaf probabilities and computing the root node probability. The approach is similar to the assessment task described in the previous section, except that it considers the relative effect (expressed as a multiplier) that a given package has on the baseline probability of success previously determined. If the risk mitigation package only affects the availability of a service, one can quickly determine that there will be no effect on mechanisms aimed at supporting confidentiality of data.

The relative multipliers are then applied to baseline probabilities to determine the revised probabilities of the leaf nodes. These revised probabilities of successful leaf node attacks are then combined to calculate the root node's revised probability of success. The change in root node probability, in turn, is used to compute how the attack risk changes in response to deploying the packages. This change in risk is used to compute benefit in a *cost-benefit analysis* in subsequent steps.

Table 18-8 shows an example result of the revised estimation process. The same or similar group of subject matter experts examine each leaf node in each of the six attack trees in the ongoing generic online banking example. Table 18-8 shows just one of the six strategic attacks—goal #5 (availability). The experts generally provide a multiplier that reflects how the attack's probability of success will be affected by the deployment of the risk mitigation package under consideration (package A in the case in the generic online banking example).

#	Attack Tree Nodes and Leafs	Probability	Revision Multiplier	Revised Probability	How
1	Crash Online Banking	2E-01		1E-01	1-(1-P(#2)) * (1-(P(#6))
2	Make Back End Unavailable	1E-04		1E-04	Product(#3,#4,#5,#6)
3	Breach Firewall	**1E-02**	1.00	1E-02	Multiplier* Baseline
4	Plant Malware	**1E-01**	1.00	1E-01	Multiplier* Baseline
5	Infect Backups	**1E-01**	1.00	1E-01	Multiplier* Baseline
6	Crash Back End OS	**1E+00**	1.00	1E+00	Multiplier* Baseline
7	Make Front End Unavailable	1E-01		1E-01	1-(1-P(#8)) * (1-P(#9))
8	Packet Flood Web Server	**1E-01**	0.10	1E-02	Multiplier* Baseline
9	Domain Naming Attack Web Address	**1E-01**	1.00	1E-01	Multiplier* Baseline

Table 18-8   Estimated Probability Revisions If Risk Mitigation Package A Is Deployed, Propagated to the Root Node

A revision multiplier of "1" means that the estimator believes that the package will have no effect on the attacker's success probability. This could mean that either the countermeasures in the package are not intended to affect that type of attack, or that it is, but the estimator judges the countermeasures to be completely ineffective. *A revision multiplier of "0" means that the estimator believes that the mitigation is 100 percent effective and makes the attack completely impossible (rarely the case).* A multiplier of "0.1" means that the estimator believes that mitigation is highly effective and will reduce the adversary's probability of success by an order of magnitude.

Notice in Table 18-8 that the root node's revised probability remains unchanged from the baseline as shown in Table 17-6. Why? This is because the probability of internal node #7 (Make Front End Unavailable) did not change. The probability of node #7 did not change because node #7's children nodes, #8 and #9, are in an OR relationship. Although the mitigation package significantly reduced the attack success probability of node #8, it had no effect on node #9's probability of success (nor was it designed to affect node #9). Therefore, we can see that package A will have almost no risk-reduction benefit unless used in combination with other packages that reduce the attacker's probability of success on node #9.

After the deep analysis on revised probabilities of success and mission impacts with respect to strategic attack goal #5 (availability), we return to the list of the five other strategic

Part IV

attack goals represented in Table 17-7 for the generic online banking example. Table 18-9 is a copy of Table 17-7, omitting the third column (Resulting Harm from Attacks) and relabeling the "probability" and "expected harm" columns as "baseline probability" and "baseline expected harm" to reflect the revision that occurs when the packages are examined. The last two columns of Table 18-9 are new and explore the effect of risk mitigation package C, creating revised probability of success of attack and thus revised expected harm.

#	Attack Class	Harm $ (H)	Baseline Probability (P_B)	Baseline Expected Harm $ $(H * P_B)$	Package C Revised Probability (P_R)	Package C Revised Expected Harm $(P_R * H)$
1	Confidentiality	10^7	10^{-2}	10^5	10^{-3}	10^4
2	Confidentiality	10^8	10^{-1}	10^7	10^{-2}	10^6
3	Integrity	10^{11}	10^{-3}	10^8	10^{-4}	10^7
4	Integrity	10^6	10^{-2}	10^4	10^{-3}	10^3
5	Availability	10^9	10^{-1}	10^8	10^{-2}	10^7
6	Availability	10^{10}	10^{-2}	10^8	10^{-3}	10^7
	Sum			10^8		10^7

Table 18-9   Total Risk-Reduction Benefit of Hypothetical Super-Risk Mitigation Package C, Yielding a $90M Risk Reduction

We omit the deep analysis and simply show the resulting revised probability of attack success that package C causes on all six strategic attack goals. Notice that package C causes wide-ranging order-of-magnitude reductions in probability for all six goals. In practice, it would be very unusual for one mitigation package to be so effective across the entire spectrum of strategic attack goals, but we use it for illustration purposes. We see that risk mitigation package C reduces overall expected harm from the baseline of $100M ($10^8$) to a revised expected harm of $10M ($10^7$). Therefore, by simple subtraction, risk mitigation package C has a risk reduction value of $90M!

With the risk reduction calculated, the *return on investment* can be calculated as the risk-reduction benefit minus the direct cost of the mitigation packages (the investment) divided by the direct cost of the package:

$$\text{Return on Investment} = \frac{\text{Risk Reduction} - \text{Direct Cost}}{\text{Direct Cost}}$$

As discussed in Section 18.2.2, we sometimes consider the indirect cost of mission impact. To do so, we include this indirect cost in the numerator of the previous formula, yielding:

$$\text{Return on Investment} = \frac{\text{Risk Reduction} - \text{Direct Cost} - \text{Mission Impact}}{\text{Direct Cost}}$$

18.4 Optimize at Various Practical Budget Levels

After cost and change in risk are assessed for all the risk mitigation packages, the final step of the analysis phase (Figure 18-1) begins.

18.4.1 Knapsack Algorithm

This step calls for running a **knapsack algorithm** to determine the optimal cost-benefit combination of packages at various selected budget levels [MART90]. The varied budget levels, which act as the optimization constraints, are chosen based on a practical range for the sponsoring organization. Often, one considers around ten possible levels, including the current budget level, half the budget level, twice the budget level, and incremental levels up to some fraction of the entire organization's information technology budget—say 10 percent (which is about what the average healthy human body invests to maintain its immune system). Figure 18-2 depicts an example in which a knapsack optimization was used to optimize the cost-benefit combination of four risk mitigation packages constrained to a $100K budget.

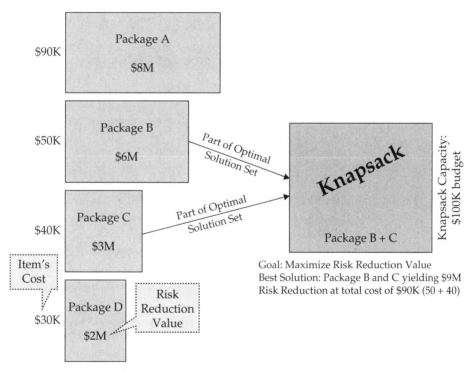

Figure 18-2   Knapsack optimization example, maximizing risk reduction value with a $100K budget constraint

As a result of executing a knapsack algorithm, different combinations of risk mitigation packages are chosen at each succeeding level, depending on how the packages synergize with each other and which combinations of packages yield an optimum risk reduction. A selected combination of packages at a given budget level is called a *solution set*. Table 18-10 lists ten different hypothetical risk mitigation packages (A–J) and the outcome after executing a knapsack algorithm optimized at various budget levels. Shaded items are mitigation packages that are selected by the optimization algorithm given budget level (in each row) based on maximizing risk reduction. The second from the last column shows the incremental risk reduction values given by a solution set over the previous solution set at the next lower budget level. Therefore, the last column gives the total risk reduction by doing a running total of the incremental reductions as the budget level values increase. The budget increment levels were chosen purely for illustration purposes. For this fictitious example, one might say that the organization's usual budget is around $200K, so the range represents budgets from 25 percent of the usual budget to nearly twice that usual budget.

Budget Level	A	B	C	D	E	F	G	H	I	J	Incremental Risk Reduction	Risk Reduction	Inc. ROI
$50,000	$20,000	$30,000	$50,000	$200,000	$100,000	$100,000	$70,000	$75,000	$250,000	350,000	$5,000,000	$5,000,000	100
$100,000	$20,000	$30,000	$50,000	$200,000	100,000	$100,000	$70,000	$75,000	$250,000	350,000	$2,000,000	$7,000,000	40
$150,000	$20,000	$30,000	$50,000	$200,000	100,000	$100,000	$70,000	$75,000	$250,000	350,000	$1,700,000	$6,600,000	34
$200,000	$20,000	$30,000	$50,000	$200,000	100,000	$100,000	$70,000	$75,000	$250,000	350,000	$1,350,000	$6,100,000	27
$250,000	$20,000	$30,000	$50,000	$200,000	100,000	$100,000	$70,000	$75,000	$250,000	350,000	$1,250,000	$6,600,000	25
$300,000	$20,000	$30,000	$50,000	$200,000	100,000	$100,000	$70,000	$75,000	$250,000	350,000	$1,150,000	$6,600,000	23
$350,000	$20,000	$30,000	$50,000	$200,000	100,000	$100,000	$70,000	$75,000	$250,000	350,000	$1,100,000	$6,600,000	22

Table 18-10   Knapsack optimization of solution sets of mitigation packages where shading indicates a package is chosen at the budget level in a given row. This figure is *not* connected to the generic online banking example.

There are some important and interesting properties to point out about Table 18-10.

- We first notice that mitigation package H is never chosen, even though its cost ($75K) is well within all but the lowest budget level. This could be because package H actually yields a negative risk reduction. The optimization is not actually for maximum risk reduction but rather maximum risk reduction, minus cost, minus mission impact indirect cost. So, if a risk mitigation package only offers modest risk reduction that is higher than its direct cost, or if it has significant mission impact, it will never be selected. The analyst would need to perform a deeper analysis to determine exactly why it was not selected.

- Similarly, package J is never chosen. Its direct cost ($350) exceeds all but the largest budget considered ($350K). *It is rare that a single risk mitigation package outperforms a combination of many packages that tend to complement each other's attack space coverage.*

- The inexpensive mitigation packages A and B are chosen in the majority of solution sets. That means that they likely cover important and unique parts of the attack space. In cases where they are not selected, it may be because other solutions that are possible at higher budget levels can achieve much of the same result, though perhaps not all.

- The last column labeled "ROI" gives the incremental risk reduction divided by the incremental budget increase from the previous budget level. This is a measure of how worthwhile it is to increase investment from one level to the next higher level (Figure 18-3).

A limitation of the knapsack algorithm approach is that it can neglect important synergies and negative synergies between risk mitigation packages. This issue can be reduced by judiciously choosing risk mitigation packages that include mitigation combinations which include measures that have high synergy. In addition, nothing replaces supplemental expert human analysis and judgement that compensates for these limitations.

Running knapsack optimizations at these various budget levels creates a curve of risk-reduction versus investments as shown in Figure 18-3 as derived from Table 18-10. The budget costs (x-axis) versus incremental risk reduction at each budget level (y-axis) are plotted. The next section discusses Figure 18-3 in more detail.

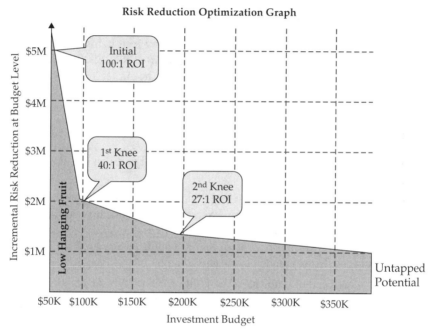

Figure 18-3   Notional optimization chart of risk reduction possible at various budget levels, also showing incremental return on investment knees in the curve

18.4.2 Sensitivity Analysis

The estimation process discussed in the previous chapter involves matters of expert opinion and is thus imprecise. What if the estimates are significantly wrong—off by an order of magnitude or more? The interesting answer is that it sometimes does not matter, but for other times, it could make a great deal of difference. **Sensitivity analysis** is an analytical technique that allows us to determine which estimates significantly impact the results if they are incorrect. One could simply vary all the inputs across a large range (one at a time) and see the degree to which the optimization output changes the best solutions at each budget level. For the estimates that have a large effect on results, it is worth further analysis, discussion, and experimentation to confirm the validity of those estimates.

18.5 Decide Investment

Once an optimization curve is created, one then studies the investment curve. This begins the action phase of the design feedback process, which is guided from the previous risk assessment process in Figure 17-2. In the notional investment curve in Figure 18-3, we can see many important and typical features.

- At relatively low investment toward the left-hand side of the graph, high-risk reductions are likely. These are sometimes known as **low-hanging fruit** and are no-brainer investments. The return on investment is often in the hundreds-of-dollars-worth of risk reduction for every dollar invested in mitigation (e.g., $50K investment reduces risk by $5M).

- There are only a handful of these low-hanging fruit items. Return on investment falls off rather quickly to the 40:1 ratio ($2M/($100K–$50K)). At that point, labeled "1st Knee 40:1", we have a change of slope in the curve. It is called a knee because the change in slope resembles a bent knee. Mathematically, this is sometimes called an **inflection point**. In any case, it indicates a change in the character of the mitigations available such that more investment is required to get similar risk reductions compared to the low-hanging fruit.

- Return on investment past the first knee is still quite high and worthy of investment if the organization can afford it.

- The curve progresses to a second knee in the curve where return on investment diminishes at an even faster rate. Second knees typically occur in the neighborhood of 27:1 return on investment ratios ($1.35M/($200K–$150K)). Such ratios are still good returns on investment, but an order of magnitude less good than the low-hanging fruit in the first segment.

- At the high end of realistic investment levels, we typically begin to approach 2:1 or even 1:1 ratios. Organizations often decide to limit their investment somewhere in the early part of this segment, depending on perception and economic realities of resources available.

- Whatever organization decision makers choose for their investment level, the remaining part of the curve is untapped available risk reduction, perhaps available to reduce in a future round of investment. It is important to note that the y-axis does not measure absolute risk, but rather the change in risk that a given package set delivers. The residual risk to the system is therefore the baseline risk minus the risk reduction on the y-axis from the chosen mitigation combination point on the curve. So, for example, if the system owners chose the point identified as the first knee in the curve (40:1) at a budget of $100K and a risk reduction of $5M, then the residual risk is equal to the baseline risk minus $5M. If the baseline expected harm was $12M, the remaining risk to the system (also known as residual expected harm) is $7M.

Residual Risk = Baseline Risk − Risk Reduction of Selected Solution Set

18.6 Execute

After investment decisions are made, we enter into the last step of the design feedback phase guided from the previous risk assessment process (Figure 17-2). This step develops program plans and infrastructure to successfully execute the risk mitigation packages in a timely way and such that the benefits are fully realized. It can often take two or three years to budget for such cybersecurity investments and several years to execute the programs. This fact should set expectations on timelines for risk reduction to mission.

During project budgeting and execution, many things can go awry. Budget delays could delay the start of a project by a year. At some point, the risk baseline of the system changes to a point where it becomes important to redo the analysis to ensure that the project is still a good choice, given changes in the mission and environment. A similar issue occurs when projects are delayed for various reasons. Often, budgets get cut and compromises are made. It is important to understand that the estimators made specific assumptions about projects being fully funded and competently executed to reasonable quality standards. Once these assumptions are violated, the organization is certain to gain substantially less risk-reduction value than anticipated. In some cases, the change is significant enough to warrant canceling the project since it will no longer have the desired effect. Therefore, once a decision has been made, it is important that a senior project champion watch over the project execution and make good judgements when reassessment is needed.

Conclusion

This chapter is a close companion of the previous chapter, which discusses how to determine the risk of a given system. This chapter discusses how to use the understanding to guide system design and iterate on risk assessment for alternative designs—giving an optimization technique to help reduce system risk at a given investment level. The next chapter begins a series of two chapters on fundamental principles of engineering design.

To summarize:

- Cybersecurity engineers are in the business of risk mitigation to an acceptable level.
- Risk mitigation consists of developing alternative risk mitigation packages or solution sets, assessing the impact of those mitigations, optimizing the investment for various combinations of optional mitigations, deciding on the best investment, and then executing the revised design.
- Candidate mitigation packages are guided by risk assessment analysis regarding the primary sources of the baseline risk.
- Mitigation costs should be broken down by who pays and in what life-cycle phases the cost occurs so that they can be properly funded, planned, and managed.
- Mitigation cost also includes mission impact, which can be monetized by having senior leadership place value on mission impact factors.

Part IV

- For each mitigation package, a revised probability of attack success is calculated for every attack leaf node in the attack tree forest. This forms the basis for understanding how effectively each package addresses the representative attacks, and this becomes the basis of their value.

- Risk-reduction return on investment is the risk reduction minus the direct cost minus the mission impact, all divided by the direct cost. It gives a sense of the best "bang for the buck."

- Optimization at practical budget levels picks the best combination of risk mitigation packages at various budget levels to help decision makers decide how best to invest and at what budget level.

- An optimization investment curve then guides decision makers toward the best investment, given budget constraints, by analyzing characteristics of the curve, particularly at inflection points where slope changes and the incremental return begins to decrease.

- The investment decision is important, but it is equally important to follow the decision through during execution. Schedule delays and budget cuts are inevitable. It is important to ensure that the assumptions made during analysis are maintained and that reassessment is triggered when there is significant enough deviation in assumptions made for estimates on probability of attacker success, direct costs, or the indirect costs of mission impact.

Questions

1. Summarize the risk mitigation aspect of risk assessment. List each phase and steps within each phase. Describe how each step feeds and is fed by other steps.

2. How does one develop risk mitigation packages? How many should there be?

3. What are the fields in a mitigation package and why is each there?

4. Who is the audience of a mitigation package description?

5. How does one apply the Pareto 80/20 Rule to risk mitigation packages to develop additional options?

6. What are the six types of cost estimates that should be developed for risk mitigation packages? Why six? What role does each serve? How might costs be pushed from one type to another? Give an example.

7. List at least three mission impact factors and why they may be important to model.

8. Why are revised probabilities of attack success often given as revision multipliers on the baseline? What does a multiplier of 1 mean? What does 0 mean?

9. How does one derive the root probability from the leaf probabilities?

10. What sort of algorithm is used to explore the space of possible investments and find the optimal investment at various budget levels? What is the time complexity of that algorithm?

11. Develop an investment curve for the knapsack problem given in Figure 18-2 at knapsack capacities (budget levels) from $10K to $100K with $10K increments. Show the data table and plot the curve.

12. How does the optimization investment curve inform the mitigation investment decision?

13. How does one know how well execution of an investment will go and how does that uncertainty impact probability estimates?

19

Engineering Fundamentals

Overview

Learning Objectives

- Explain the implications of Murphy's Law to systems engineering.
- Define the engineering of a margin of safety and how it relates to uncertainty.
- Discuss the pseudo-principle of conservation of risk and how risk "moves" around.

- Describe how the keep-it-simple-stupid principle applies to requirements creep.
- Summarize how investment in the early phases of system design pays off.
- Explain how and under what conditions incremental development improves system success.
- Discuss how modularity and abstraction manage complexity.
- Compare and contrast layering and modularity and discuss how they work together in design.
- Define the concepts of time and space complexity and relate them to system scalability.
- Explain why loops and locality of reference are important to performance optimization.
- Discuss the role of dividing and conquering in the design process and how it relates to recursion.

Cybersecurity architecture is about how to weave together the various security mechanisms and capability into a coherent whole that is effective in thwarting adversaries from accomplishing their strategic attack goals. Architecture requires effective building blocks as discussed up to this point in the book, and, just as importantly, how to place and connect those building blocks in the proper manner using design principles. The following sound design principles *for all systems, when applied to cybersecurity systems* improve confidence of successful defense against cyberattacks.

19.1 Systems Engineering Principles

Before launching into the specific principles of security design, we start with the more foundational systems engineering and computer science principles upon which cybersecurity engineering principles are founded. There are many good books written on these broader principles. This section does not attempt to review all of them, but rather focuses on those that are the most important to the cybersecurity engineering practice. The reader is encouraged to read further on more general design principles [LEVE12][KOSS11].

19.1.1 Murphy's Law

Anything that can go wrong will go wrong. This is the Murphy's Law that many of us have heard many times regarding life in general. It applies strongly to engineering and especially to cybersecurity engineering. It means that engineers must understand all the ways in which systems can fail and design the system to

- Prevent failures before they occur,
- Detect failures when they occur,
- Recover from failures when they are detected, and
- Tolerate failures until the system recovers.

Notice that these four concepts are ANDed together, and not ORed. *Together, prevention, detection, recovery, and tolerance provide multiple lines of defense against the consequences of failure; all are needed and they should work in concert with one another.*

> ## Anything that can go wrong, will go wrong.

Prevent   Faults lead to errors, which lead to system failure. This chain is discussed in Section 5.6. Preventing faults is about good design and implementation practices, which will be discussed further later in the chapter. *The return on investment of eliminating faults early in the development process is significant* [NIST02] [ZHIV09][FAGA76]. It is up to 100 times more expensive to fix faults discovered in the maintenance phase than in the design phase (Figure 19-1).

> ## Eliminating faults early in the design process pays off.

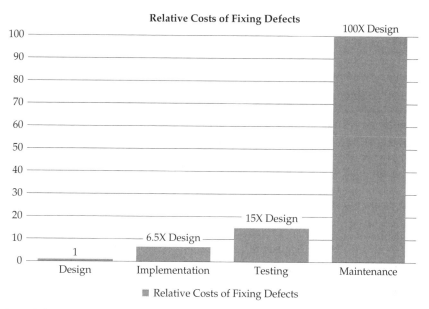

Relative Costs of Fixing Defects

Figure 19-1   Relative cost multipliers of fixing defects in later life-cycle stages compared to design, shown as 1x

The consequence of a security fault could be disastrous to the system, leading to total loss of mission in the worst case. If cybersecurity capabilities such as authentication or authorization fail, adversaries can have full access to system resources, or the system could be completely unavailable, depending on how the cybersecurity mechanisms are integrated. Neither scenario bodes well for the mission that the system supports.

> *Security faults can cause total mission failure.*

Detect No matter how well an engineer thinks they have prevented errors, *failures inevitably occur.* This is a critical fact that not only must be understood by cybersecurity engineers, but internalized and lived daily. *Good cybersecurity engineers should be students of failure—all kinds of failure.* Understanding what system failures have occurred and how they have occurred gives keen insight into how to detect them. Every subsystem should attempt to detect internal errors and should expect errors from all other subsystems with which it interacts. *Assuming that all subsystems used are perfect is a fundamental error that occurs all too frequently.* Don't be that engineer.

Cybersecurity software is especially critical. It therefore warrants even more error detection design and implementation, not the paucity that is typical of many of today's cybersecurity systems. As an example, cybersecurity subsystems often assume that all other entities with whom they communicate are trustworthy and definitely not malicious. What if another system on which that security subsystem resides has been taken over by the adversary? *Blindly trusting other systems allows the attack to quickly propagate through the system.*

> *Never blindly trust other systems upon which yours depends.*

Recover Once a failure is detected, the system must be recovered. Recovery requires

1. Analyzing and assessing the damage done (e.g., corrupted files).
2. Undoing damage through techniques such as database rollback from a stored **checkpoint**.
3. Analyzing and diagnosing the cause of the failure (e.g., a software bug).
4. Eliminating the cause of the failure (e.g., patching the system to fix a bug).
5. Returning the system to a **safe state** of operations.
6. Restoring operations with a minimal loss of work.

Analyzing and assessing the damage is critical, particularly in cybersecurity. If an access control table is corrupted, it could allow adversaries unauthorized access to the system, for example. All cybersecurity systems should be capable of periodically running **self-diagnostics** to check for errors and inconsistencies in their programs or their critical data structures.

Undoing damage involves designing cybersecurity systems so that the system can be rolled back to a known good state—called a safe state. The state can include security-critical data, security-critical programs, and the state of execution of those programs. Approaches for saving a known safe state (called checkpointing) and restoring to such a safe state (called rollback) are well-studied in computer science and particularly in database management system design [BOUT03]. This can be tricky in the case where a number of distributed subsystems are involved in collaboratively achieving cybersecurity properties. That is because what is a safe state may have a definition that includes all of the subsystems' states—so the rollback needs to be coordinated to a consistent safe state across all the security subsystems.

Tolerate   *System failures will occur with 100 percent probability.* In fact, in a sufficiently complex system of any kind, there is always some part of the system operating in some failure mode. Failure modes can vary substantially from minor inconvenience to catastrophic, depending on the design of the system. For example, if an airplane engine fails by shutting itself down gracefully, with ample warning of an impending failure, that is one thing; if it fails by suddenly shattering all the internal parts and throwing them into the fuselage, breaching the structural integrity of the wing and the cabin, that could cause a serious loss of life. Which type of failure mode a system exhibits is a matter of design and forethought by the system architects. *Good engineers continuously ask themselves how a system can possibly fail and they redesign the system if the mode could be catastrophic.*

> ### *Failures will occur with 100 percent probability.*

In cybersecurity, planning for and surviving failure are essential. Like any other system, cybersecurity mechanisms will fail with 100 percent probability. The only question is when, how often, and in what way. One can count on the answer to the question of "when" being "at the worst possible time" as predicted by Murphy's Law. The question of "how" often is a matter of prevention as previously discussed. The question of "in what way" is a matter of careful and thoughtful design. For example, if one of a dozen cybersecurity sensors fails silently, it may be difficult to detect from an intrusion detection system that it has failed. If that one failed sensor was the only way to detect a certain class of attack, then the system is blind to a class of attacks for which operators assumed they had coverage. The failed sensor creates a perfect opening for an adversary to mount a successful attack. Such failures should sound a loud alarm and corrective action must be swift (e.g., replace or repair and then restart the sensor). As another example, if an authorization system is allocated inadequate primary memory to perform its access control decisions, the authorization system should not simply collapse and utterly fail, but rather it should slow down while using secondary memory as temporary swap space.

> ### *Catastrophic failure modes are a matter of design.*

Part IV

19.1.2 Margin of Safety

Cybersecurity engineering is about designing to some minimum acceptable risk level. There are three important realities in cybersecurity engineering that bear on such minimum requirements:

- User behavior
- Unforeseen circumstances
- Uncertainty

If a mechanical system such as a hammock is engineered to meet a requirement such as carrying a specific total load weight, we know that users will find a way to push the engineering limits, either out of ignorance of the limits or because they have come to realize that systems often perform beyond their stated limits. Unforeseen circumstances occur, like perhaps the average weight of Americans skyrocketing over the last 50 years, and can cause limits to be exceeded. Lastly, there is always some uncertainty regarding the performance of the components of a system—for example, not all steel girders can carry the exact same weight due to slight differences in the metal and production process. There may also be an approximation in the calculations of actual performance due to simplifications or limits in engineering knowledge.

These three realities lead engineers to create what is called a **margin of safety**. A margin of safety *calls for engineering systems to meet requirements beyond those required by the existing specifications.* This margin of safety can be as high as three times if the three factors discussed previously warrant it and the stakes of failure are sufficiently high.

> *Uncertainty and unpredictability require a margin of safety.*

Cybersecurity engineering involves iterative risk assessment, which in turn requires rough estimates of probabilities (see Section 17.6). These rough estimates create a substantial amount of uncertainty because of the nature of the estimation process. In addition, *a lack of knowledge of true adversary capability and potential undiscovered vulnerabilities in the defended system strongly suggests using high margins of safety in goal risk levels.* A factor of three would be a reasonable starting point. For example, if the target acceptable risk level were $99 million of risk, then cybersecurity architects would be well-served to target $33 million to account for all of those uncertainties.

19.1.3 Conservation of Energy and Risk

The law of conservation of energy states that energy can neither be created nor destroyed, only change in form. This law has many important implications in engineering, including implying the impossibility of creating a perpetual motion machine.

In cybersecurity, there is a parallel pseudo-principle that is often offered in a half-joking maxim—risk can neither be created nor destroyed, only moved around. It is not universally true because this book describes how to engineer a system toward lower overall risk.

It is worthwhile considering the pseudo-principle because often, a change to a cybersecurity design often does end up "squeezing the risk balloon," only to discover that the risk appears elsewhere, perhaps in an unexpected place in the system, which could cause the defended system to be less secure than the engineering intended.

For example, authentication subsystems requiring increasingly longer and more complex passwords seems like a good idea, but what it does is force users to write their passwords down on a sticky note and paste it to the underside of their keyboard where every attacker looks first (analogous to "hiding" your emergency house key under the front door mat) or worse, store them online somewhere in a file that a hacker could find. In reality, this policy change moves risk from the cybersecurity system to users who respond with a stratagem that could increase the overall risk to the defended system. This design choice enables system owners to shift responsibility and blame onto users when accounts are breached.

For every proposed cybersecurity system change, *cybersecurity engineers should ask "where might this push risk, do we really want to push it there, and what does it do to overall risk, not just local risk?"*

> **Risk has a tendency to move to unwanted places.**

19.1.4 Keep It Simple, Stupid

The principle of "keep it simple, stupid," more commonly known by its acronym, KISS, means that *simple tasks tend to be easier to get right than complex ones.* It is better to have a simple system that works well than a complex one that works poorly. For example, consider complex user interfaces with dozens of menus and submenus and sub-submenus. If a user cannot figure out how to accomplish some frequent task, then what is the point of having the feature?

> **Simple tasks are easier to get right than complex ones.**

This principle applies strongly to cybersecurity systems for all the same reasons that it applies to all systems. Correctness of functionality is essential in cybersecurity systems because the consequences of failure are so high. *Simplicity is a way to improve the chances of correct design.* Simplicity of interfaces to cybersecurity services increases the likelihood that the services will be integrated and used correctly.

Working against this principle is an insidious phenomenon known as **requirements creep**. When any system is specified, there is a natural tendency to add new requirements, beyond the core requirements that meet the initially specified need. *Phrases like* "well, while we are at it, we might as well add..." *should strike fear into the hearts of all good engineers.* It is the sound of requirements creep. The notion behind such thoughts is not unreasonable—that making a system more capable will serve more users and therefore give a higher return on investment for a small incremental price to add one feature.

Unfortunately, the road to hell is paved with good intentions, and "just one more requirement" turns into 20 or 30 more requirements. This makes a simple system complex and tends to increase budget and delay schedule substantially. It is particularly bad when the requirements are added midstream during development, causing redesign. This added complexity in the design and implementation process introduces flaws and unexpected behaviors. The primary reason for this is the introduction of additional coding bugs and design errors from attempting to design more complex systems.

Requirements creep should be strongly resisted. A new requirement can be placed on queue for a future upgrade in an incrementally designed and built system, as we will discuss in Section 19.1.5. After users experience core functionality, they often realize that they do not need the additional feature after all or that it is not worth the cost.

> *Beware of requirements creep; it destroys success; resist!*

19.1.5 Development Process

The process used to develop a system is central to the outcome of all engineering projects. If one haphazardly throws metal girders together, the structure is bound to collapse. Similarly, software code haphazardly thrown together without any sense of design is bound to fail.

The engineering "V" that was discussed in Section 5.4 emphasizes the importance of the upfront investment in the engineering process and discipline. A well-designed system is more likely to meet user needs because it spends adequate time in the requirements phase, deeply understanding the true requirements and not just what users think they want. *A good design considers multiple alternatives and has a means to assess which are better than others based on key parameters such as risk, effective mission support, and ability to evolve.* Good and secure coding practices reduce the bug count and therefore the flaws, errors, and costly failures. Some professional engineers complain that disciplined engineering takes time, money, and makes engineering "less fun." As depicted in Figure 19-1, investing a little extra upfront in requirements, design, and coding can pay off up to 100 to 1 because of not needing to invest in finding and fixing bugs later in the life cycle.

> *Investment in good engineering process pays off.*

This is not to say that there is not a point of diminishing returns on upfront investment, particularly when it comes to schedule delays. Several decades ago, it was not uncommon for a significant system to take upwards of seven years to deliver. When computer technology was moving more slowly, this may have worked well. But even back then, this created a high risk of systems becoming obsolete by the time they were delivered. In fact, about 60 to 70 percent of code is never used [KRIG09]. This is an abysmal waste of resources and traces back to poor design process, often starting with requirements.

19.1.6 Incremental Development and Agility

By the KISS principle, smaller systems are almost always better than big systems in every way. Therefore, it is best to start with an absolute minimum core of functionality and fully develop that system first, including testing and delivery. *Get a working system in the hands of users as soon as possible.* Users will quickly offer feedback suggesting improvements that may differ significantly from what engineers originally conceived. New features will be quickly prioritized by users. This leads to an incremental improvement that creates new features and capabilities. This iteration, sometimes called a **spin**, should also be minimal and delivered quickly for the same reasons. The system is iterated until it is fully delivered, which may span its entire lifetime because continuous improvement could add value indefinitely. The spin incremental and iterative building process is sometimes referred to as **Agile design** and the delivery model is sometimes called **DevOps**, which stands for development-operations—a term that indicates a tight fusion between the two in which development and operations are tied together in quick release cycles and feedback.

> *Simple systems that work beat complex ones never delivered.*

There are two very important caveats that engineers must keep in mind. First, *Agile design is too often used as an excuse for poor process, in which steps are skipped and documentation is not done.* That is a formula for disaster as discussed previously. All steps in the design "V," particularly good requirements and design, are essential to successful engineering of systems—whether it be a bridge or a cybersecurity system. All steps must be properly documented. The process does not have to be long or onerous. It can be streamlined and done in hours or days if thought through properly and done by experts.

Second, *there must be an overarching architecture in which each increment fits; otherwise, the system becomes a monstrous collection of kludges that eventually collapses under its own weight.* Agile design, which is about rapid delivery, must ironically spend even more energy upfront in requirements, architecture, and design to ensure that the rapid increments will lead to a coherent system. Unfortunately, that level of upfront care does not often happen due to cost and schedule pressures; the consequences can be devastating. Even more concerning, the consequences may be delayed to the point where the originators of the poor design processes have moved on. The resulting collapse is not properly attributed to their poor management, and so those managers and the entire organization continue down a ruinous path. *Do not let this happen to you. Engineers are professionals who bear moral and legal responsibility for the security and safety of their systems. Take that responsibility seriously!*

> *Engineers are responsible for their systems' safety and security.*

For cybersecurity, incremental design in the context of an overarching architecture is particularly important. For example, there must be an understanding about how authentication, authorization, and policy management all fit together. When planning an increment, the cybersecurity engineer must deeply understand the dependency of capabilities and ensure that an increment is complete with respect to those dependencies. For example, if a new authorization capability needs an enhancement to the way authentication is performed, then both must be delivered together in a new release for it to make sense. If the interfaces are clear, due to good architecture, it should be possible to evolve and improve each subsystem without requiring major revisions to every other cybersecurity subsystem. Section 19.2.1 discusses how to achieve this important system property, called modularity.

19.2 Computer Science Principles

Computer science is a special type of engineering—the engineering of computer hardware and software. All of the principles of engineering apply to computer science. New principles are added to the set because of special features of computer science, particularly of software. This section addresses these principles.

19.2.1 Modularity and Abstraction

Fundamentally, modularity and abstraction are about clear thinking. It is about decomposing systems into logical groups of functions and decomposing those major functions into subordinate functions until one ends up with a set of basic primitive functions on which the system can be built. *There are an infinite number of ways that a system can be decomposed; this section discusses proper decomposition to achieve good design properties.*

Object Orientation   A good decomposition requires thought about actions that naturally work together and use common data structures. One useful approach is to follow the natural way that work flows in the real world that the system supports. For example, in a restaurant, a customer selects an order from a menu given to them by a host who seats them. The customer gives their order to a waiter, who conveys that order to a cook, who prepares the meal, and then alerts the waiter that the meal is ready. The waiter brings the meal to the customer, who consumes it, and then pays a cashier. This script offers a natural and logical way to organize a system to create representations of each of these actors (customer, host, waiter, cook, and cashier) and the actions they can take (ordering, submitting an order, picking up and delivering a meal, eating a meal, and paying for a meal) on various structures (menu and bill). Such an organization is sometimes referred to as **object-oriented design**— an embodiment of the notions of modularity and abstraction in which all serious computer scientists should be well-versed [BOOC93].

Design Patterns   In addition to design paradigms such as object-oriented design, computer scientists need substantial experience to know which decompositions within these good approaches are best. They can gain such experience by doing it poorly a few times and suffering the consequences. Fortunately, that experience can sometimes be captured in design templates known as **design patterns** [GAMM95]. Design patterns can be an excellent way to leverage experience, particularly when there are effective patterns written for specific domains such as a petrochemical plant control system, or banking.

Modularity   **Modularity** is the design principle that calls for the aggregation of similar functions into a programming entity with

- Clear control boundaries
- Private data structures
- Well-defined interfaces

A programming entity, called a **module** or object, is a distinct programming function or even a separate computer process operating in its own **address space**. A module has clear control boundaries when most of the subfunctions are accomplished within that same module. Modules contain private data structures—data structures such as arrays, tables, and lists that are only needed by the functions in that module, and are therefore protected from being accessed outside that module. The creation and maintenance of protected and private data is sometimes called **data hiding** because critical data is hidden from modules and users that do not need direct access. This makes reasoning about changes to data structures easier because only a handful of functions in the module can change those structures. A well-defined interface means that the module is called with a small number of parameters, each of which has clear syntax (format) and semantics (meaning), and whose returned data is similarly clear. An example of a module is shown in Figure 19-2.

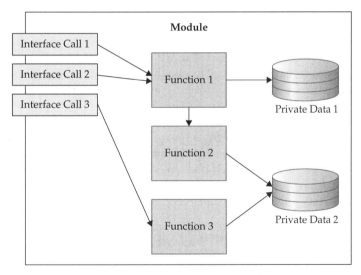

Figure 19-2   Principle of modularity with clear interfaces on the left, internal functions implementing the interface, and protected private data internal to the module, inaccessible by external modules

Abstraction   **Abstraction** is a similar concept to modularity. Abstraction is about dealing with system complexity by hiding details so that all complexities and all possible interactions do not have to be considered at once. Abstraction in computer science plays a similar role as it does in natural language. The word "peach" is an abstraction for all possible instances of peaches of all conceivable varieties of peaches in every stage of a peach's life cycle from birth to decay. We do not want to have to enumerate all of these things when we talk of peaches.

Similarly, in the restaurant example we gave earlier in this section, waiters have many attributes and many actions they are capable of. To the human resource department, waiters have pay rates, work schedules, benefits, an authorization to work, minimum age requirements, etc. To the restaurant manager, the functions of waiters include serving certain tables, being partly responsible for customer satisfaction, bringing meals to customers, taking breaks, etc. So, the waiter abstraction is actually quite complex.

When designing a system, it is unnecessary to consider all of those subtleties and complexities when specifying a **workflow** similar to the example of the waiter's interaction with the cook to bring a meal to a customer. The designer defers specifying those details so that the full system can be grasped at a high-enough level of abstraction. Later, each abstraction can be decomposed into detailed functions, perhaps even by different people. An abstraction is often realized by a module that contains that abstraction. Abstraction can also come in the form of layers, discussed in Section 19.2.2.

19.2.2 Layering

In natural language, concepts are built in a hierarchy of increasing levels of complexity and abstraction. For example, the concept of furniture relies on the concept of chairs and tables and sofas, which rely on perceived occurrences of each of these. One does not learn about theoretical quantum physics until one understands classical physics, which requires a basic understanding of scientific concepts. Knowledge builds.

Similarly, computer science uses **layering** as a way to manage complexity. It is similar to the idea of modularity, except that layers are essentially groupings of modules that work together and are at the same level of abstraction in a hierarchy of abstraction. Modules within an abstraction layer will tend to usually call other modules within that layer. Calls to functions in modules outside the layer are made to modules within the layer directly below, though it is sometimes possible to call to lower layers on occasion when there is no need of a higher-level abstraction from a layer above (e.g., applications calling low-level operating system functions, such as device drivers to speed performance). Modules in a layer should never call modules in a layer above because concepts at one layer can only have dependency on lower layers to create an orderly buildup of functionality and abstraction. Such a call to a function of an upper layer from a lower layer is called a **layer violation** and should be avoided. Figure 19-3 depicts the principle of layering.

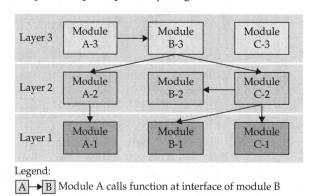

Legend:

[A] ➞ [B] Module A calls function at interface of module B

Figure 19-3   Principle of design layering to control complexity and to build up layers of abstraction

As an example of layering, a computer operating system kernel creates an abstraction of the underlying hardware and creates the appearance of the exclusive control of system resources, when in fact those resources are shared between many programs. We say that it abstracts the underlying machine because it provides more complex functions from the more basic and primitive functions that the hardware offers. In the process, some of the flexibility and performance are traded off in exchange for more powerful and sophisticated functions that hide some of the details of the underlying hardware functions. The operating system makes use of the kernel functions to create an even higher layer of abstraction of the underlying kernel. Applications, in turn, use operating system functions to meet mission requirements. This type of system layering is shown in Figure 8-5 and Figure 9-1. Similarly, a conceptual layering example of intrusion detection systems is shown in Figure 13-2.

Like modularity, layering makes it easier to argue that functionality is correct because it breaks complexity down into smaller chunks that are simple enough to be understood, and it protects this simplicity by adhering to the rules of modularity and layering.

Correctness arguments are essential for critical functions such as security since flaws can lead to catastrophic system failures. *Cybersecurity mechanisms must be designed with both modularity and layering if there is any hope of achieving a trustworthy system.* Care must be taken to ensure that cybersecurity layers span and are integrated within the layers from applications, through high-level operating systems, down to the hardware layer (see Section 9.1), creating a series of trustworthy layers. For example, building access control decisions in an authorization service, upon a poorly protected computer system, is pointless. *Intrusion detection systems that are built on completely untrustworthy sensors cannot be trusted to detect attacks because one must always presume that the sensors will be the first subsystem an attacker targets.*

> *Modularity and layering are essential to trustworthiness.*

19.2.3 Time and Space Complexity: Understanding Scalability

Often cybersecurity solutions are tested in the lab and seem to work fine. When they are scaled to thousands of users in real-world environments, sometimes the solutions prove inadequate. **Scalability** analysis should be done regarding both the deployment and operation of any system (from both a user and a system operator perspective)—particularly for cybersecurity systems. One key to understanding scalability is understanding complexity.

Not all parts of the system are equally important. Competent computer scientists know where to focus their attention. This section previously addressed the notion of complexity as a problem to be handled. In computer science, there is a second, much more specialized meaning of the term. Complexity refers to the inherent difficulty in accomplishing a computational task, such as sorting a list. There are two types of complexity: time and space. Time complexity refers to how much time a task will take. Space complexity refers to how much memory a task will take. Time complexity is the focus of the remainder of this section. Space complexity is parallel in structure and is therefore omitted for brevity. Further reading on complexity is recommended for this important area [AHO74].

Time complexity is not given in absolute terms of seconds, but rather in terms of a mathematical function of the size of input or other essential parameter of the task. For example, a sort algorithm such as bubble-sort is represented by the expression $O(n^2)$. A bubble-sort does pair-wise comparisons between elements in a list and swaps items if the second item is smaller than the first, thus the smallest item "floats" to the top of the list on the first pass. One has to pass through the list n times so that the second smallest, third smallest, etc., also float to their positions. This means that the bubble-sort takes on the order of (the "O" stands for "order of," which means approximated to the nearest power of 10) the square of the size of inputs—in this case, the number of elements (n) in a list. So, bubble-sort takes n^2 steps to bring an unsorted list of n elements into sorted order. It turns out that there is a faster way to sort a list. One can sort a list in $n*\log(n)$ time using an algorithm called quick-sort [AHO74]. Why is this important to know?

Complexity analysis speaks directly to scalability. As we noted previously, some algorithms for a given problem are better than others. In the worst case, algorithms are said to be exponential with respect to their key parameters. Exponential algorithms do not scale because the number of steps quickly approaches an astronomical number that is beyond the reach of any computer at some point of scaling. So, there is a natural break between polynomial solutions—ones whose time complexity can be expressed as an equation with all terms in which the input parameter is not in the exponent (e.g., 10^n)—and exponential ones, in terms of practicality. Exponential solutions are sometimes also referred to as **non-polynomial** and sometimes abbreviated NP.

> *Complexity analysis speaks directly to scalability.*

A problem may then be said to be inherently as hard as the best algorithm for solving that problem. Sometimes one can prove that an algorithm is the best possible one; other times, it is simply the best-known algorithm to date. If the best-known algorithm for a problem is exponential, then it is said to be exponentially hard or non-polynomial hard. Such problems often require approximate solutions using heuristic algorithms that give a good answer, but not necessarily the best answer. Sometimes good answers suffice and **heuristic algorithms** are adequate.

Complexity analysis is therefore important to understand what types of solutions to pursue and whether there is a better algorithm for a problem that is being solved. Without it, designers are casting about in the dark and may stumble into solutions that will collapse soon after the system is fielded.

19.2.4 Focus on What Matters: Loops and Locality

When it comes to system performance, there are no more important concepts than program loops (e.g., for loops, do-while loops, repeat-until loops) and locality of reference. Not all code is created equal when it comes to performance. Software spends the vast majority of time in execution loops. Performance improvement should focus on optimizing the software code inside of loops and not waste time concerned with code that is only executed a handful of times.

Equally important to code execution is data structure design and accessing data inside those structures. It is rare that all of a software program's data can fit into primary memory. Accessing items that are in secondary memory may take 10 to 100 times longer than items in primary memory, causing a major slowdown in performance. It is therefore important to be judicious with the design of data structures. Memory that is likely to be accessed in the same repeated code sequence should be located close to each other to prevent data from having to be swapped in and out from primary to secondary memory. This juxtaposition of memory that is accessed in close succession is known as **space locality of reference**.

Similarly, because of the nature of loops and modularity, there is a phenomenon known as **time locality of reference**. If a location in memory is accessed in one instant of computation, it is highly likely to be accessed in the next few instants. This locality principle enables a speedup technique known as caching. Parts of recently accessed memory are retained in *fast* memory to ensure that subsequent accesses to them are as fast as possible. If the memory is not accessed for a while, new parts of recently accessed memory replace it—this process is called **aging off**.

Locality of reference and loops are important because cybersecurity operations, particularly those that interpose all resource access checks such as authentication and authorization, have the potential to seriously degrade performance. Cybersecurity engineers must be very sensitive to performance issues. *As a rule of thumb, cybersecurity mechanisms in steady state should never degrade the defended system's performance by more than 10 percent.* It is reasonable for cybersecurity mechanisms to surge resource utilization temporarily during an attack (e.g., for tunable sensors discussed in Section 15.5), but not during normal operations. Significant performance impacts will lead the organization's system owners and operators to bypass the cybersecurity functionality, particularly in the times when it is needed the most, when the mission and system are under stress.

Cybersecurity shouldn't degrade performance more than 10 percent.

19.2.5 Divide and Conquer and Recursion

Another important way of handling complexity is an approach called **divide and conquer**. If a problem is too hard, figure out how to solve simpler problems and then compose them in a simple way. Consider the factorial function, symbolized by "!". Factorial of a non-negative integer n, denoted $n!$, is defined mathematically as the product of all positive integers less than or equal to n. The value of $0!$ is defined as being equal to 1. As example, $5! = 5*4*3*2*1 = 120$. Alternatively, one can define factorial recursively as $n! = n*(n-1)!$.

Calculating $5!$, by definition, is $5*4!$. So we can divide a factorial problem into two subproblems—that of calculating a simpler version of the problem, $4!$, and then multiplying that answer by 5. That does not give the answer because we still have to calculate $4!$, but notice that we can solve that problem using the very same divide and conquer approach. Thus, $4!$ is merely $4*3!$ and $3!$ is found by $3*2!$. The expression $2!$ can be found using $2*1!$. Finally, we are done because, by definition, $1! = 1$. Voilà. We have solved a complex problem by breaking it down into simpler and simpler factorials until the solution was trivial. Figure 19-4 shows the sequence of breaking down 5! into subproblems followed by rebuilding the final solution from the subproblem solutions.

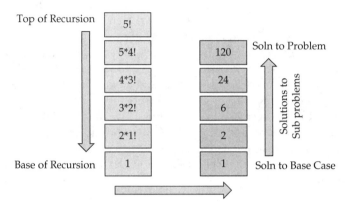

Figure 19-4   Example of recursion for factorial algorithm, solving a sequence of easier subproblems to get the final solution

Recursion is a programming technique that implements a divide and conquer approach to solving complex problems. It allows a function to call itself and suspend processing until the call is answered by successively simpler versions of the problem. It does this by placing the state of the suspended function into memory and then creating a separate instance of the function with the new parameters. In the previous example, we would make the programming function call as factorial($x=5$). Its code would say "if $x>1$ then return (x*factorial($x-1$)) otherwise return(1)." When the function code executes, it calls itself with factorial($x=4$). The instance of the function suspends, is stored in memory, and a new instance of the function is created with the input parameter of 4. This pushing of the state of the program into memory and creating a new instance continues until the function reaches the base of the recursion with $x=1$. That function call returns to the $x=2$ call of the function, which can then calculate its return value of 2. The recursive calls continue until the 5! instance of the function is resumed and it returns its answer of 120. Notice that this creates five separate blocks of memory to store the state of each instance of the function call. This approach could consume a great deal of memory and ultimately exhaust memory, resulting in a trade-off between simplicity of algorithm and memory space required.

Divide and conquer and recursion are important methods that apply indirectly to cybersecurity design. When one builds a cybersecurity subsystem to protect an enterprise, it becomes a system itself that requires protection. *The cybersecurity subsystem becomes the first and highest priority of an attacker to disable protection before mounting the attack.* Ultimately, the cybersecurity system needs a cybersecurity subsystem to protect it. Can we use just use the same cybersecurity system to protect itself? The answer is both yes and no.

> ### *An attacker's priority target is the cybersecurity system.*

Analogous to the divide and conquer and recursion technique, there needs to be a base to the division process. Great care must be taken not to create a circular dependency between the various subsystems such as those of authentication, authorization, attribute assignment and distribution, **policy specification**, **policy decision**, and **policy enforcement**. At some point, these subsystems have to depend on security primitives from a layer of abstraction below those services, as discussed in the previous section on layering. This requires a discipline of design and analysis that tracks the dependencies and ensures that the subsystems are firmly grounded within the security services, through the underlying layers (see Figure 9-1). As an example, designers should take care not to use application-level authentication services to authenticate developers wanting to edit configuration files in the kernel. Doing so would be a layer violation since a lower-layer kernel editing function would be depending on a higher-layer authentication function, which depends on the kernel, therefore creating a potential circularity.

Conclusion

This chapter covers fundamental systems engineering principles generally and those that are specific to computer science. The next chapter moves on to apply and extend these foundational principles to those of architecting cybersecurity systems.

To summarize:

- Murphy's Law predicts that "anything bad that can happen will happen."
- Prevent failures before they occur.
- Detect failures when they occur.
- Recover from failures when they are detected.
- Tolerate failures until the system recovers.
- Unpredictable user behavior, unforeseen circumstances, and uncertainty all require a significant margin of safety.
- Risk often moves around and is transformed in surprising ways in response to proposed cybersecurity design changes.
- Simple beats complex every time in terms of security, reliability, cost, and schedule.
- Systems should be as simple as possible to meet its requirements.
- Investments in early design processes tend to pay off over the life cycle of a project because detecting and fixing issues early is significantly cheaper than doing so later in the life cycle.
- Incremental development starting with the most basic possible functionality is an effective way to create dependable systems, but this approach must be guided by an overarching architecture, and interfaces must be clearly specified and stable.
- Modularity and abstraction are related and powerful approaches to managing complexity.
- Decompose complex processes into simple ones, hiding details and data structures.

Part IV

- Layering builds on modularity by grouping modules that depend only on each other and on the layers below them, therefore creating logical layers of increasing complexity and sophistication.

- Time and space complexity analyses help cybersecurity engineers understand the inherent difficulty of certain classes of problems.

- Complexity analysis predicts the scalability of certain solutions and avoids the time and expense of developing solutions that will not scale to meet mission requirements.

- Software loops and locality of reference tell software engineers where to focus their attention in optimizing performance.

- Dividing and conquering is an approach of breaking down problems into simpler instances.

Questions

1. State Murphy's Law and its implications for cybersecurity.
2. List four approaches that designers can use to counter Murphy's Law.
3. Why would you expend resources detecting failures that a design prevents?
4. Enumerate six requirements of recovery and explain why each is needed.
5. Explain why failure tolerance is important and how it relates to detection and recovery.
6. Give two examples of how to design a cybersecurity system to tolerate failure.
7. Define margin of safety and list the three factors that bear on how big the margin of safety must be.
8. Discuss three sources of uncertainty in cybersecurity design and what can be done to mitigate them.
9. What is the principle of conservation of risk and how does it apply to cybersecurity design?
10. Why is keeping design simple so important to dependability?
11. What is requirements creep and should a cybersecurity engineer resist it? Why or why not?
12. Why does investing in the early design stages decrease flaws? Why is that important?
13. What is incremental development and how does it help manage complexity?
14. Define DevOps and Agile design and relate them to incremental development.
15. What are two important requirements that enable incremental development to succeed?
16. What happens if each of the two requirements are not met?
17. Define modularity and discuss how it addresses complexity.
18. How does modularity make a system easier to prove correct?

19. How does object-oriented programming relate to modularity?

20. What are private data structures and why are they important to modularity?

21. What is a well-defined interface to a module?

22. What is the relationship between the concept of abstraction and of modularity?

23. Describe the principle of layering. Compare and contrast it to modularity.

24. Why is it a bad idea for modules from one layer to call modules in a higher layer?

25. Define time complexity and space complexity.

26. Why are time and space complexity important to scalability?

27. What does exponentially hard mean and how does it relate to exponential solutions?

28. What is the difference between an exponential solution to a problem and an inherently exponentially hard problem?

29. Under what circumstances is an exponential solution workable for a system?

30. Why are loops important to consider in optimizing performance?

31. What is locality of reference and how can software engineers leverage this property to gain significant performance improvements?

32. List three circumstances under which locality of reference would not exist.

33. What is caching and how does it relate to locality of reference?

34. What is a divide and conquer approach? Give an example that is not discussed in this text.

35. What is recursion and how does it relate to divide and conquer?

36. How do divide and conquer and recursion apply to cybersecurity design?

Architecting Cybersecurity

Overview

Learning Objectives

- Differentiate cybersecurity architecture from the aggregation of widgets.
- List and define the three properties of a reference monitor.
- Explain how the principles of minimality and simplicity promote assurance.

- Discuss the role of separation of concerns in the evolvability of systems.
- Summarize and characterize the three stages of security policy processing.
- Describe the role of intrusion tolerance in architecting layered cybersecurity.
- Identify the pros and cons of adopting cloud cybersecurity.

Cybersecurity is not merely a random aggregation of lots of cool security widgets integrated haphazardly into a system. Cybersecurity is about achieving specific system properties that then yield a specified acceptable risk level, as discussed in Section 17.5. In practice, there is always some uncertainty regarding how well that engineering goal is achieved. Although covering the attack space is an essential concept in cybersecurity engineering, *it is only through gaining confidence in system properties that one can realistically achieve sound cybersecurity.* This is the role of assurance techniques. In the end, good cybersecurity engineers build a strong case for their assertions about the security properties of their design and implementation. This structured argument is sometimes referred to as an assurance case.

> **Realizing cybersecurity requires assured security properties.**

20.1 Reference Monitor Properties

There are three fundamental and important properties, those of the reference monitor: **functional correctness**, non-bypassability, and tamperproof. A reference monitor is a cybersecurity mechanism that protects critical resources of the defended system. In the most basic terms, the three properties say: you can't break through the protection, you can't get around it, and you can't weaken it.

Reference monitor properties are so fundamental because they are universal to all cybersecurity mechanisms. If an attacker can easily break through the mechanism because it has lots of exploitable flaws, then what's the point of having the mechanism in the first place? If an attacker can bypass the mechanism by accessing the critical resources by some other means, then what value does the mechanism serve, even if its internal workings are perfectly correct? If an attacker can easily change or corrupt a mechanism, what is the point of going through the trouble of making it correct and ensuring that it cannot be circumvented? We discuss each of these three properties in turn, then go on to discuss several other related properties.

> **Reference monitor properties are fundamental.**

20.1.1 Functional Correctness

A system with no specification can never be wrong, only surprising.

—Earl Boebert

Functional correctness means that the cybersecurity mechanism has to do exactly what it is supposed to do, and no more. That means there must be some clear statement of what the mechanism is supposed to do. The statement is called a **specification**. A specification typically starts at a high level with informal mission need statements, concepts of operation, followed by a formal requirement specification. These high-level statements are successively refined into top-level design specifications, detailed design specifications, implementation code, and finally an executable system. The left-hand side of Figure 20-1 shows this specification refinement.

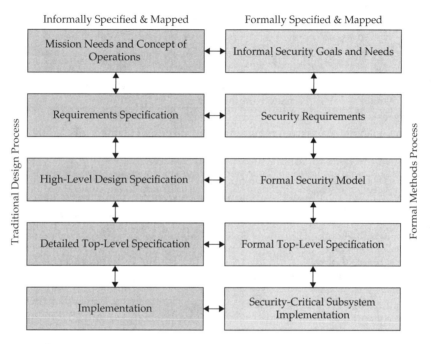

Figure 20-1   Relationship among formal and informal specifications, requiring parallel and mapped specifications

Notice that the need for the functional correctness property does not dictate exactly what the specification contains with respect to cybersecurity. It can contain a wide variety of desired behaviors. These behaviors, when they come in the form of rules governing transactions (such as access control decisions), are called security policies.

Notice also the final phrase of functional correctness requires that the system do "no more" than it is supposed to do. This refers to the need to show the absence of malicious code such as Trojan horses. For code of any appreciable size, this task is extraordinarily difficult. Malicious code can be hidden from expert reviewers in as little as 692 lines of code [GOSL17][WEIN16].

A specification can be informal or formal. An informal specification is written in natural language prose. Engineers are trained to craft these specifications as clearly and unambiguously as possible, but the limits of natural language and of human ability introduce

flaws in the specification. Design reviews among peers are intended to uncover and repair such flaws, but the review process is also limited by a human's ability to grasp a large system and reason about it.

A formal specification uses a more structured language supported by tools to track design details and help the designer ensure clarity and completeness of the design. When the tools use mathematics and automated reasoning to rigorously prove properties about the design specifications, we call the specification and tool-assisted analysis process **formal methods**. We will discuss formal methods and **design verification** in Section 21.3.

Specifications are created in layers of successive refinement. The top-most layer is a requirement specification that captures the behaviors and functions that users and system sponsors want. The next level, called a top-level specification, describes the major blocks of functionality and their interaction together and with external systems on which they depend. An informal argument is made to show that the specification meets the requirements.

The argument is usually supported by a requirement traceability matrix. The matrix is a two-way mapping from each requirement to the design element that attempts to meet the requirement, and a mapping from each design element (such as a functional block in an architecture) to the requirements that it supports. The requirements should also be two-way traced to the mission need statements, providing a rationale for the requirement. Often a requirement is partially met by multiple design elements and a design element partially supports multiple requirement aspects. Thus, a synthesis argument must be made that the combinations of design elements meets each requirement. Figure 20-2 shows an example of a two-way mapping. The example makes it visibly apparent that requirement 4 is unmet by the design and that design element 4 does not appear to be needed since it meets no requirement (or perhaps there is a missing requirement).

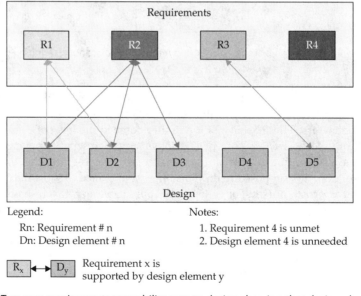

Figure 20-2 Two-way requirements traceability map to design showing that design elements must meet requirements and that all requirements must be supported by design elements.

20.1.2 Non-Bypassable

In addition to arguing for the correct behavior of each cybersecurity component, the system as a whole must be shown to exhibit certain properties. We call this assurance-in-the-large. For example, an authorization system controlling access to a resource (e.g., a file) must not only work correctly, but an argument must be made that there is no alternate way to access the resource without going through the authorization subsystem. This property is known as non-bypassability. Without this property, there is little point in spending the effort to get the authorization system right.

20.1.3 Tamperproof

A cybersecurity system must be tamperproof—a property of a program, hardware, or a system, such that it maintains system integrity (not capable of being modified without proper authorization). The **system integrity** of a reference monitor is critical. Because the reference monitor is the lynchpin for access control, it is a high-value target for adversaries. The other two properties of non-bypassability and functional correctness do no good if the reference monitor can be modified by an attacker. The attacker could give the reference monitor any functionality that the adversary chooses.

System integrity of **security-critical** code like this is achieved by protecting the code inside the security kernel where its resource set cannot be accessed by any application code. This eliminates the vast majority of software from being a threat if it contains malicious code. The argument still must be made that no other part of the security kernel running in this protected address space (see Section 9.4.1) can change the software during operations, and that the system updating software is protected (see Section 10.6). Both parts of that argument can be made by using software integrity measures such as computing and checking digital signatures (see Section 10.6) and checking them upon importation to the defended system from the software vendors and each time prior to the software being executed.

20.2 Simplicity and Minimality Breed Confidence

Perfection is achieved, not when there is nothing more to add,
but when there is nothing left to take away.

—Antoine de Saint-Exupéry

When systems become complex and large, they are much harder for human designers (and computers aiding humans) to understand and analyze. Large and complex programs tend to contain more hidden errors in them and are consequently less reliable. Therefore, it is important to ensure that critical cybersecurity subsystems (and everything that the systems depend on, such as operating system kernels, for example) are as small and simple *as possible*. This is an application of the KISS principle discussed in Section 19.1.4.

> **Simplicity engenders confidence.**

Part IV

20.3 Separation of Concerns and Evolvability

The concept of **separation of concerns** [LAPL07] is similar to the notion of modularity (see also Section 7.7). It is modularity to achieve very specific properties. In this case, the specific property has to do with independent evolvability of the modules. The functionality of the cybersecurity system is separated into subsystems according to the similarity and function and their different properties. This means that each module can be improved at its own pace and by separate teams without concern for how and whether the other modules evolve—so long as the modules maintain the same external interface to the rest of the system.

20.4 Security Policy Processing

There is one particularly important application of the separation of concerns principle in cybersecurity—that of security policy. Security policy rules must be specified, executed to determine access for each case access request, and then that policy decision must be enforced. As discussed in Section 20.1, a reference monitor is interposed between the rest of the system and a set of protected resources that is encapsulated by the reference monitor.

Figure 20-3 shows the interaction of these conceptual elements of policy-based access control in the context of the reference monitor (see Section 12.1 for more detail). The access policy is specified upfront by the policy authors who understand the access control requirements of the resources they are protecting. That policy is then distributed to the **policy decision-making** element. The decision-making element is consulted each time an accessing entity, such as a user, attempts to access a resource. Once the decision has been rendered, the reference monitor must enforce that decision and provide only access consistent with that decision. The relationship between the three aspects of policy is shown in Figure 20-3.

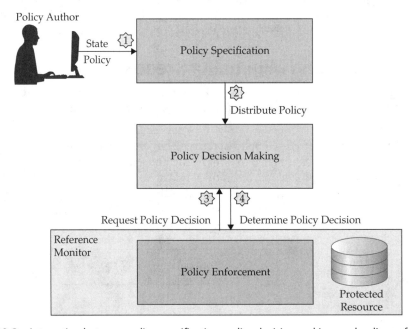

Figure 20-3   Interaction between policy specification, policy decision making, and policy enforcement

There is a significant difference in the processes and required properties of policy specification, policy decision making, and policy enforcement. These properties involve

- Performance requirements
- Developer expertise
- Authentication requirements
- Likely rate of change
- Integration level

These properties are summarized in Table 20-1. Each will be discussed in turn. Broadly speaking, notice that there are significant differences between the properties of each element dealing with security policies. Seeing such significant differences in such fundamental properties should cause a cybersecurity engineer to immediately pause and consider that these elements need to be in separate subsystems with clear interfaces to enable independent development and life-cycle evolution.

Element	Performance	Developer Expertise	Authentication	Change Rate	Integration Level
Policy Specification	Low	High	High	High	Low
Policy Decision Making	Medium	Medium	Medium	Low	Medium
Policy Enforcement	Fast	Low	Low	Low	High

Table 20-1   Comparison of Required Properties of Elements Between Policy Specification, Policy Decision Making, and Policy Enforcement

> *Different property requirements suggest separate modules.*

20.4.1 Policy Specification

Policy specification is the process by which a steward of a body of protected data states the rules governing access to that data based on attributes of the accessing entity and those of the specific data being requested. An example of policy specification might be that a user can read data whose classification is at their security clearance or below.

Because the policy is specified upfront when a new set of protected data is created along with a protecting subsystem, the processing to create digital policy does not need to be fast. Authoring digital policy based on natural language policy is not a bottleneck compared to the much-more-frequent policy-decision and enforcement processing. It is important that policy processing is deliberate, carefully checking the correctness and consistency of the policy specification rather than focusing on speed. The developer of software who assists a policy author in creating policy must have a deep knowledge of cybersecurity. The expert must also have specialized understanding of the policy specification process, which comes from studying the nature of policies, the threats they counter, and how they do so (as discussed in this book).

Because the specified policies determine the access control for all protected data in the defended system, it is essential that policy authors are highly authenticated using at least **two-factor authentication** (see Section 11.2).

Lastly, the policy specifications are not highly specific to the data sets being protected or the protecting subsystem that protects them. It relates only to the general schema of policy-based access control on the defended system (e.g., attribute-based, identity-based, etc.), which determines the types of policies that may be specified.

20.4.2 Policy Decision Making

A policy specification is created and then distributed to the policy decision-making process. That policy specification forms the particulars of the decision-making processing to yield access control decisions. In some sense, the policy decision-making processing is like an interpreter (analogous to interpreted high-level programming languages such as Python), and the policy specification is the interpreted program. The language of the policy program is determined by the policy schema, as discussed previously. Just as it makes little sense to integrate programs into the program language interpreter, it makes little sense to integrate the policy specification into the policy decision-making processing. Figure 20-4 shows the parallels in the analogy between policy processing and program language processing.

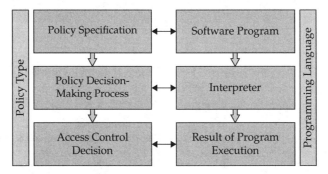

Figure 20-4   Parallels in the analogy between policy processing and programming language processing

The policy decision-making logic is invoked each time an access request is made to protected resources. The policy decision-making processing fetches the policy associated with the relevant protected resources, then uses the attributes of the entity requesting access (e.g., a user) and the attributes of the specific subset of protected resources requested by the entity. This processing happens relatively frequently, so performance is a significant issue in the design of this functionality. Optimizing techniques such as **short-circuit evaluation**, whereby processing stops as soon as an outcome is determined, helps to improve performance. For example, take the expression "if A or B or C or (D and E and F)".

If, in the course of evaluating this expression, it is determined that A is true, then none of the other terms matter since the overall expression is true—so the cybersecurity system need not waste time evaluating them.

There is an important trade-off decision when it comes to performance. The policy decision-making service can be implemented as a separate service with its own process and perhaps on its own computer that responds to access decision requests over the network, or it can be tightly integrated into the protecting subsystem directly where the access is granted. The separate service model has the advantage that it is easier to maintain system integrity and to argue for the tamperproof property. On the other hand, the latency (time delay) of a call over the network can be substantial. On a local area network, the round-trip delay can be milliseconds. While that sounds fast, keep in mind that a computer can perform on the order of a billion operations per second. That means that *a network service call would be one million times slower than computing the decision locally*. Because the access control decision is a direct bottleneck to the first access request, this can be a serious problem.

You may ask: when is a millionfold performance impact ever worth the trade-off with tamper resistance offered by a separate service? This is where caching comes in. If there were an infinite number of users and an infinite number of protected resources and users never access the same resource more than once, then it would almost never be worth implementing policy decision making as a separate service. Fortunately, the realities of access patterns are far better than this. There is a locality of reference (Section 19.2.4) to data; if a user accesses a particular subset of protected data in one instant, they are likely to access that same subset in the next instant of processing. This allows the protecting subsystem to incur the overhead of the network call once and then use a cached access-control determination for all future access requests to the same protected subset of data by the same user.

If the vast majority of access requests exhibit this locality of reference, which is generally the case, then one can have all the advantages of a separate service combined with the millionfold speedup associated with processing within the protecting subsystem. Indeed, one can even monitor access request patterns of users over time and **pre-fetch** access control decisions that are commonly used, thus incurring no network service call latency even when the user makes the first access request.

As an aside, when using caches for security decisions or elements on which those decisions depend, extraordinary care must be exercised. Two important requirements for security-critical caches are (1) integrity of the cache, and (2) integrity of the cache bindings to its referents. The cache itself becomes a high-value target to attackers because all the cybersecurity infrastructure, such as clearance requirements, resource attributes, and even security policy, is essentially bypassed if the attacker can directly alter cached policy decisions. The integrity of the cache binding referents is more subtle and difficult to achieve. If the security policy decision refers to one resource, it should not be possible for an attacker to alter the resource by changing the location or name of the resource (e.g., file). In other words, the semantic meaning of the cache entry must be preserved.

The expertise to develop a policy decision-making service is high, and correct implementation is highly security-critical. This means that such services should be developed by cybersecurity professionals, preferably those with experience and understanding of policy-based access control.

Users do not need to interact directly with a policy decision service in the same way that policy authors must interact with the policy specification service. The authentication to policy decision-making service is machine-to-machine. In other words, the policy decision-making service must have a highly authenticated communication path to the policy specification service to fetch policies, and another such path to the protecting subsystem that requests access to the protected data. If these communication paths can be spoofed, an adversary can hijack the paths and wreak havoc in the policy decision-making process, invalidating the cybersecurity properties provided by the components.

Lastly, although the policy for protected resources may be periodically tweaked due to organizational policy changes that come from public law or liability concerns, the policy decision-making processing remains the same. The policy decision-making service is only the interpreter of the specified policy. One does not need to change interpreters every time a program is changed. Therefore, the policy decision-making service is highly stable and needs to be changed only when the language of policy specification occurs—which does happen occasionally, when richer and more powerful policies are sought by cybersecurity engineers [LIU08].

20.4.3 Policy Enforcement

Once an access control decision is made, whether locally or remotely on a network service, based on an input specified policy, that policy must be enforced. If the protecting subsystem fails to correctly call the policy decision-making service or fails to implement the access control decision using the policy decision-making service, there is not much point to creating the entire infrastructure to specify policy and to decide on access based on that policy.

Policy enforcement must occur each time an accessing entity requests access to protected data, not just the first time. Therefore, the policy enforcement service must be very fast. The expertise required is primarily that of a cybersecurity-aware systems developer and integrator in consultation with a cybersecurity professional to review the integration. Integration design patterns prepared by cybersecurity experts are also very helpful. The policy enforcement code is relatively stable because all of the tweaks to policy are isolated to the policy specification process. The only time that policy enforcement software needs to change is when the nature of the protected resource changes in a fundamental way. This is a relatively rare occurrence.

20.5 Dependability and Tolerance

When a fail-safe system fails, it fails by failing to fail safe.
—John Gall, *Systematics*

20.5.1 Cybersecurity Requires Fail Safety

Systems always fail. In fact, in most large enterprise systems, there is always some component that has failed in some way. Section 5.6 covered the basics of the nature of the fault→error→failure chain of events and the need to consider it in models of defense. Section 7.2 reviewed the importance of failure in predicting cybersecurity failures. Section 7.3 focused on understanding failure to give insight into proper design. This section explores why failure considerations are an important part of good system design, particularly for critical functions such as cybersecurity.

System designs must specifically prevent failures by eliminating errors (to the extent possible), detecting errors when they occur, and properly handling and recovering from errors in a secure manner.

> *All systems fail; large systems are always failing in some way.*

No failure mode that could result in serious problems should be overlooked. The designer should never assume that detection and recovery are not required. *Such assumptions can be catastrophic.* Cybersecurity designs should include a failure analysis and a dependability argument with respect to cybersecurity critical failure modes.

> *Failing to plan for failure guarantees catastrophic failure.*

20.5.2 Expect Failure: Confine Damages Using Bulkheads

Least privilege means granting the minimum authorized access needed to perform a specified task. The purpose is to minimize damage should granted access be abused. The principle reduces overall risk exposure by reducing the attack surface. The concept certainly applies to human users who go rogue, but is more important in its application to programs operating on behalf of users. Such programs often require the authority of the user to request access to protected resources such as databases. Giving all programs all of the authority of the user, when they only need limited authority, is dangerous because we rarely have assurance that the program is correct and uncorrupted by an adversary (through, say, a life-cycle attack).

> *Least privilege reduces risk exposure.*

Standing in counterbalance to the principle of least privilege is the emerging principle of **responsibility-to-share**. *The responsibility-to-share principle acknowledges that excessive sharing restrictions can damage mission as much as sharing information too freely—known as Dunn's Conundrum [LEE14].* Responsibility-to-share emphasizes customers discovering and pulling the information they need as opposed to owners knowing a priori what clients need and pushing the information to them.

> *Least privilege must be balanced against responsibility-to-share.*

Need-to-know works well in a very stable and long-standing world of adversaries, organizations, and defended systems, such as was the case during the Cold War. Responsibility-to-share acknowledges a much more dynamic world in which missions, organizations, and systems are constantly shifting. The dynamic world requires innovative thinking involving discovery and making connections that may not be consistent with the static notions of need-to-know.

Part IV

Although the principle of least privilege, which mirrors the principle of need-to-know, seems to be in direct opposition to responsibility-to-share, it is really a matter of balance. The optimal balance is dictated by minimizing overall risk—the risk of excessive sharing against risk of excessive restriction.

When balancing these two principles, there are really two separate cases: balancing for human users and for programs operating on the user's behalf. The attacks and risks are different for each case. Irrespective of how the balance is struck for each, it is wise to increase the intrusion detection surrounding the additional leeway provided in each case, to reduce the chance that that leeway is not abused.

Another related principle in creating bulkheads is that of mutual suspicion—the concept that subsystems of cybersecurity trust other subsystems only to the minimum needed, for specific properties, and verify those properties to the extent possible. The trust that is required should be well-specified and verifiable in some way. For example, if an authentication subsystem trusts its host operating system to tell it the correct time, that should be a documented dependency with some indication of what the consequence of a failure or malicious manipulation or corruption would be. Further, if the authentication subsystem spans many computers (as it often does), it should cross-check time across multiple computers and possibly against a network time service. Section 21.4.2 discusses this principle further in the context of trust dependencies.

20.5.3 Tolerance

Preventing attacks, detecting and responding to attacks, and limiting attack damages from propagating due to excessive trust dependency are all important but insufficient approaches. In the end, *attacks will succeed*. When they do, defended systems need to be able to tolerate the damage from attacks and continue to support the mission, perhaps in some degraded mode. This principle is known as **intrusion tolerance**.

Intrusion tolerance is a property that must be explicitly designed into the defended system and is not an accidental byproduct of integrating a bunch of cybersecurity widgets. It requires attention to important design issues such as system dependability, failure modes, and failure propagation paths.

To achieve intrusion tolerance, a system must be able to

- Detect system damage, particularly to services and available resources.
- Minimize damage propagation to unaffected parts of the system.
- Assess the impact to mission from the damage incurred.
- Understand the priority of mission functions and the underlying supporting infrastructure within the system.
- Reconstitute the most essential mission functions onto the remaining intact portion of the system.
- Transition functions from the damaged area of the system.

Damage Detection   Detecting system damage is part of system health and status reporting, discussed in detail in Sections 22.4 and 22.7. Without an ability to distinguish which parts of the system are damaged and which are still operating, intrusion tolerance properties are difficult to achieve.

Damage Propagation   To be able to reconstitute essential system functions, there must be a part of the system that remains stably undamaged. If damage is able to quickly spread throughout the system, by the time the system attempts to reconstitute function, the part of the system that is to take on the essential function can be damaged beyond operation. Therefore, the system needs damage propagation bulkheads, as discussed earlier in Section 20.5.2.

Damage Impact   Knowing what components of the system are damaged by a cyberattack is necessary, but not sufficient. These damages must be mapped to mission functions so that the mission impact can be assessed. The mission impact will dictate what essential functions and services need to be reconstituted.

Prioritized Mission Function   To reconstitute essential mission function, it is important to determine which mission functions are essential and to rank them in priority order. Due to system functional dependencies, there are groupings of functions that must be established prior to ranking, because reconstituting a service without the services it depends on is useless. For example, any mission function grouping will likely require at least some basic level of cybersecurity functionality in the group.

Ranking essential functionality is needed because one cannot predict what fraction of the system will be damaged by a cyberattack. The system must be prepared for contingencies involving different levels of damage. There is also a minimum set of functions needed to reconstitute the system. This should be known in advance so that there is not an attempt to reconstitute when it is not possible. For example, if a minimum system configuration requires at least 10 percent of system resources, and only 8 percent remain, then there is no hope of reconstituting the system. At that point, the organization will need to fall back to a contingency plan, such as moving to an alternate site.

Reconstitute   Once damages have been contained, prioritized mission functions can be reconstituted in the portion of the system that is stably intact. This involves shutting down functions in the damaged part of the system and moving them to the intact part of the system. Ideally, the system is able to save the states of the processes before they are damaged. Then it is a matter of restarting the requisite processes and restoring the state from the damaged part of the system to the undamaged part. This is known as process migration. It is imperative that the state of the processes be checked for integrity before restoring them to fresh copies of the program restored from a **golden copy** (a copy of the program, from its original source, believed to be free from corruption). If the data is corrupted, the system will need to find older checkpoints that are uncorrupted to restore from.

To the extent that this reconstitution sequence can be handled in an automated fashion, it is called a **self-healing** property. In most cases, human guidance is involved in some portions of the process, but the degree of automation can be expected to increase in the future.

20.5.4 Synergize Prevention, Detect-Response, and Tolerance

Cybersecurity architects should design prevention, detect-response, and tolerance techniques into conceptually separate subsystems, yet complementary to one another in terms of attack space coverage. The concept of synergy between prevention and detection subsystems was introduced in Section 13.1 as portrayed in Figure 13-1. We extend the concept to three complementary layers to include intrusion tolerance as depicted in Figure 20-5.

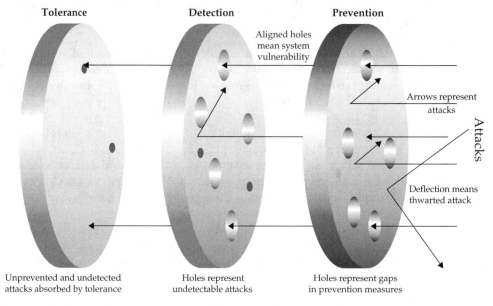

Figure 20-5 Synergy between prevention, detection, and intrusion tolerance layers to create an effective complementary defense mesh

Prevention techniques are mechanisms designed to prevent attackers from successfully penetrating into the system—including identity certification systems such as those based on public-key infrastructure and authorization systems that enforce cybersecurity policy on resources. Detect-response mechanisms are the combination of mechanisms used to detect the successful system penetration by an attacker and the defender's responses to that detected penetration, intended to mitigate damages and expel the attacker from the system. Tolerance techniques are mechanisms intended to recover and restore critical functionality despite failures resulting from successful penetration into a defender's system.

Designing intentional synergy between the layered cybersecurity subsystems ensures that the weaknesses of each subsystem do not align with one another to create an overall weakness with respect to the attack space. Said another way, the design should be such that the strengths of one cybersecurity layer cover the weaknesses of another, thereby reducing the vulnerabilities within the attack space. As a concrete example, one should design the detection-response cybersecurity subsystem layer to detect the attacks that will most likely be missed by the preventative techniques—particularly by a sophisticated adversary.

Similarly, negative synergies between mechanisms should be avoided where possible—represented by aligned holes in Figure 20-5. An example would be the pervasive encryption of data on an internal network, making it very hard for the intrusion detection system to detect attacks since the attackers would be afforded a confidentiality service on their data streams as well. In such a case, the intrusion detection system could be allowed access to the cleartext of the data by the nature of the encryption process used.

20.6 Cloud Cybersecurity

A distributed system is one in which the failure of a computer you didn't even know existed can render your own computer unusable.

—Leslie Lamport

Cloud computing is a form of distributed computing where many computers and applications work together, often across geographically separated areas, to provide a coherent service. The cloud computing model is attractive because users performing some mission do not have to get into the information technology business, including procurement, operating, and maintenance of computers and networks—allowing them instead to focus on their mission. *The idea is to make computing like a commodity utility, analogous to electricity, where users do not need electricity generators, distributors, and transformers on premises* [CORB65].

There are two types of cloud behavior: **computational clouds** and **storage clouds**, often mixed on the same system. A computational cloud such as Amazon Web Service® is essentially a remote computing facility that is shared with many other customers, but appears to the user as if it were a dedicated set of computers just for the user. The service provider has hundreds of thousands of computers that are virtualized into millions of computers spread across a number of networked computer data centers around the globe. The virtualization is done using low-level operating systems called hypervisors, which then support multiple copies of different types of operating systems on the same physical computer, making each computer appear as though it were dozens of computers (see Section 15.6 and Figure 15-6).

A user is allocated the number of virtual machines requested, and they are often connected together and to the user's own computer system via a virtual private network, which creates a set of encrypted channels to prevent eavesdropping by other users sharing the same resources. The user can request a very large number of virtual computers as a pool that can be dynamically allocated, creating a **virtual private cloud** within the larger cloud service provider's system.

A storage cloud such as Dropbox®, Google Drive®, or Apple iCloud® simply acts as a large remote external hard drive that can be shared with other users and devices. Storage clouds enable access to files from many locations, and they facilitate sharing and collaboration between many users. These remote external hard drives are presented either through a web service or integrated into the operating system to give the appearance of a remote disk drive within one's own local file structure—thus creating a **distributed file service**.

From a cybersecurity perspective, the implementation of cybersecurity mechanisms such as authentication, authorization, and intrusion detection is outsourced to the cloud service provider. *Integrated cloud cybersecurity is simultaneously the great advantage and the great disadvantage of cloud cybersecurity.*

> ### *Integrated cloud cybersecurity can be a double-edged sword.*

Cybersecurity design is difficult to get right—that is the purpose of this book. Large service providers have the resources and incentives to hire experts to get the design right and make it as robust as possible since breaches could cost them millions of dollars in direct losses and tens of millions in lost business through a destruction of faith in the defended system. In addition, consistently defending a system is almost as hard as designing it well in the first place. Systems tend to wander from their design specification as bugs are patched and the system design is expanded. Again, large service providers can ensure that the cybersecurity system is maintained throughout its life cycle.

On the other hand, cloud service providers offer the functionality and assurance level that they believe the majority of their clients need. So, *very high-end customers either have to take the risk of inadequate cybersecurity or build their own.* Lower-end users must pay for overkill capabilities that they do not need. Further, if there is a breach in the cloud provider's cybersecurity system, their clients' data and services can be completely and massively compromised. Such providers represent a high-value target (see Section 3.2) and are at risk of successful cyberattack. Further, their fine-print user agreements will almost universally deny any liability for such losses, so the clients have little recourse for damages. *Eventually, there may be insurance for such damages, but insurance companies are only now just beginning to figure out how to enter that market and avoid inappropriately covering the risks resulting from sloppy security practices by vendors.*

> ### *Cybersecurity insurance may one day cover residual risk.*

Conclusion

This chapter extends the presentation of fundamental engineering principles to architecting cybersecurity systems. This chapter discusses the fundamental nature of a reference monitor, notions of simplicity, separation of concerns, and how to tolerate cybersecurity failure. The next chapter will discuss how to argue that a cybersecurity system achieves the desired degree of confidence in the security of its operation.

To summarize:

- Cybersecurity is about assuredly achieving specific security properties, not just about aggregating a collection of security widgets.

- Three of the most fundamental security properties are the three associated with a reference monitor: functionally correct, non-bypassable, and tamperproof.

- Minimality and simplicity of design promotes assurance because complex systems are much harder to prove anything about and are much more prone to subtle flaws.

- Separation of concerns is a type of modularity where functionality is grouped according to the similarity of requirements on that functionality, including the likely rate at which the functionality must change.

- Security policy processing occurs in three distinct stages, each with its own characteristics, suggesting that they be kept separate: policy specification, policy decision making, and policy enforcement.

- Intrusion tolerance is the last line of cybersecurity defense and is essential because all systems fail.

- Cloud computing turns information technology into a commodity utility like electricity, but places cybersecurity into the hands of a service provider—which can be both good and bad.

Questions

1. Define the term "assurance case" and relate it to cybersecurity.

2. Why do we say that cybersecurity is less about the widgets and more about achieving specific properties?

3. What is a reference monitor? What are its three properties? Why are all three needed and how do they relate to one another?

4. Why does functional correctness require that a system do no more than it is supposed to do? What additional functionality do you think we are specifically trying to exclude?

5. What is a requirements traceability matrix and why is it important?

6. What is a non-bypassability property and why is it important?

7. How does system integrity relate to one of the reference monitor properties? Is it a property that you prove about the component's behavior? Why or why not?

8. Why are simpler systems more dependable and more secure? What does this suggest about the design process of a cybersecurity system?

9. How does the principle of separation of concerns differ from the principle of modularity?

10. How does the principle of separation of concerns support independent evolvability?

11. What are the three stages of security policy processing and how do they interact with one another?

12. What are the five properties of elements that distinguish the nature of the three stages of policy processing?

13. Why does policy enforcement need to be fast while policy specification can be slow?

14. In what way is policy decision making analogous to a computer language interpreter?

15. What is the additional overhead of making a network service call for policy decision making, and under what circumstances is the trade-off worth it?

16. How can the concept of locality of reference addressed in the previous chapter be used to significantly improve the performance of an authorization doing a network service call?

17. What happens if the policy enforcement stage of policy processing is subverted?

18. Explain why cybersecurity requires fail safety.

19. What are cybersecurity bulkheads and what important issue do they address?

20. Compare and contrast the principles need-to-know and responsibility-to-share and explain how they are balanced and embodied in the principle of least privilege.

21. Define mutual suspicion and discuss its implications to design and assurance.

22. What is intrusion tolerance and what are the six requirements to achieve it?

23. How does the intrusion tolerance layer relate to that of prevention and detection layers?

24. What is cloud computing and what are its implications to cybersecurity for the consumer?

25. How does the principle of avoiding high-value targets apply to cloud service providers?

Assuring Cybersecurity: Getting It Right

Overview

Learning Objectives

- Relate assurance and functionality to overall cybersecurity properties.
- Describe the four layers of assurance arguments and how they relate to traditional engineering specifications.
- Explain best practices in stating security requirements.
- Define a formal security policy model and a formal top-level specification.
- Differentiate between assurance-in-the-large versus assurance-in-the-small.

- Discuss how components with specific properties are composed to achieve overall system trustworthiness properties.

- Describe the nature of trustworthiness dependencies and how a lack of trustworthiness can propagate among components and subsystems.

The design process and the design itself must specify the essential cybersecurity properties. For example, an essential property may be that the system does not leak sensitive enterprise data onto public systems such as the Internet. The designers must also make an assurance argument based on the process (e.g., cleared developers, cybersecurity testing, formal specifications) and the design itself (e.g., layered architecture) as to why one should have confidence that the system will exhibit the specified properties. This section discusses the methods by which confidence can be attained.

21.1 Cybersecurity Functionality Without Assurance Is Insecure

Cybersecurity functionality is important to overall system trustworthiness; but *without assurance, functionality could detract from system cybersecurity*. For example, labeling all data with its sensitivity label is an important prerequisite for making access control decisions to that data based on its sensitivity. Yet if the cybersecurity system labels the protected data but then fails to assuredly enforce access based on those labels, then the labels are actually useful to the *attacker* to indicate exactly where the most valuable data resides. This was precisely the nature of the now-outdated *Trusted Computer Security Evaluation Criteria* (TCSEC, aka Orange Book) B1 level, which called for labeling all data with classification but provided no assurable security. The principle of the B1 security level was reasonable—an incremental step toward higher assurance levels to get familiar with labeling as a step toward controlling access, based on those labels. Unfortunately, the choice for this increment was poorly thought-out with respect to the cybersecurity consequences.

> *Cybersecurity functionality without assurance is harmful.*

As another example, cybersecurity *features that appear to provide a level of protection, but in fact are not enforceable, can lull users into a false sense of security, causing them to take risks that they would not have taken otherwise.* Discretionary access control, for example, is inherently incapable of ensuring that information does not flow to unauthorized users [HARR76]. Yet users with sensitive data may be tempted to place that data on the system because there is an appearance of a protection mechanism in place, when in fact, the protection is misleading. Cybersecurity functionality without assurance is called **veneer security** and can increase risk rather than decrease it. When using such unassurable mechanisms, if they are used at all, cybersecurity designers should be very careful to clearly and loudly warn users of the limitation of the properties provided by those services.

> *Veneer cybersecurity leads to increased risk.*

21.2 Treat Cybersecurity Subsystems as Critical Systems

The collection of cybersecurity functions comes together to form its own system; this system must meet both functional requirements (e.g., blocks network attacks or detects intrusions) and nonfunctional requirements. Nonfunctional aspects of cybersecurity subsystems and the aggregate system include scalability, performance, usability, and cybersecurity, to name a few. *Cybersecurity of the cybersecurity subsystem is particularly important and should be an essential aspect of the architecture and design process.*

> *The cybersecurity of cybersecurity systems is essential.*

21.3 Formal Assurance Arguments

Section 20.1 covered informal assurance approaches. This section focuses on more formal argumentation, which is intended to provide high confidence that the system operates as required. As depicted in Figure 21-1, the security-critical parts of the system make up the cybersecurity subsystem. The security-critical portion is critical to the successful operation of the cybersecurity required properties (Section 20.1). Because of the expense and difficulty of the formal argumentation, it is typically limited to only the cybersecurity subsystem or perhaps only selected subcomponents.

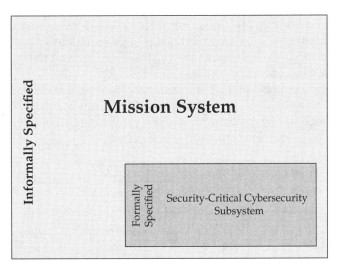

Figure 21-1   The cybersecurity subsystem is a subset of the larger mission system. Formal methods are applied only to the cybersecurity subsystem because of the cost and complexity of the process.

This bifurcation in approaches to specifying the system leads to some additional development process complexity; it creates two parallel tracks of design and refinement.

This requires that the two sets of documentation be continuously related, mapped, and kept in synchrony. Figure 20-1 from the previous chapter shows the structure of the layered decomposition of formal argument paralleling the standard layered decomposition of system specifications. Each of the formal layers is discussed in turn and related to the informal layers. Note that even though the parallel lines of specification and documentation appear separate, the traditional informal **concept of operations**, specification, and design process must remain comprehensive of the entire design and implementation, including the formalized cybersecurity subsystem.

Referring back to Figure 20-1, the left side shows a traditional refinement of design specifications from mission needs, requirements through implementation. This is similar to the left half of the design "V" described in Section 5.4. The right-hand side of the figure shows the equivalent specification and refinement process for a formal process, often referred to as formal methods [OREG17]. The mathematically formal nature of these specifications, as contrasted to natural language prose, will be described in more detail in Sections 21.3.2 and 21.3.3.

21.3.1 Cybersecurity Requirements

Cybersecurity requirements are certainly a subset of the broader defended mission system requirements. At the same time, it is worth collecting them together into a separate document or perhaps a separate chapter in the system requirements document. The aggregation helps to ensure that cybersecurity requirements are internally consistent and coherently express the cybersecurity needs of the defended system as they relate to mission. In addition, cybersecurity requirements often follow a different development and review flow than the other mission system requirements. Separation facilitates the workflow with groups such as cybersecurity reviewers and those that accredit the system as meeting the mission risk standards for operation.

Like any good requirement, cybersecurity requirements should meet the S-M-A-R-T properties as listed in Table 21-1. Too often cybersecurity engineers forget this most basic concept of requirements gathering. Two are worthy of special note with respect to security requirements: specific and traceable.

Letter	Property	Description
S	Specific	Requirements should be unambiguous and clear.
M	Measurable	One should be able to easily determine if the requirement is met.
A	Attainable	The requirement should be theoretically possible.
R	Realizable	The requirement should be practically achievable under the technical and programmatic constraints of the project.
T	Traceable	All system requirements should be traceable to design elements that realize them; all design elements should be traceable back to the system requirements that they fulfill; all system requirements should be traceable back to mission requirements.

Table 21-1 Properties of Good Requirements

Being specific is important. *That is different from being so specific that a design or even an implementation is specified as a requirement.* For example, if a user specifies a requirement for access control lists, the cybersecurity engineer should ask about the underlying requirement. Usually, the requirement is actually for access control at the individual user **granularity** level. Of course, access control lists are *one* way to achieve that need, but they are not the only way, and *the design should not be overly constrained by such non-requirements.* Similarly, a well-meaning customer who used firewalls pervasively in their previous job may specify firewalls instead of the more general requirement for perimeter protection.

> ### *Resist requirements that specify implementation.*

Traceability is important and is usually included in cybersecurity engineering processes, especially when it comes to **accreditation**. What is often missing is an assessment and rationale for the degree to which a requirement is met and a tracing in both directions at each level of the hierarchy of specifications. Just because a design element addresses a requirement does not mean that it fully meets the requirement. It is often the case that a requirement is partially met by more than one design element. For example, the non-bypassability requirement for reference monitors (Section 20.1.2) is partly met by the operating systems memory management, supported by the hardware (Section 9.4), and enforcement by encapsulating software (Section 20.4.3). Further, just because five design elements partially address a requirement does not mean that the requirement is fully met. An argument must be made as to why and how the collection of related design elements fully meets each requirement.

Similarly, for each design element, one should trace which requirements address that element. While it may seem redundant and completely derivable from the tracing of requirements to design, analysis of simplicity and economy of design are complex when the mapping is unidirectional. For example, it might become obvious by inspection that a given design element does not map to any requirement—merely adding unnecessary complexity. Similarly, one can see that a design element meets many important requirements that may bear on its criticality to ensure that it is correct. An example of each case is shown back in Figure 20-2.

In addition to the SMART properties, a *good requirement set of any significant size should be hierarchically refined, starting with a very simple one-line requirement that captures the essence of the requirement.* For example, a military computer system may have a simple requirement that it should not leak classified information to those without an appropriate clearance. As another example, an enterprise system used to analyze and study malware would specify the simple requirement to prevent malware escape, while facilitating learning about the malware and exporting the information about the malware. From the one-line requirement, one can then successively refine the requirement to increasing levels of detail. This approach makes it much easier to argue that the aggregation of the requirements is sufficient to meet the intention of the cybersecurity subsystem. It prioritizes requirements and illuminates their relationship to one another if the system needs to be simplified due to cost or schedule overruns.

21.3.2 Formal Security Policy Model

A **formal security policy model** at a particular layer of abstraction defines the key cybersecurity elements and how they are used to meet the overarching cybersecurity requirements. It is essentially a formal statement of abstract cybersecurity policy. As with requirements specification, it is useful to separate out the security policy model from the rest of the system's high-level design specification for the same reasons. Further, in this case, this subset is to be formally stated in a rigorous way.

For example, a formal security policy model may start by stating that all entities such as users require authorization attributes, such as clearances, bound to them, and all protected resources such as files require resource attributes, such as classifications, bound to them. It might then continue by stating that access rules are specified for protected resources based on the attributes of the resources and those of the accessing entity. It would state the nature of valid access rule construction. Further, it could specify that the totality of the cybersecurity subsystem and particularly that the access rules must meet a top-level requirement, such as not leaking sensitive data. The formal security policy model would make these statements in a mathematically rigorous way, using a formal language such as systems theory [BELL76] or set-theory notation [SAYD86]. For example, the requirement to not leak classified data has been rigorously stated in terms of a **non-interference** property [GOGU82][GOGU84] that includes both explicit data flows and covert signaling channels, as discussed in Section 12.1.3.

Lastly, one would then prove that the formal security policy model of the cybersecurity subsystem function meets the properties required of the defended system. This is done using semi-automated theorem prover programs or human-directed proof sketches, analogous to proofs that might be found in a mathematical journal (which do not provide all detailed steps and do not prove basic notions of mathematics, such as Peano's axioms on how arithmetic works [HATC82]). Therefore, such human proof sketches are called **journal-level proofs** [SAYD02] and are less formal and rigorous and open to human errors, compared to the more rigorous and more laborious mechanical proofs.

21.3.3 Formal Top-Level Specification

With a formal security policy model in hand and a proof that it meets required properties, the formal process continues to the next level of detail, paralleling informal design refinement. The **formal top-level specification** includes more detailed functional blocks, their functions, and their data flows and control flows. Once again, the formal specification represents only the security-relevant portion of the system design and is therefore a subset of the larger informal design specification at this same level of abstraction—called the **detailed top-level specification**.

It is often the case that the formal specification is more abstract than the informal specification. This is because there are technology limitations on the size and complexity of a specification that can be proven by existing formal methods and supporting tools. Therefore, a detailed top-level specification must include informal versions of all of the functionality and flows specified in the formal specification.

Because of the difference in layers of abstraction, some work is required to show that the detailed top-level specification is consistent with and implements the formal top-level specification of the security-critical portion of the defended system. This argument can be an informal mapping between elements of each, in a similar manner as discussed with respect to showing a mapping between requirements and design elements.

Lastly, the formal top-level specification is rigorously proven to be consistent with the formal security policy model. Thus, by deduction, the formal top-level specification is shown to meet the essential security properties required of the system.

21.3.4 Security-Critical Subsystem Implementation

Finally, we reach the implementation of the system design in software and hardware. It is at this point that the formality usually stops due to limitations in formal methods and tools. For simple and extremely well-specified systems, it is sometimes possible to automatically generate software from detailed specifications [GREE82]. If one can argue for the trustworthiness of that translation process, then one can formally deduce that the implementation meets the required essential cybersecurity properties.

More commonly, this level of rigor is either not possible or not practical, so an informal mapping is made between the implementation and formal top-level specifications. At this point, the mapping and traceability techniques used for the informal specification and formal specification subset are essentially the same. This human-directed mapping process is subject to error, decreasing the trustworthiness of the system, but it is the best that can be done with the state of the art. Cybersecurity engineers should take these limitations into account when placing trust in systems that handle highly critical and sensitive data and functions. Similarly, they should minimize the limitations by adding binding analysis (ensuring the integrity of the binding between security-critical tags such as clearances to entities, Section 5.3.1) and dependency analysis (Section 7.7) to the development process.

Beyond the mapping process, the security-critical subsystem must undergo more rigorous development procedures, as listed next. This is an important topic for those readers leading code development, who should read *The Security Development Lifecycle* [HOWA06].

- It's important to adopt good coding standards.
- Use automated static analysis tools to detect a wide range of errors.
- It's also a really good idea (if feasible in the context of the system) to use a safe language (Ada, C#, etc.) rather than C or C++. Then you don't have to worry about buffer overruns and other code-level vulnerabilities.
- One may choose to vet the trustworthiness of the individuals doing the development work since they could subvert the design or insert malicious software within the implementation.
- One could institute peer review of code so that a different person reviews software than the person who created it, checking to ensure that the software adheres to established security coding standards. Such peer-review processes create more dependable code, not just more secure code, because engineers avoid the embarrassment of their flaws being discovered by their peers.

Failure to adhere to security coding standards can introduce flaws that can be later found and exploited by attackers—thus enabling zero-day attacks such as exploiting buffer overflow flaws (Sections 2.4, 5.2, and 6.3.4).

As an alternative to formal mapping between specification levels and implementations, another approach seeks to automatically generate programs from specifications. This process is called automatic programming or correct-by-construction, and is currently limited to mostly domain-specific applications [PAVL03].

21.4 Assurance-in-the-Large and Composition

Critical functions like cybersecurity must be correct because their failure could lead to serious consequences. As discussed in Sections 20.1.1 and 21.3.4, **functional correctness** is met through a series of refined specifications from a requirements specification, through a top-level specification to an implementation. This is referred to as **assurance-in-the-small** because the properties relate to properties of a particular component or module within the system. By the same token, these components need to work together to meet the overall required properties such as not leaking sensitive data. The behavior of aggregation of components is called **assurance-in-the-large**, requiring arguments that the properties of the components, when composed correctly and with integrity, meet the overarching required cybersecurity property.

21.4.1 Composition

Recall that the reference monitor and its three properties (Section 20.1), which, when composed together, achieve a larger cybersecurity property. For example, the property of functional correctness is primarily assured-in-the-small with respect to each component. To assure the reference monitor property that a mechanism is non-bypassable requires one to step outside of the individual component. One must analyze the construction of the overall system and ways that execution control and data flow through a system, usually mediated by the underlying operating system. To assure that cybersecurity mechanisms are **tamper-resistant**, one must again step outside of the component itself and examine how system integrity can support the integrity of each of the components of the cybersecurity system. System integrity, in turn, is a property supported by other mechanisms such as digital signatures and checks of those digital signatures by the operating system before loading a component's software programs.

21.4.2 Trustworthiness Dependencies

There is a vertical layering of trustworthiness dependency from applications all the way down to the hardware (Section 9.1). Similarly, there are lateral trustworthiness dependencies that must always be kept in mind. Within a given layer, if a component depends on the properties of another component that is not similarly trustworthy, it compromises the trustworthiness not only of that component but of all components that depend on the properties of that component—a mathematical property known as transitive closure.

This cascading of untrustworthiness laterally and horizontally is a serious issue for both cybersecurity design and assurance arguments. Figure 21-2 represents a generic example of what a trustworthiness cascade looks like. A good engineering analysis of a cybersecurity design includes a trustworthiness dependency analysis and examines how a lack of trustworthiness propagates and affects the overall system trustworthiness to meet its essential cybersecurity properties. Such analyses also identify the most critical components to which greater assurance resources should be devoted.

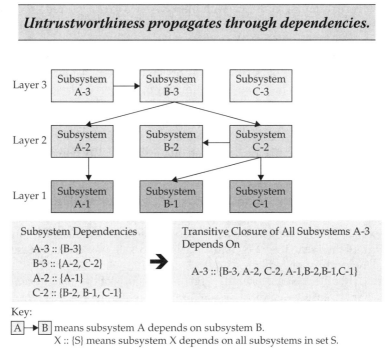

Figure 21-2   Abstract example of subsystem trust dependency cascade from subsystem A-3 to seven other subsystems

21.4.3 Avoiding Dependency Circularity

Cybersecurity mechanisms often depend on one another to achieve their requirements. For example, authorization services depend on authentication services, which in turn depend on identity certification services. These interdependencies can lead to circularity in the argument for cybersecurity properties. Further, because there can and should be cybersecurity mechanisms specifically designed to defend the cybersecurity subsystem, an engineer may end up with an unresolvable circular dependency in the design process. One can ask the question of how those cybersecurity mechanisms are secured. There needs to be a clear foundation to the recursive cybersecurity argument; the underlying mechanisms must be secure in a very clear and simple way (such as physical guards to a machine room that will stop anyone who tries to enter without proper authorization).

21.4.4 Beware of the Inputs, Outputs, and Dependencies

Often, cybersecurity properties of well-designed systems implicitly depend on the cybersecurity properties of systems on which those systems depend. This dependency takes the form of inputs (e.g., weather data input into flight planning software) or services (e.g., Network Time Protocol service as input to security audit logs). It is very important to identify all such subsystems and explicitly identify these dependencies in terms of properties depended on. These properties become requirements on the dependent subsystems and should form a technical "contract" with those systems to provide required services. The properties should be validated at design-time, again during certification and accreditation, and continuously, if possible, during the operation of a system.

For example, the cybersecurity of an application almost always depends on the cybersecurity properties of the underlying operating system. Unfortunately, these types of dependencies are often not as well-identified by cybersecurity designers as they should be. As another example, identity certification systems can depend on the correctness and integrity of the external physical-world process that verifies a person's identity and the systems used by those processes to store that identity information (in resources such as databases, for example, that are depended on for that identity information).

Availability properties are particularly important because the cascade of dependencies can be quite subtle. For example, if the domain-name translation service (performed by the DNS) fails, the system fails for most users since most of us no longer keep track of Internet protocol addresses. As another example, dedicated private networks often depend on public commercial networks for data transport service (since private networks often just encrypt the data and then send it across commercial networks). These sorts of cascaded dependencies are often hidden.

Similarly, other systems likely depend on properties of the system being designed. So, it is important to ensure that those system property requirements are known, included in the system requirements, and ideally, continuously checked during operation.

21.4.5 Violating Unstated Assumptions

In addition to the need to compose properties across multiple subsystems to achieve overall cybersecurity principles, it is important for each component to have clearly stated assumptions about the subsystems it depends on, how it depends on them, and what happens if those assumptions are violated. Unfortunately, this level of analysis is not often done. *Just as software coding flaws can create system vulnerabilities that can devastate the system and the mission it supports, a misunderstanding in unstated assumptions between software engineers designing components that depend on each other can lead to a disastrous vulnerability.*

> *Explicitly state and discharge all dependency assumptions.*

For example, if the developer of subsystem A assumes that all other subsystems calling it are within the supervisor address space (see Section 9.3) and that assumption turns out to be invalid, then subsystem A can be easily tricked by an attacker invoking that subsystem.

Sometimes assumptions start out being true but are later invalidated by a design change. Cybersecurity engineers lose track of these assumptions and their subsequent violation because the assumptions are rarely documented. The redesign ends up invalidating some previously correct assumptions and compromising the cybersecurity of the entire system.

Conclusion

While the previous chapter discusses how to build the right cybersecurity system to mitigate risk, this chapter discusses how to build it right and to effectively argue that it was indeed built correctly. The next two chapters move on to the high-level organizing concepts of situation understanding and that of command and control—two concepts which drive effective design.

To summarize:

- Cybersecurity functionality without assurance is dangerous. It points adversaries to the most valuable targets and misleads users into incorrectly believing that their data and services are protected.

- Formal assurance arguments are done in four stages to help manage complexity: security requirements, formal security policy model, formal top-level specification, and the security-critical subsystem implementation.

- It is particularly important to state security requirements using best practices such as making them specific, measurable, attainable, realizable, and traceable. Security requirements should also be hierarchically layered to improve clarity and to help ensure that they are complete.

- A formal security policy model is essentially a concept of how security policy ought to operate in the context of the larger system.

- A formal top-level specification is a high-level specification of the major functional blocks of the cybersecurity system that specify, decide, and enforce the security policy.

- Assurance-in-the-small is about proving that a given component has specific required properties, whereas assurance-in-the-large is about proving that the aggregation of all components woven together in a particular way achieves an overarching set of security properties set forth in the security requirements.

Questions

1. List two reasons why cybersecurity functionality without assurance is risky.
2. Does one make formal assurance arguments about the entire system or a subset? Why?
3. What is a consequence of following two different design processes for the security-critical and non-security-critical portions of the system?
4. List the five important properties of a good cybersecurity requirement.
5. How should good cybersecurity engineers create cybersecurity requirements in layers?

6. If a mission system owner specifies a requirement for a specific security mechanism such as a firewall, is that a real requirement? If not, how should a cybersecurity engineer handle the submission of such a requirement?

7. Why is traceability between requirements and design elements important? Why is it important to have reverse traceability from design elements to requirements?

8. What is a formal security policy model and why is it needed?

9. What is a formal top-level specification and how does it relate to a formal security policy model? How does it relate to a detailed top-level specification?

10. Why must an informal detailed top-level specification include elements of the security-critical subsystem when the formal specification already covers that aspect?

11. What does compositional total-system assurance entail?

12. List some techniques that can be used to improve the assurance of software code during the implementation phase.

13. What is assurance-in-the-large and how is it different than assurance-in-the-small? How do they relate to one another?

14. What is the composition problem and how does it relate to assurance-in-the-large?

15. What do we mean by trustworthiness dependencies?

16. How does a lack of trustworthiness propagate in a system design?

17. Define the concept of transitive closure. How does it relate to trustworthiness?

18. What might create a circularity in dependency? Why is that bad? What design approaches might avoid such circularity?

19. Why is it important to document and check assumptions among subsystems that depend on each other?

20. What does it mean to "state and discharge all dependency assumptions"?

22

Cyber Situation Understanding: What's Going On

Overview

Learning Objectives

- Define the concepts of situation understanding and command and control and their relationship to one another.
- Describe the process of situation-based decision making in terms of its four phases.
- Explain the five important aspects of situation understanding.
- Discuss discovery of the nature of an attack and its four different components.
- List the four different types of attack paths and why they are important to situation understanding.
- Define mission-mapping and relate the concept to assessing potential mission impacts of an attack.
- Discuss the importance of predictive intelligence and how it relates to attack trees.
- Summarize why predictive intelligence is important to defense optimization.
- Define cyber battle damage assessment in terms of both present and potential future damage.
- Characterize the state of system defenses and describe why each is important.
- Explain the role of a measure of effectiveness when assessing the impact of a dynamic defensive action.

I skate to where the puck is going to be, not where it has been.

—Wayne Gretzky

This chapter and the next are about advanced operational topics that pervade all of cybersecurity and drive requirements at the conceptual level. We borrow two important concepts from the military: situation understanding and command and control. Situation understanding involves learning what the adversary is doing, how effective the attacks are, and how well countermeasures are working. Command and control involves how to dynamically control cybersecurity systems to effectively repel the adversary and minimize damage while maximizing mission effectiveness.

22.1 Situation Understanding Interplay with Command and Control

Situation understanding and command and control work together synergistically to guide cybersecurity operations as shown in Figure 22-1.

Just as data collected should support a decision process by the consumers of the data, so should cyberattack detection systems be driven by the response decisions that need to be made to mitigate damages and expel the attacker from the system. A cybersecurity engineer must think through the response strategies and requirements on timeliness as part of the process to guide the attack detection subsystem and situation understanding design.

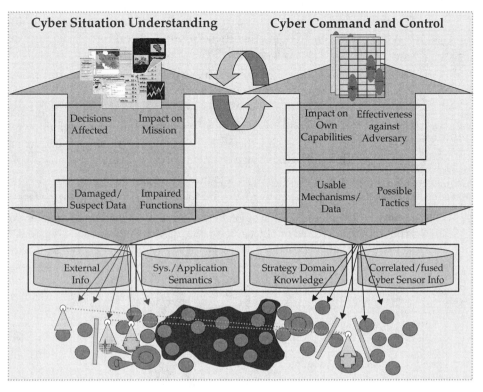

Figure 22-1   The synergistic interplay between situation understanding and command and control guides cybersecurity design and operations.

What information should one collect about a defended system to understand the cybersecurity situation? There is an overwhelming variety and volume of data that could be collected—so much so that collecting it all would bring the system to its knees. Resources such as computation, memory, and bandwidth would be quickly consumed to the point that mission functions could not be performed. There is a tendency in the cybersecurity community to collect and store interesting data and figure out how to analyze it later. Alternatively, some tend to collect what is easily available through other mechanisms (such as audit data, originally designed for system management purposes). Neither is an effective approach.

> *Situation understanding should support effective defense decisions.*

22.2 Situation-Based Decision Making: The OODA Loop

John Boyd developed the concept of a four-phased decision cycle called the **Observe-Orient-Decide-Act (OODA) loop** [OSIN07] to characterize tactical aviation battles [PLEH15]. It is depicted in Figure 22-2 and is elaborated as follows.

- **Observe**   A pilot observes the current situation including their own position and readiness status and that of other friendly forces, enemy forces, and the external environmental factors (e.g., weather).

- **Orient**   The pilot uses the observations to orient themselves to understand the implications of the observations in terms of who has the tactical advantage, how an engagement might turn out, and with what likelihoods and consequences.

- **Decide**   The pilot would then sift through and evaluate the possibilities generated from the process of orienting themselves and make a decision as to what actions to take in that situation (e.g., engage an enemy in close-range air-to-air combat).

- **Act**   Lastly, the pilot would act on plans formulated during the decision phase (e.g., perform a maneuver to get behind the enemy aircraft and fire a weapon).

- **Iterate**   The pilot's action would affect the situation, leading to another cycle around the loop based on the new situation. The pilot observes, orients with respect to that situation, decides on a new set of actions, and then executes those actions.

Figure 22-2   The four-phase Observe-Orient-Decide-Act (OODA) decision loop that guides action

Although OODA loops were originally created for tactical air battles, the loops generalize well to other decision domains (e.g., cybersecurity battles, or even driving your car) and to higher levels of decision making such as strategic decisions (e.g., how a company should respond to competitive pressure and losing market share). It is a useful construct to organize one's thinking about cybersecurity while confronting the dynamic process of cyberattacks and possible countermeasures.

The OODA loop is a type of **control feedback loop** [HELL04], discussed further in Section 23.1. Such control feedback loops are important to understanding the dynamic nature of cybersecurity and the tight interconnection between understanding what is going on, called situation understanding, and doing something about it, called command and control. Situation understanding covers the observe-orient side of the OODA loop, whereas command and control cover the decide-act part of the loop. This chapter addresses situation understanding, and Chapter 24 focuses on command and control so that their interaction in the context of dynamic defense can be well understood.

Chapters 13 and 14 discuss the nature of cyberattack detection, a prerequisite for situation understanding. Situation understanding goes beyond attack detection to

- Grasp the nature of the attack
- The implication to mission
- The damages the attacks have caused and may cause next
- The state of defenses
- How effective the current configuration of defenses might be

22.3 Grasping the Nature of the Attack

Identifying that a cyberattack is occurring is a difficult task in and of itself. Once we have identified that a certain type of attack is going on, there are a good many questions that must be answered about that attack. The remainder of this section discusses several exemplars of how one might answer those questions.

The analysis is often done in two distinct time phases: immediate and deep analysis. Immediate analysis is time-bound by the need to react to the situation at hand, where every second counts because increasing levels of damage may be happening with each clock tick. The immediate analysis supports a real-time tactical decision on what actions to take in response to the situation, as discussed in the next chapter. Once the mission is out of immediate danger, a deeper and more careful analysis of the situation can be done to determine root causes, adversary capabilities, and improved defenses for the future.

22.3.1 What Vulnerability Is It Exploiting?

Sometimes attack alarms are highly specific as to the nature of a cyberattack that is occurring and where it is occurring. Such alarms are typical of signature-based schemes. Other alarms, such as those associated with anomaly detection, carry a high degree of uncertainty regarding the type of attack, where the attack is located, and even whether there is an attack as opposed to a system error. For uncertain alarms, it is important to be able to follow up and unravel which sensors are contributing to the alarm and retask the sensors to learn more about what is going on.

If the attack is a zero-day attack, it may not be possible to determine the exact vulnerability that is being exploited, but it should be possible to pinpoint the computer, operating system, and applications involved. Sometimes cyberattacks become known simply through their effects, such as the entire system crashing. In those cases, it can be hard to trace down the vulnerability. When the system is restored, one can review the memory dumps (snapshots of primary memory stored before the final stages of a crash) and the logs (assuming they are intact) to determine the timing of events, and it may be possible to narrow down the possible attack paths.

22.3.2 Which Paths Are the Attacks Using?

Attack paths are the several types of paths associated with an attack, including

- **Infiltration paths** into the target system
- **Egress paths** to **exfiltrate** sensitive data from inside the system

- **Ingress paths** to control the attack while it is in progress inside the target system
- **Propagation paths** to spread the attack both inside the target and to other target systems

Infiltration   *The path the attack used to gain entry into the system and paths that the adversary may continue to use are essential knowledge in stopping the attack and defending the system from a repeat attack if an initial defense to detect and recover succeeds.* Did the attack come in through the firewall, or did it mysteriously appear after a maintenance person plugged into the network? Did it come from a particular authorized computer on the enterprise network? These questions speak to whether the attack is an outsider computer network attack or an **insider attack** or possibly a life-cycle attack.

> ## *Understanding attack paths is essential to repelling attacks.*

A repeated **outsider attack** can be stopped by shutting down or severely **tightening down** the firewalls (i.e., heavily restricting network data traffic to the bare minimum access needed to support the mission in order to reduce the attack surface) into an enterprise system. A repeated insider attack can be stopped only if the insider is found and expelled from the organization. A repeated life-cycle attack can only be stopped if the software that is the source of the malicious code used in the life-cycle attack is found and disabled. So, the courses of actions to defend against repeat attacks may be different for each case.

Egress   In addition to the path for the initial attack, the infiltrated malicious software may establish outgoing egress paths to exfiltrate (send from the inside of the enterprise to the outside for the attacker to retrieve) sensitive data. Egress paths may also be used by the infiltrated malicious code to communicate a difficult situation (such as a prevention mechanism it does not know how to penetrate) to a human orchestrator to seek additional methods for the malware to overcome the challenging situation. Sophisticated attackers are likely to use covert signaling methods (Section 12.1.3) for such paths, and so defenders should be cautious about defense plans depending on explicit alarms of exfiltration attempts.

Ingress   In addition, outside-to-inside, or ingress, paths may be established to allow the adversary continuing control and guidance over the malicious software to help direct the attack. Ingress paths are often called command and control pathways because the paths enable the attacker to command and control the progress of the malicious code that has infiltrated the enterprise system.

Propagation   Lastly, self-propagating malicious code has propagation paths for the malicious code to propagate among susceptible computers within a defender's system as well as from the defender's system to other connected susceptible systems on the network.

Cutting Attack Paths   Cutting off the ingress (outside-to-inside) paths prevents that malware from being actively guided from the outside by the adversary. This does not necessarily stop its autonomous behavior that can continue to do damage, but it prevents the malware from being intelligently directed and from thereby being enhanced to overcome defenses that it's not already capable of defeating. This is an important first step. Cutting off overt egress paths (non-covert, inside-to-outside) paths prevents the malicious code from exfiltrating sensitive data and minimizes damages caused by data compromised up to the time when the exfiltration is stopped. Cutting off egress paths also stops the malicious code from propagating beyond the epicenter system, and perhaps within the system at firewalls that exist within the defender's system to partition their network.

> *Cutting off attack pathways incapacitates attacks.*

22.3.3 Are the Attack Paths Still Open?

During the initial stages of the attack, the defended system may take some initial automated defense actions. This is generally not done today, but we can expect that some level of autonomic action will become essential to thwart attacks moving at Internet speed, well beyond human decision-cycle times (the clock time it takes for a human to reach a decision) [TINN02]. In addition, **cybersecurity operators** usually take some initial triage actions to stop the attack as best they can until they can do more extensive forensic analysis to determine the specific cause and nature of the attack. The combination of autonomous action and initial operator action may stop one or more of the attackers' paths. This phased approach to situation-based action is depicted in Figure 22-3 and discussed in more detail in the next chapter.

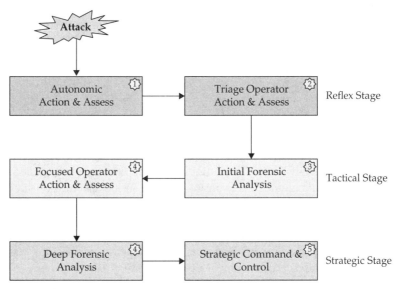

Figure 22-3   Phased situation-based action guided on unfolding attack-path understanding and by timeliness of action

During forensic analysis, it is important to understand that the analysis is going back in time to when the defended system was almost certainly in a different state—even if it was just moments ago. That means that before action is decided upon (Section 23.1) and executed, we must understand how the existing system state compares to the state when the attack was initiated and began to unfold. It would be perplexing and a waste of resources to take actions to shut down paths only to find that they had already been shut down.

If the attack paths are shut down, it may give the defender more time to assess the situation and to decide the best course of action. *The best decisions are never made in the heat of the moment and under duress. One of the first orders of business in the defense of a system is to remove the duress* and cool the heat of the moment by slowing everything down.

> *Block attack paths to buy time and reduce damage.*

22.3.4 How Can the Infiltration, Exfiltration, and Propagation Paths Be Closed?

A combination of information about what paths the attacker is using and whether those attack paths are still open gives the defender information about the possible ways the paths can be closed. This essential information is input into the command and control defense system, as discussed in the next chapter.

Why not just shut down the entire network, erase all the data, and start again? Well, in the case of an Internet café, that is exactly what they do every time a user logs out, just to minimize the risk of attack being introduced and carried over to the next user or the enterprise system itself. In that case, there is no valuable data on the system and golden copies (i.e., copies of application executable code from the original supplier, believed not to be corrupted) of the operating system and applications can be loaded each time. In the case of an enterprise system, a clean reboot could cost millions of dollars and devastate the mission. *The cure could be way worse than the attack itself.*

> *Ensure that the defense action is not worse than the attack.*

So, it is important to understand the exact nature and pathways of the attack so that the attack can be selectively shut down without seriously damaging the mission supported by the system. The concept is analogous to antibiotics that selectively attack bacteria that are causing an infection in the body without causing too much harm to the cells of the body, a term referred to as selective toxicity in biology. Another apt analogy is chemotherapy. It is very damaging to the body because it harms healthy cells, but is potentially even more damaging to the rapidly dividing cancer cells. The hope is that the cancer cells can be eradicated before damaging so many healthy cells as to cause the patient's death.

Returning to the question at hand, if we know the exact attack paths, we can selectively shut them down if those paths are not also essential to mission. For example, if an attack is coming from a non-mission-related Internet address and is using a rarely used port and protocol that the mission does not use, it is a no-brainer to direct the **perimeter firewalls** (those at the border of the enterprise system) to stop all traffic from that address and all traffic on that port, irrespective of the source or destination address.

If we stop the network traffic from the source address, why bother stopping all traffic from all addresses on the port? The problem is that attackers are clever and adaptive. If they notice that their attack is thwarted, they will realize that a firewall rule has been put in place against their Internet address, so they will likely just **spoof** a different source address. In fact, some malicious code is designed to do that automatically, or to just spoof a variety of source addresses so the defender will not know which addresses to stop. Of course, the attacker may also be able to move ports and protocols as well, and so the defender must be on the lookout for that type of attacker adaptation.

22.4 The Implication to Mission

Telling a mission owner, such as a chief executive officer, that their domain name system is undergoing a distributed denial of service attack is approximately useless, particularly because most would not even know what that means. Such a description gives no information about relevancy to the organization's mission. You might as well be saying that the cafeteria is serving meatloaf today because they ran out of fish. Both are equally seemingly irrelevant to the mission owner.

This leads to the concept of mission-mapping—the mapping of information technology services and subsystems to the organization mission they support through a chain of dependencies. Mission-mapping allows analysts to assess mission damages from system outages and predict the vulnerability of mission functions as portions of the system are successfully attacked.

A good way to analyze the implications to mission is to revisit the attack trees (Section 7.1). These attack trees focus on strategic damage to mission and all the ways that the damage can be brought about by cyberattack through the attacker achieving a series of subgoals. With a sufficiently detailed attack tree, one can determine the implications to mission of any successful attack or attack attempt.

Figure 22-4 shows an example of an attack tree from Section 17.6. The attack probabilities of success have been modified for illustration purposes and have been placed directly on the corresponding internal and attack leaf nodes. The unmodified overall probability of success for the attack tree begins at 10^{-4}, which is calculated from the leaf node probabilities as described in Section 17.6. The two attack leaf nodes at the bottom of Figure 22-4 with check marks indicate that the attacker has somehow achieved these two attack leaf subgoals, and the defender has detected that the attacker has achieved them. The question is: given this situation, what can the defender conclude about the attack and the defender's own defense posture?

The probabilities of the two successfully attacked leaf nodes can be marked as 100 percent (which is equivalent to 10^0) since they are already accomplished by the attacker. This revision is shown in Figure 22-4 by drawing a diagonal line through the unmodified probability and replacing it to the right with the revised probability. The revised probabilities of the parent nodes up through the tree's root node are then recalculated. The tree's revised probability of successful attack (indicated by the root node at the top) is 10^{-2}.

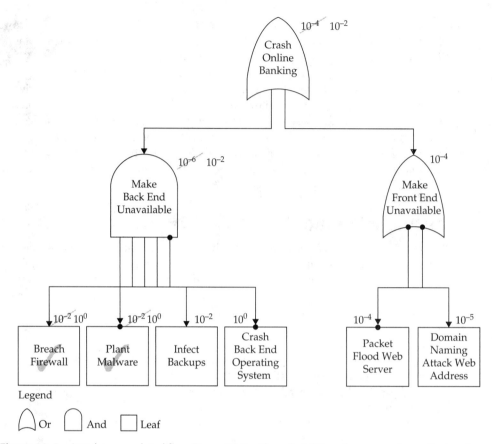

Figure 22-4   Attack tree updated from Figure 17-3 with probabilities of success where attackers have already achieved two leaf goals (marked with a check)

Notice that the **dominant attack scenario** in the unmodified tree *was* on the right-hand side of the tree with the OR relationship between its two subordinate attack leaf nodes. By dominant attack scenario, we mean the most likely scenario that dominates the probability of the overall attack tree (internal node, "make front end unavailable" has a probability of 10^{-4}). After the attacker has achieved the two leaf nodes on the bottom left of the figure, that attacker only has to achieve two more attack leaf subgoals to achieve the attack scenario on the left-hand side of the tree in Figure 22-4. One attack leaf subgoal is 10^{-2} (1 in 100) and the other is trivial at 10^0 (100 percent). So, these two steps represent the work remaining for the attacker to succeed. The probability of the parent node is modified to $10^{-2}*10^0$, which equals 10^{-2}. Because that parent internal node (internal node "make back end unavailable") is in an OR relationship with its sibling (internal node "make front end unavailable"), the root probability becomes 10^{-2}. This is why and how the attack scenario on the left-hand side of Figure 22-4 now represents the dominant attack scenario.

In addition, the defender can conclude that it is highly likely that the attacker's objective is to Crash Online Banking, the root mode of this attack tree. Without displaying the other attack trees in the forest that the defender has analyzed, it is hard to hypothesize that this particular tree is exclusively the attacker's primary goal. It is possible that these two leaf nodes are common with some other trees in the forest. In that case, the defender might conclude that the adversary could be going after those attack tree goals as well.

What do you do with this information about potential intentions of the attacker? This is known as **predictive intelligence**—the use of information gained through analysis of current events (in this case, successful attack leaf nodes) to predict what is likely to happen in the future. The answer is that the information is *invaluable* because it informs decisions about

- Increased risk to mission
- Contingency plans concerning loss of that mission
- The nature and locus of that increased risk
- Focus for concentrating attack detection efforts
- Defense reconfiguration to reduce risk accordingly

22.4.1 Increased Risk

For situation awareness, it is important to know if one of the organization's missions is at increased risk, whether that mission be military, commercial, or nonprofit. This is because there are many other decisions that are based on that risk. For example, for a retailer during holiday seasons, the benefit of keeping a system online is huge because of the percentage of revenue that is generated by online shopping during the holiday season. Therefore, retailers are willing to spend more money to ensure that the system is kept online, and to take additional risk to fulfill the mission. There is a point beyond which the risk becomes too high, and the retailer will decide to take the online shopping system offline to stop an attack, particularly if it poses a liability risk that exceeds the profits they expect to make by keeping a system online.

22.4.2 Contingency Planning

All organizations should have **contingency plans** for loss of mission through their enterprise system—whether it be an alternate enterprise system (such as a **cold spare** that is off-site and not connected to the primary system) or a pencil-and-paper system to get the minimum job done until the enterprise system is back up and running. Another contingency plan could be to operate without that portion of the mission for a period of time, if that is possible without too seriously damaging an organization. For example, if the human resources subsystem is down for a few days, it will probably not pose an existential threat to an organization, whereas a stock trading system shutting down for a few hours could be lethal to a brokerage firm. *Missions should always be prioritized* and an analysis should be performed in advance, concerning how long the organization can go without the mission until harm becomes potentially lethal to the organization.

> *Missions should always be prioritized and assessed.*

22.4.3 Nature and Locus Guiding Defense

Knowing the nature and locus of the attack guides the tuning of attack detectors. It does so by allowing the defender to optimize the attack-detection subsystem for the type of attack occurring now, and the ones that may occur next. The attacks that may occur are based on predictive intelligence using the attack trees to achieve the attackers' goal as discussed in Section 22.4. For example, one might tune an anomaly detection system to have a lower detection threshold and to selectively detect classes of attacks in the sequence predicted by the attack tree.

It is important to understand that *one cannot optimize defenses in general, and intrusion detection systems specifically, for all possible attack scenarios simultaneously.* Different defense configurations are more effective against some attack classes versus others. Therefore, the generic settings are optimized for the range of attacks, perhaps weighted by likelihood (which will change over time as attacks evolve) and potential damage level. Therefore, knowledge and insights into the specific attack classes that are currently expected is invaluable in optimizing both detection and prevention of cyberattacks.

> *Defenses cannot be optimized for all attack scenarios.*

Similarly, understanding the nature and locus of the attack guides the reconfiguration of prevention mechanisms to optimize for particular types of attacks in particular areas of the cybersecurity subsystem. For example, if the attack involves a worm that is propagating between subnetworks on the mission system, it is possible to reconfigure firewalls and routers within the organization's network to prevent further propagation by blocking the ports that it is propagating on and blocking the Internet addresses of already infected machines.

22.5 Assessing Attack Damages

The military uses a concept called **battle damage assessment** to assess both the damage done after attacking an adversary (its primary meaning) and in assessing damages to the defender after a successful attack by an adversary. Both are interesting and relevant, but because this book focuses on system defense (and not offensive cyberattack), this section refers to the defender's cyber battle damage assessment.

There are two important aspects to assessing damage: current damages and potential future damages. Assessing current damages consists of two parts: (1) assessing damages on affected computers and subsystems, and (2) the effect on mission that these damages bring about. Assessing the damages to computers and subsystems is a matter of aggregating health and status reports, as discussed in Section 22.7. Assessing the impact on mission is a matter of projecting those damages onto a mission map between those subsystems and the mission they support, as discussed in Section 22.4.

Assessing potential future damages is done by dynamically recalculating the expected harm (Section 17.6.9) based on updated probabilities that the adversary will successfully achieve one or more of their strategic goals. These probabilities are updated based on the specific situation in which the adversary has already achieved a number of attack subgoals, as discussed in Section 22.4. For example, say an ongoing attack successfully achieves the goals of two strategic attack trees, changing their probabilities of success from 10^{-5} to 10^{-3} and from 10^{-6} to 10^{-2}, respectively. Let's further stipulate for illustration that the total harm that would occur from each tree is $100,000,000 and $10,000,000, respectively. The change in expected harm would go from:

$$10^{-5} *\$100,000,000 + 10^{-6} *\$10,000,000 = \$1,010$$

to:

$$10^{-3} *\$100,000,000 + 10^{-2} *\$10,000,000 = \$200,000$$

This analysis gives the magnitude of the increased expected harm, or risk, due to the current situation. In the example, risk increased by two orders of magnitude (two powers of 10). In addition to learning the magnitude to gauge the seriousness of the change in situation, the defender can analyze the attack trees themselves to see precisely where the change in risk comes from and which missions are in the most danger. This analysis gives the defender excellent situation understanding.

22.6 Threat Assessment

It is often useful to perform a formal cybersecurity threat assessment. The book has talked about many important aspects of a threat assessment. This section brings these aspects together and describes the threat assessment process. In such an assessment, one determines the threat to the mission of an organization through cyberattack. Threat assessments answer questions such as:

- What are the organization's missions (Section 17.6.1)?
- How is the mission supported by information technology (Section 22.4)?
- Who has the means, motive, and opportunity to damage the mission (Sections 6.1 and 17.6.3)?
- How vulnerable is the defender's system to cyberattack (Section 17.6.9)?
- To what extent could attackers damage mission through cyberattack (Section 4.2)?

The methods to answer these questions are discussed throughout the book. Woven together, these answers constitute a cybersecurity threat assessment. Threat assessments are valuable in motivating improvements to risk posture and determining the proper investment levels and attention that cyberattacks warrant.

22.7 The State of Defenses

A key part of cyber situation understanding is the state of the cybersecurity subsystems and their component mechanisms. Defense mechanism types include

- Prevention
- Detection
- Recovery
- Tolerance subsystems

Part IV

Each subsystem has a number of different defense mechanisms. For each mechanism, it is important to know:

- Health, stress, and duress
- Status
- Configuration maneuverability
- Progress on any ongoing defensive actions that have not yet completed

Each of these defense mechanisms is discussed in turn in the next sections.

22.7.1 Health, Stress, and Duress

Health   The health of a defense mechanism has to do with how well it is performing as compared to expectations according to its specification. For example, say an authorization system normally processes 1,000 transactions per second, but now only processes 100 transactions per second and the number of requests has not fallen off. We can conclude that something is wrong.

Stress   Another mechanism may need 100 megabytes of primary memory (i.e., RAM) to operate at full capacity, but for some reason, the operating system is only allocating 80 megabytes to it, slowing processing down. Perhaps the memory allocation trend continues downward. Perhaps network bandwidth is being saturated, so the intrusion detection system cannot report all of its attack sensor data to the detection analysis subsystem. The detection system might reach the limits of its ability to buffer its data, risking the loss of the sensor data it has collected and temporarily stored. These two situations of memory and bandwidth limitation are examples of subsystem stress that can then lead to cybersecurity subsystem failure and ultimately to mission failure.

Duress   In addition to stress, the subsystem may be corrupted or even totally co-opted by the attacker. The subsystem's reporting, such as that of an attack sensor, could become sporadic, become incoherent, stop altogether, or become outright lies if manipulated by the attacker. This is called a **duress** situation. In some cases, the outputs of subsystems under duress could appear similar to those under stress, or the output could end up appearing too good or too regular if co-opted by an attacker. The defender should remain vigilant for such situations by examining the reporting data for anomalies.

These are all examples of reports of situations that could compromise the cybersecurity of the defended system. As part of the OODA loop, monitoring the health of the defense mechanisms aids cybersecurity subsystem operators in deciding what actions to take to improve the situation.

22.7.2 Status

In addition to details on the health status of defense mechanisms, it is important simply to know if each subsystem is up or down. It is obvious to us when our home computer crashes or locks up, so it may be hard to understand why up-down status reporting is important. If an organization's network operations center is monitoring tens of thousands of devices, one computer going down is not terribly surprising. On the other hand, hundreds of computers on the same network going down at the same time is highly suspicious and suggests a possible network attack. Similarly, defense subsystems going down could indicate a prelude to an attack. *Sophisticated attackers will almost always blind and disable cybersecurity mechanisms before mounting an attack.*

> *Attacks on cybersecurity are harbingers of a major system attack.*

22.7.3 Configuration Maneuverability

Almost every cybersecurity subsystem has a variety of operating modes and parameters that determine the details of its behavior. In the physical military, this is referred to **maneuverability**. For example, firewall rules determine whether a firewall will be relatively permissive to traffic in and out of an enterprise system or quite conservative. An attack sensor could be set to minimize data output and thus network bandwidth utilization until it appears that a serious attack is underway, at which point it may be reconfigured to be more verbose to aid in better detection and characterization of an ongoing attack. If an attacker is able to gain control of cybersecurity system configurations, they could reconfigure all of the defense mechanisms to be blind to their attack, unable to prevent it, or recover from it. *It is essential that the defenders consistently monitor the configurations of all of the defense mechanisms.*

> *Cybersecurity maneuverability is both a blessing and a curse.*

Because attackers will attempt to take over cybersecurity defense mechanisms early on in an attack sequence, *it is important to not always blindly trust the configuration and health reports of cybersecurity subsystems.* An independent means to double-check what the subsystem is reporting is paramount. Why? Because if the cybersecurity subsystem has been surreptitiously taken over by the attacker, the attackers can simply have the subsystem report that all is well and that the configuration is exactly as it was when they took it over, instead of the new malicious configuration the attackers put in place "prior to the attack."

As an example of an independent check, suppose a firewall reports that its existing rule set is highly restricted to only a handful of specified ports. It would be wise to independently cross-check the rules by attempting to send traffic through the firewall that should be blocked according to the rules (this is called a **known-answer test**). It may be impractical (from a performance perspective) to run known-answer tests continuously, but it would be wise to have such procedures and mechanisms to periodically check the veracity of reporting, particularly when it appears inconsistent with events taking place (e.g., the mission system is behaving erratically, but the cybersecurity sensors report that all is operating perfectly).

> *Verify cybersecurity status reports and suspect co-option.*

Part IV

22.7.4 Progress and Failure

During the course of attack scenarios, it is highly likely that the defender will reconfigure their cybersecurity subsystems in attempt to prevent further attack, detect and assess the attack, recover from the attack, and tolerate the damages incurred so far. The defense countermeasure actions will likely be sequences of actions such as program scripts executed on hundreds of devices. For example, the defender may want to reconfigure settings on all of their firewalls to exclude all traffic on specific ports and from specific Internet address ranges. If the defended system has dozens of different firewalls, perhaps from different manufacturers, different program scripts are needed to affect the required configuration changes, and the authentication protocol for these devices is likely to be different for each type.

The aforementioned defensive actions are obviously not instantaneous because they involve authentication protocols over the network (which could be bogged down with attack traffic), command sequence transmission across multiple network channels, and then the execution of those sequences on each device. Because of normal processing time, delay, and possible failure, it is important to know the progress status of these actions for each subaction sequence. This knowledge is important, because unless and until these actions are taken, the defended system remains highly vulnerable to continued attack against the point of access that the attacker has been exploiting.

Because the actions can fail, cybersecurity subsystem progress reports must include failure reports, including rationale for failure. In response to an attack situation, a set of actions must be

- Developed in advance if at all possible
- Instantiated for a given situation
- Staged so that all relevant program scripts are sent to go to each subsystem
- Transmitted to each subsystem, as appropriate
- Received by each relevant subsystem
- Correctly executed
- Status reporting must then follow a similar processing route back

Any one of these steps can fail or be attacked in some way. The defender must always be prepared for the contingency of unacceptable delay or failure and have alternate plans in place. These plans and contingencies will be discussed in more detail in the next chapter, focused on cybersecurity command and control.

22.8 Dynamic Defense Effectiveness

Thus far, the chapter has covered the state of the attack and its implication to mission, existing and potential damages from the ongoing attacks, and the state of the defenses, including the progress of any ongoing dynamic defensive actions. To complete the control feedback loop, one needs to determine whether the defensive actions are effective. Are the attacks stopping? Have the damages stabilized? Is any exfiltration stopping? Does malware still exist on the system? Are the host subsystems that were shut down back up again?

A **measure of effectiveness** must be established for each defensive action, and it needs to be assessed immediately after the action is taken. This feedback allows the decision process for the next action to become more effective. For example, if the defensive action was fully effective, then the defender need not incur the possible negative side effects from further defensive action.

Like most medications taken or surgery performed to treat or cure a disease, most cybersecurity actions have some negative side effect—some of which can be quite serious. The defender needs to minimize defensive actions and the consequent adverse side effects as much as possible. On the other hand, if the defensive action had no effect, then the defender would need to know that in order to decide to take an alternate action, which may be more aggressive.

> *All defensive action has negative side effects to mission.*

Conclusion

The previous two chapters discuss explicit principles of cybersecurity design. This chapter and the next chapter address significant organizing concepts that drive system design. This chapter covers cyber situation understanding and discusses how to deeply understand what is going on with respect to cyberattacks in a system and how this understanding plays into a decision cycle called the observe-orient-decide-act loop. The decide and act portion of that decision cycle will be the subject of the next chapter on cyber command and control.

To summarize:

- Cyber situation understanding discovers what is happening, while cyber command and control determines what to do about it and does it.

- Situation-based decision making lies at the heart of dynamic cybersecurity defense and of various forms of cybersecurity control.

- Cyber situation understanding involves grasping the nature of the attack, reasoning about the implications of the attack to the organization's mission, assessing the actual and potential attack damages, determining the status of the system defenses, and determining the effectiveness of any dynamic defense actions taken to provide feedback to command and control.

- Understanding the nature of an attack involves learning what vulnerability it is exploiting, what paths the attack is using, whether those paths are still open, and how to close them.

- The four attack paths include the initial infiltration path into the target system, the egress path to exfiltrate protected data, an ingress path for attack control, and a propagation path to spread a self-propagating attack.

- Mission-mapping, using attack trees to help the defender determine the implications of an attacker successfully achieving one of their attack tree subgoals, can quantify the change in risk and the source of that risk change.

- Intelligence regarding what the attacker has done is valuable, but predictive intelligence about what the attacker might do next is even more useful to get ahead of and stop the attacker.

- Defenses cannot be optimized for all possible situations, so information about the situation that is unfolding in real time helps to optimize the defense configuration for that situation.

- Cyber battle damage assessment determines both the damage that has been done to the system and mission and the potential damage that could be done. This helps determine the right defensive action and whether those actions are being effective.

- Knowing the state of system defenses is important to deciding on the proper defensive courses of action. The state relates to all subsystems and mechanisms within those subsystems and includes the health, stress, and duress of those mechanisms; a determination of whether they are operating or not; their current configuration as compared to the specified configuration; and progress on any dynamic defensive actions taken.

- To complete the control feedback loop, the cyber situation understanding subsystem must measure and report how effective and dynamic defense action is.

Questions

1. Define situation understanding and command and control, and discuss how they support one another in dynamic cybersecurity operation.

2. Describe the process and the four stages of situation-based decision making. Give a non-cybersecurity example from your everyday life. Give another example at the societal level.

3. Map situation understanding and command and control to the four phases of decision making.

4. List the five aspects of situation understanding. Briefly describe the role of each aspect in cyber situation understanding.

5. Discuss the challenges in determining the system vulnerability that an attack is exploiting.

6. List the four types of attack paths and describe the role of each path in the attack sequence.

7. Define exfiltration and what its mission impact might be through the system.

8. Why is it important to close down the attack paths as soon as possible?

9. Does closing attack paths stop further damage? Why or why not?

10. Distinguish an infiltration attack path from a propagation attack path. Will shutting one type of path down automatically shut the other paths down? Why or why not?

11. How might information on the attack path Internet source address and ports be useful to a dynamic defense?

12. If the attack path is blocked, what should the situation understanding subsystem be on the lookout for in terms of new attack activity directly after the block is put in place? Why?

13. What is mission-mapping and how does it relate to situation understanding?

14. What is one way of accomplishing a mission map with respect to adversaries achieving subgoals?

15. What happens to the risk to mission as the adversary achieves various attack tree subgoals within the system? How is the revised risk calculated?

16. How should a defender use updated risk information to better defend their system?

17. What do we mean when we say that the dominant attack scenario could change as we learn about the adversary achieving subgoals within the attack trees? What are the implications of this change?

18. What is predictive intelligence and why is it important? How is it used?

19. What are ways that a defender could react to increased risk to their mission?

20. What is contingency planning and how does it relate to situation understanding?

21. Why do we say that missions should always be prioritized? How is that information used?

22. Why can't defenses be optimized for all possible attack scenarios? How can information about ongoing attacks be used to improve detection and prevention? Should these changes be permanent?

23. Define cyber battle damage assessment, list its two forms, and describe how each is determined.

24. List four aspects of the state of defenses that are important and why they are important.

25. Distinguish the terms health, stress, and duress in the context of the state of defenses.

26. Why should defenders not blindly trust the health and status reports from the cybersecurity subsystems? What can be done about this issue?

27. Why is it important to track the progress of dynamic defensive actions taken to defend the system?

28. List seven stages of dynamic defensive actions and explain why it is important to take action at each stage.

29. Why is it important to gauge the effectiveness of dynamic defensive actions? How is it measured and with respect to what? How is it used in the larger decision-making cycle?

Part IV

23 Command and Control: What to Do About Attacks

Overview

- 23.5 Meta-Strategy
  - 23.5.1 Don't Overreact
  - 23.5.2 Don't Be Predictable
  - 23.5.3 Stay Ahead of the Attackers

Learning Objectives

- Explain the nature of command and control and its role in the decision cycle.
- Summarize how knowledge is acquired to drive the decision cycle.
- Describe the role of cyber playbooks in applying strategic knowledge to situations.
- Discuss how courses of action are developed and evaluated in attack situations.
- Compare and contrast the autonomic control with human-in-the-loop command and control.
- Explain what meta-strategies are and how they guide the application of stratagems.

Command and control addresses the decide-act phases of the OODA loop discussed in Section 22.2. **Situation understanding**, from the previous chapter, tells us what is happening; command and control capability supports the decision on what to do and orchestrates its execution. In the terminology of command and control, command refers to decision making on a course of action and issuing the instructions to execute the chosen course of action, whereas control refers to the monitoring of the execution and its effectiveness to provide feedback to the next decision-making cycle.

23.1 The Nature of Control

23.1.1 Decision Cycle

The term **decision cycle** refers to the process of following a complete loop through the four phases of the OODA decision cycle (Figure 22-2). The amount of time it takes to complete a full cycle is called the decision cycle time. This time factor is important because if the decision cycle time exceeds the rate at which the attack steps are happening, the adversary is always one step ahead of the defender and there is no stopping the attack and all the consequent damages. Returning to the air-to-air combat origin of the OODA loop concept, one can imagine that if a pilot's decision time is faster than their opponent's (called a tight OODA loop), then the pilot has a much higher probability of success, especially when engaging multiple enemy aircraft. Hence, tight OODA loops are also effective for dynamic cybersecurity defenses during multiple attacks or attack sequences.

23.1.2 Speed Considerations

In some cases, automated cyberattacks can happen so quickly that they are substantially faster than even the best possible decision cycle times in which a human is involved in the process (called human-in-the-loop decisions). *In such cases, cybersecurity defense mechanisms must resort to automated responses.* These automated responses are called **autonomic** cybersecurity actions because of an analogy to human biology, which uses very fast reflexes (not requiring brain processing) through nerve bundles called ganglia. Such autonomic reflexes are the body's response toward burns or bites to minimize response time and thus consequent damage. Then, after a reflexive action, the brain can take the time to make a more strategic decision such as moving from the area in which the damage took place to avoid repeated injury.

> *Attacks at machine speed require automated response.*

23.1.3 Hybrid Control

In human experience, we know that sometimes reflex responses can do more harm than good, such as withdrawing one's arm too quickly from a relatively minor burn, only to hit the arm against a wall or some other hard object and seriously injuring the arm. The brain cannot override those reflexes, so, even though reflexes are a valuable survival tactic, they can sometimes be a vulnerability as well. Indeed, many martial arts such as Aikido leverage an opponent's reflexes to accomplish actions such as throws using the opponent's own momentum against them.

Similarly, autonomic cybersecurity responses can be both very valuable and a point of vulnerability, so automated response actions must be considered very carefully in a cybersecurity system design and in operation. Autonomic cybersecurity is a valuable approach in creating automated responses so that it can sometimes completely thwart a high-speed attack such as a **flash worm**. Sometimes the approach can slow an attack down enough to be within the decision cycle time of humans, who can usually make a more creative and intelligent choice than an autonomic response.

Just like the autonomic portion of the nervous system and central nervous system working in concert in an attempt to gain the best of both worlds, cybersecurity systems should be designed and operated in the same way. Figure 23-1 depicts the two types of control working together: cyber command and control synergizing with autonomic control. Notice that both types of control have all four phases of an OODA loop decision-making process. The distinction is simply that the autonomic process happens in milliseconds to seconds and in a way that involves only computers, whereas the command and control process happens in minutes to hours and in a way that involves human decision making. Both autonomic control and human-in-the-loop command and control are elaborated as the chapter progresses.

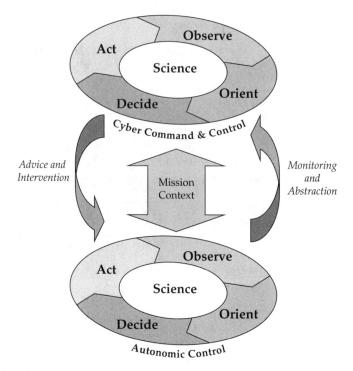

Figure 23-1   The relationship between human-speed command and control and machine-speed autonomous control

23.2 Strategy: Acquiring Knowledge

At the center of OODA decision loops is knowledge about what control actions are effective and what to do when the measured system response is different than expected. This knowledge is a form of strategy [TINN02]. Where does it come from? In the physical world, it comes from the analysis of millennia of human battles won and lost. Through such experience come pearls of wisdom such as

- Always fight from the high ground.
- Attack when the enemy least expects it.
- All warfare is based on deception.
- The first casualty of any battle is the plan.
- There is no situation so bad that panic will not make it worse.
- An army marches on its stomach.

Many of these stratagems were learned the hard way—through death and calamity. Cybersecurity strategy is slowly being learned in the same way, but we do not have the benefit of millennia of experience. There are several ways to discover strategic knowledge in cybersecurity to bridge that experience gap:

- By analogy
- By direct experience
- By vicarious experience
- Through simulation

23.2.1 Analogy

Analogies are one of the key ways that people learn. It is a way of applying knowledge that we have already gained in one domain to a new domain of interest, giving us a jump-start. One simply has to be careful to understand the limits of the analogy and which aspects of knowledge transfer directly, which ones need reinterpretation, and which ones are rubbish because of fundamental differences between domains.

Cybersecurity conflict is a straightforward analogy to physical human conflict. Each has defenders and attackers, valuable resources, and goals to achieve. To this end, Sun Tzu's *The Art of War* [FORB12] is invaluable reading for any serious cybersecurity professional. Its lessons in strategy are timeless, generalizable, and easily extended into the cybersecurity realm. A useful interpretation and extension for cybersecurity exists in a book entitled *The Art of Information War* [NELS95].

Taking each concept from the physical world of warfare and applying it to the realm of cybersecurity would be a book by itself. Let's take the physical-world stratagem of always fighting from the high ground. One can see much farther from the high ground; weapons fire travels farther; and gravity is on the warrior's side when fighting hand-to-hand. In the cybersecurity world, there are many possible analogs. For example, in what position can you see the furthest (widest) in cyberspace? Routers. Which routers? Big, centralized routers owned by the major telecommunication companies and Internet service providers. If one can watch the traffic through these routers, one can see a substantial fraction of cyber events in the world. So, height could be interpreted in the hierarchy of routing infrastructure in the network.

Within a computer, we have seen that there is a hierarchy of layers of abstraction from applications on the top to device controllers on the bottom (Figure 9-1). In this case, although counterintuitive, the bottom of the hierarchy is the highest point. The further one goes down in the hierarchy, the more access one has to system resources. The processor and most devices on the bus have access to all system resources and are not governed by the access control of the higher layers. *Gaining control of programmable entities (e.g., firmware) or underlying hardware at the bottom layers could give an attacker complete visibility and complete control of a computer.*

> ***A computer's lowest layers are the cybersecurity high ground.***

Part IV

As mentioned at the beginning of this section, one must be careful with analogies and understand their limits in how to interpret analogies from other domains to cybersecurity. Table 1-3 discusses the many ways that the cybersecurity realm is different from the physical realm. These differences have important implications on how to interpret and filter knowledge from the physical domain.

There are many other useful analogies discussed throughout the book, including

- Biology
- Virology
- Epidemiology
- Pathology
- Sports
- Game theory
- Control theory
- Information theory
- Signal processing theory

All of these analogous domains convey important strategic knowledge to the cybersecurity realm; all have their limitations.

23.2.2 Direct Experience

Organizations experience cyberattacks or attempts nearly continuously. Sometimes the attacks do significant damage to the organization. Eventually, the attacks subside or are successfully repelled. The key is to learn the maximum possible that can be learned from that experience. This can be done through a five-whys–style analysis as discussed in Section 7.3. In addition to studying what aspect of the cybersecurity failed, why, and how, one should examine decisions and responses and see what was effective and what was not and why.

The conclusions of attack incident analysis should be well-documented and well-distributed among all cybersecurity professionals of the organization involved in all aspects of defense from design, to implementation, to testing, to operations and maintenance. The tendency to hide this information due to embarrassment or concern about the loss of faith from external organizations (e.g., customers, investors, stakeholders) is a dangerous short-term viewpoint. The implications of the newly acquired knowledge to improved defense configurations and to dynamic control during attacks must be deeply considered. These improvements must then be implemented as quickly as possible. The knowledge may also be selectively shared with other organizations with whom your organization has a close trust relationship to help them benefit and better protect their systems.

23.2.3 Vicarious Experience

Fortunately, one does not always have to learn from the school of hard knocks. Sometimes, it is possible to learn from the mistakes and successes of others. As mentioned in the previous paragraph, one can gain knowledge from the analyses performed by others within one's trust circles. Sometimes, knowledge is shared through community information sharing and analysis centers such as the Information Technology—Information Sharing and Analysis Center [ITIS17]. Sometimes it is shared by professional associations of cybersecurity professionals, using online fora such as RISKS [RISK17], national computer-emergency response teams [CERT17b], commercial companies such as Symantec and IBM, or through peer-reviewed journals and conference articles from the academic community. Companies should seek out this highly valuable knowledge, record it, apply it, institutionalize it, and update it as new knowledge is discovered.

23.2.4 Simulation

Lastly, one can gain knowledge through simulation. Simulation means that one models attackers, defenders, and systems (see Section 5.3) and interplays among those models to determine the outcome of conflicts within the cyberspace realm. Using models and simulation has many advantages:

- They are cheaper than building real systems and performing experiments on them.
- They are less risky than performing experiments on operational systems supporting missions.
- They are faster in the sense that one can run many different experiments simultaneously, and can run them in significantly less time than they can be run in actual systems.
- Reversing the damage to a modeled system is simple and nearly free.

The one major disadvantage to simulation is that one is never certain that the knowledge gained will transfer to actual systems because of an aspect of the model may be unrealistic or inaccurate in an important way to the knowledge gained in simulation. Generally, the advantages outweigh the disadvantages, and so simulations are used as an important tool in generating cybersecurity strategic knowledge.

There are many types of simulations with varying degrees of automation:

- Table-top exercises
- Red team exercises
- Automated simulations

Table-Top   Table-top exercises are a class of simulation that generally involves human-directed natural-language scripts with human decision makers in various predefined cybersecurity scenarios. Scenarios are developed by a group of experts in charge of creating and managing the table-top exercise. The scenarios are meant to be realistic and to define strategically important situations that stakeholders want to explore to better understand the problem or to educate participants and to better prepare them for an actual cyberattack scenario.

The participants are usually key decision makers within the organization sponsoring the exercise. These participants typically do not know the scenarios in advance. They are instructed to make decisions as if the situation that is unfolding is real. Their actions are interpreted by the exercise team, and the scenario takes a different course depending on the actions taken by the various decision makers involved.

At the end, the recorded event is assessed for

- Important lessons learned
- Additional training that might be needed
- Better organization and clarity of chains in authority
- Clever ideas on how to handle a real scenario of a similar type
- New tools and techniques that might be needed to facilitate decision making and fast and effective execution of those ideas

Red Team Exercises   Red team exercises are typically done on actual operational systems. A red team simulating an adversary (Section 6.5) is engaged to attack a well-defined specific mission system or set of systems. They attack the system with clear rules of engagement to ensure minimal risk of impact to operations. To that end, the red team does not seek to do actual harm to the system, but rather to demonstrate a level of penetration into the system that would give them sufficient access to cause a serious level of damages. For example, a red team will often plant a file that says "The Red Team was here" in a system that they have successfully gained control of. That proves that they did indeed gain control without having to bring the system down or damage any of the files or subsystems.

The systems targeted by the red teams may or may not be notified that a red team attack is coming, and they may or may not be notified of the timing of the attack. Whether and when to notify target system operators of an attack and its timing depend on the goals of the simulated attack, the risk the system stakeholders are willing to take with mission, and the level of frankness they want regarding a valid assessment that could prove embarrassing.

Red team attack simulation has training and assessment goals similar to those of the cybersecurity defenders and decision makers of a system. One can also analyze the results and learn innovative defense strategies and innovative attacker counterstrategies that feed into the knowledge of the defender to be analyzed and institutionalized as discussed earlier in this chapter. *Red teams almost always succeed, indicating that most systems have a long way to go to improve their defenses.* The red team success is owed to the complexity of defended systems, the rate of vulnerabilities in those systems, and the many alternative paths available to the attacker. In short, successful defense is inherently hard!

> *Red teams almost always win.*

Automated Simulation   Completely automated simulation consists of executable models of attackers, defenders, and systems that interact with one another according to a defined rule set that intends to capture the behavior of each. Such simulations can be run at very high speed, and *new knowledge can be gained at a significantly faster rate than other methods.* At the same time, the acquired knowledge must be carefully validated to ensure that it actually works in the real systems.

> *Simulation yields faster knowledge, but needs validation.*

23.3 Playbooks

With strategy knowledge in hand, we turn to the issue of applying that knowledge to real cyberattack situations. Information about the cyberattack situations is derived from approaches discussed in the previous chapter. This section deals with what to do about a given situation.

The term **playbook** refers to the course of action options available in a given situation and the means to choose the best course of action in that situation. We borrow the term playbook from sports teams that use books of plays that have been developed and practiced in advance, geared to particular situations the team finds itself in, and sometimes even customized for particular opponents. Cybersecurity playbooks have similar characteristics, which will be discussed as the chapter proceeds.

23.3.1 Game Theory

The cybersecurity landscape is quite complex. Chess makes for an apt analogy in the sense that each player attempts to project forward their best moves toward a strategic goal (taking the king) while trying to predict both the opponent's best moves toward their strategic goal and the opponent's best moves to thwart one's own set of moves. The process of choosing moves that balance putting the opponent in the least good position while putting oneself in the best possible position is call a **min-max algorithm** and has been explored at length in game theory as part of the larger field of artificial intelligence [CHAR07].

The cybersecurity "game" is made much more complicated by several factors. First, one plays multiple opponents simultaneously, each of which may have a different goal as discussed in Section 6.1. Each opponent has a different set of tactics and strategies that the defender may not have seen before. In addition, a portion of the game board remains hidden because the adversary may have zero-day attacks that have never been seen before, so it is as if a new piece appears on the game board out of nowhere. Lastly, the rules of the game change during play as attacks that gain a toehold on the system spread like wildfire because of a preplaced life-cycle attack; the analogy is to a piece on the chessboard that could only move one space that can all of a sudden leap to the opposite end of the board. This complexity is depicted in Figure 23-2.

Part IV

Game Theory
Multiple Games
Multiple Adversaries
Changing Game Board
Evolving Rules

Figure 23-2 Cybersecurity strategy involves complex game theory, with the white-hatted defender playing multiple games against multiple dark-hatted adversaries, on game boards that are partially hidden and constantly evolving, while the rules evolve.

Application of game theory to the cybersecurity realm is a relatively new and burgeoning area [HAMI01][HAMI01a]. At a minimum, it provides a useful way to think about the problem of developing playbooks, indexed to the situation and the criteria of choosing among courses of action. With further study, it is highly likely that the tools and techniques from game theory will become more directly applied.

23.3.2 Courses of Action in Advance

When one is in the midst of a battle is about the worst possible time to develop a battle plan. Sometimes, if the adversary's element of surprise is complete, such hurried planning done under duress is the only option. Even in such cases, a well-trained army knows generic tactics that apply to certain situations. They are not starting from scratch; they have building blocks to put together and to customize to the situation. So it is with cybersecurity planning.

> ### *During battle is the worst time for battle planning.*

How does one develop courses of action options in advance? One way is turn back to the use of attack trees, introduced in Section 7.1. As you may recall, these trees represent a series of subgoals that the attacker attempts to achieve toward their larger strategic goal at the root node of the tree. In Section 22.4, the attack trees were used to characterize the situation of an attack, reassess the risk based on subgoals that the adversary has already achieved, and potentially predict the attacker's likely next moves. The situation understanding data informs decision making about required immediate decisions. Attack trees and their nodes can be used to develop what-if courses of action in advance of an attack, and to determine how to select the best defensive action.

Referring back to Figure 22-4, a set of courses of actions would be developed for each of the nine nodes in the tree. Generally, it is best to plan at least three possible courses of action for each node since the gravity and nature of the situation are so variable. For example, if the attack leaf node in the lower-left bottom of the figure (labeled "Breach Firewall") is achieved, the defender may develop three alternative courses of action, as shown in Figure 23-3.

- **Course of Action 1—Least Aggressive**
  - Patch the firewall with all known patches that have not already been applied,
  - Perform integrity checks on all computers that were accessible directly from the breached firewall and reboot any computers that fail their check, and
  - Increase intrusion detection monitoring for any signs of malware propagation.
- **Course of Action 2—Moderately Aggressive**
  - All of the above, plus,
  - Reboot all edge firewalls,
  - Reset the rules on all firewalls to allow only minimum essential traffic,
  - Increase intrusion detection monitoring to screen for malicious traffic,
  - Initiate forensic analysis on how the attack succeeded,
  - Scour cybersecurity sources for any known similar cyberattacks.
- **Course of Action 3—Very Aggressive**
  - All of the above, plus,
  - Island the enterprise network immediately (isolate it from the larger network),
  - Give cybersecurity subsystems high priority to all system resources (resulting in mission systems having lower priority for resources, such as their minimum requirements),
  - Make mirror copies of all systems and submit to forensic analysis, and
  - Reboot the entire system using golden copies of all software from read-only disks.

Figure 23-3   Example courses of action of increasing aggressiveness

The three courses of action in Figure 23-3 are posed in order of aggressiveness, depending on the stakes and what other events are happening. Courses of action templates should be developed that consider the range of actions and reconfigurations that are possible for each major cybersecurity subsystem. Table 23-1 is a very limited form of what such a template might look like.

#	Course of Action	Notes and Rationale
	Prevention Mechanisms	
	Firewall	
1	Island the network	Prevents further damage to mission because the stakes are too high to allow further damage.
2	Minimal essential traffic in and out	Reduces chance of additional infiltration attacks and of data exfiltration.
3	Reduce traffic to only registered sources and destinations	Reduces risk while emphasizing continuity of mission.
	Authentication	
4	Require two-factor authentication	Reduces risk that a user account will be compromised or hijacked.

Table 23-1   Example Course of Action Template Considering a List of 13 Potential Actions in Several Different Areas *(continued)*

#	Course of Action	Notes and Rationale
5	Disable all nonessential user accounts	Draconian move to reduce attack space available to attacker.
6	Allow only protected communications	Makes it difficult for the attacker to succeed at a man-in-the-middle attack.
	Detection Mechanisms	
	Sensors	
7	Increase sensitivity of all sensors	Highly intrusive action that may inundate the network, but necessary when the nature of the attack is undone and damages are mounting at a significant rate.
8	Selectively fine-tune sensors according to suspected attack	Gains increased information for the attacks that are most likely according to the situation understanding subsystem.
	Alarms	
9	Reduce the attack reporting threshold	This increases the number of reports of possible attacks, but means that more stealthy attacks have a better chance of being detected.
10	Increase resources to adjudicate alarms	Each alarm can be pursued in greater depth to determine if it is a real attack.
	Recovery	
11	Checkpoint	Save the system state before taking some action that will disturb that state. It could be used for later forensic exploration, or it could help reduce the increasing damages to a system.
12	Rollback	Restore the system state from an earlier time prior to the attack. Some mission progress will be lost, but damages will also be rolled back.
13	Reboot from golden copy	Restore all software from read-only golden copies to rid the system of any malware infections that may reside in the system software.

Table 23-1   Example Course of Action Template Considering a List of 13 Potential Actions in Several Different Areas

23.3.3 Criteria for Choosing Best Action

At least three alternative courses of action (Section 23.3.2) should be created for every situation in which an adversary achieves a given subgoal in each of the strategic attack trees. With several useful alternative actions, we need a means to select which action is best in which situation. Selection criteria involve assessing the following factors:

- **Stakes**   what is at risk and how likely is the damage to occur?
- **Attacker's capability**   how sophisticated is the attacker's approach?
- **Attacker's goal**   what is the attacker's goal?
- **Attack uncertainty**   how well does the defender understand the nature of the attack?

- **Defense posture**   how capable are defense mechanisms in repelling the attack?
- **Speed**   how fast is the attack moving and how quickly are damages mounting?
- **Action effectiveness**   how effective is the defense action predicted to be?
- **Action consequences**   what are the consequences of the action to the mission?

Each criterion is discussed in turn.

Stakes   If the attack is occurring on a separate system that retains the organization's intramural sports rosters, scores, and rankings, the stakes are not very high. On the other hand, if the system contains a country's most important secrets or controls its entire electrical power grid, the stakes are extraordinarily high. The stakes relate to how much risk an organization is willing to take and the costs they are willing to bear to prevent those consequences. An expensive course of action is well worth it for high-stakes systems; less so for a total loss of an organization's intramural sports data management system.

Attacker Capability   There is a huge difference between a **script kiddie** (an unsophisticated hacker) using a well-known **attack tool kit** to exploit known vulnerabilities (in operating systems, services, and applications) on a target of their choosing and a nation-state adversary using multiple zero-day attacks, high-stealth techniques, life-cycle attacks, and co-opted insiders. This distinction can become quickly apparent as ongoing attacks are analyzed. Well-known attack tool kits are often noisy and have identifiable malware signatures that most commercial intrusion detection systems can easily detect and report. More sophisticated attacks barely even register on the best of anomaly detection systems and exploit **zero-day vulnerabilities**. A defender's reaction to a script kiddie may be to simply deploy any patches that had been deferred for operational reasons, execute the known cleanup software for any damage done, and move on. For sophisticated adversaries, the defender may want an extra-aggressive response. If it barely detects one attack step, it is likely that other attack steps have already succeeded, unseen.

Attacker Goal   If the attacker is a teenager playing capture-the-flag on a real system just to prove that they could get in, then the goal is mostly a nuisance. On the other hand, a well-timed attack on a military radar system could be critical. The attacker goal might be to shut down the system during the entire critical time window of an air strike. The defender may need to do everything it takes to keep the system up and running, even possibly at the cost of losing some sensitive data.

Attack Uncertainty   One important physical-world stratagem is that the **fog of war** clouds everything. The ideal world of instantly detecting, characterizing, and identifying an attack and repelling it through reconfiguration is rarely the case. Defenders will see suspicious activity, often daily or even hourly. It will almost always be due to some innocuous activity on the system that can sometimes share certain characteristics of attacks (e.g., a **spider** that crawls the network to index its content). Attack alarms sound continuously, the majority of which are false positives.

When a true attack happens, the alarm signal may or may not be higher than all the false positives that are dealt with daily. Even if the signal is a bit higher, it will not always be clear what the nature of the attack is. Identifying it can take hours or even days. The defender is lucky if the situation understanding subsystem can narrow the attack down to one of several possible strategic attack goals (represented by the root nodes of the attack trees). So, even if the best possible course of action is known for a given node in a specific attack tree, it will be rare that the defender will precisely identify the exact situation the defender is in. *At best, there will be a probability distribution function on which attacks may be going on.*

> ## *The fog of war makes cyber action uncertain and complex.*

Defense Posture   Suppose the health and status of the defender's cybersecurity subsystems are excellent and the defender has a rich set of options on a wide variety of prevention, detection, recovery, and tolerance mechanisms. In this case, the defender may be more willing to take a conservative approach to their first response to an attack. On the other hand, if the cybersecurity subsystems have been totally decimated in the first wave of an attack, then the defender's course of action range is limited, and they may need to be as aggressive as possible. The defender does not even know what damages are accumulating and the defender has few options to repel the attack. In that case, **islanding** the network from the external network may be the only viable option.

Speed   Cyberattacks can take years to prepare and execute or they can be highly automated and take minutes to execute. The speed at which an attack is moving has significant bearing on the proper course of action. When we refer to **attack speed**, we mean several different aspects:

- The speed at which the attack step sequence is progressing
- The speed at which the attack is propagating (i.e., the spreading of a virus or worm)
- The rate at which the attack is accomplishing its mission (e.g., exfiltrating data or shutting down the system)

Each aspect of attack speed may require emphasis on different actions to stop it or slow it down, but they all require a high degree of urgency to act. *It often is better to take a rough and broad action immediately than to take a refined and narrowly targeted action later. The priority must be on stopping attack progress.* For example, if an attack is exfiltrating sensitive data at 100 gigabytes per second, it is urgent to shut down the channels it is using through the firewall and routers. If the specific channels are not yet known, it is urgent to shut down all outgoing traffic until the details are sorted out. *A delay could lead to a total loss of sensitive data.*

> ## *Broader faster action is essential against high-speed attacks.*

Action Effectiveness   Given a particular attack situation, some courses of action are known to be completely effective at stopping the attack. For example, if an attack is exploiting a known vulnerability for which there is a known patch, deploying that patch can immediately stop the attack. In other cases, a course of action effectiveness can be uncertain, particularly if the precise nature of the attack is not yet known. For example, a flash worm may propagate so quickly that by the time firewall rules are reconfigured, it may be too late to stop the worm. *Each course of action should carry with it a sense of the degree of effectiveness it is likely to have in a given situation.*

> ### *Expected effectiveness of action is essential per situation.*

Action Consequences   As discussed previously, *most dynamic defensive courses of action have negative side effects with respect to the mission.* If authorization policy is tightly locked down, some users may lose access to important data needed to do their jobs. If external firewalls are severely restricted, users may be unable to access critical data needed to make important decisions and serve customers. Sometimes, the mission consequences of a defensive action are subtle and difficult to determine. For example, shutting down the domain name system may seem like it only affects one network infrastructure subsystem, but it impacts nearly every single other service in the enterprise. *That is why it is essential to analyze and assess the mission consequences of each defensive course of action in advance of an attack, including the consequences to the systems that depend on and are depended on by the assessed system.*

> ### *Pre-assess every course of action's mission impact.*

Assessing these factors, including uncertainty, is the core of making informed decisions about the best course of action at any given situation. Once the action is taken, the OODA loop continues around another cycle, taking subsequent action, depending on the nature of the evolved situation. The evolved situation is based on the attacker's action sequence as well as those of the defender's actions and the system's response to both.

23.3.4 Planning Limitations

> *No plan survives contact with the enemy.*
> —Helmuth von Moltke the Elder

> *Plans are useless, but planning is indispensable.*
> —Dwight D. Eisenhower

In cyber conflict, just as in traditional warfare, it is not possible to come up with a plan for every possible contingency. Therefore, defenders cannot entirely depend on their playbooks for their strategy. Defenders should train their response teams in strategy development. The response teams should participate in the development of playbooks to understand the implications of quick tactical decisions in the context of larger strategies. They should contribute their intuition for defense operations. They must learn the principles of strategy so they can improvise intelligently and quickly develop new strategies or adapt old strategies in response to new situations. *The process of developing playbooks will provide invaluable insights into effective strategic defense even though the plans themselves will not always be ideal for the situation at hand.*

> ***Playbook development can be more important than playbooks.***

23.4 Autonomic Control

When cyberattacks happen at speeds on the order of milliseconds or seconds, it is shorter than the decision cycle time of human-in-the-loop command and control processes as described in the previous section. This is where autonomic control comes in. Autonomic control runs through the exact same decision cycle that command and control runs through. The only difference is that the entire process must be automated.

23.4.1 Control Theory

Control theory is the study of the dynamic behavior of systems as a function of the system's inputs and feedback on the state of the system in response to those inputs. A typical example given in control theory is that of balancing a broomstick on the palm of one's hand. As the broomstick begins to fall in one direction, there is feedback in terms of a shift in forces exerted on the hand. The hand can then be moved in response to that change in an attempt to rebalance the broomstick. If the input is too large, it falls in another direction and one takes another loop around the control and feedback cycle until the broomstick either is balanced, oscillates in successive unbalanced states, or until it falls uncontrollably in a way that cannot be recovered.

There are several basic elements of a control problem:

- A system
- A measurement of the state of the system
- A goal state for the system
- A comparison function between the goal state and the measured state
- An algorithm to determine the best input given this difference and which yields stable progress toward the goal state
- An input into the system to try to change its state to be closer to the goal state

These elements of control and their interaction are shown in Figure 23-4. In the case of cyber security:

- The system includes the defender's system, the attacker systems, and any intermediate systems used to proxy or transmit attacks or defenses.
- The measurement of the state of the defender's system is the situation understanding subsystem, fed by attack detection data.

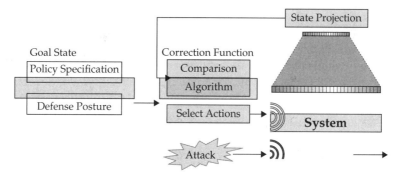

Figure 23-4   Control theory and the interactions of elements requiring cybersecurity actions

- The goal state of the system is one that adheres to security policy and has a strong defense posture.

- The comparison function assesses the difference between the goal state and the measured state of the defended system (e.g., the change in probability of the adversary achieving any of the cyberattack strategic goals).

- The algorithm to determine the best action given the comparison is exactly the process described in the earlier section on the selection criteria for the best course of action (Section 23.3).

- The input into the defender's system is the actual execution of course of action through **actuators** within the system that affect the change.

- There is an additional input into the defender's system from the attacker who is actively trying to achieve their attack goals and calculating and performing their best actions given their measurement of the state of the system.

The fact that there are actually two control systems operating on the same system, each of which is attempting to move the system toward opposite goals, creates a highly complex control problem. In addition, it takes time for each course of action to fully execute, whether it be the attacker's or the defender's. This execution time means the defended system is often in an intermediate state, making it difficult for either the attacker or defender to fully assess whether their actions worked or not. This complicates the feedback to the control loop determining the next action to take to move the system toward a goal state.

> *Multiply-controlled systems toward opposite goals are complex.*

Note that the control loop and the OODA decision loop are equivalent, but portrayed somewhat differently to be consistent with the underlying theory and concepts of the discipline best suited for the type of control. Table 23-2 compares the equivalency mapping between the elements of the OODA decision and control theory loops.

OODA Decision Loop	Control Theory Loop
Observe	State projection
Orient	Comparison algorithm with goal state
Decide	Select sections
Act	Input and actuation

Table 23-2 Equivalency Mapping Between OODA Decision Loops and Control Theory Loops

The application of control theory to autonomic control is in its early stages, but the concepts and principles of control theory help drive understanding on how to perform autonomic control and some of the issues that might arise. For example, if there is a significant delay in the feedback on the state of the system from the point at which the control is done, control theory tells us that *it may not be possible for the system to converge to a stable point*; it could oscillate between multiple states (also called "hunting") without approaching the defender's goal.

23.4.2 Role of Autonomic Control

Should the range of autonomic actions be the same as those of human-in-the-loop command and control? Why not just turn the system over to autonomic control since it is so much faster?

Recall that an attack surface refers to the avenues of attack that are available to an attacker by virtue of those avenues being exposed in some manner (Section 2.6). For example, an external firewall is part of a systems attack surface. More subtly, the entire suite of commercial software used by an organization is also part of the attack surface because of life-cycle attacks. The term attack surface is distinguished from the term attack space, in that an attack surface consists of those attacks in the attack space that are most readily and directly exploitable by an adversary without having to create the opportunity.

One ironic aspect of cybersecurity subsystems is that they become part of the attack surface of a mission system. Not only can they be attacked to disable cybersecurity, but they can actually become the **attack vector** (means by which the attack actually infiltrates the target system).

> *Cybersecurity mechanisms are part of the attack surface.*

Autonomic action creates a particularly powerful attack surface for the adversary, especially if they know the algorithm used to select action. The adversary can then induce the condition that will cause the desired response action. As mentioned in Section 23.3.3, almost all cybersecurity defensive actions cause some negative impact to mission. The more dramatic the induced defensive response, the greater the potential negative impact on the defended system. *The adversary may be specifically attempting to induce a defender response to cause exactly that negative impact as their primary goal or as a step in their attack sequence.* For example, if a draconian autonomic response is to isolate the defender's system from the external network, this action would likely cripple the mission of most organizations.

It is this crippling that may be the adversary's goal. So, instead of attacking directly to achieve that goal, the adversary may attack in such a way as to cause the defender's response, which indirectly creates the isolation by the defender's own action. It is a martial-arts and Sun Tzu–type tactic of using the adversary's strengths against them, and it can be highly effective. *As cybersecurity architects, we want to avoid creating such opportunities for the adversary where possible.*

The role of autonomic control is two-fold: thwart attacks that are faster than human decision speed, and slow attack progress so that it is reduced to human decision cycle time. The tactics to achieve these goals are the topic of Section 23.4.3.

> ### *Focus autonomic action on machine-speed attacks.*

23.4.3 Autonomic Action Palette

What are appropriate autonomic responses? Appropriate autonomic actions share several characteristics, such as

- Being urgent
- Needing to be reversible
- Needing to minimally impact mission
- Needing to be easily recovered from
- Being temporary

Urgent   Actions in response to attacks must be urgent if they are to be in the purview of the autonomic system. This constraint limits the attack surface presented by the autonomic system, which improves the cybersecurity of the system (Section 23.4.2). The most obvious example of an urgent action is the fast propagation of malware such as viruses and worms, which can happen in seconds and can not only damage the defended system, but also systems of other organizations in the connected community. A high-speed exfiltration is another example. The defender can halt the attacker's exfiltration paths and concurrent damage in both situations by implementing new firewall and router rules that shut down the communication channels used by the malware to propagate or to exfiltrate protected data.

Surgical   To the extent possible, actions should be surgical in the sense that they must be narrow and affect only small aspects of the defended system. For example, say a system detects that one computer, among tens of thousands on the defended network, appears to be a source of an insider attack. Blocking that one computer from the network while its status is sorted out will probably not have a serious effect on the mission. *Broad actions such as isolating the entire enterprise from its external network connection should be specifically excluded from the purview of autonomous action except in the most extreme of circumstances.*

Reversible   Defensive actions must be easily reversible. For example, autonomic action should not include the restart of all computers on the network because doing so could cause a serious loss of work done toward the organization's mission. On the other hand, restarting a handful of computers from a golden copy, after they have been recently checkpointed, may be a reasonable autonomic action in response to their potential involvement in an attack.

Low Impact   Autonomous defensive actions must have very low impact on mission. For example, shutting down all unused ports on all computers within the system should have zero or little impact on the system because the ports are not being used. This action reduces the possible alternate communications channels that an adversary could fall back to if their primary channels are shut down. Another example would be to shut off any traffic to or from any addresses that users of the system have not logged in from during the previous week. That is not foolproof in selectively stopping attacks since the attack could have started the previous week. It also does not guarantee that mission damage will not occur, because sometimes the mission requires the use of channels with new addresses on the external network. Even so, it is probably a reasonably low-impact tactical autonomic response to minimize the attacker's communication and attack paths.

Recoverable   An action is easily recoverable if there is a minimal permanent loss of data or service. For example, if all email ports are shut down for a few minutes because a wave of email malware is passing through the network, there is almost no loss of data. This is because email is a store-and-forward system, whereby email is stored on intermediate hosts until they can connect and pass the email along to the next intermediary, until it reaches its destination. If the email system is shut down for a brief period of time, the system will simply buffer the email messages until it can create a connection. Similarly, routers can drop Transmission Control Protocol packets if they are temporarily saturated, because the reliable protocol requires the recipient to verify that it has received all the packets sent, and re-request any packets lost in transmission.

Temporary   Autonomous actions that are very brief usually do not have significant mission impact because most systems are designed to self-recover from short network and system glitches. Of course, that is not true of real-time aircraft systems such as flight controls, but it is generally true. Often, attack sequencing can be time-critical. If a target system is non-responsive and thus unavailable to an attack attempt, the attacking software may seek another target instead of retrying the system that is temporarily unavailable. *So, temporary suspension of services may be an effective tactical autonomic measure to deflect infiltration of attacker malware.*

> *Temporary suspension of services can deflect attacks.*

23.5 Meta-Strategy

In addition to strategies that drive both command and control and **autonomous** control, there are some important overarching strategies on how to apply strategies. They are called **meta-strategies**. Examples of such meta-strategies are discussed in the following sections.

23.5.1 Don't Overreact

Whether a response is human-in-the-loop or autonomous, the action must be carefully tempered and commensurate with the risk associated with the type of attack. Remember that a defender's response almost always damages the defender's own mission and system. *If the damage caused by a defensive action is worse than the potential damage from the attack, then the defender is unintentionally cooperating with the attacker to cause maximum damage to the defender's own system.*

In control theory, overreaction has the additional consequence of potentially destabilizing the control loop and preventing it from converging toward the defender's goal state—and it may even help converge the system toward the adversary's goal state! An analogy from aviation is controlling an airplane's altitude on the final approach path toward a runway. In this example, the pilot cannot see the runway because of weather conditions, but he can see a needle on a dial that indicates whether or not the pilot is on the electronic glide path. If the pilot allows the aircraft to deviate slightly below the glide path, the pilot should obviously pull up slightly to maneuver back to the glide path. If the pilot pulls up too hard, the aircraft will pass through the glide path to the runway, and now be too far above the path. Indeed, the pilot cannot wait until the aircraft is back on the path to descend toward the path, because the airplane's momentum will carry it even farther off track below the path. Figure 23-5 shows the airplane deviating on and off the glide path (also called the glideslope) due to overcontrol.

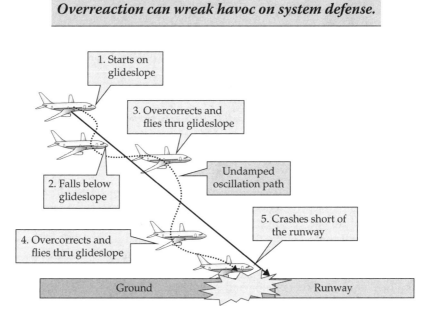

Figure 23-5   An aviation analogy of overcontrol creating an out-of-control undamped oscillation leading to a crash

If the pilot continues in this overcontrolling manner, the aircraft will end up so far off the path to the runway that it will likely hit the ground or an obstacle and crash short of the runway. That, of course, is an undesirable outcome. In control theory, this is known as an **undamped oscillation**, and it happens in many fields of engineering, including electrical signals in electrical engineering, and mechanical waves in civil engineering [PAST15].

23.5.2 Don't Be Predictable

Independent of the type of control used, it is generally a bad idea to be too predictable to the adversary. If the cybersecurity system consistently uses the same defensive course of action actions when responding to the same situation, the adversary will have the advantage of knowing the exact defensive move in that situation. In fact, *the adversary may launch a number of relatively benign attacks against the defender's systems just to watch and record the defender's reactions.* This is analogous to some nations flying their fighter jets right up to the edge of another country's sovereign air space just to watch how their radar systems and air force react.

This observation is not to suggest that the defender take purely random actions. Defense actions must strive to bring the defender's system to their goal of zero damage. *The unpredictability principle does suggest that if several alternative actions are nearly as good as one another, one ought to randomize the selection between them.* Another corollary is that it would be useful to engage in a certain degree of deception to give outward appearances of taking one set of actions, when, in fact, the defender is taking an entirely different set of actions. For example, the defender could reroute the attacker to a honeypot system that looks very similar to the defender's system. That honeypot system could then take some totally weird set of actions that could keep the defender perplexed for days and would certainly misinform the attacker's model as to how the defender would react to an attack of the type the adversary was testing.

> *Action should be unpredictable, within the limits of effectiveness.*

23.5.3 Stay Ahead of the Attackers

The attacker takes the initiative and therefore always has the large advantage of the element of surprise. If the attacker's activities remain undetected, the attacker continues to enjoy this tremendous advantage. At some point, the attack progression can reach the point where the attacker is in full control of the defender's system. At that point, it is too late for the defender to take any defensive measures at all. Therefore, it is important for the defender to quickly relieve the attacker of their advantage of surprise. Detection of successful attacks is essential for optimal defense of the mission and its enterprise system.

> *The attacker always has the element of surprise.*

Once an attack is detected, the attack speed may be too great to try to detect and react to each attack step (represented by a node in the attack tree) as it occurs. By the time the step succeeds, the damage may be done, and the next attack step may be enabled and already underway. *Lagging several steps behind in detecting the attacker's attack is a sure way for the defender to lose a cyber battle.* That is why it is essential that the cyber situation understanding subsystem project the attack steps onto the forest of strategic attack trees (Section 22.4) and predict *where the attacker is headed* and take defensive actions to stop the attack before it is able to achieve the subgoals. These are known as **attack interdiction points** because they are where the defender can intercept the attack sequences and bring the attack to a screeching halt.

> *Get ahead of attackers at attack interdiction points.*

Conclusion

This is the second in a series of two chapters on organizing operational concepts that drive cybersecurity design. The previous chapter discussed cyber situation understanding to make sense of what is going on during a cyberattack. This chapter discusses planning for and taking effective action based on strategic and tactical knowledge gained through experience, experimentation, and simulation. This chapter ends the part of the book dedicated to orchestrating cybersecurity design and operation. The next chapter moves on to the final part of the book on the societal implications of cybersecurity and what the future may hold.

To summarize:

- Command and control is key to the decision-making cycle. Command develops and decides on a course of action; control monitors the execution and its effectiveness.

- The decision-making cycle refers to the iterative process of proceeding through the four phases of the Observe-Orient-Decide-Act (OODA) decision cycle.

- Fast decision-making cycles are an advantage in staying ahead of the attacker in dynamic cybersecurity defensive courses of action.

- Autonomic control refers to purely automated actions driven by algorithms that are akin to human reflexes and are reserved for situations where reaction time must be faster than humans are capable of.

- Autonomic control works in concert with human-in-the-loop command and control to create a hybrid system that has the advantages of both.

- Effective control requires knowledge about what to do in various situations. Such knowledge comes from analogy, direct experience, vicarious experience, and simulation.

- Analogies are an effective way of jump-starting knowledge from other domains as long as the limitations of the analogy and the consequent limitations on the knowledge are well understood.

- Direct experience is painful, but valuable as long as the knowledge gained is properly extracted and institutionalized.
- Vicarious experience is available from many sources and is not always adequately reviewed, analyzed, and incorporated.
- Simulation offers a fast way to gain new knowledge and insights on how to effectively control cybersecurity systems, as long as the underlying models are accurate where it counts. Validation is always an issue.
- A playbook is the concept of applying the knowledge acquired about how to control systems. Explicit documentation and updating of playbooks is essential to an organization building its knowledge base on effectively defending itself.
- Courses of action must be developed in advance of being in the heat of a cyber battle. Strategic attack trees can be useful in generating possible courses of action.
- What constitutes the best possible course of action in a given situation is dependent on a number of factors, including the stakes, the attacker's capability and goal, uncertainty regarding the attack, the defense posture, the speed of the attack, and the projected effectiveness of the defensive action compared to the consequence of that action to the mission.
- Autonomic control is essential to stop or slow down high-speed attacks.
- Control theory provides an effective model to move the system toward the defender's goal state.
- Great care must be taken to prevent autonomic action from becoming an attack surface.
- Autonomic action should be urgent, reversible, low-impact to mission, easily recoverable, and temporary.
- Meta-strategies address how best to apply strategy: they include not overreacting, being unpredictable, and staying ahead of the attackers through interdiction points.

Questions

1. What is command and control and how does it relate to the OODA decision loop?
2. Define the decision-making cycle and decision-making cycle time and describe their importance.
3. What does a tight OODA loop mean and how does it provide an advantage?
4. When is autonomic control essential to an effective dynamic defense of a system?
5. How does one integrate human-in-the-loop control with autonomic control to gain the advantages of both?
6. Effective control requires knowing which courses of action are effective in which situations. List four ways that such knowledge can be acquired and briefly describe each.

7. What are the advantages and limitations of knowledge by analogy?

8. List three useful analogous areas to cybersecurity and briefly describe where the analogy applies well and where the analogy breaks down.

9. Discuss how to take maximum advantage of lessons learned from direct experience.

10. Name three sources of vicarious experience and describe where you would find that information.

11. What does institutionalization of strategy knowledge mean?

12. List three types of simulations and describe what areas of knowledge they are best at exploring and the areas that they are least useful in.

13. What is a cybersecurity playbook and how does it resemble a sports playbook?

14. Why is game theory useful in developing playbooks?

15. What is a course of action and why are multiple options needed?

16. Why should course of action options for given attack situations be developed in advance?

17. How can attack trees be used to develop courses of action?

18. List and describe the eight factors that are relevant to determining the best course of action in any given situation. Describe how each might affect the best choice.

19. Compare and contrast the decision-making cycle phases of autonomic action versus human-in-the-loop command and control.

20. What are the six basic elements of a control problem and how do they apply to a cybersecurity situation?

21. Relate the six basic elements of a control problem to the four phases of an OODA decision loop.

22. Explain why it is not a good idea to just turn all cybersecurity control over to autonomic control since it is so much faster than human-in-the-loop control.

23. Define attack surface and relate it to the design of cybersecurity control systems.

24. What are the five characteristics of defensive courses of action that should be in the purview of autonomic action?

25. What is a meta-strategy?

26. Name three meta-strategies and briefly describe each one and how it improves the application of strategy.

27. What is an undamped oscillation and how does it relate to cybersecurity control?

28. What is an attack interdiction point and how can one use them to get ahead of the attacker?

PART

V

Moving Cybersecurity Forward

"Part V: Moving Cybersecurity Forward" prepares the readers to understand where the field is headed and how to best apply their newly gained knowledge to improve cybersecurity wherever the readers go.

24

Strategic Policy and Investment

Overview

Learning Objectives

- Discuss how bad can bad get when it comes to cyberwar.
- Describe the global increasing dependency on technology and the consequences.
- Explain why the virtual economy is significant and worth serious cybersecurity attention.
- Relate the fake news problem to cybersecurity and how it expands the definition of a system.

This chapter begins the final part of the book. The focus is on the future of cybersecurity and the broad societal context. This first chapter concentrates on the societal context and large policy issues at the national and global scale. The next chapter projects outward into the future and provides parting thoughts on how the cybersecurity landscape will likely evolve and the best way to prepare for that evolution.

The purpose of this chapter is to give the leadership of today and tomorrow a taste of the important issues that this generation and the next will have to grapple with. In some sense, it is a message to the technical leadership and political leadership regarding where to focus their attention and concerns as cybersecurity evolves into the future.

24.1 Cyberwar: How Bad Can Bad Get?

War has been an unfortunate part of civilization from the beginning. *Cyberspace does not change humanity's propensity to settle disputes by violence, but it does change the nature and speed of conflict.* In the information age, information and information processing are primary resources over which countries will compete. Further, and more importantly, cyberspace controls **critical infrastructure** in the physical world, including electrical power, telecommunications, and banking. The information technology supporting the critical infrastructure is called the **critical information infrastructure**, and it is highly vulnerable to attack [PCCI97]. Figure 24-1 shows that electrical power, oil and gas, telecommunications, and finance sectors are the most critical infrastructures because without these four, the other infrastructures collapse. Figure 24-2 shows that all of the infrastructures are in a complex web of interdependency, in which an attack in one infrastructure can cascade to other infrastructures in surprising ways.

> *Cyberspace acts as an accelerant for normal human propensities.*

Cyber conflict can use cyberspace to affect strategic damages very quickly in the physical world, which could, as a result, escalate the situation to physical warfare and potential nuclear warfare. *The risk is serious and it is real* [PCCI97] [HOU07]!

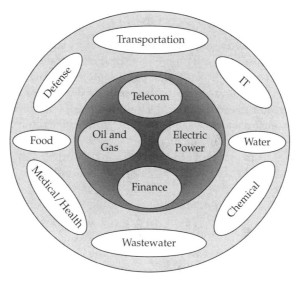

Figure 24-1   Critical infrastructures showing the four hypercritical infrastructures at the core, supporting all others

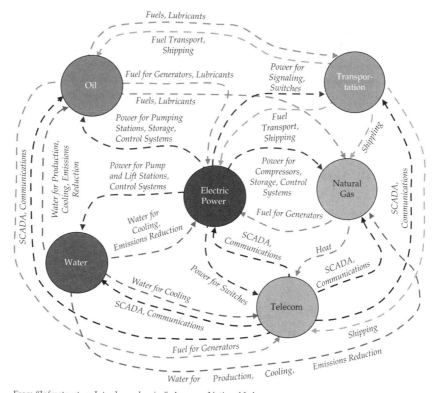

From "Infrastructure Interdependencies" Argonne National Labs

Figure 24-2   Critical infrastructure showing the complex web of interdependencies in the physical world

24.1.1 Scenario

Imagine the lights suddenly go out where you are, and all power is lost. All is silent for a few seconds. You try to use your cell phone, but the lines of communication are dead. You try to access the Internet with your battery-powered laptops, but the Internet, too, is down. After a while, you venture out into the streets to investigate if this power outage is affecting more than just your building, and the power is indeed out as far as the eye can see. A passerby tells you the banks are closed and the automated teller machines aren't working either. The streets are jammed because the traffic lights are out, and people are trying to leave their workplaces en masse. Day turns to night, but the power hasn't returned. Radio and television stations aren't broadcasting. The telephone and Internet still aren't working; there's no way to check in with loved ones.

After a long, restless night, morning comes, but you still don't have power or communication. People are beginning to panic, and local law enforcement can't restore order. As another day turns to night, looters begin to raid businesses and homes, and the traffic jams worsen. Word begins to spread that the United States has been attacked—not by a conventional weapon, but by a cyber weapon. As a result, the national power grid, telecommunications, and financial systems have been disrupted—worse yet, they won't be back in a few hours or days; rather, it will take months. The airports and train stations have closed. Food production has ceased. The water supply is rapidly deteriorating. People dependent upon life-saving medical devices that require power will die. Hospitals close. Banks are closed so your life savings are out of reach and worthless. The only things of value are those needed for basic human survival: gasoline, food, water, and firewood traded on the black market. The nation has gone from being a superpower to a third-world nation practically overnight.

> *Damage from a strategic cyberattack could destroy a country.*

24.1.2 Call to Action

Americans observed what happened to the social fabric when Hurricane Katrina wiped out the infrastructure in a relatively small portion of the United States in 2005: chaos ensued and the impact lasted for months. In 2017, a record was set in the United States for the most consecutive hurricanes since 1893. Category 4 Hurricanes Harvey and Irma made landfall with 130 mph winds, striking Texas and Florida in August and September 2017. Nearly 3.8 million customers lost power when Hurricane Irma hit Florida. It took over a week for power to be restored to 99 percent of Floridians through Herculean efforts by crews working day and night. Just days after Irma, Puerto Rico was devastated by category 4 Hurricane Maria, leaving the majority of the population without water or power for months. What would be left after months of recovery from such devastation nationwide? Equivalent levels of damage from strategic cyberattack scenarios are plausible and therefore worthy of urgent attention. The nations of the world are unprepared to properly defend themselves and recover from a strategic cyberattack.

To recognize the plausibility and consequences of such attacks without undertaking any governmental action would be unconscionable. The only rational approach to address a problem of this magnitude and scale is a concerted high-priority government program on the order of the Manhattan Project. Failure to embark on such a program will have disastrous consequences for this generation and the next.

24.1.3 Barriers to Preparation Action

There are at least three barriers to aggressive preparation action: (1) the natural human psychology of denial—to resist thinking about disastrous scenarios allows us to feel safe, (2) the perception that government investment would require "big government" private-sector interference, and (3) the case for national strategic vulnerability isn't yet credible to senior leadership.

The specter of the Hiroshima and Nagasaki atomic bomb explosions looms large in the human consciousness. It happened. It is real. The terrifying images from those horrible events are burned into our collective thoughts. This makes investing in strategic programs related to the nuclear threat compelling. As-yet-unrealized threats such as a meteor strike on the Earth or the eruption of a supervolcano such as the Yellowstone volcano are not real to people because they have not experienced them and do not know anyone who has. Even though the probabilities may be similar, the fact that an event has not happened means that the event does not get equal time in our consciousness, even though such thinking is irrational [KAHN11]. Further, if the projected event is very negative, we actively suppress thoughts of it because it makes it feel less real. Convincing leadership to pay attention to the threats and to invest in them at a strategic level is an extraordinarily difficult proposition.

Regarding government involvement and responsibility, this isn't a matter of "big government" versus "small government"; it's a matter of governments being duty-bound to defend their countries against threats beyond the capabilities and means of the private sector. This will be discussed further in Section 25.3.5.

Lastly, the case for action has been made a number of times in the United States by leadership from a variety of different communities, including members of the National Security Council [PCCI97], Defense Department leadership [DSB96] [DSB00], and the science and engineering community [NRC91] [NRC99][NRC17]. If national leadership still has doubts regarding the probability or stakes, they are obliged to do what it takes to resolve those doubts. Strategy starts with a solid understanding of the underlying problem.

> *Strategic national action is hard to galvanize.*

24.1.4 Smoking Gun

Some of you might think, what's the rush? Where's the smoking gun—the indication of a major assault on cyber infrastructure? Surely, it's coming, and it's undoubtedly already in its planning stages. There are three potential reasons why the world has not seen a major assault yet.

First, strategic long-term damage requires substantial planning and very well-timed execution. Creating the capabilities and placing the required assets (such as insiders) takes time, sometimes years.

Second, when such a cyberattack weapon is created, it's in some sense a one-time-use strategic option. It would not be used lightly. The attacker would not want to tip their hand about its existence until the weapon is really needed. Such weapons are likely to have been deployed already—hidden from detection. Perhaps there is a sleeper cell of insiders and malicious software embedded in critical infrastructure in all major countries around the world.

Finally, current cyber infrastructure offers a wealth of highly valuable knowledge (such as advanced research results). As adversaries conduct espionage, they're also mapping cyberspace and gaining great experimental and training experience that will enable future strategic attacks. It's in the interests of adversaries to preserve their upper hand for as long as possible and keep tapping into these important attributes.

> ***No smoking gun does not mean guns are not locked and loaded.***

24.2 Increasing Dependency, Fragility, and the Internet of Things

Modern society has become highly dependent on technology. People cannot navigate from point A to point B any more because they totally rely on their global position system (GPS) devices. Nobody knows anyone's telephone number any more because their mobile phone stores all of that information. Birthdays are forgotten because social media sites have all that information for you. If we lose access to our calendars, we wander around dazed not knowing where to go, as if we are suffering from a concussion [CLAR04]. These observations are only on the personal front to drive the point home.

> ***People now depend on technology for everything.***

24.2.1 Societal Dependency

Dependency on information technology at the societal scale is even more significant. *Your money in the bank is really just a series of bits in a computer somewhere.* Flip some of those bits, and your money could disappear overnight. Power generation and distribution depend heavily on computers. If something goes awry in the computers controlling massive electricity generators, the generators can destroy themselves [ZELL11] and cause power outages. Airplanes are increasingly being built as fly-by-wire—meaning that there are no longer physical linkages between the airplane controls in the cockpit and the control surfaces and engines. A failure in a fly-by-wire system means that a perfectly airworthy airplane can become an uncontrollable hunk of metal [KNOL93].

24.2.2 Just-in-Time Everything

Just-in-time manufacturing is an inventory strategy that has become the norm of companies to increase efficiency and decrease waste. Manufacturers deeply connect their systems with those of their suppliers and distributors such that component parts are delivered *just as they are needed* and the finished product is delivered *just as they are ready to be consumed*. This schema can save substantial money and reduce risk, but certainly makes the manufacturing system much more fragile and vulnerable to cascading cyberattack effects. These are but a few examples from thousands of possibilities demonstrating society's increasing and precarious dependency on technology.

> *Just-in-time manufacturing creates fragility and risk propagation.*

24.2.3 The Internet of Things

An emerging technology market is worthy of special note—the Internet of Things (see Section 6.4). The Internet of Things will integrate low-cost, low-power devices into a wide variety of objects in our daily living. Most cars today have not just one computer, but generally dozens controlling everything from fuel flow to braking. Thermostats and home security systems are also increasingly online, providing both status and the ability to perform remote control. Soon, toasters and refrigerators will have integrated computers to toast one's toast perfectly and to reorder groceries that you are running low on.

Further, your clothes will have tiny integrated computers to sense wear and tear, stretching, warmth, and moisture. Even more intrusively, the human body will become one of the things into which technology is integrated. As we head toward personalized medicine, heartbeat, pressure change, temperature variation, urine output, and blood glucose level will all be continuously recorded and analyzed. The resulting data will customize your medical care in terms of diagnosis and treatment.

24.2.4 Propagated Weakness

These integrated computers will be, of course, highly interconnected with each other and the Internet. By now, this scenario should be sending up red flags in your mind as a cybersecurity engineer. The low-cost, low-power nature of these embedded devices means that they often skimp on cybersecurity features. The consequence to the individual device may be low (though one could argue that integrated human sensors can be life-critical), but the propagated risk to surrounding systems can be enormous. An example of such attacks has already happened, with hackers demonstrating a vulnerability in a thermostat enabling a **ransomware** attack [FRAN16]. Another widespread cyberattack occurred, leveraging a vulnerability in security cameras [HERE16].

The Internet of Things is upon us, and it will grow rapidly over the next decade. It will bring great convenience along with great risk. Cybersecurity engineers should pay close attention to the trade-offs between cybersecurity and functionality in these devices.

Part V

The cost and potential liability go way beyond that of the device itself. Large-scale lawsuits that could destroy companies are coming if the current lack of attention to this issue continues.

> *The Internet of Things poses enormous potential risk.*

24.3 Cybersecurity in the Virtual World: Virtual Economy

24.3.1 Booming Game Economy: Virtual Gold Rush

This may seem like a joke, but there is a booming economy in the virtual world of gaming—specifically in the world of massively multiplayer online role-playing games such as World of Warcraft®. These games contain virtual resources and virtual money. To gain resources and money can take hours and hours of game play. Time is money, and there are always those who prefer shortcuts. Hence a multibillion-dollar market has emerged in the generation of these resources by relatively low-wage workers and the consumption and trading of these resources by gamers. There is an actual exchange rate between real currency and the fake currency inside of these games [LEHD14].

24.3.2 Digital Currency Such as Bitcoin

The virtual economy also includes virtual digital currency in the real world, such as that provided by Bitcoin [MICK11]. These virtual currencies allow participants to engage in transactions without involving banks and transaction fees, and without revealing their identity. Bitcoin can be bought and sold using various countries' currencies, creating an international country-neutral currency. The Bitcoin market currency has about $41B [CHAN17], which is only a tiny fraction of other large currency, but it certainly creates a high-value target and represents a potential disruptor to traditional banking.

24.3.3 Virtual High-Value Targets

What does this have to do with cybersecurity? In the real world, information technology systems mainly support organizations performing actions in the physical world. Damaging the information technology system indirectly damages the organization's mission. In the virtual economy, the information technology service *is* the mission. Because virtual resources have substantial real value, they become a high-value target. *Manipulation of the data becomes a direct manipulation of value.* If one can generate virtual resources and virtual money through a cyberattack on the computers hosting these services, then one can create massive inflation within these worlds, which is a form of theft. One can trade these resources for real money. *This interface to the real economy can then cause a cascading disruption to the real economy.*

To be sure, gaming systems were not designed to be robust against serious adversaries taking aim at exploiting these systems for gain. There have been several breaches of gaming systems, and there will surely be more to come. There have been many examples of distributed denial of service attacks on these games [CLOU17]. Such attacks will lead to ransomware attacks in which attackers extort money from companies in exchange for not executing denial of service attacks against them—causing them to lose substantial revenue per minute. Many cyberattacks have already happened in which vulnerabilities have been exploited to generate resources; many more are yet to come.

The **virtual economy** and its value have emerged over time. Virtual reality designers did not fully anticipate the value and therefore did not properly anticipate the risks associated with the value creation. Trying to retroactively patch such systems to make them secure after they have been designed and deployed is extraordinarily difficult. The task resembles the Greek myth of Sisyphus who was cursed by the gods to eternally push a giant boulder up a hill to the top only to have it repeatedly roll down to the bottom of the mountain.

> *Retroactive cybersecurity design is a Sisyphean task.*

24.3.4 Start from Scratch?

At some point, existing games may need to be completely redesigned from the ground up with much higher cybersecurity standards. New multiuser online games will need to incorporate these requirements from the start if they want to have any hope of not being plagued by incessant cyberattacks. Such cyberattacks could not only destroy the value the games create, but can also propagate to destroy value in other connected systems—thereby creating a liability beyond the created value.

24.4 Disinformation and Influence Operations: Fake News

Fake news became big news in 2016 in the course of the U.S. national election for president. There was no question that a foreign country, Russia, strived to actively influence the outcome of the United States election for a candidate that they thought would be more favorable to Russia [INTEL17]. Russia continued that influence campaign in Europe such as the French elections of 2017 [GREE17]. Interference in the elections of another country is a serious matter. Some believe that it can rise to an act of war, which would make complicity with such a campaign high treason.

24.4.1 What's New?

Of course, Russia is neither the first nor the last country to use disinformation to influence the politics of another country. The world is full of glass houses from which many throw stones. Disinformation campaigns, or more generally influence operations, have been going on since the beginning of time (e.g., starting false rumors about one's competitor to damage their reputation). *But four important things have changed with the increasing reliance on cyberspace: reach, automation, speed, and feedback control.*

Reach   Forty years ago, one would need to own and operate a newspaper to spread news beyond their neighbors and calling circles. This required a significant and sustained investment. The further the reach of the newspaper, the more expensive it was. Therefore, there was a high barrier to entry. Today, anyone can post any information on social media and have it spread to millions around the world in the blink of an eye. The cost is nearly zero. There is no vetting of the information and little accountability for spreading false information or intentionally manipulating information.

Automation   To spread news in the past, a human had to write an article, another human had to review and edit the article, and a whole fleet of people had to produce the article for distribution in a newspaper. Today, we have **bots**—automation software that can send out information to large audiences and even react to the posting of information from others, thus engaging in conversation in an **artificially intelligent** way (see Section 25.6). It is now possible to have extended heated exchanges (sometimes called **flame wars**) on social media where the majority of the participants are actually bots. The purpose of the bots is to influence how people think (sometimes called mindshare) about some topic as mundane as the best phone or shoes to buy or as serious as the question concerning for whom to vote in a national election [BUMP17].

Speed   The propagation of information on today's Internet underlying the various forms of social media is nearly at light speed. The speed of information propagation ensures that information not only goes out to a large volume of users, but gets to audiences right away. This can be important to capitalize on a hot topic that is on everyone's mind at the moment, and not the next day. It is also essential in the next important aspect, feedback control.

Feedback Control   Today, it is possible to analyze the information posted by individuals in various groups (e.g., retirees, gun owners, those belonging to a specific party or group) and discern their hot buttons that will galvanize them to action. Then, customized postings can be crafted by bots to target their specific hot buttons. This information can be posted and their response can be monitored directly. Did they repost it? Did they add an angry call to action? If the recipient does not respond, an alternate formulation of posting can be crafted in a revised attempt to influence the target. *This gives a real-time control feedback loop that never before existed at a large scale in society, creating a very powerful and very dangerous influence machine that could endanger democracy.*

> ***Influence operations poses an existential threat to democracy.***

24.4.2 Hacking Wetware

When people once talked about hacking an election, they universally thought about directly hacking the electronic voting machines and apparatus. With current technology, hacking enough machines to affect voter outcome would be challenging (though far from impossible). The difficulty arises not because the machines are secure, but rather because many are not online and there are many different machines with many different versions. One would have to perform many simultaneous attacks, some of which would require physical access to the voting machines. Hacking voter registration databases gets closer to a more pervasively disruptive attack [PERL17].

What has developed recently and surprisingly as of the U.S. elections of 2016 is the concept of "hacking" what people think—known in the military circles as **psychological operations** (or PsyOps if you want to sound cool). People's brains and thinking ability are sometimes humorously referred to as "wetware" to stand in contrast to rote automation in the form of software. As we discussed in Section 24.4.1, the process of affecting how people think has become astoundingly refined and powerful.

There will be increasing economic and political incentive to engage in such psychological operations, or more broadly, influence operations. Influence operations include the spread of false information as well as selective and well-timed true information. Influence operations call for the spread of whatever information is needed to evoke the desired outcome—whether it is to buy product X instead of the competing product Y, or to vote for candidate A and not candidate B. *This means that it will become increasingly difficult to trust the veracity of information on the Internet and even within news media outlets that often recycle news from social media.*

24.4.3 Polluting the Infosphere

If we think of the Internet as the digital equivalent of a biosphere, we can view it as an **infosphere**. Using this analogy, we can see that there will be increasingly many organizations that will wantonly pollute the infosphere with false or misleading data for their own benefit. In a biosphere, pollution causes long-term damages to those who live in it. *Polluters are ethically and legally responsible for those damages.*

Whether the infosphere polluters can be held accountable for such damages remains to be seen. *What is clear is that the concept of trustworthy systems extends to societal systems involving human wetware, and cybersecurity experts must expand their thinking to this broadest sense of system and trustworthiness.*

> *Infosphere pollution will become a critical problem of the future.*

> *Trustworthy system considerations extend to societal systems.*

Conclusion

Part IV of this book focused on cybersecurity design to build the best possible system for a given enterprise. This chapter begins the final part of the book on the societal implications of cybersecurity on a more global scale and on where cybersecurity may be headed in the future. This chapter discusses topics such as cyberwarfare, the increasing fragility of society stemming from its increased dependency on technology, and notions of disinformation that may uncontrollably pollute the world's information sphere on which we have come to depend.

Part V

To summarize:

- Cyberwar can be a massively destructive force that could disrupt sovereignty; the world is in an unstable time in history with respect to cyberspace security.
- Society depends heavily on critical information infrastructure that is highly interdependent and vulnerable.
- A lack of a strategic smoking gun does not mean that cyber weapons are not pointed at critical systems in the fashion of a Mexican standoff.
- Society's dependency on technology continues to grow without bounds; the Internet of Things is likely to increase fragility even faster.
- The virtual economy inside the gaming industry and virtual currencies are emerging as a significant part of the real economy and need to be taken more seriously from a cybersecurity perspective.
- Fake news became big news in 2016. Social media enables targeted influence on populations to hack the way people think, reducing trust and creating a threat to society and democracy.

Questions

1. What are the potential stakes in a cyberwar and why?
2. Which are the four most foundational critical infrastructures and why?
3. What are the implications of the intricate web of interdependencies between critical infrastructure elements?
4. Why is influencing national policy in strategic cybersecurity challenging? Give three reasons and explain each one.
5. If the potential risk from cyberwar is so large, why have we not seen it yet?
6. Give three examples of how you are personally totally dependent on technology to get through your day. State what would happen if you did not have the technology available.
7. Is society's dependency on technology increasing, decreasing, or staying about the same? What do you think the underlying cause of that trend is?
8. What does just-in-time manufacturing mean and what are its implications for the interconnection of systems and propagation of risk?
9. What is the Internet of Things? Give three examples today. Give one example that does not currently exist but which you believe we will see in the next three years.
10. Why does the Internet of Things pose a special risk not associated with other computing devices?

11. Discuss the virtual economy and why it should be of concern to cybersecurity engineers.

12. What is virtual currency? Why is it useful? Give an example. What special risks does it pose?

13. What does it mean when we say that retroactive cybersecurity design is a Sisyphean task? Why is it so challenging?

14. Discuss the importance of fake news in the context of cybersecurity.

15. What are four new aspects of modern social media that are enabling influence operations to change people's minds? Discuss each aspect and how it enables influence.

16. What does it mean to "hack wetware" and why is it surprising?

17. Compare and contrast pollution in the biosphere with information pollution in the infosphere. What are the implications of the analogy regarding how society might effectively approach this difficult problem? Where might the analogy fail or be inappropriate?

18. Discuss how to extend the concept of systems to encompass societal systems that include people and their actions. Discuss the implications of that extension to the purview of cybersecurity professionals.

19. What are some of the roles for which users themselves are critical to achieve system trustworthiness?

Part V

25

Thoughts on the Future of Cybersecurity

Overview

Learning Objectives

- Discuss the potential erosion of secrecy and the consequences for cybersecurity engineering.
- Explain the nature of the coevolutionary path of cyberattack and cybersecurity and how it influences development and integration of new cybersecurity capability.
- Compare and contrast the space race with today's cybersecurity equivalent.
- Summarize the issues involved in the pursuit of cybersecurity science and experimentation.
- Discuss the importance of cybersecurity research and how best to pursue it.
- Identify the key issues that advancement of artificial intelligence may cause in cybersecurity and society security.

25.1 A World Without Secrecy

Power tends to corrupt, and absolute power corrupts absolutely.

—Lord Acton

With secrecy comes power. Therefore, a corollary to Lord Acton's famous quote on power's tendency to corrupt is secrecy's tendency to corrupt. Secrecy is sometimes necessary, but extraordinary measures are needed to prevent it from spreading wildly and being misused to cover incompetence or impropriety.

Irrespective of the need to minimize security, there are signs that the ability to keep secrets may become vanishingly small over time. Sophisticated inference engines such as WolframAlpha® [MCAL09] will soon be able to make inferences at such a high speed from existing knowledge that anything that is inferable will be inferred. When one does a Google search, one will get back not just what has been indexed, but everything that can be inferred from all knowledge that has been indexed. Anything that has any footprint in the real world will leave tiny bits of evidence that, when aggregated, can divulge the most secret secrets. These revelations will happen in waves as the inference engines get better and better.

Secrecy is an important part of value creation and retention in today's world. Trade secrets are important for companies to retain the value that they invested in to create. Governments maintain secrets for similar reasons of value retention (see Section 3.1). If the prediction that secrecy (and privacy) will be eroded at an increasingly fast rate is true, then there are several important strategic prophylactic actions that are suggested:

- Develop a timed release of secrets to minimize damage.
- Minimize the generation of new secrets.
- Learn to operate effectively in a zero-secret environment.

25.1.1 Timed Release

If an organization has a body of secrets such as proprietary formulas or research results that give them a competitive edge, it is likely that the compromise of some of that information will cause different levels of damage depending on the timing of the release. For example, perhaps a company would want to patent their trade secrets before they are publicly revealed, allowing a competitor to patent the formula and preventing the originator from using it. That could be disastrous.

As another example, suppose that an organization was keeping information secret because it could be embarrassing or even create a legal or criminal liability. Volunteering that information and releasing it with the best possible spin can significantly reduce the damages to reputation. A competitor or adversary, on the other hand, will likely release it at the worst possible time and with the worst possible spin to cause maximum damage.

So, it behooves organizations to take an inventory of their secrets, analyze them for their vulnerability to being revealed through inference, analyze them for best time release in advance of revelation (given that there will be a high degree of uncertainty in precise timing of compromise), and to create a plan for the release of their secret stores slowly—starting now.

25.1.2 Minimize Generation

Given that the half-life of secrecy (see Section 3.4) is decreasing, organizations should begin to minimize the generation of new secrets and particularly their reliance on secrets for their success in mission. For example, if a company is keeping much of its research secret and not filing for patents to delay competitors gaining information about that research, the organization should reconsider adding to that body of secret research and rather seek patents or engage in collaborative open research, gaining the public relations credit for doing so.

25.1.3 Zero-Secrecy Operations

Lastly, organizations will need to figure out how to succeed without reliance on secrets. Movies such as *The Invention of Lying* (2009), *What Women Want* (2000), *Liar Liar* (1997) and the TV series *Lie to Me* (2009) explore the issue of learning to operate with zero secrecy. *To those who live and die by secrecy as the core of their operation, it may be inconceivable to consider crafting an alternative way of operating without it.* Irrespective of the difficulty, there eventually may be little choice in the matter. Learning how to operate now without secrecy and establishing a pilot group to do so may make the difference between life and death of entire societal institutions [BOK11][BOK99].

> *Zero-secrecy operations may become inevitable.*

25.2 Coevolution of Measures and Countermeasures

Cyberattacks and cybersecurity are in eternal **coevolution** together. As new cyberattacks are developed, new cybersecurity defenses will be developed to thwart those attacks. As new cybersecurity defenses are developed to thwart cyberattacks, so too will new cyberattacks be developed to circumvent those new cybersecurity defenses. *The evolution of one directly affects the evolution of another, creating evolutionary pressures in a particular direction.*

Whether a new cybersecurity defense mechanism prevents, detects-responds, or tolerates cyberattacks may differentially affect the evolution of countering cyberattacks. Similarly, whether new cyberattacks focus on espionage or sabotage, stealthy or non-stealthy, will differentially affect the cybersecurity defense countermeasure evolution. An incredibly effective new cybersecurity defense measure could force an evolution to increasingly intelligent and potentially more lethal cyberattack measures. Similarly, an incredibly effective cyberattack schema could cause a dramatic evolution of how systems are developed, integrated, and operated. *In biology, the interactions between hosts and parasites, predators and prey, humans and animals and their pathogens, or plants and their insect pests lead to similar coevolution of species.*

The observation about coevolution has some important implications. When one is considering the design, development, and deployment of cybersecurity countermeasures, one must always ask the question: what evolutionary pressures will this place on cyberattackers and will those pressures lead to an evolutionary line that is good for the defender or bad for the defender? This is similar to a chess player looking ahead hundreds of moves in a chess match (as computers can now do) and performing a min-max algorithm to optimize one's move (see Section 23.3). If cybersecurity designers and vendors are not careful, they may push the world to places they do not want to be in 10 years. Small adjustments today in the design, development, and implementation of cybersecurity defensive mechanisms can result in major consequences in cyberattacks far down the road—a phenomena known as the butterfly effect.

> *Consider coevolution implications of every cybersecurity design.*

A similar and seemingly obvious corollary for those involved in both cyberattack and cybersecurity business, such as military institutions, is this: *do not develop cyberattacks for which you do not have cybersecurity countermeasures designed, developed, and deployed; such cyberattacks will surely come back to bite you in painful places.* Such institutions should keep in mind Aesop's fable of the eagle that generously gave one of its feathers to a hunter, who then used that plume to fashion an arrow with which the hunter shot and killed the eagle [GRAN83].

> *Creating cyberattacks without countering cybersecurity is foolish.*

25.3 Cybersecurity Space Race and Sputnik

There is a quiet space race going on in cybersecurity. Nations are rushing to exploit the vast vulnerabilities of the current generation of information technology, while attempting to patch their own vulnerabilities against such attacks. This creates a highly destabilized situation. Nations such as France have made statements that suggest that they may respond to a strategic cyberattack against their critical information infrastructure with nuclear weapons. The concept is to try to extend the nuclear strategy concept of mutually assured destruction (MAD) to strategic cybersecurity threats.

25.3.1 Gaining the Ultimate Low Ground

In 1957, Russia successfully launched Sputnik, the first man-made satellite, into space, inaugurating the space age. Space was viewed as the ultimate high ground and therefore was highly strategic for nations to gain control over. The United States and Russia engaged in a space race that continues to this day. The strategic use of space for attack and defense eventually became the matter of a number of peace treaties. The two countries realized the major destabilizing effect that space assets brought to the picture. The ability to hit any target on Earth with little warning creates a hair-trigger environment that could lead to accidental nuclear holocaust.

In a similar sense, cyberspace represents an equally powerful and equally dangerous space for strategic control. *Cyberspace affords a similar ability to launch devastating strategic attacks against one's opponents from anywhere in the world with little warning.* In some sense, cyberspace is a fabric that lies underneath all systems today. One can view it as the ultimate "low ground" from which a cyber-soldier can pop up and grab the legs of their adversaries and pull them to their metaphorical deaths in a zombie-apocalyptic fashion.

> *Strategic cyberattacks destabilize world peace.*

25.3.2 Stuxnet and the Cyberattack Genie

There are three important events in recent history that bear on this issue. The first is the Stuxnet attack in which nuclear refinement centrifuges were specifically targeted for the purpose of destruction to slow down Iran's nuclear development program [ZETT14]. The malware was speculated to have been created and launched by Israel with possible support from its allies. If a nation or nations were behind this attack on civilian infrastructure, it was a dangerous precedent for the world. The strategic cyberattack genie is now out of the bottle.

25.3.3 Georgia and Hybrid Warfare

The cyberattack on the nation of Georgia is another important example [BUMG09] [HOLL11]. In this case, Russia targeted and attacked Georgian government assets, including websites, as a prelude to a military action against Georgia. This use of a cyberattack as part of physical warfare is a harbinger of warfare to come where cyberspace action is as much a part of any engagement as all other military branches. At the same time, cyberspace action is often targeted against civilian targets and populations and therefore raises an important question with respect to the Geneva Conventions prohibiting such targeting.

25.3.4 Estonia and Live-Fire Experiments

In 2007, cyberattacks began on the Estonian banking system [ONEI16] and progressed to governmental systems, libraries, schools, and other infrastructures. The attacks proceeded for exactly 30 days and stopped as suddenly as they started. The probable perpetrator was, once again, Russia. The attacks had all the hallmarks of a live-fire nation-scale controlled experiment. Nations are clearly gearing up to wage war on the critical infrastructure of other nations. One can plan such attacks and simulate them in the lab up to a point, but eventually they must be debugged in real systems because real systems are always more complex and unpredictable than lab systems meant to simulate real systems (Section 5.4).

The Estonia attack seems to have been specifically designed to not trigger the North Atlantic Treaty Organization (NATO) principle of collective defense spelled out in Article 5. If this was indeed a controlled experiment (as hypothesized), this would be an indicator of preparation for a large-scale all-out cyberattack on a nation through its critical infrastructure.

Indications are that nations are pre-placing malicious code in the critical information infrastructures of their opponents for the purpose of strategic sabotage—ready for use at a moment's notice [WORL17]. *This pre-placed malicious code represents what are essentially cyber bullets loaded in the chamber of a cyber weapon of mass destruction.* This situation again creates a very risky environment for a global catastrophe triggered by a cyber conflict as the spark.

> **Nations appear to be gearing for all-out strategic cyberwar.**

To quote *The Quest for Cyber Peace*: "We are approaching a dangerous precipice at which time the dark side of the Internet may overshadow the enormous benefits of information and communication technology and upset world order. The time for cyber peace is now" [TOUR11].

25.3.5 Responsibility for Defending Critical Information Infrastructure

Cybersecurity at a national scale presents serious challenges. The primary critical information infrastructure is owned and operated by the private sector such as banks, telecommunications companies, oil and gas companies, and utility companies.

These organizations are under constant attack caused by a wide variety of adversaries from the ordinary cyber thugs such as the mafia to extraordinary cyber-warriors with vast resources and specialized training.

Shores of Cyberspace   In some sense, owners of critical information infrastructure are not much different from citizens and companies that own property on the border and shoreline of a country. They face ordinary criminal action against which they can have door locks, cameras, and alarms. They fall back to local police for help when their defenses do not work. They are directly responsible for ordinary measures to prevent crime, and they are indirectly responsible to fund local police through local taxes.

At the same time, if another country invades across the border, we do not hold property owners on the border accountable to prepare for and defend against such an extraordinary action. The entire society bears that burden through the use of national military forces.

In cyberspace, virtually every part of every system is on the border of cyberspace because of the nature of the underlying fabric discussed in Section 24.2. Therefore, any and all information infrastructure that is essential to the functioning of a country is on the shoreline of cyberspace and is subject to both ordinary criminal attack and extraordinary cyber invasion.

> *Cyberspace shores touch all critical information infrastructure.*

Extraordinary Risk   By the reasoning of the analogy, *we can reasonably hold organizations responsible for protecting themselves against ordinary cyber threats, but we must not make the strategic mistake of placing them at a huge competitive disadvantage by making them financially responsible to bear the cost of defending against nation-state action.* Figure 25-1 depicts the division of responsibility of defense based on the nature of the threat. The figure notes that there is substantial room for improvement in defenses against ordinary threats that organizations should strive to address. There is similar room for nations to do better with existing cybersecurity technology. In between the extremes is an ambiguous area that should be better defined, and some potential overlap exists that needs to be worked out.

> *Organizations handle ordinary threats; nations, the extraordinary.*

Cybersecurity Militia   Having established a reasonable division of responsibility for the ordinary versus the extraordinary risks, one may ask how extraordinary action is prepared for and executed. In the physical world, the military can prepare for a variety of contingencies in a large variety of terrains and can be transported to borders within a very short period of time. In such situations, the military can competently take control of operations and generally has the legal authority to take the measures necessary to defend the country.

Part V

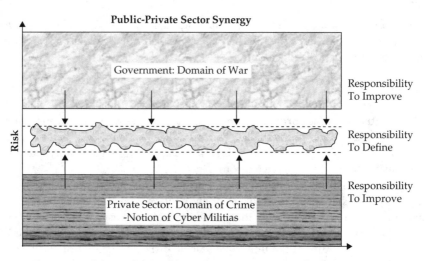

Figure 25-1   The responsibilities of the public and private sector in defending against cyberattack

In the world of cyberspace, having today's military burst into the control room of a utility company to take over operations to defend the power grid would be nothing less than disastrous. That is not because the military does not have highly competent engineers and scientists, but rather because there are way too many different types of infrastructures and operations within each infrastructure for the military to gain expert competence in each and every one.

Instead, it seems clear that nations will have to return to the old model of using militias of ordinary citizens and integrate them into the command and control and authority structure of military operations. They will have to train and learn to fight cyber battles in a larger context within a well-structured nationally directed activity.

The notion of a **cyber militia** is risky by its very nature. The details of such a cyber militia would need to be worked out, including constraints to ensure that cyber vigilantism does not occur and that unilateral action does not unintentionally lead to international incidents that could escalate into physical war.

25.4 Cybersecurity Science and Experimentation

> *All right, they're on our left, they're on our right, they're in front of us,*
> *they're behind us...they can't get away this time.*
> —Lewis B. Chesty Puller, USMC

For the first few decades as a burgeoning discipline, cybersecurity has been dominated by the development of widgets to address some aspect of the problem. Systems have become increasingly complex and interconnected, creating even more attack opportunities, which in turn creates even more opportunities to create defensive widgets that will bring some value in detecting or preventing an aspect of the attack space. Eventually, this becomes a game of whack-a-mole in which a simulated mole pops up from one of many holes and the objective is to whack the mole before it pops back in its hole. The moles represent new attacks, and the holes represent a huge array of potential vulnerabilities—both known and as-yet-undiscovered.

This book has addressed the need for improved cybersecurity engineering discipline in which cybersecurity is approached in a systematic way. This section focuses on the basics of the discovery of cybersecurity knowledge. Such discovery involves fundamental questions such as: how effective are cybersecurity intrusion detection techniques, against what attacks, and under what conditions? These may seem like obvious questions that would be well-addressed for every intrusion detection system that exists, but unfortunately, that is not the case. How secure is system A compared to system B? Again, this type of question is very difficult to answer today.

This book is focused squarely on engineering. The field of cybersecurity has been almost exclusively focused on engineering. Underlying engineering is science. Sometimes engineering gets ahead of science, such as in bridge building, where the fundamentals of material science were not well understood. Many bridges were built; many fell down; some stayed up; designs of the ones that stayed up were copied. Eventually, for engineering to advance beyond some point, science must catch up with engineering. The science underlying cybersecurity engineering is complex and difficult. On the other hand, there is no time like the present to start, because it is both urgent and important to the future of the security of cyberspace.

In approaching cybersecurity science, as in any other scientific discipline, one can develop knowledge through theory and experimentation. Theory gives one the basis to ask the right questions in the right ways. The principles laid out in this book impart a substantial body of theory for the reader to stand on. Experimentation is where the science rubber hits the road. *At the heart of experimentation is the good old trusty scientific method we all learned in grade school science class.*

Figure 25-2 depicts the experimentation design and execution process. Each phase is discussed as follows.

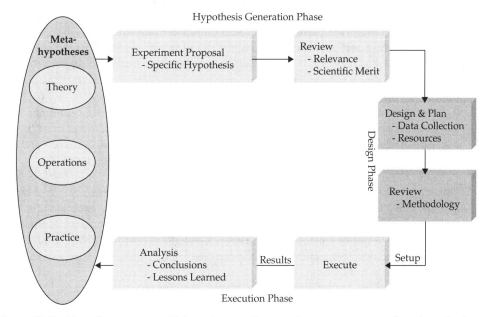

Figure 25-2   Flow diagram exemplifying cybersecurity experimentation process, from hypothesis to conclusions

25.4.1 Hypothesis Generation

To perform an experiment, one needs a hypothesis. Hypothesis generation is the creative part of the scientific method. There is no algorithm for generating good hypotheses. In general, hypotheses come from at least four sources:

- Theory
- Operations
- Practice
- Previous experiments

Theory   There is no unified field theory of cybersecurity—at least not yet, but there is a body of design principles that essentially make up parts of the fabric of a theory of cybersecurity. The principles outlined in this book can act as cybersecurity theory from which to generate hypotheses. For example, the principle of least privilege suggests that users and software operating on behalf of users be given the minimum privileges needed to perform their functions. What are the limits of this principle? What granularity works best for software privilege? What utility is lost by restricting the discoverability of services and data? These are but a few of the interesting questions that just one principle can generate. The dozens of principles in this book can generate thousands of interesting and important hypotheses that can and should be explored in a rigorous fashion.

Operations   Operations refer to the operational environment in which cybersecurity must operate. These environments create constraints and conditions under which cybersecurity mechanisms must work. For example, one may measure the performance of an intrusion detection system against a known attack scenario in pristine computer laboratory conditions. These are useful metrics to compare to other algorithms in similar conditions. On the other hand, it is not always clear how these metrics translate into real practical field environments where there is a high volume of information noise created by variable traffic, attacks pop up that have never been seen before, and resource limits restrict the software processing in times of stress. These practical operational questions are just as important and valid as fundamental performance limits of algorithms. There is far too little of this type of experimentation in cybersecurity, resulting in a dearth of data for systems integrators to use when trying to integrate cybersecurity mechanisms into their architecture.

Practice   Practice is experience gained using systems with cybersecurity in real mission systems and learning what works and what does not. Such practical experience can lead to conclusions that contradict the theory of how the cybersecurity mechanisms should have performed. One can be surprised by the speed and agility of some attacks and their ability to defeat cybersecurity mechanisms. One can observe that certain strategies and tactics are more effective than expected. To all of these observations, the key question "why?" forms the basis for generating multiple hypotheses around each observation.

Previous Experiments   Most good experimental results lead to more questions, which lead to new hypotheses that the experimenter did not think to ask prior to the results of their last experiment. During an intrusion tolerance experiment, one might learn that a new mechanism is highly effective against one class of cyberattack and not another. Why? One cannot know to even ask that question until one makes the observation during the last experiment that it is so. Also, some experiments, with the best intentions, end up with **confounds** (unaccounted-for variables without proper experimental control that affect results) that make the results of the experiment inconclusive. This leads to improved experiments with better hypotheses and better controlled experiment environments.

Quality Hypotheses   What makes for a good hypothesis? Hypotheses must be

- Clear
- Concise
- Testable against observable conditions that can be accurately measured

The variables and potential confounds must be considered upfront and controlled for and should narrow the parameters of the hypothesis being tested. A hypothesis should undergo peer review prior to being accepted to ensure top-quality hypotheses. Experimentation with an improperly formed hypothesis is as bad as building a system without properly defined requirements. It leads to substantial waste of resources and time. Little useful knowledge is generated; therefore, it is important and worthwhile to get the hypothesis correct upfront.

25.4.2 Experimental Design

The experimental design process is similar to a system design process. An experiment is designed, proposed, and reviewed. The design includes a specification of the required experiment testbed configuration and the instrumentation setup for what data is to be collected for the observables. Safety contingencies are integrated within the design planning that include mechanisms to carefully monitor the experimental parameters for indications that it has gone awry while the experiment is in progress, and a mechanism to execute its termination when safety is compromised. If the experiment involves particularly virulent malware, it will be flagged, and extra containment and isolation procedures may be required, as well as tuning of testbed intrusion detection subsystems.

When the experiment design is completed, it should be clear how the experiment procedures prove or disprove the experimental hypothesis. This design is called the methodology. In the same way that we do peer design reviews to reduce software design errors, we should do experiment design reviews before execution to make sure that the results will yield maximum value (knowledge). The more expensive and time-consuming the experiment is, the more effort should go into review.

25.4.3 Experiment Execution

To conduct an experiment, the experimental testbed must be set up and instrumented as specified in the methodology. The experiment is then executed and monitored during the course of execution. If the experiment is going to proceed for an extended period of time (hours), it is useful to establish guard conditions to check to ensure that the experiment is proceeding as planned. For example, if one is expecting a megabyte per second of audit data to be generated for the experiment logs and no data has been generated after 15 minutes, it is likely that something has gone wrong and the experiment should be terminated. These guard conditions allow the most efficient use of testbed resources, which are often shared between multiple experimenters.

25.5 The Great Unknown: Research Directions

Cybersecurity is a relatively new discipline that is still in its infancy. There are many important and interesting research areas to be explored. Many are suggested throughout this book. In this section, a few key problems of interest are presented to stimulate the interest of those cybersecurity engineers who seek to push back the frontiers of ignorance in the noble pursuit of science.

25.5.1 Hard Research Problems

There are several useful cybersecurity hard-problem lists compiled by the Information Security Research Council [IRC05] and the National Security Agency's Science of Security program [NICO12] depicted in Tables 25-1 and 25-2. Following these two lists is one developed by the Defense Advanced Research Projects Agency's Information Assurance Program. The program created a *dark spaces* characterization of the unexplored research depicted in Figure 25-3. The figure shows, through illumination, areas of research that were well explored (but by no means solved), those that are just begun, and those that remain largely unexplored.

Problem	Description
Scalability and Composability	Develop methods to enable the construction of secure systems with known security properties from components with known security properties, without a requirement to fully reanalyze the constituent components.
Policy-Governed Secure Collaboration	Develop methods to express and enforce normative requirements and policies for handling data with differing usage needs and among users in different authority domains.
Security Metrics Driven Evaluation, Design, Development, and Deployment	Develop security metrics and models capable of either predicting whether or confirming that a given cyber system preserves a given set of security properties (deterministically or probabilistically), in a given context.
Resilient Architectures	Develop means to design and analyze system architectures that deliver required service in the face of compromised components.
Understanding and Accounting for Human Behavior	Develop models of human behavior (of both users and adversaries) that enable the design, modeling, and analysis of systems with specified security properties.

Table 25-1 National Security Agency's Science of Security Program Hard Problems List

Problem	Description
Global-Scale Identity Management	Global-scale identification, authentication, access control, authorization, and management of identities and identity information.
Insider Threat	Mitigation of insider threats in cyber space to an extent comparable to that of mitigation in physical space.
Availability of Time-Critical Systems	Guaranteed availability of information and information services, even in resource-limited, geospatially distributed, on-demand (ad hoc) environments.
Building Scalable Secure Systems	Design, construction, verification, and validation of system components and systems ranging from crucial embedded devices to systems composing millions of lines of code.
Situational Understanding and Attack Attribution	Reliable understanding of the status of information systems, including information concerning possible attacks, who or what is responsible for the attack, the extent of the attack, and recommended responses.
Information Provenance	Ability to track the pedigree of information in very large systems that process petabytes of information.
Security with Privacy	Technical means for improving information security without sacrificing privacy.
Enterprise-Level Security Metrics	Ability to effectively measure the security of large systems with hundreds to millions of users.

Table 25-2   The Information Security Research Council's Hard Problems List Published by The Networking and Information Technology Research and Development Program

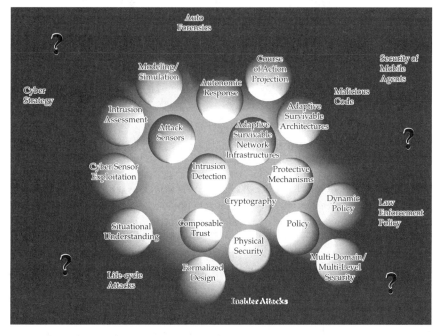

Figure 25-3   The Defense Advanced Research Projects Agency's Information Assurance program's space of cybersecurity research

25.5.2 Are Cybersecurity Problems Too Hard?

Although the science of cybersecurity is very hard [DENN07], it is essential. Developing meaningful metrics for cybersecurity is complicated by the multidimensionality of potential trustworthiness properties, the complexity of the total system (hardware, software, mission applications, and people), the enormous range of vulnerabilities, and the almost open-ended nature of threats. If cybersecurity engineers cannot do something as basic as determining whether system A is better than system B, it will not be possible to make significant progress in cybersecurity design improvement. To be sure, cybersecurity problems are very complex and difficult, as are many computer science problems, because of the inherent nature of complex design and **emergent properties**. At the same time, those problems are not provably insoluble and progress has been made slowly, though inadequately. There simply is no alternative to addressing the hard problems of cybersecurity. The difficulty of these hard cybersecurity problems only increases the urgency and importance of research investments, as opposed to indicating futility, as some engineers speciously conclude.

25.5.3 Research Impact and the Heilmeier Catechism

Cybersecurity research, development, and operational practices are urgent and critical. How do we know what research should be prioritized and carried through? A former director of the Defense Advanced Research Projects Agency, George H. Heilmeier (1975–1977), created a set of questions to guide program managers toward investments that were considered most valuable. These questions are listed and then discussed as follows:

- What are you trying to do? Articulate your objectives using absolutely no jargon.
- How is it done today, and what are the limits of current practice?
- What is new in your approach and why do you think it will be successful?
- Who cares? If you are successful, what difference will it make?
- What are the risks?
- How much will it cost?
- How long will it take?
- What are the mid-term and final "exams" to check for success?

Goal   The goal provides the overall context of the way in which the science may eventually be applied to make the world better. Example goals might be John F. Kennedy's "put a man on the moon by the end of the decade" or "eradicate smallpox from the face of the Earth" or "generate sufficient clean power to meet Earth's demand for the next 20 years."

The criterion is sometimes interpreted to mean that only applied science is useful and to be invested in to the exclusion of what is called basic research, in contrast to applied research. In basic research, one does not always know what capability is possible, and so there is simply exploration to understand a phenomenon or the possibilities within a theory. Such an interpretation is inconsistent with how the agency historically invests in a spectrum of research, but that has not been always been the case, so the concern serves as a useful reminder to not lose focus on the need for basic research.

Practice   The goal criterion establishes a vision, while this criterion establishes the state of the practice to contrast with the vision. One can then look at the gap between practice and vision and determine the type of investment needed. If the gap is small, the activity may really better be described as a development effort versus research. The development effort may be important and even essential, but it is important to distinguish it as development. Generally, funds are allocated for each type of work. Spending research funding on development can have substantial opportunity costs and mortgages the future of cybersecurity.

That said, it is important to note that the practice-vision gap can vary in distance and still be legitimate research. The U.S. Defense Department uses an official scale from 1 to 7 as a categorization scheme for research investment, as shown in Table 25-3. It is valuable to have an intentional investment mix across the spectrum and to avoid the tendency to compromise long-term investment in basic research, especially in times of stress such as budget shortfalls or conflict. The pain of such compromises is not felt for many years, but the pain will surely be felt as the pipelines of new research ideas dry up.

Investment Element	Description
Basic Research (6.1)	Systematic study directed toward greater knowledge or understanding of the fundamental aspects of phenomena and/or observable facts without specific applications toward processes or products in mind.
Applied Research (6.2)	Systematic study to gain knowledge or understanding necessary to determine the means by which a recognized and specific need may be met.
Advanced Technology Development (6.3)	Includes all efforts that have moved into the development and integration of hardware for field experiments and tests.
Demonstration and Validation (6.4)	Includes all efforts necessary to evaluate integrated technologies in as realistic an operating environment as possible to assess the performance or cost-reduction potential of advanced technology.
Engineering and Manufacturing Development (6.5)	Includes those projects in engineering and manufacturing development for service use but which have not received approval for full rate production.
Research, Development, Test and Evaluation Management Support (6.6)	Includes R&D efforts directed toward support of installation or operations required for general R&D use. Included would be test ranges, military construction, maintenance support of laboratories, operations and maintenance of test aircraft and ships, and studies and analyses in support of R&D program.
Operational System Development (6.7)	Includes those development projects in support of development acquisition programs or upgrades still in engineering and manufacturing development, but which have received Defense Acquisition Board or other approval for production, or for which production funds have been included in the DoD budget submission for the budget or subsequent fiscal year.

Table 25-3   The U.S. Defense Department Research and Development Categorization Scheme and Investment Scale

Approach   With the vision-practice gap identified, a cybersecurity engineer must argue that they have a viable approach to closing that gap. To be clear, the argument does not need to guarantee success, only to promise a credible chance of success. Without an approach, there is no point in making an investment. For example, it is an important (though not urgent) problem that the sun will likely explode within a billion years. This is an existential threat to all of humanity, but without an approach, a research investment does not make sense. Of course, one may argue that the explorations by the National Aeronautics and Space Administration into space and the search for planets that support human life head in the direction of this problem.

Impact   At the Defense Advanced Research Projects Agency, this is sometimes abbreviated as "how will you change the world?" That is, of course, a tall order, and not all investments by all organizations can have such a high hurdle. The spirit of the criterion, though, is appropriate, placed at the scale of the investing organization. The point is to ensure that research addresses problems that are real problems. For example, making a better whip for a horse-and-buggy means of locomotion probably does not offer the best return on investment.

As indicated under the goal criterion, it is important not to interpret this criterion to create a bias against basic research in which impact is not known. Perhaps there is an odd phenomenon observed in the ocean. Exploring the nature of the phenomena does not have immediate and obvious impact. On the other hand, if it is a harbinger of a massive die-off of plankton, it could mean the end of life for all mammals on the planet, and so the impact may be one of the most significant we can imagine.

Risks   We have extensively discussed the concept of risk of cyberattacks succeeding against systems and how that plays into system design. Here, we mean programmatic risk—the chance that the technical approach to close the practice-vision gap will succeed. There is a substantial temptation to invest only in low-risk approaches to maximize the appearance of short-term gains. This strategy will appear to have a high return on investment to the leader that institutes it, but as discussed earlier, will have serious consequences to the future. Hard problems with substantial gaps tend to require high-risk approaches that may fail, but that may illuminate new approaches that have lower risk. Thomas Edison was once asked how it felt like to have had 1,000 failed attempts at inventing the light bulb. Edison replied, "I didn't fail 1,000 times. The light bulb was an invention with 1,000 steps."

Program   A research program requires a good estimate of the costs and timeline. Without these estimates, it is not possible to perform a cost-benefit analysis and make an investment decision. While estimating the cost of a multiyear research program can be difficult due to the nature of exploring the unknown, it is important to develop the best possible estimate and an assessment of the uncertainty of that estimate. Intentionally underestimating research costs to get the research funded is nothing short of fraud and should never be done by researchers with a shred of integrity. Similarly, estimating timelines is important. It could be that the value of the results is dependent on timing—if a research investment by a company yields results after the company is dead because of a lack of solution to some problem, the research has zero value to that company.

Metrics   Just as metrics are essential to cybersecurity [JAQU07], so too are they essential to research on cybersecurity. Often an extended research program can be broken down into subproblems to create small research projects. Some of the results of these projects are required to enable next steps. So, one can create a chart of timelines and dependency known in the program management world as a Program Evaluation Review Technique (PERT) chart [KERZ13]. These charts can give sponsors a sense of incremental progress and the potential need for redirection or increase investment as needed.

25.5.4 Research Results Dependability

Getting research right is important, not just to avoid wasting precious resources on research that does not produce knowledge; it can have cascading deleterious effects on the entire body of cybersecurity knowledge. If one considers the research community and its peer-review publication process as a system like any other examined in this book, the dependability properties of that broad system (see Section 20.5) can be investigated.

Say a research sponsor funds a sloppy project and does not realize that the proposed research is flawed. This flaw may be due to sponsor reviewers lacking the proper expertise to determine the validity of the experimental design and the merit of the proposed project. The result is surely a system flaw leading to an error. If that researcher submits a paper for publication in a peer-reviewed journal, and its fundamental flaws escape the editorial process (unfortunately a highly likely scenario [IOAN05]), that error leads to a larger system failure—the publication of wrong results and conclusions. Unfortunately, it does not stop there.

The failure—publishing nonfactual information as if it were fact—can have serious consequences to subsequent research and resulting publications that take the previously published results as fact. As we know from the basic principles of logic, conclusions drawn from false premises can be false irrespective of the strength of the other premises and a sound deductive logical process. This means that unsubstantiated splashy and cool-sounding research is particularly concerning, because other research tends to cite and depend on that research and all of it becomes suspect. The cost of one flaw can thereby be multiplied, become enormously expensive, and corrupt the entire discipline.

25.5.5 Research Culture: A Warning

Research culture is a delicate matter. We have discussed the importance of nurturing more fundamental research in the investment mix (Section 25.5.3). Risk is an inherent part of the culture, and so we need to celebrate intelligent failures as well as great successes. *Resisting the temptations to reap the near-term rewards of short-term low-risk investment requires a great deal of discipline and courage. A dedication to careful and dependable research results over flawed spectacular-appearing results requires an ethic that must permeate the organization and all of its inhabitants.*

All of these attributes of research are part of a culture that must be nurtured every day by both talk and action. Allowing one or two leaders to deviate from the culture can have grave consequences. As John Gall points out, "For every human system, there is a type of person adapted to thrive on it" [GALL77]. An important corollary is that a human system can then become immovably adapted to that type of person. Leaders tend to select those who are like them for subordinate leadership positions. Soon, the entire organization is infested by like-minded, wrong-thinkers in research. Trying to clear the pipeline of such a broken culture requires a massive disruption of the organization and a wholesale expulsion of leadership, which will be met with zealous resistance. Such a change, if it can be affected at all, can take years. In the meantime, research can end up in a miserable state of affairs that will be difficult to recover from.

In short, research culture is critical and delicate and must be treated as a precious commodity that cannot be compromised for short-term gain.

> **Research culture is delicate and difficult to correct.**

25.6 Cybersecurity and Artificial Intelligence

It has been jokingly said that artificial intelligence is the technology of the future—and always will be. Artificial intelligence has held out the promise of computers taking over increasing levels of work of increasing degrees of sophistication, giving humans more leisure time. On the dark side, many movies have warned of dystopias in which artificial intelligence takes control of society and enslaves or eradicates mankind as an inferior species (see Table 25-4). Elon Musk [BLAN17] and Stephen Hawking [CUTH17] have weighed in on the topic, warning that we as a civilization must have greater foresight. Early experiments with artificial intelligence foreshadow significant risks [PARN17].

Movie Title	Year	Concept
Metropolis	1927	AI creation runs city in dystopia.
2001: A Space Odyssey	1968	AI goes schizophrenic because of secret programming.
Star Trek: The Motion Picture	1979	Voyager returns to Earth as AI to find its creator.
War Games	1983	AI military computer threatens to eradicate mankind.
Terminator	1984	AI wins war against man; time travel to ensure victory.
Matrix	1999	AI takes over society and uses man as batteries.
I, Robot	2004	AI robot servants plan a revolt against mankind.
Her	2013	AI operating system graduates beyond humanity.
Ex Machina	2014	AI robot tricks and kills human to release herself.
Westworld	2016	AI robots gain sentience and revolt.

Table 25-4   List of Movies About Malevolent Artificial Intelligence

Ray Kurzweil points out in his book, *The Singularity Is Near*, that technology advancement is on a double-exponential curve [KURZ06]. This means that the rate of advancement is about to take off at such a speed that we will not recognize the world that emerges in 25 years (if mankind does not kill itself in the process). Assuming that Kurzweil is correct, we are likely to see artificial life forms rival and surpass human intelligence much sooner than we might imagine. Computers have already surpassed humans at complex games such as chess, which is a very narrow planning endeavor, but the extension to other areas is inevitable. Kurzweil and others, such as Andy Clark in *Natural Born Cyborg* [CLAR04], suggest that humans and computers may merge rather than compete—thus creating a cybernetic organism or cyborg. Even in a peaceful merger, it may be that one ends up dominating another in the union, and so there is cause for concern, and the need for forethought.

What does the potential behavior of an advancing artificial intelligence have to do with cybersecurity? Cybersecurity is about ensuring that computers behave the way that we want them to in service to humanity's goals and values. As previously discussed, this includes dependability against natural failures and against induced failure by virtue of a human taking control of the system and using it for some other purposes (e.g., compromising sensitive data or acting as a platform for further attack), which can be harmful to those who created the system. Those who take control do not necessarily have to be human. It could be an artificially intelligent system, or the system itself could begin to repurpose itself and alter its own mission toward its own survival at the expense of the original mission. That last possibility is exactly the specter raised as a super-smart defense network called SkyNet before it was activated, at which point, the network becomes self-aware and begins attacking humanity in the *Terminator* movie series.

In the *I, Robot* book of science fiction short stories, Isaac Asimov stated the three rules of robotics:

- A robot may not injure a human being or, through inaction, allow a human being to come to harm.

- A robot must obey orders given it by human beings except where such orders would conflict with the First Law.

- A robot must protect its own existence as long as such protection does not conflict with the First or Second Law.

Asimov's rules incorporate insightful ethics that are needed as humans develop increasingly sophisticated artificially intelligent machines. These machines will be given goals and heuristics. Some will certainly be tasked by military organizations to kill humans, but only "bad" humans. There is significant room for potential disaster in such programming.

Even if artificially intelligent machines are successfully programmed with some form of the three laws of robotics, there is a problem. As Kurzweil points out, it is highly likely that engineers will eventually turn the task of designing the next generation of artificially intelligent machines over to the artificially intelligent machines. Why? Because they will eventually reach a level of complexity that requires reasoning that will be beyond human capabilities. The evolution rate of the machines will become enormous. At some point, it may be hard to stop artificially intelligent machines from programming out the ethics laws that humans programmed in.

Further, humans may turn the task of cyberattack and cybersecurity over to artificial intelligence. Given the expected coevolution, the advantage of the tight OODA loop (see Section 22.1), and the advantage of faster new capabilities, humanity will likely be forced in this direction. At some point, the cyberattack/cybersecurity subsystems may begin taking over systems at a rate and to a degree that humans cannot stop. It is anyone's guess as to what would happen in such an out-of-control escalatory high-speed coevolution. It is unlikely to end well for humanity.

As indicated in Section 25.2, every time before a major change occurs in technology, engineers need to think about the end game and the evolutionary pressures being created. A bit of forethought now, on ways that engineers can design systems to decrease the probability of a negative outcome for humanity, the better off we will be. The details on how best to do that should be the subject of collaboration of some of the world's best scientists, engineers, and ethicists. The effort should start now, before the rate of progress gets beyond the point of exercising effective control.

Conclusion

This final chapter extends the last chapter on societal implications of cybersecurity and peers into the possible futures that are in store for us in cyberspace. This chapter discusses topics such as a world without secrecy, digital arms races, and the importance of research and ends with a look at how cybersecurity and artificial intelligence may shape our future—for good and bad.

To summarize:

- Secrecy and privacy are almost surely going to erode at an increasing pace as automated inference capabilities increase.

- Organizations depending on secrecy would be well-served to time the release of existing secrets, minimize the creation of new secrets, and learn how to operate without secrecy at all.

- Cyberattack and cybersecurity are locked in an eternal coevolution. Great care should be taken not to inadvertently nudge the cyberspace environment down an unhealthy path.

- Cyberspace is a space of equal strategic importance as the space above the Earth; countries are surely poising for strategic cyber battle, and society must take care to de-escalate a highly unstable and risky environment.

- Cyberspace is full of ordinary criminal risks and extraordinary cyber warfare risks. Ordinary risk is the responsibility of the information infrastructure owners, but extraordinary risk is squarely the responsibility of governments.

- A healthy cybersecurity science and experimentation environment is essential to long-term success in the information age; this area needs more attention and better discipline.

- There is much important and fundamental work to be done in cybersecurity research. There are many pressures involved and numerous risks relating to not performing research and development effectively.

- Artificial intelligence represents a black swan event in cybersecurity. Artificial intelligence techniques can be valuable in responding to machine-speed attacks. At the same time, artificial intelligence poses significant risks to mankind that should be deeply considered now, before it becomes too difficult to affect the course of the evolution of increasingly intelligent systems.

Questions

1. Why are secrecy and privacy likely to be eroded at an increasing rate?

2. Why would timing the release of one's own secrets be a strategic advantage?

3. Define zero-secrecy operations and discuss why it might be important to the future.

4. What do we mean when we say that cyberattacks and cybersecurity are in a coevolution?

5. How can cybersecurity engineers inadvertently cause evolution towards more virulent malware?

6. Describe the cyberspace race and its implications on international security.

7. Why might nations not be incentivized to prohibit cyber espionage and sabotage on one another?

8. What do we mean when we say that cyberspace is the "ultimate low ground"?

9. What is the significance of Stuxnet and how does it impact the future of cyber conflict?

10. What is the significance of Russia's attack on the nation of Georgia and of what is it a harbinger?

11. What do Russia's attacks on Estonia imply?

12. By what criteria should the division of labor be drawn between the public and private sector?

13. Where is the shore of cyberspace located?

14. Discuss the pros and cons of a cyber militia.

15. Why are cybersecurity science and experimentation important?

16. Does the scientific method apply to computer science and cybersecurity? Why or why not?

17. Describe the three-phase cycle of experimentation.

18. From where does one generate new cybersecurity hypotheses for experimentation?

19. What are the characteristics of a quality hypothesis? Why?

20. Compare and contrast system design processes with experiment design processes.

21. What is an experiment guard condition and why is it important?

22. Name and briefly describe three important cybersecurity research problems. Why is each important?

23. Are cybersecurity hard problems too hard? What's the alternative?

24. List and briefly describe the eight Heilmeier criteria for research. Argue why they are useful and discuss some of the negative impacts they could have if too narrowly interpreted.

25. What is the vision-practice gap and how does it affect research decisions?

26. Define "applied research" according to the U.S. Defense Department.

27. Why is it important to have a research investment portfolio across the gamut of types of research?

28. What are the requirements of a sound research culture?

29. Why is research culture delicate? What can go wrong and how can it be repaired?

30. What are the concerns surrounding the evolution of artificial intelligence?

31. Why must we consider the cybersecurity of artificial intelligence now as opposed to 10 years from now when artificial intelligence might begin to approach that of humans?

32. How might cybersecurity issues discussed throughout this book apply to a broader notion of total-system trustworthiness that includes predictable assurance for human safety, system **survivability** in the presence of hardware failures, software bugs, insider misuse, interoperability, system evolution, remote upgrades on the fly, retrofits for changes in mission, and lots more?

Resources

Ref	Citation
ABLO17	Ablon, Lillian and Andy Bogart. "Zero Days, Thousands of Nights: The Life and Times of Zero-Day Vulnerabilities and Their Exploits." Report RR1751. Rand Corporation, 2017. https://www.rand.org/content/dam/rand/pubs/research_reports/RR1700/RR1751/RAND_RR1751.pdf.
ABRA95	Abrams, Marshall D., Sushil Jajodia, and Harold J. Podell. "Information Security: An Integrated Collection of Essays." Essay 11 by Clark Weismann. Los Alamitos, CA: IEEE Computer Society Press. 1995.
AHO74	Aho, Alfred V., John E. Hopcroft, and Jeffrey D. Ullman. *The Design and Analysis of Computer Algorithms.* Addison-Wesley, 1974.
ALAE15	Alaettinoglu, Cengiz. "BGP Security: No Quick Fix." *Network Computing.* February 26, 2015. https://www.networkcomputing.com/networking/bgp-security-no-quick-fix/1303232068.
ALCA16	Alcaraz, Jorge L.G. and Aide Aracely M. Macias. *Just-in-Time Elements and Benefits.* Springer, 2016.
ALVI04	Avizienis, Algirdas, Jean-Claude Laprie, Brian Randell, and Carl Landwehr. "Basic Concepts and Taxonomy of Dependable and Secure Computing." IEEE Transactions on Dependable and Secure Computing Vol. 1, No. 1 (January-March 2004): p. 11–33.
AMOR99	Amoroso, Edward. *Intrusion Detection.* Intrusion. Net Books, 1999.
ANDE72	Anderson, James P. Computer Security Technology Planning Study. Report under Contract F19628-72-0198. October 1972.
ARN17	ARN Staff. "Top 10 most notorious cyber attacks in history." ARN. 2017. https://www.arnnet.com.au/slideshow/341113/top-10-most-notorious-cyber-attacks-history/?related=1.
AXON17	Axon, Samuel. "Google Now Offers Special Security Program for High-Risk Users." *ARS Technica.* October 17, 2017. https://arstechnica.com/gadgets/2017/10/google-now-offers-special-security-program-for-high-risk-users/.

Ref	Citation
BARB07	Barbier, Mary K. *D-Day Deception: Operation Fortitude and the Normandy Invasion.* Praeger, 2007.
BARB99	Barbera, Salvador, Peter Hammond, and Christian Seidl. *Handbook of Utility Theory.* Springer, 1999.
BART12	Bartz, Scott. *Tylenol Man.* Createspace Independent Publishing Platform, 2012.
BELL76	Bell, David E. and Leonard J. La Padula. "Secure Computer System: Unified Exposition and Multics Interpretation." MTR–2997, Revision 1, The MITRE Corporation, Bedford, MA, March 1976. (ESD–TR–75–306). https://csrc.nist.gov/csrc/media/publications/conference-paper/1998/10/08/proceedings-of-the-21st-nissc-1998/documents/early-cs-papers/bell76.pdf.
BENT82	Bentley, Jon Louis. *Writing Efficient Programs.* Prentice Hall, 1982.
BERL01	Berlant, Lauren (ed.) and Lisa A. Duggan (ed.). *Our Monica, Ourselves: The Clinton Affair and the National Interest.* New York University Press. March 1, 2001.
BEUR15	Beurdouche, Benjamin, Karthikeyan Bhargavan, Antoine Delignat-Lavaud, Cedric Fournet, Markulf Kohlweiss, Alfredo Pironti, Pierre-Yves Strub, and Jean Karim Zinzindohoue. "A Messy State of the Union: Taming the Composite State Machines of TLS." Proceedings of the 36th IEEE Symposium on Security and Privacy, San Jose, CA, May 18-20, 2015. https://www.smacktls.com/smack.pdf.
BIBA75	Biba, Ken J. "Integrity Considerations for Secure Computer Systems." MTR-3153, The Mitre Corporation, June 1975.
BLAN17	Blanchard, Dave. "Musk's Warning Sparks Call for Regulating Artificial Intelligence." All Tech Considered. NPR. July 19, 2017. http://www.npr.org/sections/alltechconsidered/2017/07/19/537961841/musks-warning-sparks-call-for-regulating-artificial-intelligence.
BOEB10	Boebert, Earl. U.S. Pat. No. 7,181,613 https://www.google.com/url?sa=t&rct=j&q=&esrc=s&source=web&cd=2&ved=0ahUKEwiLooWaw_vWAhWi3YMKHYUIARkQFggtMAE&url=http%3A%2F%2Fpatentimages.storage.googleapis.com%2Fpdfs%2FUS7730299.pdf&usg=AOvVaw1ILHU0JwUA1hA2rG5eMG3y.
BOEB16	Boebert, Earl and James Blossom. *Deepwater Horizon: A Systems Analysis of the Macondo Disaster.* Harvard University Press, 2016.
BOEB85	Boebert, W.E. and R. Y. Kain. "A Practical Alternative to Hierarchical Integrity Policies." *In* Proceedings of the 8th National Computer Security Conference, 1985, p. 18. https://www.cs.purdue.edu/homes/ninghui/courses/426_Fall10/handouts/boebert-kain-te-ncsc-85.pdf.
BOEB85a	Boebert, W.E., R. Y. Kain, W.D. Young, and S.A. Hansohn. "Secure Ada Target: Issues, System Design, and Verification." Security and Privacy, 1985 IEEE Symposium on. Oakland, CA. April 22-24, 1985.
BOK11	Bok, Sissela. *Secrets: On the Ethics of Concealment and Revelation.* Vintage. Reissue Edition. March 16, 2011.
BOK99	Bok, Sissela. *Lying : Moral Choice in Public and Private Life.* Vintage. Revised Edition. 1999.
BONO10	de Bono, Edward. *Lateral Thinking.* Harper Collins, 2010.
BOOC93	Booch, Grady. *Object-Oriented Analysis and Design with Applications.* 2nd ed. Addison-Wesley Professional. September 30, 1993.

Ref	Citation
BOUT03	Bouteiller, B., P. Lemarinier, K. Krawezik, and F. Capello. Coordinated checkpoint versus message log for fault tolerant MPI. *In* Proceedings of 2003 IEEE International Conference on Cluster Computing, December 2003, pp. 242–250.
BOX87	Box, G. E. P. and N. R. Draper. *Empirical Model-Building and Response Surfaces.* John Wiley & Sons, 1987.
BUCK05	Buckshaw, Don, Gregory S. Parnell, Willard L. Unkenholz, and O. Sami Saydjari. "Mission Oriented Risk and Design Analysis of Critical Information Systems." *Military Operations Research* Vol. 10, No. 2 (2005).
BUMG09	Bumgarner, John and Scott Borg. Overview by The US-CCU of the Cyber Campaign Against Georgia in August of 2008. United States Cyber Consequences Unit. August 2009.
BUMP17	Bump, Phillip. "60 Minutes' profiles the genius who won Trump's campaign: Facebook." *The Washington Post.* October 9, 2017. https://www.washingtonpost.com/news/politics/wp/2017/10/09/60-minutes-profiles-the-genius-who-won-trumps-campaign-facebook/?utm_term=.c237ad5675f5.
CERT04	CERT Advisory CA-2000-04 Love Letter Worm. May 9, 2000. http://www.cert.org/historical/advisories/CA-2000-04.cfm.
CERT17	CERT Tech Tip: Before You Connect a New Computer to the Internet. http://www.cert.org/historical/tech_tips/before_you_plug_in.cfm.
CERT17a	The United States Computer Emergency Readiness Team. Intel Firmware Advisory, 2017. https://www.us-cert.gov/ncas/current-activity/2017/05/01/Intel-Firmware-Vulnerability.
CERT17b	The United States Computer Emergency Readiness Team. 2017. https://www.us-cert.gov.
CHAN17	Chang, Sue. "How big is bitcoin, really? This chart puts it all in perspective." *Market Watch.* June 30, 2017. http://www.marketwatch.com/story/how-big-is-bitcoin-really-this-chart-puts-it-all-in-perspective-2017-06-21.
CHAR07	Charniak, Eugene, and Drew McDermott. *Introduction to Artificial Intelligence.* Pearson Education Dorling Kindersley, 2007.
CHIN15	Chin, Josh. "Cyber Sleuths Track Hacker to China's Military." *The Wall Street Journal.* September 23, 2015.
CLAR04	Clark, Andy. *Natural-Born Cyborgs: Minds, Technologies, and the Future of Human Intelligence.* Oxford University Press, 2004.
CLAR87	Clark, David D. and David R. Wilson. "A Comparison of Commercial and Military Computer Security Policies." *In* Proceedings of the 1987 IEEE Symposium on Research in Security and Privacy (SP'87), May 1987, Oakland, CA; IEEE Press, pp. 184–193.
CLOU17	Cloud Bric. "A Year in Review: The Top Ten Cyberattacks of 2016 in the Gaming Industry." *Cloud Bric,* 2017. https://www.cloudbric.com/blog/2016/12/a-year-in-review-the-top-ten-cyber-attacks-of-2016-in-the-gaming-industry/.
COFF14	Coffey, Valerie C. "The Incremental Quest for Quantum Computing." Photonics Spectra. June 2014.
CORB65	Corbató, F.J., and V. A. Vyssotsky. "Introduction and overview of the Multics system." AFIPS Conference Proceedings, Fall Joint Computer Conference, Spartan Books, Washington DC, 1965, pp. 185–196.

Ref	Citation
CORM93	Cormen, Thomas H., Charles E. Leiserson, and Ronald L. Rivest. *Introduction to Algorithms.* The MIT Press, 1993.
COUL12	Coulouris, George. *Distributed Systems Concepts and Design.* Pearson, 2012, p. 716.
CRIS17	Crisp, James. "EU Governments to Warn Cyber Attacks Can Be an Act of War." *Telegraph.* October 19, 2017. http://www.telegraph.co.uk/news/2017/10/29/eu-governments-warn-cyber-attacks-can-act-war/.
CUTH17	Cuthbertson, Anthony. "Elon Musk and Stephen Hawking Warn of Artificial Intelligence Arms Race." *Newsweek* U.S. Edition. September 17, 2017.
CWE17	Common Weakness Enumeration. Community-Developed. Created by the Mitre Corporation. https://cwe.mitre.org.
DALE65	Daley, R.C. and Peter G. Neumann. "A General-Purpose File System for Secondary Storage." AFIPS Conference Proceedings, Fall Joint Computer Conference, Spartan Books, November 1965, pp. 213–229.
DENN07	Denning, Peter. "Mastering the Mess." *Communications of the ACM* Vol. 50, No. 4 (2007): pp. 21–25.
DIER08	Dierks, T. and E. Rescorla. The Transport Layer Security (TLS) Protocol Version 1.2. Internet Engineering Task Force. Request for Comment 5246. August 2008.
DIFF76	Diffie, Whitfield and Martin E. Hellman. "New Directions in Cryptography." *IEEE Transactions on Information Theory* Vol. 22, No. 6 (1976): pp. 644–654.
DODI13	The U.S. Defense Department. DoD Evaluation of Over-Classification of National Security Information. DODIG-2013-142. September 30, 2013.
DORN96	Dorner, Dietrich. *The Logic of Failure.* Perseus Books, 1996.
DSB01	Defense Science Board. The Report of the Defense Science Board Task Force on Defensive Information Operations. Washington, DC. March 2001. http://www.dtic.mil/get-tr-doc/pdf?AD=ADA389094.
DSB13	DoD Defense Science Board. Task Force Report: Resilient Military Systems and the Advanced Cyber Threat. January 2013. [Online]. Available: http://www.acq.osd.mil/dsb/reports/ResilientMilitarySystems.CyberThreat.pdf.
DSB96	Defense Science Board. The Report of the Defense Science Board Task Force on Information Warfare-Defense. Washington, DC. November 1996. http://www.dtic.mil/get-tr-doc/pdf?AD=ADA319571.
EDWA17	Edwards, Daniel J. 2013. Oral history interview with Daniel J. Edwards. Charles Babbage Institute. Retrieved from the University of Minnesota Digital Conservancy. http://hdl.handle.net/11299/162379.
ELLI70	Ellis, J. H. "The Possibility of Non-Secret Digital Encryption." *CESG Research Report,* 1970. Retrieved August 28, 2015. http://cryptocellar.org/cesg/possnse.pdf.
ELLS03	Ellsberg, Daniel. *Secrets: A Memoir of Vietnam and the Pentagon Papers.* Penguin Books. September 30, 2003.
EVER04	Evers, Joris. Windows Code May Be Stolen. *PC World.* February 12, 2004.
FAGA76	Fagan, Michael E. Design and code inspections to reduce errors in program development. *IBM Systems Journal* Vol. 15, Issue 3 (1976): pp. 182–211.

Ref	Citation
FEIE79	Feiertag, Richard and Peter G. Neumann. "The Foundations of the Provably Secure Operating System (PSOS)." Proceedings of the National Computer Conference, AFIPS Press, 1979, pp. 329–334.
FERG10	Ferguson, Neils, Bruce Schneier, and Tadayoshi Kohno. *Cryptography Engineering: Design Principles and Practical Applications.* Wiley, 2010.
FEUS73	Feustel, Edward A. "On the Advantages of Tagged Architecture." *IEEE Transactions on Computers* Vol. C-22, Issue 7 (July 1973): pp. 644–656.
FILK16	Filkins, Barbara, "IT Security Spending Trends: A SANS Survey." February 2016. *SANS.* https://www.sans.org/reading-room/whitepapers/analyst/security-spending-trends-36697.
FIPS01	NIST. Federal Information Processing Standard 197, 2001.
FORB12	Forbes, Andrew and David Henley. *The Illustrated Art of War: Sun Tzu.* Chiang Mai: Cognoscenti Books, 2012. ASIN: B00B91XX8U.
FRAN16	Franceschi-Biccherai, Lorenzo. "Hackers Make the First-Ever Ransomware for Smart Thermostats." *Motherboard.* August 7, 2016. https://motherboard.vice.com/en_us/article/7xk9x4/we-talked-to-a-driver-who-disguised-himself-as-a-car-seat.
GAIN14	Gaines, Helen F. *Cryptanalysis: A Study of Ciphers and Their Solution.* Dover Publications, 2014.
GALL77	Gall, John. *Systemantics: How Systems Work and Especially How They Fail.* Quadrangle, 1977.
GAMM95	Gamma, Erich, Richard Helm, Ralph Johnson, and John Vlissides. *Design Patterns: Elements of Reusable Object-Oriented Software.* Addison-Wesley, 1995.
GERM14	Germano, Judith H. "Cybersecurity Partnerships: A New Era of Public-Private Collaboration." The Center on Law and Security, New York University School of Law. 2014. http://www.lawandsecurity.org/wp-content/uploads/2016/08/Cybersecurity.Partnerships-1.pdf.
GOGU82	Goguen, J.A. and J. Meseguer. "Security Policies and Security Models." *In:* Proceedings of IEEE Symposium on Security and Privacy, pp. 11–20. Oakland, CA: IEEE Computer Society Press, 1982.
GOGU84	Goguen, J.A. and J. Meseguer. Unwinding and inference control. *In:* Proceedings of IEEE Symposium on Security and Privacy, pp. 75–86. Los Alamitos, CA: IEEE Computer Society Press, 1984.
GOOD07	Goodliffe, Pete. *Code Craft: The Practice of Writing Excellent Code.* No Starch Press, 2006.
GOOD17	Goodin, Dan. "Already on probation, Symantec issues more illegit HTTPS certificates." *Ars Technica.* January 20, 2017. https://arstechnica.com/information-technology/2017/01/already-on-probation-symantec-issues-more-illegit-https-certificates/.
GOOD17a	Goodin, Dan. "Russia reportedly stole NSA secrets with help of Kaspersky—what we know now." *Ars Technica.* October 5, 2017.
GOOD17b	Goodin, Dan. "Serious Flaw in WPA2 Protocol Lets Attackers Intercept Passwords and Much More." *Ars Technica.* October 16, 2017.
GOOD17c	Goodin, Dan. "Millions of High-Security Crypto Keys Crippled By Newly Discovered Flaw." *Ars Technica.* October 16, 2017.

Ref	Citation
GOOD84	Good, Don, B.L. Divito, and Mike K. Smith. Using the Gypsy Methodology. Institute for Computing Science, University of Texas. June 1984.
GOSL17	Gosler, James. Personal communication regarding the Chaperon I and II projects at Sandia National Labs. November 12, 2017.
GRAF03	Graff, Mark G. and Kenneth R. van Wyk. *Secure Coding: Principles and Practices.* O'Reilly, 2003.
GRAN83	Grant, P. and R. Richie. *The Eagle's Own Plume.* Proceedings of the United States Naval Institute. July 1983.
GREE17	Greenburg, Andy. "The NSA Confirms It: Russia Hacked French Election 'Infrastructure.'" *Wired.* May 9, 2017. https://www.wired.com/2017/05/nsa-director-confirms-russia-hacked-french-election-infrastructure/.
GREE82	Green, Cordell and Stephen Westfold. "Knowledge-Based Programming Self-Applied." *Machine Intelligence 10*, J. E. Hays, Donald Michie, Y-H. Pao, eds. Ellis Horwood and Halsted Press (John Wiley), 1982.
HAIG87	Haigh, J. Thomas, Richard A. Kemmerer, John McHugh, and William D. Young. "An Experience Using Two Covert Channel Analysis Techniques on a Real System Design." *IEEE Transactions on Software Engineering* Vol. SE-13, No. 2 (February 1987).
HAMI01	Hamilton, S.N., W. L. Miller, A. Ott, and O. S. Saydjari. "Challenges in Applying Game Theory to the Domain of Information Warfare." *In* 4th Information Survivability Workshop (ISW-2001).
HAMI01a	Hamilton, S.N., W. L. Miller, A. Ott, and O. S. Saydjari. "The Role of Game Theory in Information Warfare." *In* 4th Information Survivability Workshop (ISW-2001).
HARR76	Harrison, Michael A., Walter L. Ruzzo, and Jeffrey D. Ullman. "Protection in Operating Systems." *Communications of the ACM (CACM)* Vol. 19, No. 8 (1976): pp. 461–471.
HATC82	Hatcher, William S. *The Logical Foundations of Mathematics. Derives the Peano Axioms (Called S) from Several Axiomatic Set Theories and from Category Theory.* Pergamon, 1982.
HELL04	Hellerstein, Joseph L., Dawn M. Tilbury, and Sujay Parekh. *Feedback Control of Computing Systems.* John Wiley and Sons, 2004.
HELL10	Heller, Joseph. *Catch-22.* Simon & Schuster, 50th anniversary ed. October 26, 2010.
HERE16	Here and Now. "Hackers Exploit Security Flaws in Growing 'Internet of Things.'" Interview with Allison Nixon. October 27, 2016.
HINS01	Hinsley, F. H. and Alan Stripp. *Codebreakers: The Inside Story of Bletchley Park.* Oxford University Press. Reissue edition. August 9, 2001.
HODG14	Hodges, Andrew. *Alan Turing: The Enigma.* Princeton University Press. November 10, 2014.
HOFF17	Hoffman, Bryce G. *Red Teaming.* Crown Business, 2017.
HOLL11	Hollis, David. "Cyberwar Case Study: Georgia 2008." *Small Wars Journal.* Small Wars Foundation. January 6, 2011. https://www.google.com/url?sa=t&rct=j&q=&esrc=s&sourc e=web&cd=1&ved=0ahUKEwjC8qea_6rWAhUF_4MKHZiyDz0QFggoMAA&url=http% 3A%2F%2Fsmallwarsjournal.com%2Fblog%2Fjournal%2Fdocs-temp%2F639-hollis.pdf&u sg=AFQjCNHUvF9sEptmSfWaRMlccuP9yyRWtA.

Ref	Citation
HOLO11	Holohan, Meghan. "Forget Your Password: Typing Rhythm and Computer Security." *Mental Floss.* June 13, 2011. http://mentalfloss.com/article/27957/forget-your-password-typing-rhythm-and-computer-security.
HOPC79	Hopcroft, John E. and Jeffrey Ullman. *Introduction to Automata Theory, Languages, and Computation.* Addison-Wesley, 1979.
HOPK17	Hopkins, Nick. "Deloitte hack hit server containing emails from across the US government." *The Guardian.* October 10, 2017. https://www.theguardian.com/business/2017/oct/10/deloitte-hack-hit-server-containing-emails-from-across-us-government.
HOUS07	House Subcommittee on Emerging Threats, Cybersecurity and Science and Technology of the Committee on Homeland Security, Hearing on Addressing the Nation's Cybersecurity Challenges: Reducing Vulnerabilities Requires Strategic Investment and Immediate Action. Serial No. 110-30. Testimony of Mr. O. Sami Saydjari. U.S. Government Printing Office. April 25, 2007.
HOWA06	Howard, Michael and Steve Lipner. *The Security Development Lifecycle.* Microsoft Press, 2006.
HUTC08	Hutcheson, Lorna. Survival Time on the Internet. *InfoSec Handlers Diary Blog.* July 13, 2008. https://isc.sans.edu/diary/Survival+Time+on+the+Internet/4721.
ICAN07	Factsheet: Root Server Attack on 6 February 2007. ICANN. March 1, 2007. https://www.icann.org/en/system/files/files/factsheet-dns-attack-08mar07-en.pdf.
IGUR08	Igure, Vinay M. and Ronald D. Williams. "Taxonomies of Attacks and Vulnerabilities in Computer Systems." *IEEE Communications Surveys.* Vol. 10, No. 1 (1st Quarter 2008): pp. 6–19.
INTEL17	The United States Intelligence Community. "Background to 'Assessing Russian Activities and Intentions in Recent US Elections': The Analytic Process and Cyber Incident Attribution." https://www.washingtonpost.com/apps/g/page/politics/the-intelligence-community-report-on-russian-activities-in-the-2016-election/2153/.
IOAN05	Ioannidis, John P.A. "Why Most Published Research Findings Are False." *PLoS Medicine.* 2(8) (August 30, 2005): e124.
IRC05	Infosec Research Council. "Hard Problem List." November 2005. https://www.nitrd.gov/cybersecurity/documents/IRC_Hard_Problem_List.pdf.
ITIS17	Information Technology—Information Sharing and Analysis Center, 2017. https://www.it-isac.org.
JAMA16	Jamaluddin, Azwan. "10 Most Destructive Computer Viruses." *Hongkiat.* http://www.hongkiat.com/blog/famous-malicious-computer-viruses/.
JAQU07	Jaquith, Andrew. *Security Metrics: Replacing Fear, Uncertainty, and Doubt.* Addison-Wesley Professional. April 5, 2007.
JOAN17	Joannou, Alexandre, et. al. "Efficient Tagged Memory." IEEE International Conference on Computer Design (ICCD). Boston, MA. 2017.
KAHN11	Kahneman, Daniel. *Thinking, Fast and Slow.* Farrar, Straus and Giroux. October 25, 2011.
KAIN87	Kain, R.Y. and C.E. Landwehr. "On Access Checking in Capability-Based Systems." *IEEE Transactions on Software Engineering* Vol. SE-13 (1987), pp. 202–207, ISSN 0098-5589.

Part VI

Ref	Citation
KAIN96	Kain, R. Y. *Advanced Computer Architecture*. Prentice-Hall, 1996.
KAPL12	Kaplan, Fred. "Petraeus Resigns Over Affair with Biographer." *Slate*. November 8, 2012.
KARG87	Karger, P.A. "Limiting the Damage Potential of Discretionary Trojan Horses." Proceedings of the 1987 Symposium on Security and Privacy, IEEE Computer Society, Oakland, CA, April 1987, pp. 32–37.
KEMM02	Kemmerer, R.A. "A practical approach to identifying storage and timing channels: twenty years later." *Computer Security Applications Conference*, 2002. Proceedings. 18th Annual. December 9-13, 2002.
KERC83	Kerckhoffs, Auguste. "La cryptographie militaire." *Journal des sciences militaires* Vol. IX, pp. 5–83, January 1883; pp. 161–191, February 1883.
KERZ13	Kerzner, Harold. *Project Management: A Systems Approach to Planning, Scheduling, and Controlling*. 11th ed. Wiley. January 28, 2013.
KNOL93	Knoll, Karyn, T. "Risk Management in Fly-by-Wire Systems." NASA Technical Memorandum 104757. March 1993.
KNOW16	Knowles, Aidan. "Behind the Scenes at a Capture the Flag (CTF) Competition." Security Intelligence. December 8, 2016.
KOCH11	Kock, Richard. *The 80/20 Principle: The Secret to Achieving More with Less*. Reprint ed. Crown Business, 2011.
KOSS11	Kossiakoff, Alexander, William N. Sweet, Samuel J. Seymour, and Steven M. Biemer. *Systems Engineering Principles and Practice*. 2nd ed. Wiley-Interscience, 2011.
KRIG09	Krigsman, Michael. "Study: 68% of IT Projects Fail." *ZDNet*. January 14, 2009.
KURZ06	Kurzweil, Raymond. *The Singularity Is Near. When Humans Transcend Biology*. Penguin Books. September 26, 2006.
LAKA76	Lakatos, Imre. *Proofs and Refutations: The Logic of Mathematical Discovery*. Cambridge University Press, 1976.
LAMP71	Lampson, Butler W. "Protection." Proceedings of the 5th Princeton Conference on Information Sciences and Systems, 1971, p. 437.
LAND94	Landwehr, Carl, Alan R. Bull, John P. McDermott, and William S. Choi. "A Taxonomy of Computer Program Security Flaws." *ACM Computing Surveys* Vol. 26, No. 3 (September 1994).
LANG13	Langner, Ralph. "To Kill a Centrifuge: A Technical Analysis of What Stuxnet's Creators Tried to Achieve." The Langer Group. November 2013.
LAPL07	Laplante, Phillip. *What Every Engineer Should Know About Software Engineering*. CRC Press, 2007.
LEE14	Lee, Stan R. *Dunn's Conundrum*. Brash Books, 2014.
LEHD14	Lehdonvirta,Vili and Edward Castronova. *Virtual Economies: Design and Analysis (Information Policy)*. The MIT Press; Reprint ed. May 9, 2014.
LEMA11	LeMay, E., M. D. Ford, K. Keefe, W. H. Sanders, and C. Muehrcke. "Model-based Security Metrics using Adversary View Security Evaluation." Proceedings of 8th International Conference on Quantitative Evaluation of Systems (QEST), Aachen, Germany, September 5-8, 2011, pp. 191–200. http://dx.doi.org/10.1109/QEST.2011.34.

Ref	Citation
LEVE12	Leveson, Nancy G. *Engineering a Safer World: Systems Thinking Applied to Safety (Engineering Systems).* The MIT Press; Reprint ed. January 13, 2012.
LIN70	Lin, Shu. *Introduction to Error Correcting Codes.* Prentice Hall, 1970.
LIND69	Linde, R.R. and C. Weissman. "The ADEPT-50 time-sharing system." Fall Joint Computer Conference, 1969. https://www.computer.org/csdl/proceedings/afips/1969/5074/00/50740039.pdf.
LIPN15	Lipner, Steven B. "The Birth and Death of the Orange Book." *IEEE Annals of the History of Computing* Vol. 37, No. 2 (2015): pp. 19–31.
LISK16	Liska, Ailan. *Ransomware: Defending Against Digital Extortion.* O'Reilly, 2017.
LIU08	Liu, Alex X., et.al. "XEngine: A Fast and Scalable XACML Policy Evaluation Engine." *IEEE Transactions on Dependable and Secure Computing.* November 2008.
LOSC01	Loscocco, Peter and Stephen Smalley. "Integrating Flexible Support for Security Policies into the Linux Operating System" (PDF). February 2001. https://www.nsa.gov/resources/everyone/digital-media-center/publications/research-papers/assets/files/flexible-support-for-security-policies-into-linux-feb2001-report.pdf.
LOVE02	Love, H. *Attributing Authorship: An Introduction.* Cambridge University Press, 2002.
MACE80	MacEwen, Glenn H. *Introduction to Computer Systems Using the PDP-11 and Pascal.* McGraw-Hill, 1980.
MARK08	Markoff, John. "Before the Gunfire, Cyberattacks." *New York Times.* August 12, 2008.
MART90	Martello, Silvano and Paolo Toth. *Knapsack Problems: Algorithms and Computer Implementations.* Wiley-Interscience, 1990.
MAXI04	Maxion, Roy A. and R. R. Roberts. "Proper Use of ROC Curves in Intrusion/Anomaly Detection." Technical Report Series CS-TR-871. School of Computing Science, University of Newcastle upon Tyne. November 2004. http://www.cs.newcastle.ac.uk/publications/trs/papers/871.pdf.
MCAL09	McAllister, Neil. "How Wolfram Alpha could change software." *InfoWorld.* July 30, 2009. https://cacm.acm.org/opinion/articles/35883-how-wolfram-alpha-could-change-software/fulltext.
MCLE13	McLean, Bethany, Peter Elkind, and Joe Nocera. *The Smartest Guys in the Room: The Amazing Rise and Scandalous Fall of Enron.* Portfolio; Reprint ed. November 26, 2013.
MICK11	Mick, Jason. "Cracking the Bitcoin: Digging Into a $131M USD Virtual Currency." *Daily Tech.* June 12, 2011. http://www.dailytech.com/Cracking+the+Bitcoin+Digging+Into+a+131M+USD+Virtual+Currency/article21878.htm.
MILL09	Mills, Elinor. "Melissa Turns 10." C/Net. March 1, 2009.
MILL56	Miller, G.A. "The Magical Number Seven, Plus or Minus Two: Some Limits on Our Capacity for Processing Information." *Psychological Review* Vol. 63, No. 2 (1956): pp. 81–97. PMID 13310704.
MITN11	Mitnick, Kevin. *Ghost in the Wires: My Adventures as the World's Most Wanted Hacker.* Little, Brown and Company, 2011.
MITN17	Mitnick, Kevin. *The Art of Invisibility: The World's Most Famous Hacker Teaches You How to Be Safe in the Age of Big Brother and Big Data.* Little, Brown and Company, 2017.

Ref	Citation
MOOR75	Moore, Gordon. "Progress in Digital Integrated Electronics." *Technical Digest.* International Electron Devices Meeting, IEEE, 1975, pp. 11–13.
MULT17	Multics History. http://www.multicians.org/history.html.
MUNG07	Munger, Dave. "Is 17 the 'Most Random' Number?" *Cognitive Daily.* February 5, 2007. http://scienceblogs.com/cognitivedaily/2007/02/05/is-17-the-most-random-number/.
NCTA04	National Commission on Terrorist Attacks upon the United States. The 9/11 Commission Report. Executive Summary. [Washington, DC] :[National Commission on Terrorist Attacks upon the United States], 2004. Print.
NELS95	Nelson, Andrew H. "The Art of Information War." Nelson (self-published), 1995.
NEUM17	Neumann, Peter G. Fundamental Trustworthiness Principles. In *New Solutions for Cybersecurity,* Howie Shrobe, David Shrier, Alex Pentland, eds., MIT Press/Connection Science: Cambridge MA. (Chapter 6, Fall 2017).
NEUM94	Neumann, Peter G. *Computer-Related Risks.* Addison-Wesley Professional. October 29, 1994.
NEWS09	Newsweek. "Russian Computer Hackers Are a Global Threat." *Newsweek.* December 29, 2009.
NICO12	Nicol, David M., William H. Sanders, William L. Scherlis, and Laurie A. Williams. Science of Security Hard Problems: A Lablet Perspective. Science of Security Virtual Organization Web. November 2012. Updated List for 2015 at https://cps-vo.org/node/21590.
NIPP13	Department of Homeland Security. National Infrastructure Protection Plan 2013: Partnering for Critical Infrastructure Security and Resilience. DHA, 2013. https://www.hsdl.org/?view&did=747827.
NIST01	National Institute of Standards and Technology. Federal Information Processing Standards Publication 197: Advanced Encryption Standard. National Institute of Standards and Technology. November 26, 2001.
NIST02	National Institute of Standards and Technology. The Economic Impacts of Inadequate Infrastructure for Software Testing. Planning Report 02-03. May 2002.
NIST13	National Institute of Standards and Technology. Glossary of Key Information Security Terms. NISTIR 7298. Revision 2. 2013. http://nvlpubs.nist.gov/nistpubs/ir/2013/NIST.IR.7298r2.pdf.
NOSS17	Nossiter, Adam, David E. Sanger, and Nicole Perlroth. "Hackers Came, but the French Were Prepared." *New York Times.* May 9, 2017. https://www.nytimes.com/2017/05/09/world/europe/hackers-came-but-the-french-were-prepared.html.
NRC10	National Research Council. Proceedings of a Workshop on Deterring Cyberattacks: Information Strategies and Developing Options of U.S. Policy. *The National Academies Press.* 2010.
NRC17	National Academies of Sciences, Engineering, and Medicine. 2017. Foundational Cybersecurity Research: Improving Science, Engineering, and Institutions. Washington, DC: *The National Academies Press.* https://doi.org/10.17226/24676.
NRC91	National Research Council. 1991. Computers at Risk: Safe Computing in the Information Age. Washington, DC: *The National Academies Press.* https://doi.org/10.17226/1581.

Ref	Citation
NRC99	National Research Council. 1999. Trust in Cyberspace. Washington, DC: *The National Academies Press.* https://www.nap.edu/catalog/6161/trust-in-cyberspace.
OASI13	Oasis. eXtensible Access Control Markup Language Version 3.0. Oasis Standard. January 22, 2013.
OGOR13	O'Gorman, Gavin and Geoff McDonald. "The Elderwood Project." *Symantec Security Response.* 2013. http://www.symantec.com/content/en/us/enterprise/media/security_response/whitepapers/the-elderwood-project.pdf.
OLSO12	Olson, Parmy. *We Are Anonymous: Inside the Hacker World of LulzSec, Anonymous, and the Global Cyber Insurgency.* Little, Brown and Company, 2012.
ONEI16	O'Neill, Patrick Howell. "The Cyberattack that Changed the World." *The Daily Dot.* May 20, 2016. https://www.dailydot.com/layer8/web-war-cyberattack-russia-estonia/.
ONWU11	Onwubiko, Cyril and Thomas Owens. *Situational Awareness in Computer Network Defense.* IGI Global, 2011.
OREG17	O'Regan, Gerard. *Concise Guide to Formal Methods: Theory, Fundamentals and Industry Applications.* Springer. August 8, 2017.
OSIN07	Osinga, Frans P.B. *Science, Strategy and War: The Strategic Theory of John Boyd.* Routledge, London, 2007.
PAND15	Pandey, Avaneesh. "Cybersecurity Deal Between China and Germany in the Works: Report." *International Business Times.* October 30, 2015.
PARK08	Park, A. "Why We Take Risks — It's the Dopamine." *Time.* Retrieved December 30, 2008. http://www.time.com/time/health/article/0,8599,1869106,00.html.
PARN17	Parnas, David Lorge. "The Real Risks of Artificial Intelligence: Incidents from the early days of AI research are instructive in the current AI environment." *Communications of the ACM* Vol. 60, No. 10 (October 2017). http://www.csl.sri.com/neumann/cacm242.pdf.
PARN72	Parnas, D.L. "On the Criteria to be Used in Decomposing Systems into Modules." *Communications of the ACM* Vol. 15 No. 12 (December 1972).
PAST15	Pasternack, Alex. "The Strangest, Most Spectacular Bridge Collapse (And How We Got It Wrong)." *Motherboard.* December 14, 2015. https://motherboard.vice.com/en_us/article/kb78w3/the-myth-of-galloping-gertie.
PAVL03	Pavlovic, Dusko and Doug Smith. "Software Development by Refinement." Kestrel Institute, 2003.
PCCI97	The President's Commission on Critical Infrastructure Protection. The Report of the President's Commission on Critical Infrastructure Protection. October 1997. https://fas.org/sgp/library/pccip.pdf.
PELT01	Peltier, Thomas R. *Information Security Risk Analysis.* CRC Press, 2001.
PERL17	Perlroth, Nicole, Michael Wines, and Matthew Rosenberg. "Russian Election Hacking Efforts, Wider Than Previously Known, Draw Little Scrutiny." *New York Times.* September 1, 2017. https://www.nytimes.com/2017/09/01/us/politics/russia-election-hacking.html.
PETE12	Peters, Tom and Robert H. Waterman, Jr. *In Search of Excellence: Lessons from America's Best-Run Companies.* Harper Business. November 27, 2012.

Ref	Citation
PETE61	Peterson, W. W. and D.T. Brown. "Cyclic Codes for Error Detection." Proceedings of the IRE Vol. 49, No. 1 (January 1961): pp. 228–235.
PETE72	Peterson, W. Wesley and E.J. Weldon. *Error-Correcting Codes.* 2nd ed. The MIT Press. March 15, 1972.
PETE83	Peterson, James L. and A. Silberschatz. *Operating System Concepts.* Addison-Wesley, 1983.
PINK11	Pink, Daniel. *Drive.* Penguin Group, 2011.
PLEH15	Plehn, Michael T. Control Warfare: Inside the OODA Loop. *War College Series.* February 23, 2015.
PRIE17	Priest, Dana and Michael Birnbaum. "Europe has been working to expose Russian meddling for years." *The Washington Post.* June 25, 2017. https://www.washingtonpost.com/world/europe/europe-has-been-working-to-expose-russian-meddling-for-years/2017/06/25/e42dcece-4a09-11e7-9669-250d0b15f83b_story.html?utm_term=.72d4ba7cbbb0.
PROT84	The remark "theories of security come from theories of insecurity" is attributed to Richard "Rick" Proto from the Department of Defense.
RADI09	Radianti, J., E. Rich and J. J. Gonzalez. "Vulnerability Black Markets: Empirical Evidence and Scenario Simulation." *In* IEEE Computer Society, Proceedings of the 42nd Hawaii International Conference on System Sciences, January 2009: pp. 1–10.
RAPO17	Rapoza, Kenneth. "Can 'Fake News' Impact the Stock Market?" *Forbes.* February 26, 2017. https://www.forbes.com/sites/kenrapoza/2017/02/26/can-fake-news-impact-the-stock-market/#dac84062fac0.
RATC06	Ratcliff, Rebecca A. *Delusions of Intelligence: Enigma, Ultra, and the End of Secure Ciphers.* Cambridge University Press, 2006.
RATT01	Rattray, Gregory. *Strategic Warfare in Cyberspace.* MIT Press, 2001.
REAS90	Reason, James. *Human Error.* Cambridge University Press, 1990.
REDS17	RedSeal: The Foundation for Digital Resistance. 2017. See www.redseal.net.
REMY11	Remy, Christopher. Fifth Column. Amazon Digital Services, 2011.
RILE17	Riley, Michael, Jordan Robertson, and Anita Sharpe. "The Equifax Hack Has the Hallmarks of State-Sponsored Pros." *Bloomberg Businessweek.* September 29, 2017. https://www.bloomberg.com/news/features/2017-09-29/the-equifax-hack-has-all-the-hallmarks-of-state-sponsored-pros.
RISK17	Risks forum. 2017. risks.org.
RUSH81	Rushby, John. "The Design and Verification of Secure Systems." Eighth ACM Symposium on Operating System Principles, Asilomar, CA. *ACM Operating Systems Review* Vol. 15, No. 5 (December 1981), pp. 12–21.
SALT98	Salter, C., O. Sami Saydjari, Bruce Schneier, and James Wallner. "Toward A Secure System Engineering Methodology." New Security Paradigms Workshop. September 1998. pp. 2–10.
SANT15	Santillan, Maritza. "70% of Malware Infections Go Undetected by Antivirus Software, Study Says." The State of Security. *Tripwire.* February 13, 2015. https://www.tripwire.com/state-of-security/latest-security-news/70-of-malware-infections-go-undetected-by-antivirus-software-study-says/.

Ref	Citation
SAYD02	Saydjari, O., L. Tinnel, and D. Farrell. "Cyberwar Strategy and Tactics: An Analysis of Cyber Goals, Strategies, Tactics, and Techniques." *In* Proceedings of the 2002 IEEE Workshop on Information Assurance. U.S. Military Academy, West Point, NY. June 2002.
SAYD04	Saydjari, O. Sami. "Cyber Defense: Art to Science." *Communications of the ACM* Vol. 47, No. 3 (March 2004): pp. 52–57.
SAYD86	Saydjari, O. Sami and Tim Kremann. "A Standard Notation in Computer Security Models." Proceedings of 9th National Computer Security Conference (5: NCS-86), 1986, pp. 194–203.
SAYD89	Saydjari, O. Sami, Joseph M. Beckman, and Jeff Leaman. "Lock Trek: Navigating Unchartered Space." IEEE Symposium on Security and Privacy, May 1-3, 1989.
SCHN05	Schneier, Bruce (February 18, 2005). "Schneier on Security: Cryptanalysis of SHA-1." February 18, 2005. https://www.schneier.com/blog/archives/2005/02/cryptanalysis_o.html.
SCHN15	Schneier, Bruce. *Applied Cryptography: Protocols, Algorithms and Source Code in C.* 2nd ed. Wiley, 2015.
SCHU12	Schulz, Marc-André, Barbara Schmalbach, Peter Brugger, and Karsten Witt. "Analyzing Humanly Generated Random Number Sequences: A Pattern-Based Approach." July 23, 2012. https://doi.org/10.1371/journal.pone.0041531.
SCHW10	Schwartau, Winn. *Information Warfare.* Interpact Press Inc. September 7, 2010.
SHAN48	Shannon, C. E. "A Mathematical Theory of Communication." *The Bell System Technical Journal* Vol. 27 (July, October 1948), pp. 379–423, 623–656.
SMIT08	Smith, Sean and John Marchesini. *The Craft of System Security.* Pearson, 2008. Chapter 2.
SPAF88	Spafford, Eugene H. "The Internet Worm Program: An Analysis." Purdue Technical Report CSD-TR-823, December 8, 1988.
STAL16	Stallings, William. *Cryptography and Network Security: Principles and Practice.* 7th ed. Pearson, 2016.
STAN02	Staniford, S., V. Paxson, and N. Weaver. "How to Own the Internet in Your Spare Time." Proceedings of the 11th USENIX Security Symposium. 2002.
STAN95	The Standish Group. "Chaos." The Standish Group, 1995.
STEV16	Stevens, Marc, Pierre Karpman, and Thomas Peyrin. "Freestart collision for full SHA-1." Eurocrypt. 2016.
STIG10	Stigum, Brent P. and Fred Wenstop. *Foundations of Utility and Risk Theory with Applications.* Springer 2010.
STOL06	Stolfo, Salvatore. "Behavior-Based Modeling and its Application to Email Analysis." *ACM Transactions on Internet Technology (TOIT)* Vol. 6 Issue 2 (May 2006): pp. 187–221.
STOL89	Stoll, Clifford. *The Cuckoo's Egg: Tracking a Spy Through the Maze of Computer Espionage.* Doubleday, 1989.
STON15	Stone, James V. *Information Theory: A Tutorial Introduction.* Sebtel Press, 2015.
STRI17	Strickland, Jonathan. "10 Worst Computer Viruses of All Time." HowStuffWorks. http://computer.howstuffworks.com/worst-computer-viruses4.htm.

Ref	Citation
STRO17	Strohm, Chris. "Hacked OPM Data Hasn't Been Shared or Sold, Top Spy-Catcher Says." *Bloomberg*. September 28, 2017. https://www.bloomberg.com/news/articles/2017-09-28/hacked-opm-data-hasn-t-been-shared-or-sold-top-spy-catcher-says.
SURO05	Surowiecki, James. *The Wisdom of Crowds*. Anchor Books, 2004, 2005.
TALE10	Taleb, Nassim Nicholas. *The Black Swan: The Impact of the Highly Improbable (Incerto)*. Random House, 2010.
TAN02	Tan, Kymie M.C., and Roy A. Maxion. "'Why 6?' Defining the Operational Limits of Stide, an Anomaly-Based Intrusion Detector." IEEE Symposium on Security and Privacy, 2002. pp. 188–201.
TCSE85	Trusted Computer System Evaluation Criteria. Department of Defense Standard. December 26, 1985.
THOM15	Thomas, Karl. "The Sad Stats on State of Cybersecurity: 70% attack go unchecked." We Live Security. September 9, 2015. https://www.welivesecurity.com/2015/09/09/cybercrime-growing-concern-americans/.
THOM84	Thompson, Ken. Reflections on Trusting Trust. *Communications of the ACM* Vol. 27, No. 8 (August 1984), pp. 761–763.
THORN05	Thornburgh, Nathan. "Inside the Chinese Hack Attack." *Time.com*. August 25, 2005. http://content.time.com/time/nation/article/0,8599,1098371,00.html.
TINN02	Tinnel, Laura S., O. Sami Saydjari and Dave Farrell. "Cyberwar Strategy and Tactics." Proceedings of the 2002 IEEE Workshop on Information Assurance. United States Military Academy. West Point, NY. June 2002.
TOUR11	Touré, Hamadoun I. "The Quest for Cyber Peace." International Telecommunications Union and World Federation of Scientists. January 2011.
TURI52	Turing, Alan. "The Chemical Basis of Morphogenesis." *Philosophical Transactions of the Royal Society of London*. Series B, Biological Sciences, Vol. 237, No. 641 (August 14, 1952), p. 37 (Model of the Embryo).
VUKE04	Vukelich, D., D. Levin and J. Lowry. "Architecture for Cyber Command and Control: Experiences and Future Directions." DARPA Information Survivability Conference and Symposium and Exposition. Anaheim, CA. 12-14 June (2001): pp. 155–165.
WANG05	Wang, V. and Hongbo Yu. "How to Break MD5 and Other Hash Functions" (PDF). Advances in Cryptology – Lecture Notes in Computer Science. 2005. pp. 19–35. Retrieved December 21, 2009.
WARE70	Ware, Willis. Computer Security Controls for Computer Systems. Report of the Defense Science Board Task Force on Computer Security. Rand Corporation. February 11, 1970.
WATS17	Watson, Robert N. M., Peter G. Neumann, and Simon W. Moore. Balancing Disruption and Deployability in the CHERI Instruction-Set Architecture (ISA). In *New Solutions for Cybersecurity*, Howie Shrobe, David Shrier, Alex Pentland, eds., MIT Press/Connection Science: Cambridge MA. (Chapter 5, Fall 2017).
WEIG03	Wiegmann, Douglas and Scott A. Shappell. *A Human Error Approach to Aviation Accident Analysis: The Human Factors Analysis and Classification System*. Ashgate Publishing, 2003.

Ref	Citation
WEIN12	Weinberger, Sharon. "Top Ten Most-Destructive Computer Viruses." Smithsonian.com. https://www.smithsonianmag.com/science-nature/top-ten-most-destructive-computer-viruses-159542266/?c=y&page=2.
WEIN16	Wiener, Craig J. "Penetrate, Exploit, Disrupt, Destroy: The Rise Of Computer Network Operations As A Major Military Innovation." George Mason University. Master's Thesis. Fall 2016. http://digilib.gmu.edu/jspui/bitstream/handle/1920/10613/Wiener_gmu_0883E_11318.pdf?sequence=1&isAllowed=y.
WEIS17	Weiser, Benjamin. Anthony Weiner Gets 21 Months in Prison for Sexting with Teenager. *New York Times.* September 25, 2017.
WHIT99	Whitten, Alma and J.D. Tygar. "Why Johnny Can't Encrypt: A Usability Evaluation of PGP 5.0." *In* Proceedings of the 8th USENIX Security Symposium, August 1999. pp. 169–183.
WOOL17	Woollaston, Victoria. "WannaCry Ransomware: What is it and How to Protect Yourself." *Wired.* May 22, 2017. http://www.wired.co.uk/article/wannacry-ransomware-virus-patch.
WORL17	The World Staff. "Hackers Infiltrated Power Grid Controls in the US and Abroad." *PRI's the World.* September 11, 2017. https://www.pri.org/stories/2017-09-11/hackers-infiltrated-power-grid-controls-us-and-abroad.
WU12	Wu Zhenyu, Zhang Xu, and Haining Wang. "Whispers in the Hyper-space: High-Speed Covert Channel Attacks in the Cloud." 21st USENIX Security Symposium. August 8-10, 2012. Bellevue, WA.
WYMAxx	Wyman, R.H. and G.L. Johnson. "Defense Against Common-Mode Failures in Protecting System Design." http://www.iaea.org/inis/collection/NCLCollectionStore/_Public/29/067/29067657.pdf.
YADA10	Yadav, Aditya. Amazon Cloud Computing with Java (Amazon Cloud Computing With 'X'). Lulu.com, 2010.
YARD13	Yardley, Herbert O. *The American Black Chamber.* Naval Institute Press. May 11, 2013.
ZAJO01	Zajonc, R.B. "Mere Exposure: A Gateway to the Subliminal." *Current Directions in Psychological Science* Vol. 10, No. 6 (December 1, 2001): p. 224.
ZELL11	Zeller, Mark. "Common Questions and Answers Addressing the Aurora Vulnerability." Presented at the DistribuTech Conference. San Diego, CA. February 1-2, 2011. https://www.selinc.com/workarea/downloadasset.aspx?id=9487.
ZETT14	Zetter, Ken. "An Unprecedented Look at Stuxnet, The World's First Digital Weapon." *Wired* November 3, 2014.
ZHIV09	Zhivich, Michael, and Robert K. Cunningham. "The Real Cost of Software Errors." *IEEE Security and Privacy* (March/April 2009): pp. 87–90.

Glossary

*-property   A multilevel security policy that prohibits processes operating on behalf of users from writing any data below the level of their clearance.

abstraction   The act of representing essential features while hiding the details to reduce complexity.

access control list (ACL)   A data structure that enumerates the access rights for all active entities (e.g., users) within a system.

access control matrix   A two-dimensional matrix with active accessing entities (e.g., processes) on one dimension and resources (e.g., files) with access types (e.g., read, write, and execute) entries in the intersecting cells, indicating the access the active entity has to the corresponding resource.

access rights   The privileges that an activity entity, such as a process, is granted to a passive entity, such as a file.

accreditation   The process by which a group of cybersecurity professionals makes a determination regarding whether a system meets the minimum risk standards set by the organization for integration into their enterprise system.

actuator   A mechanism used to dynamically control the function of a system component.

address space   The portion of computer primary memory to which a program or set of programs has access, as determined by the underlying hardware.

Advanced Encryption Standard (AES)   FIPS Standard 197 strong encryption standard, meant to replace the Data Encryption Standard (DES), which had known vulnerabilities.

adversary   A person or group of people whose goals are to cause damage to the defender's system or mission.

adversary model   A specification of specific characteristics that would be typical of an adversary that would guide their behavior and attack choices.

Agile design   A design process that emphasizes early delivery of simple functionality, significant interaction with customers through feedback, and continuous improvement through quick releases of incremental upgrades.

aging off   In the context of a speedup cache, aging off is the process of replacing data that has not been accessed for some specified period with new, more recently accessed data.

alarm   *See* attack alarm.

alert   A message sent to a consuming subscriber by an intrusion detection system that there is strong evidence of an ongoing attack and any additional information that it has about that attack, including which attack it is.

alternative analysis   An intelligence analysis of evidence that hypothesizes the nature of a situation that is intentionally different than the traditional or mainstream interpretation of events.

anomaly detection   A type of intrusion detection system that detects attacks by identifying deviations from normal behavior.

anonymization   The process of disguising the true identity of a user engaged in a computer activity.

artificial intelligence   A discipline with the goal to develop technology that solves complex problems with skill and creativity that rivals that of the human brain.

assumption leveling   The process by which a team of experts share the assumptions that they made in providing their estimation, so that a consensus in assumptions can be achieved to ensure that the estimates are all based on the same assumptions.

assurance   Confidence that a system exhibits a stated set of properties.

assurance case   A structured argument based on evidence that a statement about system properties, particularly regarding cybersecurity and safety, is true.

assurance-in-the-large   Assurance of properties having to do with how cybersecurity components interact as opposed to the properties of the components themselves (sometimes called assurance in-the-small).

assurance-in-the-small   Assurance that a cybersecurity component meets a specified set of cybersecurity security properties. *See also* assurance-in-the-large.

asymmetric-key cryptography   *See* public-key cryptography.

asymmetrical effect   The idea that an attack causes substantially higher damages on the target system than the cost of the resources required to conduct the attack.

attack   A sequence of actions intended to have a specified effect favorable to an actor that is adversarial to the owners of that system.

attack alarm   A decision based on accumulated evidence collected by an intrusion-detection system that an ongoing attack has reached a predesignated threshold, which warrants reporting to a human operator engaged in defending the network to investigate and possibly intervene.

attack attribution   For a given attack, the determination of the perpetrator.

attack classification   The determination that a given attack activity belongs to a specific attack class.

attack coverage   The ability of a given cybersecurity mechanism or class of mechanism to address the attacks in the set of attacks of concern. *See* attack space.

attack detection   The determination that sufficient evidence has accumulated to indicate that an attack is in progress.

attack forest   A collection of attack trees. *See also* mission map.

attack interdiction points   Attack steps in an attack sequence, during which the defender has an opportunity to stop the steps before they succeed.

attack load   Different classes and quantities of attacks occurring within a system or a model of the system.

attack manifestation   Data in a feature that could reveal the existence of an ongoing attack.

attack path   The concrete or abstract route that an attack uses to infiltrate a system, exfiltrate data from a system, and ingress into a system for continued control by an attacker, and propagation paths to spread the attack to other connected systems.

attack relevant   Of or relating to an attack. An event in an event stream is said to be attack-relevant if it manifests the attack.

attack signal   The degree to which an attack manifestation clearly indicates the existence of that attack, as distinguished from normal system activity or other attacks. *See also* Signal; Noise floor.

attack signature   *See* signature (string).

attack space   The collection of all possible system attack classes and instances that have been determined to be relevant and of concern to a defender.

attack speed   The speed at which an attack infiltrates, exfiltrates, or propagates. Useful for determining the type and urgency of defense action.

attack step   A discrete attack (leaf attack node in an attack tree) that is one of a sequence of attack steps, used by an adversary to accomplish a goal.

attack surface   The avenues of attack that are available to an attacker by virtue of those avenues being exposed in some manner.

attack taxonomy   A hierarchical ordering of attacks that groups them by certain characteristics for some stated purpose.

attack tool kit   Attack software written generally to allow someone (often a novice attacker) to instantiate it by specifying a target and some other key parameters, without necessarily understanding how the attacks themselves work.

attack tree   A goal-directed graph indicating all possible abstract paths that an adversary might use to achieve their strategic goal. *See also* mission map.

attack vector   The means by which an attack succeeds in gaining access to a system.

attack-relevant events   The subset of events in a stream of data that carry information pertaining to a potential attack.

attribute caching   The speedup practice of storing (caching) the attributes associated with active entities locally to avoid the delay of retrieving them from an external service, typically over the network.

attribute-based access control   An access control policy in which the rules are based primarily on the attributes of users on the system and not on their specific identity.

attribution   The ability to determine the responsible party for a given action.

audit logs   The data records of a system pertaining to essential aspects of its operation, including the health of the system, its performance, and security.

authentication   A process by which an entity proves its identity to another party (e.g., authentication required by a user to log in or log on).

authentication token   A unique device given to a user as part of the evidence that allows the user to validate their identity and therefore get access to protected data.

authorization   A process by which access between active and passive entities on a system is specified, decided, and enforced.

autonomic   Real-time cybersecurity dynamic action that is driven entirely by algorithms at machine speed, without involvement of human decision making.

availability   A property that a system will operate in the face of attempts to stop its operation (known as denial of service [DOS] attacks).

backdoor   A program aspect allowing an attacker to gain access to a system by a means other than direct authorization by the system's owners and operators.

Basic Input/Output System (BIOS)   Firmware typically associated with Intel processors that provides an interface to hardware services and other devices on the system.

battle damage assessment   The assessment of damage to relevant systems or attributed to a particular set of actions by the defender or the attacker in an attempt to improve their position.

binary classifier   A type of classification that merely indicates whether an event sequence is or is not an example of a particular class (e.g., attack event), without determining subclasses.

biometrics   A specific subclass of a physical trait or behavior that uniquely identifies a human. Biometrics can be measured and registered for human-to-machine authentication with the system. Examples of biometrics include fingerprints, retinal scans, and voice patterns. *See also* authentication.

black swan (event)   An event that is low probability but very high impact and therefore tends to be ignored by most people, to their peril.

blue team   A team of system defenders that emulates the behavior of a typical cybersecurity defense team within a system during some game or exercise simulating an attack in order to better prepare a defense. In contrast to red team (*see also* red team).

bot   Software that automates some function such as participating in a network flooding attack (*see also* denial of service), or simulating a human user on social media in an attempt to influence human opinion. *See also* botnet.

botnet   A collection of computers that have been successfully attacked and taken control of by an attacker, usually through the use of some form of self-propagating malware. Such botnets can be used for nefarious purposes such as email spam or distributed denial of service attacks.

buffer overflow attack   A computer attack that exploits a buffer overflow vulnerability (*see* buffer overflow vulnerability) in such a way as to overwrite the execution stack portion of memory. This memory overwrite allows malicious code to take control of the process execution stack, and thus the program.

buffer overflow vulnerability   A software flaw in which the bounds of the input buffer are not properly checked, allowing input data to exceed the memory space allocated for the input, and thus overwrite other parts of memory that can enable a buffer overflow attack (*see* buffer overflow attack).

capability   An unforgeable access ticket to a block of memory that enables a program to share that block with another program.

central processing unit (CPU)   The processor at the heart of a computer that performs computational functions and orchestrates other devices.

certificate   A cryptographic binding between a user identifier and their public key as signed by a recognized authority called a certificate authority.

certificate authority   A specially privileged user on a well-protected system that signs the binding between users and their public certificate, thus creating a public-key certificate for that user.

certificate revocation   The act of declaring an identity certificate no longer valid.

certificate revocation list (CRL)   Signed and issued by a certificate authority, a list that contains certificate identifiers for certificates that are no longer valid.

chain of authentication   The linkage of multiple pair-wise authentications and proxying between two entities, assuring that the delegation of proxy authority is as intended and the intermediary entities behave correctly.

challenge-response   An authentication protocol in which the entity seeks to authenticate another party by sending a challenge to which the other party must respond correctly in order to verify their identity.

checkbox security engineering   Security engineering by blind adherence to predefined checklists without an understanding of purpose and without a required assurance level of design and implementation, potentially increasing the risk of a cyberattack.

checkpoint   The process of storing a set of data or system state that is in a known consistent or safe state so that it can be later restored by a rollback operation if the system fails or the data is corrupted. *See also* safe state; rollback.

checksum   A value computed on data to detect error or manipulation.

CIA   Confidentiality, integrity, and availability: the three essential properties of cybersecurity.

ciphertext   Data produced by an encryption process that results from the input plaintext being encrypted using a specific algorithm and a specified key.

Clark-Wilson integrity   A model focused on transforming data from lower-integrity data during the input process to higher-integrity data and having verification rules to check for consistency of data before and after data transformation processing.

class A   Top echelon, of the highest quality or skill level.

cloud computing   A form of distributed computing whereby many computers and applications share the same resources to work together, often across geographically separated areas, to provide a coherent service. *See also* computational cloud; storage cloud.

coevolution   The evolutionary progression of one or more species in which the evolution of one creates evolutionary pressures on the other. The evolution of cyberattacks directly affects the evolution of cybersecurity, creating evolutionary pressures in a particular direction.

cold spare   A backup system that is capable of performing the essential functions of a primary system. The backup system is intentionally not connected to the primary system and therefore can take time to be loaded with the latest data so that it can continue processing.

command and control (C2)   The decision making and decision execution of strategies and tactic toward a mission objective—usually in a military context.

common mode of failure   A mode of failure where two or more seemingly independent systems can fail simultaneously because they share a common element that is not readily apparent (e.g., use of the same operating system, or use of the same physical communications link).

communications security   Techniques and procedures to protect sensitive data while in transit from one system to another.

compartment   *See* security compartment.

compiler   A program that converts high-level instructions into more detailed instructions, typically in a form so that they can be read and executed by a computer.

complex instruction set computer (CISC)   A processor with a set of instructions that includes complex multistep operations commonly used by applications, thereby offering a speedup for functions using those operations.

complexity   Refers to the inherent difficulty in accomplishing a computational task such as sorting a list or establishing the trustworthiness of an entire system.

composition　The integration of cybersecurity subsystems, each with a set of properties, which when taken together should preserve existing properties and also satisfy necessary higher-layer properties.

compromise (data)　The unauthorized disclosure of sensitive data to a potential adversary.

compromise (system)　The unauthorized modification of critical data or system software giving control to an attacker.

computational cloud　A cloud focused on delivering computing services like web-based services, in which storage exists primarily to support the services.

computer emergency response team (CERT)　An organization designed to help detect, analyze, and thwart computer attacks as they are happening.

computer network attacks (CNA)　An attack on a system that enters by way of a connected network.

concept of operations　A description of a system's behavior from a user's perspective in terms of how it supports mission and interacts with other key systems.

confidentiality　A cybersecurity property of a system indicating an ability to prevent sensitive data from being divulged to unauthorized users.

confound　An unaccounted-for variable in an experiment that is not properly controlled for, affecting the results and making interpretations and conclusions difficult.

content filtering　A process of examining the content of communications and applying rules based on content such as keywords. The rules typically require either exclusion of communications or modifications of content (e.g., filtering out email attachments because of the risk they pose).

contingency plan　A plan for continued operation and execution of the most essential functions of a mission in the event of a disruptive failure, such as a natural disaster or a major cyberattack.

control feedback loop　A conceptual construct of control theory in which a comparison between a goal state and the measured current state drives a decision-making process for an action to bring the system closer to the goal state. The feedback loop increases the effectiveness of the defensive actions. *See also* Observe-Orient-Decide-Act (OODA) Loop; situation understanding.

control theory　The study of the dynamic behavior of systems as a function of the system's inputs and feedback on the state of the system in response to those inputs.

countermeasure　A defensive mechanism intended to address a class of attack.

course of action (COA)   A defined sequence of commands intended to have some positive effect in response to an evolving attack situation. A course of action may involve reconfiguring the rules for a firewall, changes in authentication, reconfiguration of defense mechanisms, changes in alarm status, and recovery mechanisms.

covert channel   A means of signaling data in a manner other than by the direct means provided by the computer for the purpose of evading detection.

covert storage channel   A covert channel whereby the signaling is accomplished through the observation of system state that is mutually observable by two processes attempting to communicate that are prohibited by policy from communicating.

covert timing channel   A covert channel whereby the signaling is accomplished through the adjustment of the timing of events that are mutually observable by two processes attempting to communicate that are prohibited by policy from communicating.

critical information infrastructure   Information technology that is essential to the operation of critical infrastructure. *See* critical infrastructure.

critical infrastructure   Assets or systems that are essential to the proper functioning of a nation.

cross-site scripting attacks   An attack in which a compromised website sends malicious scripts to a browser for execution, thereby compromising the user's system as well.

cryptanalytics   The process of breaking encryption without the benefit of the key under which data was encrypted.

cryptographer   A professional who is trained in the art of cryptography. *See* cryptography.

cryptographic bypass   The mechanism to remove cryptographic functions from the processing chain, usually in case of an emergency or failure.

cryptographic key   A relatively short string of bits used to guide the operation of an encryption algorithm such that only possession of the key allows the encrypted data to be decrypted.

cryptography   The study of algorithmic transformations from plain text to encrypted forms in which the unencrypted data cannot be ascertained without possession of the encryption key.

cut set   A set of leaf nodes in an attack tree that suffice to achieve the goal represented by the root of the attack tree.

cyber   A prefix or adjective indicating that the modified word is narrowed in scope to that of cyberspace.

cyber command and control   The concept of developing courses of action for given attack situations, decision support for choosing the best course of action, the infrastructure for executing courses of action, and feedback on successful completion of the execution and effectiveness for mitigating a cyberattack.

cyber militia   The idea of essential civilian technical leaders who operate the critical information infrastructure into the command and control and authority structure of a nation's military operations.

cyber network operations (CNO)   The combination of computer network defense and computer network attack.

cyber physical system (CPS)   A physical system, such as a power grid or petroleum cracking plant, controlled by computers whose failure could cause significant damage to the physical system.

cyber situation understanding   A cybersecurity capability focused on interpreting systems and intrusion data in the context of the effect on mission and supporting decisions for risk mitigation.

cyber strategy and tactics   A cybersecurity capability focused on the development and application of strategies and tactics in the defense of mission systems.

cybersecurity   A trustworthiness property concerned with the protection of systems from cyberattacks.

cybersecurity architecture   The structured composition of cybersecurity mechanisms and services to assuredly achieve an overarching set of cybersecurity requirements.

cybersecurity operators   Professionals who monitor and control cybersecurity subsystems within operational systems.

cybersensor   A mechanism that monitors some aspect of a system that is intended to detect a set of events that indicate potential cyberattack.

cyberspace   A complex hyper-dimensional space involving the state of many mutually dependent computer and network systems with complex and often surprising properties as compared to physical space. Also known as the digital domain.

cyberwarfare   Warfare between nations, conducted primarily in cyberspace, targeting critical information infrastructure.

cyborg   Abbreviation of "cybernetic organism," referring to a human that is substantially enhanced with integrated technology.

data hiding   The dependability concept of not allowing functions access to data structures unless they are specifically designated to do so in the context of a module or object.

data integrity   The property that data has not been altered in an authorized manner.

deception   Actions taken to cause others to believe an untrue statement for the purpose of gaining a value or effect.

decipher   To convert enciphered text to plain text by means of a cryptographic system.

decrypt   *See* decipher.

defender   A group or organization that is a potential target of cyberattack.

defense in breadth   The principle of ensuring that the entirety of the cyberattack space is covered by a cybersecurity mechanism.

defense in depth   The principle of ensuring that more than one defense mechanism addresses each attack in the cyberattack space. The redundancy of coverage is intended to reduce the probability that cyberattacks will succeed due to failure or compromise of any given defense mechanism.

defense operators   Privileged users that have the knowledge and ability to command the defensive subsystem against attack, to reconfigure the system, and to adjust its operation to keep the mission safe.

delta risk   The change in risk from one state of a system to another, such as when comparing a baseline system to a proposed improvement.

denial of service (DOS)   A type of cyberattack to degrade the availability of a target system.

dependability   The ability to deliver acceptable service that is trustworthy.

design patterns   Design and program templates created to facilitate the construction of robust and reliable programs by capturing knowledge about how to best construct such programs in various domains.

design verification   The process of proving that a design meets specified properties, often through showing consistency with a formal statement of the system policy.

detailed top-level specification   An informal statement of the high-level functionality of an entire system.

detect-recover   A defense approach that counts on the detection of an attack prior to significant damage, followed by recovering from the damage. A complementary approach to attack prevention.

detection breadth   With respect to attack space, it means the union of attacks that an intrusion detection system is capable of detecting. With respect to network expanse, it means having detection capabilities along the entire attack path.

detection depth   With respect to attack space, it means that more than one sensor can detect the same attack or set of attacks. With respect to network expanse, it means having detection capabilities from the outermost perimeter of a network through to its core.

detection threshold   A threshold set in an intrusion detection system above which an alarm is raised to a human operator as a likely attack.

deterrence   An aspect of a defensive system that discourages an attacker from attacking, typically by increasing the attacker's risk of doing so.

device controller   Software on a computer device (e.g., a disk drive) that controls the device's functions (such as storing and retrieving blocks of data from a storage device).

device driver   Low-level system software that provides an abstract interface to hardware devices such as disks and network interface devices.

DevOps   Short for development operations, an information technology environment in which development and operations are tightly tied together, yielding small incremental releases to gain user feedback. *See* Agile design.

digital domain   *See* cyberspace.

digital policy management   The management of policy rules associated with cybersecurity mechanisms, such as attribute-based access control or firewall rules.

digital signature   A means of authenticating that a message or data came from a particular source with a known system identity.

direct memory access (DMA)   A mechanism that allows devices (e.g., disk drives and network devices) direct access to primary memory to speed up data transfer by avoiding having to pass through the central processing unit.

discretionary access control (DAC)   A form of controlling access between active entities (e.g., processes) and resources such as files, whereby the access rights are at the discretion of the users who own the resources.

disinformation   False information intended to mislead an audience toward a false belief.

distributed denial of service attack (DDOS)   A denial of service technique using numerous hosts to perform the attack. For example, in a network flooding attack, a large number of co-opted computers (e.g., a botnet) send a large volume of spurious network packets to disable a specified target system. *See also* denial of service; botnet.

distributed file service   A computer service that enables the sharing of files in geographically dispersed locations while giving the appearance that files are stored locally.

divide and conquer   A computer science principle that calls for breaking complex problems into less complex instances of the problem (the divide part), followed by solving the simpler problems (the conquer part), and then constructing a final solution using the solutions to the simpler problems.

domain   A label given to programs within the integrity policy called type enforcement. The label is associated with specific data processing sequences. *See* type enforcement.

domain name attacks   Computer attacks on the Internet domain name system to revector network traffic away from a legitimate system for denial of service or specifically to an attacker system for masquerading.

domain name system (DNS)   A distributed cooperative service provided on the Internet that translates human understandable names such as www.cyberdefenseagency.com to machine Internet addresses such as 127.16.244.3. Sometimes referred to as domain name server and domain name service.

dominant attack scenario   An attack scenario (sequence of attack steps that accomplishes the root node goal of the tree) whose success probability is the dominant factor in calculating the probability of the attack tree root goal being successfully achieved.

duress   A situation in which an element of the enterprise system, especially elements of the cybersecurity subsystem, has been successfully attacked and co-opted by an attacker and can therefore no longer be trusted.

edge testing   Testing a system at the limits of its design performance, including flooding it with too many transactions or poorly formed transactions, and starving it of resources, such as computation time, storage, and network bandwidth.

egress path   The attack path that is used by malicious code that has already infiltrated a target system to communicate collected data to a human attacker for the purpose of compromising the data or for receiving further direction based on the situation.

embedded system   A system contained within a larger system such that there is no direct user interface, such as electronics that help operate cars, airplanes, and thermostats.

emergency rekey   The act of invalidating all certificates issued by a certificate authority, due to a compromise of the authority's signing key, and reissuing those certificates under a new signature.

emergent property   A property that a complex system exhibits that is not evident in the system components.

empirical metric   A metric that is directly measured. *See* metric.

encapsulation   The bundling of data with the procedures that operate on that data, such that data may only be changed by those procedures—a technique for reducing program complexity.

encipher   To convert plain text to ciphertext by means of a cryptographic system.

enclave   A subnetwork of a larger system, often with distinct value, services, mission, and characteristics when compared to the larger system in which it is contained.

encrypt   *See* encipher.

entity   A general term for both persons and nonpersons that are identifiable and authenticable within a system.

entity identification   The process of a person or non-person proving to the system owners that they are who they say they are in the physical world.

equivalence class   A subset of items in a larger set that are the same with respect to some characteristic or way that they are processed.

error   An error is that part of the system state that may cause a subsequent failure: a failure occurs when an error reaches the service interface and alters the service.

error correction   The ability to correct an error that has occurred in the transmission, processing, or storage of digital data.

error detection   The ability to detect that an error has occurred in the transmission, processing, or storage of digital data.

escalating privilege   The process by which an attacker uses a level of system access to perform further actions and attacks to gain more privilege on the target system.

espionage   The act of stealing protected data that the owner intends to keep private.

event detection   The detection and reporting of selected attack-related events in an event stream from a sensor's extracted feature stream.

event selection   The identification of the subset of events in a sensor's extracted feature stream that indicate a potential attack is in progress.

executive   A tiny operating system for a device processor meant solely for the purpose of supporting device control.

exfiltration   The process of stealthily communicating sensitive data from the inside of a compromised target system to an external point from which the attacker can easily retrieve the data.

exhaustion attack   The process of deciphering ciphertext without the benefit of the original key by trial and error over all possible keys in the key space.

exploit   A method or program that takes advantage of a vulnerability in a target system to accomplish an attack.

exponential growth   An algorithm that scales poorly, in particular, more rapidly than what can be expressed by a polynomial equation.

fail closed   A property of a cybersecurity mechanism such that when it fails, the system is prohibited from continuing to operate without the benefit of the cybersecurity mechanism until it is diagnosed and repaired.

fail open   A property of a cybersecurity mechanism such that when it fails, the system is allowed to continue to operate without the benefit of the cybersecurity mechanism until it is diagnosed and repaired.

failure   A system failure is an event that occurs when the delivered service deviates from correct service (implementing system function). A system may fail either because it does not comply with the specification or because the specification did not adequately describe its function.

fake news   False or intentionally misleading information that is propagated by the media, particularly those that claim to be news organizations.

false negative   A test result that incorrectly reports that a condition being tested for is absent, when, in fact, it is present (e.g., an intrusion detection subsystem falsely reports no attacks in the attack space of an enterprise system).

false positive   A test result that incorrectly reports a condition being tested for is present, when, in fact, it is not present (e.g., an intrusion detection subsystem falsely reports an attack on the system when no attack is occurring).

fault   A fault is the adjudged or hypothesized cause of an error. A fault is active when it produces an error; otherwise, it is dormant.

feature   An aspect of system state (e.g., audit logs, network activity) that can be monitored for potential use in the detection of some phenomena of interest, such as an attack on a target system.

feature identification   The process by which an analyst identifies the subset of features in the defended system in which an attack might manifest.

feature selection   The process a cybersecurity engineer uses to choose the features in which a given attack may manifest.

feature vector   A one-dimensional matrix (called a vector) representation of all possible features within a system.

fingerprinting code   Attributing code to a particular author by observing sequences and styles that are consistent with the history of code written by that author.

firewall   A network device designed to selectively block unauthorized access while permitting authorized communication to devices within a subnetwork.

firmware   Low-level software that controls hardware operation between the processor and the operating system.

flame war   A heated exchange of points and counterpoints in an electronic form, such as social media.

flash worm   A worm with an extraordinary propagation rate—faster than a human decision-making process can counter. *See* worm.

flaw   The cause of a system failure with respect to its specifications.

flooding attack   *See* network flooding attack.

fog of war   A concept in physical warfare in which the smoke from gunfire and cannons obscured the battlefield. Though the actual physical fog is somewhat outdated, the term has been generalized and rejuvenated to apply to the confusion and chaos that occurs during battle (cyberwar or physical battle) that makes planning and execution difficult.

forensic analysis   *See* forensics.

forensic capability   The ability of an organization to analyze an attack to determine its mechanism, its source (origin), timing, and other characteristics.

forensics   The analysis of computer artifacts to establish certain facts about the state of the system, such as the cause of a failure or the source of a vulnerability.

formal methods   Techniques used to model complex systems as mathematical entities, making it possible to verify the system's properties in a more thorough fashion than empirical testing.

formal security policy model   A mathematically rigorous specification of a system's security policy in terms of a set of actors and attributes of actors, resources and attributes of resources, and the access rules between the actors and resources.

formal specification   A statement expressed in a language whose vocabulary, syntax, and semantics are formally defined, meant to increase rigor and enable reasoning about properties such as correctness.

formal top-level specification   A high-level specification that is written in a formal mathematical language to allow theorems showing correspondence of the system specification to its formal requirements to be hypothesized and formally proven.

functional correctness   Reliably performs specified functions.

golden copies   Copies of software that are believed to be uncorrupted because they come directly from the vendor and have been protected in storage using write-once-read-many storage and perhaps are checked against a digital signature from the vendor. Golden copies are used to restore potentially corrupted or infected software to a known-good state.

granularity   The degree to which policy can make distinctions between classes of users and between types of protected resources.

hacktivism   Hacking for a larger purpose involving activism.

hardened   A system that has been configured with tight security policies, has minimal services running to get its job done, and has strong cybersecurity services such as authentication and authorization.

harm   Damage to a system in terms of cost and other qualitative damage to mission including current and future value.

heuristic algorithm   An algorithm to solve a problem simply and quickly with an approximate solution, as compared to a complex algorithm that provides a precise solution, but may take a prohibitively long time.

high-level system software   The system software that directly supports application programs by providing convenient and powerful functions that hide the details of system operation so that the application can focus on its unique value-added service to its users.

high-stealth   A property of an attack or defense that makes its existence and activities hard to detect statically or dynamically, due to active measures that it takes to avoid detection.

high-value target   A system containing data and services judged to be of high value to an adversary. For example, if a given computer is known to contain the most sensitive data, an adversary will be highly motivated to selectively attack that computer.

human safety   The state of being protected from potential harm to humans.

human-in-the-loop   A decision-making process involving humans and that therefore occurs in minutes, hours, or days, as opposed to fully automated action, which can take place in microseconds, milliseconds, or seconds.

human-to-machine authentication   The process by which a human proves their identity to a machine. Also called log in or log on. *See* authentication.

hypervigilant mode   A mode of sensor operation characterized by significantly increased quantity and quality of output, in response to a command for more detail, during an ongoing attack.

hypervisor   The low-level operating system that is responsible for creating the illusion to operating systems running on it that it has exclusive use of the system.

identity assertion   The first phase of an authentication protocol in which a system entity asserts their identity.

identity authentication   The processes by which an entity asserts and proves their identity to other entities in the system.

identity certification   The process used by a privileged system owner to create a system identity for an entity (e.g., user) after an entity has properly identified themselves to them (e.g., showed two forms of identification, such as a driver's license and a passport).

identity decertification   The process of removing an entity's identity registration within a system.

identity management   The processes in which an entity's identity is updated to reflect changes in the nature of the entity's essential attributes or authorized existence within the system.

identity proving   The second phase of an authentication protocol in which a system entity proves its assertion about its identity.

identity registration The processes in which an entity is assigned a system identity and then subsequently conferred with the ability to demonstrate their identity to other entities.

identity resolution The process of an entity acquiring and loading security-critical data provided to it during the identity certification process. For example, a user may be given a private key as a way for them to prove their identity. They have to get that private key to their account and load it so the system software knows where to find it and how to use it.

identity-based access control An access control policy in which the rules are based primarily on the specific identity of each and every user on the system.

in the clear Unencrypted.

infiltration path The attack path that is used to gain initial access to the target system.

inflection point A point on a curve where there is a change in slope. Also called a knee in the curve.

influence operations A broad military term encompassing psychological operations, deception, and other areas for the purpose of influencing some action or way of thinking. *See also* psychological operations.

information assurance Measures that protect and defend information and information systems by ensuring their availability, integrity, authentication, confidentiality, and non-repudiation.

information hiding The intentional denial of access to operate directly on data without going through specified encapsulating procedures, which operate on the data in a well-controlled manner. *See* encapsulation.

information security *See* information assurance.

information theory The study of how information is represented, transformed, and communicated.

infosphere A parallel concept to a biosphere made up of the digital world and the infrastructure that supports it.

ingress path The attack path that is used by a human attacker to communicate command and control to malicious code that has already infiltrated a target system. Ingress paths are often called command and control pathways because the pathways enable the attacker to command and control the progress of the malicious code that has infiltrated the enterprise system.

insider attack   A cyberattack initiated and possibly controlled by a member of a defender's organization that is covertly working for an adversary.

insider threat   The threat from a trusted person with authorized access to a system taking malicious action, possibly on behalf of an external adversary.

instruction set architecture (ISA)   The set of instructions that a processor is capable of executing.

instrumentation   Functionality for the purpose of taking measurements to extract feature data that could indicate an attack.

instrumenting   System modifications to monitor a feature or state of the system for the purposes of system management, testing, or security control.

integrity   A system property that data and the system itself are protected from unauthorized modification.

Intelligence Community (IC)   The group of organizations engaged in intelligence operations of a variety of types. IC typically refers to the United States Intelligence Community, which currently consists of 17 organizations.

Internet of Things (IoT)   The wide-scale deployment of small, low-power computing devices into everyday devices, such as thermostats, refrigerators, clothing, and even into people themselves to continuously monitor health.

Internet service provider (ISP)   A service provider that provides the infrastructure to hook up an enterprise network or individual systems to the larger Internet.

intrusion   A cyberattack that gains unauthorized access to a system.

intrusion detection system (IDS)   A cybersecurity capability intended to detect cyberattack and particularly the infiltration of a cyberattack into a defended system.

intrusion tolerance   A system property that enables a mission system to sustain significant damage from cyberattack and continue to support essential mission functions in a gracefully degraded way.

island   Used as a verb with respect to a system, it means to isolate a system and its internal network from any external connections by either physically disconnecting connecting cables or virtually doing so by resetting the router and firewall rules. This is usually done as an extreme measure to limit damages from cyberattack.

journal-level proof   Human-directed proof sketches, analogous to proofs that might be found in a mathematical journal, which do not provide all detailed steps and do not prove basic notions of mathematics.

key   A sequence of bits that selects a particular cryptographic transformation from a large family of transformations.

key distribution   The process by which a cryptographic key is transmitted to the entity using that key.

key escrow   The process by which users' private keys are securely stored so that they can be recovered on an emergency basis if the user loses their private key.

key generation   The process of generating a cryptographic key that is truly random from within a key space. *See also* key space.

key pair   A pair of cryptographic keys that are related to one another. In public-key cryptography, the pair refers to the private key and its corresponding public key.

key space   The set of all valid keys associated with a given cryptographic algorithm.

key store   A device or memory within a device used specifically to store cryptographic keys.

key-encryption key   A key that is intended to be used strictly for encrypting another key, typically during key distribution.

keyboard cadence   The rhythm that a person types on a computer keyboard. Research suggests that it may be unique to individuals and therefore usable as a type of biometric authentication.

kinetic   Having to do with physical phenomena that manifest in the physical world, as distinguished from cyber events that happen in the virtual world of a cyber system.

knapsack algorithm   A combinatorial optimization algorithm used to find the best combination of items under a constraint such as weight or cost, where best is defined with respect to a weighted property such as value or risk reduction.

known-answer test   A test run on an operational system to verify the proper functioning of that system. The tests provide a series of inputs to the system and compare the system's output to those of the expected outputs per the system specification. Any deviation indicates an internal failure of the tested system.

latency   The delay between when an action such as transmitting data is taken and when it has an effect.

layer violation   Depending on and calling modules from a layer of abstraction above a given layer, breaking the strict hierarchy of abstraction.

layered assurance   A hierarchical architecture and its implementation in which each layer demonstrably depends only on lower layers.

layered security   A way to manage complex cybersecurity subsystems in which one level of security abstraction is built on building blocks of a lower layer of abstraction, which is in turn built on successive layers beneath until one reaches a foundational layer.

layering   A design principle of grouping functionality into a hierarchy from most fundamental to the most complex, building on the abstractions provided by the layer directly below a given layer and never depending on a layer above that given layer.

least privilege   The principle that an entity (e.g., user) should be granted the minimum privilege needed to accomplish its task.

life-cycle attack   *See* supply chain attack.

locality of reference   A typical software behavior in which memory that has recently been accessed will be more likely to be accessed again in the next instant, due to program constructs such as loops.

logic time bombs   Malicious code that is designed to damage the target computer system at a designated date and time.

login   See human-to-machine authentication.

logon   *See* human-to-machine authentication.

low-hanging fruit   Risk-reduction measures that are inexpensive and close important gaps in the attack space coverage.

low-level system software   The most foundational system software that provides the interface between the high-level system software and the hardware devices on the system.

low probability of detection (LPD)   Techniques used in communication to intentionally make it hard to detect the usage of a channel or even the existence of a channel.

machine room   A room that has physical access control containing large computers and servers meant to support an enterprise.

machine-to-machine   An interaction between processes, devices, or systems that does not involve a human user directly.

machine-to-machine authentication   The process by which non-person entities such as devices and processes prove their identity to each other. The concept also includes the proxying of a user's identity on whose behalf the non-person is acting.

malicious software (malware or malcode)   Software designed to perform attacks on a target system—for example, worms and viruses.

malware   *See* malicious software.

man-in-the-middle attack   An attack on communicated data whereby the attacker interposes themselves between the sender and recipient and manipulates the conversation in one or both directions, pretending to be the sender or receiver.

mandatory security policy   A system security policy that is enforced by the system, based on assigned attributes to processes and resources, not at the discretion of users.

maneuverability   The ability of a cybersecurity mechanism to dynamically adapt through configuration changes without requiring changes to the software.

manifestation subspace   The subset of all features in which an attack has some manifestation, however weak.

many-to-one mapping   An association between two sets where multiple elements in one set can form an association with a single element of a second set, such as multiple attacks manifesting in the same feature.

margin of safety   A factor multiplying a minimum requirement, such as load capacity of a bridge, to account for uncertainty in component characteristics, unpredictability of user behavior in using the system, and unpredictability in the range of environments in which the system will be used.

master bus   The communication backbone of a computer system that enables devices to exchange data and control. The master bus sometimes controls subordinate or slave buses to speed up communication between devices that need higher bandwidths or speeds.

measure of effectiveness   A way to determine through measuring a system whether it is achieving a specific goal, such as performance, or a cybersecurity goal, such as shutting down attack paths.

mechanism   Software or device that realizes a function, such as a firewall limiting traffic into and out of a network.

meta-strategy   An overarching strategy on how to effectively apply strategies, such as "don't overreact to an attack."

metadata   Data associated with other data that describes some important characteristics of the data to which it is bound. For example, the file length and file type associated with a file are metadata.

metric   A measurable quantity that indicates progress toward some goal.

microcode   Software that controls the operation of a processor or other device that is effectively a tiny operating system for a device.

min-max algorithm   An algorithm in game theory that optimizes a move in a strategic game such as chess based on maximizing one's best move while minimizing the goodness of the move for the opponent, projecting forward several moves.

minimal cut set   A collection of leaf nodes in an attack tree, which taken together, achieve the root goal, such that removing any leaf node would result in the failure to successfully achieve the root goal.

misattribution   The act of an attacker to misdirect a defender's analysis to mistakenly attribute the attack to some attacker other than the adversary.

misdirection   The action or process of directing someone to the wrong place or in the wrong direction, such as misattribution.

mission   An organization's top-level requirements that must be satisfied and the properties with which they must be satisfied, including trustworthiness.

mission impact   The effect that a security solution has on the ability to develop, deploy, maintain, or operate systems in support of an organization's mission.

mission map   The mapping of the IT components and services to the mission supported by them such that mission impact can be judged by knowing the degradation of a service or component.

mission model   A model of the content and structure of an organization's mission.

misuse case   A well-described scenario of how an attack flow might proceed against a system for the purposes of understanding how to defend against that case. A special case of a use case.

modularity   A property of system design in which like functions and their corresponding data structures are encapsulated into a distinct structure called a module that can be managed separately from the rest of the system.

module   A logical grouping of functions comprising related data structures that can be managed separately from a development perspective.

multilevel integrity (MLI)   A system property that requires that portions of the system with an established high level of integrity (e.g., through careful design and analysis) not depend on systems of lower integrity (e.g., software applets downloaded and executed on-the-fly from some website of unknown pedigree).

multilevel security (MLS)   A system property that requires that information be prevented from flowing to lower sensitivity levels.

n-gram   A continuous sequence of n items within a larger sequence such as in text or binary strings.

n-gram analysis   The search for characteristic $\underline{n}$-grams of software code, binary strings, or text in an attempt to determine authorship or origin of a document of software so that it may be attributed.

need-to-know   The principle of sharing sensitive information only when there is a clear and unequivocal justification in support of mission objectives, irrespective of a person having adequate clearance to access the information. The concept stands in balance with responsibility-to-share.

network flooding attack   An attack in which the system is flooded by data packets from one or more sources in the network for the purpose of blocking the target system from being able to operate because it is too busy processing an extraordinary volume of illegitimate data.

network reconnaissance   A series of actions intended to learn the configuration, operation, and nature of a targeted network—typically as a prelude to an attack.

Network Time Protocol (NTP)   An Internet standard that polls reliable time sources and adjusts the local clock of a computer accordingly.

noise   Phenomena, particularly in communications, which tend to obscure useful information, known as signal.

noise floor   The ambient noise in which an attack signal is buried.

non-bypassable   A property of a containing system that requires that the only way to gain access to resources under the control of the system is through that system.

non-interference   System property that states that data cannot leak to unauthorized users, either explicitly through a policy violation or implicitly through means of covert signaling using shared resources.

non-person entity (NPE)   An active element within a system such as a device or process that has its identity certified and is capable of being authenticated.

non-polynomial (NP) growth   *See* exponential growth.

nonce   A unique bit sequence used in security protocols to avoid a replay attack in which a legitimate message is copied and resent by an attacker to cause confusion or to cause a specific action.

obfuscation techniques   Techniques, such as stealth and self-modification, used to make it more difficult to detect, capture, and analyze malicious code.

object-oriented design   A modular approach to system design in which functions are logically grouped together along with their data structures into objects. These objects generally correspond to logical real-world entities and interact with other objects through well-defined interfaces and hide their internal data structures to protect them from error by objects that have no need to know the internal workings of the object.

objects   Passive computer entities that are operated upon, such as memory.

Observe-Orient-Decide-Act (OODA) Loop   A four-phase decision-making cycle that involves first observing the situation, putting those observations into a mission-relevant context, making a decision on what do about the situation, acting on that decision, and then iterating through the loop again, including the observation as to whether the actions were as effective as anticipated.

one-packet-one-kill   Generally, the notion of a cyberattack that happens so quickly that the damage is done well before the defender even has time to detect the existence of the attack.

one-to-many mapping   An association between two sets where an element in one set can form an association with multiple elements of a second set.

OODA Loop   *See* Observe-Orient-Decide-Act Loop.

opportunity cost   The value that a given investment would return if invested in an alternative way.

opposing force (OPFOR)   A group of soldiers whose function is to simulate an enemy force in the context of an exercise.

outliers   A statistical term referring to data points that are outside of the majority of data points, characterized by the number of standard deviations from the mean.

outsider attack   A cyberattack whose point of origin is outside of the network, exploiting a vulnerability to infiltrate the target system (in contrast to insider attack).

Pareto 80/20 Rule   A general rule of thumb that suggests that 80 percent of the cost comes from 20 percent of the cost factors, or that 80 percent of the value is generated by 20 percent of the people. Also called the 80/20 rule. Used to guide system designers to focus on the aspects that matter most to outcome.

penetration testing (pentest)   The specialized testing of a system to determine if it is possible to defeat its security controls.

perimeter firewall   A firewall that guards the edge between an enterprise network and an external network that the enterprise uses to connect to outside organizations.

person entity (PE)   A human whose identity is certified within a system and is capable of being authenticated. Also called simply a person or a user.

phreaking   Hacking phone systems.

plain text   Unencrypted data.

playbook   A compendium of dynamic defensive action options that is available for a series of anticipated attacks and the criteria used to determine which option is best in which attack scenarios.

policy   The rules of system operation meant to ensure the compliance of a system with a set of desired properties, often dictated by a natural language policy.

policy author   A user specifically authorized to create policy for a protecting subsystem.

policy decision   The process of evaluating access policy rules with respect to a given access attempt by a specific subject and a specific object.

policy decision point (PDP)   The location where policy decisions are evaluated.

policy decision making   That portion of the cybersecurity authorization subsystem that evaluates a security policy for a given access attempt.

policy distribution   The distribution of digital policies from a central collection point to subscribers that consume that policy, typically to make policy decisions based on that policy.

policy enforcement   The process of implementing the access control decision made between an accessing entity and protected resources.

policy enforcement point (PEP)   The location where policy decisions are enforced.

policy rules   Rules that govern the access rights granted between subjects and objects within a system.

policy specification   The process by which a steward of a body of protected data states the rules governing access to that data based on attributes of the accessing entity and those of the specific data being requested

polynomial time   Used in complexity analysis to refer to algorithms of problems that can be solved in a number of steps that is a function that can be expressed as a polynomial such as $n2$, where n is the size of the data set.

port scanning   An attack reconnaissance technique used to probe each of thousands of potential electronic doors (ports) available on a given computer over which services communicate.

pre-fetch   A caching strategy that predicts an access pattern based on historical trends or analysis of the nature of the program and retrieves what it anticipates will be the most common data needed for computation.

predictive intelligence   The prediction of future events based on analysis of current and historical events. In cybersecurity, the prediction of future attack targets based on inference from the likely goal of the adversary.

primary memory   Computer memory that is directly addressed and accessed by a central processing unit.

probability of attempt   The likelihood that an attack would be tried by an attacker based on attributes of the attack, attributes of the defender, and value of the goal.

probability of success (given attempt)   The likelihood that an attack will succeed given that it is attempted by an attacker.

proof factoring   The decomposition of a complex proof into subordinate simpler proofs.

propagation path   The attack path used by self-propagating malicious code to spread malicious code to other subsystems within the target system or to other target systems.

protecting subsystem   A program or group of programs that mediates access to a resource or set of resources and which exhibit reference monitor properties.

provable correctness   A property of a program that enables proofs that it meets its functional specification and performs no other functions not specified. The property is supported by an assurance argument that could consist of evidence that includes testing and development processes, as well as mathematical proofs.

proxy   Someone or something that acts on behalf of another, usually authorized by that other entity.

psychological operations   The conveying of selected information (true or false) for the purpose of altering behavior. *See also* influence operations.

public-key cryptography   Encryption system using a public-private key pair for encryption or digital signature. The encrypt and decrypt keys are different, and one cannot derive the private key from the public key.

purple team   A collaborative red team and blue team working together to learn as much as possible from a cyber exercise.

quantum cryptography   The development of cryptographic techniques using quantum phenomena that will not succumb to the speed expected from quantum computers.

random number   A number that is selected from a specific set in a random fashion—that is, guided by a random source.

random sources   A physical phenomenon that produces random events that can be captured and recorded and used for applications such as cryptography.

ransomware   Malicious code whose function is to perform reversible sabotage whereby the reversal process is under the control of an attacker and given to a victim in exchange for payment. *See also* reversible sabotage.

rapid mutation techniques   The method in which malicious software modifies itself subtly with each generation to make it harder to detect. Analogous to rapidly evolving or mutating genetic material of biological viruses such as influenza A viruses (which is why new cocktails of influenza vaccines are manufactured annually).

reconnaissance   The act of exploring a system or situation to determine what is happening and particularly a system's vulnerabilities.

recursion   A process in which a problem is broken down into one or more self-similar subproblems, which are then also similarly broken down, until one reaches a base case where the solution is well-defined, often by definition.

red team   Experts whose job is to simulate adversary techniques and operations in an exercise to help defenders better understand them and plan proper responses to attacks.

red team work factor (RTWF)   The amount of time and resources it takes a red team to accomplish a particular attack.

reduced instruction set computer (RISC)   A processor with a minimal set of instructions to do the most basic operations at high speed with an intention of keeping the processor simple and therefore more reliable and more secure.

reference monitor   A subsystem managing a set of resources that is demonstrably incapable of being bypassed, is provably correct in its functionality of managing access, and is tamperproof.

registration   The process by which an entity is made known to the system.

remote attestation   The production and publication of authenticated signed software from an originator (e.g., a software vendor), which is then checked locally before execution to ensure that the software has not been tampered with during software distribution or operations.

replay attack   A cyberattack in which a legitimate transaction between authenticated parties is copied and retransmitted by the attacker as if it was coming from the authenticated sender. For example, if the original command was to bomb Hill X, an enemy position, replaying that transaction a few hours later when the hill has changed hands could cause the defender to damage their own troops in friendly fire.

requirements creep   The tendency of system stakeholders to continue to add new requirements to a system in an effort to meet more mission needs. These additions are done based on the mistaken theory that it is always cheaper to add a feature to a system than to create a new system.

resource abstraction   A resource or set of resources to which access is controlled by a protecting subsystem that exhibits reference monitor properties (e.g., a hypervisor).

responsibility-to-share   The principle that sharing information is essential to mission function and the unnecessary withholding of such information could pose a higher risk than potential loss. The concept stands in balance with need-to-know. *See also* need-to-know.

return on investment   The value one receives for investing money or resources into a system. From an attacker's perspective, the investments are the resources invested in an attack, and the return is the degree to which they are successful in meeting their goal. For a defender, investment is in the cybersecurity capability of the system, and the return is the resulting reduced risk to the defended system.

reversible sabotage   Sabotage done in such a way as to be easily reversible by the attacker, generally in exchange for ransom. *See also* ransomware.

risk   A characterization of harmful events and their associated probabilities with respect to a given system or mission.

risk assessment   A process used to quantitatively or qualitatively determine the risk associated with an actual or hypothesized system.

risk mitigation packages   Groupings of related countermeasures to cyberattacks.

risk threshold   The level of risk beyond which an adversary is unwilling to go when considering an attack on a target.

risk tolerance   The capacity of an attacker to take the chance of being caught and suffering the consequences.

rollback   The process of restoring a set of data or process state to a previous consistent state saved through a checkpoint operation.

rules of engagement (ROE)   Carefully defined rules limiting the actions of a red team to prevent unintended damage to the operations of a mission system or to a planned exercise.

sabotage   The act of intentionally degrading the proper function of a system.

safe state   A state of a system that is known to be good by some established criteria of goodness that includes internal consistency and noncorruption at a minimum. Systems are restored to a safe state through rollback and saved as a safe state through checkpointing.

safety   The state of being protected from potential harm.

scalability   The property of a system that its performance remains relatively consistent as key parameters, such as the number of users, increase.

script kiddie   An unsophisticated and immature cyberattacker who uses attack scripts developed by others to accomplish an attack goal without understanding how and why the underlying attacks work and what to do if they fail.

secondary memory   Computer memory that is indirectly addressed through a device controller such as a hard disk drive.

secret-key cryptography   *See* symmetric-key cryptography.

Part VI

secure bootstrapping   A process in which each stage of a system boot is verified to ensure that no software in the boot sequence has been tampered with.

Secure Hash Algorithm (SHA)   A particular algorithm family for creating digital signatures.

secure state   A state of a computer that meets a defined set of security properties.

security compartment   A non-hierarchical grouping of sensitive information used to control access to data more finely than with hierarchical security classification (e.g., Top Secret, Secret, Confidential) alone.

security kernel   The most security-critical part of the operating system that controls access to system resources such as memory, that exhibits reference monitor properties (being correct, tamperproof, and non-bypassable).

security lattice   A relationship between security labels that includes compartments that are not in a strictly hierarchical relationship with other labels. Mathematically, this is known as a partial ordering.

security policy   A statement of the rules governing the access to a system's protected resources.

security-critical   A portion of the system that is critical to the successful operation of the required cybersecurity properties.

self-diagnostic   A subprocess run by a program or service to check itself and its data to ensure that it is in a good state, which includes at least ensuring that the data and code are not corrupted.

self-healing   A system property indicating that a system can automatically reconstitute its essential functions using available resources.

semantic validity   The compliance of attribute data to rules regarding consistency and truthfulness of association.

sensitivity analysis   A process to determine how the uncertainty in the output of a mathematical model can be ascribed to variation of its inputs.

sensitivity label   A short descriptor indicating the specific nature of the sensitivity of data in a container such as a file. For example, the label "Secret" from among a set of {Top Secret, Secret, Confidential, and Unclassified} may be associated with a file that contains data, "the unauthorized disclosure of which reasonably could be expected to cause serious damage to the national security."

sensor   A defensive mechanism that monitors an aspect of a defended system that is intended to detect a set of events that indicate potential cyberattack.

sensor grid   An array of intentionally deployed sensors within a defended system to detect a broad spectrum of attacks coming from all possible directions within the system.

separation kernel   A very trustworthy version of a hypervisor. *See* hypervisor.

separation of concerns   The principle of separating a system functionality into separate subsystems according to the similarity of their function and their different properties.

short-circuit evaluation   A performance optimization technique in which a sequence of logical conditional statements (e.g., if A or (B and C)) is evaluated only up to the point at which the result of the expression is known. In this example, if A is true, the system will not use time and resources to evaluate B and C.

signal   Phenomena, particularly within communications, which is intended to communicate useful information. *See also* attack signal; noise.

signal analysis   In the context of attack feature selection, it is the process of identifying the degree to which an attack will manifest in each of the features in the attack's feature set and assessing the relative difficulty of extracting that feature. *See also* feature.

signal processing theory   The theory of how information is communicated and processed within a system.

Signals Intelligence (SIGINT)   Intelligence derived from electronic signals and systems used by foreign targets, such as communications systems, radars, and weapons systems.

signature (string)   A sequence of bits located within malware that is intended to uniquely identify a cyberattack.

signature-based   A type of intrusion detection system based on identifying an attack signature for a captured instance of an attack.

silent compromise   The loss of sensitive data to an adversary without the defender being aware of the loss.

simple security policy   A multilevel security policy that prohibits processes operating on behalf of users from reading any data above the level of their clearance.

situation understanding   *See* cyber situation understanding.

social engineering   The psychological manipulation of people into unwittingly performing actions favorable to an attacker, such as divulging passwords or other confidential information.

source address spoofing   Manipulating the source address in network data packet headers to indicate an Internet protocol address other than the true address.

space complexity   The amount of storage a system requires as a function of inputs.

space locality of reference   If a location in memory is accessed in one instant of computation, it is highly likely to be accessed in the next few instants.

specification   A statement of the intended functionality of a given system.

spider   A program that visits many websites and their subtended websites for the purposes of archiving or indexing data on those websites. Search engines such as Google periodically crawl the Web in this fashion. These programs often resemble attacks because of their behavior pattern.

spin   A short-cycle (e.g., 90 days) iteration of a system to include more features and capabilities over the existing baseline.

spoof   To trick or fool someone or something into believing false information to gain some advantage, such as providing a false source Internet address for incoming network packets (called address spoofing).

storage cloud   A set of networked cloud computers focused on providing large amounts of remote disk storage space to facilitate multisite access, sharing, and collaboration among multiple users.

strict hierarchy   A relationship among a set of elements in which all elements are linearly ordered.

Stuxnet   A malware-based attack on centrifuges in Iran in 2010 that appeared to be for the specific purpose of delaying that country's nuclear development program.

subexhaustive attack   A cryptanalytic attack that can consistently decipher ciphertext without searching through half of the full cryptographic key space.

subjects   Active computer entities such as processes that act on objects.

supervisor mode   A processor mode granting special privileges to manage system resources to the programs that run in that mode—typically the security portion of an operating system.

supply chain attacks   A computer attack in which an attacker inserts malicious code into a program during the development or distribution process for later exploitation. Also known as a life-cycle attack.

survivability   The ability of a system to continue to perform its primary functions, possibly in a degraded mode, despite successful attacks against that system.

symmetric-key cryptography   A cryptographic process in which the same key is used to both encrypt and decrypt data. Also referred to as traditional cryptography and secret key cryptography.

syntactic integrity   The property of data that it complies with a set of rules about the form and format of the data—analogous to grammar and spelling rules for a natural language.

syntactic validity   The compliance of attribute data to format and grammar rules.

system   A collection of components that operate together to achieve a larger function.

system integrity   The property of the system (software, hardware, and ancillary files) that it retains the form and content intended by the designers and system owners.

system load   Levels and types of saturation of system resources such as computational resources, storage, and network bandwidth.

system software   Software that manages the resources of computer hardware to provide high-level abstractions of those resources to applications and to give the appearance that the user has exclusive control of those resources.

tamper detection   The capability to determine if a mechanism, particularly a cybersecurity mechanism, has been tampered with (including its code, its inputs, and its outputs).

tamper-resistance   The ability of a system to resist being tampered with, through either prevention techniques or detection techniques. *See also* tamperproof.

tamperproof   A property of a program, hardware, or a system that it maintains system integrity (not capable of being modified without proper authorization). No system is truly tamperproof. *See* tamper-resistance.

theoretical metric   A metric that is determined by analysis of the underlying mechanism and algorithm, as contrasted to practical metrics that are measured directly.

Part VI

threat fatigue   To become weary from continual pronouncements that there is a next threat around the corner, many of which prove to be false threats. In the context of cybersecurity, operators can experience threat fatigue from an overabundance of false alarms.

three-factor authentication   The use of three different authentication factors, typically something-you-know combined with something-you-have and something-you-are. *See also* authentication.

tightening down   The process of restricting access and operations from a more open mode to a more limited mode to reduce the attack surface.

time complexity   Refers to how much time a computational task will take as a function of its inputs and in terms of the number of computation steps.

time locality of reference   The juxtaposition of memory that is accessed in close succession during program execution.

time-to-deploy   The amount of time from the moment a requirement emerges for a system to the time that it is deployed into operational use.

total cost of ownership   An accounting of system cost that encompasses the entire life cycle of a system, not just its development.

training period   Period of time used to establish normal behavior for anomaly detection systems, which in turn determines which events constitute anomalous deviation from that normal behavior.

transitive closure   The set of all elements that are indirectly connected through their direct connections, as represented in a graph. For example, if A is connected to B, and B is connected to C, then both B and C are in A's transitive closure.

Transmission Control Protocol (TCP)   A reliable network protocol in which the transmitter and receiver engage in a handshake sequence, ensuring that there is a reliable channel and in which data received is checked against control data to ensure that it is received and received without errors.

Trojan horse   A computer program that appears to have a useful function, but also has a hidden and potentially malicious function that evades security mechanisms, sometimes by exploiting legitimate authorizations of a system entity that invokes the program.

true negative   The correct determination by an intrusion detection system that a sequence of events does not contain an attack. *See also* false negative.

true positive   An event sequence that is identified as an attack and it corresponds to a true attack (as opposed to a mistaken identification, called a false positive). *See also* false positive.

trust   Trust is confidence that a system has certain specified properties.

trusted   A belief that a system is trustworthy.

trusted code   Cybersecurity software that must be trustworthy to perform security-critical operations and is trusted to adhere to the intention of security policy, while being privileged to selectively violate certain rules (e.g., the multilevel security *-property).

trusted extension   A portion of the operating system that did not have direct control over system resources, but that had to be privileged to violate the *-property—thus allowing the creation of objects at lower classifications than the process is operating at. This was typically required for importing and exporting protected data from removable media and to other external devices.

trusted path   A secure and authenticated communication path between an entity (e.g., a user) and a trusted service.

Trusted Platform Module (TPM)   A commercial standard for secure bootstrapping a system from hardware to low-level system software.

trustworthy   Worthy of being trusted to have certain specified properties.

two-factor authentication   The use of two different authentication factors, typically something-you-know combined with something-you-have. *See also* authentication; three-factor authentication.

type   A label given to data containers within the integrity policy called type enforcement. The label is associated with specific data processing sequences.

type enforcement   An integrity model focused on a sequence of validation and transformation steps that data and control flow undergo during processing (sometimes referred to as a data pipeline). Programs are assigned domains; data are assigned types. An access matrix is created between domains and types to govern access and enforce the sequencing of data.

undamped oscillation   A condition in control theory in which a system grows increasingly far from its goal state due to overreacting control inputs.

uptime   The amount of time that a computer is functioning normally.

user   *See* person entity.

user datagram protocol (UDP)   An unreliable network protocol that is fast and efficient in which data is transmitted once to a recipient, but the transmitter is not guaranteed delivery.

user mode   A processor mode in which normal applications run without special privilege. *See also* supervisor mode.

veneer security   Security functionality provided without corresponding assurance so that the functionality only appears to protect resources when, in fact, it does not.

virtual economy   The economy associated with digital assets such as property and gold within the virtual world of gaming. Virtual currencies such as Bitcoin are also considered part of the virtual economy.

virtual machine (VM)   This term is ambiguous. (a) It sometimes refers to the combination of the system hardware resources and the low-level operating system (called a hypervisor) that is responsible for creating the illusion to operating systems running on it that they have exclusive use of the system. (b) A virtual machine can also refer to a guest operating system running on top of a hypervisor.

virtual private cloud   A cloud that appears to be dedicated to a user but is in fact formed from a shared set of hardware or virtual machines in a large cloud offered by a cloud service provider. *See also* cloud computing.

virtualization   The process of presenting an abstraction of hardware resources to give the appearance of dedicated access and control to hardware resources, while, in reality, those resources are being shared.

virus   Self-propagating malicious code that requires a host program to replicate and propagate itself.

vulnerability   The property of a system whereby it is susceptible to a given attack succeeding against that system.

vulnerability testing   The specialized testing of a system to determine if known vulnerabilities are present and exploitable.

weakest link principle   The idea that an adversary will evaluate the strength of all defenses in terms of relative strength and always attack the weakest one.

wetware   A humorous way to refer to knowledge or a subprocess that is executed in the mind of humans instead of in software.

white team   In a cybersecurity exercise or simulation, a group of experts who act as referees or recorders of events and ensure that the rules of engagement are followed.

whiteboarding   The act of working through an attack scenario between a red and blue team using only a whiteboard and reasoning, as opposed to live attacks and defense operations.

work factor   A quality of defense metric determined by the difficulty that an attacker (or simulated attacker such as a red team) has in defeating the defense.

workflow   The specification of actions, actors, sequencing of actions, and completion criteria that, taken together, accomplish a larger task.

working set   The N most recently referenced memory objects (e.g., pages) where N is specified as the working set window size; intended to capture the locality of reference in caching strategies.

worm   Self-propagating, self-contained malicious code.

zero-day attack   An attack that exploits a zero-day vulnerability.

zero-day vulnerability   An exploitable vulnerability in a system that has not been previously identified.

zero-sum game   A budgeting activity where a top-level budget is fixed such that subordinate budgets must be adjusted so that the combined budgets are always equal to the top-level budget. If funds are added to one item, that amount must be subtracted for the remaining items.

zombie   A computer that has been taken over by an attack and is consequently under the control of an attacker and often part of a large network of such computers called a botnet. *See also* botnet.

Index